D1832422

INDIAN AFFAIRS ANNUAL 2008

INDIAN AFFAIRS ANNUAL 2008

(In 9 Vols.)

Vol. 4

Chronology of Events

(10-08-2007 to 11-09-2007)

Shailendra Sengar

KALPAZ PUBLICATIONS

KALPAZ PUBLICATIONS

DELHI - 110052

Indian Affairs Annual 2008

Rs. 6300 (Set)

© Reserved

ISBN: 81-7835-693-7 (Set)
ISBN: 81-7835-697-X (Vol. 4)

All rights reserved. No Part of this book may be reproduced in any manner without written permission.

Published in 2008 in India by
Kalpaz Publications
C-30, Satyawati Nagar,
Delhi-110052
E-mail: kalpaz@hotmail.com
Phone : 9212729499

Laser Type Setting by: Quick Media, Delhi
Printed at : Singhal Print Media, Delhi

INDIAN AFFAIRS ANNUAL 2008

Chronology of Events

(10-08-2007 to 11-09-2007)

2246. (10-8-2007) NEW DELHI : Mortal remains of three soldiers, killed in an AN-12 aircrash nearly four decades ago, were recovered from the remote Lahaul valley in Himachal Pradesh and moved to Chandigarh by helicopters today. Code named Operation Punaruthan-III, an expedition of the Indian Army into the 1968 crash, retrieved the bodies on 09 August from a glaciated area at an altitude of over 17,500 feet near the Chandrabhaga peak in Lahaul Valley in Lahaul & Spiti district. The expedition, led by Major Nishant Kumar of the Dogra Scouts, stumbled upon the remains on 02 August after a detailed search of the area for about five days. Efforts are being made to confirm the identity of the deceased soldiers from the documents and identity cards recovered along with the bodies. Thereafter, the next of kin of the deceased soldiers will be intimated. The AN-12 aircraft of the Indian Air Force had taken off from Chandigarh on Feb 07, 1968 on a routine logistics sortie with 102 persons on board to Leh. The aircraft was not able to negotiate the bad weather enroute and hit the towering 6264-meter high Chandrabhaga peak. There were no survivors of the crash and a detailed search of the area could not even find the remains of the aircraft. It was only in July 2003 that an expedition from the Manali Institute of Mountaineering and Allied Sports discovered the wreckage site. The team also found the mortal remains and documents of one victim,-Pioneer Beli Ram. His remains were moved to his native village in Akhnoor and cremated with full military honours. Subsequently, the army has launched expeditions every summer to recover bodies of the lost soldiers.

2247. (10-8-2007) NEW DELHI : The Union Minister for Power Shri Sushil Kumar Shinde today launched "Hydropowernet", a web based Management Information System (MIS) of the Ministry, in a function in New Delhi. Hydropowernet, an outcome of efforts put in by a dedicated team over the last one and a half years is a web based application conceptualized and operationalised by the Ministry of Power, for on-line monitoring of Hydro Power Projects and provides a platform for data sharing between various Hydro Utilities, the Central Electricity Authority (CEA) and the Ministry of Power (MOP). All major organisations which facilitate hydropower development and execution in the central sector have been integrated in the Hydropower-net namely MOP, CEA and Central Hydro Utilities viz. NHPC, SJVNL, BBMB, NTPC, NEEPCO, DVC. This web based application has been hosted at URL http://hydropowernet.gov.in on the storage Area Network of National Informatics Centre (NIC) for round the clock secured access with application level security through passwords. Hydropower-net has remote data updation facility for all the Central Hydro Power Utilities from the remote project sites itself and most of the data is made available on-line directly from the project site itself. In addition to on-line availability of extensive drilldown data on project construction activities, data is also available on generation, outages, collection of dues etc. for the Hydro stations in operations. The available information acts as a valuable Management Information Tool (MIS) and also provides inputs for informed decision making.

2248. (10-8-2007) NEW DELHI : Based on the result of the Civil Services (Preliminary) Examination, 2007 held on 20.05.2007 the names of the candidates qualified for admission to the Civil Services (Main) Examination, 2007 have been declared by the Union Public Service Commission (UPSC). UPSC has a Facilitation Centre near Examination Hall Building in its Campus.

2249. (10-8-2007) NEW DELHI : Photo Division, Ministry of Information & Broadcasting is organizing the 20th National Photo Contest on the theme "Spirit of Independent India" to mark the 60th anniversary of independence. The competition is open to all. The competition will have two sections: Black and White print (Monochrome) and colour print. Participant can send a maximum of four different photographs for both the sections. However, the entry should not be mounted. The award consists of Rs. 20,000/- as the First Prize, Rs. 15,000/- Second Prize, Rs. 10,000/- as Third Prize and ten each Commendation Prize of Rs. 2,000/- each for both the section, a memento and a certificate of merit. The last of submission of entry is September 15, 2007. The prints should be sent to Director, Photo Division, Ministry of Information & Broadcasting, Room No. 730, Soochna Bhavan, C.G.O Complex, Lodhi Road, New Delhi-110003.

2250. (10-8-2007) NEW DELHI : The Food Processing Minister, Shri Subodh Kant Sahai and Director General of Food and Agriculture Organization of United Nations Mr.Jacques Diouf discussed agricultural production in India, Value addition and inadequate post harvest management. The Secretary, Mr. P.I. Suvrathan and Joint Secretary, Mr. Gautam Sanyal were also present. During the meeting, the Minister said we want food technology revolution in India. He mentioned that DG, FAO is well aware of the huge potential of horti and agricultural produce in India. But due to low level of processing, value addition and inadequate post harvest management, India is still far behind from other developed countries. The Minister further said Government of India is committed to the growth and development of Agriculture. He said Food Processing Sector provides long term economic sustainability to the farmers by way of linking them to the industry and the market. In this regard, government has taken strategic initiatives to establish Mega Food Parks, Cold Chain, infrastructure and strategic distribution centres during the 11th Five Year Plan. Mr. Sahai said that since one of the mandates of FAO is high quality food and healthy lives, Food Processing Ministry needs FAO support in achieving the goal for the betterment of farmers. The Secretary, Mr. P.I. Suvrathan said in India organic farming is done in Himalayan ranges. This Ministry's effort to encourage and develop organic farming in a bigger way with the support from FAO. He further said FAO may consider extending assistance for establishing Organic Processing Zones in India. The Secretary further mentioned about the innovative scheme, the Ministry is going to undertake on upgrading quality of street food/food street in 11th Five Year Plan. He said FAO has been associated with the activities of improvement of hygiene, quality and safety of food products. Ministry needs assistance from FAO for upgrading the quality of food. Director General of Food and Agriculture Organization, Mr. Jacques Diouf gave assurance that every possible assistance will be provided from FAO for upliftment of farmers. He said FAO is working for achieving food security for all, higher quality of food to lead active, healthy lives. He further said FAO provides assistance in various ways for higher yield of crops, improving technical skills and legal advice on land ownership matters. Mr. Diouf discussion with President, Smt. Pratibha Patil, Prime Minister, Shri Manmohan Singh and Agriculture Minister Shri Sharad Pawar was satisfactory.

2251. (10-8-2007) NEW DELHI : The area coverage of kharif crops as compared to 9th August last year has gone up considerably as per data compiled by Agriculture Ministry. Rice area coverage is marginally less. The total coverage of kharif rice has gone up to 260.77 lakh ha as compared to 261.74 lakh hectare at this time last year, the weekly Crop Weather Watch Group meeting of the Ministry of Agriculture was informed here today. Transplanting of rice has started in the states of Andhra Pradesh, J&K, Karnataka, Kerala and Tamil Nadu. The sowing is at ending stag in the states of Haryana and Punjab. Transplanting is at peak in rest of the states. Total coarse cereals have covered an area of 193.26 lakh ha as compared to 177.75 lakh ha at this time last year. Cotton has been sown in 86.24 lakh ha as compared to 81.74 lakh ha last year. Out of this, 53.32 lakh hectare is under Bt cotton. Sugarcane coverage is reported to be 51.16 lakh hectare compared to 48.32 lakh ha last year, and jute 7.89 lakh hectare (last year 8.18 lakh ha.). The total coverage of oilseeds so far has been 159.30 lakh ha as compared to 148.78 lakh ha on August 9, last year. Soyabean has been sown in 7% and groundnut in 14% higher area as compared to that in 2006. Pulses cover an area of 104.34 lakh ha against 95.45 lakh ha during the last year.

2252. (10-8-2007) NEW DELHI : The Ministry of Rural Development has sanctioned Rs. 51.96 lakh to the State Government of Kerala towards second instalment of funds against the total approved cost of Rs. 148.47 lakh for computerization project of Rajiv Gandhi National Drinking Water Mission (RGNDWM). This grant is being provided under revised MIS guidelines during the year 2007-08. With this, the total release has become Rs. 96.50 lakh. This release is subject to the guidelines laid down in the programme.

2253. (10-8-2007) NEW DELHI : The Ministry of Rural Development has released the first instalment of Central assistance of Rs. 34.80 crore out of the Central allocation of Rs.69.60 crore under Indira Awas Yojana (IAY) to the Madhubani, District Rural Development Agency (DRDA) of Bihar, for the year 2007-08. The grant is towards the Plan expenditure and will be utilized for construction of new houses/upgradation of kutcha houses into pucca houses, subject to the conditions laid down in the guidelines under the IAY. The expenditure on the implementation of the programme is to be shared on 75:25 basis between the Centre and the State respectively. The State Government is to release its share within a month of the date of release of the Central assistance.

2254. (10-8-2007) NEW DELHI : Deptt of Animal Husbandry, Dairying and Fisheries notified an outbreak of Avian influenza in Chingmeirong Village in East Imphal District of Manipur on 25.7.2007. The Central Rapid Response Team of Ministry of Health and F.W. deputed to Imphal is assisting the State Govt. The health status of the cullers are being monitored. Today, 359 cullers/supportive staff have been examined and they are under cover of Tamiflu. The population of the infected zone [0-3 Kms] are under active surveillance on daily basis. For such purpose, the State Govt. has deployed health teams consisting of 600 health personnel. In this zone the surveillance teams could cover 44,679 houses [population of 2,33,739] on 8th August 2007. They detected 37 fever/ ARI cases some of which are follow-up of earlier cases. These cases are being monitored. Surveillance activity is also continuing with 143 health workers in the 3 to 10 Kms zone. 4,292 houses with a population of 23,951 in Karneng, Pastoi, Khumbong, Heirangoithong, Kha Imphal area, Narankonjil, Kiyamgei, Laiphansiphai, Pourabi, Kairaobitra, Langthabal, Urembarn, Khaidem areas have been covered. 3 cases of fever/ARI were detected and none of them had history of having handled sick/dead birds. As of now a cumulative population of 1,99,879 have been covered in the 3-10 Km zone. Arrangements have been made in J.N. Hospital, Imphal for isolation and critical care.

2255. (10-8-2007) NEW DELHI : The two-day high level discussions between Coast Guard and Pakistan Maritime Security Agency concluded here today. The Indian side was led by Director General Coast Guard Vice Admiral R F Contractor and the Pakistani side by the Director General of Pakistan Maritime Security Agency Rear Admiral Tayyab Ali Dogar. The discussions encompassed issues pertaining to violation of Exclusive Economic Zone (EEZ) by fishermen and procedures for their repatriation alongwith their boats, pollution incidents and response, maritime search and rescue, natural disasters and exchange of information regarding smuggling and illicit trafficking. Both sides confirmed that the regular communication on the hotline had brought down the number of apprehension of fishermen during the last nine months. Various modalities of dealing with the violations of EEZ were discussed. Both the sides reaffirmed their commitment to provide help to mariners in distress and carry out coordinated Search & Rescue Operations. The delegations also evinced interest in information sharing on matters of mutual importance. The number of fishermen and boats in custody on either side as well as the modalities of releasing those whose identities have been established were also discussed. The Indian Coast Guard and Pakistan Maritime Security Agency signed a Memorandum of Understanding (MoU) on 03 Oct 2005. Under this MoU, a hotline communication link between the two Director Generals was established on 14 Nov 06. The MoU stipulates that the heads of the two organisations meet once a year alternately in India or in Pakistan to review the progress of the MoU.

2256. (10-8-2007) NEW DELHI : The second battalion, the Royal Norfolk Regiment was the first British Army unit to leave Indian soil after the country achieved independence. The departure on August 17, 1947 from Mumbai witnessed a ceremonial function in which the Governor General Lord Louis Mountbatten delivered an emotional address to the troops. We reproduce here an article titled "Mountbatten's Good-bye to British Troops" published in the oldest Defence Journal of the country 'Fauji Akhbar' dated September 06, 1947 along with a backgrounder on the British Troops titled "Withdrawal of British Troops" published in the same issue. We also reproduce a message given by the Prime Minister Jawaharlal Nehru to the troops and which was delivered to them a short while before the ship sailed. This is the third article, which is attached.

2257. (10-8-2007) NEW DELHI : The four day festival of films on freedom movement 'Swatantrata Filmotsav' gets underway tomorrow at Siri Fort Auditorium. Organised by Films Division, Ministry of Information & Broadcasting, the festival commemorates 150th year of first war of independence. The festival would showcase our long and spirited struggle for freedom. '1857-The Beginning' directed by Bhanumurthy Alur would be the inaugural film at the festival. Shri P. R. Dasmunsi, Minister of Information & Broadcasting and Parliamentary Affairs will inaugurate the festival. Smt. Sheila Dikshit, Chief Minister of Delhi and freedom fighter, Shri Shashi Bhushan will also grace the occasion. A total of 55 films, including 15 feature films and 40 documentaries would be screened during the four-day event. The films selected for screening include classics like 'Anand Math' (directed by Hemen Gupta), 'Jhansi Ki Rani' (directed by Sohrab Modi), 'Making of Mahatma' and 'Netaji Subhas Chandra Bose-A Forgotten Hero' (both directed by Shyam Benegal), 'Train to Pakistan' (directed by Pamela Rooks) and 'Sardar' (directed by Ketan Mehta). The festival also has a film on unknown freedom fighters. The entry to the festival is free and available on 'first come first served' basis. The first screening on each day is scheduled at 10.00 a.m. and the last at 5.30 p.m.

2258. (10-8-2007) NEW DELHI : National Commission for Protection of Child Rights has directed to the State Governments to take effective steps to check incidents of corporal punishment in school. Expressing concern over recent incidents of violence in schools, the Chairman of the Commission, Smt. Shantha Sinha in a letter of chief Secretary of State Government/UT has said that all forms of corporal punishment are a fundamental breach of human rights. Citing direction of the Supreme Court regarding ban on Corporal punishment in schools, she has said that the onus of responsibility in safeguarding children from punishment lies with the schools teachers, education administration at all levels as well as all those responsible for management equally.

2259. (10-8-2007) NEW DELHI : Government of India has drawn up a very ambitious Public Private Partnership (PPP) programme in infrastructure sectors, including the roads sector. To avoid delays that have been witnessed in the approval of publicly funded projects in the past, Public Private Partnership Appraisal Committee (PPPAC) has been set-up with the mandate to fast track the appraisal and approval of central sector PPP projects where the capital costs or underlying value of the assets is more than Rs. 250 crore. PPPAC is expected to complete its due diligence within a period of four weeks for final approval and the PPPAC has been keeping to this timeline. Since its constitution in January 2006, PPPAC has received forty proposals out of which 28 have been granted in-principle or final approval. The fast track clearance of projects in the Highways sector can be assessed from the very fact that out of 29 road projects received so far, 23 have been granted in-principle or final approval. In the past, the timeline for approval of central sector projects has generally been fourteen to sixteen weeks. The decisions of the PPPAC are consensual in nature and the Administrative Ministries participate in the decision making as members. Contrary to the general belief, large contingent liabilities can devolve on the Government in PPP projects because of sharing of risks further, since they involve transfer of public assets, including land, delegation of government authority to collect and appropriate user charges, provision of services to the users in a monopoly or semi monopoly situation etc., there is a special obligation imposed on the government to ensure service quality and due diligence before approval is granted. PPPAC has been adding value by accelerating the approval process within the Government, reducing the transaction costs and acting as a central focal point for identifying and disseminating best practices in rolling out PPPs across sectors and Ministries of the Government.

2260. (10-8-2007) NEW DELHI : Anti Collision Device (ACD), which is an on-board train protection device and also the first ever device in the world indigenously developed by Konkan Railway, will be in place by 2013 on the entire Indian Railway network so as to reduce chances of collisions. Pilot implementation of ACD, indigenously developed by Konkan Railway, has been successfully commissioned on the Northeast Frontier Railway this year. Survey for expanding the system to another 10,000 route kilometres falling on the critical and busy sections of the network is almost completed. The installation of this device will go a long way in preventing accidents due to collision which is more fatal in nature. The application of this device has been refined to not only prevent mid section collisions but also to pre-empt their occurrences in station yards. The newly engineered solution is integrated with the signalling systems and interlocking to react appropriately in case collision like conditions are perceived at the time of reception and dispatch of trains from a station. In addition, the design of crash-worthy coaches and tight lock couplers with anti-climbing features has already been finalised and all future coaches are being made as per new design. Despite the phenomenal increase in traffic, the numbers of consequential train accidents have come down from 464 in 2000-01 to 234 in 2005-06, a reduction of almost 50 per cent. In the year 2006-07, the numbers of accidents have further come down to 195, which is ever lowest since sixties. Safety is the prime concern of Indian Railways and all possible measures are being taken to ensure the safety of passengers.

2261. (10-8-2007) NEW DELHI : The Union Minister of Shipping, Road Transport and Highways, Thiru T. R. Baalu has approved the construction of a new High Level bridge in km 0/6-1/4 of Old Palar Bridge Road over River Palar in Vellor District of Tamil Nadu under the Centrally Sponsored Scheme of Inter State Connectivity. The proposed Bridge would be having 29 spans of 21m and would cost of Rs. 1341.73 lakh. It was brought to the notice of Thiru Baalu that several spans of the existing old distressed arch bridge were damaged in the floods some years back and since then the bridge and the road remained defunct. Therefore, the traffic bound for Andhra Pradesh, Karnataka and the local traffic to Katpadi and other Northern villages use the Cuddalore Chittoor road which has a two-lane bridge running parallel to the Old Palar Bridge road. To ease the traffic on this section, the Highway Research Station, Chennai has recommended divided carriageway for the proposed bridge. The Minister has therefore approved the proposal for construction of the new bridge with foot-path on either side and provision for reconstruction of approaches in 350m length on Chittoor side after dismantling the existing old cement concrete pavement which is in damaged condition.

2262. (12-8-2007) NEW DELHI : In the light of recent outbreak of avian influenza in Manipur, specific steps have been suggested by the ministry of Environment and Forests to monitor the migratory birds. All Chief Wildlife Wardens have been requested to step up surveillance and monitoring of any possible emergency arising out of the arrival of migratory birds in their respective states.

2263. (12-8-2007) NEW DELHI : In the light of recent outbreak of avian influenza in Manipur, specific steps have been suggested by the ministry of

Environment and Forests to monitor the migratory birds. All Chief Wildlife Wardens have been requested to step up surveillance and monitoring of any possible emergency arising out of the arrival of migratory birds in their respective states.

2264. (12-8-2007) NEW DELHI : The Centre is in touch with the Assam Government in the wake of recent terrorist attacks in which several innocent people have been killed. The Home Minister, Shri Shiv Raj Patil has strongly condemned the attacks and conveyed his sympathies to the bereaved families. He said that militants will not succeed in their designs of disturbing the tradition harmony among different communities in the State. The Home Minister, Shri Patil has also assured the Assam Government of full cooperation from the Centre in dealing with the situations. He said that the Government would not be cowed down by such attacks and would continue to work for establishing peace and normalcy in the State.

2265. (13-8-2007) NEW DELHI : "The Private Detective Agencies (Regulation) Bill, 2007" was introduced in the Rajya Sabha today, which provides for regulation of private detective agencies through the grant of licences by the appropriate authorities. The main objective of the proposed legislation is to ensure that the private detective agencies function within legal parameters and under proper norms and that they conduct their operations with due regard to the protection of rights of individuals. The Private Detective Agencies (Regulation) Bill, 2007 is on similar lines as The Private Security Agencies (Regulation) Act, 2005, which is already in force. In the recent years, a large number of private detective agencies have come up all over the country, whose services are being availed by the private establishments and individuals for private investigation. There have been suggestions that the functioning of these private detective agencies should be regulated by a law. A suggestion to enact a central legislation was made in 2005 during discussions on "The Private Security Agencies (Regulation) Bill, 2005" in the Rajya Sabha, wherein it was suggested to bring a law to regulate the private detective agencies. Hon'ble Union Home Minister had given an assurance to come to the House with a Bill for this purpose.

2266. (13-8-2007) NEW DELHI : India is the third largest coal producing country in the world after China and USA. With 96 billion tonnes of proved coal reserves India accounts for 9.4 % of World proved coal reserves. Coal is the most abundant and sustainable energy source in India. It contributes to around 55% in India's overall energy share. India produced 662.522 billion units of power during 2006-07 of which coal based generation was 431.126 billion units, aptly defining the lead role of coal in power generation of the country.

2267. (13-8-2007) NEW DELHI : India has a rich heritage by way of its ancient systems of medicine such as Ayurveda, Siddha, Unani, Yoga & Naturopathy (AYUSH). These systems of medicines and its practices are well accepted by the

Community and have their own areas of strength. Medicines are easily available and prepared from locally available resources, economical, and comparatively safe from side effects. Because of this fact the Central Government Health Scheme, introduced in 1954 with only Allopathic dispensaries, has added AYUSH component to its net work. The National Health Policy of 1983 envisages integration of Indian System of Medicine and Health (ISM&H) with the modern system of medicine. Similarly, the National Policy on ISM &H-2002 envisages integration of AYUSH with the modern system of medicine. Mainstreaming of AYUSH is the core strategy envisaged under National Rural Health Mission with an objective to improve outreach and quality of health delivery in rural areas. The objective of the integration of AYUSH in the health care infrastructure is to re-inforce the existing public health care delivery system, with the use of natural, safe and friendly remedies, which are time tested, accessible and affordable. Under National Rural Health Mission, AYUSH doctors and facilities are being co-opted in Primary Health Centres, Community Health Centres and District Hospitals. The guidelines to include AYUSH practitioners at all levels in NRHM including state Health Mission, District Mission and Rogi Kalyan Samitis have been issued.

2268. (13-8-2007) NEW DELHI : The Government has already introduced Judges (Inquiry) Bill, 2006 in the Lok Sabha on December 19, 2006. The Bill seeks to devise a suitable legislative framework for empowering a judicial forum to deal with complaints against judges of the Supreme Court and High Courts. As far as the District and Subordinate Courts are concerned, the respective High Courts are empowered to take cognizance of complaints against the members of the lower judiciary. This was stated by the Minister of State for Law & Justice, Shri K. Venkatapathy in a written reply in Rajya Sabha today to a question whether government's attention has been drawn towards the Globe Corruption Report, 2007 of Transparency International regarding corruption in judiciary. In another written reply, Shri Venkatapathy said that the Judges (Inquiry) Bill, 2006 provides for setting up of a National Judicial Council. The National Judicial Council shall draw up a Code of Conduct for Judges, which may provide that every Judge at the time of appointment as a Judge of the Supreme Court or of the High court and thereafter shall annually give intimation of assets and liabilities to the Chief Justice of India or the Chief Justice of the High Court as the case may be.

2269. (13-8-2007) NEW DELHI : The next general elections to the Lok Sabha may be held on the basis of the newly carved out constituencies only if these delimitation orders in respect of all the parliamentary and assembly constituencies are issued by the Delimitation Commission and notified by the President by then. So far, the Delimitation Commission has completed delimitation work in respect of 22 states/union territories, namely, Kerala, Tripura, Mizoram, Goa, Pondicherry, Rajasthan, West Bengal, Punjab, Maharashtra, Sikkim, National Capital Territory of Delhi, Chhattisgarh, Uttar Pradesh, Gujarat, Orissa, Uttaranchal, Himachal Pradesh, Madhya Pradesh, Haryana, Andhra Pradesh, Karnataka and Meghalaya.

Meanwhile, the Government has received numerous representations challenging the provisions of the Delimitation Act, the procedure adopted by the Commission, the guidelines issued by it in pursuance thereto as well as the recommendations as regards delimitation of constituencies made by it. This was stated by the Minister for Law & Justice, Shri H. R. Bhardwaj in a written reply in Rajya Sabha today. In reply to another question, Shri Bhardwaj said that the Delimitation Commission has been given an extension up to the July 31, 2008, by which time, it is hoped it would complete its work.

2270. (13-8-2007) NEW DELHI : The Government has proposed expansion of National Child Labour Projects (NCLP) Scheme to all child labour endemic districts during the XI Five Year Plan. The objective is to increase the coverage of child labour under this rehabilitation scheme. However, it is subject to the necessary approvals. The districts are identified on the basis of endemicity of child labour as per the Census data and also on the recommendation of the concerned State Government. The National Child Labour Project Scheme is at present being implemented in 250 districts of the country for the rehabilitation of working children. This was stated by the Minister of State (Independent Charge) of Labour and Employment, Shri Oscar Fernandes in a written reply in Lok Sabha today.

2271. (13-8-2007) NEW DELHI : The World Bank is providing loan to improve the vocational training system in the country. International Development Association (IDA) has in June 2007 approved a credit of US $ 280 million (equivalent to Rs. 1231 crore) towards central share for taking up the 'Vocational Training Improvement Project' for upgradation of 400 Industrial Training Institutes (ITIs) in June 2007. No amount has been provided in the last three years. The project envisages upgradation of 400 Industrial Training Institutes on a cost of sharing basis between Central and State Government in the ratio of 75:25 respectively except for North Eastern States and Sikkim where sharing ratio is 90:10. The State Government would be responsible for implementation of the Scheme in the respective state. This was stated by the Minister of State (Independent Charge) of Labour and Employment, Shri Oscar Fernandes in a written reply in Lok Sabha today. In another reply, the Minister said that DGE&T under the Ministry of Labour & Employment is implementing Craftsman Training Scheme in the country.

2272. (13-8-2007) NEW DELHI : The National Commission for Enterprises in the Unorganised Sector (NCEUS) has, in its report, recommended for national minimum social security benefits for unorganised sector workers which, inter-alia, include life and disability cover, health insurance, old age protection and any other scheme as deemed necessary. The Commission has also recommended the imposition of social security tax for the benefit of workers in the unorganised sector. The proposals and the suggestions received thereon were examined. The Unorganised Sector Workers Social Security Bill is under active consideration and Government intends to introduce the Bill during the current session of Parliament. This was stated by the Minister of State (Independent Charge) of Labour and Employment, Shri Oscar Fernandes in a written reply in Lok Sabha today.

2273. (13-8-2007) NEW DELHI : There is not any proposal to increase the rate of EPF to bring it at par with the rates provided by banks. This was stated by the Minister of State (Independent Charge) of Labour and Employment, Shri Oscar Fernandes in a written reply in Lok Sabha today. He said the rate of interest declared to be credited in EPF Accounts in any particular year is determined in such a manner that there should be no overdrawal on the Interest Suspense Account as a result of debit thereto of the interest credited to members' accounts. The Minister said that while recommending the rate of interest for a particular year, the estimated liabilities on account of interest payable to members as well as estimated interest earnings are taken into consideration by the Board. The recommended interest rate is directly proportional to the earnings realised on EPF investments. The Minister said that as per the information provided by SBI, the rates of FDs offered to senior citizens have ranged between 5.50% to 8.75% during the period 1st January 2004 to 31st March 2007. Shri Fernandes said that the rate of interest declared by the Government for the years 2004-05 and 2005-06 was 9.5% and 8.5% respectively. The rate of interest recommended by the Central Board of Trustees, Employees' Provident Fund for the year 2006-07 is 8.5%. However, the rate of interest for the year 2007-08 has not so far been recommended by the Board.

2274. (13-8-2007) NEW DELHI : 549 non-Governmental organizations/voluntary organizations received grants from the Ministry of Science and Technology during the last three years namely, 2004-05, 2005-06 & 2006-07. The total amount allocated to these organizations was Rs. 84,49,68,061/- . These organizations are sanctioned funds for undertaking projects, conducting workshops and training programmes, based on proposals received from them. Each proposal is carefully evaluated by the Ministry through internal scrutiny, peer group reviews and committees of experts before sanctioning funds. Multiple criteria are applied before sanctioning projects and would include relevance of the project for societal benefits, competence and experience of organizations, competence of project investigators and need assessment for projects. This information was given by the Union Minister for Science & Technology and Earth Sciences Shri Kapil Sibal in a written reply to a question in the Lok Sabha.

2275. (13-8-2007) NEW DELHI : Government of India have announced the sale (re-issue) of "5.48 percent Government Stock, 2009" under Market Stabilization Scheme for a notified amount of Rs. 4,000 crore (nominal). The Government Stock will be sold through price based auction using multiple price method. The auction will be conducted by the Reserve Bank of India, Mumbai Office, Fort, Mumbai on August 16, 2007 (Thursday). Up to 5% of the amount notified for the sale of stock is reserved for allotment to eligible individuals and Institutions on non-competitive basis as per the Scheme for Non-Competitive Bidding Facility in the

Auction of Government Securities. Bids in the prescribed form obtainable from the Regional Director, Reserve Bank of India, Mumbai Office (Public Debt Office), Fort, Mumbai-400 001 and RBI website www.rbi.org.in should be submitted to that Office on August 16, 2007. The NDS members should submit competitive as well as non-competitive bids in electronic format using Primary Market Operation (PMO) module of NDS. All bids should be submitted by 12.30 P.M.

2276. (13-8-2007) NEW DELHI : The first Mini-Pravasi Bharatiya Diwas (Mini-PBD-2007) will be organized in New York on 23rd September 2007 by the Ministry of Overseas Indian Affairs (MOIA). This was announced by Shri. Vayalar Ravi on the occasion of signing of a Memorandum of Understanding with Confederation of Indian Industry (CII) on the Know Indian Programme (KIP) here today. He said that the PIOs and NRI's from North and South American Continents will participate in the Mini-PBD. He informed that the second largest number of PIOs are living in Caribbean countries. The Indian Associations in these Continents will also be associated in this event. The MOIA signed an MOU with the CII to organize the Know India Programme to introduce the overseas Indian youth to the culture, heritage, history, economy and development of India and to establish and maintain a website for the purpose involving a network of these youth. The Know India Program (KIP) which was earlier known as the Internship Program for Diaspora Youth (IPDY) is an on-going programme of the Ministry of Overseas Indian Affairs, which aims at associating closely the younger generation of the Indian Diaspora with India. It provides a unique forum for students and young professionals of Indian origin to share their views, expectations and experience and bond closely with contemporary India. It creates awareness about the phenomenal transformation taking place in India and the country's progress from just a destination for culture, heritage and art to an emerging powerhouse in the global economic system. The participants also meet senior dignitaries in India including the President and the Prime Minister. This is a 2/3-week comprehensive orientation programme organized by the Ministry, 2-3 times a year including one to coincide with the Pravasi Bharatiya Divas held every year around 09 January. The participants comprising of overseas Indians in the age group of 20-28 years who have distinguished themselves in any field and have abiding interest in India and links with India through parentage, are selected. In order to give the youth more exposure to the latest developments in the economic and industrial scenario of India, it has been decided to organize them in partnership with CII, which has its own youth wing and youth programme. The youth wing of the CII known as Young Indians would execute the programme on behalf of CII in Delhi and in the States. The first KIP of the current financial year is being organized in partnership with the state of Goa. KIPs are done in partnership with a State Government who host the participants and in coordination with Nehru Yuva Kendra Sangathan. The participants have had the opportunity to visit the States and understand the various facets of the States. The Ministry has organized six such programmes till now, the first in 2003-04 in Delhi, the second in 2004-05 in partnership with the states of Maharashtra and Andhra Pradesh, the third in 2005 in partnership with Uttranchal, the fourth during 2005-06 in partnership with Karnataka and Andhra Pradesh, the fifth in 2006 in partnership with Himachal Pradesh and sixth programme was held in 2006-07 in partnership with the state of Kerala and Rajasthan respectively.

2277. (13-8-2007) NEW DELHI : Government of Japan has recently introduced a Double Track Mechanism for providing ODA loan to India in two batches. An Exchange of Notes took place today between Shri Kumar Sanjay Krishna, Joint Secretary (Bilateral Cooperation), Ministry of Finance, Government of India and Mr. Yasukuni Enoki, Ambassador of Japan to India. Government of Japan would provide loan for an amount of Yen 39,555 million (Rs. 1345 crores approximately) to India as its Official Development Assistance for FY 2007 Loan Package under First Batch of Double Track. The loan has been provided to fund 2 (two) projects in power transmission, and water supply and sewerage sectors. The rate of interest for Goa Water Supply & Sewerage Project would be 1.3% per annum and the rate of interest would be 0.75% per annum for Maharashtra Transmission System Project. The repayment period would be thirty years (including a grace period of ten years) for the Goa Project and for Maharashtra Transmission System Project the repayment period would be fifteen years (including a grace period of five years). India and Japan have had a long and fruitful history of bilateral development cooperation since 1958. This is expected to be further strengthened and broad based in future. Indo-Japan bilateral development cooperation has seen remarkable and progressive expansion in recent years.

2278. (13-8-2007) NEW DELHI : The Tsunami Warning system is scheduled to be operational by the end of September 2007. Coastal areas will be identified with respect to their vulnerability to various scenarios of tsunamis using tsunami models. The warnings will be issued within an hour of Tsunami causing Earthquake, while the Tsunami alert will be generated within half an hour of the Earthquake. This will give a minimum of two hours to inhabitants in the coastal India, except for Andaman & Nicobar Islands. For the islands, the alert itself will be warning. Communication of real time data from Tide Gauges and Bottom Pressure recorders to the Early Warning Centre at Indian National Centre for Ocean Information Services (INCOIS), Hyderabad is very critical for generating timely tsunami warning and advanced communication facilities are being established. At present real-time data is being received at INCOIS through V-SAT connectivity from the already installed Tide gauges and Bottom Pressure Recorders (BPRs). The Seismic data from the Real Time Seismic Monitoring Network being installed by India Meteoroligical Department (IMD) will be received at Central Receiving Station INCOIS through V-SAT connectivity. The entire system is expected to be operational by September 2007. A Virtual Private Network for Disaster Management Support (VPNDMS) node has been setup at INCOIS that facilitates reliable connectivity to the Ministry of Home Affairs for dissemination of Warnings. This information was given by the Union Minister for Science & Technology and Earth Sciences Shri Kapil Sibal in a written reply to a question in the Rajya Sabha today.

2279. (13-8-2007) NEW DELHI : The Working Group on Power for the Eleventh Plan (2007-12) based on certain assumptions, has estimated a total fund requirement of about Rs. 10,31,600 crores for the power sector as a whole. For creation of projected capacity addition, fund requirement has been assessed at about Rs. 4,10,900 crores by the Working Group. Out of the now proposed capacity addition of about 78500 MW, 1870 MW has already been commissioned and another 50,975 MW is under construction. Power Finance Corporation and Rural Electrification Corporation have geared up to mobilize funds to ensure that viable projects do not suffer for want of funds. Further, to facilitate financial closure in respect of private sector projects, an Inter Institutional Group, comprising of leading financial institutions and banks, is functional. However, for equity contribution in respect of private sector projects, the developers have to make arrangements from their internal resources, while for meeting the equity requirements in respect of Central and State Sector projects, public sector undertaking/utilities have to make arrangements from their internal resources and /or budgetary support. With the projected capacity in place and through energy conservation measures, the gap between demand and supply of electricity is likely to be bridged gradually during the course of the 11th Plan. This information was given by the Power Minister Shri Sushilkumar Shinde in a written reply to a question in the Rajya Sabha today.

2280. (13-8-2007) NEW DELHI : 100% Foreign Direct Investment has already been permitted on the automatic approval route in respect of projects relating to electricity generation, transmission and distribution (other than Atomic Energy power plants) including hydro-based electricity projects in Sikkim and other parts of the country. In addition, fiscal incentives are also available under the mega power policy, subject to compliance of certain conditions. Under the mega policy, a lower qualifying capacity has been provided for the states of J&K, Sikkim and the North-Eastern States at a minimum 350 MW for hydel power projects and 700 MW for thermal power projects as compared to a minimum of 500 MW for hydel power projects and 1000 MW for thermal power projects in the other parts of the country. This information was given by the Power Minister Shri Sushilkumar Shinde in a written reply to a question in the Rajya Sabha today.

2281. (13-8-2007) NEW DELHI : 100% Foreign Direct Investment has already been permitted on the automatic approval route in respect of projects relating to electricity generation, transmission and distribution (other than Atomic Energy power plants) including hydro-based electricity projects in Sikkim and other parts of the country. In addition, fiscal incentives are also available under the mega power policy, subject to compliance of certain conditions. Under the mega policy, a lower qualifying capacity has been provided for the states of J&K, Sikkim and the North-Eastern States at a minimum 350 MW for hydel power projects and 700 MW for thermal power projects as compared to a minimum of 500 MW for hydel power projects and 1000 MW for thermal power projects in the other parts of the country. This information was given by the Power Minister Shri Sushilkumar Shinde in a written reply to a question in the Rajya Sabha today.

2282. (13-8-2007) NEW DELHI : The 2006 estimates released recently by the National AIDS Control Organisation, supported by UNAIDS and WHO, indicate that an estimated 2 million to 3.1 million people are living with HIV in the country. These estimates are more accurate than those of previous years, as they are based on an expanded surveillance system and a revised and enhanced methodology. The methodology adopted use of multiple data sources including National Family Health Survey-3. The new methods developed for the revised estimates have also been used to "back-calculate" the prevalence for years since 2002 based on the new set of assumptions and measures. These figures allow a fair comparison of year-on-year trends in HIV prevalence. They show an epidemic that is stable over time with marginal decline in 2006.

2283. (13-8-2007) NEW DELHI : A meeting was called in New Delhi to review the Chikungunya situation in nine states namely, Andhra Pradesh, Delhi, Goa, Gujarat, Karnataka, Kerala, Maharashtra, Puducherry and Tamil Nadu on 21st June 2007. The Chikungunya is likely to stay for 3-4 more years, however, it is expected that the disease will not occur in epidemic form after 3-4 years in areas which have been presently affected because it gives life long immunity. In addition to supply of regular logistics (Adulticides and larvicides) during 2006-07, an amount of Rs. 21.60 crore was released as emergency package to 11 States, namely, Andhra Pradesh, Andaman & Nicobar Islands, Delhi, Gujarat, Karnataka, Kerala, Maharashtra, Madhya Pradesh, Puducherry, Rajasthan and Tamil Nadu for prevention and control activities of Chikungunya. Similarly, during 2007-08, Rs. 17.29 crorre have been allotted to nine States and Rs. 8.75 crore have been released in first phase. The funds were utilized by the States for additional larvicides/Pyrethrum Extract, fogging machines, etc. for intensive prevention and control measures. The funds were also used for intensive IEC activities and social mobilization activities for community awareness to avoid mosquito breeding in domestic/peri domestic areas. This information was given by the Minister for Health & Family Welfare, Dr. Anbumani Ramadoss in a written reply to a question in the Rajya Sabha.

2284. (13-8-2007) NEW DELHI : Chikungunya fever was reported first time in Kerala during 2006 with a total 70731 suspected cases and no death. Out of the total 235 samples tested, 43 (18.29%) were confirmed serologically for Chikungunya. In the year 2007, there were 21590 suspected Chikungunya fever cases. However, no death has been reported till 5th August. Out of the 3845 samples tested, 550 (14.30%) have been confirmed serologically for Chikungunya. The State had also reported 981 cases of dengue in 2006 and 188 cases in 2007 till 5th August. In addition to supply of regular logistics (Adulticides and larvicides), an amount of Rs. 220.50 lakh was released to the State during 2006-07, as emergency package for prevention and control activities of Chikungunya. During 2007-08 also, Rs. 403.90 lakh has been released to the State as emergency package for prevention and control of Chikungunya. Central teams visited the State during May, June and July this year to provide technical guidance to the State Government. In 2007, four deaths have been reported due to dengue. However, no deaths have been reported due to Chikungunya. This information was given by the Minister for Health & Family Welfare, Dr. Anbumani Ramadoss in a written reply to a question in the Rajya Sabha.

2285. (13-8-2007) NEW DELHI : There is no such thing as "artificial milk/ synthetic milk." The term "synthetic milk" is a misnomer. Under the Prevention of Food Adulteration (PFA) Rules, 1955, milk is defined as the normal mammary secretion derived from complete milking of an healthy milk animal without either addition thereto or extraction there from. It shall be free from colostrum. Milk of different classes and of different designations shall conform to the standards laid down under the provisions of PFA Rules, 1955. As per rule 44(l) of the PFA Rules, 1955, sale of milk and milk products containing substances not found in milk except as prescribed in the Prevention of Food Adulteration Rules, 1955, is prohibited. The existing law is enough for curbing such menace. Sale of any adulterated and misbranded article of food is an offence punishable with minimum imprisonment of six months and with fine, which shall not be less than Rs.1000/ - . In case adulterated foodstuff causes death or grievous hurt, the offence is punishable with imprisonment, which may extend to term of life and with fine which shall not be less than Rs.5000/- . All State Governments have been requested to take necessary action to keep strict vigil on the quality of milk particularly for presence of chemical substances. This information was given by the Minister of State for Health & Family Welfare, Smt. Panabaka Lakshmi in a written reply to a question in the Rajya Sabha.

2286. (13-8-2007) NEW DELHI : Under Indira Awas Yojana (IAY), the Ministry of Rural Development has released the first instalment of Central assistance of Rs. 71.94 lakh out of the Central allocation of Rs.143.89 lakh to the Thoubal, District Rural Development Agency (DRDA) of Manipur, for the year 2007-08. The grant is towards the Plan expenditure and will be utilized for construction of new houses/upgradation of kutcha houses into pucca houses, subject to the conditions laid down in the guidelines under the IAY. The expenditure on the implementation of the programme is to be shared on 75:25 basis between the Centre and the State respectively. The State Government is to release its share within a month of the date of release of the Central assistance.

2287. (13-8-2007) NEW DELHI : Replying to a question about the procedure for seeking assistance from Government for unemployed youths of minority communities for their self-employment and the amount of assistance provided to them, the Minority Affairs Minister, Shri A.R. Antulay has informed the Rajya Sabha today that the National Minorities Development and Finance Corporation (NMDFC) provides loans at concessional rates for self employment/income generating activities to persons belonging to the minority communities living below double the poverty line. He further informed that under the term loan scheme of NMDFC, a maximum loan amount of Rs. 5.0 lakhs is admissible to the beneficiary. Similarly, under the micro-credit scheme a loam amount of Rs.25,000 is available per member of the Self Help Group (SHG). A statement showing the amounts disbursed, State/UT wise, for the last three years is enclosed as Annexure. This information was given in reply to an Unstarred Question in the Rajya Sabha today.

2288. (13-8-2007) NEW DELHI : The Minority Affairs Minister, Shri A.R. Antulay has informed the Rajya Sabha that Government has already considered the report submitted by Justice Rajendra Sachhar Committee for upliftment of the Muslim Community and a decision taken regarding the follow up action.

2289. (13-8-2007) NEW DELHI : The Regional Deputy Directors of Wildlife Preservation and Officers of the Wildlife Wing reviewed the progress of Wildlife Crime Control Bureau, today. The meeting has taken important decisions regarding staff deployment and filling up of posts as well as procurement of necessary infrastructure. It was decided that till a full time Officer is appointed, Regional Deputy Director (WR) will look after the functioning of the newly created Regional Office of the Crime Control Bureau, at Jabalpur, Madhya Pradesh. Out of six posts of Assistant Directors, three will be posted at Sub-Regional Offices and three will be posted at Headquarters. Out of these six posts, two will be selected from Police and four from Forests. Eighteen posts of Inspectors will be filled. Regional Offices at Chennai, Kolkata and Mumbai will have two persons each and New Delhi and Jabalpur, one person each. Three Sub-Regional Offices as well as Five Border Stations will have one Inspector and one Person respectively. Headquarter will have two Inspectors. The posts of Inspectors will also be filled. Seven new Inspectors will be taken, two from Forests and five from Police Departments. Twenty-five posts of Guards/Constables will have 17 persons from Police and Eight from Forests Department. Southern, Eastern, Western, Northern and Central Region will have three Guards each, Sub-Regional Offices at Cochin, Amritsar and Guwahati will have two Guards each and Headquarter will have four Guards. The jurisdiction of Regional Offices also has been defined. Wildlife Crime Control Bureau, Regional Office (WCCB-RO), Mumbai, will look after Goa, Gujarat, Maharashtra, Daman and Diu and Dadara and Nagar Haveli. WCCB-RO, Delhi, will cover Haryana, Himachal Pradesh, Rajasthan, Uttar Pradesh, Uttarakhand and

Delhi. WCCB-RO, Kolkatta, will cover Bihar, Meghalaya, Mizoram, Nagaland, Sikkim, Tripura and West Bengal. Andhra Pradesh, Karnataka, Tamil Nadu and Pondicherry under WCCB-RO, Chennai. Chhatisgarh, Jharkhand, Madhya Pradesh and Orissa will fall under jurisdiction of the new Office of WCCB-RO Jabalpur at Madhya Pradesh, Pubjab, Jammu and Kashmir and Chandigarh, under WCCB-Sub-RO, Amritsar, Arunachal Pradesh, Assam and Manipur under WCCB-Sub-RO and Guwahati and Kerala, Lakshadweep and Andaman and Nicobar Islands will fall under WCCB-Sub-RO, Cochin. These Offices will assist and advise Custom Authorities in the inspection of consignments of flora and fauna as per the provisions of Wildlife (Protection) Act, CITES and Exim Policy. They will collect and collate intelligence related to organised wildlife crime activities and disseminate them to State and other enforcement agencies for immediate action. They will develop infrastructure and capacity building for scientific and professional investigation into wildlife crimes.

2290. (13-8-2007) NEW DELHI : The existing Gross Enrolment Ratio (GER) for the relevant age group is 9.7% (2006-07). It is proposed that enrolment in the higher education be increased to achieve the targeted GER of 15% by the end of the XIth Five Year Plan. The UGC provides grants to those Institutions, which meet the minimum standards prescribed by it. In addition, the UGC provides assistance to Universities, Departments/Centres and Colleges with potential for excellence. The National Assessment and Accreditation Council (NAAC), an inter-university Centre of the UGC, accredits Universities and Colleges. The NAAC has so far assessed 50% of the Universities and 20% of the Colleges. Accreditation by NAAC is not compulsory. Private not-for-profit participation in higher education is permissible under the national policy. This was stated by the Minister of State for Human Resource Development Smt. D. Purandeswari in a written reply in the Rajya Sabha today.

2291. (13-8-2007) NEW DELHI : The Gross Enrolment Ratio (GER) of higher education is at present 9.7% (2006-07), which is lower in comparison to many developing countries. Various schemes of development assistance to eligible colleges and universities for improving quality of higher education are being implemented. These schemes aim, inter-alia, at improving curriculum, strengthening infrastructure, orientation and in-service training of the teachers and encourage research. The University Grants Commission provides Special Development Grant for universities in Backward Areas. It is also proposed to assist State Government's, to incentivise them to establish one college in each district which has a low Gross Enrolment Ratio, during the XI Plan, subject to availability of resources. This was stated by the Minister of State for Human Resource Development Smt. D. Purandeswari in a written reply in the Rajya Sabha today.

2292. (13-8-2007) NEW DELHI : A proposal for setting up of 16 Central

Universities-one each in such States as have no Central University-is in the process of being finalized. Orissa being one of such States, its request for establishment of a Central University in the tribal dominated KBK region shall receive due consideration. Further, a Bill for setting up a Central Tribal University is in the process of being introduced in the current session of the Parliament. The proposed University shall have power to establish its Regional Centres in the areas inhabited by tribal population, which could include KBK region of Orissa. This was stated by the Minister of State for Human Resource Development Smt. D. Purandeswari in a written reply in the Rajya Sabha today.

2293. (13-8-2007) NEW DELHI : Subject to availability of resources, it is proposed to establish new Central Universities and to develop existing Universities to world standards. The XIth Plan is yet to be finalized. This was stated by the Minister of State for Human Resource Development Smt. D. Purandeswari in a written reply in the Rajya Sabha today.

2294. (13-8-2007) NEW DELHI : It is proposed to establish 30 Central Universities during the XIth Plan and the first two years of the XIIth Plan period, subject to the Plan being finalized. While a common entrance test would be desirable, in keeping with the NCMP commitment of the autonomy, any such decision would be taken by the concerned Universities after they come into existence. An estimated 20% of the budgeted expenditure on higher education is met currently by the Central Government. Action for establishment, in the first phase, of one Central University in each of the 16 States which do not have a Central University so far has already been initiated. The financial requirement of these Universities is estimated at Rs.4,800 crore during the 11th Plan period at an average of Rs.300 crore per University. This was stated by the Minister of State for Human Resource Development Smt. D. Purandeswari in a written reply in the Rajya Sabha today.

2295. (13-8-2007) NEW DELHI : It is proposed to establish during the XIth Plan, one Central University in each State with no such University and provide assistance for establishing one college in each district with low Gross Enrolment Ratio in higher education. As at present, 23 Central Universities in 14 States/Union Territories have been functioning under the purview of Ministry of Human Resource Development. Action for establishment of a Central University in each of the remaining 16 States, namely Bihar, Chhattisgarh, Goa, Gujarat, Haryana, Himachal Pradesh, Jammu and Kashmir, Jharkhand, Karnataka, Kerala, Madhya Pradesh, Orissa, Punjab, Rajasthan, Tamil Nadu and Uttarakhand, has already been initiated. This was stated by the Minister of State for Human Resource Development Smt. D. Purandeswari in a written reply in the Rajya Sabha today.

2296. (13-8-2007) NEW DELHI : Ministry of Human Resource Development in collaboration with National AIDS Control Organization (NACO), has launched Adolescence Education Programme which is meant for secondary and higher secondary classes with the objective to empower the adolescent population to make informed choices and develop life skills for addressing psychological, social and health concerns. According to information received by National Council of Educational Research and Training (NCERT), State government of Gujarat has decided not to implement Adolescence Education Programme, and the State Government of Kerala has decided to review the content of the programme. The State Government of Maharashtra is in the process of reviewing the content of the programme. The State Government of Rajasthan has informed that it has decided not to implement the programme in its present form. Reasons for refusal are not uniform, but the main cause for opposition has been some of the material for use under the Programme. (c): Before introduction of Adolescence Education Programme, A National seminar involving various stakeholders including experts, educationists, State Govt. representatives, teachers, parents and the adolescent was held to elicit opinion. These were followed by regional seminars. This was stated by the Minister of State for Human Resource Development Shri M.A.A. Fatmi in a written reply in the Rajya Sabha today.

2297. (13-8-2007) NEW DELHI : The Government have decided to set up three new Indian Institutes of Technology (IITs), one each in the States of Andhra Pradesh, Bihar and Rajasthan, for which 'in principle' approval of the Planning Commission has been obtained. When fully developed, each IIT will have about 3000 students in various programmes. For the new IITs, respective State Governments will provide land free of cost. The recurring and non-recurring costs will be borne by the Central Government. No public-private partnership is contemplated in setting up of new IITs. This was stated by the Minister of State for Human Resource Development Smt. D. Purandeswari in a written reply in the Rajya Sabha today.

2298. (13-8-2007) NEW DELHI : The Press Information Bureau has made special arrangements for webcast of President's Address to the Nation on the eve of Independence Day and also the Prime Minister's Independence Day Address on its website in collaboration with the National Informatics Centre. These webcasts will be available simultaneously with their telecast on Doordarshan. The President's address will be available on www.pib.nic.in. starting at 7 p.m. on 14th August and the Independence Day celebrations starting from 7 a.m. on 15th August. PIB's website is widely used website for authentic information relating to the Government's initiatives and policies. On an average, it receives nearly 2 lakh hits per day. It caters to the information needs of mediapersons and also the general public. PIB took this initiative of making available the above important speeches starting from 2005 with a view to disseminate them to a larger audience using advances in modern technology. PIB and NIC have been collaborating for webcasts of Prime Minister's addresses and other important events. An audio visual archive has been created on PIB's website for video on demand.

2299. (13-8-2007) NEW DELHI : As there is a substantial requirement for the armed forces for special clothing and sleeping bags in high altitude locations, OFB has been exploring the possibility of setting up a suitable manufacturing facility. They have contacted the major manufacturers in the field including a company from Switzerland. After evaluation of the capabilities of different manufacturers, OFB plans to take steps for technical collobaration for manufacturing the items, after inviting tenders as per the prescribed procedure.

2300. (13-8-2007) NEW DELHI : Government proposes to set up two new defence production units of which one is for the production of Bi-Modular Charge System (BMCS), and the other is for production of new generation carbines. The project for production of BMCS at Nalanda has already been approved by the Government. The revision in project cost is now pending approval. The unit for production of new generation carbines is under consideration of the Government. Private sector companies can obtain industrial licence for production of arms and ammunition and set up manufacturing facilities. This information was given by the Minister of State for Defence Production Rao Inderjit Singh in a written reply to Shri Rayapati Sambasiva Rao and others in Lok Sabha today.

2301. (13-8-2007) NEW DELHI : A Memorandum Of Understanding (MOU) was signed on 29 May 2006 between the Ministry of Defence of the Republic of India and the Ministry of National Defence of the People's Republic of China for exchanges and cooperation in the field of Defence. The MOU, inter alia includes provision that both the countries will endeavour to hold joint military exercises in the fields of search and rescue, anti-piracy, counter terrorism and other areas of mutual interest. This information was given by the Defence Minister Shri AK Antony in a written reply to Shri Rajnarayan Budholia in Lok Sabha today.

2302. (13-8-2007) NEW DELHI : The Bharat Sanchar Nigam Ltd (BSNL) has plans to introduce WiMAX services in the country, which will support mobility in future. BSNL will be floating a tender for procurement of WiMAX systems based on IEEE 802.16e-2005 standard. Mobility feature will be supported by these systems in future. BSNL has plans to provide WiMAX services through Franchisees. This information was given by Dr Shakeel Ahmad, Minister of State in the Ministry of Communications and Information Technology in the Lok Sabha today in a written reply to Shri Sanjay Dhotre and Smt. Bhavana P.Gawali.

2303. (13-8-2007) NEW DELHI : A committee has been constituted to study the present structure of taxes and levies applicable in the telecom sector. This information was given by Dr. Shakeel Ahmad, Minister of State in the Ministry of Communications and Information Technology in the Lok Sabha today in a written reply to a question by Shri Prahlad Joshi.

2304. (13-8-2007) NEW DELHI : The special Incentive Package Scheme to encourage investments for setting up Semi-conductor Fabrication and other micro and nano technology manufacture industries in India, has been announced by the Government vide Gazette Notification No. 78, Part I, Section I dated 21st March 2007. A copy of the Notification is available on the website http://www.mit.gov.in. As per para 7.1 of the above Notification, an Appraisal Committee has been set up by the Department of Information Technology. This information was given by Dr.Shakeel Ahmad, Minister of State in the Ministry of Communications and Information and Technology in the Lok Sabha today in a written reply to a question by Shri K.S.Rao.

2305. (13-8-2007) NEW DELHI : The Independence Day celebrations on 15th August are synonymous with the unfurling of the national flag by the Prime Minister on the Red Fort, in Delhi in the morning. As we celebrate the 61st Independence Day, we take a look at the ceremony at the Red Fort down the years. Pandit Jawaharlal Nehru, the first Prime Minister of independent India, unfurled the national flag for the first time on the Red Fort on August 16, 1947. Since then the hoisting of the tricolour atop the Red Fort has become a symbol of Indian independence and our pride. Figuratively speaking, Pandit Nehru hoisted the flag atop the Red Fort 17 times since 1947, the maximum number of times by any Indian Prime Minister during the sixty-one years of our independence. His daughter Indira Gandhi comes a close second, unfurling the tricolour 16 times. Next in the line, Shri Atal Behari Vajpayee has hoisted flag atop the Red Fort six times, followed by Rajiv Gandhi and PV Narasimha Rao-five each, Lal Bahadur Shastri in 1964 and '65, Morarji Desai in 1977 and '78, Charan Singh in 1979, Shri VP Singh-1990, Shri HD Deve Gowda-1996 and Shri Inder Kumar Gujral-1997. Interestingly, Gulzari Lal Nanda, in his two brief tenures as interim Prime Minister, never hoisted the flag, besides Chandra Shekhar. The present Prime Minister Dr. Manmohan Singh will be hoisting the national flag atop the Red Fort for the 4th time on August 15, 2007. We are releasing herewith photographs of the 12 different Prime Ministers who have unfurled the National Flag from the Ramparts of the Red Fort.

2306. (13-8-2007) NEW DELHI : Twenty-five insecticides and their formulations and four insecticide formulations are banned for import, manufacture and use in the country. In addition, two insecticides have been banned for use in the country except their manufacture for export. Restriction has been imposed on use of nine insecticides. The usage of 37 pesticides has been reviewed recently by an Expert Group, constituted by the Registration Committee, under the Insecticides Act, 1968. The recommendations of an Expert Group regarding twenty-one pesticides have been accepted by the Government. Consequently, the use of Fenthion is banned in agriculture except for locust control in scheduled desert area and public health and the use of Diazinon has been banned in agriculture except for household purposes. The use of Metoxuron has also been withdrawn. The recommendations regarding remaining pesticides are under consideration of the Government.

2307. (13-8-2007) NEW DELHI : Lok Sabha The central government has provided Rs 520 during 2006-07 for promotion of Drip Irrigation. Under the Centrally Sponsored Scheme on Micro Irrigation, which was launched during 2005-06 the implementing agencies prepare Annual Action Plan for taking up Drip and Sprinkler Irrigation. 50% of the system cost is provided as subsidy out of which, 40% is borne by the Central Government and 10% by the State Government. The remaining 50% is borne by the beneficiary either through his/her own resources or soft loan from financial institutions. As a result of this Scheme, 71662 ha. area has came under Drip Irrigation last year, 65155 ha. in Maharashtra and 39700 ha. in Rajasthan, followed by other States. This information was given by Shri Kanti Lal Bhuria, Minister of State for Agriculture in written reply to a question in the Lok Sabha today.

2308. (13-8-2007) NEW DELHI : The Coconut Development Board (CDB) has submitted a project proposal on "Replanting and Rejuvenation of Coconut Gardens in Traditional States" for revival of coconut gardens with main emphasis on Kerala to be implemented during XI Plan. The Proposal has been reviewed by Agriculture Ministry in consultation with representatives of Government of Kerala, Karnataka, Orissa, Tamil Nadu, Indian Council of Agricultural Research and CDB. The Board has accordingly revised the project for in-principle approval of the Planning Commission.

2309. (13-8-2007) NEW DELHI : Secretary of Ministry of Tourism, Shri Shilabhadra Banerjee, here today launched a Brand Channel on You Tube to help communicate the wonders of India to a worldwide audience. The Ministry, known worldwide for its "Incredible India" campaign, have made promotional Incredible India videos available to the YouTube community at www.youtube.com/India. Speaking on the occasion, Shri S. Banerjee said that Incredible India Campaign is well recognized all over the world and efforts are being made to maximize our reach. He said we have to show the world the progress India has made since its Independence 60 years ago. He said using YouTube website for promotion of Incredible India Campaign is an effort in that direction. YouTube one of the leaders in online video, and the premier site to watch and share original videos worldwide through the Web experience. As per the Neilsen NetRatings. www.youtube.com (main site) has about 48 million unique users in US only and it is the 8th most trafficked website in the world. Every minute, videos of six hours in combined are uploaded on www.youtube.com This Channel www.youtube.com/India will give further international exposure to "Incredible India" (which includes content related to India's Independence) and, with its dynamic video content, will complement the already content-rich web presence of the Ministry of Tourism's website http://www.incredibleindia.org. By creating this Brand website on YouTube, the Ministry of Tourism will enable people around the world to experience and engage with the marvels of India through the power of Incredible videos. Presently there are 18 Films/Videos uploaded on the site and more will be added in due course of time. Shri Shailesh Rao, Managing Director, Google India was also present on the launching ceremony.

2310. (13-8-2007) NEW DELHI : Department of Posts has made special arrangements for handling of Rakhi Mails from 16.8.2007 to 3.9.2007. Special posting counters are being set up in 34 important Post Offices in Delhi and Delhi Railway Station and New Delhi Railway Station during this period. Specially designed Rakhi Envelopes are also available for sale at Post Offices. Department of Posts has advised the public to post their Rakhis well in time to avoid last minute rush.

2311. (13-8-2007) NEW DELHI : The Public Sector Bharat Earth Movers Limited (BEML) under the Ministry of Defence has paid the second and final dividend cheque of Rs. 18 crores to Government of India for the financial year 2006-07 against its 61.23 per cent shareholding in the company. The cheque was handed over to Defence Minister Shri AK Antony by BEML Chairman and Managing Director Shri VRS Natarajan in New Delhi, today. With this BEML paid a total dividend of 120 percent for the financial year 2006-07 to the Government totalling Rs. 27 crores. BEML has already paid Rs. 9 crores being 40 % Interim Dividend to Government of India in February 2007. BEML has also reported improved results for the first quarter of the current financial year with sales turnover of Rs. 421.78 crores and profit before tax of Rs. 36.36 crores. BEML is poised to achieve total turnover of about Rs. 3000 crores for the current financial year with improved profitability. The company has an order book position of Rs. 1621 crores at the end of the first quarter of the current financial year and more orders including metro are in the pipeline.

2312. (13-8-2007) NEW DELHI : The Prime Minister, Dr. Manmohan Singh, felicitated the Vice-President and Chairman, Rajya Sabha, Shri Mohammad Hamid Ansari, here today. The following is the text of Prime Minister's welcome speech: "Mr. Chairman, Sir, I welcome you to this August House with great joy and pride. I have been a Member of this House for over 16 years. So I say with all sincerity that you come in a long line of distinguished Chairpersons, and you come with great distinction. You have had a distinguished service as a diplomat, representing our country in important capitals of the world and the United Nations. More recently, you have also served the cause of education as Vice Chancellor of the Aligarh Muslim University, and the cause of empowerment of all our minorities, as Chairperson, Minorities Commission. Your professional record, your sincere commitment to the ideals and values that define our Republic, your patriotism and your concern for the well being and welfare of our people have earned you the respect and admiration of our people. I am sure all of this will stand you in good stead in the years to come as you discharge your onerous responsibilities. Sir, this

House has a unique position in our Republic. It is both a House of States and a House of Elders. As House of States it offers a unique platform for every region of our country to have its voice heard in the highest councils of Government. As House of I Elders we are called upon to reflect, with patience and sobriety, on the issues of the day and legislation at hand. I am sure with your wide-ranging experience you will provide guidance and balance to the proceedings of the House. Sir, I have witnessed the proceedings of this House for many years, as its Members for the past 16 years, and as an official of the Government of India for almost two decades before that. This House has been witness to some very enriching and enlightening debates. However, in recent years we have also witnessed, with profound concern and sadness, repeated disruptions of proceedings and a regrettable unwillingness, on occasions, to engage in informed discussion. I hope all of this can be put behind us and we can restore to this House a sense of dignity and decorum that is expected of a House of Elders. Sir, I stand here to assure you the sincere cooperation of our government and the constituents of the United Progressive Alliance. All of us must work together to ensure that this House echoes the heartbeat of the Indian people and lives up to their expectations. Sir, I wish you well and wish you the best in discharging your constitutional responsibilities."

2313. (13-8-2007) NEW DELHI : Government has launched training programmes through its field institutions by reserving 22.5 per cent in Entrepreneurship Development Programmes (EDPs) and Entrepreneurship & Skill Development Programmes (ESDPs) for SC, ST, women and physically handicapped persons, as also giving them a stipend of Rs.500/- per candidate per month. Besides, the Ministry of Micro, Small & Medium Enterprises has decided that all SC, ST, women and physically handicapped candidates who are trained in EDPs and ESDPs, other than the reserved 22.5 per cent of programmes, shall also not have to pay any fees. A sum of Rs. 99.30 lakh will be utilized by the field institutes of the Ministry of MSME for this purpose from the Annual Plan allocation for the Ministry for the financial year 2007-08 under Scheduled Caste Sub Plan & Tribal Sub Plan. This information was given by the Minister of Micro, Small & Medium Enterprises, Shri Mahabir Prasad in a written reply to a question in Lok Sabha today.

2314. (13-8-2007) NEW DELHI : Under the Rural Employment Generation Programme (REGP) implemented through Khadi & Village Industries Commission (KVIC), entrepreneurs can establish village industries in rural areas and small towns with a population upto 20,000, by availing of Margin Money Assistance from KVIC and loans from Public Sector scheduled commercial banks, selected regional rural banks, cooperative banks, etc. for projects with a maximum cost of Rs.25 lakh. As per the guidelines of the REGP, only new projects are to be considered by banks for providing loans by them in combination with Margin Money Assistance through KVIC and the banks cannot assist any ongoing or already existing units. This information was given by the Minister of Micro, Small & Medium Enterprises, Shri Mahabir Prasad in a written reply to a question in Lok Sabha today.

2315. (13-8-2007) NEW DELHI : The State Government of Karnataka has detected 3027 cases of illegal mining which involves seizure of 3.05 lakh Metric Tonnes of ore/minerals and 3378 vehicles seized, lodging 427 FIRs, filing of 277 court cases and realizing Rs. 719.76 lakhs as fine during the year 2006. The Central Government has also directed State Governments to frame rules, constitute task forces at State/district level for preventing of illegal mining and furnish quarterly return on illegal mining for review by the Ministry of Mines. The State Government of Karnataka has constituted State Level and District Level Task Force Committee to curb the instances of illegal mining. State Governments have been empowered under Mines & Mineral (Development & Regulation) Act, 1957 to curb illegal mining, transportation & storage etc. This was stated by the Minister of State for Mines Dr. T. Subbarami Reddy in a written reply in the Rajya Sabha today.

2316. (13-8-2007) NEW DELHI : Deptt of Animal Husbandry, Dairying and Fisheries notified an outbreak of Avian influenza in Chingmeirong Village in East Imphal District of Manipur on 25.7.2007. The Central Rapid Response Team of Ministry of Health and F.W. deputed to Imphal is assisting the State Govt. The health status of the cullers are being monitored. Today, 359 cullers/supportive staff have been examined and they are under cover of Tamiflu. The population of the infected zone [0-3 Kms] are under active surveillance on daily basis. For such purpose, the State Govt. has deployed health teams consisting of 600 health personnel. In this zone the surveillance teams could cover 44,423 houses [population of 2,32,273] on 9th August, 2007. They detected 20 fever/ ARI cases some of which are follow-up of earlier cases. These cases are being monitored. Surveillance activity is also continuing with 143 health workers in the 3 to 10 Kms zone. 4,292 houses with a population of 23,951 in Tengdongyang, Maklang, Langthabal Lap, Sangomsang, Keirao Bitra, Keirao Bitra, Keirao Makting, Urembam, Shamushang, Singjamei Chirom Leikai, Chongtham Leikai, Thongju Part I, Ningombam, Kudompokpi, Kiyamgei Awang Lei, Konjeng, Hajari Leikai, Thochom Lei, Paurabi, Langjing Kolom/Achouba, Awang Khunou, Chingamakha areas have been covered. No cases of fever/ARI were detected. As of now a cumulative population of 2,34,013 have been covered in the 3-10 Km zone. Arrangements have been made in J.N. Hospital, Imphal for isolation and critical care. This is in addition to the critical care facilities available at Regional Institute of Medical Sciences, Imphal. Adequate supply of logistics [Tamiflu (25,000 caps), N-95 masks (1000) and personal protective gears (2000)] have been made available to the State Government. As of now, there is no suspected human cases of Avian Influenza. As the situation is reported to be normal, daily status report is being discontinued. However, the situation would continue to be monitored.

2317. (13-8-2007) NEW DELHI : Indian Railways have carried 247.05 million tonnes of revenue earning freight traffic during the first four months (*i.e.* April-July 2007) of the current financial year 2007-08. The freight carried shows an increase of 13.84 million tonnes over the freight traffic of 233.21 million tonnes actually carried during the corresponding period last year, reflecting an increase of 5.93 per cent. During the month of July 2007, the revenue earning freight traffic carried by Indian Railways was 61.80 million tonnes. There is an increase of 4.43 million tonnes over the freight traffic of 57.37 million tonnes actually carried by the Indian Railways during the same period last year, reflecting an increase of 7.72 per cent.

2318. (13-8-2007) NEW DELHI : The Ministry of Health & Family Welfare would like to refer to the new item that appeared on page 1, captioned, "Health in for ban on cola ads, I&B resist" and on page 16, captioned, "Ban on ads will hurt industry badly" in the Times of India dated 7th August 2007 and would like to clarify that the proposed meeting on 16.8.2007 is for considering appropriate mechanism to regulate advertisements for carbonated water and other provisions which could be misleading or contravening the existing provisions of the Prevention of Food Adulteration Act, 1954. The representative of the Ministry of Information & Broadcasting has also been invited to attend the meeting on 16.8.2007. The meeting does not deal with cola only as shown in the news item, nor is it concerned with legitimate advertisements. The group proposes to examine the possibility of regulating misleading advertisements of all carbonated drinks.

2319. (14-8-2007) NEW DELHI : The President of India, Smt. Pratibha Devisingh Patil, has congratulated the Indian Cricket Team for wining the just concluded three test series against England. The President has said that the Nation is proud of their achievement and has wished success to them in future.

2320. (14-8-2007) NEW DELHI : On the eve of Independence Day, Md. Hamid Ansari, Vice President of India greets all the coutrymen. Following is the text message of Mr. Ansari. " I convey my greetings and good wishes to the people of our country on the historic occasion of 60th Anniversary of our Independence. My respectful homage to our valiant freedom fighters who laid down their lives during the long and arduous struggle for Independence. During the sixty years of our Independence, the country has made remarkable progress in many areas of our national life. Many of the problems of underdevelopment, however, remain within us and need to be addressed urgently. This Independence Day inspires us to strive towards realizing the goal of making India a strong and prosperous country free from the scourge of poverty, illiteracy and underdevelopment. May this historic occasion instill in all citizens the true spirit of patriotism to take our country to new heights of glory."

2321. (14-8-2007) NEW DELHI : The Government provides free food supplements to children (6 months to 6 years) and pregnant and lactating women under the

Integrated Child Development Services (ICDS) Scheme. Children suffering from severe malnutrition receive double the quantity of supplementary food for 300 days in a year. This was stated by the Minister for Women and Child Development, Smt. Renuka Chowdhury in a reply to a question by Shri Raghunath Jha in Lok Sabha today. She further stated that undernourished adolescent girls weighing less than 35 kg receive 6 kg of wheat/rice per month under the Nutrition Programme for Adolescent Girls implemented in 51 districts. About 12 crore children are receiving mid day meals in schools under the national Programme for Nutritional Support to Primary Education, she added.

2322. (14-8-2007) NEW DELHI : Minister for Information & Broadcasting and Parliamentary Affairs, Shri P. R. Dasmunsi today released the special issue of magazine 'Yojana', brought out by Publications Division, Ministry of Information & Broadcasting, in commemoration of 150 years of First War of Independence and 60th year of India's freedom. An audio CD of the book '1857' by Shri S. N. Sen was also released on the occasion. Speaking on the occasion, Shri Dasmunsi said the magazine has been of tremendous utility for the students, youth and administrators. During its 50 years, it has retained its relevance despite not being governed by the profit motive. Noted film personality and Member Parliament, Shri Shyam Benegal in his remarks said that the magazine has proved its worth during all these years. Issues concerning evaluation of our development need to be given due importance in the magazine to make it still more acceptable in the changed scenario. Speaking on the occasion, Smt. Asha Swarup, Secretary (I&B), said that the magazine has retained its popularity by adding new features from time to time. A regular column detailing opportunities in Jammu & Kashmir, articles by eminent private sector personalities and launch of 'Do You Know' series are some of the special features added in the recent past. Smt. Deepak Sandhu, DG, PIB, Ms. Nafisa Ali, Chairman, Children Film Society, India and Smt. Veena Jain, Director, Publications Division also graced on the occasion. Yojana is a monthly devoted to socio-economic issues. It started its publication in 1957 with the blessings of Pt. Jawaharlal Nehru. The magazine is now published in 13 languages viz. English, Hindi, Urdu, Punjabi, Marathi, Gujarati, Bengali, Assamese, Telugu, Tamil, Kannada, Malayalam and Oriya. One of the main features of the special issue is the contribution by noted lyrist Gulzar in the form of a poem on 1857 movement, written specifically for the occasion. The poem was sung by artists of Song & Drama Division. Yojana is an official venture. It tries to accommodate plurality of views and opinions on varied issues on national importance to give a balanced picture. Yojana endeavour has been to be a journal of mass circulation and communicate with the common people in their languages and be available at a price they can afford. On the occasion, the Division launches a new initiative in the field of book publishing. It brings out an audio CD on the popular book '1857' for the visually challenged. This is one more step in line with the social mandate of the Division, to reach out to those sections, which are not covered by the market oriented publishing houses. The Audio CD has been especially designed to allow easy navigation between chapters, pages and even paragraphs. This would be extremely useful for the visually impaired who are deprived of such books on an important issue like 1857. The original book was brought out in 1957 by Publications Division and the audio version is based on the abridged Hindi version of the book by Shri S. N. Sen. A very popular book, the audio CD is likely to be extremely useful for the visually impaired even though common people may also like it in the audio format.

2323. (14-8-2007) NEW DELHI : The Sarva Shiksha Abhiyan covers children of 6-14 years of age. The Gross Enrolment Ratio for primary and upper primary level for SC and ST children from 2001-02 to 2004-05 is at Annexure. The aim of the Sarva Shiksha Abhiyan is to provide Universal Elementary Education to all children in age group of 6-14 years. SSA supports elementary education free of cost to children studying in Government schools. This was stated by the Minister of State for Human Resource Development Shri M.A.A.Fatmi in a written reply in the Lok Sabha today.

2324. (14-8-2007) NEW DELHI : The Union Budget for 2007-08 has announced the extension of the Mid-Day Meal Scheme to the Upper Primary stage in Educationally Backward Blocks. A budget provision of Rs. 7324 crores has been made for lower and upper primary stage for the MDM Scheme in the current year. The State wise allocation of funds for the primary stage is annexed. The actual quantum of funds for Upper Primary stage to each State/Union Territory will be finalized after formal approvals are received for extension of the programme to Upper Primary stage. The Mid-Day Meal Scheme guidelines, 2006 stipulate a provision of a cooked mid day meal to children studying in classes I-V with nutritional content of 450 calories and 12 grams of protein. The National Steering-cum-Monitoring Committee for Mid Day Meal Scheme has recommended a nutritional norm of 700 calories with about 20 grams of protein for Upper Primary stage. The MDM Scheme covers children studying in classes I-V in schools run by Government, Local Body and Government aided schools and EGS/AIE centres. As reported by the States/Union Territory Administrations, all eligible schools/ institutions have been covered under the Scheme As and when complaints come to the notice of the Government about inferior quality/unhygienic food or irregular supply of midday meal or black marketing of food grains, State Governments/UT Administrations are asked to conduct suitable enquiry and initiate corrective actions. States/UTs are continuously advised and encouraged to establish systems to avoid recurrence of such incidents and give full attention to the issues of quality and regular supply of food and prevent misuse of resources. States have also been urged to involve the parents, community members, Village Education Committee members and Panchayati Raj Institutions to supervise the cooking and serving of mid day meal to children. This was stated by the Minister of State for Human

Resource Development Shri M.A.A.Fatmi in a written reply in the Lok Sabha today.

2325. (14-8-2007) NEW DELHI : The Government today decided upon a slew of measures to ensure both qualitative and quantitative supply of rations to Jawans deployed in far flung and difficult terrains. Based on the recommendations of the Army, the Defence Minister Shri AK Antony instructed higher prescriptions of rice and different kinds of pulses for the Jawans. He has also directed that better quality tea should be procured in consultation with Tea Board. Furthermore, to improve the quality of milk being supplied to the Jawans in the far flung areas of Northern and Eastern Commands, it has been decided that the same may be procured in Tetra packs from National / State Federations. Similarly, improved packaging standards for edible oil have been prescribed. Procurement of salt will be decentralised. It is expected that these measures will go a long way in improving the quality of rations for the troops.

2326. (14-8-2007) NEW DELHI : The Ministry for Women and Child Development is working on an integrated child protection programme to take care of welfare and developmental needs of the children. The programme will have a component for development and rehabilitation of mentally challenged children. This was disclosed by Smt. Renuka Chowdhury, Minister for Women and Child Development here today at 'TAMANNA', school for mentally challenged children. Interacting with the children in the school, she said the Government and society has to ensure that the children, specially the children of special needs and mentally challenged are provided all opportunities for development. If given enough opportunities, these children can also make significant achievements in various walks. She said that her Ministry is very sensitive about the rights, needs and overall welfare of children. A number of programmes have been launched and are in pipeline with this objective. Child Right Commission has been set up to see that there is no violation of rights of the children. The Government wants active participation of society and people at the grass root level to monitor various programmes and policies related with the children. She appreciated the activities of Tamanna and said there was need to set up such schools in each and every district of the country. She urged the founder of the school, Smt. Dr. Shyama Chhona to take the initiative in this regard that would be supported by the Government in all possible manners. On the occasion, mentally challenged children presented cultural programme and patriotic songs.

2327. (14-8-2007) NEW DELHI : Youth Parliament Competitions are not held in all the schools and colleges of the States every year. However, the All India Whips' Conference had recommended that all States should take steps to implement the Youth Parliament Scheme on the pattern adopted by the Central Ministry of Parliamentary Affairs. The Central Scheme envisages the conduct of the

Competitions in selected schools only and not in all the schools. Further, it is not mandatory on the part of States to conduct Youth Parliament Competitions in the schools and colleges.

2328. (14-8-2007) NEW DELHI : The Minister for Social Justice and Empowerment Smt. Meira Kumar said that we want a right based inclusive society where persons with disabilities should be equal partners in the development of our country. She was speaking at the regional consultation meeting for amendments in the Persons with Disabilities (Equal Opportunities, Protection of Rights and Full Participation) Act, 1995, in New Delhi today. The Minister said there was a demand from many stakeholders that the amendment of the Act may be taken up only after the UN Convention on the Rights for the Persons with Disabilities was finalized. India has signed the Convention on the very first day of its opening on 30th March, 2007 and now we are progressing very well to ratify the convention. She expressed hope that the stakeholders will consider all aspects and many other critical areas of UN Convention including the role of private sector while recommendation for the amendment in Persons with disabilities Act. She also suggested that while making recommendations, we should keep ground realities in view and we have to remember that basic purpose of the whole exercise is to empower the persons with disabilities specially those living in remote, inaccessible and rural areas. Earlier two meetings were held at Patna and Chennai. The consultation process has been initiated after passage of a more than decade after the enactment of landmark legislation in 1996, to make it more effective. The Persons with Disabilities (Equal Opportunities, Protection of Rights and Full Participation) Act, 1995 was enacted in 1996 on the initiative of the Ministry of Social Justice & Empowerment. The Act deals with seven disabilities and provides the legal basis of a rights based inclusive society wherein the Central and State governments have to play the lead role in making the rights actionable. The spectrum of activities that this Act enjoins is very broad and of multi-dimensional nature of rehabilitation. Inter-alia, the Act covers prevention and early detection of disabilities and aspects of rehabilitation like early intervention, education, employment and vocational training, reservation of jobs in the state sector, non-discrimination, research and manpower development and development of barrier-free environment. The Ministry of Social Justice and Employment is the nodal Ministry in the Government of India for the implementation of the Act. The Ministry has also formulated a National Policy and is being implemented. After the enactment of the Act, a number of initiatives have been taken to create an inclusive environment for persons with disabilities in all walks of life. There have been achievements in ensuring reservation to persons with disabilities in Government establishments, ensuring admission of children and students with disabilities in educational institutions, especially higher education institutions and creation of awareness about the need for an accessible physical environment. A scheme for facilitating regular employment of persons with disabilities in the organized sector has been announced by the Finance Minister in his Budget Speech. This will enhance employment opportunities for persons with disabilities and will provide them life of dignity and self-respect.

2329. (14-8-2007) NEW DELHI : Oil & Natural Gas Corporation Limited (ONGC) has recently undertaken a review of crime situation, especially issue related to theft and pilferage in Gujarat, and has prepared an action plan to curb the theft/pilferage of oil in the State. Recently, a Memorandum of Understanding (MoU) has been signed between the Government of Gujarat and ONGC for deployment of one Battalion of State Reserve Police (SRP), exclusively for the protection of ONGC installations and pipelines. ONGC keep a strict vigil on safety and security of oil pipelines. Safety of the pipeline is the responsibility of the ONGC and the State Government. However, wherever required, in addition to State Police & CISF, Central Forces have also been deployed. All cases of theft are reported to jurisdictional Police stations and investigations are undertaken. Above information was given by the Minister of State for Petroleum and Natural Gas Shri Dinsha Patel in a written reply in the Rajya Sabha today.

2330. (14-8-2007) NEW DELHI : The Minister of State for Petroleum and Natural Gas Shri Dinsha Patel today informed the Rajya Sabha in a written reply to a question that the Ministry of Petroleum & Natural Gas has keenly pursued the import of natural gas from Myanmar. Government of Myanmar issued a Letter of Intent on February 11, 2004 and subsequently signed an MoU on March 9, 2006 during the visit of President of India to Myanmar, acknowledging GAIL as a preferential buyer of gas from A1 and A3 blocks in Myanmar. He added, "However, in August 2006, Myanmar invited bids for selling 15.8 MMSCMD natural gas from A1 and A3 offshore blocks through the pipeline route. GAIL submitted its bid. Subsequently, Government of Myanmar reviewed their decision to sell this gas through the pipeline route and invited bids for sale of 3.5 MMTPA of Liquefied Natural Gas (LNG). GAIL again submitted its bid. The matter was discussed in various meetings held between Government of Myanmar and Consortium in January, February and March, 2007." Shri Patel further said that in the meeting held in February 2007 between Myanmar Government and PetroChina, Myanmar Government decided that the gas from A1 and A3 blocks would be sold to China through the pipeline route. This development was conveyed to the consortium partners by Myanmar Government during a meeting held at Nay Pyi Taw (NPT) on March 16, 2007. GAIL impressed upon the other partners and Myanmar Government that GAIL's pipeline offer was still the most competitive and offered optimum value for them due to proximity of India to these fields. However, Myanmar Government stuck to their decision to sell the gas to China. The Minister emphasized that in order to achieve energy security for the country, India will continue to make efforts for import of natural gas/LNG from all possible sources, including Myanmar.

2331. (14-8-2007) NEW DELHI : The total sales of auto-LPG through Auto LPG Dispensing Stations (ALDS) set up by the Public Sector Oil Marketing Companies (OMCs) during the year 2006-07 is 8751 Metric Tonnes (MTs) and during April-June, 2007 is 3447 MTs in the State of Tamil Nadu. OMCs are presently operating 34 ALDS in the State of Tamil Nadu. The district/town-wise details are: Chennai (22), Madurai (4), Tiruvallur (2), Kanchipuram (2), Coimbatore (2), Salem (1) and Erode (1). OMCs propose to set up 37 more ALDS in the State of Tamil Nadu. Above information was given by Shri Murli Deora, Minister of Petroleum and Natural Gas in a written reply in the Rajya Sabha today.

2332. (14-8-2007) NEW DELHI : Being the most attractive and effective mass media, it is an accepted fact that television can play an important role in socio-economic development of the people. Doordarshan being the sole public service television broadcaster has been playing a leading role in the socio-economic development of the country since its beginning in 1959. At present when about 300 TV channels are beaming programmes from within and outside the country and are competing for attracting more and viewers by adopting all sorts of methods, the responsibility of Doordarshan in providing healthy media support to socio-economic development of the country has gained more importance. Presently Doordarshan has 30 channels and a DTH service. These channels include: Five national channels (DD1 National, DD News, DD Sports, DD Bharati, DD Urdu), 11 regional language satellite channels (DD Bangla, DD Oriya, DD Saptagiri, DD Podhigai, DD Chandana, DD Malayalam, DD Sahyadri, DD Gujarati, DD Punjabi, DD Kashir, DD North-East), 1111 regional service state network (Rajasthan, Uttar Pradesh, Madhya Pradesh, Bihar, Jharkhand, Chhattisgarh, Haryana, Himachal Pradesh, Uttarakhand, Mizoram, Tripura), one international channel (DD India), DD Rajya Sabha, DD Gyandarshan and a DTH service (DD Direct Plus). Two of these channels viz. DD1 National and DD News are in both terrestrial and satellite modes. Besides this, there are regional networks and regional language satellite channels which have terrestrial support. The rest three channels namely DD Sports, DD Bharati and DD India are satellite channels telecasting in satellite mode only. Present terrestrial coverage of Doordarshan is 79.1 per cent area and 91.4 per cent population of the country. In the bouquet of Doordarshan DTH service (DD Direct Plus) there are 36 TV channels and 20 Radio channels and it is a free to air service. In order to provide backup to programme production as well as telecast Doordarshan has 64 Doordarshan Kendras/ Studios, 126 Maintenance Centres, 1399 Transmitters of various categories and 24 Regional News Units all over the country, besides two Central Production Centres-one at Delhi and another at Guwahati. According to Indian Readership Survey TV Report 2006 (Round 2) there are 212.7 mn. TV homes in the country. About 56 per cent TV homes in the country have cable connections. The corresponding percentage in urban and rural areas is 70 and 42 respectively. Doordarshan is trying to reach those TV homes having no cable & satellite connection, through its DTH service 'DD Direct Plus'. From the very beginning Doordarshan has earmarked a sizable chunk of its time for telecasting various programmes to provide media support to socio-economic development activities of the country. Agriculture programme, programmes for rural development, women, children, family welfare, adult education, youth, civic sense and public awareness, science & technology, special programmes during natural calamities like flood, earth quake, epidemics etc. are some of important programmes for socio-economic development of the country. DD News channel provides news and current affairs programmes on the development taking place in different parts of the country and in various fields. In order to manage these development programmes more efficiently Doordarshan has created two separate wings namely Development Communication Division, and Narrowcasting. Development Communication Division concentrates on health and sanitation and other development issues; while Narrowcasting deals with agriculture and allied subjects.

2333. (14-8-2007) NEW DELHI : Following is the English rendering of the Defence Minister Shri AK Antony's address to the Armed Forces personnel broadcast over All India Radio on the eve of Independence Day:-"Dear Jawans and members of our Armed Forces, We are celebrating our 61st Independence Day. On the eve of this auspicious day, I offer my humble tributes and heartiest greetings to all uniformed and civilian employees of the three wings of the Armed Forces and their near and dear ones. You guard our nation's frontiers-on land, in air and sea, at great personal risk. It is difficult to live away from one's families and work in adverse climatic conditions. I visited some of the forward areas and have for myself seen the tough conditions of work. It will be my endeavour to increase my interactions with you in the future too. While performing your duties, you have to face several other challenges on the personal and professional front. Some months ago, I had written to the Chief Ministers and taken up the matter with the State Governments to quickly dispose off petitions regarding various problems being faced by you and your families. The urgent need of the hour is to take all possible steps to reduce stress on jawans. I want to urge the officers and commanders to emphasise the humanitarian side through a more humane man management. Senior officers must provide more opportunities for enhanced interaction with junior officers. The officers and commanders must become more accessible to jawans. Our Government is fully committed to support our Armed Forces by providing latest arms, ammunition and equipment to help them perform their duties more effectively. However, the real strength of our Armed Forces lies in enhancing the quality and well being of its human component. Thus, we remain firm in our resolve to ensure the welfare of Armed Forces personnel. We want that the defence personnel should get the best available material and resources. Recently, the Union Cabinet has increased the allowance for personnel posted in remote areas to Rs. 3, 734 per month and that of officers to Rs. 5, 600 per month. The Cabinet has also decided to remove the restriction of 1450 kms on availing Leave Travel Concession and make all service personnel eligible to undertake leave journey to their choice station without any restriction on distance. Besides, Army personnel deployed in field areas will be eligible for an additional railway warrant every year. I am sure that the Sixth Pay Commission will favourably consider the extremely difficult circumstances of service faced by you. The Defence Ministry is discussing with the Sixth Pay Commission the issue of providing valid facilities to you. Our forces are engaged in fighting terrorism and anti-national elements. I understand the stressful conditions under which our jawans operate, particularly in areas affected by insurgency. Though the provocation can be extreme at times, I request you all to respect the human rights of innocent civilians. The task is really difficult and utmost patience and tact is required to meet these and other such challenges. The Ministry of Defence has under its supervision more estates than any other ministry. Several steps have been initiated for digitization of land records. With this process, it will be possible to develop land for residential quarters, defence installations and firing ranges on identified excess land, in a more meaningful way. Our Government is also committed to improve the status of women in the Armed Forces. Recently, an anomaly in promotions for women officers has been removed. Women officers will now be eligible for promotion at par with Short Service Commissioned Officers to the posts of Captain, Major and Lieutenant Colonel on completion of two, six and 13 years of service respectively. To ensure equitable distribution of work, the tenure of training of women officers has been raised to 49 weeks. Ex-servicemen are an important part of our Armed Forces. We should make every possible effort to utilise their vast experience more productively and help them in leading a more meaningful retired life. Today, we once again salute them for the service rendered by them. Preserving world peace, security and unity among the comity of nations has always been the guiding principle of our foreign policy. The efforts of our Armed Forces personnel deployed in the United Nations peace missions have been appreciated the world over. Our Armed Forces personnel have also excelled in the arena of international sports. It is the Government's resolve to provide state-of-the-art facilities to our sportspersons to enable them to keep our flag flying high in international sporting events. India will be hosting the World Military Games in October. It is hoped that by hosting these Games, will induce the interest of youth and Armed Forces personnel in sports and games. Dear friends, you guard our frontiers, even while living away from your families. Hence, it is equally our responsibility to take care of your families and dependents, so that you can render your responsibilities with sincerity, devotion-and most importantly, a free mind. On this auspicious day, I want to give you all my solemn assurance that your family members and loved ones can approach me without hesitation for any grievance that is just, or right. I once again extend my heartiest greetings and best wishes on the eve of Independence Day to all uniformed and civilian personnel and their family members. Jai Hind."

2334. (14-8-2007) NEW DELHI : To further facilitate the import of cement, MMTC Limited, has been mandated to import cement from such foreign manufacturers of cement, whose applications have been recorded by Bureau of Indian Standards (BIS) as per provisions of the Cement (Quality Control) Order.

2335. (14-8-2007) NEW DELHI : The Government of India today announced the Prime Minister's Shram Awards for the year 2005. 65 workers employed in the public and private sectors share the 32 awards in recognition of their distinguished performances, innovative abilities, outstanding contribution in the field of productivity and exhibition of exceptional courage and presence of mind. They include 46 workers from the public sector and 19 workers from the private sector. Among them are 6 women workers.

2336. (14-8-2007) NEW DELHI : Smt. Sudha Chobe has taken over the charge of the office of Financial Commissioner, Railways. Prior to joining Railway Board, she was General Manager, Metro Railway Kolkata. She joined the Indian Railway Accounts Service (IRAS) in 1971 and attended almost all the major in-service training programmes. She had undergone training on Mechanized Maintenance of Track under World Scheme in USA and Sweden for 6 weeks in 1993. She also participated in Advance Leadership Programme from 10.10.2006 to 18.10.2006 held in Stern School of Business, New York. She has also worked as General Manager, Rail Wheel Factory, Bangalore. She served as Financial Adviser & Chief Accounts Officer (FA&CAO) in different Zonal Railways including Western, North Eastern, Central, Northeast and North Western Railways.

2337. (14-8-2007) NEW DELHI : The Minister of State for Textiles, Shri E.V.K.S. Elangovan, informed the Lok Sabha today, in a written reply to a question by Shri G. Karunakara Reddy that the Government has launched a new scheme called "Integrated Handloom Cluster Development Scheme" in the year 2005-06 for holistic and integrated development of 20 handloom clusters in a timeframe of four years at a total cost not exceeding Rs. 2 crore per cluster. These clusters are spread in 12 States, including the State of Karnataka each covering about 5000 handlooms. This cluster approach will not replace the cooperative approach for the development of handloom sector, the Minister said. The Minister further informed the House that the Integrated Handloom Cluster Development Scheme will be replaced by the proposed new "Integrated Handloom Development Scheme (IHDS)", which has been formulated by merging the components, with or without modifications of the Deen Dayal Hathkargha Protsahan Yojana, Integrated Handloom Cluster Development Scheme, Integrated Handloom Training Project and Workshed-cum-Housing Scheme implemented during the Tenth Five Year Plan. Shri Elangovan further stated that in the State of Karnataka, Gadag is one of the 20 handloom clusters where the cluster development programme is under implementation. Additional five handloom clusters *i.e.* (i) Mahalingapur-Bagalkot District; (ii) Challoakere Town—Chitradurga District; (iii) Kollegal-Chamarajnagar District; (iv) Thimmasandara-Kolar District and (v) Mulakalamuru-Chitradurga District have been selected in the State of Karnataka and their diagnostic study has been conducted. The proposed new Scheme will cover the weavers both in and outside the cooperative fold.

2338. (14-8-2007) NEW DELHI : On the eve of Independence Day this year 737836 Sergeant Jai Prakash Shukla Clerk General Duties has been awarded Shaurya Chakra (Posthumous) for displaying exceptional courage in the face of severe adversity with disregard to his personal safety in attempting to rescue fellow citizens. Barmer District of Rajasthan experienced incessant rains and flash floods from 18-23 Aug 06. On 23 Aug 06, Sgt Shukla along with other Air Warriors of the unit proceeded to surrounding villages to assist the families of some civilians working at Air Force Station Utarlai (Barmer). While returning, some villagers requested the Air Warriors to rescue four persons perched on tree tops and struggling for life in the flood. The task of rescuing the persons from dangerously high levels of the turbulent flood waters was extremely challenging and evidently hazardous. It required extraordinary courage for any person to under take such a risk. While other members of the team did not dare to enter torrential current of flood waters, Sgt Shukla in a true tradition of soldier, readily volunteered to rescue these persons though it involved a great risk to his own life. He swam in the strong current in 20 feet deep flood waters, with the single-minded purpose of rescuing the helpless persons, who were under the threat of being washed away. However, after swimming for about 100 meters, he got sucked down in the swirling water and could not extricate himself. His body was recovered after two days. Sgt Shukla displayed extraordinary courage and valour in extreme circumstances, and made the supreme sacrifice while trying to save fellow citizens. For displaying exceptional courage in the face of severe adversity with utter disregard to his personal safety in attempting to rescue fellow citizens, Sergeant Jai Prakash Shukla is being awarded Sahurya Chakra (Posthumous). The President is also pleased to award Vayu Sena Medal (Galantary) to Wg Cdr Subroto Kundu, Wg Cdr Jitender Yadav, Wg Cdr Sartaj Bedi, Wg Cdr Rajesh Ranwan, Sqn Ldr Bhupender Singh Sehrawat and Corporal Prasanta Kumar Pati.

2339. (14-8-2007) NEW DELHI : During the year 2007-08, the Central allocation for the State of Andhra Pradesh is Rs. 934.29 crore under major allocation based schemes. So far, Rs. 1132.45 crore has already been released. Statement of financial progress is given in the Annexure. For the year 2006-07, the Central allocation for Andhra Pradesh for allocation-based programmes of the Ministry of Rural Development was Rs. 772.18 crore and against this allocation Rs. 923.92 crore was released. However, the total release including the demand-based programmes (NREGA) from the Centre was Rs. 2139.80 crore and an amount of Rs. 1826.23 crore was reported to have been spent.

2340. (14-8-2007) NEW DELHI : The Appointments Committee of the Cabinet has approved the appointment of Shri S.R. Mehra, IPS (AM: 70), presently Commissioner, Bureau of Civil Aviation Security (BCAS) as Secretary (Security), in the Cabinet Secretariat vice Shri N.C. Padhi, IPS (MP:68).

2341. (14-8-2007) NEW DELHI : The Appointments Committee of the Cabinet has approved the additional charge of the post of Commissioner, BCAS to Shri J.K. Dutt, IPS (WB:71), presently Director General, National Security Guard, with immediate effect for a period of six months or till the post is filled on regular basis, whichever is earlier.

2342. (14-8-2007) NEW DELHI : The Minister of State for Textiles, Shri E.V.K.S. Elangovan, informed the Lok Sabha today, in a written reply to a question by Shri K.C. Pallani Shamy that it has been decided to seek private partnership to modernize and run some of NTC mills through joint venture route. The proposal for Joint Venture has been approved by the Board for Industrial and Financial reconstruction (BIFR) and Group of Ministers (GOM) as part of the Revival Scheme for NTC, to implemented by the year 2008. Shri Elangovan further stated that it has also been decided to set up Indian Textile Plaza on the vacant land of Jehangir Textile Mills, Ahmedabad which includes setting up of Textile Museum, Training Centre and Exhibition Centre, etc. To implement the project a Memorandum of Understanding has been entered into with the National Building Construction Corporation for developing the Indian Textile Plaza at a cost of Rs. 180 crore, he added.

2343. (14-8-2007) NEW DELHI : A number of steps are being taken to meet the requirement of additional trained Air Traffic Controllers to man the newly established ATC workstations to handle the increased growth in air traffic. This information was given by Shri Praful Patel, Minister for Civil Aviation in the Parliament today. The Minister said that during the last two and half years, 371 Junior Executives (ATC) have been inducted in Airports Authority of India (AAI). Steps are being taken to fill up 148 additional posts of JE (ATC). AAI is also utilizing the services of retired ATCOs whenever possible. It has also been programmed to recruit 100 ATCOs every six months by the AAI for a period of two years to meet the additional requirement.

2344. (14-8-2007) NEW DELHI : Air India Express, the budget carrier launched by Air India's subsidiary company, is planning to commence domestic operation from October 2007. This information was given by Shri Praful Patel, Minister for Civil Aviation in the Parliament today. The Minister also said that these operations would be in addition to existing international operation. The fares charged by Air India Express would be competitive and comparable to the other low cost carrier operating on the same route.

2345. (14-8-2007) NEW DELHI : The estimated loss incurred by Indian Airlines and Alliance Air during the flash strike by the employees of Indian Airlines in the month of June 2007, is Rs. 3.5 crores by way of loss of contribution, additional expenditure on hotel, food and conveyance charges for disrupted flights etc. This information was given by Shri Praful Patel, Minister for Civil Aviation in the

Parliament today. Employees of Indian Airlines covered by Air Corporation Employees Union (ACEU) had gone on flash strike w.e.f. night shift of 12th June, 2007 all over India. The strike was called off on the afternoon of 14th June, 2007. ACEU had been demanding revision of wages and allowances w.e.f. 1.1.1997 and better career progression. The negotiations in this regard were initiated in February, 2007 but, when no satisfactory agreement was reached and the ACEU adopted an agitational approach, the matter was seized with Chief Labour Commissioner (Central). Even as the conciliation proceedings were underway with the Chief Labour Commissioner(Central), the ACEU suddenly called for a flash strike. Memorandum of Settlement covering revision of pay scales and allowances, payment of arrears, career progression of specified category of workmen etc. has been signed in conciliation with the representatives of ACEU on 15th June 2007. The revision of pay scales will be effected in the salary of August, 2007. However, the first installment of arrears has already been paid in July 2007.

2346. (14-8-2007) NEW DELHI: The Indo-U.S. civil nuclear deal issue disrupted proceedings in the Lok Sabha on Monday, but Prime Minister Manmohan Singh made his statement in the afternoon amid vociferous protests by the National Democratic Alliance (NDA) and the United National Progressive Alliance (UNPA). Later, in the Rajya Sabha, he chose to table the statement in view of the loud protests by the entire Opposition and Left parties after which the House was adjourned for the day. The day's proceedings underlined the United Progressive Alliance Government's political isolation on the issue. While the Left parties were the first to walk out of the Rajya Sabha in protest soon after the Prime Minister began to speak, their party members heard Dr. Singh out in the Lok Sabha till the fag end and did not join the NDA and UNPA in picketing the well of the House and raising slogans. The Left members raised their voice of protest in the Lok Sabha when Dr. Singh reached the last paragraph and walked out of the House. The NDA and UNPA, however, continued with their siege of the well as Speaker Somnath Chatterjee proceeded with the morning's business that could not be taken up due to two quick adjournments.

2347. (14-8-2007) NEW DELHI: Goa Speaker Pratap Singh Rane, has refused to accept the Supreme Court notice on the petitions challenging his interim order that restrained two MLAs of the Maharastrawadi Gomantak Party from voting in the floor test on July 30. In a brief affidavit, Mr. Rane said: "Out of deference to this court's order on August 6, but without accepting service [of the notice] of the same or without accepting the jurisdiction of this court to determine matters arising within the House, I would only like to state that the allegations made in the petitions that the impugned order was actuated by bias or that I had passed the order mala fide as alleged is specifically denied. It is also denied that the order is perverse, mala fide, unreasonable or capricious. I reserve the right to file a detailed affidavit if so desired at a later date."

2348. (14-8-2007) NEW DELHI : The Minister of State for Textiles, Shri E.V.K.S. Elangovan, informed the Lok Sabha today, in a written reply to a question by Dr. Chinta Mohan and Shri Rajiv Ranjan Singh "Lalan" that the production in apparel sector during 2005-06 was of the order of Rs. 93328 crore including Rs. 37208 crore for exports and Rs. 56120 crore for the domestic market. No definite figure of any gap between demand and supplv of garments can be indicated in the absence of official estimates of demand of garments in the country. However, there have been no reports of shortage in the supply of garments in the country. Shri Elangovan further informed the House that imports of readymade garments during 2004-05, 2005-06 and 2006-07 (April to December) have been of the order of Rs. 149.54 crore (7705000 pieces), Rs. 251.59 crore (8133000 pieces) and Rs. 236.96 crore (8816000 pieces) respectively. The total imports of readymade garments during the last three years are thus less than one per cent of the total domestic production of apparel during 2005-06 alone.

2349. (14-8-2007) NEW DELHI : Youth Parliament Competitions are not held in all the schools and colleges of the States every year. However, the All India Whips' Conference had recommended that all States should take steps to implement the Youth Parliament Scheme on the pattern adopted by the Central Ministry of Parliamentary Affairs. The Central Scheme envisages the conduct of the Competitions in selected schools only and not in all the schools. Further, it is not mandatory on the part of States to conduct Youth Parliament Competitions in the schools and colleges.

2350. (14-8-2007) NEW DELHI : In pursuance of Article 21A of the Constitution, which makes education a Fundamental Right for children in the age group of 6-14 years by providing that "the State shall provide free and compulsory education to all children of the age of six to fourteen years in such manner as the State may, by law, determine", a draft Model Right to Education Bill, 2006 was formulated and circulated as framework to the States/UTs with a view seek their comments thereon. In order to motivate and incentivise the State governments to adopt the Model Right to Education Bill, 2006, it was proposed that the scale of funding under Sarva Shiksha Abhiyan (SSA) be made contingent upon enactment of appropriate State Acts on free and compulsory education where none exist, or suitable adaptation of existing Acts. The comments from 23 States/UTs have been received.

2351. (14-8-2007) NEW DELHI : The present policy of the Government permits Foreign Direct Investment (FDI) upto 100% on the automatic route in the education sector. A legislative proposal on entry and operations of foreign education institutions in the country is under consideration of the Government. Amendment of the University Grants Commission Act, is not contemplated, for this purpose. This was stated by the Minister of State for Human Resource Development Smt. D. Purandeswari in a written reply in the Lok Sabha today.

2352. (14-8-2007) NEW DELHI : Out of the total financial package of Rs.13596 crore, for strengthening the Short Term Rural Cooperative Credit Structure (STCCS) in the Country comprising State Cooperative banks (SCBs), District Central Cooperative Banks (DCCBs) and Primary Agriculture Credit Societies (PACS), the Asian Development Bank and World Bank have agreed to provide an assistance of US$1000 million and US$600 million respectively to the Government of India. The World Bank assistance is proposed in the form of loan of US$300 million from International bank for Reconstruction and Development (IBRD) and a credit of SDR 196.8 million (equivalent to US$300 million) from International Development Assistance (IDA). The Government has approved a revival package to strengthen Short Term Rural Cooperative Credit Structure (STCCS). The States willing to implement the package are required to sign a Memorandum of Understanding (MoU) with Central Government and NABARD for carrying out certain legal and institutional reforms. Financial assistance for STCCS under the package is available for cleansing of Balance Sheet as on 31st March 2004 and increasing the capital to a specified minimum level subject to legal and institutional reforms. In order to ensure that STCCS continues on sound financial managerial and governance norms, technical assistance is to be provided to upgrade institutional and human resources of STCCS, computerization and setting up proper internal control and accounting systems. This information was given by Shri Pawan Kumar Bansal, Minister of State for Finance in reply to a question raised by Shri Pyarelal Khandelwal in Rajya Sabha today.

2353. (14-8-2007) NEW DELHI : In accordance with the existing FDI policy, FDI up to 100 per cent is permitted under the automatic route in Floriculture, Horticulture, Development of seeds, Animal Husbandry, Pisciculture, Acquaculture and Cultivation of Vegetable and Mushrooms under controlled conditions and services related to Agro and allied sectors. FDI upto 100 per cent, with prior Government approval, is permitted in Tea plantation subject to the conditions of divestment of 26 per cent equity of the company in favour of an Indian partner/ Indian public within a period of five years and with the prior approval of the State Government concerned in case of future land use change. FDI upto 100 per cent under the automatic route is also allowed in the Food Processing Industry and for infrastructure facilities like Cold storage, transportation etc. There is no proposal to further ease the FDI norms in agro processing and agro infrastructure. This information was given by Shri Pawan Kumar Bansal, Minister of State for Finance in reply to a question raised by Shri Rajkumar Dhoot in Rajya Sabha today.

2354. (14-8-2007) NEW DELHI : The President has approved three Ashok Chakras, six Kirti Chakras and 20 Shaurya Chakras to Armed Forces personnel and others. This year Ashok Chakra has been awarded to Col Vasanth Venugopal of 9 Maratha Light Infantry, Capt Harshan R of the 2 Parachute Regiment (Special Forces) and Naib Subedar Chunni Lal of 8 Jammu and Kashmir Light Infantry.

All of them have been honoured posthumously. Col Vasanth Venugopal was the commanding officer of his battalion deployed along the Line of Control in Uri Sector of J&K. On 31 July, 2007, he personally took command of a body of troops to intercept a group of terrorists who were attempting to escape back across the Line of Control. Out flanking the terrorists, Col Vasanth engaged them from close quarter, killing one of them. However, he himself was injured in this action. Unmindful of this, he exhorted his men to block all escape routes of the terrorists and killed two more terrorists before succumbing to his wounds. A total of eight foreign terrorists were killed in this operation by his group. Earlier in the same general area, he had led an operation from 27 to 30 June, 2007 in which his battalion had eliminated four terrorists. Col Venugopal was born in Bangalore and had his schooling from Udupi. Capt. Harshan R killed two hardcore terrorists at very close range in Lolab (North Kashmir) on 20 March, 2007. For over two months preceding the operation, this gallant officer had been relentlessly tracking foreign terrorists. The officer first killed one terrorist but was injured due to a gunshot wound on his thigh in this action. Unmindful of this injury he went on to kill another terrorist. In the process he received another gunshot, this time on his neck. He later succumbed to his wounds. Capt. Harshan R belonged to Manacaud, Thiruvananthapuram, Kerala. Naib Subedar Chunni Lal who belonged to Bhaderwah (J&K) killed three terrorists on 24 June, 2007 before laying down his life in countering an infiltration bid by terrorists in Kupwara sector of J&K. This courageous junior commissioned officer was decorated twice for bravery on earlier occasions. As a young soldier he had taken part in the capture of Bana Top in Siachen Glacier in 1987 for which he was awarded a Sena Medal. He was also awarded Vir Chakra for beating back an attempted intrusion in Poonch sector in 1999.

2355. (14-8-2007) NEW DELHI : India is interested in a long-term contract with Syria for import of rock phosphates and phosphoric acid. This was conveyed by the Minister for Steel, Chemicals and Fertilisers. Shri Ram Vilas Paswan to the visiting Syrian Foreign Minister Mr. Walid Mouallem who called on him here this morning. Shri Paswan said, fertilizer consumption in the country is growing and the demand for all varieties of fertilizers like Urea, DAP and MOP is on the rise. He said, the country is looking for a long-term stable arrangement for the supply of raw materials. He said a long-term agreement will be to the mutual interest of the two countries which enjoy a very friendly relation. Shri Paswan said, India can also consider strengthening mining infrastructure and help upgrade railways and ports if such a long term contract is worked out. The Syrian Minister said, he will convey the offer to the concerned Minister and follow it up. Mr. Walid Mouallem said, he is looking forward to increased economic ties between the two countries. Secretary Department of Fertilisers Dr. J. S. Sharma and other senior officials were present during the meeting.

2356. (14-8-2007) NEW DELHI : In its ongoing drive against tax evasion, the

Income Tax department conducted surveys at nine premises of different institutions engaged in imparting coaching for competitive examinations (coaching institutes), deployment of manpower in various institutions (placement agencies), air-services institutes and foreign-education placement agencies in Delhi and Mumbai on 9.8.2007. Based on the evidence collected during these surveys and subsequent investigations, various concerns have already admitted tax evasion amounting to Rs.26.75 crore. Further investigations in these cases are in progress and detection of more tax evasion is likely.

2357. (14-8-2007) NEW DELHI : The President has approved 140 gallantry awards to Armed Forces & Coast Guard personnel and others. This includes three Ashok Chakras, six Kirti Chakras, 20 Shaurya Chakras, two Bars to Sena Medal (Gallantry), 99 Sena Medals (Gallantry), four Nao Sena Medals (Gallantry) and six Vayu Sena Medals (Gallantry). Out of the six Kirti Chakras, three have been awarded to civilians, posthumously. The President has also approved one President's Tatrakshak Medal (Distinguished Service), two President's Tatrakshak Medals (Gallantry) and two Tatrakshak Medals (Meritorious) to Coast Guard personnel.

2358. (14-8-2007) NEW DELHI : Government of Japan would provide loan for an amount of Yen 39,555 million (Rs. 1345 crores approximately) to India as its Official Development Assistance for FY 2007 Loan Package under First Batch of Double Track. Japan has recently introduced a Double Track Mechanism for providing ODA loan to India in two batches. The loan would fund two projects in power transmission, and water supply and sewerage sectors. An Exchange of Notes on this package took place here today between Shri Kumar Sanjay Krishna, Joint Secretary, Ministry of Finance and Mr. Yasukuni Enoki, Ambassador of Japan to India. The rate of interest for Goa Water Supply & Sewerage Project would be 1.3% per annum and the rate of interest would be 0.75% per annum for Maharashtra Transmission System Project. The repayment period including a grace period of ten years would be thirty years for the Goa Project and for Maharashtra Project it would be fifteen years including a grace period of five years. India and Japan have had a long and fruitful history of bilateral development cooperation since 1958. This is expected to be further strengthened and broad based in future. This bilateral cooperation has seen remarkable and progressive expansion in recent years. The Government of Japan provided Yen 184,893 million (equivalent to Rs. 6916 crores approximately) for projects in FY 2006 ODA package. The total ODA loan commitment including this batch of loan has become Yen 2476.985 billion (Rs. 93967 crores approximately). At present, 54 projects are being implemented in India with Japanese loan assistance of Yen 839.042 billion (Rs. 28527 crores approximately).

2359. (14-8-2007) NEW DELHI : TV channels and radio stations are held responsible for advertisements which are misleading or wrong. The Central Government has also constituted an Inter-ministerial Committee (IMC) under section 20 of the Act to look into the violation of Programme and Advertising Codes prescribed under the Act and Rules framed thereunder. The Committee either suo-motu or on receipt of complaint, examines cases of violation of the Codes. Show cause notices are issued in the first instances to TV channels for telecasting objectionable programmes/advertisements in violation of Codes. Further action is taken as per the rules. The committee constituted for reviewing Programme and Advertising Codes prescribed under the Cable TV Networks (Regulation) Act 1995 and rules framed thereunder and drafting a new content code and guidelines in order to give them greater specificity and details and introduce new provisions as found necessary as per contemporary community standard and to facilitate self regulation among the channels, have not submitted its Report. A draft of the proposed Code has also been posted on the website of the Ministry of Information & Broadcasting but it is not final and representations are still being received. The Committee itself was constituted to protect the interests of the viewers. This information was given by Minister of Information & Broadcasting and Parliamentary Affairs, Shri P. R. Dasmunsi in written reply to a question in Lok Sabha today.

2360. (14-8-2007) NEW DELHI : Government has signed an agreement with Indira Gandhi National Open University (IGNOU) for operationalisation of FM stations for education broadcast at 40 places. Out of this, 26 are presently operational. In addition, the Government has also agreed for setting up of FM stations for educational broadcasts by IGNOU at 15 more places. The FM stations set up by IGNOU are called Gyan Vani, a "Radio Cooperative" devoted exclusively to education and community development. These inter-active participatory educational stations are aimed at great empowerment of the people particularly the disadvantaged sections of the Society located in the remote and distant areas of the country. The programmes include information relevant to students of pre-primary, primary, secondary and higher secondary, as well as enrichment programmes to build environmental awareness, women's empowerment, legal literacy, professional education and science education. This information was given by Minister of Information & Broadcasting and Parliamentary Affairs, Shri P. R. Dasmunsi in written reply to a question in Lok Sabha today.

2361. (14-8-2007) NEW DELHI : The Minister for Tourism and Culture Smt. Ambika Soni has said, the number of foreign tourist arrival to India during 2006 is provisionally estimated to be 4.45 million, recording an increase of 13.5% over the corresponding figures of 3.92 million during 2005. The Working Group on Tourism for the 11th Five Year Plan (2007-2012) has set a target of 10 million international visitors in 2011 at the end of 11th Plan.

2362. (14-8-2007) NEW DELHI : The Minister of Tourism and Culture Smt. Ambika Soni has said that during the Tenth Five Year Plan, the Ministry of Tourism has sanctioned Rs.2011.68 crore for 1160 projects for development of Destinations, Circuits, Rural Tourism, Events, Fairs & Festivals and IT projects. The unique tourism products developed in the last 3 years in the whole of the country include Medical tourism, Cruise tourism, Eco-tourism, Convention tourism etc.

2363. (14-8-2007) NEW DELHI : The Minister for Tourism and Culture Smt. Ambika Soni has informed the Rajya Sabha today that a project 'Floodlighting of monuments in Rajasthan' has been sanctioned for Rs. 800.00 lakh in the current financial year. This project covers 28 monuments spread across different districts such as Jaipur, Karauli, Udaipur, Ajmer, Dausa, Churu, Dholpur, Madhopur, Jaisalmer, Bharatpur, Jhalawar, Bikaner and Kota. In a written reply she said implementation of projects is the responsibility of the State Government. Ministry of Tourism monitors the progress of the projects from time to time. She said development of tourist places in the country is undertaken primarily by the State Governments/ UT Administrations. The Ministry of Tourism extends financial assistance to the State Governments/ UT Administrations for tourism related projects under the schemes for Product/ Infrastructure Development of Destinations/ Circuits and Assistance to Large Revenue Generating Projects.

2364. (14-8-2007) NEW DELHI : Minister for Tourism and Culture Smt. Ambika Soni has said that no such directions have been received from the Madras High Court to declare Ram Setu (between India and Sri Lanka) as national monument under the National Monument and Archaeological Place Law, 1958.. In a written reply in the Rajya Sabha today she said, no archaeological study has been made in respect of Ram Setu by the Archaeological Survey of India by the Archaeological Survey of India. As per the scientific evidence available so far, Ram Setu does not fulfill the criteria to be declared as a monument of national importance under the provisions of the Ancient Monuments and Archaeological Sites and Remains Act, 1958.

2365. (14-8-2007) NEW DELHI : The total number of land oustees for National Aluminium Company Limited (NALCO)'s Mines & Refinery Complex, Damanjodi is 600 and for its Smelter & Power Complex, Angul is 35. As a part of rehabilitation policy, NALCO at its initial stage, had formulated a policy for providing employment to one able bodied member of each oustee family subject to suitability of candidate and availability of vacancy. Out of 600 land oustees at Damanjodi, one member each from 591 land oustees has been provided employment and out of 35 at Angul, 34 have been given employment in the Company. NALCO has intimated that the Company stands committed to provide employment to at least one member of each land oustee family. However, the Company has not been able to provide employment in respect of the remaining oustees as on date due to reasons like non-determination of bonafide nominees, lack of response from the families, etc.

2366. (14-8-2007) NEW DELHI : The famous tourist train, hauled by world's oldest working steam engine 'Fairy Queen', taking passengers from Delhi to Alwar (Sariska Tiger Reserve) is scheduled to commence its run for the tourist season 2007-08. Ministry of Railways has issued instructions for making necessary arrangements for run of the Fairy Queen on 27th October, 10th and 24th November, 8th and 22nd December 2007, 12th and 26th January, 9th and 23rd February and 8th March 2008. The itinerary of the train with revised timing is: Delhi Cantt departure 0900 hrs. arrival Alwar 1600 hrs. and in return direction on the next day Alwar departure 1300 hrs. and arrival Delhi Cantt. 1845 hrs. The Fairy Queen, the famous steam locomotive of Indian Railways, which completed its 150 years in the year 2005, will take the tourists from Delhi to Alwar and back to Delhi giving them the sounds, smells and experience of the bygone era. The coaches have been specially designed for comfort of the tourists and the services include on-board catering, guide, piped music entertainment, magazines etc. Finding its pride of place in the Guinness Book of World Records and also capturing the National Tourism Award, this Fairy Queen steam engine is the oldest working steam engine in the world. It was in 1855 when the majestic Fairy Queen rolled out for the erstwhile East Indian Railway. This locomotive also hauled troop trains to Raniganj during the famous 1857 War of Independence. This beautiful locomotive retired from services in 1908 and was the first locomotive to be brought and conserved in National Rail Museum in 1971. To improve the quality of services to the tourists, National Rail Museum has also obtained ISO 9001-2000 certification for operation and maintenance of the Fairy Queen locomotive and coaches.

2367. (14-8-2007) NEW DELHI : In order to optimize intelligence flow and co-ordination between multifarious agencies at the Centre and in the States in the field of counter-terrorism and counter-intelligence, a Multi-Agency Centre and Joint Task Force on Intelligence have been created in the Intelligence Bureau at Delhi, supported by Subsidiary Multi-Agency Centres at almost all State capitals. For strengthening counter intelligence apparatus in the Intelligence Bureau, additional manpower has been given. The states have been advised to earmark up to 5% of the annual total allocations under the Modernization of State Police Forces Scheme towards strengthening training and technical capabilities of Special Branches. This information was given by the Minister of State for Home, Shri Sriprakash Jaiswal in a written reply to a question in the Lok Sabha today.

2368. (14-8-2007) NEW DELHI : Since the inception of the Freedom Fighters' Pension Scheme in 1972, the Government has sanctioned pension to approximately 1.70 lakh freedom fighters and their eligible dependents till 31st July, 2007. 310 applications, received through State Governments with their verification reports, were under process as on 31st July, 2007. In addition, 438 cases of Maharashtra and 98 cases of Goa pertaining to the Goa Liberation Movement (Phase II) were also under process as on 31st July, 2007. Complaints containing allegations of bogus/fraudulent claims for freedom fighter's pension are received from time to time. All such complaints are examined with reference to the applicable provisions of pension scheme in consultation with the concerned State Governments. In cases, where the allegations are substantiated, the claims are rejected and if the pension has been sanctioned, the same is suspended/cancelled and recovery of pension ordered after following the prescribed procedure. This information was given by the Minister of State for Home, Shri Manikrao Hodlya Gavit in a written reply to a question in the Lok Sabha today.

2369. (14-8-2007) NEW DELHI : Lok Sabha Conditional Access System (CAS) has been reviewed in consultation with TRAI. As on 31 July, 2007, 5.12 lacs Set Top Boxes (STBs) have been reported to be deployed by Multi System Operators (MSOs)/cable operators. A meeting with the concerned State Government officials and nodal officers has been held in the ministry in June 2007.The State Governments have been requested to come up with their formal views on the extension of CAS and to get a survey conducted by a professional agency to understand the issues and problems, if any faced by the viewers. TRAI has issued a regulation on Quality of Service to be provided by the service providers in the CAS notified areas. To assess the implementation of Quality of Service norms, TRAI has engaged Broadcast Consultant India Limited (BECIL), to carry out an audit of Quality of Service (QoS) performance in CAS notified areas. No committee has been constituted by Government on implementation of CAS. Extension of CAS requires evaluation of first phase & large scale consultations with stakeholders, consumer organisations & States. Hence, no time limit can be given. TRAI has intimated that 47 complaints have been received by TRAI regarding poor quality and non-availability of channels selected by the subscribers. Out of these, 40 complaints have been resolved, and for the rest, the matter is being pursued with the service providers. This information was given by Minister of Information & Broadcasting and Parliamentary Affairs, Shri P. R. Dasmunsi in written reply to a question in Lok Sabha today.

2370. (14-8-2007) NEW DELHI : Lok Sabha Doordarshan has produced 558 and 446 documentaries/films during 2006-07 & 2005-06 respectively and expenditure incurred on this was Rs. 10.08 crore & 4.39 crores. Documentaries/ films are made on a wide range of topics including those of scientific, technical, medical, cultural, historical, etc.nature.No separate and comprehensive list is maintained as to which topics concern which specific State. However, Doordarshan Kendra Lucknow has produced a documentary on the First War of Indian Independence 1857 namely, "Bhartayan", which is UP related. This is being telecast since January 2007 on every Thursday of the month and will continue during the current financial year. This information was given by Minister of Information & Broadcasting and Parliamentary Affairs, Shri P. R. Dasmunsi in written reply to a question in Lok Sabha today.

2371. (14-8-2007) NEW DELHI : Several steps have been taken by the Reserve Bank of India (RBI) in the recent past to step up credit flow to minorities. In its Circular dated 1.09.2006, RBI had instructed all Scheduled commercial Banks to ensure that the minority communities receive a fair and equitable portion of credit within the overall targets of Priority Sector and sub-targets of 10% earmarked for Weaker Section. The Master Circular on Priority Sector lending was amended on 18.05.2007 to include minority communities under "Weaker Section". In their consolidated Master Circular dated 5.07.2007 on lending to minorities, the RBI has advised the banks to take care to ensure that minority communities secure in a fair and adequate measure, the benefits flowing from various Government sponsored special programmes and create a separate cell in each bank to ensure smooth flow of credit to minority communities. In its circular dated 16.07.2007, RBI has issued a consolidated list of 121 minority concentration districts to Scheduled Commercial Banks for specially monitoring credit flow to minorities. This information was given by Shri Pawan Kumar Bansal, Minister of State for Finance in reply to a question raised by Ms. Sushila Tiriya in Rajya Sabha today.

2372. (14-8-2007) NEW DELHI : Shri Kamal Nath, Commerce & Industry Minister, while responding to a request from Swaziland for capacity building for SMEs (small & medium enterprises) assured that an expert delegation could be sent for exploring the modalities. This was stated by Shri Kamal Nath when Mr. Lutfo E. Dlamiai, Minister of Enterprise and Employment of Swaziland, called on him here last evening. While referring to a Framework Agreement on Economic Cooperation between India and South African Customs Union (SACU), Shri Kamal Nath sought the assistance of Swaziland for its early finalisation and signing of the Agreement paving the way for expansion of flow of two-way trade. The Indian Commerce Minister informed that India and SACU have agreed in principle to move forward with negotiations for a Preferential Trade Agreement (PTA) and hoped that PTA would help provide market access to both the sides facilitating growth of trade between India and SACU. Expressing satisfaction over the bilateral trade between India and Swaziland which has increased almost 5-fold during the last 5 years achieving a level of US $ 66.04 million, Shri Kamal Nath observed that it does not reflect the true potential which exists and can be further exploited to mutual advantage. Shri Kamal Nath mentioned about the rapid strides made by India in the knowledge sector and stated that Indian expertise can be utilised by Swaziland in sectors like IT, agro & food processing, SMEs development, infrastructure & human resource development.

2373. (14-8-2007) NEW DELHI : Shri Kamal Nath, Commerce & Industry Minister, has called for achieving a vibrant trade basket for improving upon the existing bilateral trade ties between India and Syrian Arab Republic, when Mr. Wallid Mouallem, Minister for Foreign Affairs of the Syrian Arab Republic called on him here last evening. The Commerce and Industry Minister appreciated the help of Syrian authorities in assisting Indian companies like KEC, ABB India, Champdany, BEML and IRCON for getting contracts in Syria and hoped that further help would be forthcoming in future as well. He also apprised the Syrian Foreign Minister as regards difficulties faced by some of the Indian companies in submitting bids for tenders floated by Syria in view of the problems between Commercial Bank of Syria and some of the Indian banks. Shri Kamal Nath expressed confidence that the prospects for Indian investments in rock phosphates and fertilisers, cement, power sector, IT, education and agro-industries appear to be bright and with the support of Syrian government such investments would increase in future. During the discussions, the Syrian Foreign Minister offered to export pulses to India. Exports to Syria during 2006-07 amounted to US $ 408.39 million as against exports of US $ 276.67 million during last year showing a growth of 47.61%. Imports from Syria during this period amounted to US $ 79.55 million (inclusive of import of petroleum products of US $ 67.49 million). The prominent export items from India include machinery & instruments, manmade yarn, fabrics, made-ups, manmade staple fibre and drugs, pharmaceuticals & fine chemicals while the major import items consist of petroleum & crude products, fruits & nuts (excluding cashew nuts), raw wool, leather and spices.

2374. (14-8-2007) NEW DELHI : 291 vacancies of judges in High Courts in 21 States were filled from 2004 to 2006. Of these 95 vacancies were filled during 2004, 86 during 2005 and 110 vacancies during 2006. During the current year, 35 vacancies of judges in High Courts have been filled till 6th August. In pursuance of the judgement of the Supreme Court in the Supreme Court Advocates on Record & Anrs. Vs. the Union of India, the judge strength of the High Courts is reviewed every three years. The last triennial review was undertaken in the year 2006 whereby it is proposed to increase the judge strength by 106 in 8 High Courts, subject to concurrence of the respective State Governments.

2375. (14-8-2007) NEW DELHI: Leader of Opposition in the Lok Sabha L.K. Advani has sought the cooperation of Left and other parties to take on the Government on the nuclear agreement with the United States. Copies of a fresh notice by Mr. Advani for a discussion under a rule that mandates a vote were sent to Communist Party of India (Marxist) general secretary Prakash Karat and Samajwadi Party leader Ram Gopal Yadav, BJP deputy leader in the Lok Sabha V.K. Malhotra told *The Hindu*. Earlier, the former External Affairs Minister Yashwant Sinha confirmed that Mr. Advani spoke to Mr. Karat and leaders of other parties seeking coordination in Parliament on the issue. The notice under Rule 184 has been sent by Mr. Advani and other NDA leaders, including Prabhunath Singh and Anant Geete.

2376. (14-8-2007) NEW DELHI : Based on the complaints received and suo-motu on the basis of the information given on the website of Indian Institute of Planning & Management (IIPM) offering free international study tours and free laptops to students of MBA/BBA, the Monopolies and Restrictive Trade Practices (MRTP) Commission has initiated action against the IIPM. The matter has been referred to the Director General (Investigation & Registration) to investigate and file the Preliminary Investigation Report. The MRTP Commission can take cognizance of such advertisements under the provisions of MRTP Act. All India Council for Technical Education (AICTE) has issued a show cause notice to the Indian Institute of Planning and Management, New Delhi and has placed the name of the Institution in the list of Institutions which are running technical courses without their approval, on their web-site. This information was given by Shri Prem

Chand Gupta, Minister of Corporate Affairs in reply to the questions raised by Shri Dharam Pal Sabharwal in Rajya Sabha today.

2377. (14-8-2007) NEW DELHI : The National Defence Academy and Naval Academy Examination (II), 2007 will be held by the Union Public Service Commission on 19th August, 2007 as scheduled and there is no change in the schedule of this examination.

2378. (14-8-2007) NEW DELHI : The AICTE has justly recognized that the gravest problem bedeviling our country's system of technical education is the woeful shortage of competent teaching staff. The number of technical institutions imparting education and research skills in Engineering & Technology has risen to 1475 with an annual intake of nearly 5,00,000. It is likely that the magnitude of the intake will be about 15,00,000 *i.e.*, threefold by the year 2011-12 (at a projected annual growth rate of 20%). Currently, based on the established AICTE norms of student : teacher ratio (1:15) and the cadre ratio of 1:2:6 for Professors : Readers : Lecturers, the total shortage of teaching staff is over 40,000 and the shortage in the different cadres is Professors-4531, Readers-9063 and Lecturers-27187. The shortage of Ph. D.s exceeds 30,000 while the Masters' shortfall is over 24,000. The shortage in the faculty and the inadequacy of the existing faculty in several instances are further reflected in the alarming failure rate in a large number of technical institutions. For example, in about 150 of the 229 engineering colleges in Tamil Nadu, the failure rate was as large as nearly 65%. In order to address the shortage of qualified faculty, a Committee was appointed under the Chairmanship of Prof. P. Rama Rao.

2379. (14-8-2007) NEW DELHI : The Prime Minister, Dr. Manmohan Singh and the External Affairs Minister, Shri Pranab Mukherjee met Shri Prakash Karat, General Secretary of the CPI (M), here today and discussed the issues connected with the bilateral Civil Nuclear Cooperation Agreement between India and the United States. Some of the points regarding the agreement were discussed. The CPI (M) General Secretary stated that he would put it to the party's politburo which will meet over the week end. Shri. Karat and the Prime Minister reiterated that efforts would be made to sort out the issues.

2380. (15-8-2007) LUCKNOW: After the Presidential and Vice-Presidential elections, the Congress in Uttar Pradesh finds itself in a dilemma. There is a strong feeling in the party that its "appeasement" policy toward Chief Minister Mayawati may cost it dearly. Murmurings on this count have reportedly reached the Congress central leadership. After Ms. Mayawati supported the United Progressive Alliance-Left candidates in the two elections the Congress is weighing the options for an approach toward the Chief Minister. In the current scenario in the State, the Congress is unable to define its stand - as that of an Opposition party or as an ally of the Bahujan Samaj Party (BSP). Uttar Pradesh Congress Committee president Salman Khurshid told The Hindu that "in the overall context it was too soon to predict the exact contours of the Congress' relationship with Ms. Mayawati." He, however, st ressed that the party was sensitive to the opinions from different parts of the State. "The Congress cannot shut its eyes toward these opinions, we are awaiting guidance from the Central leadership," the State Congress chief said.

2381. (15-8-2007) MUMBAI: The demand to implement the Srikrishna Commission report on the 1992-93 communal riots in Mumbai could not have come at a worse time for the Congress-Nationalist Congress party (NCP) Government in Maharashtra. Its relations were at an all-time high with the Shiv Sena. On the eve of the Presidential polls on June 18, the Chief Minister and the Deputy Chief Minister of Maharashtra actually paid a never-before visit to Matoshri, the home of Shiv Sena leader Bal Thackeray to thank him for supporting the UPA candidate for President. The Sena broke ranks with its alliance partner in Maharashtra of 21 years, the Bharatiya Janata Party (BJP), to back Ms. Pratibha Patil. Ms. Patil since then has called Sena executive president Uddhav Thackeray on his birthday and last week, her husband Devisingh Patil paid a courtesy visit to the Thackeray senior. The Sena-BJP alliance is on the rocks and even though a glimmer of hope was felt after the Sena voted for NDA candidate Najma Heptullah in the elections to the post of Vice-President, things are not hunky dory. On Monday, the district chiefs of the Shiv Sena held a meeting at the Sena Bhavan and decided to pass a unanimous resolution saying that the alliance with the BJP must be broken off. The Sena rank and file feels that the BJP calling their support to a Maharashtrian woman for President as a "betrayal" was an insult to the party. However, late on Monday night Uddhav Thackeray who was cornered by the press while attending the 47th anniversary celebration of the weekly magazine, Marmik, said he still had to see the resolution. While the central leadership of the BJP does not seem too keen on the break, State BJP president Nitin Gadkari has continued to indicate that the ties are strained.

2382. (15-8-2007) NEW DELHI : The Vice President, Mohammad Hamid Ansari has said that sixty years after 1947, India's progress is evident. Doubts about our capability have given way to certitude. Our achievements in every sector of national activity are noteworthy. Addressing at the function to commemorate 60th Anniversary of India's Independence at the Central Hall of Parliament House today, Shri Ansari said that there was an apprehension in the early years of independence of physical balkanization which proved to be unfounded. A more distressing trend, increasingly evident, is the balkanization of the mind, that needs to be addressed. The challenge is to promote Indianness in all its diversity, he said.

2383. (15-8-2007) LUCKNOW: India is a country of more than a billion people. Hence, the world's largest democracy is getting set to celebrate its 60th year of political Independence. The people of Uttar Pradesh, the most populous and politically mighty State, however, have a different reason to rejoice in the year of 2007. The rise of the Bahujan Samaj Party (BSP) or the Majority People's Party to power after the March-May election to the 403-member Uttar Pradesh Legislative Assembly is clearly a great phenomenon for ushering in an era of 'Social Democracy.' Truly, the U.P. Assembly election-2007 results have created strong undercurrents and a wave in Indian politics. Think of it as a positive and progressive sign as the Shashan Mantra of "Sarwajan Hitai, Sarwaja n Sukhai" (Progress and Prosperity For All) is under way. Moreover, I would not like to speak about the BSP's superb electoral victory merely in terms of politics, as people say: "Whoever gets to lord over the Legislative Assembly [of Uttar Pradesh] will have a bearing on who rules at the Centre." True, the road to Parliament passes through Uttar Pradesh. It is also true that Uttar Pradesh has been dominating the Indian political scene right from Independence. But the bitter fact is that the majority of the people of this Hindi heartland State of U.P. remain in misery and abject poverty and are socially downtrodden. Naturally, people have remained grossly disenchanted and disillusioned with the Congress-like politics and Manuvadi-type of politicians. The BJP too was never different in the eyes of the people. It is a known fact that victory by majority has been elusive for any so-called high and mighty political party for the past 16 years in Uttar Pradesh for one reason or another. In such circumstances and given the heightened public outcry for good governance, a grand electoral success by the BSP against all odds in the crucial Assembly election in Uttar Pradesh was unprecedented. Social scientists termed this success of the BSP 'social engineering' and my political strategy. However, in broader terms, it was a surgical social strike, through political and electoral moves with the best of intentions. This was an uphill and risky task as our country is so orthodox, so archaic in its thoughts and its social structure that very few could even attempt to think of it. We all know that after Independence the rulers were at liberty to reform our social system - which is so full of inequities, so full of inequalities, discriminations, and of other things, which conflicts with our fundamental rights. But they lacked a strong political will. To be fair, we all know that an honest, committed, and well-intentioned attempt to serve the greater cause of 'Social Transformation and Economic Equality' among its people had never been a fair and honest play in Indian political governance. Disenchantment was thus inevitable. Moreover, social acrimony and caste hatred perpetuated by the Manuvadi politicians guided by vested political and electoral interests played a negative, rather a devastating role in eroding the credibility of a party in a democratic system despite knowing fully well that the failure of parliamentary democracy would result in rebellion, anarchy, and communalism. In such an atmosphere, we tried our best with solid groundwork.

2384. (15-8-2007) NEW DELHI: The Communist Party of India (Marxist) on Tuesday reiterated its stand that the Government should not proceed with the India-U.S. civil nuclear agreement. It said Prime Minister Manmohan Singh's statement in Parliament "does not shed any new light" that calls for a reassessment by the party. Hours after CPI(M) general secretary Prakash Karat met Dr. Singh and External Affairs Minister Pranab Mukherjee, the party Polit Bureau said the more important issue that the Left parties had been raising from the beginning was the link that the agreement had with India's foreign policy.

2385. (15-8-2007) NEW DELHI : Following is the text of the Prime Minister, Dr. Manmohan Singh's speech on the occasion of commemoration of the 60th Anniversary of India's independence: "Sixty years ago the voice of the people of India found its true and free expression in these hallowed premises. In the early hours of that historic day Pandit Jawaharlal Nehru asked the people of free India to march forward "with faith and confidence in this great adventure" of building a secular, democratic and modern India. Inspired by the unique personality of a great soul, Mahatma Gandhi, our freedom fighters gave us a Constitution of which we are all truly proud. As Babasaheb Ambedkar said in the last session of the Constituent Assembly, our Constitution has given us not just a political democracy, but also a social democracy, guaranteeing equality of all and empowerment of the weak and the marginalized. Every citizen of this great Republic has cherished our hard won freedom because it is only as a secular democracy committed to social justice that we have been able to empower the poorest of the poor in this ancient land of ours. The building of a free, democratic India has been one of the greatest adventures of humankind this past century. In these sixty years we have done much and we have achieved much. Yet, we have some distance to travel before we can say that we have fulfilled Gandhiji's dream of wiping the last tear of the poorest of the poor. This remains our sacred duty as representatives of our people. Today, when we look back and look around I believe we can say with some sense of satisfaction that India is on the move. There is a new dynamism in our people. A new sense of confidence in their capabilities. A new sense of hope in their collective future. They recognize we have a long road ahead in our tryst with destiny; and more to be done to redeem our pledge in full measure.

2386. (16-8-2007) NEW DELHI : The National Development Council in its resolution of 29th May, 2007 decided that an Additional Assistance Scheme be launched to incentivise States that increase the share of agriculture in their State Plans. Hence, in view of the above, the Cabinet Committee on Economic Affairs today gave its approval for a new Additional Central Assistance Scheme. The objectives of the scheme are (i) to enhance public investment in agriculture and allied sectors, (ii) to incentivise States to draw up comprehensive State and District Agriculture Plans and (iii) to help the States to achieve the targeted agricultural growth rates. The scheme will enable the States to draw up plans for their agriculture sector more comprehensively, taking agro climatic conditions, natural resources, and technology into account, and by integrating livestock, poultry and fishery sectors. The outlay under the scheme would depend upon the amount provided in the State Budgets for agriculture and allied sectors, over and above the base line percentage expenditure incurred by the State Governments. The funds under the ACA would be provided to the States as 100% grant by the Central Government. An outlay of Rs.1500 crore for the Scheme for 2007-08, along with an allocation of Rs.25,000 crore for five years has also been approved by the CCEA. It would result in quantifiable increases in agriculture and allied sector production, productivity and farm incomes and reduction in yield gaps.

2387. (16-8-2007) NEW DELHI : In view of the stagnating food grain production and an increasing consumption need of the growing population, National Development Council in its 53rd meeting adopted a resolution to enhance the production of rice, wheat and pulses by 10, 8 and 2 million tons respectively by 2011. Hence, in view of the above, the Cabinet Committee on Economic Affairs today gave its approval for launching a Centrally Sponsored Scheme 'National Food Security Mission (NFSM)' to operationalise the resolution. The Mission aims at increasing production of rice, wheat and pulses through a set of measures such as area expansion, productivity enhancement in selected districts; restoring soil fertility; creating employment opportunities; and enhancing farm level economy to restore the confidence of the farmers of the targeted districts. In addition to the above, CCEA also approved the revision in the existing norms governing ISOPOM (Integrated Scheme of Oilseeds, Pulses, Oil Palm and Maize) and Distribution of Quality Seeds, addition of more implementing agencies and inclusion of new components. NFSM will have three components-(i) National Food Security Mission-Rice (NFSM-Rice); (ii) National Food Security Mission-Wheat (NFSM-Wheat); and (iii) National Food Security Mission-Pulses (NFSM-Pulses). Total financial implications for the NFSM will Rs.4882.48 crores during the XI Plan (2007-08-2011-12). Beneficiary farmers will contribute 50% of cost of the activities / work to be taken up at their / individual farm holdings. Beneficiaries can choose to draw loans from the Banks, in which case subsidy amount prescribed for a particular component for which the loan availed will be released to the Banks. 133 districts of 12 States (A.P., Assam, Bihar, Chhattisgarh, Jharkhand, Karnataka, M.P., Orissa, Tamil Nadu, U.P. and West Bengal) will be covered under NFSM-Rice. 138 districts of 9 States (Punjab, Haryana, U.P., Bihar, Rajasthan, M.P., Gujarat, Maharashtra and West Bengal) will be covered under NFSM-Wheat. 168 districts of 14 States (A.P., Bihar, Chhattisgarh, Gujarat, Karnataka, M.P., Maharashtra, Orissa, Rajasthan, Tamil Nadu, Punjab, Haryana, U.P. and West Bengal) will be covered under NFSM-Pulses. 20 million hectares of rice, 13 million hectares of wheat and 4.5 million hectares of pulses are included in these districts that roughly constitute 50% of cropped area for wheat and rice. For pulses, an additional 20% cropped area would be created. The implementation of the NFSM would result in increasing the production of rice by 10 million tones, wheat by 8 million tones and pulses by 2 million tones by 2011-12. It would also create additional employment opportunities.

2388. (16-8-2007) NEW DELHI : The Union Cabinet today gave its approval for concluding a Bilateral Investment Promotion and Protection Agreement with the Macedonia. This Agreement would likely to increase investments between India and Macedonia.

2389. (16-8-2007) NEW DELHI : The Union Cabinet today gave its ex-post-facto approval to the Extradition Treaty singed between India and Portuguese on January 11,2007 and to authorize the ratification of the Extradition Treaty. The proposed Treaty would provide a legal framework for seeking extradition of terrorists, economic offenders, and other criminals from and to Portugal.

2390. (16-8-2007) NEW DELHI : A dividend cheque for Rs.5.04 crore was presented by Mrs. Neera Saggi, Chairperson-cum-Managing Director, Hindustan Diamond Company Private Limited (HDCPL) to Shri Kamal Nath, Union Minister of Commerce & Industry, here today. HDCPL, the supplier of rough diamonds to small and medium manufacturers-exporters of polished diamonds in India, has registered a turnover of Rs.907.58 crore in 2006-07. In its 29th Annual General Meeting held on 6th August, 2007, the company has declared 18% dividend to its shareholders.

2391. (16-8-2007) NEW DELHI : The Chairman Chiefs of Staff Committee and Army Chief, General JJ Singh is on a two-day visit of prestigious defence training institutes and Public Sector Units in Hyderabad and Bangalore. On arrival at Hyderabad today (16 Aug 07), he addressed participants viz the Colonels and equivalents of the three services attending the Higher Defence Management Course (HDMC) at the College of Defence Management (CDM)-a premier tri-Services Institute involved in imparting institutionalized training and education in development of concepts and application of scientific disciplines in various facets of management of national military security at the operational and strategic levels. The theme of his address to the participants of the HDMC was "Vision 2020 for the Indian Army". He later interacted with the officers of an infantry division, formations and units of the Secunderabad military garrison. On his arrival in Bangalore on 17 Aug 07, Gen JJ Singh will inaugurate the newly constructed ultra modern complex and associated state-of-art training and residential facilities for the Army Institute of Hotel Management & Catering Technology (AIHM&CT). The AIHM&CT has been established under the Army Welfare Education Society (AWES) which is involved in development and management of a large number of technical education institutes, as part of the Army's contribution in developing the nation's human capital and the national resource pool of technically qualified youth. The AWES runs a large number of Army Public Schools across the length and breadth of the country as well as the premier technical education institutions viz, the Army Institute of Law (AIL) and the Army College of Dental Sciences (ACDS). While in Bangalore, the Chief of Army Staff will also be visiting the Madras Engineering Group (MEG) Training Centre and the Hindustan Aeronautics Ltd (HAL). At the HAL, he is to critically appraise the state of progress made on various current projects including the Light Combat Aircraft (LCA); the Jaguar

Assembly Line; Advance Light Helicopter (ALH) and various Training Simulators. The two-day visit will help Gen JJ Singh appraise the state of progress made in various key areas of force modernization and training that he had set for the Indian Army.

2392. (16-8-2007) NEW DELHI : The Minister of Petroleum & Natural Gas Shri Murli Deora held a wide ranging discussions with the President of Kyrgyztan Mr. Kurmanbek Bakiev for enhancing cooperation between the two countries. Leading a high level Indian delegation to participate as observer at the meeting of the Council of the heads of Shanghai Cooperation Organisation (SCO), Shri Deora late yesterday called upon the President of the host country at Bishkek (the capital city of Kyrgyztan). During the meeting Shri Deora emphasized the warm and friendly relations between the two countries and expressed satisfaction at the institutional framework established for bilateral relations. He also conveyed India's desire to further explore possibilities of cooperation in oil and gas sector while underlining India's considerable experience in human resources development. Shri Deora added that India would consider requests for adding new areas of studies including in the oil and gas sector. Earlier, Shri Murli Deora inaugurated the Indo-Kyrgyz IT Centre at Bishkek. Speaking on the occasion Shri Deora said "Indian skills and capacity in the IT are now globally acknowledged and we are happy to share our expertise in this area with your country". This project has been executed by one of the prestigious organizations of India-HMT International. Indian assisted projects such as Potato Processing Plant and Mountain Medical Centre are in advanced stages of planning and are expected to be executed soon.

2393. (16-8-2007) NEW DELHI : The eleventh plan proposals envisage start of work on eight indigenous Pressurised Heavy Water Reactors (PHWRs) of 700Mwe each to be set up on a twin unit basis. Two units are planned to be located at Kakrapar (Gujarat) and two at Rawatbhata (Rajsthan). Site Selection Committee set up by the Department of Atomic Energy has evaluated a number of sites including a site in the state of Orissa for locating 700Mwe PHWRs or PWRs with capacity of 100MWe and above. The annual Power Production from a 2 x 700 MWe station is about 10,000 Million Units of electricity. This information was given by the Minister of State in the Prime Minister's Office, Shri Prithviraj Chavan in the Rajya Sabha today.

2394. (16-8-2007) NEW DELHI : The Critical Design Reviews of Chandrayaan-1 Space Craft and payload systems have been completed. The flight units of space systems and scientific instruments are in advanced stage of realization. Commisioning the Indian Deep Space Network 9IDSN), required to track the Chandrayaan-1 is progressing satisfactorily. The 18m antenna has successfully undergone testing and evaluation and is ready for use. The critical design review for 38m antenna was completed. This information was given by the Minister of State in the Prime Minister's Office, Shri Prithviraj Chavan in a written reply to a question in the Rajya Sabha today. The Chandrayaan-1 Mission is presently scheduled for launch in the first half of 2008.

2395. (16-8-2007) NEW DELHI : Government have approved project proposals of the Sports Authority of India amounting to Rs.1000 crores (± 10%) for the upgradation/creation of sports venue infrastructure; the upgradation of the tennis venue by the All India Tennis Association at a cost of Rs.30 crores (± 15%) and the expenditure budget of the Organizing Committee on a revenue neutral basis of Rs.767 crores (± 15%) for the 'Conduct of Games'. The Expenditure Finance Committee have recommended the proposal of the Delhi Development Authority for Rs.325.00 crores (± 25%) for the international zone etc. in the Games Village (which is being developed on the Public Private Partnership Mode) and sports infrastructure. The Planning Commission have approved a proposal of the Government of the NCT of Delhi for an amount of Rs.770.00 crores for the up-gradation of the civic infrastructure in the context of the Commonwealth Games. The Planning Commission have also approved an amount of Rs.110.00 crores to the Govt. of Maharashtra as Special Central Assistance for sports infrastructure for the Commonwealth Youth Games, 2008 to be held in Pune, as a sub-event of the main Commonwealth Games 2010. No amount has been allocated by the Government for developing accommodation in the Games Village, which is being developed on the public-private-partnership mode for housing all Indian/foreign accredited athletes, coaches, medical/administrative staff, managers etc. Other foreign nationals, who may include technical officials/visitors would be accommodated in existing hotels or those coming up from investment by private entrepreneurs. This information was given by Shri Mani Shankar Aiyar, Minister of Panchayati Raj, Youth Affairs & Sports and DoNER in the Rajya Sabha today in a written reply to a question by Shri Jai Parkash Aggarwal.

2396. (16-8-2007) NEW DELHI : Suspension of Operations (SoO) agreement with the United People's Democratic Solidarity (UPDS) has been extended for six months beyond 1.8.2007. This follows a tripartite meeting of the representatives of the Government of India, Government of Assam and UPDS, held on 30.07.2007. The meeting reviewed the functioning of the Suspension of Operations (SoO) arrangement and observance of agreed ground rules.

2397. (16-8-2007) NEW DELHI : Central Board of Excise and Customs (CBEC), Department of Revenue issued Notification no. 83/2007-Cus (N.T), here today, notifying tariff values of edible oils and brass scrap (all grades) as shown in the Table below. The tariff values of six palm group oils and crude soyabean oil remain unchanged. However, tariff value of brass scrap (all grades) has been raised.

2398. (16-8-2007) NEW DELHI : During current financial year (2007-08) an allocation of Rs. 65.00 crores has been provided for protection and conservation of tiger under the Centrally Sponsored Scheme of Project Tiger. This includes Rs. 30.00 crores for relocation of villages from the core areas of tiger reserves. Based on the recommendations of the National Board for Wildlife under the Chairmanship of the Prime Minister, a Tiger Task Force was constituted to review the problems of tiger conservation in the country. The said Tiger Task Force had submitted its report with urgent recommendations, which have been accepted for implementation to strengthen tiger conservation, based on ground reality. This information was given by the Minister of State in the Ministry of Environment and Forests, Shri S. Regupthy in a written reply to question by Shri Karnendu Bhattacharjee in the Rajya Sabha today.

2399. (16-8-2007) NEW DELHI: Addressing the nation from the ramparts of the Red Fort on the 60th Independence Day, Prime Minister Manmohan Singh hailed that "we have built the firm foundations of an open society and an open economy," and reiterated the "quest for a caring, sharing and an inclusive society." While stressing the "unity in diversity" theme, he said "those who profess hatred and extremism, those who spread the virus of communalism and those who believe in violence and terrorism have no place in our society." He reiterated that "let there be no doubt in anyone's mind that the Government is firm in its resolve to fight all forms of extremism and terrorism." The Prime Minister's 40-minute address was devoted entirely to showcasing the Government's concern for the "aam aadmi." However, it was conspicuously silent on the most controversial issue of the day—the nuclear agreement with the U.S. Dr. Singh highlighted the "significant increase in public expenditure in the social sectors" in the last three years, including the "historic" National Rural Employment Guarantee Act. He announced that a special programme entailing an investment of Rs. 25,000 crore in agriculture would soon be launched." "Farmers are the backbone of our nation. Unless they prosper, the nation cannot prosper. I reassure our farmers that their welfare lies at the core of all our concerns," he said. "Our economy is now growing at historically unprecedented rates. However, we cannot become a nation with islands of high growth and vast areas untouched by development, where the benefits of growth accrue only to a few. This is good neither for our society nor for our polity." Dr. Singh made public the Government's commitment to the "social safety" and "economic security" of the vast work-force in the unorganised sector. The Prime Minister also devoted considerable attention to the need to create an educated India.

2400. (16-8-2007) NEW DELHI : The works of pollution abatement in rivers started with the launching of the Ganga Action Plan (GAP) Phase-I in the year 1985 which was completed in March 2000. Subsequently, GAP Phase-II (GAP-II) was approved in stages from 1993 onwards which included the works on the tributaries of the river Ganga namely, Yamuna, Gomti and Damodar and Mahananda. The programme was broad based in 1995 and renamed as the National River Conservation Plan (NRCP) which presently covers 160 towns along identified polluted stretches of 34 major rivers spread over 20 States at an approved cost of Rs.4783 crore. The rivers covered under the Plan, and the river-wise expenditure incurred till March, 2007 is given at Annexure. Conservation of rivers through pollution abatement works is a continuous activity under NRCP and are aimed towards ameliorating the water quality in rivers. With the pollution abatement works completed so far in both the phases under GAP, the water quality of the river Ganga has shown discernible improvement at major locations over its pre-GAP quality as per the water quality monitoring undertaken by independent reputed institutions of the country. Also, as per an independent evaluation study conducted by University of Bath, and Metroeconomica, United Kingdom and the Institute of Economic Growth, New Delhi, published in the year 2000, the Ganga Action Plan compares favourably, both in terms of cost and time taken, with those of other major rivers of the world like Thames, Rhine, Danube etc. A total of sewage treatment capacity of 1747 mld. (million litres per day) has been created so far for Ganga and its tributaries namely, Yamuna, Gomti, Damodar and Mahananda. As regards Yamuna, the tributary of Ganga, the quality of river water has not shown the desired improvement owing to the large gap between the demand and the availability of the sewage treatment capacity particularly in Delhi, and lack of availability of fresh water for ensuring minimum flow in the river.

2401. (16-8-2007) NEW DELHI : Integrated Forest Protection Scheme (IFPS) was initiated during Xth plan. This scheme provides financial assistance on sharing basis for protection of existing forests. The financial assistance is made available for strengthening of infrastructure, preparation of working plans and other protection related measures. The allocation of funds to States is determined by various factors such as demand projected by States, past performance in terms of utilization of funds, availability of funds etc. The grant is not given on the basis of the forest areas of different States This information was given by the Minister of State in the Ministry of Environment and Forests, Shri S.Regupathy in a written reply to question by Smt Sushma Swaraj :in the Rajya Sabha today.

2402. (16-8-2007) NEW DELHI : The river Ganga is changing its course in the town of Allahabad. The river Ganga was shifting towards the Phaphamau side during the last 3-4 years. It has formed a meandering loop and it was observed that about 1.5-2.0 kms. upstream of the bridges, some erosion has taken place. However, the extent of erosion could not be found out. A Technical Team comprising officers from Government of Uttar Pradesh, Ganga Flood Control Commission (Patna), Ministry of Railways and the Central Water Commission which was constituted by the Ministry of Water Resources visited Allahabad in May, 2007 to study the matter relating to this change in trend The Team also observed that the approach to the road and railway bridges is quite protected and stacked boulders placed there will also dampen the river flow. The river flow is still 600 to 700 metres away from the existing road and the Phaphamau town is protected by the road itself. Some protection works have also been carried out by the Government of Uttar Pradesh earlier at the junction of straight and curved portions of guide bund of upstream of the railway bridge. Thus, no immediate danger to the guide bund, road and railway bridges or Phaphamau town from floods is anticipated. The Team has recommended the need for (i) close monitoring of the flow pattern of the river during the current monsoon season, (ii) conducting a model study on the behaviour of the river in the vicinity of the bridges, and (iii) carrying out morphological studies with remote sensing techniques in the 20 kms. reach of the river (10 kms. upstream and downstream of the bridges) by the State Government. The Ministry of Water Resources has already suggested to the Government of Uttar Pradesh to undertake the required studies and remedial measures. This information was given by the Minister of State in the Ministry of Environment and Forests, Shri Namo Narayana Meena in a written reply to question by Smt Jaya Bachchan :in the Rajya Sabha today.

2403. (16-8-2007) NEW DELHI : Protection measures under Wildlife Crime Control Bureau have come into action for protection of wild tigers. India has banned trade in the body parts (and their derivatives) of tiger and other wild animals included in Schedule I and Part II of Schedule II of the Wildlife (Protection) Act 1972, so requesting China to lift the ban on trade in tiger parts does not arise. The Wild Life Protection Act, 1972 has been amended during 2006 to provide enabling provisions for creating the National Tiger Conservation Authority and the Tiger and Other Endangered Species Crime Control Bureau, which have already been constituted for strengthening tiger conservation and protection of our wildlife. The penalties for offences relating to tiger reserves have been made more stringent. Amendment of the Wild Life (Protection) Act, 1972 for providing enabling provisions for constitution of the National Tiger Conservation Authority and the Tiger and Other Endangered Species Crime Control Bureau have been made. Under this the punishment in cases of offence within a tiger reserve has been enhanced. The Act also provides for forfeiture of any equipment, vehicle or weapon that has been used for committing any wild life offence. Regarding Administrative steps, antipoaching activities, including special strategy for monsoon patrolling, by providing funding support to Tiger Reserve States have been strengthened. For deployment of antipoaching squads involving ex-army personnel / home guards, apart from workforce comprising of local people, in addition to strengthening of communication / wireless facilities have also been considered. The National Tiger Conservation Authority constituted with effect from 4.09.2006, which will take care to strengthen tiger conservation by, interalia, ensuring normative standards in tiger reserve management, preparation of reserve specific tiger conservation plan etc., Constitution of a multidisciplinary Tiger and Other Endangered Species Crime Control Bureau (Wildlife Crime Control Bureau) with effect from 6.6.2007 comprising of officers from Police, Forest, Customs and other enforcement agencies to effectively control illegal trade in wildlife. At International level India has a Memorandum of Understanding with Nepal on controlling trans-boundary illegal trade in wildlife and conservation, apart from a protocol on tiger conservation with China. A Global Tiger Forum of Tiger Range

Countries has been created for addressing international issues related to tiger conservation. India introduced a resolution along with China, Nepal and the Russian Federation, which contains directions to Parties with operations breeding tigers on a commercial scale, for restricting such captive populations to a level supportive only to conserving wild tigers. The resolution was adopted with minor amendments during the 14th meeting of the Conference of Parties to CITES at the Hague in last June. This information was given by the Minister of State in the Ministry of Environment and Forests, Shri S.Regupathy in a written reply to question by Shri R. Shunmugasundaram:in the Rajya Sabha today.

2404. (16-8-2007) NEW DELHI : Hundred thousand tones of solid wastes is generated in the country is per day, of which about 20% is recycled. This has been reported in the manual prepared by the Ministry of Urban Development As per the Export and Import Policy, 2004-2009, amended from time to time and the Hazardous Wastes (Management & Handling) Rules, 1989 amended 2000 and 2003, import of garbage and chemical waste respectively for dumping are prohibited. No report of such dumping has been received by the Ministry of Environment and Forests. Further, a per the Municipal Solid Wastes (Management and Handling) Rules 2000, bio-degradable wastes which produce methane are not permitted to be disposed off in landfills. No project to utilize methane has been prepared by this Ministry. This information was given by the Minister of State in the Ministry of Environment and Forests, Shri Namo Narayana Meena in a written reply to question by.

2405. (16-8-2007) NEW DELHI : The Minister of Tourism and Culture Minister Smt. Ambika Soni informed the Lok Sabha today that Manuscripts are kept in various government and private collections across the country, in libraries, museums, matts, madrasas, temples etc. Most of these institutions, especially the private ones, have very little funds for preserving manuscripts. Both in terms of infrastructure and skill, these institutions are lagging behind. The general lack of awareness about manuscripts are also responsible for sufficient funds not flowing in for the preservation of the manuscripts in the smaller and often unknown collections of manuscripts. The Government started the National Mission for Manuscripts in February 2003 with the aim of locating, documenting and preserving the manuscript collections across the country. The Mission has networked with as many as 80 partner institutions throughout the country as Manuscript Resource Centres and Manuscript Conservation Centres, which are given financial assistance in documenting the regional manuscript collections, as well as conserving them. Special projects are being taken up and funded, in association with reputed institutes for conservation of manuscript collections.

2406. (16-8-2007) NEW DELHI : To meet the enhanced requirements of rolling stock and components, works have been approved to increase production capacities in locomotives and coach building production units at Diesel Locomotive Works,

Chittaranjan Locomotive Works, Integral Coach Factory & Railway Coach Factory. In addition, the Ministry of Railways, are setting up a Rail Coach Factory, a Diesel Locomotive Factory, an Electric Locomotive Factory & a Wheel Manufacturing Plant.

2407. (16-8-2007) NEW DELHI : The Minister of Tourism and Culture Smt. Ambika Soni has said that the Taj Mahal is already the most visited centrally protected monument. In the year 2006-07, 26,03,571 tourists (Indian: 20,71,243 and Foreigner: 5,32,328) visited Taj Mahal. Some increase in these numbers is anticipated as a result of the recent declaration of the Taj Mahal as one of the seven wonders of the world. In a written reply in the Lok Sahha today, she said, in addition to the regular watch and ward, the security and safety of the Taj Mahal is assigned to the Central Industrial Security Force. Basic tourist amenities like drinking water, toilets, wheel chairs for physically challenged persons, lockers etc. have been provided.

2408. (16-8-2007) NEW DELHI : In order to attract the foreign tourists, Indian Railways introduced Indrail Pass Scheme in the year 1977 as a tourism promotion measure. These passes are issued to the foreign nationals and Non Resident Indians (NRIs) against payments in the US dollars, Sterling pounds and Euro currency. The pass holder is entitled to travel throughout the Indian Railway's Network within the period of its validity in a class it is issued for. Further, Indian Railways have also run six luxury tourist trains for tourists including foreign tourists *i.e.* Palace on Wheels, Heritage on Wheels in Rajasthan sector, Steam Safari Train-the Fairy Queen on Delhi-Alwar sector, Deccan Odyssey in Maharashtra Sector and Buddhist Special by covering places linked with Lord Buddha. In addition to above, two new luxury tourist trains in Karnataka and Rajasthan may also be launched in the tourist season 2007-08. One luxury tourist train in the Punjab sector has also been approved. These luxury tourist train facilities are available by foreign tourists. This information was given by the Minister of State for Railways Shri R.Velu in written reply to a question in the Lok Sabha today.

2409. (16-8-2007) NEW DELHI : The Sky Bus Metro Technology Project is currently in developmental stage. A test track for a length of about 1.6 kilometres for conducting trials has been constructed at Madgaon. The Ministry of Urban Development had appointed an Expert Committee headed by Dr. P.V. Indiresan, former Director, IIT, Chennai, for evaluation of the Sky Bus Technology. The Committee's report, submitted in August 2005, recommended formation of a Technological Advisory Group (TAG) to evaluate the novel system and guide for further development of the technology. The TAG has already been constituted and has had three meetings so far. The Ministry of Railways have allocated an amount of Rs. 25 Crores under Plan Head "Railway Research" for conducting further trials of Sky Bus Metro leading to Certification of Technology under the guidance of Technical Advisory Group. Specific time frame for a technology development project cannot be stipulated as the success of the project will depend upon the results of the trials and opinion of Commissioner of Railway Safety or any other agency appointed for the designated purpose. This information was given by the Minister of State for Railways Shri R.Velu in written reply to a question in the Lok Sabha today.

2410. (16-8-2007) NEW DELHI : Railways provide hygienic food to the passengers at stations and in trains. Regular inspections are conducted by Railways as well as Indian Railway Catering and Tourism Corporation (IRCTC) officials to ensure the quality of service. Appropriate action is taken against staff/licensees found overcharging the passengers. Catering services provided through private licensees at D, E and F category stations, are directly administered by Zonal Railways. Catering service at A, B and C category stations and in trains are provided by private licensees and departmental staff of IRCTC, a wholly owned company of Indian Railway. During 2006-07, a total of 2656 number of complaints were received. Appropriate actions like warning, fine, termination, counselling etc. have been taken on the complaints found substantiated. IRCTC is setting up multi-cuisine state-of-the-art food Plazas, Automatic Vending Machines to dispense hot and cold beverages, and modernizing railways' existing base kitchens. Regular monitoring of catering services is done by Railways and IRCTC official. IRCTC has engaged independent food audit agencies to ensure quality of food being supplied to the passengers of Indian Railways. All good practices like, progressive ISO (International Organization for Standardization) and HACCP (Hazard Analysis and Critical Control Points) certification of catering units are being followed by Railways through IRCTC. In addition, dedicated quality inspectors have also been engaged for constant monitoring of quality of food. This information was given by the Minister of State for Railways Shri R.Velu in written reply to a question in the Lok Sabha today.

2411. (16-8-2007) NEW DELHI : Indian Railways have identified 185 Railway Stations including 17 metro stations as vulnerable where security systems are proposed to be upgraded. X-Ray machines are proposed to be installed at very important railway stations. Procurement process has been started for installing X-Ray machines for screening luggage/baggage of passengers at very important Railway Stations. One such machine has been installed at Kolkata Terminal Railway Station (Chitpur) and another Machine has been procured for platform No. 18 at Delhi Main station. Moreover, procurement of 29 numbers of X-Ray machines are under process with Zonal Railways. This information was given by the Minister of State for Railways Shri R.Velu in written reply to a question in the Lok Sabha today.

2412. (16-8-2007) NEW DELHI : Gauge conversion of Manamadurai-Rameswaram including Pamban Bridge has already been completed and the converted broad gauge section is commissioned for passenger train services on

12.08.2007 by running three pairs of trains viz. 6713/6714 Chennai Egmore-Rameswaram Express, 751/752 and 753/754 Madurai-Rameswaram Passengers. Introduction of 8495/8496 Bhubanswar-Rameswarma express (Weekly) and Madurai-Rameswaram passenger train has been announced in the Railway Budget for 2007-08 and 2006-07 respectively. Southern Railway has planned to seek World heritage status for Pamban Bridge. This information was given by the Minister of State for Railways Shri R.Velu in written reply to a question in the Lok Sabha today.

2413. (16-8-2007) NEW DELHI : In reply to a question raised in Lok Sabha, the Minister of State for Railways informed the House that introduction/extension of trains including Garib Rath services, is an on going process on Indian Railways subject to operational feasibility, resource availability and traffic justification. Indian Railways is alive to the needs of tribal regions and has proposed the following Garib Rath services which will serve these regions.

2414. (16-8-2007) NEW DELHI : Due to joint efforts of Railway Protection Force (RPF), Vigilance and Commercial staff, 1015 touts have been apprehended over Indian Railways during 2006 and 655 touts upto June 2007 under the provisions of the Railways Act.

2415. (16-8-2007) NEW DELHI : Strengthening of security measures at Railways Stations including installation of Close Circuit Televisions and Cameras is an on going process. The expenditure to be incurred thereon is Rupees 34,99,10,006/- (approximately) for the year 2007-08. The selection of Railway stations for installation of Close Circuit Televisions and Cameras have been done on the basis of terrorists threat perception and during the year 2006-07, the following stations have been covered with the facilities of Close Circuit Televisions and Cameras. Remaining important Railway Stations of Zonal Railways will be covered subject to availability of adequate funds.

2416. (16-8-2007) NEW DELHI : The Ministry of Housing & Urban Poverty Alleviation has approved 169 projects under the Basic Services to the Urban Poor (BSUP) and 257 projects under Integrated Housing and Slum Development Programme (IHSDP). These projects have been approved by the Central Sanctioning and Monitoring Committee (CS&MC) and Central Sanctioning Committee (CSC) out of the total 232 projects under BSUP and 700 projects under IHSDP respectively, received as on 6th August, 2007. This information was given by the Minister of State for Housing & Urban Poverty Alleviation, Kumari Selja in the Rajya Sabha today, in a written reply to a question by Shri Balavant Alias Bal Apte and Shri Vinay Katiyar. The State-wise details of the projects received & approved under Basic Service to the Urban Poor (BSUP) and Integrated Housing & Slum Development Programme (IHSDP) are given at Annexure-I & Annexure-II respectively.

2417. (16-8-2007) NEW DELHI : 60th Anniversary of India's independence was celebrated at the Indian Research Station, Maitri in Antarctica and at Ny-Ålesund in the Arctic, with great warmth and gaiety. This is for the first time that the event was marked together in both the polar regions. India has sent its first Arctic expedition to the Svalbard archipelago inside the Arctic Circle, which was flagged off on 3rd August by Shri Kapil Sibal, Union Minister for Science & Technology and Earth Sciences. In the Antarctic the National flag was hoisted at the Station by the Leader and Station Commander, Shri Jayapaul D in presence of all the 23 members of the 26th Indian Antarctic Expedition. The ceremony was conducted under severe blizzard conditions, which was blowing over Maitri at the time, showing dedication and high spirits of the team members who are spending the dark Antarctic winter in total isolation. This was followed by distribution of sweets and a cultural programme. The 5-member team of the Indian Arctic expedition under the leadership of Shri Rasik Ravindra, Director NCAOR, Goa, planted the flag in the Arctic island of Spitbergen, where they are currently conducting scientific experiments.

2418. (16-8-2007) NEW DELHI : Since the Government is yet to announce spectrum policy for 3G services, Board of Bharat Sanchar Nigam Ltd (BSNL) had taken a review of the GSM tender with the possibility to restrict order to 2G compnent. BSNL employees had also raised their concern against possible restriction of order on 3G component and requested for immediate release of purchase order. However, based on the legal opinion, BSNL Board has decided to maintain the provision of the tender including 3G component. This information was given by Dr. Shakeel Ahmad, Minister of State in the Ministry of Communications and Information Technology in the Rajya Sabha today in a written reply to a question by Shri T.T.V.Dhinakran.

2419. (16-8-2007) NEW DELHI : The Minister for Tourism and Culture Smt. Ambika Soni has said that no survey has been conducted by the Government to estimate the extent of loss of manuscripts in the Kashmir Valley due to terrorism. In a written reply in the Lok Sabha today she said, National Mission for Manuscripts (NMM), under Ministry of Culture, has collaborated with Directorate of State Archaeology, Archives and Museums to locate and document the manuscripts in the State of Jammu & Kashmir. The Mission has collected information on more than 22,000 manuscripts in 163 manuscript repositories in the State, which has been incorporated in the National Database of the Manuscripts of the Mission. In order to protect the knowledge contained in manuscripts for long term preservation, the Mission has started a programme for digitization of manuscripts under which more than 14 lakh folios of rare manuscripts from the State of Jammu & Kashmir have already been digitized. Public awareness programmes are also organized by the Mission to train owners of repositories on the methods of preserving their manuscript collections.

2420. (16-8-2007) NEW DELHI : The Master Plan for Delhi-2021 aims to ensure housing and shelter options for all categories of people. The proposed housing strategy incorporates specific approaches for development of new housing areas, upgradation and re-densification of existing housing areas including unauthorised colonies, housing in villages and Special Area. The housing strategy recommends four categories of Dwelling Units (DU) sizes with different density norms. Keeping in view the socio-economic composition of the population, around 50-55% of the housing requirement would be for urban poor and the economically weaker sections in the form of house of two rooms or less with average plinth area of about 25 square metres to 40 square metres.

2421. (16-8-2007) NEW DELHI : Sanction of building plan can be done by the local body concerned only on regularization of unauthorized colonies. Municipal Corporation of Delhi (MCD) and Delhi Police has reported that no such complaint has been received/ is under investigation except one case where a vigilance enquiry is under process in Delhi Police. A firm date can not be given at this stage in view of the legal and administrative issues involved. This information was given by Shri Ajay Maken, Minister of State in the Ministry of Urban Development in the Rajya Sabha today in a written reply to a question by Shri Amar Singh and Shri Abu Asim Azmi.

2422. (16-8-2007) NEW DELHI : Delhi-Gurgaon Access Controlled Highway was conceived in 1997, and Detailed Project Report (DPR) completed in October, 2001. Work commenced in January, 2003 and the entire project is likely to be completed by December, 2007. The reasons for delay in completion of project include value additions incorporated on the suggestions of Government of Delhi and Government of Haryana and to cater for increased traffic; delay in handing over of land by Airport Authority of India, Defence and Government of Haryana; delay in shifting of utilities; and poor performance by the concessionaire. The likely date of completion of the project is December, 2007. This information was given by the Minister of State for Shipping, Road Transport and Highways, Shri K.H. Muniyappa in a written reply in the Rajya Sabha today.

2423. (16-8-2007) NEW DELHI : Steel Authority of India Ltd (SAIL), India's largest steel producer and a Navratna PSU, and POSCO, Korea's largest steel company, today signed a memorandum of understanding (MoU) to establish a strategic alliance for aligning and cooperating with each other in a wide range of strategic business and commercial interest areas. Mr. G. Ojha, Director (Personnel), SAIL, and Mr. Soung-sik Cho, Senior Executive Vice President and Member of Board, POSCO, signed the MoU here in the presence of SAIL Chairman Mr. S.K. Roongta.

2424. (16-8-2007) NEW DELHI : The Ministry of Labour and Employment has invited applications from eligible workers in public & private sectors for the Prime Minister's Shram Awards for the year 2007. The applications should reach the

Ministry of Labour and Employment, Government of India, Shram Shakti Bhawan, Rafi Marg, New Delhi latest by August 31, 2007. A total number of 33 Prime Minister's Shram Awards are to be given away to workers both in the private and public sectors in recognition of their outstanding contribution towards production and for showing exemplary zeal and enthusiasm in discharge of their duties. These awards are given under different titles like Shram Ratna, Shram Bhushan, Shram Vir/Shram Veerangana and Shram Shree/Shram Devi. While the Shram Ratna is common to workers both form public and private sector, all the other 32 awards, are shared equally by the worker from both the sectors.

2425. (16-8-2007) NEW DELHI : A ten days workshop on management of patients with AIDS and HIV was inaugurated at Army Hospital (R&R) Delhi Cantt today. This is being attended by delegates from various Military and Civil Hospitals. The theme of the workshop, "Call of the Century-Global threat from HIV, a human approach to management of patients with HIV & AIDS" will focus on the role of Nursing Officers in understanding the innate attributes of human behaviour to formulate strategies for prevention, control and management of HIV/AIDS. Lt Gen J Jayaram, Director General Health Services (Armed Forces) inaugurated the training programme. Maj Gen Shashi Bala, Additional Director General Military Nursing Service and Maj Gen O P Mathew, Comdt Army Hospital (R&R) were present at the inaugural ceremony. Speaking on the occasion, the Chief Guest, Lt Gen J Jayaram, intimated that prevalence of HIV and AIDS amongst Armed Forces if far lesser than the civil. He advised the delegates on the need to develop good communication skills to unravel the cultural, social and personal values and beliefs of each patient which will help in formulating further effective prevention and control measures against HIV/AIDS. He released a souvenir to mark the occasion. Two compact discs containing training material were also released for distribution to the participating delegates.

2426. (16-8-2007) NEW DELHI : The UPSC has declared the results of Combined Defence Services Examination-II, 2006. 361 candidates have finally qualified on the basis of the results of the Combined Defence Services Examination-II, 2006 conducted by the Union Public Service Commission and the Interviews held by the Services Selection Board of the Ministry of Defence for admission to the Officers Training Academy, Chennai (Madras) for 86th Short Service Commission Course commencing in Oct., 2007. The complete list is available on PIB website www.pib.nic.in. The list also includes the names of the candidates who were recommended earlier on the basis of results of the same examination for admission to Indian Military Academy, Dehradun/ Naval Academy Goa-Course, Air Force Station, Begumpet, Hyderabad Course(s). The number of vacancies for Short Service Commission Course is 163.

2427. (16-8-2007) NEW DELHI : The following is the text of the Statement by the Union External Affairs Minister, Shri Pranab Mukherjee in Parliament today relating to the Indo-US Bilateral Civil Nuclear Cooperation Agreement: "Questions have been raised about India's right to test when the bilateral civil nuclear cooperation agreement with the US enters into force. The factual position is as follows: India has the sovereign right to test and would do so if it is necessary in national interest. The only restraint in our voluntary unilateral moratorium on nuclear testing, declared by the previous government and being continued by the successor government. There is nothing in the bilateral agreement that would tie the hands of a future government or legally constrain its options. A decision to undertake a future nuclear test would be India's sovereign decision, resting solely with the Government of India. Nowhere in the bilateral agreement on Cooperation for Peaceful Uses of Nuclear Energy with the United States of America is testing mentioned. The bilateral cooperation agreement contains elaborate provisions in Articles 5 and 14 to ensure the continuous operation of India's reactors. These include fuel supply assurances, the right to take corrective measures, and a strategic fuel reserve for the lifetime of India's reactors in case of cessation of cooperation."

2428. (16-8-2007) NEW DELHI : A delegation of German parliamentarians, led by Dr. Norbert Lammert, President of the German Bundestag called on Minister of Information and Broadcasting and Parliamentary Affairs, Shri P.R. Dasmunsi today. They deliberated on issues related to the functioning of parliamentary democracy in the two countries. Shri Dasmunsi said that India's cooperation with Germany in the technological and investment sector has been very important, and they continue to have extremely rich bilateral ties. Shri Dasmunsi also gave them an overview of the functioning and systems of Indian parliament. The visiting dignitary expressed the view that there are some astonishing similarities in the working of the two democracies.

2429. (17-8-2007) NEW DELHI : A project to computerize and network state consumer commissions and district fora will be completed by the end of this year. Shri Sharad Pawar, Minister for Agriculture, Food & Public Distribution and Consumer Affairs said this here today while inaugurating a conference of the Presidents, State Commissions and the Secretaries in-charge of consumer affairs in the States and Union Territories. The scheme executed at an estimated cost of Rs. 49 crore is in its final phase, he added. Shri Pawar informed that Central Government has been extending liberal grants for infrastructural improvement of the fora. The government has already sanctioned Rs. 98 crore for 18 states and over Rs. 47 crore to 16 State governments as the first tranche of assistance despite the fact that State Commissions and District Fora are the responsibility of the States concerned. The Minister stated that the process of increasing the number of members of the National Commission from 5 to 9 is currently on, to further strengthen the commission. Also, law has been amended to enable the senior most member to act as the President in the absence of the President to ensure uninterrupted functioning of the fora. The Minister asked the conference to deliberate and consider adoption of some uniform formula with regard to remuneration to the members. Observing that "the need of the hour is to change the common man's perception that the Consumer Fora have slipped onto the path of civil courts, making litigation long drawn out and taking several years to dispose of even cases involving small compensation", Shri Pawar called upon presiding officers of the Fora to take a pledge that they would dispose of the cases within the time norm. Organized by the National Consumer Disputes Redressal Commission, the function was presided over by Shri H.R. Bhardwaj, Minister for Law and Justice.

2430. (17-8-2007) NEW DELHI : Shri B. K. Handique, Minister of State for Parliamentary Affairs and Chemicals and Fertilizers gave away the prizes to winning students/vidyalayas for their meritorious performances in the Youth Parliament Competition. On this occasion, the students of Kendriya Vidyalaya, IIT, Kharagpur, West Bengal which stood first in the competition also presented a short sitting of Youth Parliament. Speaking on the occasion, Shri Handique said that the competition promotes in students the values like leadership, discipline, responsibility and accountability. It also develops democratic spirit and temper in the students. Through such competitions, they get groomed into the culture of all-inclusiveness, tolerance, debate and deliberations which is the essence of democracy, he added. The Minister praised the high level of debate displayed during the enactment of Youth Parliament by the winning team. Dr. Rekha Bhargava, Secretary, Ministry of Parliamentary Affairs, in her remarks said that this competition works in two ways-it provides the participants knowledge and enlightens them about the functioning of our Parliament and Parliamentary institutions. It also provides them a platform to express themselves about various important social, national and international issues and to disseminate their ideas. Ministry of Parliamentary Affairs have been organizing Youth Parliament competitions in the schools under the Directorate of Education, Government of NCT of Delhi and NDMC every year since 1966. In 1988, a separate National Youth Parliament Scheme for Kendriya Vidyalayas was introduced. In 1997-98, two more national competitions, one for Jawahar Navodaya Vidyalayas and the other for Universities and Colleges were introduced as a part of the celebrations to commemorate 50 years of Indian's Independence. The Youth Parliament Scheme aims at inculcating among the younger generations the spirit of self-discipline, tolerance of diverse opinion, righteous expression of views and other virtues of democratic way of life. In accordance with the scheme, the competition was held in two stages, first at the regional level and then at the national level. The position of zonal first is also determined on the basis of evaluation of performance for the national level. The Vidyalayas, which stood first in their respective regions, then competed at the national level. The Vidyalayas and students who secured positions in the competitions were awarded, shields, trophies, books and certificates during the prize distribution function. The running parliamentary shield and trophy for standing first at the national level was awarded to Kendriya Vidyalaya, IIT, Kharagpur, West Bengal. Besides, trophies were also be awarded to 5 vidyalayas which stood first in their respective zones and 12 vidyalayas which stood first in their respective regions.

2431. (17-8-2007) NEW DELHI : Government of India have announced the sale (re-issue) of "7.27 per cent Government Stock, 2013 for a notified amount of Rs. 5,000 crore (nominal) through a priced based auction using multiple price method. Government of India have also announced the sale (re-issue) of "7.99 per cent Government Stock, 2017" for a notified amount of Rs. 2,000 crore (nominal) through a price based auction using multiple price method. The auctions will be conducted by the Reserve Bank of India, Mumbai Office, Fort, Mumbai on August 24, 2007 (Friday). Up to 5% of the notified amount of the sale of both the stocks will be allotted to eligible individuals and Institutions as per the Scheme for Non-Competitive Bidding Facility in the Auction of Government Securities. Bids in the prescribed form obtainable from the Regional Director, Reserve Bank of India, Mumbai Office (Public Debt Office), Fort, Mumbai-400 001 and RBI website www.rbi.org.in should be submitted to that Office on August 24, 2007. The NDS members should submit competitive as well as non-competitive bids in electronic format using Primary Market Operation (PMO) module of NDS. All bids should be submitted by 12.30 P.M. The result of the auctions will be announced on August 24, 2007 and payment by successful bidders will be during banking hours on August 27, 2007 (Monday). Both the Stocks will be eligible for "When Issued" trading in accordance with the guidelines on 'When Issued transactions in Central Government Securities' issued by the Reserve Bank of India vide circular No.RBI/ 2006-07/178 dated November 16, 2006.

2432. (17-8-2007) NEW DELHI : The area coverage of kharif crops as compared to 17th August last year has gone up considerably as per data compiled by Agriculture Ministry. Rice area coverage is marginally less. The total coverage of kharif rice has gone up to 278.37 lakh ha as compared to 281.26 lakh hectare at this time last year, the weekly Crop Weather Watch Group meeting of the Ministry of Agriculture was informed here today. Transplanting of rice is in progress in Andhra Pradesh, J&K, Karnataka, Kerala and Tamil Nadu. The sowing is at ending stage in Gujarat and Haryana. Transplanting is at peak in rest of the states. Total coarse cereals have covered an area of 195.27 lakh ha as compared to 186.57 lakh ha at this time last year. Cotton has been sown in 87.45 lakh ha as compared to 82.49 lakh ha last year. Out of this, 53.32 lakh hectare is under Bt cotton. Sugarcane coverage is reported to be 51.04 lakh hectare compared to 48.32 lakh ha last year, and jute 7.89 lakh hectare (last year 8.18 lakh ha.). The total coverage of oilseeds so far has been 164.65 lakh ha as compared to 152.25 lakh ha on August 16, last year. Soyabean has been sown in 8% and groundnut in 15% higher area as compared to that in 2006. Pulses cover an area of 107.1 lakh ha against 98.46 lakh ha up to this time the last year.

2433. (17-8-2007) NEW DELHI : Shri Kamal Nath, Union Minister of Commerce & Industry, will be laying the foundation stone of the new National Institute of Intellectual Property Management (NIIPM), at Nagpur tomorrow, 18th August 2007, in the presence of Shri Vilasrao Deshmukh, Chief Minister of Maharashtra.

The NIIPM will cater to the needs of an Intellectual Property (IP) regime that is in line with the global norms while at the same time safeguarding national interests. The setting up of the NIIPM closely follows on the launch of the e-Filing facility for patent and trade mark applications by Shri Kamal Nath on 20th July, 2007. Its functions will encompass training, education and research, besides being a think tank of the government on important IP policy matters. It will conduct training programmes for Examiners of Patents, Designs, Trade Marks and Geographical Indications, IP professionals such as agents, attorneys and lawyers, and IP managers in business enterprises and research organisations. Its education programmes will cover government officials, enforcement agencies such as police and customs and judicial officers, besides academics. Research will be carried out in a wide variety of subjects relating to Intellectual Property Rights (IPRs) which have topical relevance. Inputs will be provided by the Institute based on analytical and empirical research to facilitate government decision-making in the area of IP policy and legislation. The NIIPM will be a unique institute combining all the four functions. The establishment of the NIIPM will cost about Rs.22 crore. While the construction of the building, etc. may take about an year or so, it is proposed to commence academic programmes in the premises of the existing Intellectual Property Training Institute at Nagpur. The Government has recently completed the implementation of a Rs.153 crore modernisation programme which has seen the establishment of state-of-the-art modern integrated intellectual property offices at the four metros of Chennai, Delhi, Kolkata and Mumbai. Computerisation has also been introduced at all levels of functioning of the Intellectual Property Offices. This has resulted in an increase in patent and trademark applications as well as their grants. Government is also planning to invest another Rs.300 crore in the next five years on further modernisation of the IP Offices so as to make them world class. It has already moved an application with the World Intellectual Property Organisation to recognise the Indian Patent Office as an International Search Authority and an International Preliminary Examining Authority under the Patent Cooperation Treaty administered by that organisation. Currently there are only 12 such offices. On the trademark side, it is planning to become a Member of the Madrid Protocol, a facilitative system for international trademarks.

2434. (17-8-2007) NEW DELHI : Shri Kamal Nath, Union Minister of Commerce & Industry, while briefing the media persons here today informed that during the financial year 2006-07, the FDI equity inflows have been US $ 15.7 billion as compared to US $ 5.5 billion received during 2005-06. This is a growth of 185% as compared to the previous year. This is also the first time that FDI equity inflows into India have crossed the US $ 10 billion mark. If reinvested earnings and other capital inflows are also included, the total inflows in 2006-07 add up to US$ 19.5 billion compared to US$ 7.7 billion during the same period last year showing a growth of 153%. During the first quarter of the Financial Year 2007-08, the FDI inflows have been US$ 4.9 billion as against US$ 1.7 billion received during the corresponding quarter of 2006-07, registering a growth of more than 185%. The first six months of the current calendar year (January-June 2007) have witnessed FDI inflows of US$ 11.4 billion as against US$ 3.6 billion received during the same period in 2006. This indicates a growth of 218%. With regard to industrial production, Shri Kamal Nath stated that as per the Quick Estimates of Industrial Production released by the Central Statistical Organization, the industrial production registered a double-digit growth of 11% in the first quarter of the current fiscal as compared to the corresponding period of the previous year. The Manufacturing Sector, which has around 80% weightage in the Index of Industrial Production, has also shown a double-digit growth of 11.9% during the first quarter of Financial Year 2007-08 (April to June 2007) as compared to a growth of 11.7% in the previous year. For the Financial Year 2006-07, Manufacturing Sector registered a growth of 12.5%, up from 9.1% in 2005-06. This was the highest growth registered by the Manufacturing Sector since 1995-96.

2435. (17-8-2007) NEW DELHI : Indian systems of Medicine mainly Ayurveda is getting acceptance and popularity through out the world mainly because of its holistic approach. As per the findings of WHO more than 75% of the population in developed countries are using complementary and Alternative Traditional Medicine like Botanicals, Herbals which is part and parcel of Ayurveda. Ayurveda is having much more potential in some areas like minimal invasive Para-surgical measure and so on. The Anushastra Karma *i.e.* minimal invasive Para-surgical measure of Ayurveda, particularly Ksharasutra is gaining acceptance and popularity in fistula-in-ano and other selected ano-rectal disorders. In India, many general surgeons and proctologists are also practicing this art routinely, considering the cost-effectiveness and safety of this unique approach. In view to mainstream this measure among surgeons of other systems of medicine and to popularize the role of Ksharasutra, the Central Council for Research in Ayurveda and Siddha (CCRAS) in the Department of AYUSH has initiated a National campaign on Ksharasutra from 24th August 2007 throughout the country. The campaign will be launched with national level workshop in association with ICMR to be held on 24th and 25th of August in the auditorium of AIIMS, New Delhi. The practicing general surgeons, proctologists, academicians from premier Medical Colleges will be participating in this Two days workshop.

2436. (17-8-2007) NEW DELHI : A site has been selected near latitude 69o South and longitude 76o East for the Third Research Station at Larsemann Hill Area in Antarctica. A comprehensive Environment Evaluation (CEE) report mandated under the Environmental Protocol of the Antarctic Treaty was prepared by the National Centre for Antarctic and Ocean Research, NCAOR, Goa in November 2006. It has been accepted during the XXXth Antarctic Treaty Consultative Meeting held in New Delhi this year. NCOAR has now initiated action on developing detailed design of the building of the new research centre which is required for obtaining necessary administrative approval for taking up construction work during the 11th Five Year Plan. The total allocation for polar Science Programme during the 10th Plan period was Rs. 160 Crores. The proposed outlay for the 11th Plan for Antarctic Research and logistic activities is about Rs. 320 Crores. The increased outlay is to strengthen the research and logistic facilities at Maitri, construction of the new research base and to further develop the in-house research facilities at NCAOR. In addition the Ministry of earth Sciences has also proposed to construct an ice-breaker class research-cum-logistic vessel. The Union Minister of Science and Technology and Earth Sciences Shri Kapil Sibal gave this information in the Lok Sabha today.

2437. (17-8-2007) NEW DELHI : The Planning Commission has set up a High Level Committee on Financial Sector Reforms with a view to outlining a comprehensive agenda for the evolution of the financial sector indicating especially the priorities and sequencing decisions which the Government must keep in mind. Shri Raghuram G. Rajan will be the Chairman of the 12-Member Committee. The Committee will identify the emerging challenges in meeting the financing needs of the Indian economy in the coming decade and to identify real sector reforms that would allow those needs to be more easily met by the financial sector. It will also examine the performance of various segments of the financial sector and identify changes that will allow it to meet the needs of the real sector, identify changes in the regulatory and the supervisory infrastructures that can better allow the financial sector to play its role, which ensuring that risks are contained. The terms of reference also include identify changes in other areas of the economy-including the conduct of monetary and fiscal policy, and the operation of the legal system and the educational system-that could help the financial sector function more effectively. The Committee will submit report by 31st March, 2008. Other members of the committee include : Suman Berry, Director General NCAER, Uday Kotak of Kotak Mahindra Bank, Rajeev Lall of IDFC, Vijay Mahajan, Chairman Basix, Zia Modi Senior Partner, AZB Partners, O.P. Bhatt State Bank of India, K.V. Kamath ICICI Bank, Chitra Ramakrishna, Deputy MD. NSE, R. Ravimohan, CRISIL, J.R. Varma, of Indian Institute of Management Ahmadabad, and R. Sridharan, Adviser (FR), Planning Commission will be the Convener of the committee.

2438. (17-8-2007) NEW DELHI : In exercise of its powers under section 233B of the Companies Act, 1956, the Central Government issues Cost Audit Orders on select companies, where it considers necessary, covered in the list of 44 industries as per Annexure enclosed for which Cost Accounting Record Rules (CARR) have been prescribed under section 209 (1) (d) of the Act. The intent of the legislative provision provides discretion to the Central Government in the matter and the statute does not imply mandatory application to all industries. No discrimination is made between domestic and multinational companies producing, processing or manufacturing various items for the purpose of issue of cost audit orders. The Central Government examines the application of provisions relating to Cost Audit under the Companies Act, 1956 to companies producing different kinds of items depending upon need and issues appropriate orders from time to time.

2439. (17-8-2007) NEW DELHI : It is proposed to enable Limited Liability Partnerships (LLPs) to be formed and regulated in the country on the basis of legislation. The Government has introduced a Bill, namely, the Limited Liability Partnership (LLP) Bill, 2006 in the Rajya Sabha on 15th December, 2006. The Bill is under the consideration of Parliamentary Standing Committee on Finance. The Limited Liability Partnership (LLP) is viewed as an alternative corporate business vehicle that would provide the benefits of limited liability but allows its members the flexibility of organizing their internal structure as a partnership based on a mutually arrived agreement. Once the proposed legislation is enacted, this form would enable entrepreneurs, professionals and enterprises providing services of any kind or engaged in scientific and technical disciplines, to form commercially efficient vehicles suited to their requirements. Owing to flexibility in its structure and operation, the LLP would also be a suitable vehicle for small enterprises and for investment by venture capital. This information was given by Shri Prem Chand Gupta, Minister of Corporate Affairs in reply to a question raised by Sh. Joachim Baxla in Lok Sabha today.

2440. (17-8-2007) NEW DELHI : Telecom Consultant India Limited (TCIL) and Sudan Technology City (STC) have signed a Memorandum of Understanding for award of feasibility study of STC and its implementation to TCIL. The MoU was signed in New Delhi during the visit of a high level STC delegation led by the Sudanese Minister of Science & Technology Shri Abdel Rahman Saeed to India from 13 to 16 August, 2007. The MoU was signed by Mr. R.K. Upadhyay, Chairman & Managing Director TCIL and Mr. Gamal M. Hassanien, President & CEO of STC. Sh. Saeed had a meeting with the Minister of Communications and Information Technology, Shri A. Raja on Thursday. It may be mentioned that TCIL has earlier completed Feasibility Study of Sudan Electronic City which was very much appreciated by Ministry of Science and Technology, Republic of the Sudan.

2441. (17-8-2007) NEW DELHI : 4 Projects of Maharashtra at the cost of Rs.52.60 crores have been sanctioned for implementation for Phase-I of Rajiv Gandhi Grameen Vidyutikaran Yojana. Total funds released to Maharashtra under the scheme since April, 2005, when the scheme was introduced, uptil 10.08.2007 are Rs.10.02 crores. This information was given by the Union Power Minister Shri Sushilkumar Shinde in the Lok Sabha today.

2442. (17-8-2007) NEW DELHI : According to schedule approved in November, 2004 for the 1000 MW Tehri Dam & HPP, Stage-I, three units of 250 MW each were to be commissioned in June '05 and the last unit of 250 MW in July '05. However, due to Rehabilitation and Resettlement (R&R) issues and rock fall in tunnel shafts, the commissioning schedule was again revised in February/March,

2006 to June 2006, July, 2006, August, 2006 and September, 2006 for each of the four units respectively. All the four units (unit IV, III, II & I) of Tehri Hydro Project Stage-I have, however, been synchronized with the Grid on 17.07.2006, 25.10.2006, 30.01.2007 and 19.03.2007 respectively. During 2006-07, 891 MU of energy has been generated from the project against the target of 1384 MU from the project. The target for energy generation for the year 2007-08 is set at 2773 MU and Generation of 780 MU against the proportionate target of 713 MU has been achieved so far. The First Phase of the 2400 MW Tehri Hydro Complex *i.e.* the Tehri Dam & HPP (1000 MW) has already commenced power generation as mentioned in the reply to (a) & (b) above. Power generation from balance two projects of Tehri Power Complex viz. the Koteshwar HEP (400 MW) and the Tehri Pumped Storage Scheme (1000 MW) is scheduled for June, 2010 and June, 2011 respectively. This information was given by the Union Power Minister Shri Sushilkumar Shinde in the Lok Sabha today.

2443. (17-8-2007) NEW DELHI : Since the Polio eradication programme was launched in 1988, a significant number of political leaders and individuals pledged commitment and spearheaded the campaign along with the global polio eradication partners. To honour these leaders, heads of State, health agency leaders and others who have made a significant contribution to the global eradication of polio, the Rotary Foundation of Rotary International established the Polio Eradication Champion award in 1995. The Award recognizes past achievements and the promise of continuing activity and improvement from these individuals to make the world Polio free. Leaders who have been honoured with Rotary's Polio Eradication Champion Award include past United States President William Jefferson Clinton, former Prime Minister of the United Kingdom, John Major and Tony Blair, First Lady of Egypt, Mrs. Suzanne Mubarak, President of Nigeria, Olusegun Obasanjo, UN Secretary-General Kofi Annan, President of Angola Jose Eduardo dos Santos and Heidemarie Wieczorek-Zeul, Germany's Minister of Economic Development and Cooperation, Organisation of Islamic Conference (OIC) Secretary-General, Professor Ekmeleddin Ihsanoglu, the Gates foundation co-chair, Bill Gates Sr. and the Prime Minister of India, Dr. Manmohan Singh. In recognition of the outstanding efforts made by Dr. Anbumani Ramadoss in controlling the polio cases in the country and the support provided for the polio eradication programmes in India, Rotary International has decided to confer this year's Polio Eradication Champion Award to the Union Minister for Health & Family Welfare, Dr. Anbumani Ramadoss.

2444. (17-8-2007) NEW DELHI : Cabinet Committee on Economic Affairs in its meeting held on 02.11.2006 has approved the implementation of Central Sector Reform-Linked Scheme for setting up of modern Terminal Markets Projects under National Horticulture Mission. The Operational Guidelines of the Scheme have been circulated to those States, which have amended their laws dealing with agricultural marketing to allow setting up of markets in private and cooperative sector and direct marketing. Under this scheme, the setting up of Terminal Markets is not location specific and can be set up by the State Government, or if preferred by the State Government, then by the selected Enterprise, at any suitable location on the basis of specificities of that area and the economic viability of the project. Accordingly, the State Governments of Andhra Pradesh, Bihar, Karnataka, Madhya Pradesh, Maharashtra, Orissa, Punjab, Rajasthan, Tamil Nadu and Union Territory of Chandigarh have initiated action for setting up of terminal markets. These Terminal Markets would provide state of the art infrastructure facilities for electronic auction, cold chain and logistics and operate through primary collection centres conveniently located in producing areas to allow easy access to farmers. The terminal markets are envisaged to operate on a "hub-and-spoke" format wherein the terminal market (the hub) would be linked to a number of collection centres (the spokes), conveniently located in key production centres to allow easy access to farmers for the marketing of their produce. The Terminal Market would be built, owned and operated by a Corporate/Private/Cooperative entity either by itself or through adoption of an outsourcing model. The enterprise could be a consortium of entrepreneurs from agri-business, cold chain, logistics, warehousing, agri-infrastrucutre and related background. The enterprise would charge user charge for the services provided. Implementation and successful operation of this path-breaking initiative would necessitate State Government support. The Central/State Government will lend its support to the initiative by providing financial support to the project by way of equity participation upto maximum 49%, which would be determined through a competitive bidding process. The disinvestments of Government equity shall be done at an appropriate time at market/fair value and not at face value. So far, no financial assistance has been released under the scheme as the projects are only at the initial stages. This information was given in the Rajya Sabha today by the Minister of State for Agriculture, Shri Kanti Lal Bhuria in a written reply. Modern Terminal markets being set up for handling agricultural produce.

2445. (17-8-2007) NEW DELHI : Cabinet Committee on Economic Affairs in its meeting held on 02.11.2006 has approved the implementation of Central Sector Reform-Linked Scheme for setting up of modern Terminal Markets Projects under National Horticulture Mission. The Operational Guidelines of the Scheme have been circulated to those States, which have amended their laws dealing with agricultural marketing to allow setting up of markets in private and cooperative sector and direct marketing. Under this scheme, the setting up of Terminal Markets is not location specific and can be set up by the State Government, or if preferred by the State Government, then by the selected Enterprise, at any suitable location on the basis of specificities of that area and the economic viability of the project. Accordingly, the State Governments of Andhra Pradesh, Bihar, Karnataka, Madhya Pradesh, Maharashtra, Orissa, Punjab, Rajasthan, Tamil Nadu and Union Territory of Chandigarh have initiated action for setting up of terminal markets. These Terminal Markets would provide state of the art infrastructure facilities for electronic auction, cold chain and logistics and operate through primary collection centres conveniently located in producing areas to allow easy access to farmers. The terminal markets are envisaged to operate on a "hub-and-spoke" format wherein the terminal market (the hub) would be linked to a number of collection centres (the spokes), conveniently located in key production centres to allow easy access to farmers for the marketing of their produce. The Terminal Market would be built, owned and operated by a Corporate/Private/Cooperative entity either by itself or through adoption of an outsourcing model. The enterprise could be a consortium of entrepreneurs from agri-business, cold chain, logistics, warehousing, agri-infrastrucutre and related background. The enterprise would charge user charge for the services provided.

2446. (17-8-2007) NEW DELHI : NTPC Ltd. is setting up a coal based thermal power project of 750 MW (3x250 MW) at the site of Assam's existing non-operational Bongaigaon Thermal Power Station (TPS) (4x60 MW). In this regard, a Transfer Agreement has been executed amongst NTPC Ltd., Government of Assam and Assam Power Generation Corporation Ltd. (APGCL) for transfer of the existing infrastructure of 240 MW (4x60 MW) Bongaigaon Thermal Power Station of APGCL in Assam to NTPC Ltd. and setting up of new 3x250 MW power station at same location by NTPC Ltd. Power Purchase Agreement (PPA) has been signed by NTPC Ltd. with Assam State Electricity Board (ASEB) on 30.05.2007 for power supply from the project. Feasibility Report of Bongaigaon TPS (750 MW) with an estimated cost of Rs.4496.24 crore (at 3rd Qtr. 2006 Price Level) has been prepared by NTPC Ltd. All key linkages/clearances for the project including Environmental Clearance have already been obtained. Project is identified for benefits starting in 2010-11. This information was given by the Union Power Minister Shri Sushilkumar Shinde in the Lok Sabha today. In a written reply to another question related to NTPC, Shri Shinde said that it does not have necessary expertise to undertake power equipment manufacturing activities on its own. However, NTPC can partner with a strategic partner who can bring the expertise in manufacturing which in combination with NTPC's strength in planning, Engineering, Project Management, Operational Expertise can be used to develop a viable equipment manufacturer and EPC contractor. NTPC has decided to take 44.6% stake of Government of Kerala in Transformers and Electricals Kerala, Ltd. (TELK) Kerala. An agreement to this effect has been signed amongst NTPC, TELK and Government of Kerala on 23.06.2007. TELK is a state owned Company in the business of manufacturing of Transformers. TELK, which is located at Angamali in Ernakulam District of Kerala is already manufacturing Transformers of different types and capacities.

2447. (17-8-2007) NEW DELHI : Reserve Bank of India has issued Master Circular on Credit Card Operations of the banks on 02.07.2007 advising banks/NBFCs/their agents not to resort to intimidation or harassment of any kind, either verbal or physical, against any person in their debt collection efforts. Banks have been especially advised against acts intended to humiliate publicly or intrude the privacy of the credit card holders' family members, referees and friends, making threatening and anonymous calls or making false and misleading representations. This information was given by Shri Pawan Kumar Bansal, Minister of State for Finance in reply to a question raised by Shri G. Karunakara Reddy in Lok Sabha today.

2448. (17-8-2007) NEW DELHI : The Government proposes to populirize the concept of E-taxation in the North East Region. As far as direct taxes are concerned, various initiatives undertaken by the Government for e-governance in the Income Tax Department are being implemented in the North East Region also. For this purpose, Income-tax Department has set up a Regional Computer Centre at Shillong. As far as indirect taxes are concerned, the Government has provided the facility of electronic filing of monthly/quarterly excise returns, namely, ER-1, ER-2. ER-3 under Central Excise Rules, 2002 and dealers return prescribed under sub-rule (6) of rule 7 of the CENVAT Credit Rules, 2002 to all manufacturers of excisable goods, EOUs and registered dealers with effect from 30.06.2004. The facility to file excise returns electronically is optional, and is available to all assesses. Similarly E-payment of excise duty became operational from 11th May, 2005, to all assesses. However, it has now been made mandatory for major assesses that is, those paying annual duty of more than Rs. 50 lakh, w.e.f. April, 2007 in Central Excise. This information was given by Shri S.S. Palanimanickam, Minister of State for Finance in reply to a question raised by Shri Anwar Hussain in Lok Sabha today.

2449. (17-8-2007) NEW DELHI : The Central Board of Direct taxes have further extended the last date of filing of income tax returns from 16th August to 15th September 2007 in the state of Bihar. This decision has been taken in view of the continued disruption caused by floods in the state. The due date for filing returns of income was 31st July, 2007.

2450. (17-8-2007) NEW DELHI : Minister of State for Finance Shri S.S. Palanimanicham affirmed in the Lok Sabha today that the income tax department has issued revised guidelines for allotment of Permanent Account Number (PAN) to Indians living abroad, foreign citizen or a company, trust or firm not having an office in India. The requirement of having a representative assessee in India by a non-resident for allotment of PAN has been dispensed with. Further, the procedure for allotment of PAN to non-residents has been streamlined.

2451. (17-8-2007) NEW DELHI : Reserve Bank of India, vide Circular dated 30th April, 2007, has issued instructions to the Chairman & Managing Director/ Chief Executive Officer of All Scheduled Commercial Banks (including Regional Rural Banks) that banks may dispense with the requirement of No-Due Certificate for small loans upto Rs. 50,000/- to small & marginal farmers, share croppers and the like and, instead, obtain self declaration from the borrower. This information was given by Shri Pawan Kumar Bansal, Minister of State for Finance in reply to a question raised by Shri Harisinh Chavda in Lok Sabha today.

2452. (17-8-2007) NEW DELHI : Farakka Super Thermal Power Station (STPS) has not faced any shortage of water during the current year 2007-08 till the end July, 2007. In order to mitigate the impact of drop in water levels in the feeder canal, National Thermal Power Corporation Ltd. under Capital Addition Scheme for the existing Station and in line with the approval from Central Water Commission (CWC), has awarded the work of Lift Pump House which will pump the water from feeder canal to intake channel of Circulating Water (CW) pumps. This information was given by the Union Power Minister Shri Sushilkumar Shinde in the Lok Sabha today. Farakka STPS had been incurring generation loss due to low water availability on account of the water level in the feeder canal dropping below the intake channel during the regulation period of 1st March to 10th May, since the implementation of Indo-Bangladesh Treaty 1996 on sharing of Ganga water.

2453. (17-8-2007) NEW DELHI : As a general practice, issues, if any, raised in respect of the functioning of the Institute of Chartered Accountants of India (ICAI) from any quarter are looked into by the Government and the Institute to ascertain facts and to take action as warranted under the Chartered Accountants Act, 1949. There is no finding of manipulation in declaration of the results of the examinations conducted by the Institute. Recently on receipt of information pertaining to leakage of the question paper for the Common Proficiency Test (CPT) examination scheduled for 05th August, 2007, the examination in its entirety was cancelled by the Institute and in its place a fresh examination is scheduled to be held on 26th August, 2007. The ICAI is a statutory body required to function, in terms of the provisions of the Chartered Accountants Act, 1949 as amended from time to time and the rules and regulations framed thereunder. The Chartered Accountants Act, 1949 has been amended in 2006 with a view to, inter-alia, further improve the functioning of the Institute. ICAI is also a public authority in terms of the provisions of the Right To Information Act, 2005. This information was given by Shri Prem Chand Gupta, Minister of Corporate Affairs in reply to a question raised by Sh. Subrata Bose in Lok Sabha today.

2454. (17-8-2007) NEW DELHI : In reply to a question regarding irregularities in the implementation of Pradhan Mantri Gram Sadak Yojana (PMGSY) the Minister of State for Rural Development, Smt. Suryakanta Patil informed the Lok Sabha that no Complaint from State Governments including the Government of Rajasthan regarding irregularities being committed in Pradhan Mantri Gram Sadak Yojana (PMGSY) has been received. For ensuring high level of quality in works, PMGSY programme guidelines have the provision for three tier Quality Control Mechanism. The first two tiers of the Quality Control Structure are overseen by the State Quality Coordinators, appointed by the State Governments. The first tier of quality control mechanism is in-house quality control at the level of the executing agencies. Field laboratories are established by the Contractors and mandatory tests on the quality of material and workmanship are conducted under the supervision of Programme Implementation Units (PIUs). The second tier provides for quality monitoring by the State Governments through independent State Quality Monitors (SQMs). SQMs are deployed to ensure that quality issues are properly being attended to at the first tier. The third tier of this arrangement consists of quality monitoring of works through random inspections by independent National Quality Monitors (NQMs). In addition, measures like Standard bidding document, Online monitoring, display of Citizen's information board etc. have been put in place for ensuring quality and transparency in execution of PMGSY projects.

2455. (17-8-2007) NEW DELHI : National Rural Employment Guarantee Act (NREGA) is demand driven and not allocation based. Employment is to be provided to a registered job seeker holding a job card within 15 days of the demand. Therefore, States are permitted to apply for incremental funds upon utilization of 60% of the available funds so that there is an adequate fund balance available to meet the demand. National Level Monitors have visited all the 200 phase one districts. The reports submitted by National Level Monitors have been shared with the concerned State Governments for taking necessary remedial/ corrective measures. Out of 130 districts included in the 2nd phase of expansion of NREGA, National level Monitors have recently visited 113 districts.

2456. (17-8-2007) NEW DELHI : In the year 2006 the Ministry of Corporate Affairs referred two matters relating to cement prices to the Monopolies and Restrictive Trade Practices (MRTP) Commission. The details of matters relating to cement prices referred by Ministry of Corporate Affairs to the Monopolies and Restrictive Trade Practices (MRTP) Commission are as under: 1. The Builders Association of India, in September, 2006 made a representation alleging that the cement manufacturers have increased the prices unduly without any corresponding increase in excise duty, limestone, royalty, sales tax, railway freight, etc. This representation was forwarded to the Commission. 2. The Ministry of Corporate Affairs (then Ministry of Company Affairs) referred matters relating to an agreement entered into between ACC Limited and M/s Bulk Cement Corporation (India) Limited, which, on the basis of an inspection carried out under the provisions of the Companies Act, 1956, prima facie appeared to contain, inter-alia, certain restrictive trade practices as defined under sub-section (o) of section 2 and section 33 of the MRTP Act, 1969. The Commission, in exercise of its powers under the MRTP Act, 1969 has directed the Director General (Investigation and Registration) to carry out an investigation and submit a report on the references in question. This information was given by Shri Prem Chand Gupta, Minister of Corporate Affairs in reply to a question raised by Sh. Ravi Prakash Verma and Sh. Adhalrao Patil Shivajirao in Lok Sabha today.

2457. (17-8-2007) NEW DELHI : In reply to a question regarding the details of road works under Pradhan Mantri Gram Sadak Yojana (PMGSY) sanctioned by the Ministry of Rural Development, Government of India, constructed up to June 2007 in the States of Bihar and UP the Minister of State for Rural Development, Smt. Suryakanta Patil informed Lok Sabha that the State Governments as well as central agencies have been requested to expedite the submission of DPRs and execution of projects under the Scheme.

2458. (17-8-2007) NEW DELHI : Government has approached Ministry of Communications and Information Technology, Department of Posts to explore the possibilities of disbursement of wages under National Rural Employment Guarantee Scheme through post offices. However, Department of Posts has asked for service charges @ 2%. The matter is under discussion. This was stated by the Minister of State for Rural Development, Shri Chandra Sekhar Sahu in reply to a written question in Lok Sabha today.

2459. (17-8-2007) NEW DELHI : The provisions of the Companies Act, 1956 regulate a large number of corporate processes. The statutory obligations of a company include filing of annual returns and various other event based filings. The interests of investors are primarily associated with the listed public companies where the compliance rate, including in filing of annual returns and balance sheets etc. is found to be considerably higher than 50%. Prosecutions are filed against the non-compliant companies, when detected on the basis of inspections/ investigations etc., in the courts of competent jurisdiction. Under the provisions of section 621A of the Companies Act, 1956, any offence punishable under this Act (whether committed by a company or any officer thereof), not being an offence punishable with imprisonment only, or with imprisonment and also with fine, may either before or after the institution of any prosecution, be compounded by the Central Government on payment or credit, by the company or the officer, as the case be. In case the option of compounding of offence is not resorted to, the petitions are filed before the Competent Court of Law. This information was given by Shri Prem Chand Gupta, Minister of Corporate Affairs in reply to a question raised by Sh. Joachim Baxla in Lok Sabha today.

2460. (17-8-2007) NEW DELHI : The Ministry of Rural Development through the State Governments/UT Administrations is implementing some major progrmames namely, Swarnjayanti Gram Swarojgar Yojana (SGSY), Sampoorna Grameen Rozgar Yojana (SGRY), Indira Awaas Yojana (IAY) and National Rural Employment Guarantee Scheme (NREGS) for the poor households living in rural areas of the country. The implementation of these schemes is done in accordance with the respective programme guidelines. The implementation of various poverty alleviation programmes of the Ministry is monitored strictly for which a comprehensive multi tool monitoring mechanism has been put in placed. There has been a direct interaction with the State Governments and the district level officers involved in the implementation of these programmes. Thus a system of getting feed back continuously on the implementation of these programme both from the official and independent sources, such as research institutions and National Level Monitors is existing. Restructuring of various programmes on the basis of experiences is continuous process. Decision of enhancing the units cost of an IAY house, taking up of the issue of flow of more credit to the rural poor etc. are the steps which have been taken. Presently, the Ministry of Rural Development does not propose to subsume any schemes in single scheme for poverty alleviation. This was stated by the Minister of State for Rural Development, Smt. Suryakanta Patil in reply to a written question in Lok Sabha today.

2461. (17-8-2007) NEW DELHI : A large number of persons were given employment during the construction of various projects of Damodar Vally Corporation in the State of Jharkhand. Land losers/displaced persons were given preference in employment in work-charged and master roll establishments and most of them were finally absorbed in the regular establishment of DVC. Some of them left DVC after availing retrenchment benefits as per their own option. Of the remaining 1239 displaced persons of Jharkhand a panel was prepared out of which, 528 persons have been absorbed in DVC till date. In respect of the remaining displaced persons, it has been decided to offer a lump sum amount of Rs. 3 lakhs in lieu of employment over and above the compensation already paid. All the land acquired by DVC has been developed and utilised for the purpose it was acquired. This information was given by Union Power Minister Shri Sushil Kumar Shinde in the Lok Sabha today.

2462. (17-8-2007) NEW DELHI : Ratnagiri Gas & Power Private Limited (RGPPL) which is implementing the Dabhol power project have informed that the R-LNG (Regasified Liquefied Natural Gas) supply to RGPPL has commenced. The Dahej-Dabhol pipeline constructed by GAIL India Limited for supply of R-LNG from Petronet's Dahej terminal was completed on 11th July, 2007 and R-LNG was made available at RGPPL's power block on 23rd July, 2007. Thereafter, RGPPL switched from naphtha to LNG for power block-II (740 MW) on 4th August, 2007. As regards Power block-III (740 MW), revival work is under progress and is likely to be available for generation on gas by 31st August, 2007. RGPPL has been supplying power generated on R-LNG as per requirement of the Maharashtra State Electricity Distribution Company Limited (MSEDCL). In the absence of demand for power from MSEDCL, the power block-II is being maintained under reserve shut down. Further, the hon'ble High Court of Gujarat have granted stay on 31.07.2007 for sale of R-LNG at pooled price. The MSEDCL have not confirmed power off-take at the higher R-LNG price/spot market rates. This information was given by the Union Power Minister Shri Sushilkumar Shinde in the Lok Sabha today.

2463. (17-8-2007) NEW DELHI : The Minister of State for Housing & Urban Poverty Alleviation, Kumari Selja informed the Lok Sabha today, in a written reply to a question by Dr. M. Jagannath, Shri Bhartrunhari Mahtab and Smt. Rupatai Dilprao Nilangakar Patil that a Technical Group on estimation of Urban Housing Shortage constituted by the Ministry of Housing and Urban Poverty Alleviation has estimated housing shortage as 24.71 million in urban areas of the country as in 2007 (at the beginning of 11th Five Year Plan), which is likely to go upto 26.53 million during the 11th Five Year Plan. The major part of this housing shortage pertains to the economically weaker section. Kumari Selja further informed the House that the Government has launched the Jawaharlal Nehru National Urban Renewal Mission (JNNURM) to provide necessary amenities to the urban poor in 63 select cities under the Basic Services to the Urban Poor (BSUP) programme. For non-Mission cities, for taking up housing and slum upgradation programmes and providing other civic amenities, the Integrated Housing and Slum Development Programme (IHSDP) has been launched. Both BSUP and IHSDP are under implementation since December, 2005 the Minister added.

2464. (17-8-2007) NEW DELHI : On the recommendations of National Human Rights Commission and National Commission for Women and as per the judgement of the Supreme Court, the proposal to enact a suitable legislation relating to Compulsory Registration of Marriages is under consideration with the Government. In view of the importance and complexity of the matter, it may take some more time before a Bill could be brought before the Cabinet. The Supreme Court in its judgement dated 23.7.2007 in Smt. Seema Vs. Ashwani Kumar, has reiterated its earlier judgement dated 14.2.2006 that marriages of all persons who are citizens of India belonging to various religions should be made compulsorily registrable in their respective States, where the marriage is solemnized. This was stated by the Minister of State for Law & Justice, Shri K. Venkatapathy in a written reply in Lok Sabha today.

2465. (17-8-2007) NEW DELHI : The Government is not facing shortage of Electronic Voting Machines (EVM). The Government has entered into an agreement for the purchase of EVMs. EVMs are being purchased from two public sector manufacturing firms, namely, Bharat Electronics Limited, Bangalore and Electronics Corporation of India Limited, Hyderabad under separate agreement with them. These public sector companies are indigenously manufacturing EVMs. This was stated by the Minister for Law & Justice, Shri H.R. Bhardwaj in a written reply in Lok Sabha today.

2466. (17-8-2007) NEW DELHI: The country has the sovereign right to conduct a nuclear test and would do so if it is in the national interest, External Affairs Minister Pranab Mukherjee told the Lok Sabha on Thursday. "The only restraint is our voluntary unilateral moratorium on testing declared by the previous government and continued by the successor government," he said. Mr. Mukherjee's statement was in response to the turmoil in both Houses of Parliament over reports of the U.S. State Department spokesperson, Sean McCormack, comments on Wednesday that the nuclear deal would be terminated if India conducted a test.

2467. (17-8-2007) NEW DELHI : A scheme for computerisation of seven hundred courts in the four metropolitan cities has been completed. In addition, computerisation of city courts in State capitals or in cities where High Courts are located was taken up under which 781 courts are reported to have been computerised by the National Informatics Centre (NIC), the implementing agency. Government approved a scheme in February 2007 for computerisation of around 13,000 District and Subordinate courts in the country, the first phase of which is to be implemented at a cost of Rs. 442 crore. The Scheme is being implemented by the NIC and an amount of Rs. 187 crore has been placed at its disposal till March 2007. The NIC has commenced implementation of the scheme by providing laptops to all Judicial Officers involving an expenditure of Rs. 36 crore approximately. All the three phases of the scheme are likely to be completed in five years. This was stated by the Minister of State for Law & Justice, Shri K. Venkatapathy in a written reply in Lok Sabha today.

2468. (17-8-2007) NEW DELHI : Article 348(1) of the Constitution of India provides that all proceedings in the Supreme Court and in every High Court shall be in English language until Parliament by law otherwise provides. No law has since been made in this regard by the Parliament; therefore English continues to be the language for all the proceedings of the Supreme Court. The matter of use of Hindi in the proceedings of the Supreme Court has been examined by the Department of Official Language in consultation with the Registry of the Supreme Court. With respect to a reference made by Department of Official Language, the Registrar, Supreme Court of India intimated that the point of introduction of optional use of Hindi in the hearing and proceedings in the Supreme Court has been considered by the full court twice *i.e.* on 10.4.1990 and 26.9.1996. However, after ascertaining the views of the Bar Council of India, Supreme Court Bar Association and the Supreme Court Advocates-on-Records Association, it was unanimously resolved that it was not practically feasible to introduce Hindi in the proceedings of the Supreme Court on the ground that matters in this court are filed from all parts of the country and Hindi Language is used only in Northern India. If introduced, it will cause great difficulties to the litigants, Judges as well as Bar members, particularly to those who hail from Southern region of the country. Under Article 348(2), the Governor of the State may with the previous consent of the President, authorise the use of the Hindi language or any other language used for any official purpose of the State, in the proceedings of the High Court having its principal seat in that State. In four states namely Bihar, Uttar Pradesh Madhya Pradesh and Rajasthan the use of Hindi language has been authorised for the proceedings of the High Courts. This was stated by the Minister for Law & Justice, Shri H. R. Bhardwaj in a written reply in Lok Sabha today.

2469. (17-8-2007) NEW DELHI : Union Minister of Human Resource Development, Shri Arjun Singh has thanked the Prime Minister, Dr. Manmohan Singh for the magnanimity he has shown to the education sector during his address to the nation on the 60th Anniversary of the Independence. In a Statement he said, "The nation is grateful to the Hon'ble Prime Minister Dr. Manmohan Singhji for his magnificent gift to the education sector on the 60th Anniversary of our Independence. We are delighted that the wish-list of the Ministry of Human Resources Development for expansion and strengthening of public institutions in education during the 11th Five Year Plan-namely, new IITs, new IIMs, new IISERs, new IIITs and new Central Universities, universalizing secondary schooling, high quality schools, colleges and vocational institutions-would now be realized. Hon'ble Prime Minister has reiterated the UPA Government's commitment, under the NCMP, to facilitate affordable access to educational opportunities. Indeed, not since the decade of the fifties' when our First Prime Minister Pt. Jawahar Lal Nehru envisioned new institutions of learning has such a giant leap been proposed. While all those who believe in the essentiality, nay compulsion, of higher public outlays in education should be reassured. The Prime Minister's generous announcement, in my humble opinion, is also an exciting challenge for our academic community and those responsible for academic administration to rise to the immense possibilities of guiding our youth to realize their true potential and attain even loftier heights in the global knowledge society. I am sure they would be up to it. We in the Ministry of HRD have an onerous task to perform which we will do with single minded dedication."

2470. (17-8-2007) NEW DELHI : The details of World Bank assistance during the Financial Years 2005-06 and 2006-07 is at Annex A. The Annual borrowing from World Bank is about US $ 2.5-US $ 3billion for various projects, both in Central and State sectors. The current year level is also expected to be of this order. A list of posed projects is at Annex B. This information was given by Shri Pawan Kumar Bansal, Minister of State for Finance in reply to a question raised by Shri Harikewal Prasad and Shri Dalpat Singh Parste in Lok Sabha today.

2471. (17-8-2007) NEW DELHI : Based on design standards and laid down norms, passenger amenity items are provided in the coaches and efforts are made to ensure proper upkeep and functioning. Indian Railways have more than 8000 stations. It has always been the endeavour of the Railways to provide adequate amenities to the passengers at the stations. Based on the passenger earnings of the stations, these have been categorized into 7 categories, *i.e.* A-1, A, B, C, D, E & F. Minimum essential amenities have been prescribed depending upon category of the station. Minimum essential amenities have been provided at all stations. Certain amenities are provided at the time of construction of new stations based on anticipated traffic. Amenities are further augmented from time to time based on the needs and subject to availability of funds. This information was given by the Minister of State for Railways Shri R.Velu in written reply to a question in the Rajya Sabha today.

2472. (17-8-2007) NEW DELHI : Modern Generation light weight Stainless Steel coach design was acquired under Transfer of technology with M/s Alstom.

Indigenous manufacture of such coaches has already commenced at Rail Coach factory, Kapurthala since 2002 and till date about 400 such coaches have already been manufactured and have been inducted in service. Besides being light weight, the average passenger carrying capacity of these types of coaches is higher than the corresponding conventional design coach by about 12 per cent thereby earning extra revenue. This information was given by the Minister of State for Railways Shri R.Velu in written reply to a question in the Rajya Sabha today.

2473. (17-8-2007) NEW DELHI : Indian Railway Catering and Tourism Corporation (IRCTC) have awarded contract to M/s. Hindustan Coca-Cola Beverages Pvt. Ltd. for setting up of 67 Automatic Vending Machines (AVM) at Lucknow (NR), Lucknow (NER), Varanasi, Allahabad, Kanpur, Tundla, New Delhi, Hazrat Nizamuddin, Delhi, Meerut City, Okhla, Kishanganj, Sarojini Nagar, Ghaziabad Junction, Subji Mandi, Darjeeling and Guwahati Railway Stations. This information was given by the Minister of State for Railways Shri R.Velu in written reply to a question in the Rajya Sabha today.

2474. (17-8-2007) NEW DELHI : The Ministry of Railways has received a proposal to run Luxury Tourist Train on the line of 'Palace on Wheels' from the State Government of Karnataka. Approval has been given by the Ministry to run Luxury Tourist Train in the Karnataka. The tentative itinerary of the proposal is Bangalore-Srirangapatna-Mysore-Shravanabelagola-Hassan-Hospet-Gadag-Vasco/Dabolin-Bangalore. The manufacturing of the coaches is almost completed. The train is likely to become operational in tourist season 2007-08. This information was given by the Minister of State for Railways Shri R.Velu in written reply to a question in the Rajya Sabha today.

2475. (17-8-2007) NEW DELHI : Railways already have a Passenger Insurance Scheme, wherein insurance cover of Rs. 4 lakhs is provided to rail passengers in case of death and of Rs. 32 thousand to Rs. 4 lakhs (depending on the gravity of injury) in case of injuries resulting from train accident or untoward incident. However, there is no provision of insurance for belongings of the passengers. During the last two year, *i.e.* 2005-06 and 2006-07 a total of 167 cases of compensation claims have been finalized by Railway Claim Tribunal, where the next of kin of the deceased passengers have been awarded compensation. Compensation is paid only after a decree is awarded on a claim filed in this regard in Railway Claims Tribunal. This information was given by the Minister of State for Railways Shri R.Velu in written reply to a question in the Rajya Sabha today.

2476. (17-8-2007) NEW DELHI : It is proposed to develop industrial infrastructure around Delhi-Mumbai Rail Freight Corridor to leverage the rail and road connectivities. As per the concept report, the Industrial Corridor may have 24 Industrial Nodes (12 investment Regions and 12 Industrial Areas). Investment opportunities would be presented to domestic and overseas investors alike. Government of India is discussing with Government of Japan about the possibilities of their contribution in the Project development Fund. The project is expected to start in January 2008, while the Concept Paper is in the final stages of preparation. Details pertaining to estimated cost of expenditure and time-frame for completion would be decided after the detailed project report is finalised. This information was given by the Minister of State for Railways Shri R.Velu in written reply to a question in the Rajya Sabha today.

2477. (17-8-2007) NEW DELHI : Twenty-five private satellite TV channels were permitted to be uplinked from India during the year 2005, thirty-seven channels were permitted during the year 2006 and thirty-one channels have been permitted during the current year up to 31.7.2007. Complete list of channels permitted is available on the Ministry's website. Receipt of applications under the uplinking guidelines is an on-going process. No record is kept in the Ministry of incomplete applications, which are closed or returned. As on 31.7.2007, applications of 59 companies to uplink 99 TV channels from India are at various stages of scrutiny. These also require inter-Ministerial comments and hence, no definite time frame can be indicated. Permission for starting a News Channel are given as per the procedure prescribed in the 'Guidelines for Uplinking from India' which were issued on 2.12.2005. These guidelines and application form are available on the Ministry's website (www.mib.nic.in). The eligibility criteria is as prescribed in para 3.1, for News and Current Affairs TV Channels. This information was given by Minister of Information & Broadcasting and Parliamentary Affairs, Shri P. R. Dasmunsi in written reply to a question in Lok Sabha.

2478. (17-8-2007) NEW DELHI : A high-level business delegation is scheduled to visit India on August 21-22, 2007 to participate in business meetings being organised by the Industry Association, Chambers of Commerce in coordination with the Department of Industrial Policy & Promotion, Ministry of Commerce & Industry, Government of India. Mr. Fujio Mitarai, Leader of the Japanese business delegation along with the Presidents of Confederation of Indian Industry (CII), Associated Chamber of Commerce & Industry (Assocham) and Federation of Indian Chambers of Commerce & Industry (FICCI) would be participating in the preliminary discussions with Shri Kamal Nath, Minister of Commerce & Industry, on August 21, 2007. Mr. Toyoda, Vice Minister, Ministry of Economy, Trade and Industry (METI) would be addressing the Indian industry on Japanese government's efforts to support Japanese business at the inaugural session of India-Japan Business Seminar on August 22, 2007. On the same day, Shri Kamal Nath would be inaugurating the Business Leaders Forum. Representatives from the top Japanese companies and officials expected to attend the 2-day meetings include: Nippon Keidanren, Canon Inc., Toyota Motor Corporation, Mitsubishi Corporation, Matsushita Electric Industrial Co. Ltd., Hitachi Limited, Fujitsu Ltd., Suzuki Motor Corporation, Japan Airlines, Japan chamber of Commerce & Industry, Japan Bank for International Cooperation.

2479. (17-8-2007) NEW DELHI : The National Pharmaceutical Pricing Authority (NPPA) has issued 376 notices to drug companies during this year. Out of this 229 cases are those in which the price increase is beyond 20 percent and 147 cases in which price increase is over 10 per cent. This information was given in a written reply in the Rajya Sabha today by the Minister of State for Chemicals & Fertilisers and Parliamentary Affairs Shri B.K. Handique.

2480. (17-8-2007) NEW DELHI : The pricing policy for new and expansion projects in urea section has been notified by the Government in January 2004. The existing policy has not been successful in attracting investments in this sector. Moreover, the availability of gas, which is the critical feedstock for production of urea, has been a major constraint in attracting investments in this sector. In view of the projected improvement in availability of gas in future and the limitations of the existing policy, the review of existing policy is under consideration of the Government. The fertiliser industry is being consulted to decide upon the broad contours of the new investment policy. The fertiliser industry through FAI has suggested a new investment policy based on import parity price for brownfield/ greenfield plants as well as for expansion through revamp of existing units. The Government is examining all possible options including the above option as suggested by the fertiliser industry for finalising the new investment policy. This information was given by the Minister of State for Chemicals & Fertilizers and Parliamentary Affairs Shri B.K. Handique in a written reply in the Rajya Sabha today.

2481. (17-8-2007) NEW DELHI : The Union government is soon going to setup an independent regulatory authority.There is a plan to setup scientific panels in consultation with consumers, investors and industry. The Union Minister of State for Food Processing, Mr. Subodh Kant Sahay while inaugurating the first ever three days Indian Animal Industry Exposition at Pragati Maidan called upon the scientists and experts of the livestock industry as well as technical people to provide a "business plan" to the government for helping the livestock industry. The Expo has attracted people from the livestock industry from far and wide. Foreign delegates from Thailand, Malaysia, Germany, and Middle East Industry attended the inaugural session. The Three days Expo was organized by Pixie Publication Indian Pvt. Ltd. The Minister also stated that if India could act on such a business plan and tap the resources available in the agriculture and livestock sector, India would "become a food factory of the world in the near future". He also maintained that if business in the livestock industry is to be improved, the captains in the industry needed to update processing, marketing, health plan and farming in the country. Specific plans for all this should be chalked out. Mr. Sahay held that if such plans could be executed, livestock sector' would prove to be a big sector for providing employment to the farmers. The need of the hour, however, is to motivate the farmers to enter this segment for economic sustainability. Mr. Sahay wanted the industry, the experts the technical people and the scientist to join their heads together and come out with solutions and layman's outlay which the farmers could understand so that they could be persuaded to make investments. It is because of the fact that livestock sector is going to provide largest employment not only to the landless farmers but to the unemployed youth also. Mr. Sahay said that efforts are underway to make the livestock industry and the processed food products and Dairy items as totally tax less items. This is being done to attract more and more people for investment in the food processing industry. He regretted that processed food items in India were rejected by the foreign countries on their soil when exported. He said that he had asked countries like UK, Italy, France and United States to reject the Indian processed food items on the Indian soil itself:

2482. (17-8-2007) NEW DELHI : The total consumption of chemical fertilisers in 2006-07 is estimated at approximately 449.1 lakh metric tonnes. The production of fertilisers in terms of N+P (nitrogen & phosphates) in the country during 2006-07 has been about 354.30 lakh metric tonnes. An amount of Rs. 12,650.37 crore on indigenous urea and Rs. 6648.16 crore was paid on indigenous decontrolled fertilisers as subsidy, produced in the country during 2006-07. Urea is the only fertilizer, which at present is under partial movement and distribution control of the Government of India. During Kharif 2007, approximately 31.80 lakh metric tonnes of urea is planned to be imported to bridge the gap between demand and indigenous production. Subsidized fertilisers are made available to the farmer at Maximum Retail Price which is much cheaper than the actual cost of production/ import. This information was given by the Minister of State for Chemicals & Fertilisers and Parliamentary Affairs Shri B.K. Handique in a written reply in the Rajya Sabha today.

2483. (17-8-2007) NEW DELHI : Doordarshan transmission is not affected by the foreign TV signals although Chinese TV signals are received in some areas of Arunachal Pradesh during favourable seasonal conditions. Similarly, though Chinese radio channels are audible on different frequencies in Arunachal Pradesh, but coverage of AIR transmitters in Arunachal Pradesh has not been affected by Chinese transmitters. A special package for expansion of Doordarshan and All India Radio Coverage in North East Region and Island territories of Andaman & Nicobar and Lakshadweep has been approved by the Government in May, 2006. With the launch of "DD Direct Plus" (free to Air DTH service of Doordarshan) both AIR and TV signals can be received all over the country including NE Region except Andaman & Nicobar Islands with the help of small size dish receive system. This information was given by Minister of Information & Broadcasting and Parliamentary Affairs, Shri P. R. Dasmunsi in written reply to a question in Lok Sabha.

2484. (17-8-2007) NEW DELHI : Eleven All India Radio Stations and 164 private FM radio stations are expected to go on air till the end of the year. Of these, 27 are in Maharashtra, 17 in Kerala, 14 in Tamil Nadu, 12 in Rajasthan,

10 each in Gujarat and Uttar Pradesh, 9 each in Andhra Pradesh and Madhya Pradesh, 8 in Karnataka and West Bengal, 7 each in Punjab and Jharkhand, 6 in Chattisgarh, 3 each in Himachal Pradesh, Sikkim and Pondicherry, 2 each in Orissa, Meghalaya and Assam and one each in Arunachal Pradesh, Mizoram, Tripura, Bihar and Daman & Diu. A new policy of expansion of FM broadcasting through private operators was notified in July, 2005. Subsequently, 337 channels including 217 channels of class-C and class-D cities were put on bid. Out of these 217 channels, agreements were signed with successful bidders for 139 channels in 57 cities. For the remaining 78 vacant channels of class-C and class-D, pre-qualification bids have been invited from private companies through tender notification dated 8.6.2007. This information was given by Minister of Information & Broadcasting and Parliamentary Affairs, Shri P. R. Dasmunsi in written reply to a question in Lok Sabha.

2485. (17-8-2007) NEW DELHI : The Empowered Committee of the Ministry of Steel has cleared a proposal from the Indian Institute of Technology, Kharagpur, to set up a Steel Technology Centre at a cost of Rs.20 crore approximately. The Centre will play a catalytic role for higher learning and research in the field of steel making. The Empowered Committee which met under the chairmanship of the Secretary, Ministry of Steel, Shri R.S. Pandey also cleared a few proposals for augmenting the availability of qualified manpower for the steel industry in future. The Committee also reviewed the progress of the ongoing research projects. The proposed Steel Technology Centre would be run according to the rules and regulations applicable to such Centres already existing at IIT Kharagpur. IIT Kharagpur will provide facilities like manpower, administrative and infrastructure support and available equipment and laboratory. The centre will encourage faculty members to offer more courses on iron and steel, take up research projects relevant to steel industry in India and to encourage students to take up projects relevant to steel sector for dissertation. It will also carry out laboratory trials of technology developed jointly by the faculty of IIT, Kharagpur, scientists from NML and scientists and engineers from steel industries in which pilot plant trials can be taken up by NML, Jamshedpur and shop floor trials by the concerned industry. The estimated expenditure of Rs. 20 crore (approx) for setting up the centre includes, among others, installation of laboratory facilities to address problems in iron and steel making and related areas. The Department of Science and Technology will bear 20 percent of the cost including the expenditure on the Chair professor and five research fellows. After five years, the recurring expenditure will be taken care of by the income generating activities of the centre. The Empowered committee also cleared a proposal to create a post of Chair professor in the Department of Metallurgy in IIT, Kharagpur, Benaras Hindu University and NITS at Rourkela, Durgapur and Jamshedpur and other institutes, where study of Metallurgical Engineering is pursued at a salary at par with the individual institute's norm. These institutions will also provide scholarships to five undergraduate students in each of them to pursue studies in areas related to iron and steel. The undergraduate scholarships will carry a monthly stipend of Rs.4000 per month during the entire period of the course. The Empowered Committee has also approved a proposal for conducting a study for assessing the manpower requirement for the growing steel industry in the country. The study to be undertaken by the Indian Institute of Metals, Kolkata, will project the manpower requirement of different skills from technicians to Engineers over the next decade. The report will be submitted by the end of December this year. The Empowered Committee has so far approved 54 projects in the field of basic and applied research amounting to Rs.476.4 crore with Steel Development Fund contributing Rs.211 crore. The SDF has so far released Rs.97 crore. 24 projects have been completed and the research findings have been implemented by the industry yielding significant benefits. Six more projects are currently under review besides 24 other on going projects.

2486. (17-8-2007) NEW DELHI : The Tourism and Culture Minister Smt. Ambika Soni will pay a day-long visit to Kolkata on August 18, 2007. During her stay in the city, Smt. Soni will inaugurate the Travel and Tourism Fair at Netaji Stadium, interact with the West Bengal Minister of Tourism Sh. Manabendra Mukherjee, who is hosting a lunch in her honour. Before returning to Delhi Smt. Soni is also scheduled to inaugurate Handicrafts Museum "Karu Angan" in the premises of the Eastern Zonal Centre, Salt Lake and Ganga Festival at Rajiv Mancha. Karu Angan has been set up exclusively for preserving the exquisite crafts and crafts based handloom heritage of the State. This will also provide exposure to the artisans for market support and quality improvement.

2487. (17-8-2007) NEW DELHI : The Directorate General of Civil Aviation (DGCA) will soon be issuing Civil Aviation Requirement (CAR) stating that no airline should refuse to carry incapacitated persons or physically challenged persons if such carriage does not pose a threat to safety. This information was given by Shri Praful Patel, Minister for Civil Aviation in the Parliament. The DGCA has issued a draft CAR on the subject of carriage of physically challenged persons by air. The draft CAR will be finalized after considering the public comments, which have been invited for by the DGCA. The CAR when published will be mandatory for all airlines and airport operators. Meanwhile Airports Authority of India and major airlines have provided facilities for the sick and disabled persons at the airports. All airlines have published the facilities to be provided to passengers including the sick and the disabled persons on their respective websites.

2488. (17-8-2007) NEW DELHI : The Secretary, Ministry of Civil Aviation, Shri Ashok Chawla, yesterday announced that the free time given to exporters and importers as "dwell time" for their cargo at the airports would be reduced to 3 days from the existing 5 days. This policy would be implemented from 1st October 2007. In case of exports this would mean two days for the airlines and one day for the exporter. This announcement was made during the fourth meeting of the

'Civil Aviation Core Group' (CACG), which is headed by the Secretary, Civil Aviation and has representatives from the various stakeholders of the Air Cargo Industry as well as representatives from Airports Authority of India, BCAS, Customs and the Ministry of Commerce. The CACG was formed to suggest ways to remove the bottlenecks for the growth of cargo industry. An Inter-Ministerial Group (IMG) under the Chairmanship of Secretary, Ministry of Civil Aviation too has been constituted specifically to consider issues relating to dwell time at airports and the IMG has been meeting to consider issues relating policies, procedures and infrastructure to make recommendations on these issues. These steps are being taken by the Ministry of Civil Aviation to improve the efficiency of Indian Airports as well as to give an impetus to the Air Cargo industry, which is expected to undergo a high rate of growth in the coming years. Dwell time of cargo at Indian airports does not compare favourably with the world standards. Hence policies, systems and procedures, infrastructure etc. are being upgraded to bring India at par with international standards.

2489. (18-8-2007) NEW DELHI : The first ever Indian Animal Husbandry Expo concluded at Pragati Maidan, here this evening. The Union Minister for Food Processing Industry, Shri Subodth Kant Sahai in his address called upon the scientists and experts to evolve a comprehensive business plan to help the livestock industry of the country. Outlining his vision for India to become the food factory of the world, the Minister urged the captains of industry to update the farming, processing, marketing and health plan for all breeds of livestock. The first ever event of this kind, the Expo was very unique with delegates from Asian and European countries dotting their presence. For students from 21 veterinary and universities in the country, participating in this unique Expo was a lively experience, which helped them to directly relate theoretical knowledge with practical knowhow. It was for the first time that all the segments of livestock were exhibited under one roof. Shri Sahai also released a Hindi book titled "Thalella Ki Roktham" published jointly by the Animal Husbandry Department of Delhi Government and All India Radio.

2490. (18-8-2007) NEW DELHI : Addressing the Rotarians at the National Polio Plus Orientation and Planning Meet, after accepting the 'Polio Eradication Champion Award' the Union Minister for Health & Family Welfare, Dr. Anbumamani Ramadoss said that the Government of India is fully committed to undertake all possible measures, notwithstanding the cost, for eradicating polio from the country. Now our goal is to achieve zero transmission by 2008. During this year Government of India has allotted more than Rs. 1300 crores for the pulse polio Programme and more than 80% programme expenditure are met from our domestic budget. Shri Deepak Kapur, Chairman, Indian National Polio Plus Committee, Rotary International, Mr. Robert S. Scott, Chairman, the Rotary Foundation & Polio Plus Committee, Rotary International and other senior leaders from the Rotary were also present at the function. The following is the summary of the Health Minister's speech: I am happy to be with you all here today afternoon. I thank the Rotary International for playing the crucial role of the Global Polio Eradication partnership and contributing to the programme by donating large funds and also support in kind. In our resolve to eradicate polio, India has been consistently and steadfastly supported by various partners, in terms of funds, technical support, advocacy, etc. Rotary International has been a long-term and valued partner in this endeavor. No words are enough for describing the contribution of Rotary towards this goal. I would like to express my thanks to the Rotary International for organizing the meet with districts governors which will apprise them on the strategy being followed in our country to achieve the goal of polio eradication. I would also like to place on record my appreciation for the admirable role-played by the India Expert Advisory Group, which comprise of national and international experts. The Group takes stock of the epidemiological situation in the country from time to time and advises the Government about the Strategy. My Ministry has valued the advice of the Group and has followed the same. I hope the Group will continue to guide the implementation of our polio eradication programme under the aegis of the World Health Organization. I hope the meeting will provide good opportunity to discuss the strategies being adopted in our country and would go a long way in motivating the participants to work with greater commitment and dedication for achieving the goal. I am thankful to the Rotary Foundation of Rotary International for conferring on me the Polio Eradication Champion Award.

2491. (19-8-2007) NEW DELHI : The Indian Air Force's microlight aircraft flown by Wg Cdr Rahul Monga and Wg Cdr Anil Kumar arrived at Air Force Station Hindon today creating a 'New World Record' of fastest round the world trip. The expedition was flagged in by the Chief of Air Staff, Air Chief Marshal FH Major. Round the World microlight expedition was flagged off on 01 Jun 07 by Chief of the Air Staff from Air Force Station Hindon as a part of Platinum Jubilee Celebrations of the Indian Air Force. The aim was to circumnavigate the earth (Minimum distance of 36889 kms) in the shortest period of time. The Air Chief in his address at the time of Flag-Off ceremony had directed them to go "Around the World in eighty days". The expedition has covered a total distance 40,497 kms in 80 days flying over 19 countries. Wg Cdr Rahul Monga and Wg Cdr Anil Kumar have achieved a speed of 21.092 km/h, which is far better than the existing record of 16.53 km set by Mr. Colin Bodil of UK in 2001. The crew comprising two pilots, were all by themselves during the entire expedition and carried out all the necessary maintenance and servicing on the microlight. The crew faced many challenges while flying over various kinds of terrain ranging from plains, dense forests, deserts and seas including the harsh terrain of Siberia, lofty Rockies, Alps and even over frozen waters of the North Atlantic. The expedition experienced their share of bad weather on route. At times they had to fly longer duration sorties to avoid weather. In Russia Wg Cdr Rahul Monga flew along with a Russian navigator as per the regulations of that country. The crew crossed the International date line over Bering Strait on 06 Jul 07. In USA, the situation with respect to weather was no different. The expedition got stuck at Anchorage in Alaska for Six days. Not withstanding the weather, the crew maintained their josh and entered Canada and then to Iceland often making quick alterations to the original planned routes. The crossing of the formidable North Atlantic was done solo by Wg Cdr Rahul Monga where he negotiated inclement weather flying over frozen land and sea of icebergs for a considerable period of time. From Iceland, they reached Germany through UK. The weather kept them on ground for four days in Germany. The crew then crossed the icy peaks of Alps and entered Italy. This expedition never had a dull movement with a minor unserviceability occurring in Italy, causing them to do an unplanned landing. The crew handled each and every situation in very professional manner. The next challenge was the encountering of High temperatures and consequent high Density altitudes (a condition of reduced air density) which pose difficulties in flying. The hot weather coupled with mountainous terrain also led to excessive turbulence which made the flying conditions uncomfortable. The brief stop over for refueling at Karachi in Pakistan was an unique experience for the crew prior to arriving at Ahmedabad. The last leg was flown from Ahmedabad to Hindon, to complete the arduous journey, which was required to terminate at the same location from where the aircraft was flagged off 80 days earlier, to qualify for the Record. The pilots have under taken the task with courage and fortitude. Enroute they interacted with civil and military personnel from 19 countries and have been Goodwill ambassadors of India in general, and the Indian Air Force in particular.

2492. (19-8-2007) NEW DELHI : The Prime Minister, Dr. Manmohan Singh, has greeted the nation and especially the members of the Parsi community on the joyous occasion of Navroz-the Parsi new year, which is being celebrated on August 20th. In his message, the PM has said that Navroz is a festival of renewal and happiness. He hoped that the new year would bring joy, happiness and prosperity to all Parsis and to Nation.

2493. (19-8-2007) NEW DELHI : The Government of India has accorded in-principle approval to the "Delhi Mumbai Industrial Corridor" Project. It may be recalled that the Prime Ministers of India and Japan had announced the Project in December 2006 during the visit of Prime Minister Mr. Manmohan Singh to Japan. The Ministry of Commerce & Industry, Government of India and the Ministry of Economy, Trade and Industry, Government of Japan had constituted a Task Force for developing the Project. The approval covers project outline developed in consultation with all stake holders including State Governments as well as Indo-Japanese Task Force set up under an MOU between the two Governments.

2494. (19-8-2007) NEW DELHI : The Vice President of India, Md. Hamid Ansari, has greeted the people on the occasion of Parsi New Year, Navroj. The following is the text of the message. "I convey my greetings and good wishes to the people of our country on the auspicious occasion of Navroj. The New Year is celebrated with great fervour and traditional gaiety. The mood of rejoicing and gaiety is vividly captured in the rituals and the festivities, which transcend all barriers and unite us all in a common brotherhood. May the Parsi New Year bring peace, prosperity and happiness in the lives of all."

2495. (20-8-2007) NEW DELHI : The Tourism and Culture Minister Smt. Ambika Soni and Chairman, China National Tourism Administration, Mr. Shao Quwei jointly inaugurated the China National Tourist Office here today. Speaking on the occasion Smt. Soni said the opening of the CNTA office is in conformity with the Action Plan adopted by the two countries in February this year during the launch of 'India-China Year of Friendship Through Tourism'. She said it is also an indication of the importance that the Govt. of China attaches to expanding people to people links with India through tourism. She said her ministry will provide all necessary support for the smooth functioning of the Chinese Tourist Office. Smt. Ambika Soni said UNWTO survey has placed China and India amongst the fastest going outbound destinations in the world. A very interesting feature of outbound statistics reveals that 78% of outbound traffic from Asia is within the region itself. The Minister said she is confident that if India and China can manage their two way tourist traffic, it will make a significant contribution to the Asia region. Smt. Soni said the Beijing Olympics next year is a major event for China. Massive infrastructure has been created and Chinese people are working round the clock to make it a success. India too is gearing itself to hosting the Commonwealth Games in 2010. Smt. Soni said these mega events have enormous touristic value both during and after the event. We need to share our experiences and learn from each other, she added. Chairman of the National Tourism Administration of China, Mr. Shao Qiwei said on the occasion that the opening of Tourist Office in India will further promote bilateral relations. He said his country is looking tourists from India during Olympics and World Expo in Shanghai. Earlier, the India-China Tourism Forum met to exchange information for future cooperation in the tourism sector between the two countries. More than 120 delegates from India and China attended the meeting. Smt. Soni and Mr. Shao Qiwei also held a brief meeting to discuss ways to further promotion of bilateral relations in tourism sector. A high level Chinese Tourism Delegation led by Chairman of the National Tourism Administration of the People's Republic of China (CNTA) is currently in India at the invitation of the Minister of Tourism and Culture, Smt. Ambika Soni. A series of events will be held in New Delhi and Mumbai during the stay of the Delegation in India which include China Tourism Night in New Delhi and Mumbai. Over 200 travel industry representatives in each place have been invited to meet with their Chinese Counterpart and explore business opportunities with them.

2496. (20-8-2007) NEW DELHI : The Rajiv Gandhi National Sadbhavana Award-2006 was presented to Shri Hem Dutta on the occasion of 63rd birth anniversary of late Shri Rajiv Gandhi here today. Following is the text of the Prime

Minister, Dr. Manmohan Singh's address on the occasion : "I sincerely believe that the Rajiv Gandhi Sadbhavana Award has come to truly symbolize the inner core of the personality of our great beloved leader, late Shri Rajiv Gandhi. Over the years we have honoured ourselves by honouring some of the great sons and daughters of our nation through this prestigious award. Each year, as I have sat here and reflected on the qualities of the award winners, I have been heartened by the thought that Rajiv Gandhi would have been proud to honour these men and women. That is why, this year too, I feel a deep sense of satisfaction that we are doing justice to the memory and the living legacy of Rajivji by honouring Shri Hembhai. Shri Rajiv Gandhi once said that "Non-violence comprises the values of truth and tolerance, compassion and concern for all humanity, coexistence and celebration of diversity". I do believe that Hembhai, from my adopted state of Assam, is a living example of non-violent mass action for peaceful social transformation. He is a truly deserving recipient of this prestigious award for translating into action, the ideals for which Shri Rajiv Gandhi lived for and laid down his life. Deeply influenced by India's ancient ethos of co-existence, Hembhai became its exponent and practitioner right from his youth. During his college days, he resolutely stood for non-violent direct action in opposition to compulsory military training. He emerged victorious in that struggle and established his credentials at an early age, as a man wedded to the cause of non-violence, peace and understanding. He organized the Peace Soldiers in Assam and worked for national integration and peaceful social change. Hembhai, and people like him, symbolize hope in our troubled times. At a time when Assam was going through the pain of social turmoil and the nation was appalled by the barbarism at Nelli, Hembhai gave us reason to hope. His deep humanism was like a ray of sunshine in a dark place. It was at that terrible time that Hembhai was asked to go to Assam from Vinobaji's Ashram to spread the message of peace and non-violence. He exemplified the voice of sanity. His Peace Mission sought to remove the fear psychosis gripping the minds of people at the time. Like a true Gandhian he went and camped in areas devastated by bloody violence, facing great threats to his life. His non-violent act assuaged a wounded people and restored their hope and confidence in themselves. Through such acts of Sadbhavana, he was able to win the hearts and minds of a people living in fear and in an atmosphere of anger and frustration. The Peace Mission Padyatra he undertook revitalized the spirit of the people of Assam.

2497. (20-8-2007) NEW DELHI : Government of India have announced the sale (re-issue) of "5.48 percent Government Stock, 2009" under Market Stabilization Scheme for a notified amount of Rs. 4,000 crore (nominal). The Government Stock will be sold through price based auction using multiple price method. The auction will be conducted by the Reserve Bank of India, Mumbai Office, Fort, Mumbai on August 22, 2007 (Wednesday). Up to 5% of the amount notified for the sale of stock is reserved for allotment to eligible individuals and Institutions on non-competitive basis as per the Scheme for Non-Competitive Bidding Facility in the

Auction of Government Securities. Bids in the prescribed form obtainable from the Regional Director, Reserve Bank of India, Mumbai Office (Public Debt Office), Fort, Mumbai-400 001 and RBI website www.rbi.org.in should be submitted to that Office on August 22, 2007. The NDS members should submit competitive as well as non-competitive bids in electronic format using Primary Market Operation (PMO) module of NDS. All bids should be submitted by 12.30 P.M.

2498. (20-8-2007) NEW DELHI : The 8th Sectoral Summit of NEC began in New Delhi today at Vigyan Bhawan. This Summit focuses on issues pertaining to Education, Sports and Art & Culture in the Northeastern region. The Human Resource Development Ministry representatives made various presentations on policies and programmes in the northeast region related to education, like Sarva Shiksha Abhiyan, National Literacy Mission etc. The issues were discussed by the representatives of Northeastern states present at the Conference. Projects and Programmes related to Sports and Youth Affairs were also discussed on the Day one of the Summit. The Ministry of Sports and Youth Affairs made presentations on various programmes being implemented in the northeastern regions. The representatives of the northeastern States brought out their perspectives and progress and the need for further development in the area of sports and youth affairs. The Summit is being attended by S/Shri S.S.Sidhu (Governor, Manipur), S.K. Singh (Governor Arunchal Pradesh), B.L Joshi, (Governor Meghalaya), Lt. Gen. (Retd.) Ajay Singh (Governor, Assam), D.N. Sahaya (Governor, Tripura), Neiphiu Rio (Chief Minister, Nagaland), Sushma Singh, Secretary (DoNER), Falguni Rajkumar, Secretary NEC and senior State Government officials from the Northeast, among others. Shri Mani Shankar Aiyar, Minister for Panchayati Raj, Youth Affairs & Sports and DoNER is chairing the Summit. There will be presentations and discussions on Art and Culture on day two of the Summit *i.e.* tomorrow.

2499. (20-8-2007) NEW DELHI : The World Bank is currently financing a number of projects aimed at modernizing irrigation system in India. However, with regard to the news item published in "The Hindu" dated June 8, 2007, the World Bank has informed that World Bank has neither committed nor received any official proposal to modernize any further irrigation systems in Tamil Nadu besides the recently approved Tamil Nadu Irrigated Agriculture Modernization and Water-bodies Restoration and Management (TNIAMWARM) Project.

2500. (20-8-2007) NEW DELHI : Ministry of Water Resources has requested all the concerned States/UTs for adoption of artificial recharge to ground water and promotion of rain water harvesting in all the over-exploited areas and ensure inclusion of roof top rain water harvesting in the Building Bye-Laws. The Central Ground Water Board (CGWB), under the Ministry of Water Resources, has prepared and circulated manual and guidelines on Artificial Recharge to Ground Water covering investigation techniques for selection of sites, planning and design of artificial recharge structures, economic evalution and monitoring of recharge facility. A demonstrative scheme on "Rain Water Harvesting and Artificial Recharge to Ground Water" is being implemented by the CGWB at a total cost of Rs. 5.95 crores for 8 identified areas of the States of Andhra Pradesh, Karnataka, Madhya Pradesh and Tamil Nadu. However, State-wise allocation are not made. However, the report on Mid-Term Appraisal of X Plan has recommended that States should set up water regulators. This information was given by the Minister of State for Water Resources, Shri Jai Prakash Narayan Yadav in a written reply to a question in Lok Sabha today.

2501. (20-8-2007) NEW DELHI : The Rural Infrastructure Development Fund (RIDF) was set up with NABARD in 1995-96 by Government of India with contributions from Commercial Banks by way of deposits to the extend of shortfall in their agriculture/priority sector lending. A portion of shortfall in agriculture sector lending target of 18% of net bank credit is being deposited by the Commercial Banks with NABARD as part of their contributions to the RIDF. The purpose of the fund is for assisting State Governments in the completion of ongoing Rural Infrastructure Projects and to take up new Infrastructure Projects. Flood Control is an eligible activity for funding under RIDF. During the current financial year (2007-08), no project has so far been sanctioned for control of floods as reported by NABARD, Mumbai. This information was given by the Minister of State for Water Resources, Shri Jai Prakash Narayan Yadav in a written reply to a question in Lok Sabha today.

2502. (20-8-2007) NEW DELHI : The Ministry of Steel will request the Finance Ministry to review the five per cent customs duty on imported scrap. The Minister for Steel, Chemicals and Fertilisers Shri Ram Vilas Paswan said this while talking to newsmen after addressing the Steel Consumers Council meeting here today. Secondary steel producers made a demand for abolishing the five percent import duty at the council meeting saying that there is already a 4 percent CVD on scrap barring a few exceptions. Shri Paswan said, the positioning of stockyards of SAIL and Rashtriya Ispat Nigam Limited (RINL) across the country will be reviewed to ensure availability of steel. He said, SAIL has already established a dealership network of about 1100 outlets across 602 districts and its product is now available at district headquarters at the same price as the state capitals. The Minister said, SAIL is now implementing an expansion plan of over Rs. 49,000 crore which will take its capacity to 26.18 million tonnes by 2010 and RINL's modernization and expansion programme will cost about Rs. 9,000 crore and will be completed by 2010 also. He said, strict monitoring of implementation of the expansion programme is being done to ensure timely completion. On Chiria mines issue, the Minister said, SAIL will set up a 15 million tonnes plant in Jharkhand if the lease for 2 billion tonnes iron ore is renewed in favour of SAIL by the state government. He said steel is a deregulated sector but a price monitoring committee has been set up with officials, steel producers and consumers as its member to keep a watch over the price movements and the committee will work on plans to avoid volatility in the steel price movements. Earlier delivering the inaugural address at the meeting of the Council, the Minister said, in order to contain the prices, the steel producers have been requested by the committee to keep a check on the ex-factory prices of long products and also to balance their exports keeping in view the domestic demand and not to commit exports at the cost of domestic demand. He said, the steel sector which contributes about two per cent of the GDP is set for rapid growth. The production of steel has gone up form 35 million tonnes to 51 million tonnes during the last three years making India the 5th largest producer in the world. He said, India will produce about 85 million tonnes by 2011-12 and may reach 200 million tonnes by 2020. Shri Paswan said, India will become the second largest steel maker in the world by 2015. The Minister said, the Steel Consumers Council will henceforth meet once in six months to ensure better coordination. Secretary Steel Shri R. S. Pandey, Chairman SAIL, Shri S.K. Roongta, Chairman and Managing Director of RINL, Shri P.K. Vishnoi, representatives from Tata Steel, Essar Steel. JSW and Ispat Industries, representatives of 51 industry associations, representatives from various states attended today's meeting.

2503. (20-8-2007) NEW DELHI : In exercise of the power conferred by clause (2) of article 124 of the Constitution of India, the President is pleased to appoint Shri Justice Palanisamy Sathasivam, Judge of the Punjab & Haryana High Court to be a Judge of the Supreme Court of India with effect from the date he assumes charge of his office.

2504. (20-8-2007) NEW DELHI : The All-India Consumer Price Index for Agricultural and Rural Labourers (Base 1986-87 = 100) increased by five points and four points respectively during July 2007 to stand at 404 points for both the series. The rise and fall in index varied from state to state. In case of Agricultural Labourers 17 states reflected an increase in indices ranging between 2 to 9 points, in two states the indices went down by 1 to 2 points while in one state the index remained constant. In case of Rural Labourers, 17 states reflected an increase ranging between 1 to 9 points while in two states the indices fell by one to two points. The Indices remained constant in one state. Manipur and Orissa experienced the highest increase of 9 points each in respect of Agricultural Labourers and Rural Labourers. The rise has been mainly due to increase in the prices of Rice, Wheat Atta, Arhar Dal, Onions, Vegetables & Fruits, Bidi, Firewood and Leather Chappal. On the other hand, the indices in respect of Meghalaya showed a decrease of two points each for Agricultural Labourers and Rural Labourers mainly due to decrease in the prices of Rice, Turmeric, Sugar and Kerosene Oil. Punjab with 432 points for Agricultural Labourers and 433 points for Rural Labourers figured at the top of the index table. Manipur with 362 points for Agricultural Labourers and 363 points for Rural Labourers remained at the bottom of the index.

2505. (20-8-2007) NEW DELHI : Under the National Project for Cattle and Buffalo Breeding, a sum of Rs. 412.79 crore has been released to States up to

March 2007 for genetic upgradation of cattle and buffaloes. At present 28 States and one UT are participating in the project. Phase I of the programme started in year 2000. To consolidate the gains made in Phase-I, Phase-II of the NPCBB has also been initiated from December, 2006 for further five years with an allocation of Rs. 775.87 crore. Under Phase-II, major emphasis is on improving the availability of quality bulls for breeding, quality assurance programmes for all aspects of artificial insemination, development and conservation of indigenous bovine breeds. This information was given by Shri Taslimuddin, Minister of State for Agriculture in written reply to a question in the Lok Sabha today.

2506. (20-8-2007) NEW DELHI : The Government has constituted an Expert Committee involving the State Governments, technical experts and representatives of the poultry industry to examine the strategy to be adopted by the industry and trade in the event of a single stray incidence of avian influenza in the country. This committee has been set up on the request of the All India Poultry Breeders Association for a joint meeting of different stakeholders to evolve such a strategy.

2507. (20-8-2007) NEW DELHI : The Prime Minister Dr. Manmohan Singh has emphasized the need for developing all our energy resources viz. coal, gas, oil, hydro and nuclear along with renewable, such as wind and solar. Speaking at the Foundation Stone Laying of ONGC's Rajiv Gandhi Urja Bhavan here today Prime Minister recognized the deep and abiding commitment of former Prime Minister late Shri Rajiv Gandhi to India's energy security. Dr. Singh added that India's economic development is vitally dependent on energy security and on the promotion of sustainable and environment friendly technologies. He said there are many options for using alternative fuels and technologies. "From a long term perspective, nuclear energy and solar energy can play an important role in addressing our energy security needs", he added. Calling for more investment in R&D for commercial use of solar energy, the Prime Minister said that country is blessed with an abundance of this resource and it could be a major source of energy in coming years. The Prime Minister Dr. Manmohan Singh laid the foundation stone of Oil and Natural Gas Corporation's (ONGC) new high-tech corporate office cum energy research centre at Vasant Kunj in South Delhi on the birth anniversary of former Prime Minister Rajiv Gandhi. Stating that Rajiv Gandhi Urja Bhawan will undertake holistic research in all forms of clean and renewable energy sources to make Rajivji's dream come true, he emphasized that the technologies that emerge from here will have to be commercially viable. The Chairperson of UPA Smt. Sonia Gandhi, the Minister of Petroleum and Natural Gas Shri Murli Deora, the Minister of State for Petroleum & Natural Gas Shri Dinsha Patel, Lieutenant Governor of Delhi Shri Tejinder Khanna, Chief Minister of Delhi Smt. Shiela Dikshit were among those present on the occasion. In his address on the occasion, Shri Murli Deora informed that Government is actively considering a scheme under which an Energy Efficient Lighting Lamp "Nutan Deep" will be marketed and distributed to the rural masses. This will help them save further money on kerosene as the Lamp will come in the form of more than 50% saving in kerosene due to higher efficiency. Expected to be launched by Diwali, Shri Deora said that this scheme will benefit crores of rural households who use these lamps for lighting their houses. The lamps will be supplied to the people at a subsidized price. Shri Deora also said that his Ministry is implementing Shri Rajiv Gandhi's vision of an environment friendly and an equitably distributed energy provisioning to sustain our rapid economic growth. As part of this, Ethanol Blended Petrol (EBP) Programme was launched in November, 2006 for a 5% blend of Ethanol in petrol in the first phase. Approximately 60 crore litres of ethanol will be procured per year and approximately 9 crore litres have been procured. Complimenting ONGC and the Architect for coming up with an innovative and modern design for Rajiv Gandhi Urja Bhavan, Shri Deora said that the proposed building will be unique and will emerge as a benchmark for "green" and "intelligent" buildings in India. This Centre will house the corporate office of ONGC and more importantly, also a dedicated R&D centre for development of futuristic perspectives on energy.

2508. (20-8-2007) NEW DELHI: The Congress and Left leaders remained engaged on Sunday in trying to find a way out of the impasse created by the Communist Party of India (Marxist) demand that the India-United States civilian nuclear deal be put on hold. One suggestion, according to a participant of a meeting between CPI(M) Polit Bureau member Sitaram Yechury and senior Congress leaders, was to evolve a mechanism to evaluate the implications of the Hyde Act on India's sovereignty. At the meeting, External Affairs Minister Pranab Mukherjee, Defence Minister A.K. Antony and senior Congress leader Ahmed Patel sought a clarification from Mr. Yechury on the statement issued by the Polit Bureau on Saturday after its two-day meeting. In particular, the Congress leadership wanted a clarification on the demand that the Government should not take the next step of negotiating a safeguards agreement with the International Atomic Energy Agency until all objections to the deal are considered and the implications of the Hyde Act evaluated. It is to evolve clarity on these issues that a mechanism was suggested. Now, according to Mr. Yechury, it was for the United Progressive Alliance (UPA) to evolve a mechanism and inform the Left parties about it. Conceding the difficult situation facing the government, Mr. Mukherjee told journalists that allies in the UPA felt "a way out is possible." The Congress leadership was prepared to discuss what — if any — "confidence-building measures" could be instituted that would meet the demands of independence in foreign policy. However, CPI(M) general secretary Prakash Karat told The Hindu that "any committee [by way of a mechanism] can be set up" to discuss the implications of the 123 agreement and the Hyde Act but the UPA government must R 20;first tell us whether it is prepared not to proceed with the operationalisation of the deal." After his meeting with the Congress leaders, Mr. Yechury said there was no "compromise formula" on the table to ease the stand-off. Apart from Mr. Yechury's meeting, back-channel efforts were on to iron out the rough spots. And, it was not just Congress leaders who were engaged in this. Other leaders of the UPA were also roped in: Railway Minister Lalu Prasad (Rashtriya Janata Dal); Union Surface Transport Minister T. R. Baalu (Dravida Munnetra Kazhagam); and Pattali Makkal Katchi leader S. Ramadoss spoke to CPI national secretary D. Raja in a bid to find a middle path. The four Left parties supporting the UPA are scheduled to meet in the Capital on Monday afternoon to assess the situation and chalk out the course of action. All of them oppose the deal and want its operationalisation kept on hold. Prominent leaders of the United National Progressive Alliance—Chandrababu Naidu of the Telugu Desam Party and Amar Singh of the Samajwadi Party—are understood to have spoken to Mr. Karat about the situation. Both parties are opposed to the deal. The BJP senior leadership also met during the day to take stock of the situation and prepare itself for the possible situations that may arise, particularly a mid-term poll. It will discuss the issue and strategy to be adopted in Parliament with other constituents of the National Democratic Alliance on Monday morning.

2509. (20-8-2007) NEW DELHI : The bidding process has been completed in respect of the Ultra Mega Power Projects (UMPPs) in Mundra and Sasan. In the case of Mundra, M/s. Tata Power Ltd. and in the case of Sasan, M/s. Reliance Power Ltd. have been selected as the project developers. In addition to the above, the bidding process has been initiated in respect of the UMPPs at Krishnapatnam (Andhra Pradesh) and Tilaiya (Jharkhand). Commencement of the bidding process in respect of the remaining five locations is contingent upon the requisite clearances from the State Governments. The Ministry of Power has taken up with the concerned State Governments to provide the requisite clearances/examine the feasibility of alternate sites for development of the Ultra Mega Power Projects in their respective States.

2510. (20-8-2007) NEW DELHI : The capacity of the National Grid (inter-regional power transfer capacity) has been enhanced by 2000 MW with the commissioning of the "East-North Tala Transmission System" which was dedicated the to the Nation by the Prime Minister on 20.06.2007. The present aggregate capacity is 14600 MW. As decided by the Central Electricity Regulatory Commission (CERC), the transmission tariff for the project is recovered from beneficiaries on a monthly fixed cost basis. Based on the same, the average time frame of recovery of the entire cost, approximately Rs.2800 crore, is about 35 years.

2511. (20-8-2007) NEW DELHI: The key constituents of the United Progressive Alliance (UPA) on Sunday night threw in their lot with coalition chairperson Sonia Gandhi and Prime Minister Manmohan Singh and expressed full confidence in their ability to address "all legitimate concerns" voiced by the Left parties. A statement to this effect was issued by the UPA leadership after a 90-minute meeting convened at the Prime Minister's residence to address the situation arising out of the Communist Party of India (Marxist) demand that the government put on hold the India-United States nuclear agreement.

2512. (20-8-2007) NEW DELHI : Under the Rajiv Gandhi Grameen Vidyutikaran Yojana (RGGVY) electrification works have been carried out in 1,327 unelectrified villages and in 570 electrified villages for intensive electrification in Rajasthan up till 10.08.2007. Under the scheme, during 2005-06, Rural Electrification works were carried out in 230 unelectrified villages. During 2006-07, works were carried out in 765 unelectrified villages and in 570 electrified villages for intensive electrification. During 2007-08, up till 10.08.2007, Rural Electrification works have been carried out in 332 un-electrified villages. This information was given by Union Power Minister Shri Sushilkumar Shinde in the Rajya Sabha today. In a written reply to a question regarding rural electrification in Bihar, the Minister said that electrification works have been completed in 11,401 un-electrified villages and 29,959 rural households including 22,115 Below Poverty Line (BPL) households have been given electricity connections. RGGVY envisages electrification of 24,703 un-electrified villages reported by Bihar through its Detailed Project Reports (DPRs) submitted under the scheme.

2513. (20-8-2007) NEW DELHI : The National Electricity Policy envisages that the per capita availability of electricity will be increased to over 1000 units by 2012. The per capita consumption of power in the country in 2005-06 as calculated by the Central Electricity Authority has been about 631 Kilowatt Hours. This information was given by Union Power Minister Shri Sushilkumar Shinde in the Rajya Sabha today. The state-wise details are given at Annex-I.

2514. (20-8-2007) NEW DELHI : Maneri Bhali Stage-II HE Project of capacity (4x76 MW = 304 MW) is programmed to be commissioned during the year 2007-08 in Uttarakhand. A target of 304 MW of hydro capacity addition was set by the State from Maneri Bhali Stage-II HE project in the State Sector during Tenth Five Year Plan. However, this target could not be achieved due to delay in completion of major civil works viz. head race tunnel, surge shaft, etc. of Maneri Bhali Stage-II HE Project. The completion of civil works is being expedited and generating units are likely to be commissioned during the current year in December 2007, January, February and March, 2008 respectively. This information was given by Union Power Minister Shri Sushilkumar Shinde in the Rajya Sabha today.

2515. (20-8-2007) NEW DELHI : The Integrated Child Development Services (ICDS) Scheme provides all the six services including supplementary nutrition to children who come to Anganwadi centres (AWCs). As reported by the States, 54.07% children (6 months-6years) received supplementary nutrition (as on 31st march, 07). Further, it is the mandate of the Government as enunciated in its National Common Minimum Programme (NCMP), to universalize the ICDS Scheme to provide a functional Anganwadi in every settlement and ensure full coverage of all children, below 6 years of age. This was stated by Smt. Renuka Chowdhury, Minister for Women and Child Development in a reply to a question by Ms. Mabel Rebello in Rajya Sabha today. She further stated that with a view to achieve an inclusive universalisation of ICDS and to reach the most vulnerable and disadvantages beneficiaries; the States have been addressed to furnish their requirements for additional Projects/AWCs for the 3rd phase of expansion of the Scheme. In doing so they have also been requested to identify SC and ST hamlets/ habitations for setting up AWCs and also to ensure that no habitation/settlement with predominantly SC/ST Minority population, is left out, she added.

2516. (20-8-2007) NEW DELHI : The Ministry of Tribal Affairs implements several Central Sector/Centrally /Sponsored Schemes/Programmes for the welfare of tribal people in the country including the States in the North Eastern Region. The schemes of the Ministry relate to income and employment generation, infrastructure development, educational development and improvement in literacy of all the tribal people. Some schemes pertain to insuring fair prices for minor forest produce besides the promotion of voluntary efforts in the area of tribal welfare. This was stated by Shri P.R. Kyndiah, Minister for Tribal Affairs in a reply to a question by Shri O.T. Lepcha in Rajya Sabha today.

2517. (20-8-2007) NEW DELHI : A pilot project on combating trafficking of women and children for sexual exploitation is being implemented. A 'Comprehensive Scheme for Prevention of Trafficking and Rescue, Rehabilitation and re-integration of Victims of Trafficking and Commercial Sexual Exploitation' has been included in the Annual Plan, 2007-08. The scheme has specific components for prevention of trafficking, rescue, rehabilitation and repatriation of victims. This was stated by Smt. Renuka Chowdhury, Minister for Women and Child Development in a reply to a question by Dr. K. Malaisamy in Rajya Sabha today. The Central Advisory Committee on combating Child Prostitution headed by Secretary, Ministry of Women and Child Development, reviews the State's activities in combating trafficking and prostitution every quarter. The Ministry has also conducts advocacy, awareness generation, sensitization programme for prevention of trafficking, she added. She further stated that the Ministry of WCD runs Swadhar Shelter Homes which provide shelter, food, clothing, emotional support, counselling, rehabilitation and other facilities to women in difficult circumstances including victims of trafficking.

2518. (20-8-2007) NEW DELHI : The Department of Posts is selling the air tickets of Deccan Aviation Limited in Karnataka Postal Circle. The scheme of selling air tickets of Deccan Aviation Limited through 511 e-enabled post offices in Karnataka Postal Circle has been started with effect from July 2, 2007. This is a pilot project which has been implemented in select post offices of Karnataka Circle. As such it would be too early to assess the revenue likely to be generated through the initiative. There is no proposal to extend the scheme at present. This information was given in the Lok Sabha today by Dr. Shakeel Ahmad, Minister of State for Communications and Information Technology in a written reply to a question by Shri K.C. Pallani Shamy.

2519. (20-8-2007) NEW DELHI : A scheme has been launched by Universal Service Obligation Fund (USOF) for provision of subsidy support for setting up and managing 7,871 number of infrastructure sites (towers) for providing mobile services spread across 500 districts in 27 States. A Group of Districts with two or more Districts have been clubbed together to constitute a Cluster for the purpose of bidding. Each cluster has been assigned a unique Cluster Number of 81 such Clusters have been formed in the country for setting up these towers. A total number of 2,12,304 villages are likely to be covered under the Scheme. USOF has entered into an agreement with the successful bidders, which has become effective from June 1, 2007. Mobile services through these shared towers are targeted to be made operational in a phased manner by May, 2008. This information was given in the Lok Sabha today by Dr. Shakeel Ahmad, Minister of State for Communications and Information Technology in a written reply to a question by Shri Haribhau Rathod.

2520. (20-8-2007) NEW DELHI : As on June 30, 2007, 18,118 eligible villages, excluding villages having population less than 100, villages lying in thick forest areas/naxalite infested areas etc., remain to be connected with Village Public Telephones (VPTs). The telephone exchanges, from which these VPTs have been provided, are equipped with STD/ISD/Fax facilities. However, as per the present policy these facilities are extended to the VPT on the request of its custodian and subject to the completion of the requisite formalities by the custodian. This information was given in the Lok Sabha today by Dr. Shakeel Ahmad, Minister of State for Communications and Information Technology in a written reply to a question by Shri G.M. Siddeswara.

2521. (20-8-2007) NEW DELHI : Telecom Regulatory Authority of India (TRAI) has been monitoring performance of Cellular Mobile Operators against the bench marks laid down for the various parameters (vide Regulation on Quality of Service of Basic and Cellular Mobile Telephone Service, 2005) through Quarterly Performance Monitoring Reports submitted by all the service providers including BSNL. TRAI had also undertaken independent assessment of the Quality of Service through an independent agency. Performance of BSNL is comparable to the private mobile companies in respect of quality of service of Cellular Mobile Telephone Service. This information was given in the Lok Sabha today by Dr. Shakeel Ahmad, Minister of State for Communications and Information Technology in a written reply to a question by Shri Raghuraj Singh Shakya.

2522. (20-8-2007) NEW DELHI : The Scheme for development of the core e-Governance Infrastructure entitled "State Wide Area Network" (SWAN) was approved by the Government in March, 2005, with an estimated outlay of Rs.3334 crore for the entire country, out of which estimated expenditure of Rs.2005 crore would be met as Grant-in-Aid from DIT (Department of Information Technology) Budget, to be expended over 5 years. Under SWAN scheme, it is envisaged to establish minimum 2 Mbps capacity intra-State Wide Area Networks (SWAN), linking the State Hqrs. right up to the Block Hqrs., in order to create a secure Government network for the purpose of delivering G2G and G2C services. Out of 35 States/UTs the Empowered Committee on SWAN, constituted by the Government, has so far approved 28 projects and they are at various stages of implementation. The SWAN proposals from the State of Jammu & Kashmir and UT (Union Territory) of Lakshadweep have been submitted to DIT for scrutiny. The proposals from UT of Daman & Diu, Dadra & Nagar Haveli and State of Arunachal Pradesh are likely to be submitted to DIT shortly. UT of Andaman & Nicobar Island has opted out of the SWAN scheme and State of Goa has initiated its own Broadband Network in collaboration with private sector. Regular follow-up actions have been undertaken by the DIT SWAN team to facilitate preparation and submission of SWAN project proposals by the States/UTs to Empowered Committee. For the remaining State/UTs also, DIT team had visited State of Arunachal Pradesh and UTs Daman & Diu and Dadra & Nagar Haveli to facilitate preparation of project proposals. This information was given in the Lok Sabha today by Dr. Shakeel Ahmad, Minister of State for Communications and Information Technology in a written reply to a question by Shri Prabodh Panda.

2523. (20-8-2007) NEW DELHI : Under the provisions of Gender Budgeting, the Government is considering various programmes for Gender Empowerment through Information and Communication Technology. This information was given in the Lok Sabha today by Dr. Shakeel Ahmad, Minister of State for Communications and Information Technology in a written reply to a question by Shri Rayapati Sambasiva Rao.

2524. (20-8-2007) NEW DELHI : Appreciating the requirement for promoting the cause of women entrepreneurs, the Government has announced a slew of measures for supporting enterprises owned or managed by women in the Package for promotion of micro and small enterprises in February/March, 2007. These measures include, inter alia, commencing exclusive EDPs/ESDPs, offering Government of India assistance upto 90% of the project cost for setting up of clusters developed exclusively for women owned enterprises, establishing exhibition centres, offering 80% guarantee cover for all eligible loans sought by women owned micro and small enterprises, 50% concession in fee for management development programmes and facilitating their participation in 25 international exhibitions for marketing facilitation, etc. This information was given by the Minister of Micro, Small & Medium Enterprises, Shri Mahabir Prasad in a written reply to a question in Lok Sabha today.

2525. (20-8-2007) NEW DELHI : A 'Technology Mission' has been set up to assist micro, small and medium enterprises in technology development, energy conservation and pollution mitigation. The said Mission will be implemented and monitored by a Governing Body under the Chairmanship of the Secretary, Ministry of Micro, Small & Medium Enterprises. No training institute is set up or is proposed to be set up under the Technology Mission. An amount of Rs. 35 lakh has been allocated for the functioning of Technology Mission during the current financial year (2007-08). This information was given by the Minister of Micro, Small & Medium Enterprises, Shri Mahabir Prasad in a written reply to a question in Lok Sabha today.

2526. (20-8-2007) NEW DELHI : The Coir Board, a statutory body under the Ministry of Micro, Small & Medium Enterprises (MSME), has been implementing the Coir Workers Group Personal Accident Insurance Scheme since 1st December, 1998 for the welfare of the coir workers all over the country. Under the Scheme, the coir workers engaged directly or indirectly by the employer, dealer or producers of coir and coir products and under any person employed by or through a contractor or through an agent and depends mainly on coir industry for his livelihood are eligible for compensation in case of death or disability caused by an accident. Further the coir workers may be self employed in the organized coir industry or working in the organizations of any of the recognized or unrecognized coir sector. Since the inception of the Scheme, 186 claims have been settled and an amount of Rs. 47, 37,500/- has been paid as compensation by Coir Board. An amount of Rs. 2.60 crore has been allotted for implementation of Welfare Measures for coir workers during 2007-2008. This information was given by the Minister of Micro, Small & Medium Enterprises, Shri Mahabir Prasad in a written reply to a question in Lok Sabha today.

2527. (20-8-2007) NEW DELHI : Recruitment rules for selection of officers in the Defence Forces are already designed to identify candidates who are prone to stress. The officers' selection is based on personality assessment carried out at the Services Selection Boards, which includes Group Testing, Psychological Test and Interview. Psychological Test, comprises of Situation Reaction Tests, Thematic Appreciation Tests, Word Association Tests and Self Description Test. For recruitment of Personnel Below Officer Rank in the Army the Defence Institute of Psychological Research has been engaged to develop a system for psychological testing of the candidates. There is no such proposal in the Navy and the Air Force.

2528. (20-8-2007) NEW DELHI : Defence Research and Development Organisation (DRDO) had equipped Services with state-of-the-art technologies in the field of strategic systems, battle tanks, electronic warfare and communication systems, armour and armaments, life support systems, naval systems, missile systems etc.

2529. (20-8-2007) NEW DELHI : Construction or repair and re-equipping of an aircraft carrier is a complex exercise. It not only involves construction / repair of the platform but also fitment of a large number of systems, assemblies, and subassemblies. In any project of such nature, coordination with a large number of agencies is involved. At times problems arise due to various reasons which are resolved through interactions between the agencies concerned. It is apprehended that some delay may take place in the project due to unforeseen problems. For supervising the project for repair and re-equipping of the aircraft carrier Vikramaditya (earlier called Admiral Gorshkov), an apex level committee under Defence Secretary and a Steering committee under a Vice Admiral have been set up. A team has also been stationed at the shipyard where the repair and re-equipping work is going on. From time to time, teams comprising senior officers are also sent to monitor progress of the project. At present, the Russian authorities are seized of the issue of timely delivery of the ship. This information was given by the Defence Minister Shri AK Antony in a written reply to Shri Anandrao V Adsul and others in Lok Sabha today.

2530. (20-8-2007) NEW DELHI : There is no nominee representing the Armed Forces in the Sixth Pay Commission. Ministry of Defence had made a request to the Ministry of Finance and Sixth Central Pay Commission to appoint a person with Service background in the Sixth Central Pay Commission. Ministry of Finance observed that the Members of the Pay Commission do not represent any particular service or organisation but would be working on various issues concerning the overall service conditions of the Central Government employees. The Sixth Central Pay Commission also felt that Armed Forces would be given full opportunity to place their views before the Commission and therefore, it will not be necessary to have a representative of the Armed Forces in the Commission. The three Services have been permitted to have direct interaction with the Pay Commission. The three Service Chiefs and representatives of Ministry of Defence also had a discussion with the Sixth Central Pay Commission on 19 April 2007 wherein the issues concerning the Services were also raised. The Services have submitted a Joint Memorandum to the Commission projecting their demands and aspirations. The representatives of the services and Ministry of Defence are regularly interacting with the Pay Commission on specific issues. This information was given by the Defence Minister Shri AK Antony in a written reply to Shri Jyotiraditya M Scindia in Lok Sabha today.

2531. (20-8-2007) NEW DELHI : The amounts for which the Annual Work Plan & Budgets 2007-08 have been approved by Government of India (GoI) for States/ Union Territories (UTs) under Sarva Shiksha Abhiyan (SSA).

2532. (20-8-2007) NEW DELHI : The Ministry of Human Resource Development under various schemes during the years 2004-05, 2005-06 and 2006-07 are given in the enclosed statement. With the help of Sarva Shiksha Abhiyan (SSA) and Mid-Day Meal Scheme, the State of Sikkim has managed to substantially reduce the number of out of school children at the elementary stage. The dropout rate has been reduced from 8.74% to 0.58% for the primary level and from 9.92% to 3.98% at the Upper Primary level. Under SSA 45 primary / upper primary schools and 48 AIE / EGS Centres have been opened, 37 school buildings constructed and

377 teachers recruited. 885 schools and 83602 children were covered under the Mid-Day Meal Scheme in 2004-05; 871 schools & 98000 children in 2005-06 and 899 schools & 102520 children in 2006-07. To provide good quality secondary education, 2 Kendriya Vidyalayas and 4 Jawahar Navodaya Vidyalayas have been opened in the State. A new Central University, viz Sikkim University has been established with effect from 2.7.2007 to cater to the higher education needs in the State. Under the programmes of Indira Gandhi National Open University (IGNOU), 4523 students have been enrolled, 455 in-servive teachers were trained in B.Ed and 151 teachers were issued Certificate in Primary Education (CPE). 425 students completed Computer Literacy Programmes (CLP). One Statellite Interactive Terminal (SIT) has been set up at Regional Centre, Gangtok and three at different Study Centres in the State. All major programmes being offered by the University have been activated in the region.

2533. (20-8-2007) NEW DELHI : The Government, at present, has no specific proposal to set up specialized training centres for providing training in the area of cyber crimes to judges. However, the Government conducts regular awareness and training programmes on cyber laws and cyber crimes for Judicial Officers. National Judicial Academy at Bhopal also conducts programmes to train judges in cyber laws and cyber crimes. 43 judges participated in each of the workshop conducted by the Academy in 2004 and 2006. This was stated by the Minister of State for Law and Justice, Shri K. Venkatapathy in a written reply in Rajya Sabha today.

2534. (20-8-2007) NEW DELHI : With the objective of evolving a consensus on Women Reservation Bill, a meeting was called by the Chairperson of United Progressive Alliance (UPA) on 22.8.2005 in which the constituents of UPA and Left Parties participated and subsequently the Prime Minister held a meeting with the Leaders of national Democratic Alliance (NDA) and other Leaders on 24th August, 2005. However, there was no consensus on the provisions of the Bill in both the above meetings. The main objection to the concept of reservation for women in Lok Sabha appears to arise from the rotational phenomenon which would break the link between the Member of Parliament and his/her constituency. These apprehensions are required to be removed before the Government could bring a new Bill in the Parliament. This was stated by the Minister of Law and Justice, Shri H. R. Bhardwaj in a written reply in Rajya Sabha today.

2535. (20-8-2007) NEW DELHI : Appointments of Judges of the Supreme Court of India and High Courts are made under articles 124 and 217 of the Constitution of India, respectively, which do not provide for reservation for any caste or class of persons. After the Supreme Court judgement of October 6, 1993 in the Supreme Court Advocates-on-Record & Anr. Vs. Union of India, read with the Advisory Opinion of October 28, 1998, the entire process of initiation of proposal for appointment of a Judge of a Supreme Court lies with the Chief Justice of India and for the appointment of a Judge of a High Court, with the Chief Justice of that High Court. The Government have, however, addressed letters to the Chief Ministers and the Chief Justices of the High Courts, from time to time, requesting them to locate persons from the Bar belonging to Scheduled Castes, Scheduled Tribes, other Backward Classes, Minorities and amongst Women who are suitable for appointment as High Court Judges. This was stated by the Minister of State for Law and Justice, Shri K. Venkatapathy in a written reply in Rajya Sabha today.

2536. (20-8-2007) NEW DELHI : The Delimitation Commission has so far issued orders in respect of 25 States/Union Territories. These are Kerala,Tripura, Mizoram, Goa, Pondicherry, Rajathan, West Bengal, Punjab, Maharashtra, Sikkim, National Capital Territory of Delhi, Chhattisgrh, Uttar Pradesh, Gujarat, Orissa, Uttaranchal, Himachal Pradesh, Madhya Pradesh, Haryana, Andhra Pradesh, Karnataka, Meghalaya, Tamil Nadu, Bihar and Jharkhand. The High Court of Guwahati has passed its two different interim orders to suspend the delimitation work in Arunachal Pradesh and Assam. The High Court of Guwahati in another interim order directed the Delimitation Commission not to publish the final order in respect of Nagaland. Further, in respect of the State of Manipur the work of delimitation has been resumed after the stay given by the Hon'ble Supreme Court on the order dated 19.01.2007 of the Guwahati High Court. The term of the Delimitation Commission has been extended till July 31, 2008 to complete its work. The population criteria for undertaking delimitation have been set down by the Parliament itself. Government has, however, received representations challenging the delimitation exercise on various grounds including inter alia that it would threaten the ethnic structure of political representation of North-Eastern States and some other states as well. This was stated by the Minister of Lawr and Justice, Shri H. R. Bhardwaj in a written reply in Rajya Sabha today.

2537. (20-8-2007) NEW DELHI : There is no proposal to constitute a Tripartite Committee for ensuring proper implementation of labour laws. Whenever violations of labour laws come to notice, either on the basis of complaints or at the time of periodical inspections made by the enforcement sphere, action is taken by the appropriate Government concerned as per provisions of the respective enactments.

2538. (20-8-2007) NEW DELHI : Employment of children in agriculture and farming sector has not been prohibited under the Child Labour (Prohibition & Regulation) Act, 1986 except in the processes where tractors, threshing and harvesting machines are used and chaff cutting is involved as also handling of insecticides and pesticides. No adverse reports have been received with regard to a critical situation in these sectors in respect of engagement of children. Under the programmes of the Labour Ministry, rehabilitation of children withdrawn from hazardous occupations is being provided. Under these programmes, children withdrawn from work are admitted to special schools where they are provided with education, vocational training, stipend, nutrition as well as health check-up facilities. At present, this programme is being implemented in 250 districts covering 20 States in the country under the National Child Labour Project Scheme. An expansion in the Scheme alongwith the enlargement of its scope through additional components during the XI Plan is under consideration. This inter alia covers the children working in notified hazardous occupations in the agricultural and farming sectors also. In addition, a scheme of Grants-in-aid to voluntary agencies for the benefit of children withdrawn from hazardous occupations is being implemented in the uncovered districts. This was stated by the Minister of State (Independent Charge) of Labour and Employment, Shri Oscar Fernandes in a written reply in Lok Sabha today.

2539. (20-8-2007) NEW DELHI : An externally aided 'Vocational Training Improvement Project (VTIP)' has been taken up during Eleventh Plan Period for up-gradation of 400 Government ITIs with the objective to produce multi-skilled workforce of world standard. 100 Government ITIs were taken up for up-gradation during the year 2006-07 and the remaining 300 ITIs are being upgraded during 2007-08 and 2008-09. The average allocation per ITI is Rs. 3.0 crore for establishment of infrastructure for multi-skill courses and up-gradation of related trades. Minimum of 100 trainees per year per ITI selected for upgradation would be benefited under the scheme.

2540. (20-8-2007) NEW DELHI : The Central Vigilance Commission (CVC) disposed of 393 cases referred to it for advice in July, 2007. Further, the investigations by the CTE unit of the Commission resulted in recoveries to the tune of Rs. 3.82 crores during the month to the Government.

2541. (20-8-2007) NEW DELHI : The Railways have generated Rs. 14378.80 crore of revenue earnings from freight traffic during the first four months (*i.e.* April-July 2007) of the current financial year 2007-08 as compared to Rs. 13222.09 crore during the corresponding period last year, registering an increase of 8.75 per cent. Railways carried 247.05 million tonnes of freight traffic during April-July 2007 as compared to 233.21 million tonnes carried during the corresponding period last year, reflecting an increase of 5.93 per cent. The Net Tonne Kilo Metres (NTKM) went up from 154082 million during the months of April-July 2006 to 158662 million during April-July 2007, with an increase of 2.97 per cent. The earnings from freight traffic during the month of July 2007 was Rs. 3482.16 crore, compared to Rs. 3262.25 crore during the corresponding period last year showing an increase of 6.74 per cent. Railways carried 61.80 million tonnes of freight traffic during the month of July 2007 as compared to 57.37 million tonnes of freight traffic during the corresponding period last year, registering an increase of 7.72 per cent. The Net Tonne Kilo Metres (NTKM) went up from 37202 million during the month of July 2006 to 38790 million during July 2007, showing an increase of 4.27 per cent. Of the total earnings during the month of July 2007, Rs. 1255.35 crore came from transportation of 25.72 million tonnes of coal, followed by Rs. 310.80 crore from 4.58 million tonnes of iron ore for exports, Rs. 308.03 crore from 6.29 million tonnes of cement, Rs. 264.19 crore from 3.07 million tonnes of petroleum oil and lubricant (POL), Rs. 222.96 crore from 2.67 million tonnes of foodgrains, Rs. 196.52 crore from 3.35 million tonnes of fertilizers, Rs. 182.21 crore from 1.70 million tonnes of iron & steel for steel plants, Rs. 144.59 crore from 4.17 million tonnes of raw material for steel plants and Rs. 597.51 crore from 10.25 million tonnes of other goods.

2542. (20-8-2007) NEW DELHI : In 2007, Polio cases have been reported from Andhra Pradesh, Bihar, Gujarat, Haryana, Maharashtra, Rajasthan, Uttar Pradesh and Uttarakhand. There are no polio cases reported from Kerala and Punjab in 2007. Kerala reported the last polio case in the year 2000. Last polio case in Punjab was in 2006. There were 28 polio cases with onset of paralysis in December 2006. The total polio case count in 2006 is 676. During 2005 only 66 polio cases were reported in the country Prior to 2006, there was an outbreak in 2002 when 1600 cases of polio were detected. The four-year cycle is due to accumulation of susceptible children during this period. The poliovirus survived in Western UP and Bihar during the period between 2002 and 2006 and got enough susceptible children in 2006 to start another outbreak. The polio virus survived in Moradabad and JP Nagar due to environmental factors such as high population density, poor sanitation, high incidence of diarrhoea that require more doses of polio vaccine to be given to children in these areas compared to other areas of the country. However, since the overall immunization status of children in 2006 was much better than what it was in 2002, the number of polio cases seen in 2006 was only 676 (compared to 1600 in 2002). The polio outbreak in 2006 started from two districts of West UP-Moradabad and JP Nagar, from where it spread to other districts in West UP, districts of Central and Eastern UP, Bihar and other states.

2543. (20-8-2007) NEW DELHI : As per existing population norms, there is a post of Medical Officer at a Primary Health Centre (PHC) covering a population of 20000 in tribal/hilly areas and 30000 in plain areas. As on 31st March 2006, the number of Medical Officers available in the PHCs are 22273 as against the requirement of 22669. The State-wise position of doctors in PHCs can be seen at Annexure. Under National Rural Health Mission (NRHM), every PHC in the country is being strengthened with provision of an AYUSH practitioner in addition to the Medical Officer, subject the State planning for it. There is a shortfall of 1793 Medical Officers, 16938 Nurse Midwives at Primary Health Centres (PHCs) and Community Health Centres (CHCs) and 18318 Auxiliary Nurse Midwives (ANMs) as on 31.03.2006. Under NRHM, the States have been provided funds for setting up of Sub-centres, PHCs, CHCs as per 2001 population norms and also for construction of buildings. A Sub-centre has been provided with an additional ANM and a PHC with 3 Staff Nurses on contractual basis to make it functional for 24 hours for all seven days. Support is also provided under NRHM to States to appoint doctors/specialists in PHCs/CHCs/District Hospitals on contract basis

States have to incorporate in their annual Programme Implementation Plan (PIP) the requirement of funds for the activities. This information was given by the Minister of State for Health & Family Welfare, Smt. Panabaka Lakshmi in a written reply to a question in the Rajya Sabha.

2544. (20-8-2007) NEW DELHI : As per Medical Council of India, the total number of registered allopathic doctors in the country is 6, 83, 582. Thus the allopathic doctor-population ratio at present works out to 1:1634. In addition, there are more than 6 lakhs practitioners of Indian Systems of Medicine and Homoeopathy in the country. Taking all these numbers together, the doctor-population ratio comes to 1: 870 approximately. The data relating to the doctor-patient ratio in rural as well as in urban areas in the country is not maintained. However, the doctor-patient ratio varies from case to case depending upon various factors like the type of disease, nature of specialization, type of patient-care required *i.e.* indoor/outdoor. There are 269 medical colleges in the country with annual intake of 30,922 students who add up to the existing medical manpower. The National Rural Health Mission has been operationalised with the main aim of providing accessible and reliable primary health care facilities especially to the poor and the vulnerable sections of the population. This information was given by the Minister of State for Health & Family Welfare, Smt. Panabaka Lakshmi in a written reply to a question in the Rajya Sabha.

2545. (20-8-2007) NEW DELHI : As per data collected through National Cancer Registry Programme (NCRP) by Indian Council of Medical Research (ICMR), an estimated 4.4 lakhs people die of cancer every year and about 7-9 lakh new cancer cases are detected every year. At any given point of time there are 2.5 million cancer patients in the country. According to International Agency for Research on Cancer (WHO), Lyon, France it is estimated that about 74% of cancer deaths occur in low and middle-income countries. The report of Registrar General for the survey in 1998 has placed cancer as the 4th commonest cause of the death in India. Considering the fact that about 50% cancer deaths are due to Tobacco use, the Central Govt. has enacted a comprehensive tobacco control legislation titled 'The Cigarettes and other Tobacco Products (Prohibition of Advertisement and Regulation of Trade and Commerce, Production, Supply and Distribution) Act, 2003' to discourage the consumption of tobacco. National Tobacco Control Programme has been launched recently with a view to ensuring effective implementation of Law & Rules and also for creating awareness on the ill effects of Tobacco & providing Tobacco cessation services for the users. In addition, the Central Govt., under National Cancer Control Programme is supplementing the efforts of the State Governments by providing financial assistance for setting up of Oncology Wings in Govt. Medical Colleges/Hospitals for providing treatment facilities. Under NCCP special emphasis is now being laid on early detection of Cancer through screening, promoting health education, creating awareness etc. under District Cancer Control Programme. In addition, the comprehensive cancer detection and management facilities including testing facilities in respective region/ States are provided by 25 Regional Cancer Centre recognized under NCCP. This information was given by the Minister of State for Health & Family Welfare, Smt. Panabaka Lakshmi in a written reply to a question in the Rajya Sabha.

2546. (20-8-2007) NEW DELHI : The matter regarding qualified practitioners of Ayurveda, Unani, Siddha and Homoeopathy systems prescribing allopathic medicines has been examined in depth by the Hon'ble Supreme Court of India in Civil Appeal No.89 of 1987 Dr. Mukhtiar Chand & Others versus State of Punjab & Others. Representations have been received from time to time on this matter and accordingly Department of AYUSH entrusted the study of the contemporary acts on medical practice in the light of judgement of Hon'ble Supreme Court in 1987 Dr. Mukhtiar Chand & Others versus State of Punjab & Others and other similar judgements. Drugs can be sold and supplied by a Pharmacist or a Druggist only on a prescription of a Registered Medical Practitioner and who can also store them for treatment of patients.

2547. (20-8-2007) NEW DELHI : The Prime Minister Dr. Manmohan Singh said that there is a need to develop all our energy resources, viz, coal, gas, oil, hydro and nuclear along with renewables, such as wind and solar power. He was speaking at the laying of foundation stone of Rajiv Gandhi Urja Bhavan here today. Dr. Manmohan Singh said that there are many options of using alternative fuels and technologies. He said, "from a long-term perspective, nuclear energy and solar energy can play an important role in addressing our energy security needs. Our Government is committed to the development of nuclear energy". The Prime Minister said that we are blessed with an abundance of solar energy, it could be a major energy source in the coming years and we must invest in Research and Development for commercial use of solar energy. He said that several non-conventional energy sources fall in the domain of high technology and are presently commercially not viable. "The immediate need is to develop these technologies to make such energy available to the masses in the shortest possible time", he added. Underlining the need of energy, Dr. Manmohan Singh said that real energy security implies assured supply of good quality energy at affordable prices. He said, when we aim for a 10% growth rate, we must recognize the critical importance of energy security. "India's energy needs, which will grow with the pace of economic development, cannot be met with oil and gas for long", the Prime Minister added. Expressing his concern over the growing import bills for imported crude oil, he said that as we grow, import oil bill will put an unbearable and an unsustainable burden on our economy.. The Chairperson of UPA Smt Sonia Gandhi, the Union Minister for Petroleum & Natural Gas Shri Murli Deora, the Minister of State for Petroleum & Natural Gas Shri Dinsha Patel, Lieutenant Governor of Delhi Shri Tejinder Khanna, Chief Minister of Delhi Smt Shiela Dikshit were among those present on the occasion.

2548. (20-8-2007) NEW DELHI : A Joint Business Meeting with Japanese Prime

Minister, Mr. Shinzo Abe, is scheduled to be held on August 22, 2007. This is jointly organised by the Confederation of Indian Industry (CII), Federation of Indian Chambers of Commerce & Industry (FICCI) and Associated Chambers of Commerce & Industry (Assocham) in coordination with the Ministry of Commerce and Industry. During the Business Meeting, Shri Kamal Nath, Union Minister of Commerce & Industry, will deliver a special address and the Prime Minister of Japan will deliver the keynote address. To coincide with the Joint Business Meeting, there will be India-Japan Business Seminar on 22nd August, 2007, where Shri Kamal Nath and Mr. Toyoda, Vice Minister, METI, is scheduled to address. During the seminar, there will be presentations on: "Macro Business Environment in India and Opportunities for Investment" by Mr. Ajay Shankar, Secretary (DIPP); "Investment Opportunities in the Delhi-Mumbai Industrial Corridor" by Indian side; "Investment Opportunities in Infrastructure" by Mr. Russell Parera/CEO of KPMG India; and "Doing Logistic Business in India" by Mr. Hiroshi Maniwa, MD/NYK Ltd.

2549. (20-8-2007) NEW DELHI : The Ministry for Women and Child Development has announced Rajeev Gandhi Manav Seva Awards for the year 2007 to recognise outstanding contribution towards child development, child protection and child welfare. Smt. Mahzabeen of Andhra Pradesh, Smt. Shobhna Ranade (Maharashtra) and Shri Ahanthem Tolen Singh(Manipur) will be awarded Rupees one lakh each and a citation later in a function in New Delhi. In order to support and promote voluntary efforts in the area of child welfare and development, the Ministry of Women and Child Development instituted these awards in 1994 and every year awards are conferred on 3 individuals who make outstanding contribution in the fields of (i) child protection, (ii) child development and (iii) child welfare. Smt. Mahzabeen of Hyderabad (Andhra Pradesh), is a sociologist, feminist writer and a lawyer. She is a founder member of an organisaiton working for women and children at Hyderabad. For the last 15 years, she focused on child protection. Smt. Shobhana Ranade of Pune (Maharashtra), is a veteran and dedicated social worker. She is working for destitute women and children with a view to making them self-sufficient. She is running 25 balwadies and crèches in the villages of Maharashtra through Kasturba Trust. Shri Ahanthem Tolen Singh, Chindgeirong (Manipur), render his untiring service in the field of welfare protection and development of children. He established a Destitute children home at Nonggpok Inghkhot, a leprosy colony and 20 bedded community care centre for HIV affected children.

2550. (20-8-2007) NEW DELHI: The Bharatiya Janata Party (BJP) on Sunday indicated its preference for a wait-and-watch policy in the wake of the strain in the relations between the United Progressive Alliance (UPA) and Left parties over the India-U.S. civilian nuclear deal. However, it will continue to press for a discussion in Parliament on the deal and on the Quattrocchi issue. The 'core group' of the BJP met at the residence of the former Prime Minister, Atal Bihari Vajpayee, to take stock of the political situation. One view is that nothing ought to be done that will allow the Left and the UPA to close ranks. Besides Mr. Vajpayee, the meeting was attended by L.K. Advani, Rajnath Singh, Jaswant Singh, Sushma Swaraj, V.K. Malhotra, Arun Jaitley, Yashwant Sinha, Arun Shourie, Bal Apte and Ram Lal. On speculation that the BJP is planning to bring a no confidence motion against the government in Parliament, Mr. Malhotra told The Hindu that this issue was not discussed at the meeting. Briefing mediapersons later, BJP spokesman Mukhtar Abbas Naqvi described the UPA government as a "paralysed" administration as its principal crutches had crumbled. "A mid-term poll appears to be a possibility. As a responsible Opposition, we are concerned about the fluid situation." As to whether the BJP would bring a no-confidence motion against the Government, Mr. Naqvi said: "That will be decided by the National Democratic Alliance (NDA)." The NDA is slated to meet at Mr. Advani's house on Monday morning ahead of the day's proceedings in Parliament to evolve the coalition's strategy in both Houses.

2551. (20-8-2007) NEW DELHI : Shri Jairam Ramesh, Minister of State for Commerce will launch the electronic auction (e-auction) system, a new initiative of the Spices Board (Board) to ensure transparency in cardamom trading in the country for the benefit of small growers on August 23 at Bodinayakanur in Tamil Nadu. Bodinayakanur accounts for 80% of the Traders in this commodity and 21% of the total cardamom auctioned. It has traditionally been a major assembling centre for cardamom. The e-auction system has been developed with the support of the Tata Consultancy Services, Bangalore to provide transparency in transactions and to promote healthy competition for purchases. The Board has proposed introduction of e-auction in cardamom to revamp the existing manual procedures at par with modern technologies. The new system will provide a calm platform to make the transaction smooth and hassle-free. Proper and error-free documentation is done in e-auctions facilitating speedy billing/ invoicing eliminating the chances for hidden costs. As the identity of the bidder is not revealed during the process of auction, the chances of speculation is also discouraged. The moisture and bulk density of every lot offered for sale will be displayed on the main screen at the auction centre, which will help the bidders to assess the quality. The Board is planning to establish common cleaning/grading/packing facilities in association with auctioneers which will help the traders/bidders to sell the material bought in the auction to the buyers with out further cleaning/grading thereby save time and costs. The new system is designed to replace the traditional manual auction system of shouting out of bids now being followed in all auction centres. This method conducted by licensed auctioneers at the approved centres in Kerala, Tamil Nadu and Karnataka, according to farmers lacked clarity as regards bids concluded. It is from these centres that cardamom is purchased in bulk by cardamom dealers and exporters. The introduction of the e-auction system will set a new trend in cardamom marketing since this is expected to bring in increased benefits to the farming community in terms of bringing in transparency that would curtail the formation of cartels that is the bane of the present system.

2552. (20-8-2007) NEW DELHI : Shri Kamal Nath, Minister for Commerce & Industry, will inaugurate the India-Japan Business Leaders Forum at a Business Seminar on 22nd August, 2007 in New Delhi during the forthcoming visit of the Japanese Prime Minister. The India-Japan Business Leaders Forum would emphasise the major role of the private sector in strategic economic engagement. The prominent members from the Indian side include CEOs of Bharat Forge Ltd, Infosys, Moser Baer Ltd, Toyota Kirloskar Ltd, Wockhardt Ltd. while those from the Japanese side include CEO's of Canon, Hitachi Limited, Mitsui & Co, Mitsubishi Corpn., Matsushita Electric Industrial Co. Ltd., Sumitomo Chemical Co., and Toyota Motor Corporation.

2553. (20-8-2007) NEW DELHI : Shri Murli Deora, Hon'ble Minister (P&NG) has appealed to Officers' Associations of Oil PSUs not to resort to the strike and pointed out that this path to seek resolution of issues is not only illegitimate but also against public interest. Various Hon'ble High Courts have directed the concerned Associations/Officers to refrain from going on strike rendering such an action liable for contempt of Court. It may be pointed out that there are more than 250 Central PSUs in the country whose pay revision is being looked into by the Pay Revision Committee set up by the Ministry of Heavy Industries and Public Enterprises. The officers "least of all" are not only not expected to resort to such an approach but this is against the service rules and amounts to contempt of the Court orders. The officers should appreciate that such a course of action would cause immense hardship and inconvenience to the public at large to whom the Oil industry is expected to maintain uninterrupted fuel supply. The Oil sector officers are amongst the highest paid in Government/Public Sector. Therefore, for them to repeatedly seek reddressal through the means of strike threat is totally incorrect and not in keeping with the best tradition of public service. The Ministry of Petroleum & Natural Gas and the PSUs under its administrative control have put in place a contingency plan to maintain the supplies to all sections, including aviation and defence. Simultaneously, Oil PSUs' management is considering disciplinary action against the officers joining this illegal and unjustified strike. They have also deployed retired officers and sought the services of Territorial Army to maintain normalcy. In view of this, Shri Deora has made a strong appeal to the officers to withdraw their strike call as Government has always been sympathetic to the genuine demands of officers and employees of the public sector in general and oil sector in particular.

2554. (21-8-2007) NEW DELHI : Following is the text of the Prime Minister, Dr. Manmohan Singh's address to the Japanese Business Delegation, which came with the Prime Minister of Japan, Mr. Shinzo Abe, here today: "It is a great pleasure and honour to welcome you all to this capital city of our country. I thank Prime Minister Abe for taking the initiative of bringing such a distinguished business delegation to India. I express my admiration for the ambitious vision that you have often set out in your speeches-of close economic engagement between

India and Japan. I sincerely believe that such an engagement, between Asia's largest democracy and its most developed country, will create an 'arc of advantage and prosperity' through out Asia. In December 2006, during my visit to Japan, Prime Minister Abe and I decided that the time had come for our two countries to raise our ties to the level of a global and strategic partnership. In today's changed international system, the political, economic and strategic interests of India and Japan have never been so convergent as they are today. The core element of our global and strategic partnership is a comprehensive economic engagement between our two countries. To accelerate this process, we decided to establish a Special Economic Partnership Initiative. This initiative will focus on key projects in areas ranging from the transport sector to industrial infrastructure, technology and education. There are enormous complementarities and commercial potential that exists in a strategic alliance between a technologically advanced, mature industrial economy like Japan's and a rapidly growing developing country like India's. The Japanese automobile industries like Toyota, Honda and Suzuki have located parts of their global production chains in India. We need more such models and examples of mutually beneficial collaboration in other sectors. We will do all that is in our power to facilitate their entry and also to ensure that they share our prosperity. Today, the Indian economy is in a position to sustain GDP growth rates that are close to 9%. Foreign Exchange reserves stand at over US$ 200 billion. We expect to receive Foreign Direct Investment of about US$ 30 billion this year. Our savings and investment rates are close to 35% of our GDP. Our foreign trade constitutes 33% of our GDP, which is a testimony to India's growing integration into the global economy. We have a very favourable demographic profile and a strong educational system to support rapid industrialization.

2555. (21-8-2007) NEW DELHI : Shri Kamal Nath, Union Minister of Commerce and Industry, while addressing the 400-strong Japanese business delegation here today evening, said that both India and Japan were engaged to conclude the Comprehensive Economic Partnership Agreement (CEPA) at the earliest. "The dialogue is on the fast track and we expect to have the agreement in place by the designated time", Shri Nath said. Mr. Fujio Mitarai, Leader of the Japanese delegation expressed optimism at the growing Indo-Japan economic relations and looked forward to a fruitful business engagement with Indian counterparts. Pointing out on the strategic importance of the engagement of business leaders from both sides, Shri Kamal Nath stated that the two governments will require the active participation of business leaders from both sides to make the comprehensive economic engagement between the two countries successful. "It is your support and dynamism that will propel the economic relations of India and Japan", he added. The meeting was also attended by the representatives of Indian business chambers including CII, FICCI and Assocham, apart from officials from both the countries. Japan is the 5th major investor in India with cumulative inflow of US $ 2.58 billion since 1991. Indian exports to Japan in 2006-07 were US $ 2812.83 million while imports from Japan were to the tune of US $ 4560.84 million. Major items of exports to Japan include gems & jewellery, iron ore, marine products while major import items are machinery, electronic goods, iron & steel and transport equipment.

2556. (21-8-2007) NEW DELHI : The 8TH Sectoral Summit of NEC ON 'EDUCATION, SPORTS, ART & CULTURE' concluded in New Delhi today. Issues related to education, sports and Art and culture were discussed at the summit. Several important decisions and conclusions were reached in each of these sectors. In the HRD sector it was decided that since most North East States have a high percentage of untrained teachers, IGNOU along with NEC and with the support of the NCERT would undertake a massive Teachers' training through distance training programme and double the figure of trained teachers in the next two years in the region. Teachers Training through Teachers' Training College would also continue. Given the geographical condition of Arunachal Pradesh, it was felt that the problems of the State are unique. Their infrastructure particularly residential accommodation is not available in remote areas, therefore teachers do not go to these distant places. It was decided to form a Committee with HRD, NEC and DoNER to seek solution to specific problems of Arunachal Pradesh. The recommendations would be applicable to other States which have similar areas. It was decided that for recruitment of teachers for schools the institution of village Panchayats may be used on the lines of Punjab State. Initial recruitment may be done from the Village Panchayat area first and then from Anchal area and lastly from the district etc. Community Polytechnics should be involved for vocational training along with conventional system.

2557. (21-8-2007) NEW DELHI : An Academic Dialogue was conducted here today between presidents and vice presidents of 12 major Universities in Japan and Vice-Chancellors of major Indian Universities, Directors of IITs and IIMs on the occasion of the visit to India by the Prime Minister of Japan. The meeting agreed to strengthen the relationship between Universities and Institutions of Higher Learning, to identify common research interests and to work towards increasing the volume of faculty and student movement between the countries, teaching Japanese language in India, etc. Both sides agreed to hold such Dialouges regularly in the future. This gathering was addressed by the Prime Minister of Japan Mr.Shinzo Abe and the Minister of Human Resource Development, Shri Arjun Singh. In his remarks the HRD Minister called attention to the request formally posed to the Government of Japan for assistance towards a new IIT. The Japanese Prime Minister in his remarks emphasised the need for people to people contact and increased relations between the institutions of Higher Learning in the two countries.

2558. (21-8-2007) NEW DELHI : The Prime Minister, Dr. Manmohan Singh, has condoled the death of eminent Urdu writer Qurratulain Hyder. In a condolence message, the Prime Minister said: "I am deeply grieved to learn about the sad demise of Smt. Qurratulain Hyder. She was a great teacher and scholar famous in India and abroad. She was one of the most celebrated and prolific writers of Urdu literature. Aag Ka Dariya, her magnum opus, is a landmark novel that explores the vast sweep of time and history. In her unfortunate passing away the country especially Urdu literature has lost a towering literary figure. She will be truly missed in literary circles in the country.

2559. (21-8-2007) NEW DELHI : The Minister of State for Textiles, Shri E.V.K.S. Elangovan, informed the Lok Sabha today, in a written reply to a question by Shri *E.G.* Sugavanam that the Government has revised the Duty Drawback and DEPB rates, which will benefit the textile sector. The Government is aware of the problems being faced by the garment exports in the wake of appreciation of the rupee. As per reports received from Export Promotion Councils, Garment/ Textile Industry has been adversely affected due to appreciation of rupee, he said. Shri Elangovan further stated that during the eight years of operation of Technology Upgradation Fund Scheme (TUFS), differential level of benefits has been observed in different segments. Certain segments like spinning and composite upgradation have benefitted to the desired level leaving scope of focus in segments like processing, garments etc.

2560. (21-8-2007) NEW DELHI : The Minister of State for Textiles, Shri E.V.K.S. Elangovan, informed the Lok Sabha today, in a written reply to a question by Shri Magunta Sreenivasulu Reddy that the National Institute for Fashion Technology (NIFT) and the Apparel Training & Design Centres (ATDCs) are running various courses/programmes at various places in the country to meet the skilled manpower requirement of the textiles industry, especially apparel, in the field of design, merchandising and marketing. The Minister further informed the House that the readymade garments is an important segment for augmenting production and export of textiles and clothing. It accounts for approximately 43% of the country's total textile exports. During the year 2006-07, the readymade garment exports have amounted to US$ 8.08 billion, recording an increase of 1.12% over the exports during the corresponding year of 2005-06.

2561. (21-8-2007) NEW DELHI : In a significant move to ensure effective implementation of rural development schemes through greater participation of elected representatives, Union Ministry of Rural Development has started a novel practice of convening interactive group conferences during the Parliament session with the Members of Parliament in different batches. The objective of these group meetings is to apprise the MPs about different provision of the rural development schemes, the status of implementation of various programmes in the concerned State, physical and financial progress and also to get their valuable feedback/ suggestions based on their Review meetings as Chairman of District Vigilance & Monitoring Committees. The first such interactive session was held yesterday in which the MPs belonging to West Bengal and North East States participated. The Speaker, Lok Sabha, Shri Som Nath Chatterjee was among those who attended the meeting and addressed the participants. Highlighting the importance of the District Vigilance & Monitoring Committees and extremely important role assigned to the Members of Parliament as Chairmen of the Committees, the Speaker impressed upon the MPs to convene the meetings on regular basis and to undertake rigorous review of the progress of various programmes. Lauding the efforts of Dr. Raghuvansh Prasad Singh, Union Minister of Rural Development in implementation of rural development programmes with zeal and commitment, Shri Chatterjee appreciated the achievements of the Ministry and complimented the efforts. Addressing the session, Dr. Raghuvansh Prasad Singh, Union Minister of Rural Development, urged the MPs to regularly undertake the monitoring committee meetings and also to take out field visits for ascertaining ground level realities in implementation of various programmes. He specifically requested the MPs to look into the implementation of the flagship programmes of the Government, namely, NREGA, PMGSY, IAY, Sanitation and Drinking Water Supply. Under NREGA, it was requested that MPs may visit work sites and look into few muster rolls so as to see their correctness and also with a view to ensure awareness in the community. Under PMGSY, the quality of roads built is to be inspected by MPs for ensuring their proper quality. Such other conferences are scheduled for all States in groups for 21st, 22nd, 23rd, 24th, 29th & 30th August, 2007 and 3rd, 5th & 6th September, 2007. The Ministry expects to receive innumerable valuable feedbacks from the MPs during the interactive session for looking into the policy formulation of the programmes being implemented.

2562. (21-8-2007) NEW DELHI : The Officers of Oil PSUs who had given a strike call from, today has called off their strike this morning responding to the appeal of Shri Murli Deora, Minister of Petroleum & Natural Gas. Shri Deora expressed his happiness over the development saying that the step is in right direction as a strike in the petroleum sector causes avoidable hardship and inconvenience to the people. He pointed out that this path to seek resolution of issues should always be avoided and added that his endeavour is to promote harmonious working in the oil sector and maintain smooth and uninterrupted supply of petroleum products to the people. The Minister emphasized that Government is always sympathetic to the genuine demands of officers and employees of the public sector in general and oil sector in particular. It may be pointed out that a Pay Revision Committee set up by the Ministry of Heavy Industries and Public Enterprises is already looking into the issues concerning pay revision in the Central PSUs.

2563. (21-8-2007) NEW DELHI : Commercial Banks, Regional Rural Banks and Cooperative Banks issue Kisan Credit Card (KCC) to farmers for accessing adequate and timely credit in a hassle free and cost effective manner. The credit limit of a farmer is fixed on the basis of his operational land holding, cropping pattern followed by the farmer, agriculture practices adopted in the area, scale of finance approved by District Level Technical Committee and the repaying capacity of the farmer. A total of 4,05,706 KCCs (provisional figures) have been issued in Haryana by various banks during the year 2005-06, 2006-07 and 2007-08 (upto 30.06.2007) The Banks have robust internal grievance redressal mechanism to address all customer complaints including those relating to KCC. Various instructions have been issued to banks from time to time in this regard. Any customer who has a grievance, which may relate to KCC loans, needs to be attended by the concerned bank. Besides, as and when NABARD receives any complaint from the Government/any other agency in regard to irregularities committed by banks in issuance of KCCs to farmers, the matter is examined/taken up with the concerned bank, for taking suitable remedial measures. This information was given by Shri Pawan Kumar Bansal, Minister of State for Finance in reply to a question raised by Shri Ajay Singh Chautala in Rajya Sabha today.

2564. (21-8-2007) NEW DELHI : Keeping in view the extreme conditions of the farmers in the 31 districts in Andhra Pradesh, Karnataka, Kerala and Maharashtra, Government is implementing a comprehensive Rehabilitation Package which, inter-alia, includes ex-gratia assistance from Prime Minister National Relief Fund and Debt Relief Package for farmers. The main items of the package are as under:- (i) The entire interest on overdue loans as on 01.07.2006 will be waived in the 31 affected districts such that all farmers will have no past interest burden as on that date. This should immediately make them eligible for fresh loan from the banking system. The burden of interest waived will be shared equally by the State Government and the Central Government in the ratio 50:50. (ii) The overdue loans of the farmers as on 01.07.2006 will be rescheduled over a period of 3-5 years with a one year moratorium. (iii) A credit flow of Rs.13,817.78 crore, Rs.3,076.20 crore, Rs.1,945.07 crore and Rs.1275 crore will be ensured in the above debt stressed districts of Andhra Pradesh, Karnataka, Kerala and Maharashtra respectively in 2006-07. This information was given by Shri Pawan Kumar Bansal, Minister of State for Finance in reply to a question raised by Dr. Vijay Mallya in Rajya Sabha today.

2565. (21-8-2007) NEW DELHI : Pursuant to the announcement made in the Union Budget speech 2007-08, that "National Housing Bank will introduce a novel financial product for senior citizens; a 'reverse mortgage' under which a senior citizen who is the owner of a house can avail of a monthly stream of income against the mortgage of his/her house, while remaining the owner and occupying the house throughout his/her lifetime, without repayment or servicing of the loan", the National Housing Bank (NHB) formulated the Operational Guidelines for Reverse Mortgage Loan (RML), after taking into account the feedback and suggestions of the senior Citizens, the public and the Technical Working Group constituted by NHB, in this regard.

2566. (21-8-2007) NEW DELHI : A revolving fund with a corpus of Rs. 100 crore to quicken the pace of preparation of a shelf of bankable projects which can be offered for competitive bidding was announced by Finance Minister in the Budget Speech 2007-08. India Infrastructure Project Development Fund scheme, to operationalise the Fund is under consideration of the Government. This information was given by Shri Pawan Kumar Bansal, Minister of State for Finance in reply to a question raised by Shri Dara Singh in Rajya Sabha today.

2567. (21-8-2007) NEW DELHI : The Pension Fund Regulatory and Development Authority, through a competitive bidding process has identified three public sector entities viz State Bank of India, Life Insurance Corporation of India and UTI-Asset Management Company Private Ltd. As sponsors of pension funds to manage the funds of the New Pension System in respect of Government of India employees who have joined on or after 1,1.2004. The pattern of permissible investments for non-government provident funds, superannuation funds and gratuity funds is prescribed by Government. With a view to providing wider avenues for investment by such funds this pattern of investment is periodically revised. There is no compulsion to invest in stock market as per this pattern. Investment decisions are taken by trustees of each fund based on their assessment of risk-return trade-off, and not by the Government. This information was given by Shri Pawan Kumar Bansal, Minister of State for Finance in reply to a question raised by Shri C. Ramachandraiah in Rajya Sabha today.

2568. (21-8-2007) NEW DELHI : Government has proposed to set up a Special Purpose Vehicle (SPV) in a separate country with a mature financial system in order to give a shape to the idea of using the burgeoning forex reserves for country's infrastructure development. Government is examining the legal and regulatory aspects in consultation with RBI and the details have not yet been chalked out. This information was given by Shri Pawan Kumar Bansal, Minister of State for Finance in reply to a question raised by Shri Ekanath K Thakur in Rajya Sabha today.

2569. (21-8-2007) NEW DELHI : Government had launched a Senior Citizens Savings Scheme, 2004 with effect from 2nd August, 2004. Persons of age 60 years and above and those retired persons who are 55 years of age and above but less than 60 years are eligible to invest in the scheme. The deposit under the scheme carrying interest rate of 9 per cent per annum payable on quarterly basis, compared favourably with the yield on Government security of comparable tenor. While the small savings schemes provide a secure avenue for investment, enjoys a number of incentives and are designed keeping in view the needs of different segment of investors. The de-regulation of interest rates relating to banks, financial institutions and debt market have made available various alternative options to all investors. This information was given by Shri Pawan.Kumar Bansal, Minister of State for Finance in reply to a question raised by Shri Tariq Anwar in Rajya Sabha today.

2570. (21-8-2007) NEW DELHI : Based on the recommendations of Foreign Investment Promotion Board (FIPB) in its meeting held on 17th August, 2007, Finance Minister, Shri P. Chidambaram has approved 20 proposals of Foreign Direct Investment amounting approximately to Rs. 1078.6526 crore. The proposals related to Ministries/Departments, namely, Commerce, Information & Broadcasting, Industrial Policy & promotion, Bio-technology, Micro, Medium & Small Enterprises, Telecommunications and Economic Affairs.

2571. (21-8-2007) NEW DELHI : The Government is open to talks with any militant groups including United Liberation Front of Asom (ULFA), provided they shun violence. The Government has not received any formal proposal from ULFA for direct talks. Ceasefire Agreement/Suspension of Operations (SoO) Agreement are in operation with National Socialist Council of Nagaland (Issac/Muivah) ((NSCN(I/M)}, National Socialist Council of Nagaland (Khaplang) ((NSCN(K)}, United People's Democratic Solidarity (UPDS), Dima Halam Daogah (DHD), National Democratic Front of Boroland (NDFB) and Achik National Volunteer Council (ANVC). Several rounds of tripartite talks with UPDS, DHD and ANVC on their Charter of Demands have been held and the talks are inconclusive. A Group of Minister (GoM) has been constituted to hold talks with NSCN(I/M). The latest round of talks was held on 31.7.2007. The talks are inconclusive. The NDFB and NSCN(K) have not submitted their charter of demands. This information was given by Smt. V. Radhika Selvi Minister of State in the Ministry of Home Affairs in reply to a question raised by Shri Hansraj G. Ahir in Lok Sabha today.

2572. (21-8-2007) NEW DELHI : As per the reports of the State Government of Jammu and Kashmir, there has been a continuous declining trend in the level of violence during the last three years. The number of terrorist related violent incidents has come down by 16% in 2006 as compared to 2005 and by 33% in 2007 (till July) over the corresponding period of 2006.

2573. (21-8-2007) NEW DELHI : A Committee constituted under the Chairmanship of Prof. Madhava Menon has submitted a Draft National Policy on Criminal Justice to the Government on 1st August, 2007. The Draft Policy has recommended classification of all offences under Indian Penal Code into four codes, namely, Social Welfare Offences Code, Correctional Offences Code, Penal Code and Economic Offences Code. The Draft Policy has also recommended changes in criminal law and procedure, the institutions of police, prosecution, judiciary and prisons including correctional services etc. for streamlining the Criminal Justice System in the country. It has also been suggested that Draft Policy should identify all such crimes affecting the unity and integrity of the country and create a united National Agency to undertake prevention, investigation and prosecution of such crimes with the support and cooperation of the State machinery concerned. The Draft Policy is being circulated to all the State Governments for their views/ comments as the Criminal Law and Criminal Procedure are on the Concurrent List of the Seventh Schedule to the Constitution of India and are administered by the

State Governments. On receipt of the same, a final view will be taken by the Government on the Draft Policy. This information was given by Smt. V. Radhika Selvi, Minister of State in the Ministry of Home Affairs in reply to a question raised by Shri Chandra Bhushan Singh in Lok Sabha today.

2574. (21-8-2007) NEW DELHI : Out of 185 km, a stretch of only 38.015 km fence was erected at a distance of 400 meter to 1.5 km away from IB (Zero Line) due to certain constraints. The Government has decided to shift this stretch closer to International Border and CPWD has been appointed to execute the work. There are some restrictions due to security consideration. However, all the farmers who own their land across the fence are being allowed by BSF to cultivate their land for which timings for opening and closing of gates are fixed in consultation with locals. This information was given by Smt. V. Radhika Selvi Minister of State in the Ministry of Home Affairs in reply to a question raised by Shri Chaudhary Lal Singh in Lok Sabha today.

2575. (21-8-2007) NEW DELHI : As per reports received from the State Government, in the wake of an incident of alleged rape and subsequent murder of a young Kashmiri girl at Langate, Handwara, on July 20, 2007 in which 4 persons, including 2 from outside the State of Jammu and Kashmir were accused/ arrested, threats and calls were given by certain secessionist groups asking Non-State subjects (mainly workers from outside the State) to leave the State. As a result, movement of a sizeable number of non-local workers and labourers from the Valley was observed. The Government has issued an advisory to the State Government and conjointly monitored the emerging security scenario. The State Government took immediate steps, including statements and appeals by the Chief Minister and a number of other functionaries of various parties and organizations, to instill confidence among the Non-State subjects. Under pressure from various sources, the secessionist groups also made statements retracting the threats. The steps taken by the State Government included, strengthening of security arrangements and operations in areas inhabited by labourers and workers from outside, constitution of Joint Committees comprising the Deputy Commissioner, Superintendent of Police and Assistant Labour Commissioner in each District to look into various aspects of the issue including a survey of such workers, meetings with respectable persons of the areas with the aim of generating public opinion against any such movement and creating a feeling of security amongst Non-State workers. As a result of the various measures taken, outward movement/exodus of Non-State subjects has substantially receded and, according to available information, a number of persons who may have left the Valley have also returned. This information was given by Shri Sriprakash Jaiswal Minister of State in the Ministry of Home Affairs in reply to a question raised by Shri A. Sai Prathap, Shri Mohan Singh and Shri Kailash Baitha in Lok Sabha today.

2576. (21-8-2007) NEW DELHI : The expansion of the telecom sector was accelerated with an increase of 7.56 million in the number of telecom subscribers during the month of July 2007. As a result, the total number of telephones in the country is more than 232.77 million, as compared to 158.05 during July 2006, *i.e.*, a growth of 47% during August 2006-July 2007. The GSM segment has shown an increase of 5.75 million during the month of July 2007, the CDMA segment of 1.92 million while the fixed segment has decreased by 0.11 million. The overall teledensity improved further to 20.50% in July 2007 as compared to 14.10% as on July 31, 2006. In the GSM segment, Tamilnadu telecom circle added more than 5.6 lakh subscribers during July 2007. In the CDMA segment, Delhi added more than 2.08 lakh subscribers during the period. Tamilnadu, Andhra Pradesh, Uttar Pradesh (E) and Maharashtra telecom circles have added more than 6 lakh subscribers each. The growth of broadband connections improved further and at the end of June 2007, about 2.46 million broadband connections were provided and coverage of broadband connectivity by public sector service providers has reached 1039 cities. Further, the total number of existing ISP licencees is 373. Under Bharat Nirman Programme, of the 66,822 villages remaining to be covered on November 2004, a total of 48704 villages have been provided with VPTs till June 2007. The remaining 18118 villages having more than 100 population and not lying in thick forest area etc. are to be covered by November 2007.

2577. (21-8-2007) NEW DELHI : Shri A.V. Muralidharan, Chairman and Managing Director, Export Credit Guarantee Corporation of India Limited (ECGC), presented a dividend cheque of Rs.100 crore to Shri Kamal Nath, Union Minister of Commerce & Industry here today. ECGC has already paid an interim dividend of Rs.25 crore earlier, thus totalling an amount of Rs.125 crore for the financial year 2006-07. This is the highest ever dividend paid by ECGC, since its inception in 1957. ECGC is currently in its 50th year of operations and is the only insurance company in India operating exclusively in the export credit insurance sector under 'non-life' category. One of the initiatives in the golden jubilee year is for setting up of an institute of international standard for credit insurance and credit risk management. ECGC is getting excellent support from international credit risk insurers and the Berne union, the international association of export credit risks insurers for this project. ECGC has earned a gross premium income of Rs.617.66 crore during 2006-07 as compared to Rs.578.44 crore of previous year registering a growth of over 6 percent. ECGC achieved recoveries of Rs.210.20 crores crossing the Rs.200 crore mark for the first time. The net profit after tax for the year was Rs.369.70 crore as against the previous year's profit of Rs.221.76 crore. ECGC has covered exports aggregating Rs.51733.77 crore and has covered export finance aggregating Rs.377107.03 crore. ECGC's new initiatives include insurance cover for exports made against Cargo Forward Receipts. A specific cover to suit the requirements of financial Institutions/ Factors was also designed and introduced during the year. The Corporation has on the anvil, proposal to introduce new products to cover Bio-technology and IT sectors. The designing of a cover to protect the exporters of Commodities against the risks of rejection is on the top of the agenda. The Corporation hopes to introduce these products in the current financial year with due approvals. Another significant development in the matter of Government's support to facilitate exports, especially the medium and long-term exports is in approving the National Export Insurance Account (NEIA), which has been made fully operational. The NEIA has been provided with funds by the Government of India and operated by a public trust, set up jointly by the Department of Commerce and ECGC. An amount of Rs.66 crore was released in the financial year 2005-2006; Rs.180 crores in 2006-07; and Rs.150 crore is expected to be added to the corpus of NEIA during 2007-08.

2578. (21-8-2007) NEW DELHI : The National Capital Region (NCR) Planning Board at its meeting today has approved a total plan outlay of Rs.1469 crore for 2008-09 on account of providing loan assistance to the participating states of U.P, Haryana, Rajasthan and NCT of Delhi and for undertaking studies, surveys and meeting expenses incurred in preparation of sub-regional plans and functional plans. This was stated by Shri S.Jaipal Reddy, Minister of Urban Development who chaired today's meeting. The borrowing programme of Rs 900 crore for the above purposes has also been approved. The Board approved the proposed financing plan for the 11th Five year Plan involving loan assistance of Rs. 11000 crore for infrastructure projects for which the Board will be accessing funds to the extent of Rs. 8000 crore from the International Aid Agencies like World Bank and Asian Development Bank. The Meeting also reviewed the progress of preparation of sub-regional plans for different sub-regions of the NCR viz. U.P sub-region consisting of five districts, Haryana Sub-region comprising eight districts and Alwar district of Rajasthan besides NCT of Delhi. The sub-regional plans are detailed blueprint of plan proposals contained in the Regional Plan of the Board. The Regional Plan provides a framework within which the State governments concerned will prepare Sub-regional plans and Master plans/Development plans. The State governments expressed their commitment to implement the plan in right earnest so as to make joint efforts for accelerating the development of the NCR. The Meeting was attended by Shri A.Raja, Minister of Communication and Information Technology, Shri Tejendra Khanna, Lt. Governor NCT-Delhi, Smt. Sheila Dikshit, Chief Minister NCT-Delhi, Shri B.S. Hooda, Chief Minister Haryana, Dr. Naseemuddin Siddiqui, Minister of Housing, Uttar Pradesh, Sh. Jayant Malaiya, Minister for Urban Administration and Development, Madhya Pradesh and the Chief Secretaries and other senior officials of Central and State Governments. The NCR Planning Board, an autonomous body under the Ministry of Urban Development, was set up in 1985 by an act of the Parliament with the twin objectives of preparing Regional Plan for the National Capital Region and also to finance selected infrastructure development projects in the region. Towards this objective, the Board has prepared Regional Plan 2021 and has financed 171 urban infrastructure development projects involving an outlay of over Rs. 11300 crore in the areas of water supply, sanitation, sewerage, transport and power etc. The Board has disbursed loans amounting to Rs. 2628 crore for these projects as on 31-3-2007. During the last financial year, the Board disbursed loans amounting to Rs. 416 crore, which was the highest disbursement in a year since inception of the Board. The Board has set disbursement targets of Rs. 700 crore for the current financial year (2007-08) and Rs. 1375 crore for 2008-09. In order to push infrastructure development in the NCR as per the thrust areas identified in the Regional Plan-2021, the Board has made plans to finance projects involving outlay of Rs. 15000 crore during the Eleventh Five Year Plan (2007-12).

2579. (21-8-2007) NEW DELHI : The Ministry of Tribal Affairs implements various Central Sector/ Centrally Sponsored Schemes/ programmes for the socio-economic development of tribal people in the country. Funds under the schemes of the Ministry are allocated to the State/ UT Governments based on the ST population in the State/ UT as a percentage of the total ST population in the country. This was stated by the Minister for Tribal Affairs, Shri P.R. Kyndiah in a reply to a question by Shri Rasheed Masood in Lok Sabha today.

2580. (21-8-2007) NEW DELHI : A central fact finding team will leave for Jammu & Kashmir tomorrow to enquire into the August 11 fire at the Army's biggest Ammunition Depot at Khundroo in Anantnag district. The four member team led by Shri Binoy Kumar, Joint Secretary (Ordnance), Defence Ministry includes a high level official from the union Home Ministry. The team will look into various aspects of the mishap, especially those related to safety and security of the personnel and civilian population living in and around the depot area. The team will also hold talks with State Government officials.

2581. (21-8-2007) NEW DELHI : Various reports indicate that the average temperature values of the earth has in last decade shown increasing trend. As reported by Defence Research and Development Organisation (DRDO), the seasonal snow cover has been melting in the last few years, the same way it was in the past and it seems that effect is more pronounced on Glaciers. Geological Survey of India (GSI) and it seems that effect is more pronounced on Glaciers. Geological Survey of India (GSI) have reported that most of the glaciers of Himalayas as well as in the other parts of the world are receding and the recession of the glaciers may result due to subnormal snowfall, higher temperature during summer, less severe winter or a combination of all of them. The GSI has further reported that it may also be due to global warming a topic which is still debatable. As per GSI, if the present scenario of receding glaciers is accelerated, there may be some reduction in the river discharge. However, it may be noted that the major part of the river discharge is contributed by snow fall and precipitation which is likely to go up with global warming. More melting of glaciers will generate more water initially. Hence there is no likelihood of northern rivers drying up in the near future. This information was given by the Minister of State in the Ministry of Water Resources Shri Jai Prakash Narayan Yadav in a written reply to question by Smt. Maya Singh :in the Rajya Sabha today.

2582. (21-8-2007) NEW DELHI : The Ministry of Water Resources has set up a Sub-Committee to formulate a policy for water for industries which provides the framework for regulation as well as incentive for economic use for large users of ground water. The Sub-Committee has submitted its report to the Ministry. Water being a state subject, any action about regulation in respect of various 'uses' is to be taken by respective State Governments. This information was given by the Minister of State in the Ministry of Water Resources Shri Jai Prakash Narayan Yadav in a written reply to question by Shri P.R.Rajan :in the Rajya Sabha today.

2583. (21-8-2007) NEW DELHI : In past 20 years Oil & Natural Gas Corporation Limited (ONGC) has accreted 3,990 Million Metric barrels of oil and oil equivalent gas (MMboe) (O+OEG) of recoverable reserves equivalwent to eight 'majors' within and around discovered fields. The contribution from new finds is 1.78 Million Metric Tonne (MMT) oil per annum including condensate which is 6.83% of annual production and 2299 Million Standard Cubic Metre (MMSCM) of gas which is 10.34% of the total annual gas production of ONGC. ONGC was awarded 47 blocks with operatorship in New Exploration Licensing Policy (NELP) rounds I to IV. ONGC has reported 8 oil/gas discoveries in 40 drilled wells as on 1stJuly, 2007. The success ratio is 20%. Oil/gas blocks under NELP are offered through international competitive bidding where all companies-Government, private, foreign or national can bid on equal terms and conditions. This was stated by the Minister of State for Petroleum & Natural Gas Shri Dinsha Patel in a written reply in the Rajya Sabha today.

2584. (21-8-2007) NEW DELHI : The Minister for Tourism and Culture Smt. Ambika Soni has said that the increase in foreign tourist arrivals to India during the year 2005 in comparison to 2004, and the year 2006 in comparison to 2005, is 13.3% and 13.5% respectively. In a written reply in the Rajya Sabha today, she said, the details of foreign tourist visits to different States/UTs during 2005 and 2006 are given in the Annexure. A study has been commissioned by the Ministry of Tourism to examine the various aspects of tourism covering existing policies, infrastructure, marketing strategies, etc., and prepare a plan for increasing the flow of foreign tourists in the country. Development of Tourism is primarily the responsibility of the State Governments/UT Administrations. The Ministry of Tourism provides Central Financial Assistance to States/UTs, including Himachal Pradesh, for development of Destinations/ Circuits under its Scheme 'Product Infrastructure Development for Destinations and Circuits'.

2585. (21-8-2007) NEW DELHI : The Minister for Tourism and Culture Smt. Ambika Soni has said that the Government has established a National Culture Fund (NCF) in which National and International Corporate Houses can contribute for various cultural activities including conservation and restoration of monuments. The total amount committed in the last three years is Rs. 1.00 Crore from Steel Authority of India (SAIL) and US $43900 from World Monument Fund (WMF). In a written reply in the Rajya Sabha today, she said, separate Memoranda of

Understanding are entered into with the donors for NCF projects and the donors are associated in restoration or conservation activities through representation on Project Implementation Committees. The NCF project with association of SAIL, relating to conservation of monuments at Lodi Garden, New Delhi is being implemented through Indian National Trust for Art and Cultural Heritage (INTACH). The NCF project with WMF relates to restoration of parts of Jaisalmer Fort. The responsibility of supervising restoration works lies with the Archaeological Survey of India.

2586. (21-8-2007) NEW DELHI : Indian Air Force successfully completed a casualty evacuation at night using Night Vision Goggles through a narrow valley close to the border for the first time in the history of the Indian Air Force. Headquarters Eastern Air Command of Indian Air Force was approached by an operational division of the Indian Army with an emergency request at 1630 hrs on 20 Aug 07 for evacuating two casualties, one with a serious head injury. The helipad being located in the narrow valley close to the international border, the late hours of the day, marginal weather conditions and the deteriorating health of the casualty necessitated a prompt decision to undertake the evacuation in a helicopter using Night Vision Goggles. 12 minutes after the request was received the most qualified aircrew from Air Force Station Mohanbari were launched using a Mi-17 helicopter, after a meticulous planning and co-ordination. Surmounting low visibility conditions and turbulent weather during monsoons, the attempt was made to evacuate the patient from Kibitoo helipad to Jorhat Air Force Hospital. The professional flying which involved about four hours of flight time was courageously undertaken. This enabled the saving of the lives of two critically injured soldiers. This type of casualty evacuation at night using Night Vision Goggles through a narrow valley close to the border was undertaken for the first time in the history of the Indian Air Force. The professionalism and execution of this mission has been a morale booster for our troops deployed in difficult and inhospitable terrain.

2587. (21-8-2007) NEW DELHI : The Government is committed to create a network of world-class airports in the country with a view to establishing India as a global aviation hub. Measures have been taken to augment capacity as a result of which additional capacity to handle 601.05 lakh passengers per annum on the domestic sector and 301.80 lakh passengers per annum on international sector is under construction and is likely to be commissioned within the next two-three years. This information was given by Shri Praful Patel in a written reply to a question.

2588. (21-8-2007) NEW DELHI : A total of 67,744 new companies have been formed in the country online through MCA21 programme. Information regarding the number of companies formed on-line as on August 14, 2007, indicating the ROC jurisdiction and the State(s) is annexed. The promoter(s) / interested person(s) is/are required to file Memorandum of Association (MOA) and Articles of Association (AOA), duly signed by the Subscribers, in terms of Section 15 and 30 of the Companies Act, 1956 for the formation of a company. The Act does not prescribe filing of a prospectus or Statement in lieu of prospectus at the time of formation of a company. The MOA and AOA are detailed documents and furnished by the promoter(s)/ subscribers under their signatures as attachments to e-Form 1 prescribed for the purpose. The attachment, consisting of the MOA and the AOA are scanned images. The e-Form is digitally signed and the complete set of documents is filed in a secure environment whereby the interests of the promoters are fully secured. These are available in the electronic registry for viewing by the stakeholders at all times.

2589. (21-8-2007) NEW DELHI : Guwahati Regional Centre of Song and Drama Division has prepared new programme packages on 150th year of First War of Independence. Twenty-two registered cultural troupes and two departmental/ empanelled troupes were deployed with the newly developed programme packages on the above theme. So far, 130 programmes have already been presented in coordination with Nehru Yuva Kendra and District Administrations of the concerned Districts of Assam and Manipur. As part of the commemorative programme of 150th year of First War of Independence 1857, the Government is implementing an exhibition project on a mobile train, with DAVP as the implementing agency. The total cost of the project is estimated at Rs. 14.84 crore inclusive of all participating Ministries/Organisations. Government of India has constituted a National Committee under the Chairmanship of Hon'ble Prime Minister and a National Implementation Committee under the Chairmanship of Hon'ble Minister of Human Resource Development to chalk out the programmes and activities for commemoration of 150th Anniversary of First War of Independence, 1857 in a befitting manner. This information was given by Minister of Information & Broadcasting and Parliamentary Affairs, Shri P. R. Dasmunsi in written reply to a question in Lok Sabha today.

2590. (21-8-2007) NEW DELHI : The National Association of Software and Service Companies (NASSCOM) made a presentation before the Prime Minister on 19.12.2005 on the vision for IT Industry, based on the NASSCOM-Mckinsey Report, 2005. According to this report, India will need a 2.3 million IT and BPO workforce by the year 2010 to maintain its current market share. NASSCOM's supply projections indicate a shortfall of nearly 0.5 million employees, nearly 70 percent of which will be concentrated in the BPO industry. AICTE has, however, forecast that at an anticipated growth in enrolment in engineering courses at 15% there would not be any shortage of manpower for IT job. The Government has set up a working group, on 27.06.2006, under the Chairmanship of Secretary (Higher Education) and with representatives from the Department of IT, CSIR, Department of Economic Affairs, AICTE, NASSCOM, industry, etc. to make recommendations on improving the supply of talent to the IT/BPO sector. As recommended by the Working Group, AICTE is updating curriculum and syllabi of undergraduate engineering courses to make them more compatible with the requirements of the IT & ITeS and related industries. As also recommended by the Working Group, finishing schools have been organized in some National Institutes of Technology and IIT Roorkee to enhance the employability of engineering graduates of other Engineering Colleges. The Ministry of HRD has also taken up a major initiative to establish 20 new Indian Institutes of Information Technology (IITs) in the country during the 11th Five Year Plan. This was stated by the Minister of State for Human Resource Development Smt. D. Purandeswari in a reply to a question by Shri Jyotiraditya M. Scindia in Lok Sabha today.

2591. (21-8-2007) NEW DELHI : A committee consisting of representatives of Ministry of Home Affairs, Ministry of External Affairs, Association of Indian Universities (AIU), Council of Board of School Education (COBSE), National Council of Education Research & Training (NCERT), Central Board of Secondary Education (CBSE) and eminent educationists, was constituted by the Ministry of Human Resource Development in February, 2006 to suggest a policy, inter-alia, regarding setting up of schools affiliated to foreign boards in India and appointment of foreign teachers in such schools. The main recommendations of the Committee relate to designation of a schools as "International" school, affiliation to foreign Borads, need to have respect for values relating to Indian culture, secularism, diversity and tolerance of differences as enshrined in Indian Constitution and appointment of foreign teachers. The recommendations are under consideration of the Government. This was stated by the Minister of State for Human Resource Development Smt. D. Purandeswari in a reply to a question by Shri Vijoy Krishna in Lok Sabha today.

2592. (21-8-2007) NEW DELHI : Lakshdweep native students who are original inhabitants belonging to Scheduled Tribes are provided concessions including financial assistance under the Lakshdweep Scholarship Rules. All ST students of Lakshdweep who pursue recognized post-matriculation courses in recognized institutions are also entitled to the Post-Matric Scholarship for STs, which is a shceme of Ministry of Tribal Affairs. Under this scheme, the full amount of the fee charged by Government schools/colleges is reimbursed. In respect of seats in private institutions filled up on merit or competition basis, fees are reimbursed to the extent equal to that for students in Government institutions. For management quota seats, fees reimbursed are the same as for comparable courses in Government institutions, but the number of students is limited to the reservation quota for STs in the concerned State/UT. This was stated by the Minister of State for Human Resource Development Smt. D. Purandeswari in a reply to a question by Dr. P.P.Koya in Lok Sabha today.

2593. (21-8-2007) NEW DELHI : While there is no scheme of government loans to students for education, the Indian Banks' Association has an Education Loan

Scheme to provide financial support from the banking system to deserving meritorious students for pursuing higher education in India (for upto Rs. 7.5 lakh) and abroad (for upto Rs. 15 lakh). No security is required for loans upto Rs. 4 lakh and only simple interest is charged during the Repayment holiday/moratorium. The Central Government through its various Ministries, has a number of scholarship schemes, such as National Scholarship Scheme (for Post Matric studies in India), Post-Matric Scholarships for Scheduled Castes, Scheduled Tribes and Other Backward Classes, Post-Graduate Indira Gandhi Scholarship Scheme for Single Girl Child, Post-Matric Merit Scholarship Scheme for University Rank Holders in General and Honours course at Under-graduate level, as well as Fellowships for studies abroad. The proposal for setting up a Refinance Corporation has been reconsidered, on the basis of inputs received from the Planning Commission and the Department of Financial Services, and an alternative scheme is being worked out. This was stated by the Minister of State for Human Resource Development Smt. D. Purandeswari in a reply to a question by Shri Anandrao V. Adsul in Lok Sabha today.

2594. (21-8-2007) NEW DELHI : The Committee constituted by this Ministry under the Chairmanship of Dr. G. Sanjeeva Reddy has since submitted its report in December, 2006. The report recommended establishment of a Workers Technical University for inter-alia training the students from workers family and those belonging to economically poor sections of the society particularly form rural areas to make them more relevant to the needs of today's technology intensive and knowledge driven industrial society. The Committee recommended the industry to contribute a small percentage of their gross profit (ranging from 0.5% to 2%) as the education cess for the proposed university. The Committee recommended that the jurisdiction of the proposed National Workers Technical University shall be the whole of the country, having the main campus at Hyderabad with regional centres at different major cities in the country. The Ministry has constituted a Core Committee to work out the details of establishment of the National Workers Technical University. The XIth plan has not been finalized. This was stated by the Minister of State for Human Resource Development Smt. D. Purandeswari in a reply to a question by Shri Ravi Prakash Verma in Lok Sabha today.

2595. (21-8-2007) NEW DELHI : The Ministry of Human Resource Development, in collaboration with National AIDS Control Organisation (NACO) has launched an educational programme, known as Adolescence Education Programme (AEP) for implementation by States and Union Territories in secondary and higher secondary school. It is focused on three major concerns of adolescence: (i) Process of Growing up during adolescence, (ii) Prevention of HIV/AIDS and (iii) Prevention of Substance (Drug Abuse). According to information with National Council of Education Research and Training (NCERT), there have been some objections to the contents in the Toolkit, which is meant for the teachers. National AIDS Control Organization (NACO) under the Ministry of Health and Family Welfare (MOHFW) has set up a Committee to critically review the material pertaining to Adolescence Education Programme. Besides, all the States and Union Territories have also been advised to review the material to align the same in the context of local environment and the socio-cultural ethos. This was stated by the Minister of State for Human Resource Development Smt. D. Purandeswari in a reply to a question by Shri P.S.Gadhavi in Lok Sabha today.

2596. (21-8-2007) NEW DELHI : The Government proposes to set up 20 new Indian Institutes of Information Technology (IITs) in the country during the 11th Five Year Plan. As advised by the Planning Commission, a Task Force has been constituted to deliberate on the setting up of new IIITs in a Public-Private Partnership mode. The Task Force is yet to submit its Report. Details regarding places, time schedule, location etc. will be finalized after getting "in principle" approval of the Planning Commission. At present, there are four IIITs set up by the Government of India and operating in the Country. These institutes are:-Indian Institute of Information Technology, Allahabad; Atal Bihari Vajpayee-Indian Institute of Information Technology & Management, Gwalior; Pandit Dwarka Prasad Mishra Indian Institute of Information Technology, Design & Manufacturing, Jabalpur and Indian Institute of Information Technology, Design & Manufacturing, Kancheepuram, An extension Centre of IIIT Allahabad has also been set up at Amethi. This was stated by the Minister of State for Human Resource Development Smt. D. Purandeswari in a reply to a question by Shri Chandrakant Khaire in Lok Sabha today.

2597. (21-8-2007) NEW DELHI : The Minister of Social Justice and Empowerment, Smt. Meira Kumar inaugurated the training programme for Backward Classes youth, sponsored by National Backward Finance and Development Corporation (NBCFDC) at Apparel Training and Design Centre (ATDC), Gurgaon today. On the occasion, the Minister said that the training in skill up-gradation is important for the target group of Backward Classes as the group is mostly connected with the traditional economic activities, which need continuous up-gradation to match the market requirement. She expressed hope that after the successful completion of training, the beneficiaries will get an opportunity to work with the garment industry and will mitigate their hardship by enhancing their income level. Smt. Meira Kumar said that NBCFDC has developed the training schemes, in skill development, which promise a new future to the young members of the Backward Classes. It has established linkages with the best institutions of the country. ATDC is one among them and Ministry has also sanctioned Rs. 99 lakh to ATDC through NBCFDC for these training programmes for 1150 Backward Class beneficiaries. The NBCFDC is providing financial assistance to the eligible members of Backward Classes through SCA's in various trades and occupations and providing loans under various schemes in the country and so far disbursed over Rs.1200 crore to cover more than eight lakh beneficiaries in the country. The Corporation has provided training to over 60,000 beneficiaries in skill up gradation through various training programmes, which include about 2200 beneficiaries through ATDC at their 16 training centres in different states.

2598. (21-8-2007) NEW DELHI : Given the safety, cost-effectiveness and the success rate of Ksharasutra in the treatment of anal fistula, the Department of AYUSH, in collaboration with the ICMR and the CCRAS, is organizing a National Campaign to promote the use of Ksharasutra in ano-rectal diseases. A National Workshop is being organized on 24-25 August 2007 in the auditorium of the All India Institute of Medical Sciences, New Delhi. Eminent experts in Ksharasutra will be participating in the Workshop. In keeping with the increased interest in Ksharasutra in foreign countries, a renowned Japanese expert Dr. Kenji Tazawa will also be participating in the National Workshop.

2599. (21-8-2007) NEW DELHI : Direct tax collections during fiscal 2007-08 recorded a growth of 44.39% up to 15th August, 2007. Tax collections stood at Rs.59,210 crore, up from Rs.41,006 crore during the same period last fiscal. Corporate tax recorded a growth of 52.25% at Rs.33,164 crore, up from Rs.21,783 crore during last fiscal, while personal income tax (including FBT, STT and BCTT) grew by 35.57% at Rs.25,989 crore, up from Rs.19,170 crore last fiscal. Securities Transaction Tax (STT) grew by 36.30% at Rs.2,495 crore and Banking Cash Transaction Tax (BCTT) grew by 29.71% at Rs.207 crore. The continued buoyancy in direct tax collections is a reflection of the robust growth in the economy, better tax compliance and improved tax administration.

2600. (21-8-2007) NEW DELHI : The Institute of Company Secretaries of India is examining the concept of Labour Laws Compliance Report (LLCR) by Practising Company Secretaries for corporate entities. Under this concept, a periodical compliance report of labour laws by a professional Practising Company Secretary could be made to the Board of Directors/shareholders of a company for taking appropriate steps and making disclosures. If found operationally feasible and reasonable in terms of compliance costs, suitable amendments in respective labour laws, where such a requirement is warranted, would be required. This information was given by Shri Prem Chand Gupta, Minister of Corporate Affairs in reply to a question raised by Shri Jai Parkash Aggarwal in Rajya Sabha today.

2601. (21-8-2007) NEW DELHI : The Ministry of Corporate Affairs proposes to set up an Indian Institute of Corporate Affairs during the Eleventh Five Year Plan period. The institute would start its' operations only after the detailed Project Report has been prepared and the requisite financial sanctions issued. The proposal submitted to the Planning Commission contained an estimate of Rs. 211.00 crore for the setting up of the institute. An amount of Rs. 47.00 crore has been allocated during the current financial year for this purpose. The broad objectives of the institute include capacity building/training for the Indian Company Law Service (ICLS) and subordinate cadres, provision of value added services with the implementation of MCA21 e-Governance Project and service delivery in areas like investor education/awareness, Corporate Governance etc. The institute is also envisaged to serve as a think-tank for the Ministry to provide for a dynamic response to the ever changing business environment and support the Ministry in taking up initiatives that are responsive to the expectations of the stakeholders in general and the corporate sector in particular. This information was given by Shri Prem Chand Gupta, Minister of Corporate Affairs in reply to a question raised by Shri C. Ramachandraiah in Rajya Sabha today.

2602. (21-8-2007) NEW DELHI : In a unique experiment to reach out to beneficiaries directly Dr. Raghuvansh Prasad Singh, Union Minister for Rural Development linked up to over 1100 Panchayats in Orissa through the "Gram SAT- An ISRO Satellite" and interacted on the rural development schemes under operation in Orissa with about 75,000 rural development functionaries/ PRIs/ villages directly. The Ministry of Rural Development stands committed to bring about transparency and efficiency in implementation of its various schemes all over the country. As a part of this effort the Ministry has of late been initiating different proactive measures like online monitoring, social auditing, etc. In yet another measure in this direction the Ministry organized a direct interaction with the beneficiaries of Rural development schemes in Orissa spread in 30 districts, 314 blocks and 1179 Panchayats through Gram SAT. Addressing the beneficiaries of various rural development schemes, the field level implementers of rural development schemes, the elected representatives of Panchayati Raj Institutions (PRIs) Dr. Raghuvansh Prasad Singh told that this experiment would go a long way in taking the Government machinery to the doorsteps of the beneficiaries and mitigating their problems and issues. Dr. Singh also gave a detailed account of the financial and physical achievements of rural development schemes in Orissa in his address through the satellite. Dr. Singh informed that stern measures will be taken to stamp out any attempt at any level to deprive the beneficiaries from their rights and corruption shall not be tolerated in implementation of the rural development schemes. He urged the State Governments to ensure that benefits of the schemes are reached to the masses without any hindrances. The Minister had a face to face interaction with about 75,000 rural development functionaries/ PRIs/ villages directly. Also present in the occasion was Shri Chandra Shekhar Sahu, Union Minister of State for Rural Development. Sh. Sahu emphasized on the need of cooperation between the State and the Central Governments for effective implementation of rural development schemes. The event which is first of its kind evoked tremendous enthusiasm and response from participants down up to the Panchayat level and nearly one lakh people were present at the Gram SAT centres. Some of the districts from where questions were asked are in the remote areas like Malkangiri, Nuapara, Kalahandi and Phulbani. This effort of the Ministry is also aimed at enhancing the awareness of the beneficiaries about their entitlement and various processes involved for getting the benefit of schemes. Through interaction, Ministry could get insight into field level problem, which shall help, in further planning and drawing up strategy in future. Gram SAT pilot projects are being run in some select states of the country and are being utilized very effectively to reach out development messages directly to the villagers by ensuring community listening, viewing and linking up large body of villagers. In view of the high potential of this media the IEC Division of MoRD has initiated this unique experimentation. Appreciating the initiative, Dr. Singh directed to arrange for such conferences once in a month on rotational basis. The Minister shall discuss other technical options with ISRO to reach to the common masses including exploring the possibilities of creating a dedicated television and radio channel for rural development.

2603. (21-8-2007) NEW DELHI : The total approximate earnings of Indian Railways on originating basis during the period 1st August-10th August 2007 were Rs. 1665.20 crore compared to Rs. 1479.31 crore during the same period last year, registering an increase of 12.57 per cent. The total goods earnings have gone up from Rs. 980.69 crore during 1st August-10th August 2006 to Rs. 1131.92 crore during 1st August-10th August 2007, showing an increase of 15.42 per cent. The total passenger revenue earnings during the period 1-10 August 2007 were Rs. 473.72 crore compared to Rs. 443.07 crore during the same period last year, reflecting an increase of 6.92 per cent. The revenue earnings from other coaching amounted to Rs. 47.30 crore during this period compared to Rs. 43.95 crore during the same period last year, showing an increase of 7.62 per cent. The total sundry earnings have gone up from Rs. 11.60 crore during 1-10 August 2006 to Rs. 12.26 crore during 1-10 August 2007, showing an increase of 5.69 per cent. The total approximate number of passengers booked during the period 1-10 August 2007 were 177.20 million compared to 168.66 million during the same period last year, showing an increase of 5.06 per cent. In the suburban and non-suburban sectors, the number of passengers booked during 1-10 August 2007 were 100.36 million and 76.84 million compared to 93.82 million and 74.84 million during the same period last year, registering an increase of 6.97 per cent and 2.67 per cent respectively.

2604. (22-8-2007) NEW DELHI : The government has not decided on a joint venture with Israel for the production of missiles. The Defence Research and Development Organisation (DRDO) has earlier entered into a contract with M/s. Israel Aerospace Industries (IAI), Israel to jointly develop a Long Range Surface to Air Missile (LRSAM) system for the Indian and Israeli Navy in January 2006. The Government of India pursues bilateral cooperation with Israel in many fields, keeping in mind our national interests. Cooperation in the field of defence is one of the many dimensions of bilateral cooperation. This is based on our sole national interest and does not come in the way of the warm and mutually beneficial cooperation that we share with friendly Muslim countries. This information was given by the Defence Minister Shri AK Antony in a written reply to Shri D Raja and Shri Syed Azeez Pasha in Rajya Sabha today.

2605. (22-8-2007) NEW DELHI : Co-development of a Fifth Generation Fighter Aircraft (FGFA) has been identified as an important area of cooperation between the Indian and Russian governments. Technical discussions to work out the details are in progress. Efforts are on for finalizing the draft Inter-Governmental Agreement in this regard. The US government has not proposed to provide a fifth generation fighter F-35 aircraft to India. This information was given by the Defence Minister Shri AK Antony in a written reply to Shri D Raja in Rajya Sabha today.

2606. (22-8-2007) NEW DELHI : A total number of 10 MiG 21 aircraft of the Indian Air Force (IAF) have crashed during the last three financial years from 2004-05 to 2007-08 (till 13.8.2007). In these accidents a total number of 7 persons lost their lives. Besides the loss of aircraft, compensation amounting to Rs.40,49,853/- has also been paid on account of service personnel /civilian killed / injured and loss to the civil property in these accidents. Each aircraft accident in the IAF is investigated through a Court of Inquiry (CoI) and remedial measures as per the recommendations of the CoI are taken. Besides, a continuous and multifaceted effort is always underway to enhance and upgrade flight safety. Measures to enhance the quality of training to improve the skill levels, ability to exercise sound judgment and situational awareness of pilots are being pursued. Constant interaction with Original Equipment Manufacturers (OEMs), both indigenous and foreign, is also maintained to overcome the technical defects of aircraft. Besides, anti-bird measures are also undertaken. This information was given by the Defence Minister Shri AK Antony in a written reply to Smt Prema Cariappa in Rajya Sabha today.

2607. (22-8-2007) NEW DELHI : There are 41 court martial cases pending against army personnel which require disposal by a forum higher than summary court martial. However, the number of cases pending against army personnel in various courts is 25 only which includes 6 cases filed before special court of CBI. Out of 41 court martial cases, 35 cases are related to serious offences such as property, murder, rape and other offences of physical assault. Trial proceedings by courts martial or civil courts in such matters is an ongoing process. No amendment is contemplated as the existing law/rules are considered adequate. However, to provide a meaningful opportunity of appeal against verdicts of court martial to the officers and other ranks in courts in various parts of the country, the government has decided to set up an Armed Forces Tribunal (AFT) which would also be empowered to deal with service matters. Once the AFT and its regional branches are fully functional, it is expected to reduced the burden of the courts significantly. This information was given by the Defence Minister Shri AK Antony in a written reply to Shri Surendra Lath in Rajya Sabha today.

2608. (22-8-2007) NEW DELHI : The Union Government has made an additional allocation of 3.00 lakh tons of foodgrains to the Bihar Government for distribution among the flood affected people in the State. The Food Corporation of India has been directed to release 2.00 lakh tons of rice and 1.00 lakh tons of wheat to the state to meet the emergency in the wake of the recent floods.

2609. (22-8-2007) NEW DELHI : The Union Territory of Lakshadweep (UTL)

Administration signed a contract with M/s. Hindustan Shipyard Limited (HSL), Visakhapatnam on 14.09.2000 for construction of one 700 Passenger-cum-160 M.T. Cargo Vessel at a total cost of Rs.129.62 crores with a delivery period of 29 months *i.e.* by February, 2003. Due to severe financial crunch, HSL could not construct the vessel in time. HSL has now informed that the overall completion of the vessel is around 91% and the vessel is planned for handing over to Lakshadweep Administration in September this year.

2610. (22-8-2007) NEW DELHI : The Merchant Shipping (Amendment) Bill, 2004 further to amend the Merchant Shipping Act, 1958 and Indian Ports Act, 1908 was introduced in the Lok Sabha on 14th August, 2007 and the Bill was passed by the House. The International Maritime Organisation (IMO) has introduced new Maritime Security Regulations-International Code for the Security of Ships and of Port facilities (ISPS Code) from 1st July, 2004. India also implemented ISPS Code from this date. Enforcement of ISPS Code requires legislative measures which have necessitated amendments in certain provisions of the Merchant Shipping Act and Indian Port Act to incorporate safety related provisions. The enhanced security measures will add to maritime safety and security in the Indian shipping industry so that the country's EXIM trade is not effected due to non-compliance of ISPS Code in its ports and ships engaged in International trade. The amendments will come into force after the Bill is considered and passed by the Rajya Sabha and assented to by the President. This information was given by the Minister of Shipping, Road Transport and Highways, Thiru T.R. Baalu in a written reply in the Lok Sabha today.

2611. (22-8-2007) NEW DELHI : The Government of India received requests from some State Governments for setting up of Maritime Universities in their States. The Indian Maritime University Bill, 2007 was introduced in the Lok Sabha on 13.3.2007. The Bill envisages that the headquarters of the University shall be at Chennai with its campuses at Mumbai, Kolkata, Vishakhapatnam and such other places within its jurisdiction as it may deem fit. The Bill now has been referred to Department-related Parliamentary Standing Committee on Transport, Tourism and Culture for examination. This information was given by the Minister of Shipping, Road Transport and Highways, Thiru T.R. Baalu in a written reply in the Lok Sabha today.

2612. (22-8-2007) NEW DELHI : The Union Minister of Shipping, Road Transport and Highways, Thiru T. R. Baalu has reiterated in a written reply in the Lok Sabha today that the Detailed Environmental Impact Assessment Study and Detailed Feasibility Report have concluded that there is no impact on ecology and environment in the dredging and dumping areas of Sethusamudram Ship Channel Project. As such, there is no adverse impact on the livelihood of people living in the vicinity of the project site, he added in his reply. Adequate arrangements to provide sustainable livelihood opportunities to the coastal communities, including fishermen, have been made as per the Order of the Ministry of Environment and Forests dated the 31st March, 2005,. About 2% of the project cost has been made available for such activities.

2613. (22-8-2007) NEW DELHI : A Task Force has been set up under the chairmanship of Shri Anwarul Hoda, Member, Planning Commission to examine Tariff Setting Mechanism and Bidding parameters for Public Private Partnership projects in Major Ports. The report of the Task Force is being finalised. This information was given by the Minister of Shipping, Road Transport and Highways, Thiru T.R. Baalu in a written reply in the Lok Sabha today.

2614. (22-8-2007) NEW DELHI: Proceedings in Parliament were disrupted for the whole day on Tuesday as Left parties joined the Opposition benches in protesting against the reported remarks by India's Ambassador to the United States, Ronen Sen, in an interview to Rediff India Abroad on the political turmoil over the nuclear deal with Washington. Though External Affairs Minister Pranab Mukherjee came out with a clarification — coupled with an expression of regret — in the morning and the envoy tendered an "unqualified" apology by afternoon, there was no let-up in the Opposition and Left's demand for his recall. They also submitted privilege notices against Mr. Sen. Mr. Mukherjee, in the clarification to both Houses, said: "These comments, if made by our Ambassador, and reported correctly, are totally unwarranted and unacceptable. In a democracy, there will always be dissension and divergence of opinions. Noone can accuse others who hold divergent views. I regret the alleged comments which have hurt the members' feelings." The Minister made the clarification after he contacted Mr. Sen. The envoy told him that "certain comments, either deliberately or through misunderstanding, were published by the correspondent." Mr. Mukherjee said the Ambassador was "misquoted in several respects" and he was asked to issue a clarification. Mr. Sen's apology came post-lunch — again read out by Mr. Mukherjee in both Houses. Admitting that his comment "running around like headless chicken, looking for a comment here or comment there," was a tactless observation, Mr. Sen said it was a reference to some of his media friends and not to any Member of Parliament. "It was certainly not my intention to cast an aspersion on any individual or organisation. Some of the comments attributed to me in this off-the-record conversation were, however, made by me in my personal capacity and do not reflect the positions of the government."

2615. (22-8-2007) NEW DELHI : The Power Finance Corporation Ltd (PFC) and Karnataka Renewable Energy Development Ltd. (KREDL) signed a Memorandum of Understanding (MoU) on 20th August, 2007 for facilitating financing of non-conventional renewable energy projects such as wind, small. hydro, solar, biomass, etc. recommended by KREDL to PFC. The MoU was signed by Sh. M.K.Goel, Director (Institutional Appraisal & Development), PFC and Dr.B.Shivalingaiah, MD, KREDL in the presence of Shri H.D. Revanna, Minister for Energy and PWD, Govt. of Karnataka and Shri Dilip Rau, Additional Chief

Secretary and Principal Secretary to Govt. of Karnataka. KREDL is a State Nodal Agency for promotion and development of non-conventional and renewable sources of energy and is implementing renewable energy programmes of Ministry of New and Renewable Energy (MNRE), New Delhi in the State of Karnataka. MNRE has set for itself a goal to add an additional 14,000 MW capacity of grid quality power through non-conventional renewable resources from commercially exploitable resources by the end of 11th Five Year Plan. It is estimated that Karnatka has a potential to add 11150 MW through renewable energy sources. At present, the installed capacity of electric power from non-conventional renewable energy sources in Karnataka is 1630 MW. In addition to this, KREDL has drawn an action plan to add 1500 MW of power through renewable energy sources by the end of 11th Five Year Plan period in the State. PFC and KREDL shall cooperate to leverage their respective strengths and competencies built over the years for development of non-conventional and renewable sources of energy, avail Clean Development Mechanism (CDM) benefits from the small scale renewable energy power projects and for promoting energy efficiency in all sectors for mutual benefit.

2616. (22-8-2007) NEW DELHI : The Constitution 79th Amendment Bill 1992 disqualifying a person having more than two children to be a member of either house of Parliament and State Legislature (with prospective effect) was introduced in Rajya Sabha in December 1992. The Bill was later referred to Parliamentary Standing Committee on Human Resource Development. On the recommendations of Parliamentary Standing Committee on Human Resource Development the Government convened meetings of leaders of various political parties in Parliament to ensure the passage of the Bill. No consensus emerged in favour of the Bill. As such the Bill is pending in Rajya Sabha due to lack of unanimity on the subject among various political groups/parties. This information was given by the Minister of State for Health & Family Welfare, Smt. Panabaka Lakshmi in a written reply to a question in the Lok Sabha.

2617. (22-8-2007) NEW DELHI : National AIDS Control Organisation (NACO) has set up a National Adolescence Education Programme toolkit review committee comprising of academicians, educationists, child psychologists, child psychiatrists, Communication Experts, Non-governmental Organisations, National Council of Educational Research & Training and Central Board of Secondary Education to review the existing educational material. The first meeting of the committee was held on 08th August 2007. At this meeting it was decided to prepare a guideline on content and pedagogical aspects of the AEP for guidance to State Governments and implementing agencies. This guideline will be based on a review of the Adolescence Education Programme materials developed by (a) NACO, UNICEF, Ministry of Human Resource Development and NCERT, (b) NCERT (c) CBSE in collaboration with Vidyasagar Institute of Mental Health & Neurosciences (VIMHANS); and (d) YUVA module developed by Delhi State Council of

Educational Research & Training. In a letter addressed to the Chief Ministers of the States that have discontinued this programme, it was recommended that a committees be constituted consisting of teachers and parents to review the modules in order to suggest changes, if any. NACO has offered to provide technical assistance, if required. This information was given by the Minister of State for Health & Family Welfare, Smt. Panabaka Lakshmi in a written reply to a question in the Lok Sabha.

2618. (22-8-2007) NEW DELHI : The first meeting of the Governing Council of the Overseas Indian Facilitation Centre (OIFC) was held at CII House, New Delhi under the Chairmanship of Mr. Nirmal Singh, Secretary Ministry of Overseas Indian Affairs. The meeting was attended by trustees. The Governing Council approved the broad policy framework for the programmes and activities of trust in consonance with the objectives of trust. The trust decided that OIFC would play an important role in PBD being organized at New York on 23 September, 2007 and later in PBD to be held on 8-9 January 2008 in India. In addition of providing information across the sectors, initially OIFC will focus on few sectors including providing handholding services. The knowledge partner will ensure the services are provided to the Clients to their satisfaction. OIFC will have a panel of three knowledge partners in each sector. Selection of partner from the panel will be left to the clients. Ministry would be acting as a facilitator. The trust also decided that the OIFC should be promoted and publicized globally through various channels. Mr. Vayalar Ravi, Minister of Overseas Indian Affairs also met the trustees at CII house and reiterated that OIFC will serves as a "one stop shop" for the Overseas Indians. He extended full support in to the OIFC from the Ministry and called upon the trustees to infuse the innovative ideas to address issues concerning Overseas Indians and connect them to India. The trust is chaired by Mr. Nirmal Singh, Secretary Ministry of Overseas Indian Affairs and Co-Chaired by Mr. Tarun Das, Chief Mentor, CII. Apart from Secretary (DEA), Secretary (DIPP) and Financial Advisor to the Ministry, eminent Overseas Indians like Mr. Yussufali from UAE, Mr. Thomas Abraham & Mr. Sam Pitroda from USA and Mr. Rajaram from Singapore are the trustees. Eminent businessman from India Such Mr. Analjit Singh, Chairman Max India Ltd and Mr. Sunil Kant Munjal Chairman, Hero Corporate Services are also trustees of OIFC. In recognition of the potential of Overseas Indians to invest in the emerging opportunities in their home country, the Ministry of Overseas Indian Affairs has established a not-for-profit trust, in partnership with the Confederation of India Industry and register in under the Indian Trust Act, 1882 under the title 'Overseas Indian Facilitation Centre'. The OIFC serves as a "one stop shop" for the Indian Diaspora. The trust will function with the objective of Promoting Overseas Indian Investment in India and facilitating Business-to-Business partnership between Indian Business and Overseas Indians

2619. (22-8-2007) NEW DELHI : The Infant Mortality Rate is decreasing in the country. The State wise details of infant mortality for the last five years can be seen at Annexure. On perusal, there has been a decline in infant mortality for the country as well as in all the major states of the country. Major measures undertaken to get over the problem of infant mortality are implementation of the Integrated Managemnet of Neonatal and Childhood Illnesses (IMNCI) strategy, which adopts a holistic approach to the management of the commonest causes of neonatal and childhood mortality-sepsis, acute respiratory infections, diarrhea, measles and malaria, all compounded by malnutrition. IMNCI shall be implemented throughout the country in a phased manner. At the current point in time, 154 districts from all across the country have initiated IMNCI implementation.

2620. (22-8-2007) NEW DELHI : The agricultural and processed Food Products Export Development Authority (APEDA) of Ministry of Commerce and Industry has conducted study on medicinal and aromatic plants. The objective of the study was to identify, market opportunities for India in the medicinal and aromatic plants domain and to coin strategies to promote exports. India is the second largest exporter of medicinal plants.

2621. (22-8-2007) NEW DELHI : The Government proposes to include Hepatitis B in the schedule under the National Immunization Programme. Hepatitis B disease does not have any effective treatment but there is a highly safe and effective vaccine, which can prevent hepatitis B infection and its serious consequences like liver cirrhosis and liver cancer. Administering Hepatitis B vaccine to all infants in National Immunization Programme would save more than 1.5 million (15 lakhs) chronic Hepatitis B infections and more than 0.2 million (2 lakhs) deaths due to Hepatitis B. The country would need more than 6 million doses of Hepatitis B vaccine per year. To vaccinate all infants the country would require approx 100 million doses. At present five-vaccine manufacturing institutions are manufacturing the Hepatitis B vaccine in the country. The combined installed capacity of the five institutions is 5160 lakhs doses per annum. This information was given by the Minister of State for Health & Family Welfare, Smt. Panabaka Lakshmi in a written reply to a question in the Lok Sabha.

2622. (22-8-2007) NEW DELHI : The Ministry of Health & F.W. has made BIS Certification mandatory in respect of 11 food articles under the PFA Rules, 1955, the details can be seen at Annexure. Under Section 33 of the BIS Act, 1996, the BIS takes action in case of violations of provisions under Section 11 & 12 of the BIS Act, 1996. As far as PFA Act is concerned, the Food (health) Authorities of States/UTs are responsible for the implementation/enforcement of the Prevention of Food Adulteration Act, 1954 and Rules, 1955. The enforcement staff draw random samples of various articles of food and take penal action against the offenders where the samples are not found to be conforming to the provisions of the PFA Act, 1954 and Rules, 1955. The Food (Health) Authorities of the State/ UTs have been advised from time to time to keep a strict vigil on the quality of food articles sold in the market and take penal action where the provisions of Prevention of Food Adulteration Act, 1954 and Rules, 1955 are violated. This information was given by the Minister of State for Health & Family Welfare, Smt. Panabaka Lakshmi in a written reply to a question in the Lok Sabha.

2623. (22-8-2007) NEW DELHI : The Panchayat Empowerment and Accountability Incentive Scheme (PEAIS) was introduced and implemented by the Ministry of Panchayati Raj during the year 2005-06 with an allocation of Rs. 5 crores. This scheme aimed to provide incentives to the States to devolve powers upon Panchayats in accordance with the recommendations of the Seven Round Tables and for Panchayats empowered by such reforms to effectively assume the responsibilities devolved upon them. Release of funds under the Scheme were made in accordance with the progress achieved by States against milestones and bench marks in the reform aspects identified. During the year 2006-07, the Panchayat Empowerment and Accountability Incentive Scheme had an allocation of Rs. 10 crore. Based on the rankings of States/Union Territories in the Devolution Index prepared by NCAER, Rs. 8 crores were released to the first 10 States and Rs. 2 crores were released to the 6 UT's, in accordance with their rankings. The NCAER presented an interim devolution index to the Ministry in August 2006. Thereafter, based on the data available with the Ministry of Panchayati Raj and as obtained from different States/ other Sources, NCAER measured the assessing environment for PRIs in different States and assigned scores and rankings to all the States and Union Territories. Panchayat Empowerment and Accountability Incentive Scheme was operationalized during 2006-07 on this basis. The Index prepared last year is now sought to be further refined and nuanced to measure the progress on Devolution over time. Towards this end, a concept paper has been prepared by NCAER giving details of the construction of the Devolution Index information or data needs and the application of the Index. This comprehensive index is proposed to be utilized for implementation of the Panchayat Empowerment and Accountability Incentive Scheme during the current year. This Comprehensive index is a substantial improvement on the Index formulated last year. The previous Index measured the States on three broad indicators viz. Devolution of funds, functions and functionaries. The present Index has included a distinct "Framework" sub Index which will take into account the mandatory provision of the Constitution containing Part IX. Continuing their work on refining and making more nuanced the Devolution Index with the view to undertaking in the miserable manner all indicators relating to the empowerment of PRIs. It is hoped to give the final shape to this Devolution Index during the course of the current financial year. This information was given by Shri Mani Shankar Aiyar, Minister of Panchayati Raj, Youth Affairs & Sports and DoNER in the Lok Sabha today in a written reply to a question by Shri S.K Kharventhan.

2624. (22-8-2007) NEW DELHI : The Indian delegation led by Minister of Panchayati Raj visited Pakistan from the 1st July to the 3rd July 2007. The Pakistan India Joint Working Group on Local Governance (JWG) met on the sidelines of the Pakistan-India Symposium on the 2nd July, 2007 and recommended the following activities for consideration of the Forum in consultation with the respective Governments: (i) The two sides will continue to share their evolving experience particularly with a view to facilitating people to people contact in the areas such as:-Outcomes of local Government system in Pakistan and India-Achievements and Challenges ahead; Fiscal decentralization, fiscal capacity and financial management at the local level; Decentralised planning; Economic development through local Government, including rural-urban integration; and Women, Youth and Citizen empowerment including capacity building and training. (ii) To facilitate these exchanges Pakistan and India should each host one meeting each year, besides arranging face-to-face encounters in each others' country of elected representatives to local self-government institutions. (iii) All stakeholders, including elected representatives, think tanks, government officials, academia, researchers and civil society representatives should be invited to these meetings to share and disseminate best practices and innovations in service delivery at the local level. (iv) Best practices and innovations should be regularly shared between the two countries through the National Reconstruction Bureau in Pakistan and the Ministry of Panchayati Raj in India. (v) Stakeholders will be encouraged to exchange views on issues surrounding local governance and to participate in action research and in developing comparative studies. (vi) Experts and officials on local governance from both the countries should be invited, under an Exchange Programme, to participate as Resource Persons in the Academies, Schools and Institutions in Pakistan and India, to impart training and disseminate emerging developments in the field of local governance.

2625. (22-8-2007) NEW DELHI : The Backward Regions Grant Fund Programme (BRGF) was approved in the financial year 2006-07. The Programme has three components, namely, Special Plan for Bihar, Special Plan for the KBK districts of Orissa and the district component covered by the Backward Districts Initiative of the Rashtriya Sam Vikas Yojana (RSVY) subsumed into the Backward Regions Grant Fund Programme from 2006-07. Special plans for Bihar and the KBK districts of Orissa are handled by the Planning Commission. The allocation under the district component of BRGF consists of two funding windows (a) funds for capacity building of Panchayati Raj Institutions and (b) an untied developmental grant. According to the extant policy, the districts covered under the Rashtriya Vikas Yojana must complete their allocation of Rs. 45 crore per district under the earlier programme before these shift to the BRGF mode of funding. A statement showing the funds released under these three components, State wise from 2005-06 onwards is annexed.

2626. (22-8-2007) NEW DELHI : The existing National Youth Policy 2003, provides for a review after 5 years from the date of commencement of implementation. There is now a clear recognition in the Prime Minister's policy statements, the approach to the Eleventh Five Year Plan and the 2007 World Development Report on "Development and the next Generation" all underline the critical inter-connection between youth development and overall national development. The review will take into account this overarching objective. Developments in the filed of technology, particularly Information Technology and communication network necessitate reworking of the priorities and thrust areas for youth. The role of youth in Panchayati Raj Institutions (PRIs) and of PRI in the amelioration of the condition of the rural youth needs to be strengthened in the review of the policy.

2627. (22-8-2007) NEW DELHI : The Sports Authority of India (SAI) runs 126 National Sports Talent Contest (NSTC) Centres, 10 Special Area Games (SAG) Centres, 57 SAI Training Centres (STC), 18 Army Boys Sports Company Scheme (ABSC) Centre and 10 Centre of Excellence (COX) where sportspersons are given training in different sports disciplines. State-wise details are at Annexe-I. Besides, SAI has an Academic Wing at the Netaji Subhas National Institute of Sports, Patiala.

2628. (22-8-2007) NEW DELHI : The Government is making multi-pronged efforts to improve the performance level of Indian sportspersons at international level. The efforts of National Sports Federations (NSFs) for the development of various sports disciplines and excellence therein are being significantly supplemented by Government through the 'Scheme of Financial Assistance to National Sports Federations' for organizing national and international tournaments in India; participation of Indian teams in tournaments and events abroad; provision of coaching through Indian and foreign coaches; backed-up with requisite technical support; procurement of equipment, etc. Meritorious sportspersons are also being assisted directly by the Ministry for the purchase of equipment, the provision of scientific support and training and participation within the country and abroad, under the 'Scheme relating to Talent Search & Training' and through the 'National Sports Development Fund'. In addition, action is being taken under various schemes of the Sports Authority of India (SAI) to establish state-of-the-art training infrastructure and facilities in different parts of the country, as also for spotting and nurturing sports talent in their Centres spread across the country, including in areas with special potential for different identified sports disciplines. With a view to broad-basing sports and creating avenues to provide access to organized sports and games facilities for vast sections of youth, particularly in the rural areas, both as an essential ingredient of youth development and for significantly expanding the catchment for spotting talent, the Ministry is also at an advanced stage of promoting a Scheme titled "Panchayat Yuva Khel avam Krida Abhiyan" (PYKKA). This information was given by Shri Mani Shankar Aiyar, Minister of Panchayati Raj, Youth Affairs & Sports and DoNER in the Lok Sabha today in a written reply to a question by Shri Ranen Barman.

2629. (22-8-2007) NEW DELHI : At the instance of Cabinet, the Ministry has framed a draft Comprehensive Sports Policy, which has been posted on its website since 26 July 2007. Consultations are being held with stakeholders and, after the draft is revised in the light of the consultations, a final draft will be submitted to Cabinet. In recognition of the fact that the overwhelming majority of our children, adolescents and young people have no access to organized sports and games, the revised Twenty Point Programme adopted on Gandhi Jayanti 2006 has set the national goal of "Sports for All". The draft makes provision to fill this gaping lacuna in a time-bound manner. Various lacunae identified in the pursuit of the second overarching goal of "Excellence in Sports" have been identified and measures proposed toward building on "Sports for All" to achieve "Excellence in Sports". Contingent Constitutional, Legal and Institutional measures have been identified and steps in this regard suggested. The draft indicates that approximately 72 crore out of an estimated 77 crore of our population below the age of 35 has little or no access to organized sports and games, thus indicating the extent to which previous sports policies have not succeeded in promoting "Sports for All". Secondly, as regards "Excellence in Sports", the draft indicates how far behind most other countries is our performance in Olympic and other sports disciplines, indicating the requirement for a reappraisal of previous policies which have left us so far behind in the pursuit of "Excellence in Sports". Thirdly, the process of rectifying identified lacuna has indicated the Constitutional, Legal and Institutional measures that appear to be required.

2630. (22-8-2007) NEW DELHI : The Government is a signatory to the Copenhagen Declaration against doping in sports and follows the World Anti-Doping Agency (WADA) guidelines to deal with doping in sports. The Government of India has set up the National Anti-Doping Agency (NADA), which is the nodal agency for test planning, result management and out reach programmes relating to anti-doping in the country. The Government has also set up a National Dope Test Laboratory, which is at present under probation for WADA Accreditation. This information was given by Shri Mani Shankar Aiyar, Minister of Panchayati Raj, Youth Affairs & Sports and DoNER in the Lok Sabha today in a written reply to a question by Shri N.S.V. Chitthan.

2631. (22-8-2007) NEW DELHI : The Minister of State for Textiles, Shri E.V.K.S. Elangovan, informed the Rajya Sabha today, in a written reply to a question by Shri Datta Meghe that under the Scheme for Integrated Textile Park (SITP), Industry Associations/Groups of Entrepreneurs are the main promoters of Textile Park. To facilitate development of infrastructure for setting up of textile units, Government of India provides assistance @ 40% of the project cost of common infrastructure and facilities subject to the limit of Rs. 40 crore. During the Tenth Five Year Plan, 30 Textiles Park projects were approved. Locations of these projects are-Mahboob Nagar, Ananthpur, Pochampally and Vishakhapatnam in Andhra Pradesh, Ahmedabad, Surat (3 projects), Kutch, Kheda and Sanand in Gujarat, Ichalkaranji (3 projects), Baramati, Tarapur and Wada in Maharashtra, Perundurai, Cuddalore, Palladam, Komarapalayam, Karur and Madurai in Tamil

Nadu, Kishangarh (2 projects), Pali and Hasteda in Rajasthan, Dodaballapur in Karnataka, Dhaula (Barnala) in Punjab and Kolkata in West Bengal. The Minister further informed the House that during the Tenth Five Year Plan, no proposal was received from any Industry Association / Group of Entrepreneurs to set up Textiles Park in Nagpur. Government is not averse to consider any proposal to develop Textiles Park in Nagpur region.

2632. (22-8-2007) NEW DELHI : The Minister of State for Textiles, Shri E.V.K.S. Elangovan, informed the Rajya Sabha today, in a written reply to a question by Smt. Hema Malini that the Government is envisaging plan for developing and promoting textile industry in the country. The Government is implementing schemes like Technology Upradation Fund Scheme (TUFS), Scheme for Integrated Textiles Park (SITP), Mill Gate Price Scheme (MGPS) and Technology Mission schemes, namely Technology Mission on Cotton (TMC) and Jute Technology Mission (JTM) to facilitate Indian textiles industry to grow at the rate of 16 percent in value terms to reach level of US$ 115 billion (comprising of US$ 55 billion of exports and US$ 60 billion of domestic market) and attain 7 percent share in global textile trade by the terminal year of the Eleventh Plan period. These will generate ample employment opportunities.

2633. (22-8-2007) NEW DELHI : The Minister of State for Coal Dr. Dasari Narayana Rao informed the Lok Sabha in a written reply today that the exploration activity has established additional resources during Xth Plan period in several coalfields including Orissa and West Bengal. Giving details, he said during the period January, 2006 to March, 2007, 4080 million tonnes of new coal resources have been estimated in the country.

2634. (22-8-2007) NEW DELHI : The Chief of Army Staff Gen JJ Singh and other senior officers of the Indian Army will be attending the Mechanised Forces Conference scheduled from 23 to 25 of August at the Mechanised Infantry Regimental Centre, Ahmednagar. The Armoured Corps, the Mechanised Infantry Regiment and the Brigade of the Guards are together addressed as the Mechanised Forces. The three Regiments have to remain integrated in peace to be successfully applied for a decisive victory against any adversary challenging or threatening the sovereignty of our nation. The Mechanised Forces Conference validates this integration as a necessary adjunct to the war fighting principles that applies to Mechanised Warfare concepts. The First Mechanised Forces Conference was held in 2005 under the aegis of the Armoured Corps Centre and School, Ahmednagar. In keeping with the tradition set by the inaugural session, the Second Mechanised Forces Conference is being hosted by the Mechanised Infantry Regimental Centre at Ahmednagar. The conference will be attended by a large number of distinguished senior officers of the Mechanised Forces fraternity. This conference is being organized as a brainstorming session for the Army top brass to discuss a number of issues relevant to the Mechanised Forces and also the Army as a whole. The issues being addressed include the visualized challenges for the mechanized forces in 2020, integration of Battle Field Management Systems with special reference to Revolution in Military Affairs, upgrading reconnaissance assets, those already in service and as well advance versions planned for the future and Networking.

2635. (22-8-2007) NEW DELHI : The Union Rural Development Minister, Dr. Raghuvansh Prasad Singh has said that 'Jaankari' (awareness) and 'Bhaagidari' (participation) are the two most important ingredients for the successful implementation of any welfare programme of the Government. He called upon to make vigorous efforts to increase awareness about various schemes of Ministry of Rural Development among the masses living in rural areas. The Minister was addressing a group conference of Members of Parliament (MPs) from Madhya Pradesh and Chhattisgarh, here yesterday. These group conferences have been started by the Ministry of Rural Development for close interaction with the MPs in separate batches to ensure effective implementation of rural development schemes through greater participation of elected representatives. The objective of these group meetings is to apprise the MPs about different provision of the rural development schemes, the status of implementation of various programmes in the concerned State, physical and financial progress and also to get their valuable feedback/suggestions based on their review meetings as Chairman of District Vigilance & Monitoring Committees. This was the second such interactive session held yesterday in which the MPs belonging to Madhya Pradesh and Chhattisgarh participated. Shri Chandra Shekhar Sahu, Union Minister of State for Rural Development and Shri Kanti Lal Bhuria, Union Minister of State for Agriculture were among those present on the occasion. Dr. Raghuvansh Prasad Singh said that MPs can play a major role in monitoring the implementation of rural development programmes. Underscoring the importance of the Gram Sabha in the whole scheme of things, the Minister pointed out that Gram Sabha is a Constitutional unit and has the foremost responsibility in the implementation of rural development schemes. These have been empowered to ensure maximum transparency in the entire implementation process. Dr. Singh emphasized the need to create greater awareness at the Gram Sabha level for better results. The Minister said that the District Vigilance & Monitoring Committees have an important role to play under the guidance of concerned Member of Parliament in removal of corruption in the implementation of rural development schemes. The Minister said that constant monitoring, supervision, site visits and use of RTI Act by the MPs can ensure effective implementation. Participating in the Conference the MPs lauded the initiative of the Ministry of Rural Development for organizing such interactive conferences. They said that the National Rural Employment Guarantee Scheme (NREGS) is playing a crucial role in improving the lot of rural masses. The MPs requested the Minister not to allow use of heavy machinery for the works under NREGA. A request has also been made to increase the number of beneficiaries under the Indira Awas Yojaya (IAY). Some members also suggested that the permanent wait list in IAY should be prominently displayed on the walls and on the Internet. The Members also pointed out that sub-standard materials are being used at some places for building roads under the Pradhan Mantri Gram Sadak Yojana (PMGSY). They said that centre's guidelines for implementing the rural schemes are not always being followed and quality of work done is poor. A suggestion was also made to give more powers to the area MPs in the supervision of implementation of rural road schemes. The inaugural interactive session of this series was held on Aug. 20 this year, in which the MPs belonging to West Bengal and North East States participated. The Speaker, Lok Sabha, Shri Som Nath Chatterjee was among those who attended the meeting and addressed the participants. Such other conferences are scheduled for all States in groups for 22nd (J&K, Punjab, H.P., Haryana & Rajasthan), 23rd (Karnataka & Orissa), 27th (Andhra Pradesh), 29th (Tamil Nadu & Kerala), 30th August, 2007 (Gujarat, Goa, UTs and Uttarakhand) and 3rd (Bihar & Jharkhand), 5th (Uttar Pradesh) & 6th September, 2007(Maharashtra). The Ministry expects to receive innumerable valuable feedbacks from the MPs during the interactive session for looking into the policy formulation of the programmes being implemented.

2636. (22-8-2007) NEW DELHI : India is ranked Number Second in bio-gas and Number Four in Wind Energy Development globally. Giving a key-note address during the celebration of State level function of Rajiv Gandhi Akshay Urja Diwas today, Shri Vilas Muttemwar, Minister of State for New and Renewable Energy further said that solar water heating system has become very popular in urban, commercial and industrial sectors. Over 20 lakh sq. meter solar collector area has been installed for solar water heaters and other solar thermal applications. Addressing a gathering of more than 2500 school children from various schools in and around in Delhi, the Minister explained that solar photovoltaic technology has been used for number of applications such as lighting, communication, water pumping, power generation etc. Over 10 lakh photovoltaic systems have been promoted from this application. The Minister said that excessive use of fossil fuels were creating environmental problems in the form of global warming and climate change. India is blessed with plenty of renewable energy sources such as solar, bio-energy, wind and hydel energy. Shri Muttemwar described them as non-depleting, environmental friendly sources and available in most parts of the country all the time. With such a vast pool of renewable sources available, the ministry is striving to provide energy in every village and lighting in every house. Encouraging people and especially children to increase the use of renewable energy to protect the environment, the Delhi Chief Minister, Ms. Sheela Dikshit said that Rajiv Gandhi Akshay Urja Diwas serves to educate and mobilize people across the country for environmental protection, to inspire action on personal, community, national and international levels. She said that each of us can join in voluntary action to build a productive land in harmony with nature. Dr. R.K.Pachauri, Head of TERI and Chairman of United Nation's Intergovernmental Panel on Climate Change said that at TERI, they want to rekindle their commitment to the cause and nation to develop and promote technologies for efficient and sustainable use of natural and renewable resources. More than 2500 students from public, private and Government Schools of Delhi participated in this event. Students administered Akshay Urja Pledge to the audience to avoid excessive consumption of energy derived from conventional sources and to follow the path of renewable energy. A week-long series of events were organized which include essay writing competition, inter-school banner and caricatcher, painting competition, songs, skits and signature campaign. Solar torches and educational kits developed by TERI were given as prizes to students and schools.

2637. (22-8-2007) NEW DELHI : The Ministry of Environment and Forests had constituted an Expert Committee under the Chairmanship of Prof. M. S. Swaminathan in July, 2004, to review and make recommendations with regard to implementation and amendments if necessary, of Coastal Regulation Zone Notification, 1991. The Expert Committee submitted its report alongwith the recommendations, which were accepted by the Ministry of Environment and Forests in April, 2005.

2638. (22-8-2007) NEW DELHI : The Central Pollution Control Board (CPCB), has been conducting inspections to ensure compliance by industrial units to various pollution control norms. The number of inspections of industrial units carried out by the CPCB were 76 in the year 2005, 203 in the year 2006 and 27 in 2007 (upto June 2007). Based on the inspections carried out, 65 industrial units in 2005, 107 industrial units in 2006 and 15 industrial units in 2007 (upto June, 2007), have been identified by the CPCB to be violating the pollution control norms. The CPCB has issued directions under Section 5 of the Environmental (Protection) Act, 1986 for closure of 2 industrial units in 2005, 63 industrial units in 2006 and 11 industrial units in 2007 (upto June, 2007). The CPCB also issued directions under Section 18 (1) (b) of the Water (Prevention and Control of Pollution) Act, 1974 and the Air (Prevention and Control of Pollution) Act, 1981 to the concerned State Pollution Control Boards (SPCBs) for closure of 1 industrial unit in 2005, 1 unit in 2006 and 6 units in 2007 till installation and satisfactory operation of requisite pollution control system, in order to meet the prescribed norms. The CPCB, through the concerned SPCBs, regularly monitors the compliance of directions issued to industrial units for controlling pollution. The industrial units against which the directions were issued have been either closed down or have upgraded the pollution control system as per directions issued. This information was given by the Minister of State in the Ministry of Environment and Forests, Shri Namo Narayana Meena in a written reply to question by Dr. Ramkrishna Kusmaria in the Lok Sabha today.

2639. (22-8-2007) NEW DELHI : Conservation of rivers is a dynamic activity with the ever increasing pollution load due to increase in population. Review of the strategies of conservation policy and identification of additional towns and rivers is a continuous process. Water being a State subject, it is the responsibility of State Governments to create proper sewerage infrastructure to prevent pollution from entering the rivers. Central Government is only supplementing the efforts of the State Governments by providing one time grant for capital works for identified polluted stretches. The pollution abatement works are implemented through Implementing Agencies nominated by the State Governments for the purpose. A multi-tier monitoring mechanism at the Centre and State level reviews the policy issues, funding pattern and progress of works from time to time. The States have been advised to ensure coordination among various Departments/ agencies at the implementation level through holding regular meetings by Pr8incipal Secretary/Chief Secretary and to sort out inter-sectoral issues like acquisition of land, power supply, mobilization of resources among others. This information was given by the Minister of State in the Ministry of Environment and Forests, Shri Namo Narayana Meena in a written reply to question by Shri Ravi Prakash Verma and Shri Anandrao V. Adsul: in the Lok Sabha today.

2640. (22-8-2007) NEW DELHI : The Ministry of Environment and Forests had constituted an Expert Committee under the Chairmanship of Prof. M. S. Swaminathan in July, 2004, to review and make recommendations with regard to implementation and amendments if necessary, of Coastal Regulation Zone Notification, 1991. The Expert Committee submitted its report alongwith the recommendations, which were accepted by the Ministry of Environment and Forests in April, 2005.

2641. (22-8-2007) NEW DELHI : No notification /order/ instruction / guideline has been issued by the Government for setting up of a Tribunal for Environment Impact Assessment (EIA). However, the Government has issued an Environment Impact Assessment Notification No. S.O. 1533 dated 14th September, 2006 which provides for constitution of State Level Environment Impact Assessment Authority (SEIAA) and State Level Expert Appraisal Committee(SEAC) for the States and Union Territories for grant of environmental clearance to Category 'B' Projects listed in the Schedule of the said Notification. The detailed Proforma Resume has been circulated to all the State Governments/ UT Administrations for sending the nominations for constitution of State Level Environment Impact Assessment Authority (SEIAA) and State Level Expert Appraisal Committee (SEAC) as per the criteria laid down in the EIA Notification, 2006. So far, SEIAA/ SEAC have been constituted for six States namely Andhra Pradesh, Gujarat, Karnataka, Meghalaya, Uttar Pradesh and West Bengal. This information was given by the Minister of State in the Ministry of Environment and Forests, Shri Namo Narayana Meena in a written reply to question by Shri Raghuveer Singh Koshal in the Lok Sabha today.

2642. (22-8-2007) NEW DELHI : An amount of about Rs. 5,400 crore has been received by the Ad-hoc body of CAMPA from various States / Union Territories towards Compensatory Afforestation, Net Present Value (NPV), Protection and

Conservation of National Parks / Sanctuaries, etc. No funds have been released from the ad-hoc CAMPA to the States, so far. The Supreme Court of India, vide order dated 29.10.2002 in WP(C) No. 202 of 1995, directed that the Net Present Value (NPV) of the forest land diverted for non-forestry purposes with the prior approval of the Central Government, shall be paid by user agencies in addition to other usual payments for Compensatory Afforestation, Conservation and Protection of National Parks / Sanctuaries etc. The Court also directed that a body shall be constituted for management of the funds received on account of diversion of forest land. In compliance of the above order, the Ministry of Environment and Forests issued a notification dated 23.04.2004 for constitution of the Compensatory Afforestation Fund Management and Planning Authority (CAMPA). The process of obtaining Cabinet approval to the CAMPA notification is under way. Meanwhile, the Hon'ble Supreme Court, on 05.05.2006, observed that CAMPA had still not become operational, and constituted an Ad-hoc Body of CAMPA in the Ministry of Environment and Forests for transfer of all the funds lying unutilized with the State / Union Territory Governments. The funds deposited in ad-hoc CAMPA are meant for utilization for protection and conservation of forests and wildlife, etc. as directed by the Hon'ble Supreme Court of India. These funds shall be utilized after obtaining the Cabinet approval to the CAMPA Notification. This information was given by the Minister of State in the Ministry of Environment and Forests, Shri S. Regupathy in a written by Smt. Rupatai Diliprao, Nilangakar Patil and Shri Asaduddin Owaisi in the Lok Sabha today.

2643. (22-8-2007) NEW DELHI : The Ministry of Environment and Forests has taken action under the Environment Protection Act, 1986 against four parties who had started construction without obtaining prior permission. This information was given by the Minister of State in the Ministry of Environment and Forests, Shri Namo Narayana Meena in a written reply to question by Shri Prabhunath Singh :in the Lok Sabha today.

2644. (22-8-2007) NEW DELHI : Occasional killings of wildlife animals have been reported on Railway Tracks through accidents, particularly in Assam and North Bengal. This issue has been brought to the notice of Railway Authorities to regulate the speed of trains. Several precautionary measures have also been identified in this regard in consultation with Railway authorities. West Bengal Government has conducted awareness programmes to sensitise the drivers and guards of trains passing through the forests. This information was given by the Minister of State in the Ministry of Environment and Forests, Shri S. Reghupathy in a written reply to question by Shri M.K.Subba :in the Lok Sabha today.

2645. (22-8-2007) NEW DELHI : The services in the Bhartiya Reserve Bank Note Mudran Limited, Mysore (Karnataka) and Salboni (West Bengal) have been declared public utility under the Industrial Disputes Act, 1947 for six months with immediate effect. The Labour Ministry in a notification issued here has said that this has been done in public interest. The employees in this industry, as a result, would among other things be required to give notice to their employer six weeks in advance of proceeding on strike so that conciliatory proceedings could be started. During the conciliatory proceedings and seven days after their completion, the employees cannot go on strike.

2646. (22-8-2007) NEW DELHI : Representations have been received from All India Motor Transport Congress (AIMTC) raising a number of issues which, question the levy of road tax and user's fee (toll) on the road users. The levy of road tax falls under the purview of State Governments. User's fee is however, levied for the use of National Highways, bridges, etc. which is not in the form of a tax. The levy of user's fee is governed by National Highway (Rate of fee) Rules, 1997, the National Highways (collection of fees by any person for the use of section of National Highways/Permanent Bridge/Temporary Bridge on National Highways) Rules 1997 and the National Highways (Fees for the use of National Highways section and permanent Bridge-Public Funded Project) Rules, 1997. Certain categories of vehicles are exempted from payment of user's fee which include the vehicles of Member of Parliament, Member of Legislative Assembly and Member of Legislative Council etc.

2647. (22-8-2007) NEW DELHI : Six laning of 6,500 km of National Highways comprising 5,700 km of Golden Quadrilateral and 800 km of other sections on Build, Operate and Transfer (BOT) basis following, Design, Build, Finance and Operate (DBFO) pattern has been approved at an estimated cost of Rs.41, 210 crore under National Highways Development Project (NHDP) Phase-V, scheduled for completion by December 2012.

2648. (22-8-2007) NEW DELHI : National Highways Authority of India (NHAI) has so far received a good response from the private sector for construction of highway projects under Public Private Partnership (PPP) mode. The Government has assessed the efficacy of Public Private Partnership (PPP) in execution of projects under NHAI. NHAI has so far awarded 79 projects aggregating to a length of 4606 km at an estimated cost of Rs. 30,535 crore on PPP mode, out of which 16 projects aggregating to a length of 902 km have been completed and remaining 63 projects are in progress. Projects already awarded are progressing as per schedule. The projects are monitored by consultants appointed through international competitive bidding by NHAI to act as Independent Engineer for the project. In order to carefully monitor all projects, NHAI has set up Project Implementation Units (PIUs) at suitable locations along the stretch, which is headed by Project Director (PD) alongwith other Officers for his assistance. Senior officers regularly visit project sites for monitoring of projects. Projects are also monitored in the Ministry of Shipping, Road Transport and Highways as well as by Ministry of Statistics and Programme Implementation, Planning Commission and Committee on Infrastructure (CoI) headed by the Prime Minister. This information was given by the Minister of State for Shipping, Road Transport and Highways, Shri K.H. Muniyappa in a written reply in the Lok Sabha today.

2649. (22-8-2007) NEW DELHI : The Government has taken up a massive progarmme for development of National Highways in the country. The programme is executed through various phases of National Highways Development Projects (NHDP). A policy decision has been taken to implement the NHDP Phase III and onwards through Public Private Partnership (PPP) mode. A Special Accelerated Road Development Programme for the North East Region (SARDP-NE) has also been drawn up for development of National Highways and state roads of the North Eastern Region of the country. A few projects under SARDP-NE have also been identified for implementation by PPP mode. The National Highway projects implemented through PPP mode are executed through the concessionaire. However, the Government bears only the expenditure of feasibility studies, land acquisition, utility shifting and viability gap funding wherever required for such projects. This information was given by the Minister of State for Shipping, Road Transport and Highways, Shri K.H. Muniyappa in a written reply in the Lok Sabha today.

2650. (22-8-2007) NEW DELHI : The Government of India takes up the development works of National Highways through five year plans. However, the Ministry in 2001 had prepared, through Indian Roads Congress (IRC), 'Road Development Plan VISION: 2021' for a period of 20 years (2001-2021). This document provides the vision for the next 20 years for development and maintenance of all categories of roads *i.e.* National Highways, State Highways, Major District Roads and Rural Roads. The urban roads as well as the roads for specific need *e.g.* tourism, forestry, mining and industrial areas etc. have also been considered. The research and development, mobilisation of resources, capacity building and human resources development, quality system, environment and energy considerations for the highway sector and highway safety are also included in this document which serves as only a valuable guide to the Centre and the State Governments for planning purpose. This information was given by the Minister of State for Shipping, Road Transport and Highways, Shri K.H. Muniyappa in a written reply in the Lok Sabha today.

2651. (22-8-2007) NEW DELHI : As against the sanctioned strength of 5959 in the CBI, the number of vacant posts is 1341. The occurrence of vacancies and their filling up is an ongoing process. With effective use and deployment of existing personnel, the vacancies have not affected the performance of the CBI adversely. In order to attract officers to join CBI, the Government has introduced a Special Incentive Allowance to all the officers from Constable to Director level in the CBI. The Recruitment Rules of various posts are also amended, as and when necessary to ensure that vacancies are filled up speedily. This information was given by the Minister of State in the Ministry of Personnel, Public Grievances and Pensions, Shri Suresh Pachouri in reply to a question raised by Smt. Sumitra Mahajan in Lok Sabha today.

2652. (22-8-2007) NEW DELHI : The Central Government has issued notifications on 24th August 2006 amending the Indian Administrative Service (Cadre) Rules, 1954, Indian Police Service (Cadre) Rules, 1954 and Indian Forest Services (Cadre) Rules, 1966 to provide for minimum tenure, in consultation with the State Governments concerned, of all or any of the cadre posts specified for the State concerned, in item 1 of the Schedule to the Indian Administrative Service (Fixation of Cadre Strength) Regulation, 1955, Indian Police Service (Fixation of Cadre Strength) Rules, 1955 and Indian Forest Services (Fixation of Cadre Strength) Rules, 1966. All the States have been asked to forward their comments for fixing the minimum tenure of the postings of the members of IAS of the States concerned. Himachal Pradesh, Jammu & Kashmir, Karnataka, Arunachal Pradesh, Daman & Diu, Goa, Chandigarh and Manipur have agreed to the proposal and minimum tenure of two years has been fixed for the cadre posts of the IAS for Himachal Pradesh, Jammu & Kashmir and Karnataka. The States, which have not agreed to the proposal of providing minimum tenure of the postings of the IAS officers, are Tamil Nadu, Rajasthan, Punjab, West Bengal, Madhya Pradesh, Andhra Pradesh, Gujarat and Tripura. The other States have not given their final comments. This information was given by the Minister of State in the Ministry of Personnel, Public Grievances and Pensions, Sh. Suresh Pachouri in reply to a question raised by Dr. M. Jagannath in Lok Sabha today.

2653. (22-8-2007) NEW DELHI : As per the information received from the State/ UT Governments, 67,691 prosecutions have been launched against the offending employers during the period 1997-98 to 2005-06 under the provisions of Child Labour (Prohibition & Regulation) Act. Government is implementing the National Child Labour Project (NCLP) Scheme in 250 districts of 20 states of the country for the rehabilitation of children withdrawn from hazardous occupations. Under the scheme, these children are put into special schools where they are provided with accelerated bridging educations, vocational training, midday meal, stipend and health care facilities etc. Under the scheme, at present, 3.43 lakh children are enrolled in the special schools and 4.57 lakh children have already been mainstreamed into formal education system since the inception of the scheme. This was stated by the Minister of State (Independent Charge) of Labour and Employment, Shri Oscar Fernandes in a written reply in Rajya Sabha today.

2654. (22-8-2007) NEW DELHI : A representation by Central Trade Unions, addressed to the Prime Minister has been received. The representation contains issues relating to (i) the entry of foreign cigarettes companies and MNC and its impact on beedis and local producers of cigarettes, (ii) MNC domination of soft drink sector, (iii) rosy assurances given by MNCs, (iv) once entry is given, MNCs cannot be ejected, (v) anti-tobacco legislation and MNCs. No study has been conducted on allowing FDI in tobacco sector. FDI up to 100% with prior Government approval is allowed in the tobacco sector subject to industrial licensing, where applicable. This position is in existence since 1998. An administrative decision was taken in 1999-2000 not to grant industrial licence for cigarette manufacturing and, resultantly, no FDI proposal is being considered. This was stated by the Minister of State (Independent Charge) of Labour and Employment, Shri Oscar Fernandes in a written reply in Rajya Sabha today.

2655. (22-8-2007) NEW DELHI : The Government has taken cognizance of the study on Industrial Training Institutes (ITIs) conducted by FICCI. The main conclusions of the study carried out by FICCI show that while situation with regard to physical infrastructure and availability of power supply remains comfortable, factors like non-availability of computerized numerically controlled machines, inadequate supplies of raw material and lack of focus on staff training and development are key impediments in the strengthening of these institutions. Some of the suggestions given by FICCI are—introduce courses which have larger employment potential, fill up vacancies of instructors, have effective and vigilant monitoring system, strengthen industry-institute linkage, provide functional autonomy to the Institute, update syllabi of trades, train instructors and staff of institutes, introduce training in soft skills and strengthen testing and certification norms to global standards etc.

2656. (22-8-2007) NEW DELHI : There has been an increase in the number of workers in the unorganised sector. According to the survey conducted by National Sample Survey Organisation (NSSO) during 1999-2000, the total number of workers in the unorganised sector was about 37 crore (93% of the total workforce in the country). The number has increased to 43.3 crore ((4%) as per recent survey conducted by the same organisation during 2004-2005. This was stated by the Minister of State (Independent Charge) of Labour and Employment, Shri Oscar Fernandes in a written reply in Rajya Sabha today. In another written reply, Shri Fernandes said that the Unorganised Sector Workers' Social Security Bill, 2007 is under active consideration and Government intends to introduce the Bill during current session of the Parliament. The details of the Bill are yet to be finalised. He said some of the States like Kerala, Tamil Nadu, Madhya Pradesh, Gujarat, Punjab, West Bengal, etc. are implementing social security schemes for the unorganised sector workers under their respective legislations/schemes.

2657. (22-8-2007) NEW DELHI : The Railway Sports Promotion Board (RSPB) will be organizing the 54th Senior National (Men) Boxing Championship at Karnail Singh Stadium, New Delhi from 25th to 30th August 2007. In this mega event around 600 players/officials across the country will be participating. RSPB has got the honour of organizing such national championships in the past also like the Senior National Weightlifting Championships in 2003 and Senior Women Hockey Championships in 2005. Railways have traditionally been a major force in the field of Boxing and have been dominating the sports of Boxing at National and at International levels. Railways have been runners up in the year 2005 and 2006 and also were the winners in the year 2004. Recently Railways won the

Boxing Federation titles both in Men and Women in Chennai in July 2007 with Shri Dilbagh Singh from North Western Railway being adjudged as the best Boxer of the tournament. Railways have star boxers namely; Akhil Kumar from Northern Railway, Vijender from North Western Railway, Diwakar from Eastern Railway, Dilbagh Singh from North West Eastern Railway, Harpreet Singh and Jitender from Northern Railway in men section. In women section, Ms. Chotto Loura from Northern Railway, Ms. Sunita Yadav and Sushma Yadav from North Western Railway and Kalpana Chaudhry from Northeast Frontier Railway are the world class Boxer.

2658. (22-8-2007) NEW DELHI : A Workshop on Modern Terminal Markets got underway here today. Inaugurating the Workshop Dr. P.K. Mishra, Secretary, Department of Agriculture and Cooperation said that central government has recently initiated the process of promoting terminal markets in the country under a Central Sector Scheme. He urged upon potential investors to take advantage of the scheme and requested the state governments to play a proactive role in creating an investor-friendly atmosphere for this purpose. Modern Terminal Markets would go a long way towards integrating domestic producers with food processing industries, retail chains and emerging global markets, while offering premium prices to farmers based on quality, in a competitive environment and transparent manner, he added. Organised by National Institute of Agricultural Marketing and US Agency for International Development, the two-day Workshop will deliberate on a range of issues involved in the development of marketing facilities. There will be direct interaction between the US experts on terminal markets and the stakeholders from India in the technical sessions of the Workshop.

2659. (22-8-2007) NEW DELHI : Shri Murli Deora, Minister for Petroleum & Natural Gas today flagged off a motorbike expedition to Daulat Beg Oldi in Jammu & Kashmir from M/s Engineers Service Station, IndianOil's Retail Outlet in Delhi. Sponsored by IndianOil, the expedition has been organized by the Bikers for Integration and Conservation of Environment (BICE). Shri Murli Deora, also released the expedition commemorator in the presence of Shri V.C. Agrawal, Director (HR) and other senior officials of IndianOil. On this occasion, Shri Murli Deora emphasized that this expedition titled 'Peaks Of Freedom' will be a tribute to the courage, patriotism and resilience of our armed forces as the members of the expedition are scheduled to touch those Himalayan ranges where our men in uniform have made some of the greatest sacrifices during Chinese War and Kargil conflict. He was hopeful about the expedition members forging a closer bond with the people of those regions through which they pass, promoting national integrity and spreading the message of peace. On their way, the expedition members will touch the Himalayan ranges passing through Rohtang, Baralacha La, Nakee La Lachalung La, Tanglang La, Chang La, Khardung La reaching Daulat Beg Oldi near Karakoram Pass at an approximate height of 18,000 feet, criss-crossing several Trans Himalayan passes and arduous terrain. The members of the team which comprises journalists, photographers and other professionals have chosen a village located at the northernmost tip of Ladakh as their summit. While wishing the expedition team members all success in their thrilling venture, Shri Murli Deora complimented the nation's premier oil company, IndianOil, for sponsoring such an adventurous mission. The Minister added that powered by IndianOil's world class engine oils and their own undaunted spirit, these young men will surpass all obstacles and stand up to any challenge that nature presents. Shri V.C. Agrawal, Director (HR), IndianOil in his address congratulated BICE on their resoluteness, their spirit of adventures and unquenchable desire to better themselves in leading daredevil expeditions up the treacherous slopes of the indomitable Himalayas. He said that the 13 member team which aimed to travel through difficult terrain included four ladies whom he specially saluted for showing the world that women were every bit as capable and daring as men. He further said that we at IndianOil respect such spirit, determination and dedication because we can fully empathize with it. The Bikers for Integration and Conservation of Environment endeavours to promote the spirit of adventure, exploration of nature and promotion of ecological consciousness.

2660. (22-8-2007) NEW DELHI : The Ministry of Railways has decided to constitute a Core Group for monitoring of Public Private Partnership (PPP) projects related to development of World Class Railway Stations including New Delhi Railway Station. The Committee will set up clear timeframe for each of the 22 railway stations, which will be upgraded to world-class stations. The Group will take stock of the progress and also devise a format for compiling a monthly progress report. The move will give further flip to the modernization activities aimed at improving passenger amenities. The Group will review and strengthen other related departments of Railway Board to enable them to deliver results as per the targets laid down for PPP projects. The Group will also formulate a list of preparatory activities to be completed by the Zonal Railways before any station is taken up for developing as a world class and this would include the dedicated organizational set-up that needs to be created with in the Zonal Railways for this purpose. Earlier, in a move to make Indian Railways world's number one Railway network, the Committee on Infrastructure approved the proposal for completing the first phase of modernization of the New Delhi railway station into a world-class station through Public Private Partnership before the Commonwealth Games, 2010. In addition to New Delhi, the other stations would be developed as world class stations are: Agra, Ahmedabad, Amritsar, Anand Vihar, Bangalore, Bhopal, Bhubaneshwar, Bijwasan, Chandigarh, Chennai, Mumbai CST, Howrah, Jaipur, Lucknow, Mathura, Patna, Pune, Secunderabad, Thiruvananthapuram, Varanasi and Gaya. The Core Group will consist of high-ranking officials of Railway Board. These are; Member (Engineering), Additional Member (Commercial), Adviser (Infrastructure) and Adviser (Finance). Adviser (Land and Amenities) will function as the Convener of the Committee.

2661. (22-8-2007) NEW DELHI : Shri A.Raja, Minister of Communication and Information Technology urged upon private service providers to promote the use of indigenous equipment in their network and contribute in the growth of telecom equipment manufacturing in the country to cater to domestic demand & exports. Shri Raja was speaking at the launch of the TEMA Export Promotion Forum here today. An export target of US $ 10 billion has been set for the next 5-6 years. A collaborative effort between all stakeholders will steer us towards this target. He added that he was sure that Export Promotion Forum will work hard to achieve this target. Shri Raja said that to achieve projected target of 650 Million by 2012, we would need telecom equipments of the order of US $ 84 Billion. The TEMA has projected an indigenous production of the order of US$ 75 Billion. That's an ambitious target to achieve. He called upon equipment manufacturers to work out strategies to achieve the same. He assured that the Department of Telecom will provide all enabling factors for this purpose. Creation of world class telecom manufacturing facilities is important step towards making India a Hub for telecom equipment manufacturing. India has the potential to emerge as a manufacturing hub of international standards, he said. Shri Raja said that with the present level of more than 230 millions subscribers and addition of over 7 million subscribers per month, we are all set for achieving the target of 250 million well ahead of the year end. Our next targets are 500 Million connections and 20 million broadband connections by 2010 to achieve our goals.

2662. (22-8-2007) NEW DELHI : Shri Kamal Nath, Union Minister of Commerce and Industry, has called upon the Japanese business leader s to benefit from the investment opportunities available in the Indian economy and highlighted the enormous contribution that Japan could make for infrastructure development. "Our need for infrastructure is massive, and we estimate that in the next five years, we will need US $ 384 billion to bridge the infrastructure gap", he informed the participants at the India-Japan Business Seminar here today. Shri Kamal Nath highlighted the lead given to Indo-Japan economic engagement through the Delhi-Mumbai Industrial Corridor Project and hoped that apart from benefiting the country's industrial infrastructure development, it would also become a new springboard for the Japanese companies for accessing the US and EU markets. The Minister also highlighted the tremendous strides made by India on trade front as well as in achieving a record growth in foreign direct investment (FDI) and in propelling the manufacturing revolution in the country. He invited the Japanese business leaders to look at some of the sectors with high potential in manufacturing such as textiles & apparels, food processing, chemicals & petrochemicals, automobiles, electronics & IT hardware etc. The Indo-Japan Business Seminar was also addressed by Shri Masakazu Toyoda, Vice Minister, Ministry of Economy, Trade and Industry, Government of Japan; Shri Ajay Shankar, Secretary (DIPP); and representatives from Mitsubishi Electric, KPMG, NYK Ltd. The Seminar was jointly organised by DIPP, JETRO, FICCI, CII and Assocham. Later, while addressing the inaugural session of the India-Japan Business Leaders Forum here,

Shri Kamal Nath hoped that the Business Leaders Forum would be able to bring to the notice of the two governments the particular roadblocks being faced for doing businesses in the two countries. Shri Nath highlighted the resurgence of the manufacturing sector in India which has now become the growth driver of the economy. “The resurgence of manufacturing is visible in the sustained interest of overseas companies in establishing production centres in India. Factories for Suzuki, Mitsubishi, Toyota, Honda, Asahi and others are going online rapidly, making a range of products for domestic as well as international sales”, he said. The Minister also noted the emergence of India as one of the fastest growing markets in the world. According to McKinsey, by 2025, India will have quadrupled its markets, with discretionary spending comprising 70% of all spending. Rural spending will increase to almost US $ 600 billion, lowering poverty to 29% of the rural population by 2025. The Business Leaders Forum was also addressed by Shri Masaharu Kohno, Deputy Minister of Foreign Affairs, Government of Japan; Shri Fujio Mitarai, Leader of the Japanese business delegation and Shri Mukesh Ambani, Chairman/Reliance Industries and co-chair of India-Japan Business Leaders Forum. The Prime Ministers of India and Japan had announced the constitution of the Business Leaders Forum in their Joint Declaration in December 2006 in Tokyo and today’s meeting was the first meeting of the Forum.

2663. (22-8-2007) NEW DELHI : Following is the text of the Prime Minister, Dr. Manmohan Singh’s speech at the Banquet hosted in honour of Japanese Prime Minister: “On behalf of the Government and people of India it gives me immense pleasure to welcome you, along with all the distinguished members of your delegation, to India. Your visit marks a historic milestone in our bilateral relations. Fifty years ago your grandfather, the late Prime Minister Nobusuke Kishi, made his path-breaking visit to India. That visit laid the foundation of our partnership in the modern era. Today, it is our privilege to welcome you not only as the inheritor of a great legacy, but also as an architect of strong Indo-Japan relations. We deeply appreciate your personal commitment to realizing our common vision of building a strong bilateral relationship of lasting value. We applaud your efforts to make Japan a ‘beautiful’ country. Our two ancient cultures have had exchanges as far back as recorded history takes us. We admire the Japanese way, which emphasizes harmony, balance and moderation. We strive to emulate the individual and social attributes that have made Japan the shining light of modern Asia. You have been a valuable partner in our economic progress and a friend in times of need. Our contemporary bilateral relationship is on the verge of full bloom. Our talks today give us the confidence that the strategic dimension of our relations will be further consolidated in the years ahead. On the pillars of this strong bilateral relationship, we stand as two major powers ready to play a commensurate global role in dealing with challenges such as terrorism, climate change and energy security. We believe that a strong and dynamic Japan is a factor of peace and stability in Asia. As two leading democracies of Asia, who share common values, our combined voice can contribute decisively towards the building of a new Asia and a new economic community that is open and inclusive. We have turned a new page in our ties with the dawn of this century. We have added vitality and depth to our ties through enhanced political understanding, economic partnership, cultural exchange and cooperation in emerging areas such as environment and energy security. We have today laid out a Roadmap for our future partnership. Let us pledge to walk resolutely on this path and usher in a glorious era in our age-old ties. This is what we owe to our people, and to future generations. We must make up for lost time. Your inspiring address to our Parliament this morning left a deep impact. A strong India and a strong Japan will work together in harmony and peace to build a perfect partnership.

2664. (23-8-2007) NEW DELHI : The Cabinet Committee on Economic Affairs today gave its approval for setting up of a uranium mine and processing plant at Tummalapalle, Cuddapah, Andhra Pradesh at a total cost of Rs.1106.29 crore. The plant will be set up by the Uranium Corporation of India. Setting up of uranium mine will meet the uranium fuel requirements of the nuclear power programme. Besides developing the area, the project will also provide direct employment to about 934 persons in various categories including employment to Project Affected Persons (PAPs). The mine is likely to be commissioned within 30 months and the Processing Plant in 36 months.

2665. (23-8-2007) NEW DELHI: A crucial two-day meeting of the central committee of the Communist Party of India (Marxist) began here on Wednesday, amid indications that it would reiterate the Left parties' stand on the India-U.S. civilian nuclear agreement asking the United Progressive Alliance (UPA) government to "press the pause button" on the deal. "All we are asking from the government is to press the pause button on the deal and properly evaluate all the implications and objections before proceeding further," a senior CPI(M) leader said. The CPI(M) central committee meeting, convened in the wake of the ongoing stand-off between the Left parties and the government over the Indo-U.S. civilian nuclear deal, is discussing all aspects of the deal as well as taking a critical look at the government response so far and the prevailing political situation in the country. On Monday, the four Left parties reiterated their August 7 stand that in view of the widespread opposition to the 123 agreement with the U.S. and the fact that a majority in Parliament was against it, the government should not proceed further with the agreement. It means not taking the next step of safeguards negotiations with the International Atomic Energy Agency (IAEA) at Vienna. On Wednesday, CPI(M) Polit Bureau member and MP Sitaram Yechury said that his party did not have any objection to India participating in the IAEA meet in September but asserted that there should be no talks on India-specific safeguards on the nuclear deal with Washington.

2666. (23-8-2007) NEW DELHI : The Cabinet Committee on Economic Affairs today gave its approval for the following: (a) Continuation of the Centrally

Sponsored Scheme relating to 'Establishment of new Industrial Training Institutes (I.T.I.s) in North Eastern States and Sikkim [outlay Rs.100 crore] and incur expenditure of Rs.18.31 crore under various components, till 31.3.2008, after which the State Governments will bear the recurring expenditure. (b) Continuation of the other scheme component on strengthening / modernization of ITIs in the State of Jammu & Kashmir [outlay Rs.37.00 crore] and incur expenditure of Rs.30.49 crores for J&K, under various components including recurring expenditure 1.4.2007 till 31.03.2009. (c) To incur expenditure of Rs.13.70 crore for setting up of three new I.T.I.s-two in Sikkim and one in the State of Assam. As additional allocation, within the existing North East scheme, for next two years during the XI Plan from 1.4.2007 till 31.03.2009. (d) Building in flexibilities for change of trades in the identified I.T.I.s within the State and for allocation of funds from one scheme of the project to another and from one component of the scheme to another and between the major components, within a upper limit of 10%. Secretary, M/o Labour and Employment will have the power for approving such changes within the original project cost of Rs.100 crore for North Eastern states and Rs.37.00 crore for J & K. The project aims at creating and developing infrastructure for training of youth in the identified skill areas as per the demand pattern of Sikkim, North Eastern States and J&K.

2667. (23-8-2007) NEW DELHI : The Cabinet Committee on Economic Affairs today gave its approval for the continuation of the 'Nutrition Programme for Adolescent Girls' in the year 2007-08 in 51 Districts as per existing guidelines except that two cut off weights viz. 30 kg for those in the age group of 11-15 years and 35 kg for beneficiaries in the age group of 15-19 years would be used for selection of beneficiaries under this programme. The CCEA also approved the releasing of funds to the tune of Rs.124.09 crore for the current financial year as Special Central Assistance (on 100% grant basis) to States/UTs. With the implementation of this project, it is expected that the nutritional status of the adolescent girls in the selected districts would improve.

2668. (23-8-2007) NEW DELHI : The Union Cabinet today gave its approval to make amendments to the Payment and Settlement Systems Bill, 2006 based primarily on the recommendations of the Standing Committee of Parliament on Finance, already introduced in Lok Sabha. The amendments would ensure a safe, secure and sound payments system.

2669. (23-8-2007) NEW DELHI : The Union Cabinet today gave its approval for revival of company M/s NEPA Limited through a Joint Venture Partner in private sector by disinvestment of Government of India's equity, preferably to the extent of 74% or 100% and introduction the NEPA Limited (Disinvestment of Ownership) Bill, 2007. The Cabinet also gave its approval for requesting BIFR to locate a Joint Venture partner and issue appropriate orders in this regard. A Bill namely, the NEPA Limited (disinvestments of Ownership) Bill, 2007 will be introduced in the coming session of the Parliament.

2670. (23-8-2007) NEW DELHI : The Union Cabinet today gave its approval to the following proposals: (i) Setting up of six National Institutes of Pharmaceutical Education and Research (NIPER) at Hyderabad (Andhra Pradesh), Ahmedabad (Gujarat), Hajipur (Bihar) Guwahati (Assam), Raibareilly (U.P.) and Kolkata (West Bengal). (ii) Commencing some courses at four locations of New NIPERs from the current academic session *i.e.* September, 2007 with the assistance of Mentor Institutes. (iii) Continuation of courses under the present arrangements from the plan budget for two years *i.e.* 2007-08 and 2008-09 and preparation and preparation and approval of the Detailed Project Reports (DPRs) by the Competent Authority. (iv) Appointment of a Consultant of repute to prepare the DPR for each NIPER wherever possible on the Public Private Partnership model. (v) Pending the constitution of board of Governors under the NIPER Act 1998, an Apex Steering Committee under the Chairmanship of Secretary (C&PC) to oversee the functioning of these NIPERs may be set up. This decision will facilitate training of high caliber pharmaceutical experts and award of Masters degrees to cater to the demand of pharmaceuticals industry, academic institutes and the pharmacy profession.

2671. (23-8-2007) NEW DELHI : The Union Cabinet today gave its approval to signing of Mutual Legal Assistance Treat in Criminal Matters between India and Vietnam and also ratification of the said Treaty. The Treaty will enhance effectiveness of cooperation between the two countries in the field of mutual legal assistance in criminal matters. It will provide the widest measure of mutual legal assistance in connection with investigations, prosecutions and other proceedings related to criminal matters. Similar Treaties on Mutual Legal Assistance in Criminal Matters have been entered into with Switzerland, Turkey, United Kingdom, Canada, Russian Federation, France, Kyrgyzstan, Kazakhstan, United Arab Emirates, Uzbekistan, Mongolia, Tajikistan, Ukraine, United State of America, South Africa, Bahrain, Thailand, Kuwait, South Korea, Singapore, Belarus, Mauritius and Spain. The Treaty shall enter into force from the date of exchange of the instruments of ratification.

2672. (23-8-2007) NEW DELHI : Maharashtra Natural Gas Limited (MNGL) would commence CNG supply in Pune from November 2007. It is planning to set up 29 CNG stations in Pune progressively by end of 2008. MNGL would take up City Gas Distribution projects in other cities of Maharashtra in a phased manner, depending upon availability of gas and economic viability. Mahanagar Gas Limited (MGL) presently has 127 CNG stations in Mumbai, Thane and Mira-Bhayander. The above information was given by the Minister of State for Petroleum & Natural Gas Shri Dinsha Patel in a written reply in the Lok Sabha today.

2673. (23-8-2007) NEW DELHI : Shri Dinsha Patel, the Minister of State for Petroleum & Natural Gas informed the Lok Sabha in a written reply today that Under New Exploration Licensing Policy (NELP), 43 oil and gas discoveries have already been made. In Gujarat, 3 lakh cubic metres of gas per day is being provided from one block operated by Niko Resources. In another block operated by Gujarat State Petroleum Corporation (GSPC), crude oil of the order of 500 barrels per day has started recently from July, 2007 onwards. Gas production of 40 Million Metric Standard Cubic Metres per Day (MMSCMD) from Krishna Godavari basin is likely to commence in July 2008 with peak production of 80 MMSCMD. He pointed out that a total 90 exploration blocks have been awarded under first four rounds of NELP. Further, 72 more blocks have been contracted in fifth and sixth rounds of NELP bidding. Shri Patel also said that blocks under various rounds of NELP are contracted for carrying out exploration activities for a period of seven to eight years during which operator completes Exploration Work Programme. Time taken for oil/gas discovery to come on production is normally about 3 to 8 years depending upon the location of discovery, availability of infrastructure and markets in and around the discovery area.

2674. (23-8-2007) NEW DELHI: Key constituents of the United Progressive Alliance (UPA) joined the Opposition and the Left parties on Wednesday in demanding action against the Indian Ambassador to the U.S., Ronen Sen, for his remarks on the political debate over the India-U.S. civilian nuclear deal. In the Rajya Sabha, the Dravida Munnetra Kazhagam (DMK), the Nationalist Congress Party (NCP) and the Rashtriya Janata Dal (RJD) made common cause with the Opposition and Left parties on this issue. In the Lok Sabha, the demand for his recall came from RJD member Devendra Prasad Yadav. Mr. Sen's remarks held up proceedings in both Houses of Parliament for the second day as members insisted on his recall and admission of their privilege notices against him. While both Houses adjourned for an hour within minutes of meeting in the morning as members wanted to raise the matter before the question hour, the Lok Sabha returned to schedule thereafter as members were allowed to make brief interventions on the issue. The Rajya Sabha saw another adjournment and could return to business only post-lunch; again after a short discussion on the issue. The two Houses also witnessed walkouts by the NDA–barring the Shiv Sena—after the discussion over the Government's non-committal stance on the demand for Mr. Sen's recall. Prior to the first adjournment, Bharatiya Janata Party (BJP) Deputy Leader in the Lok Sabha, V. K. Malhotra, wanted to know from Prime Minister Manmohan Singh—who was present in the House—whether a decision had been taken to recall Mr. Sen. As for the fate of the privilege notices, Speaker Somnath Chatterjee said he needed more time. Later, responding to the demand for Mr. Sen's recall–raised by Rup Chand Pal (Communist Party of India-Marxist), Mohan Singh (Samajwadi Party) B. K. Tripathi (Biju Janata Dal), Gurudas Dasgupta (CPI), Sukhdev Singh Dhindsa (Shiromani Akali Dal), Subrato Bose (All India Forward Bloc), P. C. Thomas (Kerala Congress), Anant Geete (Shiv Sena) and M. Shivanna (Janata Dal-Secular).

2675. (23-8-2007) NEW DELHI : The Central Government has increased the rate of abatement to 75% for the purpose of levy of service tax on taxable services provided by tour operators in relation to package tours. To this effect, the Central Government has issued Notification No.38/2007-ST dated 23.8.2007 amending Notification No.1/2006-ST dated 1.3.2006. Services provided by tour operators, in relation to a tour, are leviable to service tax under Tour Operators Service. At present, tour operator, providing package tour which includes provision of transportation, accommodation for stay, is liable to pay service tax on 40% of the gross amount charged for such tour. In other words, 60% of the gross amount charged is provided as abatement for the purpose of levy of service tax. The Indian Association of Tour Operators (IATO) requested to increase the rate of abatement on package tour services provided by tour operators. The suggestion has been recommended by Ministry of Tourism. The request of the Indian Association of Tour Operators was examined by the Advisory Committee on Service Tax Abatement and the Committee has recommended to prescribe the rate of abatement of 75% on package tours where the gross amount charged includes cost of accommodation, food, transport arrangement, tourist guide, entry to monuments and other similar categories of expenditure. The recommendation of the Committee was accepted by the Government and a notification prescribing abatement rate of 75% to services provided by tour operators in relation to a package tour wherein cost of accommodation, food, transport arrangement, tourist guide, entry to monuments and other similar services are included as part of the package tour has been issued. As a result of this Notification, the tour operator is required to pay service tax only on 25% of the gross amount charged on such package tour.

2676. (23-8-2007) NEW DELHI : The Minister of State for Housing & Urban Poverty Alleviation, Kumari Selja informed the Rajya Sabha today, in a written reply to a question by Shri Sanjay Raut that 21 State Governments have submitted 232 projects under Basic Services to the Urban Poor (BSUP) and 18 State Governments have submitted 700 projects under Integrated Housing and Slum Development Programme (IHSDP) for construction of houses including the provision of basic amenities in urban areas for the weaker sections. The state-wise details of total project cost, approved project cost and the Central assistance approved are given in the Annexure, the Minister told the House.

2677. (23-8-2007) NEW DELHI : As per the policy of Ministry of Shipping, Road Transport and Highways, no advertisements or hoardings are allowed on National Highways land except informatory signs of public interest. However, under the policy of private sponsorship of road signs and greening of National Highways, the private entrepreneurs are allowed to depict the name and logo of their company in a sign of specified dimension. Instructions have been issued to executing agencies for removal of unauthorized hoardings. This information was given by the Minister of State for Shipping, Road Transport and Highways, Shri K.H. Muniyappa in a written reply in the Rajya Sabha today.

2678. (23-8-2007) NEW DELHI : The National Highways Authority of India (NHAI) is planning to start collection of user fee by introducing Smart Cards and

On Board Units to further reduce the time taken in collection of user fee. This information was given by the Minister of State for Shipping, Road Transport and Highways, Shri K.H. Muniyappa in a written reply in the Rajya Sabha today.

2679. (23-8-2007) NEW DELHI : The Chief Labour Commissioner initiated conciliation proceedings on the issue of raising the age of retirement from 58 to 60 years of the employees of Major Ports on representations received from certain Labour Federations. The conciliation proceedings have not been closed. The Ministry of Shipping, Road Transport & Highways had also constituted a Committee to look holistically into the matter relating to retirement age of Port and Dock employees. The Committee has submitted its report but no decision has been taken. This information was given by the Minister of Shipping, Road Transport and Highways, Thiru T.R. Baalu in a written reply in the Rajya Sabha today.

2680. (23-8-2007) NEW DELHI : The Government has taken several steps to modernize the functioning of the Mercantile Marine Departments and also for ensuring efficiency and transparency in the working of its five Regional level Mercantile Marine Department (MMD) offices and 13 District level MMD offices covering all the major ports in the country.

2681. (23-8-2007) NEW DELHI : The National Highways Authority of India (NHAI) has taken initiative to combat menace of HIV/AIDS on projects funded by World Bank (WB) and the Asian Development Bank (ADB). NHAI is implementing HIV/AIDS awareness campaign through Non-Governmental Organizations (NGOs) alongwith National AIDS Control Organization (NACO) as part of their loan commitments. Accordingly, the NHAI has set up a HIV/AIDS Prevention and Control Unit with experts and implementing HIV/AIDS awareness campaign along NH-2 (Delhi-Kolkata) and NH-28 (Lucknow-Muzaffarpur) through World Bank Loan. Further, it is proposed to implement HIV/AIDS awareness campaign along North-South Corridor [NH-26 and NH-7 (Lalitput to Anantpur-Andhra Pradesh/Karnataka Border)] and East-West Corridor [NH-76 and NH-25 (Chittorgarh {Rajasthan}-Orai{Uttar Pradesh})] through ADB Loan. Presently, four NGOs have been awarded contracts for implementing HIV/AIDS awareness campaign along NH-28 (Lucknow-Muzaffarpur). This information was given by the Minister of State for Shipping, Road Transport and Highways, Shri K.H. Muniyappa in a written reply in the Rajya Sabha today.

2682. (23-8-2007) NEW DELHI : Fishing vessels are registered under Section 435 of Merchant Shipping Act. These vessels are used solely for fishing and their use for any other purpose is not contemplated under the said Act. As per available information, the Major Ports do not permit fishing vessels to operate as supply vessels for oil companies. This information was given by the Minister of Shipping, Road Transport and Highways, Thiru T.R. Baalu in a written reply in the Rajya Sabha today.

2683. (23-8-2007) NEW DELHI : The Government has increased the rate of abatement to 75% for the purpose of levy of service tax on taxable services provided by tour operators in relation to package tours. To this effect, the Finance Ministry has issued a notification today. Services provided by tour operators, in relation to a tour, are leviable to service tax under Tour Operators Service. At present, tour operator, providing package tour which includes provision of transportation, accommodation for stay, is liable to pay service tax on 40% of the gross amount charged for such tour. In other words, 60% of the gross amount charged is provided as abatement for the purpose of levy of service tax. The Tourism and Culture Minister Smt. Ambika Soni had taken up this matter with Finance Minister, Shri P. Chidambaram in a letter dated August, 30th 2006 and followed it up with a series of meetings at the official level between the two ministries. A presentation in this regard was made by the Tourism Ministry representatives to the Advisory Committee on service tax abatement in mid July. The request of the Ministry of Tourism was examined by the Advisory Committee on Service Tax Abatement and the Committee has recommended to prescribe the rate of abatement of 75% on package tours where the gross amount charged includes cost of accommodation, food, transport arrangement, tourist guide, entry to monuments and other similar categories of expenditure. The recommendation of the Committee was accepted by the Government and a notification prescribing abatement rate of 75% to services provided by tour operators in relation to a package tour wherein cost of accommodation, food, transport arrangement, tourist guide, entry to monuments and other similar services are included as part of the package tour has been issued. As a result of this Notification, the tour operator is required to pay service tax only on 25% of the gross amount charged on such package tour.

2684. (23-8-2007) NEW DELHI : The National Highways Authority of India (NHAI) is currently implementing four National Highways projects with loan assistance from World Bank. The planning and outlining of these projects, which includes preparation of detailed project report (from technical and environmental point of view), have been finalized with the concurrence of World Bank. For execution of the work, the agencies for supervision and construction are also finalized following guidelines of procurement of World Bank with their concurrence. World Bank Mission have been undertaking regular visits to above projects to monitor progress and compliance of various loan covenants. The inputs provided by the World Bank mission through various aide-memoires are duly considered by NHAI for effective monitoring of project progress and appraised to World Bank from time to time. This information was given by the Minister of State for Shipping, Road Transport and Highways, Shri K.H. Muniyappa in a written reply in the Rajya Sabha today.

2685. (23-8-2007) NEW DELHI : In exercise of the power conferred by article 224-A of the Constitution of India, the President is pleased to appoint Shri Justice

Om Prakash Srivastava, a retired Judge of the Allahabad High Court, to sit and act as a Judge of the Allahabad High Court for hearing Ayodhya matters, for aperiod of one year with effect from the date he assumes charge of his office or till the disposal of Ayodhya matters, whichever is earlier.

2686. (23-8-2007) NEW DELHI : A Total Eclipse of the Moon will occur in the evening of Tuesday, the 28th August 2007 (6 Bhadrapada, 1929 Saka Era) from 1421 Hrs to 1754 Hrs IST. The eclipse is visible in the region covering Americas except the eastern part of South America and northeastern parts of North America, the Pacific Ocean, eastern parts of Asia, Australasia and Antarctica. The beginning of the umbral phase will be visible from South Atlantic Ocean, northeastern part of Brazil, northern part of Atlantic Ocean, New Found Land, extreme northeast of Canada. The ending will be visible from southern part of Indian Ocean, northeastern part of India, China, western part of Mongolia, central part of Russia.

2687. (23-8-2007) NEW DELHI : The Minister of State for Housing & Urban Poverty Alleviation, Kumari Selja informed the Rajya Sabha today, in a written reply to a question by Shri Vedprakash P. Goyal that the Government has launched the Jawaharlal Nehru National Urban Renewal Mission (JNNURM) to assist cities and towns to check rapid increase in slums in 63 select cities under the Basic Services to the Urban Poor (BSUP) Programme. Kumari Selja further informed the House that under the JNNURM, Central assistance support is provided to cities and towns for undertaking slum upgradation including houses at affordable cost to the urban poor. It is a demand driven scheme and no targets are fixed. For other cities, for taking up housing and slum upgradation programmes, the Integrated Housing and Slum Development Programme (IHSDP) has been launched. Both BSUP and IHSDP are under implementation since December, 2005. The duration of the Mission is seven years. Projects are being executed by the State Governments/ Urban Local Bodies (ULBs), the Minister added.

2688. (23-8-2007) NEW DELHI : A number of institutional arrangements have been made for ensuring proper planning and timely preparation for the Commonwealth Games, 2010. These include a Core Group of Minister (GOM) under the Chairmanship of the Minister for Human Resource Development for coordinating the various works related to the conduct of the Games; an Apex Committee headed by Minister for Youth Affairs and Sports for overseeing and coordinating various matters related to CWG 2010; the Organizing Committee (OC) headed by the President, Indian Olympic Association for the conduct of the Games; and a Committee of Secretaries headed by Cabinet Secretary which is responsible for monitoring the implementation of the decisions of the GOM and taking decisions on other related matters. In addition to these arrangements at the Central level, there is a sub-committee under the Chief Minister of Delhi to take decisions in respect of all matters pertaining to infrastructure and other preparations for the Games within the jurisdiction of the Government of NCT of Delhi. The Lt. Governor Delhi has been entrusted with the overall responsibility with specific reference to security, law and orders and matter coming under DDA. The locations for the various competitions/training venues, and the major non-competition venue viz. International Broadcasting Centre (IBC)/Main Press Centre (MPC), have been agreed to among the stakeholders. All the stakeholders have indicated their specific time lines with reference to key milestones, viz., finalization of detailed design and estimates, commencement of tendering process, award of work, commencement of work, completion of work and handing over to OC. It is expected that work on all the major sports venue infrastructure projects will commence between August-December, 2007 and the venues will be handed over to the OC by the end of 2009. An Empowered Committee has been set up under the chairmanship of Chief Secretary, GNCTD with representatives from all the concerned agencies/ authorities to facilitate speedy clearances in respect of the Games related projects. Another Committee has been set up under the Secretary, Ministry of Urban Development to facilitate clearances pertaining to Delhi Urban Arts Commission (DUAC). Keeping in view the need for developing adequate tourist accommodation in the context of the Commonwealth Games, an inter-Ministerial Task Force has been set up under the Ministry of Tourism (MoT) for monitoring and coordinating further action in this regard by all the agencies concerned. A Committee for expediting the Central Government clearance in respect of Hotels coming up in Uttar Pradesh has also been set under the Chairmanship of Secretary, Ministry of Youth Affairs and Sports.

2689. (23-8-2007) NEW DELHI : According to the 86th Amendment to the Constitution Act, 2002, Right to Education is a fundamental right and therefore, elementary education shall be free. According to Article 21 A, "The State shall endeavour to provide free and compulsory education to all children of the age of six to 14 years in such manner as the State may, by law, determine". The endeavour therefore of Sarva Shiskha Abhiyan (SSA), is to provide universal primary education to all in the country. The Prime Minister heads the National Mission for SSA, which monitors the progress made under the scheme. SSA is expected to provide relevant elementary education for children in the country between the age group of six and 14 years by 2010. The Finance Minister, Shri P. Chidambaram during this Budget period, 2007-08 has increased the allocation for school education by about 35 per cent from Rs.17, 133 crore in 2006-07 to Rs.23, 142 crore in 2007-08. He said: "Out of this amount, Sarva Shiksha Abhiyan (SSA) will be provided Rs.10, 671 crore. Further, I propose to increase the provision for strengthening teachers training institutions from Rs.162 crore to Rs.450 crore. Next year, we will appoint 2,00,000 more teachers and construct 5,00,000 more classrooms." The performance audit of SSA carried out by Comptroller and Auditor General (CAG) of India (March 2005) mentions specifically the aim of SSA: "to ensure that all children complete five years of primary schooling by 2007; to ensure that all children complete eight years of elementary schooling by 2010; bridge all gender and social category gaps at the primary stage by 2007 and at the elementary educational level by 2010 and achieve universal retention by 2010". By March 2007, under the scheme the Government has already opened 1,10,217 schools, touching 83 per cent of the target for 2006-07, which is 1,33,928. Supply of free textbooks has been to the tune of 6.40 crore and appointment of teachers has been to the tune of 7.95 lakh during the same period, which has sufficiently met the targets. Covering the period from 2003-04 to 2007, SSA has received external funding to the tune of Rs 4,700 crore ($ 1bn) from World Bank's International Development Association; Department for International Development, UK and the European Commission. Sarva Shiskha Abhiyan is an ambitious programme meant to cover 19.2 crore children in the country. It evolved from the recommendations of the State Education Ministers' Conference held in October 1998 to start Universal Elementary Education. The programme was launched in 2001-02. Allocation of funds under SSA, since its inception has shown high growth from Rs 350-crore in 2000-01 to Rs 7,800 crore in 2005-06, and to Rs 11,000 crore in 2006-07, representing an increase of 41 per cent over the previous year (2005-06). The World Bank Aide-Memoire (January 2006) on the third joint-review mission of SSA mentions that the target of reducing out of school children by 3 million per year is being exceeded. It mentions that the number of out of school children has fallen from 25 million in 2003 to 13.5 million as on March 2005 and that "the positive trend will continue in 2006" whereas the CAG report says that, "Even after 4 years of the implementation of the scheme and utilisation of almost 86 per cent of funds available with the implementation agencies, the revised target of SSA to enroll all children in schools, education guarantee scheme, alternative schools, back to school camps by 2005 was not achieved as 1.36 crore (40 per cent of the total 3.40 crore children out of school) remained out of school in the age-group 6-14 years." A lot requires to be done. As per the World Bank Report, there are 48 districts in the country where more than 50,000 children are out of school, the highest being in Bihar (20), Uttar Pradesh (15) and West Bengal (4). According to the CAG report, nationally, there were 71 children out-of-school per thousand. So efforts need to be speeded up in this direction too. The World Bank Report also mentions that the gender parity continues to improve, which is within the reach at the primary level.

2690. (23-8-2007) NEW DELHI : As per Cellular Mobile Telephone Service/ Unified Access Services (CMTS/UAS) License provisions, Delhi Service Area is defined as "Local Areas served by Delhi, Ghaziabad, Faridabad, Noida and Gurgaon Telephone Exchanges." Therefore, Greater Noida, Gurgaon and Noida areas are part of Delhi service area. BSNL is not licensed to operate Cell One mobile services in Delhi service area. Hence, the applicable roaming charges is to be paid by BSNL Mobile (Cell One) subscribers for using mobile services in these areas in roaming mode. Recently, on 24th January 2007 vide Telecommunication Tariff (forty fourth amendment) Order, 2007, (1 of 2007), Telecom Regulatory Authority of India (TRAI) has reduced the ceiling tariff for mobile roaming. There is no proposal to waive off roaming charges in these areas. This information was given by Dr.Shakeel Ahmad, Minister of State in the Ministry of Communications and Information Technology in the Rajya Sabha today in a written reply to a question by Shri Raj Nath Singh.

2691. (23-8-2007) NEW DELHI : Total estimated quantity of hazardous waste generation in the country is more than five million tonnes per annum, which includes wastes that are recyclable, incinerable and disposable to landfill. As per the information available, there are eighteen Hazardous Waste Treatment Storage and Disposal Facilities (TSDFs) operational in eight States, namely-Gujarat, Maharashtra, Andhra Pradesh, Uttar Pradesh, Rajasthan, Madhya Pradesh, and West Bengal. Of these, six have been provided the Central and State Government subsidies. It has been estimated that the existing facilities take care of 40% of the total waste generation. Ministry of Environment and Forests, Government of India has provided a Central Scheme wherein financial assistance is given for setting up of Treatment Storage and Disposal Facilities (TSDFs). Under this scheme, the Ministry of Environment & Forests provides a grant to the tune of Rs.2 crores with a proportionate contribution from the State Government for setting up of TSDF on a Public Private Partnership involving the Central and State Government and a private enterprise through Build Operate Own (BOO) principle. This information was given by the Minister of State in the Ministry of Environment and Forests, Shri Namo Narain Meen in a written reply to question by Shri C. Perumal in the Rajya Sabha today.

2692. (23-8-2007) NEW DELHI : The India Meteorological Department (IMD) maintains a network of Global Atmospheric Watch (GAW) stations that follow the World Meteorological Organization (WMO) norms. Rainwater samples collected at 10 locations are analyzed regularly and this data is available for about 28 years now. The study was conducted by the IMD using this data and statistical analysis has shown an increasing acidity of the rain samples collected from Pune and Nagpur. However, the rain water at these places is still in the alkaline range due to the dominance of neutralizing agents in the dust. This information was given by the Minister of State in the Ministry of Environment and Forests, Shri Namo Narayan Meena in a written reply to question by Shri Syed Azeez Pasha and Shri D. Raja :in the Rajya Sabha today.

2693. (23-8-2007) NEW DELHI : The Ministry of Environment and Forests notified the Municipal Solid Wastes (Management and Handling) Rules, 2000 for the sound management of Municipal Solid Wastes vide S.O. 908 (E) dated 25th September, 2000. These rules provide for and lay down detailed compliance criteria., for the collection, storage, segregation, transportation, processing and disposal of municipal solid wastes. As per these rules the municipal authority is responsible for the implementation of the provisions of the rules and for any infrastructure development for management of municipal wastes. The municipal authorities are required to seek authorization for setting up of waste processing and disposal facility including landfills from the State pollution Control Boards. The overall responsibility for the enforcement of these rules rests with the Secretary incharge, Department of Urban Development in the State. As per the provision of the Municipal Solid Wastes (Management and Handling) Rules, 2000 the State Pollution Control Boards (SPCBs) and the Pollution Control Committees (PCCs) of the Union Territories are required to prepare and submit an annual report on the implementation status of the rules to the Central Pollution Control Board (CPCB). The CPCB prepares a consolidated annual review report on the management of municipal solid wastes and forwards the same along with its recommendation to the Ministry of Environment & Forests. As per the consolidated annual review report on the management of Municipal Solid Waste forwarded by the CPCB, many local bodies have set up / streamlined waste collection, storage and transportation system. 2339 local bodies have applied for grant of authorization to set up waste processing and disposal facility to the respective SPCBs / PCCs and 1220 authorization have been granted. 65 compost plants are in operation and 56 are proposed to be set up. Seven landfills have been constructed and local bodies in 17 states have identified new sites for development of sanitary landfills. A regional waste processing and disposal facility for a cluster of 11 municipalities is under completion by the Ahmedabad Urban Development Authority.. This information was given by the Minister of State in the Ministry of Environment and Forests, Shri Namo Narayan Meena in a written reply to question by Shri. K.E. Ismail and Shri. D. Raja in the Rajya Sabha today.

2694. (23-8-2007) NEW DELHI : Bharat Sanchar Nigam Ltd as a policy does not provide GSM handsets to its subscribers and does not procure the same. However, present tender of 45.5 M GSM lines of BSNL is operational and an Advance Purchase Order has been issued to successful bidder. The equipment procurement efforts for BSNL's new mobile network expansion project received a setback with one of the bidder approaching the Hon'ble High Court against the decision of BSNL rejecting his bid. BSNL's loss is merely on account of opportunity lost. An APO has since been issued to one of the successful bidders. The bidder has accepted the offer by submitting Purchase Bank Guarantee (PBG) with some conditions, which are under evaluation. Equipment is expected to be progressively available in about six months time from the date of acceptance of Purchase Order. This information was given by Dr.Shakeel Ahmad, Minister of State in the Ministry of Communications and Information Technology in the Rajya Sabha today in a written reply to a question by Shri Sitaram Yechury.

2695. (23-8-2007) NEW DELHI : A project titled 'Integrated Sewerage Project' has been approved for Bhubaneshwar under Sewerage sector by Central Sanctioning and Monitoring Committee in its meeting held on 22.2.07 at an approved cost of Rs.49891.35 lakh. Central share committed for this project is Rs.39913.08 lakh (being 80%). Out of this, a sum of Rs.5158.40 lakh has been released towards first instalment on 24.04.07. The implementation period of this project is 48 months. A project titled 'Conservation of the Heritage Tank of Bindusagar' has also been approved for Bhubaneshwar under 'Urban Renewal Sector' by Central Sanctioning and Monitoring Committee in its meeting held on 9.02.07 at an approved cost of Rs.601.31 lakh. Central share committed for this project is Rs.481.04 lakh (being 80%). Out of this, a sum of Rs.120.26 lakh has been released towards first instalment on 7.3.07. The implementation period of this project of this project is 24 months. These are not entirely centrally funded projects and only 80 percent of the approved cost is provided as Additional Central Assistance as central share. This information was given by Shri Ajay Maken, Minister of State in the Ministry of Urban Development in the Rajya Sabha today in a written reply to a question by Shri B.J.Panda and Ms. Pramila Bohidar.

2696. (23-8-2007) NEW DELHI : The Wildlife (Protection) Act enacted in the year 1972 has been amended from time to time, the latest being in the year 2006. The amendments in the Act are resorted to as per the exigency and requirements of the matter. There is no plan to overhaul the "Wildlife Protection Act, 1972." Under the provisions of the Wildlife Protection Act, 1972, there is no earmarking of funds for relocation of the villagers. However, financial assistance is provided to the State Governments under the Centrally Sponsored Schemes, viz, 'Assistance to Development of National Parks & Sanctuaries', 'Project Tiger' and 'Project Elephant' for relocation of villagers. This information was given by the Minister of State in the Ministry of Environment and Forests, Shri S.Regupathy in a written reply to question by Shri Vijay J.Darda and Shri Gireesh Kumar Singh :in the Rajya Sabha today.

2697. (23-8-2007) NEW DELHI: A crucial two-day meeting of the central committee of the Communist Party of India (Marxist) began here on Wednesday, amid indications that it would reiterate the Left parties' stand on the India-U.S. civilian nuclear agreement asking the United Progressive Alliance (UPA) government to "press the pause button" on the deal. "All we are asking from the government is to press the pause button on the deal and properly evaluate all the implications and objections before proceeding further," a senior CPI(M) leader said. The CPI(M) central committee meeting, convened in the wake of the ongoing stand-off between the Left parties and the government over the Indo-U.S. civilian nuclear deal, is discussing all aspects of the deal as well as taking a critical look at the government response so far and the prevailing political situation in the country.

2698. (23-8-2007) NEW DELHI : Ministry of Power have issued Energy Conservation Building Code (ECBC) for new commercial buildings having a connected load of 500 KW or above, has been launched. The major components of the building which are being addressed through this Code are walls, roofs and windows; lighting system; air-conditioning system; electrical distribution system; and water heating and pumping system. The Energy Conservation Building Code is intended for new commercial buildings only and is not applicable for residential buildings. The ECBC has been framed for addressing the energy performance standards for new commercial buildings and therefore, are not applicable to residential buildings. This information was given by Shri Ajay Maken, Minister of State in the Ministry of Urban Development in the Rajya Sabha today in a written reply to a question by Shri Santosh Bagrodia and Shri Harish Rawat.

2699. (23-8-2007) NEW DELHI : The Government of India launched Jawaharlal Nehru National Urban Renewal Mission (JNNURM) on 3rd December 2005 aiming at reforms driven, fast track, planned development of identified cities with focus on efficiency in urban infrastructure/services delivery mechanism, community participation and accountability of Urban Local Bodies (ULBs)/Parastatals towards citizen. A sum of Rs.50,000 crore has been committed as Additional Central Assistance from Government of India under JNNURM for its two sub-missions, namely, Urban Infrastructure & Governance (Sub-Mission-I) and Basic Services for the Urban Poor (Sub-Mission-II) and two omnibus schemes, namely, Urban Infrastructure Development Scheme for Small and Medium Towns (UIDSSMT) and Integrated Housing and Slum Development Programme (IHSDP). The Mission is for a period of seven years beginning from 2005-06. Decision to keep number of cities covered under JNNURM around 60 was taken with the approval of Government. However, cities which are not covered under Sub-Mission-I Urban Infrastructure & Governance of the JNNURM have been covered under UIDSSMT of JNNURM. This information was given by Shri Ajay Maken, Minister of State in the Ministry of Urban Development in the Rajya Sabha today in a written reply to a question by Shri Kanjibhai Patel and Shri Keshubhai S.Patel.

2700. (23-8-2007) NEW DELHI : Import of highly pollutant useless material is not permitted as per the Hazardous Waste (Management and Handling) Rules, 1989 as amended in 2000 and 2003 notified under the Environment (Protection) Act, 1986. import of hazardous wastes is regulated under rules 11 to 14 of the said rules. According to these rules, any import of hazardous waste into India for dumping and disposal is prohibited. Any hazardous waste containing or contaminated with the hazardous waste categories listed in Schedule 8 of these rule is also prohibited for imports. However, imports of such wastes other than those listed in Schedule 8 of these rules, is permitted into the country for recycling by the registered recyclers, registered with the Central Pollution Control Board and having environmentally sound management facilities for reprocessing such wastes. The import of hazardous waste is also regulated under the Export Import Policy of the Ministry of Commerce and Industry, Government of India. This information was given by the Minister of State in the Ministry of Environment and Forests,

Shri Namo Narayan Meena in a written reply to question by Shri Ram Jethmalani and Dr. Murli Manohar Joshi the Rajya Sabha today.

2701. (23-8-2007) NEW DELHI : A part of the radio frequency spectrum required for mobile services is in use by Defence services. The Defence services have been requested to release this spectrum for growth of public mobile telecom services by shifting some of their wireless links between fixed locations, to alternate media like Optical Fibre Cable. The spectrum so released by the Defence services would be allotted for growth of mobile services, to the new as well as existing mobile service providers appropriately. This information was given by Dr.Shakeel Ahmad, Minister of State in the Ministry of Communications and Information Technology in the Rajya Sabha today in a written reply to a question by Shri Virendra Bhatia.

2702. (23-8-2007) NEW DELHI : As per Society of Indian Automobile Manufacturers (SIAM) during the year 2006-2007, a total number of 12.38 lakh passenger cars were produced by the Indian Automobile Industry. During the first quarter of current year (April to July, 2007), a total number of 4.47 lakh passenger cars have been produced by the industry.

2703. (23-8-2007) NEW DELHI : As per Public Enterprises Survey, 2005-06, the Central Public Sector Enterprises (CPSEs) had a cash and bank balance of Rs. 1,50,680 crore, Rs. 1,29,428 crore and Rs. 84,979 crore as on 31.3.2006, 31.3.2005 and 31.3.2004 respectively. Boards of concerned CPSEs take decision for deployment of surplus funds in specific areas as stipulated in the guidelines issued by the Government from time to time. Recently the Government have decided to allow Navratna and Miniratna CPSEs to invest their surplus funds in SEBI regulated public sector mutual funds subject to the condition that not more than 30% of the available surplus funds would be invested by these CPSEs in public sector equity mutual funds. Board of Directors of the CPSEs would decide the guidelines, procedures and management control systems for investment in public sector mutual funds in consultation with their administrative Ministries. This information was given by the Minister for Heavy Industries & Public Enterprises, Shri Sontosh Mohan Dev in a written reply to a question in Lok Sabha today.

2704. (23-8-2007) NEW DELHI : The Government has issued guidelines on the appointment of Chief Executives and Functional Directors in sick/loss making Central Public Sector Enterprises (CPSEs) under approved revival package. These guidelines, issued in July 2007 inter alia, state that any Board level incumbent who has contributed exceedingly well in the turn around of the sick CPSE, his tenure may be extended till he attains the age of 65 years and in case of fresh appointment of a Chief Executive or any Functional Director, relaxation of cut-off age for applying, to 62 years, with minimum tenure of 3 years, could be considered. Further, Chief Executives and Functional Directors of these CPSEs would be considered for a lump-sum incentive up to maximum of Rs.10 lakh out of the profits of the CPSE besides usual pay, allowances and perks attached to the post. The incentives to Chief Executives/ Functional Directors will enable the Government to attract Board level executives capable for turning around sick CPSEs and give them continuity of tenure for the revival package to succeed. This information was given by the Minister for Heavy Industries & Public Enterprises, Shri Sontosh Mohan Dev in a written reply to a question in Lok Sabha today.

2705. (23-8-2007) NEW DELHI: Seven years after Bill Clinton spoke in Parliament to a tumultuous reception, it was the turn of another overseas head of state, Japanese Prime Minister Shinzo Abe, to address a joint session of Parliament during which he set out his vision of a "Broader Asia" with India as a prominent participant. Speaking in the Central Hall of Parliament on Wednesday, Mr. Abe called on India to contribute to the concept's success by aligning more closely with Japan on a range of issues. In pursuit of the "Broader Asia" concept, Japan is promoting several other concepts. One of them, in which India would be a crucial element, is building an "arc of freedom and prosperity" along the outer rim of the Euroasian continent. Freedom, democracy and the respect for basic human rights would be the common fundamental values of all participating countries. (Mr. Abe's close aide had said on Tuesday that China needed to work more on the democracy and human rights fronts.) In case Japan and India come together in a strategic relationship, Mr. Abe felt the "Broader Asia" concept would then span the entire Pacific Ocean along with two non-Asian entities, U.S. and Australia.

2706. (23-8-2007) NEW DELHI : Central Public Sector Enterprises (CPSEs) are expected to pay the wages/ salaries and statutory dues to their employees regularly out of their own resources. Government, however, provides financial assistance by way of non-plan loan to certain CPSEs to supplement their efforts for payment of wages and salaries and statutory dues when they are unable to generate enough resources. As per information available, during 2004-05 and 2005-06, Government sanctioned Rs.1804.21 crores for payment of wages and salary and statutory dues to sick/loss making CPSEs. During 2006-07 Government sanctioned Rs.305.51 crores. This information was given by the Minister for Heavy Industries & Public Enterprises, Shri Sontosh Mohan Dev in a written reply to a question in Lok Sabha today.

2707. (23-8-2007) NEW DELHI : The Prime Minister, Dr. Manmohan Singh has approved funding of the Bogibeel Rail-cum Road Bridge and the Rangia-Murkongselek gauge conversion projects at a cost of Rs1980 crores. Additional Budgetary support will be given to the Railways to complete the projects. A detailed milestone map with target dates is to be prepared for these projects with indication of annual requirement of funds. The Ministry of Railways will set up a dedicated fund for these projects to ensure timely implementation. The cost overruns will be funded by the Railways from internal resources. The Prime

Minister has directed that a uniform funding pattern, on the same lines, be extended to the remaining five-sanctioned National Projects for the North East Region. A dedicated fund called the " North East Rail Development Fund" will be set up for the timely completion of these projects. The projects will be completed in five years. The Ministry of Railways will submit a proposal for the approval of the Cabinet.

2708. (23-8-2007) NEW DELHI : As per the Society of Indian Automobile Manufacturers (SIAM), during April-July, 2007, the domestic sale of passenger and commercial vehicle segments has registered a positive growth rate of 12.6% and 3.5% respectively while that of two-wheelers and three wheelers segment has registered negative growth rate of 7.3% and 9.2% respectively.

2709. (23-8-2007) NEW DELHI : The Minister of Tourism and Culture Smt. Ambika Soni informed the Lok Sabha today that her ministry promotes a number of tourism related themes including Monsoon Tourism through its Incredible India Media Campaign in the International markets as well as through the India tourism Offices abroad. In a written reply she said, there is no separate data regarding tourists who have come for Monsoon Tourism.

2710. (23-8-2007) NEW DELHI : The Minister for Tourism and Culture Smt. Ambika Soni informed the Lok Sabha today that the Government proposes to create anintegrated bibliographic database of National Library, Kolkata, Central Secretariat Library, New Delhi and other major Libraries. In a written reply she said, towards this end, electronic bibliographical database is being created at select libraries which will be subsequently linked. The project is anticipated to cost about 10 crores during the 11th Plan. The Minister said, the project is in its preliminary stage.

2711. (23-8-2007) NEW DELHI : The Minister for Tourism and Culture Smt. Ambika Soni informed the Lok Sabha today that as per the requirement of the UNESCO World Heritage Conventions, 1972, the World Heritage Committee has established a list of World Heritage Sites considering the outstanding universal value of the sites nominated by the states parties. No network is launched by UNESCO for preserving living heritage of Indian cities. In a written reply she said, Archaeological Survey of India protects and maintains 3667 centrally protected monuments/sites, including 19 World Heritage sites located in different parts of the country. Activities of conservation, preservation and environment development are undertaken as per the available resources. To contain the effect of development around the protected monuments/sites, a notification was issued by the Government in 1992, declaring 100 meters from the protected limits of the protected monuments / sites as prohibited area, where no construction / mining activity is allowed, and further 200 meter area beyond the prohibited limits has been declared as regulated area wherein height of construction is regulated and owners /agencies are required to obtain N.O.C. from the Archaeological Survey of India. Further, in order to prevent encroachment, fencing is provided around the protected area of the monument/site, wherever necessary.

2712. (23-8-2007) NEW DELHI : The Minister of Tourism and Culture Smt. Ambika Soni has said that As per the existing provision, Pakistani nationals consisting a group of not less than ten persons are entitled for fourteen days non-extendable group tourist visa. However, in the proposed revised draft visa agreement between India and Pakistan, which is yet to be finalized by Ministry of Home Affairs, there is a provision that Group Tourist Visa can be used by the tourists as well as pilgrims of the two countries. Smt. Soni gave this information in a written reply in the Lok Sabha today.

2713. (23-8-2007) NEW DELHI : The Tourism and Culture Minister Smt. Ambika Soni has said the tourism sector is now being considered as an industry which would create a large number of employment opportunity as well as help in uplifting the standards of the local population. Inaugurating the first ever Hotel Association of India Conclave, 2007 here today she said according to a study, 42 million jobs have been generated directly or indirectly in past three years through tourism. She said we need 150,000 rooms in all categories of hotels by 2010 and for services in these rooms more than 2 lakh jobs have to be created. Smt. Soni said her Ministry has worked out the requirement of Tourist Guides till 2010 in consultation with the Travel Trade and an action plan has been launched to meet the goal. A scheme has also been launched to induct part-time guides so that we can cater to special interest groups in various foreign languages. These guides would be specialists in their respective fields and the educational qualifications expected from them is either a doctorate or a published paper in a university. She called upon the Hotel Industry to create a pool of young Tourist Guides under the "Earn While You Learn" scheme of the Ministry to meet the growing demand of Guides. The Minister said our endevaour should be to attract a large number of foreign tourist as well as give due focus to promotion of domestic tourism within the country. Hence, with the objective to provide better services to the tourists and to inculcate a sense of responsibility among the local population, a capacity building scheme has been launched under which the service providers, like the immigration staff, custom staff, porters, tax drivers and police etc. are being trained in various spheres so that our product can match the expectations of the demanding tourists. She said air, rail, surface transport and road connectivity, sewage disposal and sanitation must be on the top priority of all the stake-holders in the tourism sector to strengthen the sector. Smt. Soni said she has written to all the Chief Ministers about creating land banks to build new hotels in view of the shortage of land and high prices. She said, so far Haryana has responded positively and Uttar Pradesh has started work in this direction. The Minister said the Government is open to expansion of tourism sector through public private partnership. She said the hotel industry should come forward to adopt atleast two historical monuments per hotel for illuminating. The two-day meeting will discuss among other things, strategy: balancing development with operations and other matters related to the hotel industry.

2714. (23-8-2007) NEW DELHI : Retail prices of essential commodities monitored by the Department of Consumer Affairs at four metropolitan cities have remained stable or shown mixed trend in the week ending 17.8.2007. Prices of atta, sugar, vanaspati, tea, milk and salt were steady over the week. Prices increased in respect of wheat by 50 paise per kg at Mumbai, groundnut oil by Re. 1 per kg at Delhi and Rs. 2 per kg at Chennai. Potato prices rose by Rs. 2 per kg at Delhi and Chennai and 50 paise per kg at Kolkata. Onion prices increased by Rs. 2 per kg at Delhi and Chennai and Rs. 1 per kg at Mumbai. Prices declined in the case of gram dal by Re. 1 per kg at Kolkatta, tur dal by Rs. 2 per kg at Mumbai and Kolkata, groundnut oil by Re. 1 per kg at Kolkata and mustard oil by Rs. 2 per kg at Kolkata. At Delhi prices of rice, atta, tur dal, tea loose and salt remained steady over the month, sugar and milk over the fortnight and gram dal, mustard oil and vanaspati over the week.

2715. (23-8-2007) NEW DELHI : The number of children who have been withdrawn from hazardous jobs and have been admitted to special schools under the National Child Labour Project (NCLP) Scheme has more than doubled during the last three years. Their number has increased from 1,67,825 in 2004-05 to 3,37,269 in 2006-07. These children in the age group of 9 to 14 years are provided with accelerated bridging education and other benefits like stipend, midday meal, vocational training, health check-ups, etc. in special schools for a maximum period of three years to enable them to join regular mainstream education system.

2716. (23-8-2007) NEW DELHI : Ministry of Steel had constituted a Committee under the Chairmanship of Director (Finance), Rashtriya Ispat Nigam Limited (RINL) to submit a Status Paper on "Securing Coking Coal Supplies for Steel Authority of India Limited (SAIL) and Rashtriya Ispat Nigam Limited (RINL)". Based on the recommendations of the Committee, an Empowered Special Purpose Vehicle (SPV) comprising Steel Authority of India Limited (SAIL), Coal India Limited (CIL), Rashtriya Ispat Nigam Limited (RINL), National Thermal Power Corporation (NTPC) and National Mineral Development Corporation (NMDC) has been proposed for incorporation for the purpose of acquisition of coal mining companies/properties in overseas territories. The proposed SPV would specifically cater to meet the requirements of coking and thermal coal of the participant companies. SAIL and RINL are also making efforts to acquire coking coal mines abroad. Discussions are underway. However, no proposals have been finalized so far. Both SAIL and RINL are currently purchasing coking coal against long term and spot coking coal contracts. No serious difficulty in obtaining the requisite quantities of coal has been faced so far. However, acquisition of mines would confer overall long term advantage to both the companies. Efforts are being made to identify suitable coal mining companies/properties in countries from where landed cost of coal to India would be competitive. SAIL is in discussions with its long term suppliers of coking coal in Australia and New Zealand for acquisition of equity stakes in their existing or new mine development projects. RINL is also negotiating with parties in Australia and USA. No specific proposals have been finalized so far. This information was given by the Minister of State for Steel, Dr. Akhilesh Das in a written reply in the Lok Sabha today.

2717. (23-8-2007) NEW DELHI : National Pharmaceutical Pricing Authority (NPPA) regularly takes action against pharma companies who do not implement the prices fixed/notified by NPPA under the provisions of Drugs (Prices Control) Order, 1995 (DPCO,95) and this is a continuous and ongoing process. Since, inception in Aug' 1997, NPPA has raised a total demand of Rs. 1427.37 crore for recovery towards overcharged amount in 425 cases, under the provisions of DPCO' 1995 read with Essential Commodities Act' 1955. NPPA has recovered Rs. 100.43 crore (upto 31.7.07) from the defaulting companies. NPPA continues to take appropriate action regularly for recovery of the overcharged amount. The major amount is under litigation and recovery of the same depends upon the outcome of the Court cases. Since inception of NPPA (August, 1997) till date, NPPA is handling/dealing 75 court cases filed by Pharma Companies against NPPA/Union of India in various parts of the country with respect to recovery of overcharged amount. An estimated overcharged amount of Rs. 1333.85 crores is being contested by the said Pharma units against which NPPA has recovered Rs. 81.14 crore (upto 31.7.2007). NPPA continues to take regular and appropriate action for recovery of overcharged amount. In some cases, recovery is affected, due to orders from the courts such as the Hon'ble High Courts and Hon'ble Supreme Court of India. This information was given by the Minister of State for Chemicals & Fertilisers and Parliamentary Affairs Shri B.K. Handique in a written reply in the Lok Sabha today.

2718. (23-8-2007) NEW DELHI : The Union Rural Development Minister, Dr. Raghuvansh Prasad Singh has said that the National Rural Employment Guarantee Scheme (NREGS) has to be monitored very closely by the people's representatives. The people's participation and monitoring by the elected representatives will make it a highly successful programme of the Government of India to make the dreams of 'Bharat Nirman' a reality. He said that the programme has already been implemented in 330 districts of the country. Dr. Singh said that the District Level Vigilance Committees are doing a very good job for awareness generation and ensuring the transparency and accountability of rural development programmes. He requested the Members of Parliament to play a cardinal role in successful implementation of all the poverty eradication programmes being implemented by the Government in the rural areas of the country. He laid special emphasis on National Rural Employment Guarantee Scheme (NREGA), Pradhan Mantri Gram Sadak Yojana (PMGSY), Total Sanitation Campaign(TSC) and Accelerated Rural Water Supply Programme (ARWSP). The Minister said that only with the successful implementation of these programmes we will be able to eradicate poverty and to provide basic comfort to all our people, which will ultimately lead to a developed India by 2020.

2719. (23-8-2007) NEW DELHI : It has been decided by the Government that smaller airlines having 7 services or less to India may be exempted from the Mandated Commercial Agreement, w.e.f. 1st January 2008.This information was given by Shri Praful Patel, Minister for Civil Aviation in a written reply to a question in the Parliament today. In December, 2004 it was decided that all existing Government Mandated Commercial Agreements would be reviewed and phased out over the next five years and all new operations by foreign carriers, both on new destinations as well as on existing routes would be free from the obligations of Mandated Commercial Agreement. The decision for smaller airlines was taken subsequently. This new system is expected to bring about a level playing field between the national carriers and the foreign carriers on the international operations. Answering to whether after doing away with the existing system the air fares were likely to come down, the Minister replied that while air fares are determined by market forces, it would be reasonable to expect that the airlines would be in a position to lower the fares once the Mandated Commercial Agreements cease to exist.

2720. (23-8-2007) NEW DELHI : The Directorate General of Civil Aviation (DGCA) has received 37 proposals for setting up flying training institutes in various parts of the country. This information was given by Shri Praful Patel, Minister for Civil Aviation in a written reply to a question in the Parliament today. Of the 37 proposals received by the DGCA, 5 are from Maharashtra, 5 from Tamil Nadu, 4 from Rajasthan, 3 each from Bihar, Punjab, Andhra Pradesh, Haryana and Gujarat, 2 each from Karnataka and Chhatisgarh and 1 each from Uttranchal, West Bengal, Madhya Pradesh and Orissa. These proposals are being processed by the DGCA. There are 42 flying training institutes in the country of which 26 are operational which provide training for various licences like Private Pilot Licence, Commercial Pilot Licence etc. 14 of these operational institutes are run by various State Governments, while the Indira Gandhi Rashtriya Uran Akademi (IGRUA) is an autonomous society under the Central Government. The remaining 11 institutes are run by private entrepreneurs. All the institutes have to conform to the requirements laid down by DGCA. 16 flying training institutes were found to be not conforming to the guidelines laid down by DGCA. Their licences have therefore not been renewed. These institutes have been advised by DGCA to take corrective measures for their revival.

2721. (23-8-2007) NEW DELHI : Based on specific intelligence inputs, the Investigation wing of the Income Tax department yesterday recovered Rs.4.92 crore cash in a search conducted on persons / concerns engaged in mobilizing deposits for investment schemes and auto finance at Thane in Maharashtra. The cash was found stacked in the residence of an employee of the main concern. Further investigations and scrutiny of seized documents are in progress.

2722. (24-8-2007) NEW DELHI : The Defence Minister Shri A K Antony and his Japanese counterpart Ms Yuriko Koike have expressed happiness on the enhanced defence cooperation between the two countries in the recent years. During their meeting in New Delhi today, both sides reaffirmed their commitment to further enhance this cooperation in various fields like maritime security, research and development and exchange of information on technology aspects. Japan is participating in the multilateral naval exercise scheduled to be held early next month. The Japanese Defence Minister informed Shri Antony about the role played by Japan in the fight against international terrorism. Shri Antony sharing the views of his counterpart, also emphasised upon the need to combat terrorism of any kind. Japan is sending their military officers for training in Indian Defence institutions like the National Defence College. Japan also invited Indian representatives to participate in the Tokyo Defence Forum. Earlier in the day Ms. Koike paid homage to the martyrs at Amar Jawan Jyoti and was accorded a ceremonial inter-services Guard of Honour at defence headquarters. The three Service Chiefs also called on the visiting dignitary. Shri Antony hosted a dinner in the honour of Ms Koike last evening.

2723. (24-8-2007) NEW DELHI : Country's first Speed Post Call Centre with a four digit Toll Free Code was inaugurated at the Delhi Postal Circle here today. Smt. K. Noorjehan, Member (Operations & Marketing) Postal Services Board inaugurated the Call centre. Today is the 21st Anniversary of the introduction of Speed Post Service by the Department of Posts. Two departmental Mail Motor Service Vehicles with illuminated advertisements on Speed Post and Business Post Services were also flagged off on the occasion. The Call Centre is located at Speed Post Centre, Bhai Vir Singh Marg, New Delhi-110001. The exclusive Toll Free numbers allocated to the Call Centre are 1256 for local calls and 1800-11-9888 for national calls. The Call Centre established to provide value added services will cater to the demands of all the prospective customers to pick up their Speed Post articles at their doorstep throughout Delhi. In addition to free pick up service, the Speed Post Call Centre will provide all basic information regarding Speed Post Service and respond to customers' queries relating to Speed Post rates, quality of service, destinations covered, delivery norms etc. It will also intimate the status of Speed Post articles booked under the Track and Trace system and register complaints of the customers. The Call centre will be manned round the clock by departmental officials.

2724. (24-8-2007) NEW DELHI : Adequate steps have been taken to ensure confidentiality of information relating to Permanent Account Number. No instances have come to the notice of the Government, wherein data relating to PAN is leaked out, thus putting the holder of PAN to a great harassment from bank agents. This information was given by Shri S.S. Palanimanickam, Minister of State for Finance in reply to a question raised by Shri Kinjarapu Yerrannaidu in Lok Sabha today.

2725. (24-8-2007) NEW DELHI : Excise duty exemption schemes have been extended by the Government for specified goods produced by specified units in the States of Jammu and Kashmir, Uttarakhand, Himachal Pradesh, Sikkim and North East Region and Kutch district of Gujarat, subject to certain conditions. All the above exemptions, except that for Kutch district of Gujarat, have been extended as per specific Industrial Policies announced by the Government. In the case of Kutch district of Gujarat, however, the exemption was given following an earthquake in January, 2001 leading to loss of industrial assets. The exemption is for a period of ten years from the date of commencement of commercial production by eligible units located in NER, Jammu & Kashmir, Uttarakhand and Himachal Pradesh and for five years in case of Kutch.

2726. (24-8-2007) NEW DELHI : As on 31st July, 2007, Public Sector Banks (PSBs) have 115 branches abroad, consisting of Punjab National Bank-1, Allahabad Bank-1, State Bank of India-33, Bank of India-22, Bank of Baroda-42, Indian Bank-3, Indian Overseas Bank-6, Uco Bank-4, Canara Bank-2 and Syndicate Bank-1. Reserve bank of India (RBI) has received applications from 3 PSBs for opening overseas branches in 7 countries viz., South Africa, Germany, Oman, Bahrain, Qatar, UAE and New Zealand. RBI has not received any complaint in regard to functioning of these branches from regulators of the host countries. RBI monitors the functioning of Indian banks' branches abroad by way of Off-site monitoring through quarterly returns, quarterly letters from the Chief Executives of the banks and monthly compliance certificates from the banks reporting incidents of overseas regulatory violations, if any, etc. Further, in case of no violation, banks are required to certify to RBI that no violation on any regulations had been reported/observed in any of the countries where the concerned bank has its branch/ office. RBI also carries out On-site inspection of these branches occasionally. This information was given by Shri Pawan Kumar Bansal, Minister of State for Finance in reply to a question raised by Shri Asaduddin Owaisi in the Lok Sabha today.

2727. (24-8-2007) NEW DELHI : Government of India has not received any proposal from North Eastern States for more loans for Centrally Sponsored Schemes. The States have only been requesting permission to raise the loan component (10% of Normal Central Assistance/Additional Central Assistance/ Non Lapsable Central Pool of Resources etc.) from the market. Whenever the State Governments have requested, Government of India have given its consent under Article 293(3) of the Constitution of India for raising the loans from the market. This information was given by Shri Pawan Kumar Bansal, Minister of State for Finance in reply to a question raised by Shri Kiren Rijiju in the Lok Sabha today.

2728. (24-8-2007) NEW DELHI : WHO is Pandit K. Santanam of Lahore? Few Indians and Pakistanis will probably know the answer today 58 years after the death of the Tamilian Congress Leader, who made Lahore in the undivided Punjab his home in the early 1900's and lived there. He was a close associate of Lala Lajpat Rai and had worked with both Hindu and Muslim leaders of the freedom movement. Pandit Santanam's life and times are all the more relevant in the context of current efforts at improving relations between India and Pakistan and the ever-increasing people-to-people contact. Every year on April 13, as Punjab celebrates its festival of Baisaki, the nation remembers the Jallianwala Bagh massacre of April 13, 1919. But the one man who dug out details of the massacre to present them to the outside world is hardly ever remembered. He was Pandit Santanam of Lahore, originally a native of Kumbakonam, a temple town on the banks of Cauvery in Tamil Nadu. Born into a conservative Tamil Brahmin family on August 25, 1885, Santanam lost his parents in childhood. He was helped by his elder brothers to go to England for higher studies. Santanam studied Economics and Law in Cambridge. A meeting with Lala Lajpat Rai in London resulted in a life-long association.

2729. (24-8-2007) NEW DELHI : The Department of Health in the Ministry of Health & Family Welfare, Government of India has issued a draft Prevention of Food Adulteration (Amendment) Rules, 2007 published vide notification GSR 451 (E) dated 28.06.2007 in the Gazette of India, section 3, sub-section (i) Extraordinary dated 28.06.2007. The amendments in rules are in respect of labeling of chewing tobacco, condition for sale of package food without staple pins, lowering the limit of caffeine in carbonated water and amendment to standards of dehydrated garlic and dehydrated onion. The draft rules have been published for inviting objections/suggestions within sixty day's time. The comments may be forwarded to Secretary, Ministry of Health & Family Welfare, Nirman Bhawan, New Delhi-11. The details of the notification shall be available on the Ministry of Health & Family Welfare's.

2730. (24-8-2007) NEW DELHI : The Government has formulated a National Urban Transport Policy (NUTP) in April, 2006 for urban area which envisages integration across different modes and operators of public transport system so as to provide seamless travel across different modes and operators. This information was given by Shri Ajay Maken, Minister of State in the Ministry of Urban Development in the Lok Sabha today in a written reply to a question by Shri Anandrao V. Adsul.

2731. (24-8-2007) NEW DELHI : Master Plan for Delhi (MPD) 2021, as notified on 7.2.2007, provides for regularization of construction upto 100% ground coverage and 350 FAR which were already existing as on September 22, 2006 on plot measuring upto 175 sqm. on payment of charges, as notified. However, the Hon'bla Supreme Court in the matter of "M.C. Mehta vs. Union of India & Others" has restrained MCD from granting permission for construction of additional floor (third floor) in plotted development except those cases where construction was permissible on the basis of the Master Plan-2001 (notified on 1.8.1990), as modified in 1998. Regularization is subject to payment of charges. MCD has intimated that no action is being taken against buildings which have been got regularized as per the provisions of MPD-2021. This information was given by Shri Ajay Maken, Minister of State in the Ministry of Urban Development in the Lok Sabha today in a written reply to a question by Shri P.Rajendran.

2732. (24-8-2007) NEW DELHI : The Delhi Development Authority (DDA) has informed that the allotment of land is pending in the case of about 238 Cooperative Group Housing Societies in Delhi. DDA has further informed that as per Rule 6 of the Delhi Development Authority (Disposal of Developed Nazul Land) Rules, 1981, the allotment of land to Cooperative Group Housing Societies is governed by the seniority determined on the basis of registration of the Societies with the office of Registrar Cooperative Societies (RCS), Government of NCT of Delhi (GNCTD) and verification of membership by that office. The recommendation of RCS, GNCTD for allotment of land to those societies against which no criminality has been found by CBI has not yet been received in DDA. This information was given by Shri Ajay Maken, Minister of State in the Ministry of Urban Development in the Lok Sabha today in a written reply to a question by Shri Mohan Jena.

2733. (24-8-2007) NEW DELHI : There is scope to increase the area under coastal aquaculture and thereby the production of shrimp by bringing in an additional area of about one lakh hectare to produce about one lakh tonnes of shrimp in the next five years. However, no target in terms of value can be fixed for the next five years due to the fluctuations in the shrimp price in the international market and the exchange rate of rupee.

2734. (24-8-2007) NEW DELHI : Contract farming is practiced in various parts of the country for crops like sugarcane, cotton, tea, coffee, etc. The main feature of contract farming is that farmers grow selected crops under a buy-back agreement with an agency engaged in trading or processing. By now, in 17 States/ Union Territories, relevant provisions have been made in the concerned Agricultural Produce Marketing Regulation Acts for providing a legal framework to contract farming and in seven States/ Union Territories there are no regulatory laws preventing such by-back arrangements. However, in other States also various forms of contract farming do exist in practice. The exact extent of land covered under contract farming in the country is not known. The contract farming is reportedly beneficial to the farmers as it takes care of price risk and also helps in mitigating production risk. In order to make contract farming arrangements beneficial for the farmers, as well as, the sponsoring companies under a legal framework, suitable provisions were included in the Model Agricultural Produce Market Committeo (APMC) Act formulated by the Ministry of Agriculture in 2003 and circulated to State Governments for considering suitable amendments in their concerned Act by adopting those provisions. The Model Act circulated by the

Ministry is suggestive in nature, and, since Agriculture is a State subject, it is for the State Governments to decide on the implementation of the contract farming arrangements in their State. This information was given in the Rajya Sabha today by the Minister of State for Agriculture, Shri Kanti Lal Bhuria in a written reply.

2735. (24-8-2007) NEW DELHI : The President,Smt. Pratibha Devisingh Patil has asked the students of the Villa Marie Degree College for Women, Hyderabad to give back to society. The students and staff of the college called on her at Rashtrapati Bhavan today. The President said the girls could engage in social service along side their careers, as they have the benefit of education. The students are on a visit to New Delhi to have a practical exposure to government, after learning about the theory of government in their college course. During their visit they have so far visited the Lok Sabha and the Rajya Sabha to see their functioning. Smt. Patil said it is very necessary for educated women to spread the message that educating the girl child is essential especially in rural areas and in the urban slums, so that their condition is improved. Tee President observed that today educated women from urban gbackgrounds are making their mark in various fields. It is necessary for educated women to be socially aware and help those who are not fortunate to have education. The President also emphasised that women must work hand in hand and shoulder to shoulder with men. Earlier the students of the college were taken on a guided tour of Rashtrapati Bhavan, which the President has described as the People's House.

2736. (24-8-2007) NEW DELHI : The services in the Copper Mining industry will continue as a public utility under the Industrial Disputes Act, 1947 for another six months with immediate effect. In a notification issued here today, the Labour Ministry said that this has been done in public interest. The employees in this industry, as a result, would among other things be required to give notice to their employer six weeks in advance of proceeding on strike so that conciliatory proceedings could be started. During the conciliatory proceedings and seven days after their completion, the employees cannot go on strike.

2737. (24-8-2007) NEW DELHI : Central Potato Research Institute, Shimla, has developed two new potato varieties, Kufri Himsona for cultivation in the Himachal Pradesh Hills and Kufri Sadabahar for Uttar Pradesh plains. Both the varieties have been released by the respective state agencies. Kufri Himsona, a processing variety, contains high levels of dry matter and low sugar content. It produces excellent white chips on frying. On-line' testing of Kufri Himsona in the industry produced excellent flawless chips. Cultivation of this variety in the hills of Himachal Pradesh will prove to be boon to potato farmers particularly in Kangra region. Till now, this region was dependent on Kufri Jyoti variety which has now become susceptible to late blight. Kufri Himsona has very high degree of late blight resistance. In spite of release of three exclusive varieties for potato processing by CPRI for cultivation in the plains *i.e.* Kufri Chipsona-1, Kufri Chipsona-2 and

Kufri Chipsona-3, there was urgent need for development of a suitable processing variety for cultivation in the hills so as to maintain round the year availability of raw material for processing units located in the plains. The cultivation of Kufri Sadabahar will boost potato production in Uttar Pradesh which has already the record of highest potato production in the country. New table potato variety Kufri Sadabahar produces more than 10% higher yield over Kufri Bahar. The variety is capable of yielding about 35-40 tones/hectare under optimum agronomical practices. The added advantage of this variety is field resistance to late blight. CPRI released white skin potato variety Kufri Bahar in 1980 for cultivation in plains of Uttar Pradesh. It is the most popular variety of the State occupying as much as nearly 70 per cent of potato area in the state of UP. Though the farmers are satisfied with the productivity of this variety, it is susceptible to late blight.

2738. (24-8-2007) NEW DELHI : Following is the text of the speech delivered by the Minister of State for Defence Shri M M Pallam Raju at the Seminar on 'Defence Offset Policy: Opportunities For IT & Electronics Industry'. "With the opening of the Indian economy since 1990s, there has been a remarkable growth in the industrial and core sectors. Foreign Companies are now increasingly looking at India as an attractive investment destination. Global players are outsourcing work orders to the Indian companies, benefiting from the high degree of skills available here especially in the Information Technology sector. Doing business in India is also proving to be more cost-effective for the foreign companies. I would like to thank CII for inviting me to address today's seminar on offsets. As a logical outcome of economic liberalisation initiated in 1991, the private sector industry in India is playing a greater role in production and development of different equipment and products in the country. I am confident that this increased participation of the industry, now also in the defence production, would enable us to establish a world-class defence manufacturing industrial base in the country, comprising of public and private sectors, which would be technologically self-reliant to be able to meet the short term and long term requirements of the defence forces. Such a strong industrial base would also assure life cycle support including periodic up-gradation to enhance operational life of the equipment and to develop capabilities in the defence Industry for technological upgrade of various existing weapon systems. In the Union Budget of 2007-2008, Rs. 96,000 crore is earmarked for national defence. Within the Defence Budget, about Rs 42,000 crore is under the capital head and would be spent on "acquisitions" which means buying new weapon systems and equipment. This also includes acquisitions and procurement from DPSUs. Of the remaining amount also, which is earmarked under the revenue head, a portion would be spent on "purchases", which relate to buying of spares, general stores, fuel, clothing, food and medical stores etc. As is evident, we are talking of a large scale defence acquisition programme. If a major share of the defence purchases and acquisition could be made from within the country, this would have a salutary effect on the overall economic growth and create more employment; saving valuable foreign exchange as also reduce dependence on foreign sources for strategic requirements; provide benefits in terms of R&D; technological spin offs, higher industrial growth, enhanced exports etc. This would be a major step towards our national defence preparedness.

2739. (24-8-2007) NEW DELHI : Government will ensure a level playing field for private sector in defence manufacturing, the Minister of State for Defence, Shri MM Pallam Raju told a seminar in New Delhi today. Encouraging private sector to take advantage of the Defence Offset Policy, he said foreign vendors in big ticket defence deals were free to choose an Indian partner. In the union budget for the year ending March 2008, nearly 42,000 crores (over $10 billion) would be spent on buying weapons, systems and equipment. The Confederation of Indian Industry (CII) estimates India will spend about $45 billion in arms purchases, making it amongst the most attractive defence markets in the world. Benefits to the tune of 10,000 crore rupees are expected to accrue to the Indian industry as a result of the new offset policy, as spelled out in the Defence Procurement Procedure, 2006. Shri Pallam Raju said the aim was to build such indigenous capabilities in defence industry that would be export oriented over a period of time. Interacting with entrepreneurs, Shri PK Rastogi, Additional Secretary (Department of Defence Production), Defence Ministry, admitted exports by just a couple of defence PSUs were still a small fraction of the country's huge defence budget of 96,000 crore rupees. The minister earlier released the book, "Indian Defence Procurement Opportunities-A Guide", written by Major General Bhupinder Verma. Over a hundred entrepreneurs attende the day-long seminar on "The Defence Offset Policy: Opportunities for Indian IT and electronics industry", orgainsed jointly by the Defence Offset Facilitation Agency (DOFA) and CII. The DOFA was set up by the Defence Ministry in September last year to act as bridge between Indian defence industry and potential vendors, both foreign and Indian. It also helps private industry obtain industrial license for manufacture of defence products from the Department of Industrial Promotion and Policy (DIPP). There is enormous potential as only 37 such licenses have been granted, Shri Rastogi pointed out.

2740. (24-8-2007) NEW DELHI : The Minister of State for Housing & Urban Poverty Alleviation, Kumari Selja informed the Lok Sabha today, in a written reply to a question by Shri Kashiram Rana and Shri Anjan Kumar M. Yadav that the Target fixed for achievement during the Eleventh Five Year Plan for eradication of poverty viz reducing the headcount ratio of consumption poverty by 10 percentage points has not been changed. The Minister further informed the House that with a view to ameliorate the living conditions of the urban poor, an employment-oriented Urban Poverty Alleviation programme named Swarna Jayanti Shahari Rozgar Yojana (SJSRY), is already being implemented by the Ministry of Housing & Urban Poverty Alleviation on all India basis, with effect from 1.12.1997. The programme strives to provide gainful employment to the urban unemployed and underemployed poor through, firstly, encouraging the setting up of self-employment ventures by those who have not studied beyond 9th standard and, secondly, by providing wage employment by utilizing their labour for construction of socially and economically useful public assets.

2741. (24-8-2007) NEW DELHI : Rajiv Gandhi Grameen Vidyutikaran Yojana (RGGVY), a rural electrification programme launched by Government of India in April, 2005 has so far been progressing on the expected lines. As compared to earlier rural electrification scheme where average rate of electrification has been 3,000 villages per year, under RGGVY, 9,819 unelectrified villages were electrified in 2005-06 and, 28,706 unelectrified villages were electrified in 2006-07 besides intensive electrification of around 12,000 electrified villages in these two years. In 2007-08, so far 4,467 unelectrified villages have been electrified and 7,708 electrified villages have been intensively electrified. Also, since the introduction of the scheme in April, 2005, 13 lakh electricity connections have been released to Below Poverty Line (BPL) free of charge.

2742. (24-8-2007) NEW DELHI : The Satluj Jal Vidyut Nigam Limited, the implementing agency of the Rampur Hydro-electric Project, has informed that only one joint venture company of two Chinese firms has submitted its bid for electro-mechanical works of Rampur Hydro-electric Project in Himachal Pradesh. The joint venture is between (i) M/s Harbin Power Engineering Company Ltd., No.-39, Sanda Dongli Road, Dongli District, Harbin, China, and (ii) M/s Harbin Electric Machinery Company Ltd., No.-99, Sanda Dongli Road, Dongli District, Harbin, China. The matters related to security concerns have been deliberated upon in an inter-ministerial meeting with security agencies. Shri Sushilkumar Shinde, Union Power Minister, gave this information in a written reply in Lok Sabha today.

2743. (24-8-2007) NEW DELHI : Production of chemical fertilisers during April-July, 2007 has been of the order of 108.03 Lakh Metric Tonnes (LMT) as against production plan of 119.21 LMT submitted by the producing units for this period in the beginning of the year. Slight decline in production vis-à-vis the plan has been on account of temporary shutdown of plants of some of the producing units due to technical problems, shortage of gas, liquidity problems faced by some of the companies and constraints in availability of inputs like phos. Acid, etc.

2744. (24-8-2007) NEW DELHI : NTPC Ltd. has signed Memorandum of Understanding (MoU) with Bhabha Atomic Research Centre (BARC) on 26.07.2007 for collaborative research to Develop and Deliver Automated Boiler Tube Inspection System for Coal Based Thermal Power Plants. This is a project to develop a prototype crawler for Automated Boiler Tube Inspection in Coal Based Power Station. NTPC Ltd. will supply inspection probes. The BARC will develop the technology and assemble the prototype Automated Boiler Tube Inspection System in their robotic lab at BARC. The prototype will be tested in one of the power stations of NTPC Ltd. Preliminary estimated cost of this collaboration research project is Rs.170 lakhs and total time envisaged for completion of this project is 26 months. Shri Sushilkumar Shinde, Union Power Minister, gave this information in a written reply in Lok Sabha today.

2745. (24-8-2007) NEW DELHI : Out of the proposed XI Plan capacity addition of 78,577 MW, 52,905 MW is proposed to be coal based, of which projects totalling 1350 MW are envisaged to use imported coal. The Ministry of Power has launched an initiative for the development of coal based Ultra Mega Power Projects (UMPPs) each of about 4000 MW capacity. Under the initiative, four pit-head sites and five sites at coastal locations have been identified by the Central Electricity Authority in consultation with the concerned States. The UMPP at Mundra in Gujarat is one of the coastal sites. The developers, that is, M/s. Tata Power Company Ltd. in respect of this project had been selected through a tariff based competitive bidding process, and the Special Purpose Vehicle *i.e.* Coastal Gujarat Power Limited (CGPL) which had been set up for the Project has also been transferred to the developer. CGPL has informed that the contracts have been entered into for supply of boiler and steam turbine generator packages. The Project is expected to give full benefits during the 12th Plan. Shri Sushilkumar Shinde, Union Power Minister, gave this information in a written reply in Lok Sabha today.

2746. (24-8-2007) NEW DELHI : The expansion plan of Rashtriya Ispat Nigam Ltd. (RINL), VSP which is currently under implementation, will enhance the capacity of the plant from the present levels of operation of 3.6 million tonnes to 6.3 million tonnes of liquid steel by March 2010. The approved project cost is Rs. 8692 crore. Concurrently, it is also envisaged to increase the liquid steel capacity additionally by 0.5 million tonnes from the existing production facilities by March, 2010 through introduction of various Addition, Modification and Replacement (AMR) and Non-AMR Schemes at an estimated cost of Rs. 500 crore under Medium Term Plan. Subsequent to implementation of both, Phase-I expansion and Medium Term Plan Schemes, the capacity of the plant will be increased to 6.8 million tonnes of liquid steel per annum from the existing levels of operation of 3.6 million tonnes. The iron ore requirement upto 6.3 million tonnes has almost entirely been tied up with M/s National Mineral Development Corporation. RINL has also applied for mining lease for iron ore reserves in the States of Orissa, Chhatisgarh and Andhra Pradesh. No iron ore reserve has so far been allocated to RINL. This information was given by the Minister of State for Steel Dr. Akhilesh Das in a written reply in the Rajya Sabha today.

2747. (24-8-2007) NEW DELHI : The Minister of State for Housing & Urban Poverty Alleviation, Kumari Selja informed the Lok Sabha today, in a written reply to a question by Shri Subhash Sureshchandra Deshmukh that with a view to ameliorate the living condition of urban poor, Ministry of Housing & Urban Poverty Alleviation is implementing an urban poverty alleviation programme named Swarna Jayanti Shahari Rozgar Yojana (SJSRY) on all India basis since

1.12.1997. The scheme strives to provide gainful employment to the urban unemployed and underemployed poor through, firstly, encouraging the setting up of self-employment ventures by those who have not studied beyond 9th standard and, secondly, by providing wage employment by utilizing their labour for construction of socially and economically useful public assets, the Minister informed the House. The State-wise release of Central funds, as well as physical progress under Swarna Jayanti Shahari Rozgar Yojana (SJSRY) during the last three years are given at Annexure-I & Annexure-II respectively.

2748. (24-8-2007) NEW DELHI : 231 appointments were made for filling the vacant posts of Judges in High Courts from 2005 to 2007 (till 21.8.2007). 38 proposals are at various stages of consideration as on 21.08.2007. The proposal for filling up of vacancies in the High Courts are made to the State Constitutional authorities who, along with their comments send the proposal to the Union Government. The Union Government refers the proposal to the Chief Justice of India for advice. The advice tendered by the Chief Justice of India is submitted for consideration and approval of the Prime Minister and the President. Since the appointment of Judges in the High Courts is through a consultative process amongst the Constitutional Authorities, no time frame can be fixed. This was stated by the Minister of State for Law and Justice, Shri K. Venkatapathy in a written reply in Lok Sabha today.

2749. (24-8-2007) NEW DELHI : In recent past, the Representation of the People (Amendment) Act, 2002 and the Representation of the People (Third Amendment) Act, 2002 have been enacted with a view to making the electoral process clean and free from criminal and corrupt influences. The Government, however, continues to strive and explore further ways and means aimed at bringing about further reforms. In this regard, the Government has before it the recommendations made by different bodies/individuals like the Dinesh Goswami Committee, the Indrajit Gupta Committee, the Election Commission of India, the Law Commission of India, the Department-Related Parliamentary Standing Committee on Personnel, Public Grievances, Law and Justice, etc. Since the process of electoral reforms is a continuous and ongoing process and can be carried out only through consensus among the political parties, which is a time-consuming process, no time frame can be given. The evolution of Code of Conduct for legislators is a matter for the Legislatures to decide and the Government has no intention to interfere in the matter. This was stated by the Minister of State for Law and Justice, Shri K. Venkatapathy in a written reply in Lok Sabha today.

2750. (24-8-2007) NEW DELHI : The Supreme Court of India in its judgement delivered on the 21st July, 2003 in the matter of John Vallamattom Vs. Union of India and Anr. [2003(5) SCALE 384] has made certain observations in respect of enactment of Uniform Civil Code. Bringing in a Uniform Civil Code involves changes in the Personal Laws including those of the minority communities. It has been the consistent policy of the Central Government not to interfere in the Personal Laws of the minority communities unless the necessary initiatives for such changes come from a sizeable cross-section of such communities themselves. This was stated by the Minister of State for Law and Justice, Shri K. Venkatapathy in a written reply in Lok Sabha today.

2751. (24-8-2007) BANGALORE/RAMANAGARA: "Enough is enough" is the message that the BJP Ministers, led by Deputy Chief Minister B.S.Yediyurappa, sought to convey here on Thursday. They reportedly threatened to quit en masse from the Cabinet if Chief Minister H.D. Kumaraswamy did not adhere to the "coalition dharma". Mr. Kumaraswamy in turn defended his actions and told the coalition partner to refrain from repeatedly seeking assurances on transfer of power. An upset Chief Minister at one stage (during a meeting of the Cabinet) reportedly even threatened to seek the dissolution of the Legislative Assembly. With just a month to go for the transfer of power to it, an edgy BJP sees in any action or statement by the Chief Minister a reneging of commitment to hand over power. It took umbrage at the appointment of a member to the Karnataka Public Service Commission (KPSC) by the Chief Minister without consulting the coalition partner. The differences between the two parties were patched up with the Chief Minister saying that he had not criticised the BJP in Gulbarga on Wednesday, as reported in a section of the media, and that in fact, the secular credentials of the Janata Dal (S) had taken a beating after he led party legislators into an alliance with the BJP. The Chief Minister also agreed to summon regular meetings of the coordination committee of the two parties, with the next meeting fixed for Friday. The meeting of the Cabinet, scheduled to commence at 9 a.m., was delayed with the BJP Ministers first meeting at the residence of Mr. Yediyurappa and on reaching the Vidhana Soudha, staying away in protest from the Cabinet hall for over an hour until the Chief Minister came out with a clarification. The Chief Minister said he would produce the video and audio tapes of his press conference in Gulbarga as proof that he did not say what had been ascribed to him. He also said that appointment of G.T. Chandrashekharappa as KPSC member was his prerogative as it was the Janata Dal (S) that had ensured that the strength of the KPSC was increased from six to seven members. BJP Ministers Ramachandra Gowda, Govind M. Karjol, Shashikanth Akkappa Naik, Shivanand Naik, S.A. Ravindranath, B. Nagaraj Shetty, Appasaheb Pattanashetty and S. Shivanna remained inside the Chief Minister's chamber for more than an hour protesting the appointment. Minister for Health R. Ashok and Minister for Higher Education D.H. Shankaramurthy mediated between the Deputy Chief Minister and the Chief Minister and succeeded in finding a solution after which the Cabinet meeting began. Later in the day, the Chief Minister publicly reinforced his assurance to transfer power to the BJP. "I will be free after October 3 and will be able to interact personally with you," he told the gathering in Ramanagara, his Assembly constituency, where he had gone to inaugurate the new district. Mr. Yediyurappa said that the ruling coalition partners were united. "We will complete the remaining 21-and-a-half months without any problems," he said.

2752. (24-8-2007) NEW DELHI : The Ministry of Corporate Affairs, Government of India has approved the application for merger of Air India and Indian Airlines into a new company called National Aviation Company of India Limited (NACIL), earlier incorporated under the Company's Act 1956 on 30th March 2007. With the filing of this approval today with the Registrar of Companies, the legal process for merger of Air India Limited and Indian Airlines Limited in National Aviation Company of India Limited will stand completed. Shri V. Thulasidas takes over as the Chairman and Managing Director and Shri Vishwapati Trivedi as the Joint Managing Director of the merged company. The merged airline will fly under the brand of 'Air India' both domestically and internationally. The new airline will have a combined fleet size of over 112 aircraft, comparable to the best airlines in the Asian region and will rank among the top 30 airlines in the world. As part of its fleet acquisition programme of 111 aircraft, the new airline will be inducting 21 new aircraft (7 Boeing 777, 10 A-320 family aircraft and 4 Boeing 737-800) this year itself. 'Air India' launched its inaugural daily, non-stop Mumbai-New York flight with the first Boeing 777 200 LR aircraft. This is the first non-stop India-US flight by a domestic carrier. The new Boeing 777 aircraft was the first of the series to sport the new branding. The merger of Air India and Indian will provide an integrated international and domestic footprint, which will significantly enhance customer proposition and allow easy entry into a global airline alliance. The merged airline has given them the opportunity to unlock significant synergies on account of optimal utilization of resources through improvement in load factors and yields on commonly serviced routes as well as deployment of 'freed up' aircraft capacity on alternate routes. Leveraging the combined network and route rationalization will result in improved product offering to consumers. The merger will provide an opportunity to fully leverage strong assets, capabilities, infrastructure and skilled and experienced manpower available with both the companies to the optimum potential. It will also provide a large and growth oriented company for the people in larger public interest; provide maximum flexibility to achieve financial and capital restructuring through revaluation of assets; and provide an increased thrust and focus on airline support businesses. Overall, over Rs 800 crores of annual synergies are expected to be realized once the integration is completed. Domestic and international flights will seamlessly integrate, allowing passengers to check in for their international flight from any domestic point in India. The new fleet brings in a product and service level that is the best in class, and will now include in-flight entertainment, better seats and enhanced in-flight service. A combined schedule now means better connectivity to the largest international airline in India as well as improved service to various domestic points in India. An improved frequent flier programme is in the pipeline along with a dedicated holiday packages website with new offerings to various global destinations. The consumer is a clear winner in the merger, having a much-improved product and superior service quality. Apart from the main Passenger Airline, other revenue generating divisions such as Cargo, Low Cost Carrier (LCC), Ground handling and MRO will gain increased focus in the merged entity. They will be able to unlock significant value in the new structure where each will be managed as a separate Strategic Business Unit (SBU) under the corporate umbrella of the merged organization. The new cargo airline, Air India Cargo is in the process of acquiring freighter aircraft by way of conversion of B-737 and A-310 passenger aircraft. The first A-310 freighter aircraft has already started operations to the Gulf and Europe while the B-737 freighter will be operating in the North-East Region. The new Cargo airline is targeting a freighter fleet of almost 10 aircraft over the next year. Under the brand of Air India Express, the low cost carrier will fly on both domestic and international routes. Positioned as a value airline, it will serve markets that require point to point connectivity at a lower price point. Air India Express will have a brand new fleet with in-flight entertainment, meal service and other services that distinguish it from traditional low cost carriers.

2753. (24-8-2007) NEW DELHI : During the Budget speech 2007-08, it was announced that Ministry of Railways will conduct prefeasibility studies for construction of high speed passenger corridors, equipped with state of the art signalling and train control systems, for running high speed trains at the speed of 300 to 350 kms per hour; one each in the Northern, Western, Southern and Eastern regions of the country. In this regard, various State Governments were approached by Railways to find out their willingness for participating in pre-feasibility studies. Government of Andhra Pradesh, Maharashtra, Gujarat, Haryana, Punjab, Kerala, Karnataka, Tamil Nadu and West Bengal have agreed 'in principle' to participate in any pre-feasibility studies. Ministry of Railways have also conducted Financial and Economic Analysis for Mumbai-Ahmedabad and Delhi-Amritsar high speed rail corridors. This proposal is in its initial stages. Hence, it is not possible to predict the actual time of implementation of this scheme. This information was given by the Minister of State for Railways Shri R.Velu in written reply to a question in the Rajya Sabha today.

2754. (24-8-2007) NEW DELHI : In Sikkim, Survey for new line from Sivok to Sangpo has been completed recently. As per survey report, cost of construction of this 52 kms. long line has been assessed as Rs.1329 crore. New Lines have been taken up from Dimapur to Zubza (Kohima) in Nagaland, Harmuti-Itanagar in Arunachal Pradesh and Azra-Byrnihat, Dudhnoi-Depa in Meghalaya. Survey for new line in Mizoram from Bairabhi to Sairang has been completed and proposal has been processed for necessary clearances. This information was given by the Minister of State for Railways Shri R.Velu in written reply to a question in the Rajya Sabha today.

2755. (24-8-2007) NEW DELHI : Ministry of Railways has withdrawn 10 percent Supplementary surcharge on commodities having classification above Class 130 when transported in Mini-rakes and Two Point Rakes w.e.f.. 20.5.2007. Ministry of Railways has announced 30 percent freight discount on incremental earning in traditional empty flow directions under the Incentive Scheme for Traditional Empty Flow Direction. The above two measures were undertaken to attract more traffic and optimum utilization of railway wagons in traditional empty flow direction. Accordingly, Railways do not anticipate any loss due to these measures. This information was given by the Minister of State for Railways Shri R.Velu in written reply to a question in the Rajya Sabha today.

2756. (24-8-2007) NEW DELHI : The percentage increase in budget allocation for health sector during 2006-07 as compared to 2005-06 had been 21.87%. Funds are allocated to States in the form of Grants-in-aid under Health and Family Welfare in respect of the admissible activities under National AIDS Control Programme (NACO) and the National Rural Health Mission (NRHM). Besides these programmes, grant-in-aid is also released under certain other programmes like Cancer, Mental Health, etc., based on proposals received from State Governments. Data on the extent of utilization of funds by states reveals that of the eighteen States having weak public health indicators/weak infrastructure, identified for special attention under the NRHM, eight states viz., Arunachal Pradesh, Assam, Chhattisgarh, Himachal Pradesh, Madhya Pradesh, Mizoram, Rajasthan and Sikkim have utilized more than 50% of allocated funds on Family Planning Programmes while others have utilized funds of a lower order.

2757. (24-8-2007) NEW DELHI: The stand-off between the Left parties and the government over the nuclear deal with the United States continued, with the Central Committee of the Communist Party of India (Marxist) reiterating on Thursday that the government should not proceed further to operationalise the deal. At the end of its two-day meeting, the Central Committee authorised the Polit Bureau to take "whatever necessary measures" to block the agreement. It means that India can attend the International Atomic Energy Agency in Vienna next month as a member-country but there should not be any India-specific safeguards negotiations. The stand of the Central Committee has put the onus on the government of making its choice: go ahead with the deal or count on the Left support. "We do not want this [current] crisis to affect the government; it depends on how this government or in particular the Congress leadership responds. As long as the government does not take the next step to operationalise the deal, it is fine," CPI(M) general secretary Prakash Karat said at a press conference.

2758. (24-8-2007) NEW DELHI : National AIDS Control Programme-III (NACP-III) has commenced with effect from 1st April 2007 with a three-pronged strategy prevention, care & support including treatment and institutional strengthening. Under the NACP-III, synergy with programmes under National Rural Health Mission (NRHM) including Revised National Tuberculosis Programme (RNTCP) and Reproductive & Child Health (RCH) programme has been ensured. At district level, all activities will be implemented by the District Health Society. Services for HIV testing and counselling and other preventive measures will be available under NACP-III in rural areas through NRHM set-up. Antiretroviral treatment will be made available upto district or sub-district level based on prevalence of HIV/AIDS and number of persons on treatment. This information was given by the Minister of State for Health & Family Welfare, Smt. Panabaka Lakshmi in a written reply to a question in the Rajya Sabha.

2759. (24-8-2007) NEW DELHI : The Government is providing Central assistance to the States/UTs under National Rural Health Mission (NRHM) and second phase of Reproductive and Child Health (RCH-II) programme for implementation of various family welfare activities to achieve population stabilisation in the country as envisaged in the National Population Policy (NPP), 2000 through responsible and planned parenthood, voluntary and informed choice of Family Planning method best suited to acceptors. Under the National Rural Health Mission (NRHM) emphasis has been laid to provide accessible, affordable, accountable, effective, reliable, and quality primary health care through creation of a cadre of Accredited Social Health Activities (ASHA), improved hospital care measured through Indian Public Health Standards (IPHS), decentralization of programme to district level to improve intra and inter-sectoral convergence and effective utilization of resources. As a part of NRHM, fixed day services both for terminal and spacing methods of family planning in all the upgraded Primary Health Centres, Community Health Centres, District Hospitals and Sub-District Hospital has been taken in all the States/Uts. During the last three years the family planning measures like sterilization and IUD have shown a downward trend. A drop in sterilization by 4.1% in 2005-06 over 2004-05 and drop in IUD by 1.2% in 2005-06 over 2004-05 has been reported. However temporary methods of family planning like the condom users have gone up by 8.07% during 2005-06 over 2004-05. The sterilization and IUD have further fallen down by 10% in 2006-07. Some of the factors contributing to the gradual fall in the achievements of Family planning during last few years inter-alia include :(1) Directions of Hon'ble Supreme Court of India in March 2005 that the doctors performing the surgery should have minimal 5 years gynaecological experience. There was also a restriction of number of sterilization operations by a Team of Doctor in a day as per Government of India Guidelines. This had lead to reduction in the number of providers drastically and affected the Family Planning measures adopted by the government, as 5 year gynaecological experience clause is not there in the guidelines. (2) Non-availability of adequate number of working Laparoscope's at the health facilities in the States for conducting Female Sterilization.

2760. (24-8-2007) NEW DELHI : National Rural Health Mission (NRHM) envisages setting up of Primary Health Centres (PHCs) and Community Health Centres (CHCs) as per 2001 population norms in a phased manner by the State

Governments. The requirement of funds for the purpose is to be incorporated by the State Governments in their annual Programme Implementation Plan (PIP) under NRHM. The State wise shortfalls of PHCs and CHCs as per 2001 population norms can be seen at Annexure. The biggest challenge in the delivery of rural health care services is to ensure the availability of services of doctors in PHCs and CHCs. NRHM envisages provision of one AYUSH Doctor in PHC in addition to an Allopathic Doctor for co-locating AYUSH facilities in PHCs. NRHM also envisages support for upgradation of PHCs and CHCs to Indian Public Health Standards (IPHS). The States are being encouraged to appoint doctors on contractual basis. Multi-skill training of doctors in anesthesia and newborn care is being done. A number of States have taken various initiatives to ensure services of doctors in rural areas such as giving cash incentives, difficult area allowance, walk-in interviews for recruitment of doctors etc. Some States have also adopted policy of compulsory rural/difficult area posting for admission to post-graduate courses and as a pre-requisite for promotion, foreign assignment or training abroad; compulsory rotation of doctors etc. The States have also been adopting various Public-Private Partnership models for health care delivery. This information was given by the Minister of State for Health & Family Welfare, Smt. Panabaka Lakshmi in a written reply to a question in the Rajya Sabha.

2761. (24-8-2007) NEW DELHI : Number of cases of foeticide registered during 2003, 2004 and 2005 was 57, 86, and 86 respectively in the country. State wise number of cases registered can be seen at Annexure. In order to check female foeticide, the Government has enacted the Pre-Conception and Pre-Natal Diagnostic Techniques Act (PC&PNDT Act). The technique of pre-conception sex selection has been brought within the ambit of this Act so as to pre-empt the use of such technologies, which significantly contribute to the declining sex ratio. Use of ultrasound machines has also been brought within the purview of this Act more explicitly so as to curb their misuse for detection and disclosure of sex of the foetus lest it should lead to female foeticide. The sale of ultrasound machines has been regulated through laying down the condition of sale only to the bodies registered under the Act. At the district level, as per the Pre-Conception and Pre-Natal Diagnostic Techniques Act (PC&PNDT Act), the Appropriate Authority which is the Chief Medical Officer (CMO) of the district has been empowered to implement the Act. The Appropriate Authority is aided and advised by the Advisory Committee in the discharge of its functions. The Advisory Committee is consists of three medical experts, a legal expert, a publicity expert and three social workers/NGOs (out of which one is from women's organization). In addition, a 'National Support and Monitoring Cell' has been set up for effective implementation of the Act.

2762. (24-8-2007) NEW DELHI : The Union Rural Development Minister, Dr. Raghuvansh Prasad Singh yesterday interacted with a group of Members of Parliament from Karnataka and Orissa about the implementation of various Rural development schemes initiated by the Ministry of Rural Development. This was fourth such interactive session of the Minister with the Members of Parliament of various States. The Minister laid emphasis on monitoring of the schemes at District level so that the schemes are successfully implemented. The Minister has asked the elected representatives to ensure that the village, district and state level Vigilance and Monitoring Committee meetings are held regularly and should take place every quarter. This will lead to people's participation, close monitoring, transparency and accountability for the successful implementation of the rural development programmes. Shri Chandra Shekhar Sahu, Union Minister of State for Rural Development and former Chief Minister of Orissa, Shri Girdhar Gomango, MP were among those present on the occasion. Such interactive sessions are scheduled on 29th (Tamil Nadu & Kerala), 30th (Gujarat, Goa, UTs and Uttarakhand) and 3rd September (Bihar & Jharkhand), 5th (Uttar Pradesh) & 6th September, (Maharashtra & Andhra Pradesh).

2763. (24-8-2007) NEW DELHI : The Government continuously promotes 'Swadeshi' as one of the principal objectives in so far as khadi, village industry and coir products are concerned through its programmes and measures implemented by the Khadi and Village Industries Commission (KVIC) and Coir Board. The steps taken in this direction by the Ministry of Micro, Small and Medium Enterprises include the implementation of the following schemes through KVIC and Coir Board, in the country: (i) Schemes for development of Khadi and Polyvastra activities: For this purpose, Interest Subsidy Eligibility Certificate (ISEC) is issued in favour of implementing agencies for availing institutional finance to meet working capital requirement of khadi and polyvastra activities, at 4% rate of interest and the difference between 4% and actual lending rate is subsidized by KVIC. 10% Rebate is provided on retail sales of Khadi/Polyvasta products as normal rebate throughout the year and another 10% special rebate for 108 days in the year. (ii) Scheme of Product Development, Design Intervention and Packaging (PRODIP) has been launched in order to diversify and develop products under Khadi & Village Industries and also to improve the packaging of the various KVI products. (iii) Scheme of Fund for Regeneration of Traditional Industries (SFURTI) has been launched in October, 2005 for regeneration of traditional industries in 122 identified clusters in khadi, village industries and coir sectors. (iv) A Rural Industries Service Centre (RISC) scheme is in vogue for providing common facility services to KVI programmes on a cluster based manner. (v) Rural Employment Generation Programme (REGP) is being implemented for establishing village industries projects with margin money assistance from KVIC and loan from public sector scheduled commercial banks. (vi) Mahila Coir Yojana, Development of Production Infrastructure and Domestic/ Export Market Development Assistance are some of the programmes under implementation in Coir sector through Coir Board. (vii) Development of Production Infrastructure Scheme for coir production through supply of equipment and machinery at subsidised rates. (viii) Research and Development Schemes. (ix) Financial assistance for participation in national and international exhibitions. This information was given by the Minister of Micro, Small & Medium Enterprises, Shri Mahabir Prasad in a written reply to a question in Rajya Sabha today.

2764. (24-8-2007) NEW DELHI : The Government has proposed the formulation of a new welfare scheme for the weavers of the khadi sector, namely, "Workshed Scheme for Khadi Weavers and Artisans". The scheme is in the conceptual stage and drawn on the lines of one under implementation in the Ministry of Textiles for the benefit of handloom weavers. The Ministry of Micro, Small and Medium Enterprises has been implementing a welfare scheme for the artisans of the khadi sector, including khadi weavers, namely, "Khadi Karigar Janashree Bima Yojana" with effect from 2003-04. This information was given by the Minister of Micro, Small & Medium Enterprises, Shri Mahabir Prasad in a written reply to a question in Rajya Sabha today.

2765. (24-8-2007) NEW DELHI : There are no findings available with the Ministry of Corporate Affairs of siphoning of funds by the pharmaceutical companies through licensing arrangement with their associate/subsidiary companies. Cost audit of the companies is carried out under section 233B of the Companies Act, 1956 and the compliance thereof is monitored in the Ministry of Corporate Affairs. National Pharmaceutical Pricing Authority has also been availing cost audit reports from this Ministry for regulatory action by them as appropriate in respect of pharmaceutical companies. This information was given by Minister of Corporate Affairs, Shri Prem Chand Gupta in reply to a question raised by Shri Subrata Bose in Lok Sabha today.

2766. (24-8-2007) NEW DELHI : The services in Industrial Establishments manufacturing or producing Nuclear Fuel and components, Heavy Water and Allied Chemicals and Atomic Energy will continue as a public utility under the Industrial Dispute Act, 1947 for another six months with effect from 26th August 2007. In a notification issued here, the Labour Ministry said that this has been done in public interest. The Central Government had earlier declared the services in the above said industry as a public utility for six months from 26th February 2007. The employees in this industry, as a result, would among other things be required to give notice to their employer six weeks in advance of proceeding on strike so that conciliatory proceedings could be started. During the conciliatory proceedings and seven days after their completion, the employees cannot go on strike.

2767. (24-8-2007) NEW DELHI : In partial modification of the Department of Justice's notification dated 22nd August, 2007, the President, in exercise of the powers conferred by article 224-A of the Constitution of India, is pleased to appoint Shri Justice Om Prakash Srivastava, a retired Judge of the Allahabad High Court, to sit and act as a Judge of the Allahabad High Court, for a period of one year with effect from the date he assumes charge of his office.

2768. (25-8-2007) NEW DELHI : Vice-President of India, Mohammad Hamid Ansari has greeted the people of our country, especially the people of Kerala, on the joyous occasion of Onam. In his Onam greetings, the Vice-President said "Onam is celebrated with traditional gaiety and enthusiasm. The mood of rejoicing is vividly captured in the rituals and festivities associated with the festival, transcending all barriers and uniting us in a common brotherhood". Vice-President hoped that this festival would foster unity, harmony and prosperity in the lives of all Indians.

2769. (25-8-2007) NEW DELHI : The Vice President of India Mohd. Hamid Ansari has strongly condemned and expressed profound shock at the twin blasts that occurred in Hyderabad today evening that has caused loss of innocent life and injured many people. In his condolence message the Vice President has expressed his sympathy for the families of those killed and injured in the blasts and called for maintenance of peace and harmony at this juncture.

2770. (26-8-2007) NEW DELHI : Union Minister for Science and Technology and Earth Sciences Shri Kapil Sibal today called for a dedicated satellite for providing health services to the people in remote areas. Speaking after formally launching the Telemedicine facility for the rural areas at Sir Ganga Ram Hospital in New Delhi he said the country with 17000 hospitals and half a million doctors has the potential to give its people the best health care facilities. Lauding the efforts of the technologists from ISRO, doctors from Sir Ganga Ram Hospital and administrators from both Central and State Governments who made it possible to take good health care to the doorstep of the poor in some rural areas, the Minister assured all assistance from the Ministry of Science and Technology in terms of installation of hardware to reach out to the rural areas. Later, in a teleconference with the Chief Minister of Haryana, Shri Bhupinder Singh Hooda and the Health Minister of Rajasthan, Shri Digambar Singh who were present at the Medical Kiosks in Gohana and Kaithun respectively, Shri Sibal congratulated the State Governments for taking forward the initiative for the benefit of the rural masses. A project entitled 'Village Resource Centre', which aims at providing specialized (tertiary level) health services at the Community Health Centre (CHC) level, was funded to Sir Ganga Ram Hospital (SGRH), New Delhi in March, 2006. Three such centres have been set up in the first phase in Gohana (Haryana), Kaithun (Rajasthan) and Dasmal (Himachal Pradesh). The centres at Gohana and Kaithun are now working in full swing. Each centre provides some modern diagnostic facilities to people coming from rural areas and they are also attended by a qualified doctor. In addition, through a satellite link, each centre is connected to SGRH, New Delhi for providing online consultation and medical diagnosis. In case further consultation is needed, patients are referred to SGRH, New Delhi where they do not have to pay any consultation fee to specialist at SGRH. Initially, the proposal from SGRH was for setting up 16 such centres. It was, however, decided to do a pilot at three centres and then consider setting up more centres.

2771. (26-8-2007) NEW DELHI : The Prime Minister, Dr. Manmohan Singh, has greeted citizens in India and abroad on the occasion of Onam, which is being celebrated on August 27. In a message, Dr. Manmohan Singh has said that Onam, which heralds the beginning of the harvest season, gives us an opportunity to salute our farmers for their contributions to our economy. He has also wished that the festival may bring peace, prosperity and happiness to all.

2772. (26-8-2007) NEW DELHI : The President, Smt. Pratibha Devisingh Patil in her message on the occasion of Onam, which is being celebrated tomorrow, has said:-"On the auspicious occasion of Onam, I greet all my people in India and abroad. The auspicious festival is a symbol of unity and oneness of people belonging to various religions. May this harvest festival herald a new year of happiness and prosperity for the people and promote harmony and brotherhood in the country."

2773. (27-8-2007) NEW DELHI : The Meeting of the full Planning Commission scheduled to be held tomorrow (28.8.2007) under the chairmanship of the Prime Minister has been postponed. New date will be intimated later. Inconvenience caused is regretted.

2774. (27-8-2007) NEW DELHI : In exercise of the powers conferred by clause (1) of article 224 of the Constitution of India, the President is pleased to appoint Shrimati Veena Birbal to be an Additional Judge of the Delhi High Court, for a period of two years, with effect from the date she assumes charge of her office.

2775. (27-8-2007) NEW DELHI : The Prime Minister Dr. Manmohan Singh has requested Chief Ministers to prepare time-bound action plans for providing all basic services for the urban poor in major cities in their States. Dr. Manmohan Singh sought their personal attention to promote the concept of inclusive cities in which every citizen has reasonable and affordable access to basic amenities. The Prime Minister in a letter to the Chief Ministers has said that while the states have responded to the challenges offered by the Jawaharlal Nehru National Urban Renewal Mission (JNNURM), there is a need to focus on the component of Basic Services to the Urban Poor to implement the charter of the JNNURM. This component relates to provision of basic entitlements and amenities to urban poor in terms of security of tenure, affordable housing, potable water, and sanitation facilities while envisaging convergence of health, education and social security. The Mission also seeks internal earmarking in Urban Local Body budgets for provision of basic services to the urban poor. He has also urged the Chief Ministers to direct each city to develop these plans using innovative resource mobilization models to finance the projects by combining funds provided by the Central and State Governments with community and private resources.

2776. (27-8-2007) NEW DELHI : In partial modification of the Department of Justice's notification dated 22nd August, 2007, the President, in exercise of the powers conferred by article 224-A of the Constitution of India, is pleased to appoint Shri Justice Om Prakash Srivastava, a retired Judge of the Allahabad High Court, to sit and act as a Judge of the Allahabad High Court, for a period of one year with effect from the date he assumes charge of his office.

2777. (27-8-2007) NEW DELHI : The President, Smt. Pratibha Devisingh Patil in her message on the occasion of Raksha Bandhan which is being celebrated tomorrow, has said :-"On this auspicious occasion of Raksha Bandhan, I extend my greetings and good wishes to all my people in India and abroad. Raksha Bandhan is a unique festival of love, affection and trust between sisters and brothers. May this festival strengthen the spirit of kindness and goodwill and spread the message of fraternal feelings and oneness among our people".

2778. (27-8-2007) NEW DELHI : Another multi organ transplant has been carried out at Army Hospital (R&R), here yesterday. Leela Devi aged 26, lost the battle with her brain tumor but even in her death she gave life to three others. Her husband, Lance Naik GS Bisht of 26 Rashtriya Rifles, consented to donate her organs after she was pronounced brain dead. A combined team of over 40 doctors and para-medical staff from Army Hospital (R&R) and Base Hospital at New Delhi successfully transplanted her liver into a serving soldier with terminal cirrhosis due to Hepatitis B and one kidney into a 12 year old daughter of a soldier suffering from end stage kidney disease. The other kidney was handed over to AIIMS, where it was transplanted into a 45 years old with chronic kidney failure. Organ donation after brain death is rare in India. The Armed Forces has launched the Armed Forces Organ Retrieval and Transplantation Authority (AORTA) earlier this year to increase awareness on organ donation. As per Col AK Seth, Director of AORTA, hundreds of serving personnel and their families have already pledged to donate their organs.

2779. (27-8-2007) NEW DELHI : The Army Chief General JJ Singh has called for increased synergies among the three Armed Forces. Inaugurating the Centre for Joint Warfare Studies in New Delhi today, General Singh said despite rich experience, the three services have a long way to go in launching Joint Operations. He said the centre has come up in a short time after the Defence Minister Shri AK Antony granted it approval on priority, based on a report of the Group of Ministers. The Army Chief hoped that the Centre would go a long way in achieving synergies in operations, formulation of joint policies and concepts and integrating procurements. The Centre for Joint Warfare Studies will function under the Chief of Integrated Staff to the Chiefs of Staff Committee (CISC), headed by Lt Gen HS Lidder. The creation of the centre is a logical step to achieve integration and training of joint warfare professionals. It will train military and civilian professionals in the field of Joint Warfare and Practices. An independent think tank of the Defence Ministry, the Centre will act as a semi autonomous body promoting Joint Warfare Studies at the strategic, operational and tactical levels. It will also cater to various Ministries, Intelligence Agencies and other Government departments associated with Integrated Defence Staff Headquarters in matters of national security. The prime objectives of the Centre are promotion of joint strategies among the three services and conduct studies and research in joint war-fighting.

2780. (27-8-2007) NEW DELHI : The Vice President of India Mohd. Hamid Ansari has greeted the people of our country on the occasion of Rakshabandhan. In his Rakshabandhan greetings the Vice President said "Rakshabandhan is celebrated across the country by tying of Rakhis around the wrists of brothers by sisters, thus strengthening the bonds of love and affection. The festival reminds us of the enduring importance of the brother-sister relationship in our family and social structures in this day and age." The Vice President hoped that this festival would foster the true spirit of love, goodwill, love and compassion in the society.

2781. (27-8-2007) NEW DELHI : With a view to construct the state-of-the-art rail tunnels with ventilation, monitoring device, control room for safe operation in the challenging terrain between Udhampur to Baramula in the state of Jammu and Kashmir, the Ministry of Railways has decided to constitute a four-member Committee to formulate the policy guidelines. The Committee will study various practices in electrified and non-electrified rail tunnels in India and different parts of the world and to suggest various aspect of working in tunnels that could help improve passenger safety and comfort including operation and maintenance strategy. The Committee will submit its recommendations within a period of three months from the date of its constitution. The Committee will study various monitoring devices installed in the tunnels and control room for same operations and identify the best suited system for Udhampur-Baramula project and will have interaction with consultants/agencies specializing in ventilation in different world railways and to identify the technology best suited for Indian conditions. The Committee will also share the experience of different world railways in maintaining these tunnels, to understand the operational and maintenance needs, the infrastructure requirements and also to study various guidelines of International Union of Railways (UIC) on the subject. Besides studying the existing code of practices as well as laying down the criteria for ventilation in tunnels for normal operation on electric traction, the Committee will also study the measures being adopted for relief and rescue operations in case of fire accidents/disaster inside the tunnel. With a view to provide an alternative and the reliable transportation system to Jammu & Kashmir, Government of India has planned a 345 km. long railway line joining the Kashmir valley with the Indian Railway network. The Project has been declared as a Project of National Importance. The rail link between Jammu and Udhampur has been opened to public since April 2005. Shri Sudhir Kumar, Executive Director, Engineer Energy Management, Railway Board will be the Convener of the Committee. S/Shri R.K.Chowdhary, Chief Electrical Engineer/Construction (J&K), Northern Railway, B.P.Awasthi, Deputy Chief Engineer/Construction, Northern Railway and Sanjay Kubba, Director/Safety, Railway Board will function as Members of the Committee.

2782. (27-8-2007) NEW DELHI : The Prime Minister, Dr. Manmohan Singh, has greeted citizens in India and abroad on the auspicious occasion of Raksha Bandhan, which is being celebrated on August 28. In a message, the Prime Minister has said, "the festival is a special occasion to celebrate the bond of love between brother and sister. It also marks a re-affirmation of traditional family values."

2783. (27-8-2007) NEW DELHI : In view of the present security threat perception prevailing in the country, ports and shipyards are also considered as possible targets by anti-social elements. X-ray machines or Gamma scanners are installed by Customs Department at Ports which primarily handle container traffic. Gamma scanner have been installed at Jawaharlal Nehru Port. Some of the ports have identified locations for installing the container scanners and the Custom Department has been informed about it. A High Powered Committee has been set up headed by Chairman, Cochin Port Trust with Deputy Chairman Chennai Port Trust, Deputy Chairman Paradip Port Trust, Deputy Chairperson Jawahalal Nehru Port Trust, Traffic Manager Mumbai Port Trust, Joint Director Intelligence Bureau and Deputy Inspector General Central Industrial Security Forces as members to review the security aspects of all Major Port Trust and shipyards under the control of Department of Shipping. The Committee has visited all the major ports and its recommendations are awaited. This information was given by the Minister of Shipping, Road Transport and Highways, Thiru T.R. Baalu in a written reply in the Lok Sabha today.

2784. (27-8-2007) NEW DELHI : The Government has been taking various measures from time to time for the development of Shipping Industry and growth of Indian Tonnage. The Government has constituted a Group to review the Tax Regime for Indian Shipping Industry. The Group is in the process of finalising its report which is expected to include some recommendations relating to exemption of Income Tax for Indian Seafarer sailing on foreign going Indian flag ships. The Indian Shipping Industry is liable to a variety of taxes. Even after the introduction of Tonnage Tax from 2004-05, there are still about 12 direct and indirect taxes. There is wide disparity in the salary structure of the Indian Seafarer sailing on board foreign going Indian flag ships where the salary is taxable and Indian Seafarer on board foreign flag ships, where the salary is tax free. This situation induces preference among Indian seafarers for opting to some foreign flag vessels. This information was given by the Minister of Shipping, Road Transport and Highways, Thiru T.R. Baalu in a written reply in the Lok Sabha today.

2785. (28-8-2007) NEW DELHI : The Prime Minister Dr. Manmohan Singh called on the President Smt. Pratibha Devisingh Patil at Rashtrapati Bhavan today. The meeting lasted for about 40 minutes. They reviewed the recent developments.

2786. (28-8-2007) NEW DELHI : The Prime Minister today reviewed the Thrust Areas for the power sector. Dr. Manmohan Singh directed that urgent steps be taken to operationalise the decisions taken in the Chief Ministers' Conference on Power Sector in May 2007. He stressed that the UPA Government was fully committed to Bharat Nirman and the Rajiv Gandhi Grameen Vidyutikaran Yojana and that all steps should be taken in this regard. The Prime Minister was also keen to continue and strengthen the efforts being made towards the accelerated development and reforms of the distribution sector and directed the Ministry of Power to ensure that formal clearances to both the initiatives are completed in the next fortnight. He expressed the hope that with the constitution of the Standing Committee of State Power Ministers and the Sub-Committee under the Finance Minister to look into financing issues, the power sector would be able to achieve the full momentum necessary to sustain high rates of economic growth.

2787. (28-8-2007) NEW DELHI : The Request for Proposal (RFP) for the procurement of 126 Medium Multi-Role Combat Aircraft (MMRCA) at an estimated cost of Rs. 42,000 crores for the Indian Air Force was issued today to six vendors- Russia's MIG-35(RAC MiG); Swedish JAS-39 (Gripen);Dassault Rafale (France); American F-16 Falcon (Lockheed Martin); Boeing's F/A-18 Super Hornet and Eurofighter Typhoon (Made by a consortium of British, German, Spanish and Italian firms). The 211-page document deals with various issues relating to initial purchase, transfer of technology, licensed production and life-time maintenance support for the aircraft. The RFP contains the selection model that would involve an exhaustive evaluation process as detailed in the Defence Procurement Procedures (DPP)-2006. The proposals from the likely contenders would first be technically evaluated by a professional team to check for compliance with IAF's operational requirements and other RFP conditions. Extensive field trials would be carried out to evaluate the performance. Finally, the commercial proposal of the vendors, short-listed after technical and field evaluations, would be examined and compared. The aircraft are likely to be in service for over 40 years. Great care has been taken to ensure that only determinable factors, which do not lend themselves to any subjectivity, are included in the commercial selection model. The selection would be transparent and fair. Under the terms of purchase, the first 18 aircraft will come in a 'fly away' condition while the remaining 108 will be manufactured under Transfer of Technology. The vendor finally selected would also be required to undertake 50% offset obligations in India. The ToT and offset contracts would provide a great technological and economic boost to the indigenous defence industries which would include Defence Public Sector Undertakings, Raksha Udyog Ratnas and other eligible private sector industries. Foreign vendors would be provided great flexibility in effecting tie up with Indian partners for this purpose. It may be recalled that the Defence Minister Shri A K Antony while chairing the Defence Acquisition Council Meeting on June 29, 2007 had outlined three guiding principles for this procurement scheme. First, the operational requirements of IAF should be fully met. Second, the selection process should be competitive, fair and transparent, so that best value for money is realized.

Lastly, Indian defence industries should get an opportunity to grow to global scales.

2788. (28-8-2007) NEW DELHI : Shri B. K. Handique, Minister of State for Parliamentary Affairs and Chemicals and Fertilizers gave away the prizes to winning students/Vidyalayas for their meritorious performances in the Youth Parliament Competition. On this occasion, the students of Jawahar Navodaya Vidyalaya, Sukhasan, Distt. Madhepura, which stood first in the competition, also presented a short sitting of Youth Parliament. Speaking on the occasion, Shri Handique said that the competition promotes in students the values like leadership, discipline, responsibility and accountability. It develops democratic spirit and temper in the students. Through such competitions, they get groomed into the culture of all-inclusiveness, tolerance, debate and deliberations, which is the essence of democracy, he added. It also provides them a platform to express themselves about various important social, national and international issues. Ministry of Parliamentary Affairs have been organizing Youth Parliament competitions in Jawahar Navodaya Vidyalayas for the past ten years. Under the scheme of National Youth Parliament Competition for Jawahar Navodaya Vidyalayas, the 10 th competition in the series was organised during 2006-2007 among 78 Vidyalayas spread over eight regions all over India. The Youth Parliament Scheme aims at inculcating among the younger generations the spirit of self-discipline, tolerance of diverse opinion, righteous expression of views and other virtues of democratic way of life. Besides, the scheme also acquaints the students with the practices and procedures of Parliament, techniques of discussion and debate and develops in them the self-confidence, the quality of leadership and the art and skill of effective oratory. Team of judges comprising of MPs/Ex-MPs and officers of the Ministry of Parliamentary Affairs and Navodaya Vidyalaya Samiti evaluated these competitions. The Running Parliamentary Shield and Trophy for standing first in the competition was awarded to Jawahar Navodaya Vidyalaya, Sukhasan, Distt. Madhepura, Bihar. Merit trophies were awarded to seven Vidyalayas for standing first in their respective regions.

2789. (28-8-2007) NEW DELHI : Prime Minister Dr. Manmohan Singh will present National Awards to the Micro Small and Medium Entrepreneurs here on 30th August, 2007. The Awards will be in three categories: a) Outstanding Entrepreneurs of Micro & Small Enterprises, Khadi and Village Industries and Coir Industries; b) Special Awards to Women and SC/ST Entrepreneurs and c) Banks for Excellence in Small Enterprises Lending. The Government instituted a Scheme of National Awards under the title 'National Award for Research & Development Efforts in Small Scale Industries' in 1999. The objective of the scheme is to encourage in-house R&D efforts and to promote this spirit in the larger interest of qualitative development in Small Scale Industries. Under this scheme First, Second and Third Awards are conferred to deserving registered small scale industries which may be in continuous production for at least four years before the year of Award. The First, Second and Third Awards carry a Cash Prize of Rs. 1,00,000/-, Rs.75,000/- and Rs. 50,000/- respectively; besides a Certificate and a Trophy. With a view to encouraging the banks to enhance credit flow to the MSE Sector, a scheme of National Awards to the Banks in recognition of their outstanding performance in financing the micro and small enterprises sector was introduced from the year 2001-02. Further, the National Awards for Excellence in Lending to Micro Enterprises have also been instituted from the year 2005-06.

2790. (28-8-2007) NEW DELHI : A Chair on Consumer Law and Practice will be set up at National Law School of India University (NLSIU), Bangalore. An agreement to this effect was signed here today between Department of Consumer Affairs and NLSIU in the presence of Shri Sharad Pawar Minister for Consumer Affairs, Food & Public Distribution and Agriculture. Shri Sanjay Singh, Joint Secretary, Deptt. of Consumer Affairs and Dr. A. Jayagovind, Vice Chancellor, NLSIU signed the MoU. Speaking on the occasion Shri Sharad Pawar observed that with the signing of this MoU a new vista has been opened which would be effective in developing and incorporating perspective of academia in the initiatives of the Ministry. Consumer welfare and awareness is an area that impinges on the life of every citizen and the Government has been earnestly trying to ensure that these rights are not trampled upon, he added. The Department of Consumer Affairs will provide an endowment grant of Rs. 90.00 lakh to the NLSIU to meet the annual recurring cost of the Chair and also Rs. 15.00 lakh as cost for setting up the Chair during the first year of the award. The primary objective of the chair is to act as a think tank for the Research and Policy related issues on consumer law and practice and also develop Consumer Affairs as a distinct subject for study at the undergraduate and postgraduate levels.

2791. (28-8-2007) NEW DELHI : The President, Smt. Pratibha Devisingh Patil, has stressed the need for special attention to the girl child and children in distress. The President was speaking at Rashtrapati Bhavan today on the occasion of Raksha Bandhan. Children from various parts of the country were present on the occasion, which was also an opportunity for cultural integration. The President said, it is on such occasions that society can in a small way fill the void existing in the lives of children affected by distress. She said, "Generally, financial support is available for these children, but perhaps it is the emotional support of society which can lift their spirit and morale to succeed against all odds. Let us reaffirm our commitment as a society to provide them with a bright future by all means on this occasion of Raksha Bandhan and "tie the bond of love, affection, care and concern" with all these children who are not fortunate to have their natural childhood." Smt. Patil further emphasised on the role of education and said, " Education is a tool through which a person gets self-respect and confidence. On this day of Raksha Bandhan, I would also like to emphasise that every effort should be made to prevent practices, which have an adverse impact on the male-female population balance. The girl child has as much rights as a male child." This year's

Raksha Bandhan gathering at Rashtrapati Bhavan brought together nearly 100 children from different parts of the country. These children were from the militancy affected areas of Jammu & Kashmir and the North East, children who lost their parents in communal riots, children who lost their fathers or mothers serving in the Armed Forces and the Police, HIV positive children, differently abled children and those suffering from Thalassaemia. The children also had an interaction with the President during breakfast in the morning and were also taken on a guided tour of Rashtrapati Bhavan. For many of them this was their first ever visit to a place outside their state. The children were from the following organisations:- Help Foundation-Srinagar, Muskan-Jammu, All India Quami Mahaz-Ahmedabad, Maitri Gram-Guwahati, Plan India-Tamil Nadu, Aman Biradari-Action India and Prayas, SOS Care India, Hostel and Vocational Training Institute for Blind all from Delhi and Foundation Against Thalessaemia-Faridabad, Balgram-Sonepat. Children. In addition students from Residential Colleges run by the Bharatiya Netraheen Kalyan Parishad, Residential Schools run by the Delhi Arya Pratinidhi Sabha and Mother's Pride School all from Delhi and the Special School for Mentally Retarded and Hearing Impaired from Rewari were present.

2792. (28-8-2007) NEW DELHI : The Ministry of Environment & Forests has successfully completed the State of Environment (SoE) Reporting process under the Xth Plan. It was initiated with all the State Governments across the country since last five years. The basic objective of the process is to bring out an overview of the environmental scenario in the States and Union Territories (UTs), streamlining the existing data collection and collation system and to prepare the State of Environment (SoE) Reports. These reports would serve as baseline documents and to assist the administrators and planners in overall policy formulation and logical decision-making. The ministry in association with The Energy and Resources Institute in a workshop will deliberate on the issues of sharing experiences of the achievements and weaknesses of the exercise of the SoE Reporting, dissemination of SoE Reports and Products produced so far, discussion on how could SoE reports be used as a tool to mainstream the environment vis-à-vi sustainable development, capacity building on the SoE reporting system, preparation of National SoE Report and the way forward for SoE reporting in the 11th Five Year Plan.

2793. (29-8-2007) NEW DELHI : Prasar Bharati has set up an exclusive Marketing Division at Guwahati in 2006, which is working as a Single Window for catering to the needs of Advertisers/Clients of Assam and the entire North-Eastern region. This division accepts bookings for and on behalf of all the AIR stations of Assam and North-Eastern Region. With the help of the Marketing Division at Guwahati, the AIR stations in Assam and North-Eastern Region have been able to increase their commercial revenue. Besides, All India Radio has already allowed concession up to 50% on commercial rates to NGOs/Voluntary Organisations for promoting Public Service Broadcasting on various radio stations of Assam and the North-Eastern Region viz. Halflong, Jorhat, Diphu, Kokrajhar, Belonia, Gangtok, Jowai,

Kailashahar, Mokokchung, Kohima, Tezu, Tura etc. in order to make the stations of this region commercially viable to some extent. This information was given by Minister of Information & Broadcasting and Parliamentary Affairs, Shri P. R. Dasmunsi in written reply to a question in Rajya Sabha.

2794. (29-8-2007) NEW DELHI : As per National Mineral Inventory prepared by Indian Bureau of Mines (IBM), the total resources of copper ore are estimated at 32,00,000 tonnes with metal content of 34,880 tonnes and the total resources of gold ore are estimated at 32,00,000 tonnes with metal content of 4.93 tonnes in Dausa district of Rajasthan as on 1.4.2005. Geological Survey of India (GSI) carried out systematic geochemical sampling in Dhani-Basri Copper-Gold prospect in Dausa district of Rajasthan from October, 1999 to September, 2000, followed by test drilling in November, 2000. A resource of 3.2 million tonnes of Gold-Copper ore of possible category at 1.56 ppm Au (gold) and 1.09% Cu (copper) of which 0.89 million tonnes is of probable category with 1.04% Cu and 1.54 ppm. Au has been estimated in Dhani-Basri area. The above information was given by the Minister of State for Mines Dr. T. Subbarami Reddy in a written reply in the Rajya Sabha today.

2795. (29-8-2007) NEW DELHI : Minister of Corporate Affairs, Shri Prem Chand Gupta introduced the Competition (Amendment) Bill, 2007 in the Lok Sabha today after withdrawing the Competition (Amendment) Bill, 2006. The Government had enacted the Competition Act in 2002 keeping in view the economic developments in the nineties which required that the Indian market be geared to face competition from within the country and outside. The Act provided for the establishment of a Commission to prevent practices having adverse effect on competition, to promote and sustain competition in markets, to protect the interests of consumers and to ensure freedom of trade carried on by other participants in markets. However, the Compettition Commission of India (CCI) could not be made fully functional due to filing of a writ petition before the Hon'ble Supreme Court against certain provisions of the Act, Rules framed there under and the selection of the Chairperson and Member. The Hon'ble Supreme Court, delivering its judgement, closed the writ petition declinig to pronounce on the matters argued before it and left open all questions regarding validity to be decided after the proposed amendment of the Act. Keeping in view the judgement of the Hon'ble Supreme Court, the Competition (Amendment) Bill, 2006 was introduced in Lok Sabha on the 9th March, 2006 and the same was referred for examination and report to the Parliamentary Standing Committee on Finance. The Committee presented its report to both the Houses of Parliament on 12.12.2006. Taking into account the recommendations of the Committee and the legal challenges and to make the CCI fully operational on a sustainable basis, the Competition (Amendment) Bill, 2007 has been introduced.

2796. (29-8-2007) NEW DELHI : Government has detected some major defects in the Main Battle Tank 'Arjun' during the course of its field trial. The main defects noticed during trials by Army were related to failure of piston rods of hydro pneumatic Suspension Unit, Gunner Main Sight & Gun Control System. These defects were noticed during the trials in 2005 and 2006. The cause of defects have been analysed and corrective action has been taken to eliminate the defect. Defect related to premature warning of Air filter of the engine fitted in MBT Arjun was noticed during the trial in 2005. The cause of the defect was analysed and rectified in consultation with the specialists from Germany, Belgium and France. The remedial measures have been implemented at the production stage. This information was given by the Minister of State for Defence Production Rao Inderjit Singh in a written reply to Shri Abu Asim Azmi in Rajya Sabha today.

2797. (29-8-2007) NEW DELHI : About 54 missing defence personnel of 1971 War are believed to be in the custody of Pakistan. Pakistan has however been consistently denying the presence of any such personnel in its custody. The Government has been pursuing this issue with Pakistan for a long time. This issue was taken up with the Pakistan Government at various levels on a number of occasions. Recently, during the visit of External Affairs Minister to Islamabad in January 2007, the matter was again raised with the President of Pakistan and the latter in turn agreed to a visit by a small group of relatives of missing personnel to Pakistan. Accordingly, a delegation of 14 relatives of missing defence personnel visited 10 jails in different cities of Pakistan from 1st June, 2007 to 14th June 2007, but they could not find any missing defence personnel of 1971 War. As per laid instructions, a missing person is presumed to be killed if he is not found for 7 years and thereafter his family is given liberalized pensionary awards, which include liberalized family pension, gratuity and education allowance for children. Actions accordingly have been taken in case of missing defence personnel of 1971 War. The Government will continue to pursue the issue of missing defence personnel with the Govenment of Pakistan as it has been doing in the past. This information was given by the Defence Minister Shri AK Antony in a written reply to Smt Surendra Lat in Rajya Sabha today.

2798. (29-8-2007) NEW DELHI : In a glittering ceremony at Rashtrapati Bhawan today, President, Smt. Pratibha Devisingh Patil gave away sports and adventure awards. Rajiv Gandhi Khel Ratna Award for the year 2006 was conferred upon Shri Manavjit Singh Sandhu for his outstanding performance and achievements in Shooting He was presented a Citation and Rs.5 lakhs. Shri R.D. Singh (Athletics, Paralympic Games), Shri Damodaran Chandralal (Boxing) and Shri Koneru Ashok (Chess) were conferred Dronacharya Award for the year 2006 in recognition of their meritorious achievements in the field of coaching. This award carries an amount of Rs. 3 lakhs, a Memento and a Citation. Shri Jayanta Talukdar (Archery), Shri Kalyathumkuzhiyil Mathew Binu (Athletics), Shri B. Chetan Anand (Badminton), Shri Vijender (Boxing), Shri Pentala Harikrishana (Chess), Ms. Anjum Chopra (Cricket), Ms. Jyoti Sunita Kullu (Hockey), Shri Vijay Kumar (Shooting), Shri Saurav Ghosal (Squash), Shri Subhajit Saha (Table Tennis),

Smt. Geeta Rani (Weightlifting), Ms. Geetika Jakhar (Wrestling), Shri Navneet Gautam (Kabaddi) and Shri Rahit Bhakar (Badminton-Disabled category were conferred Arjuna Award for the year 2006 in recognition of their outstanding achievements in the field of Sports. The Award carries an amount of Rs. 3 lakhs and a Citation. The President also gave away Dhyan Chand Award for the year 2007 to Shri Varinder Singh (Hockey), Shri Shamsher Singh (Kabaddi) and Shri Rajendra Singh (Wrestling) to honour these sportspersons for their contribution to sports by their performance and efforts to promote the sports. Maulana Abul Kalam Azad Trophy 2005-2006 has been awarded to Guru Nanak Dev University, Amritsar. The winner receives a cash prize of Rs.2 lakh and the MAKA Rolling Trophy alongwith a small replica of the MAKA Trophy for retention by the University. The President also conferred Tenzing Norgay National Adventure Awards for the year 2006 to recognize the contribution and performance of the awardees in the field of adventure sports. Shri Gurdial Singh was given Life Time Achievement Award, Sub. Palden Giachho, was awarded for Land Adventure, Wg.Cdr. Motuku Indra Kanth Reddy got the award for Air Adventure while Shri Tapas Chowdhury was awarded for his performance in Water Adventure.

2799. (29-8-2007) NEW DELHI : Comptroller and Auditor General (CAG) pointed out delays in some defence buys in the report for the year ended March 2006, submitted in 2007. Contributions made by the Defence Research and Development (R&D) have been acknowledged from time to time by various agencies. Wherever there are delays in products being realized byDRDO, import option is considered to fill the gap. While attention has been drawn to delay in some defence buys in the CAG report for the year ended March 2006, there does not appear to be a specific reference to re-emphasise accountability aspect. Defence Procurement Procedure (DPP-2006) has further streamlined the procurement procedure and also included a broad timeframe for procurement activities. Recommendations of the CAG have also been taken into account while formulating the DPP-2006. This information was given by the Defence Minister Shri AK Antony in a written reply to Smt Shobhana Bhartia and Shri Vijay J Darda in Rajya Sabha today.

2800. (29-8-2007) NEW DELHI : The High Altitude (Uncongenial Climate) Allowance is payable to the Armed Forces personnel deployed in High Altitude (Uncongenial Climate) areas. The government has recently decided to grant enhanced rates of High Altitude (Uncongenial Climate) Allowance to troops deployed in more difficult, hazardous and isolated areas above 14,000 ft within the existing High Altitude (Uncongenial Climate) Areas at the rate of Rs. 5,600 per month for Officers and Rs. 3,734 per month for Personnel Below Officer Rank with a view to rationalize the High Altitude Allowance. The enhanced allowance is 80% of Siachen allowance and is comparable to Siachen allowance in proportion to the physical hardships being faced by the Armed Force Personnel.

2801. (29-8-2007) NEW DELHI : For occupation of lands during Operation

Parakram, the number of farmers for whom compensation is yet to be released to Deputy Commissioners are approximately 790 in districts Jammu and Poonch of J&K and districts Gurdaspur and Ferozepur of Punjab. Government has sanctioned an amount of Rs. 296,93,230/- in June/July 2007 for payment as compensation to approximately 684 farmers in districts Ferozepur and Jammu. This amount will be placed shortly with concerned Deputy Commissioners by the Defence Estate officers. For the remaining cases in districts Jammu, Poonch and Gurdaspur, the formalities for assessing/sanctioning of compensation are underway. This information was given by the Defence Minister Shri AK Antony in a written reply to Shri T S Bajwa in Rajya Sabha today.

2802. (29-8-2007) NEW DELHI : The purchase of light helicopter for the army is being processed under the Defence Procurement Procedure and an appropriate decision would be taken after following all the stages of procurement process. As such, no definite time limit could be given at this stage. The exact value of the procurement would be known only thereafter. This information was given by the Defence Minister Shri AK Antony in a written reply to Shri Amar Singh and Shri Abu Asim Azmi in Rajya Sabha today.

2803. (29-8-2007) NEW DELHI : The state of Jammu and Kashmir is facing the menace of militancy, aided and abetted from across the border, for quite some time. To counter the militancy in the State, Army and Central Para Military Forces have been deployed to assist the state administration. Army undertakes operations against the militants based on hard intelligence. In such operations, at times firings take place, especially when the militants are armed and they use fire arms against the force or innocent public. Such encounters are unavoidable in the situation prevailing in the state. However, there are strict guidelines prescribed for the forces for honouring human rights during discharge of their duties. Do's and Don'ts to be followed while acting under the Armed Forces Special Powers Act have also been laid down by the Army. The force personnel are also sensitized from time to time to discharge their duties with a humane face and with minimum inconvenience to the public. All reported cases of alleged human rights violations are investigated promptly by the Army and stringent punishments are awarded to those found guilty. During last 3 years (2005 onwards), four cases of alleged killing of civilian personnel by the Army in fake encounter have been reported. In all these four cases, a Court of Enquiry has been instituted and a number of witnesses have been examined. In two of the cases, criminal cases have been filed against some Army personnel in the district court by the state police. The State Government of J&K has also appointed a Commission of Enquiry on 2nd April, 2007 to enquire into alleged fake encounters/custodial killings in the state and to give its report within six months. In order to sensitize the troops deployed in Counter Insurgency/Counter terrorist operations, Human Rights Cells have been established at various levels. The troops are sensitized at regular intervals regarding the importance of upholding human rights and avoiding collateral damage. Regular foundation and refresher training in human rights is also carried out. This information was given by the Defence Minister Shri AK Antony in a written reply to Shri Janardhana Poojary in Rajya Sabha today.

2804. (29-8-2007) NEW DELHI : There are 39 Ordnance Factories in the country and one factory is being set up at Nalanda, Bihar. Their specialized area of production are Troops Comfort Items, Small Arms, Ammunitions, Chemicals and Explosives, Weapon, Main Battle Tanks, Armoured Personnel Carrier, Towed Guns, Mine Protected and Bullet Proof Vehicles, Naval Guns, Anti-aircraft Guns, Transport Vehicles, Optics, Equipments etc. Ministry of Defence, Ministry of Home Affairs, Ministry of Surface Transport, Ministry of Railways, all the State Police Departments and Forest Department are customers of the product of Ordnance Factories. Government has opened Defence sector for 100 % Indian private sector participation in May 2001 subject to licensing. Since then, 38 letters of intent/ industrial licenses have been issued to various companies in the private sector for manufacture of wide range of defence items.

2805. (29-8-2007) NEW DELHI : So far eleven rounds of Defence Secretary level talks have been held with Pakistan on the Siachen issue. Both sides have reaffirmed their commitment to the November 2003 cease-fire between the two countries which is holding successfully and have agreed to continue the discussion to resolve the issue in a peaceful manner. This information was given by the Defence Minister Shri AK Antony in a written reply to Shri Rasheed Masood and Shri Naveen Jindal in Lok Sabha today.

2806. (29-8-2007) NEW DELHI : Heavy Vehicles Factory has so far supplied 181 T-90 tanks to Army. No technical problems viz barrel bursting has been observed in T90 tanks. The problem of barrel bursting was noticed earlier in T-72 tank. The bursting of barrel in T-72 tanks occurred in barrels of Russian origin as well as of Indian origin. The problem was analysed in consultation with Russian experts and remedial action towards modifying the chemistry of material has been taken. This information was given by the Minister of State for Defence Production Rao Inderjit Singh in a written reply to Shri A Krishna Swamy and Shri Kuldeep Bishnoi in Lok Sabha today.

2807. (29-8-2007) NEW DELHI : Co-development of a Fifth Generation Fighter Aircraft has been identified as an important area of cooperation between the Indian and Russian Government. Technical discussions to work out the details are in progress. Efforts are on for finalizing the draft Inter Governmental Agreement in this regard. This information was given by the Minister of State for Defence Production Rao Inderjit Singh in a written reply to Shri Gurudas Dasgupta and Shri CK Chandrappan in Lok Sabha today.

2808. (29-8-2007) NEW DELHI : The women offices are appointed both in Short Service and Permanent Commissions in the Medical, Nursing and Dental Services.

In these Services, SSC women officers are also eligible for Permanent Commission. The women officer's are also appointed as SSC officers in some select branches in the three Defence Forces. They are, however, not eligible for Permanent Commission. Women officers are treated at par with similarly placed male counterparts in terms of recruitment, training, tenure of service, promotion etc. Writ petitions have been filed by three women officers of Air Force against non-grant of Permanent Commission, extension of Commission. The matter is subjudice. Similarly, one retired women officer of Navy has lodged a complaint for the same.

2809. (29-8-2007) NEW DELHI : As per National Mineral Inventory prepared by Indian Bureau of Mines, as on 1.4.2005, the total resources of gold ore (primary) and diamond are estimated at 390.29 million tonnes (with a metal content of 490.81 tonnes) and 4.58 million carats respectively. The import of gold in the last few years has been in the range of 700-800 tonnes per annum. Apart from the regional exploration for gold and diamond undertaken by Geological Survey of India (GSI), since the year 2000 the Government has been giving prior approvals for grant of reconnaissance permits for regional exploration of gold and diamond to various applicants, including private companies. These may convert into mining leases based on the outcome of the exploration, including detailed prospecting. As per available information, the Central Government has given prior approval for grant of mining lease for gold in favour of three private companies, viz, M/s Manmohan Industries Private Limited in Jharkhand, M/s Ramgad Minerals and Mining Private Limited in Karnataka and M/s Geo Mysore Services India Private Limited in Andhra Pradesh. As informed by the Indian Bureau of Mines, no mining lease for diamond has been granted to a private sector company. The above information was given by the Minister of Mines Shri Sis Ram Ola in a written reply in the Rajya Sabha today.

2810. (29-8-2007) NEW DELHI : Maharashtra State Power Generation Company Limited (Mahagenco) have requested supply of coal on tapering basis for their future expansion projects till their coal blocks come into production. These expansion projects include Bhusawal-3, Parli-3, Paras-3, Koradi-1 (Replacement), Chandrapur-1 and Koradi-2. The request of Mahagenco was considered by the Standing Linkage Committee (Long-term) on Power in its meeting held on 2.8.2007 which approved grant of Letter of Assurance (LOA) to Mahagenco on "tapering basis" to the tune of maximum quantity of 2 million tonnes per annum, keeping in view actual requirement/shortfall from captive mines of Mahagenco. However, the commercial arrangements in this regard would be worked out between the consumer and CIL/specifically linked company for supply of coal on short term tapering basis. In addition, Mahagenco has also been granted LOA to the tune of about 10 million tones during 2006 for their power projects. The request from the Government of Maharashtra was for supply of coal from Western Coalfields Limited (WCL) area. The Committee has approved LOA to Mahagenco on "tapering basis" on "cost plus basis" from Coal India Limited/specifically linked company, to the tune of maximum quantity of 2 million tones per annum keeping in view actual requirement/shortfall from the captive mines of Mahagenco. The above information was given by Dr. Dasari Narayana Rao, Minister of State for Coal in a written reply in the Lok Sabha today.

2811. (29-8-2007) NEW DELHI : The Government has reviewed the policy regarding necessity of obtaining No Objection Certificate (NOC) from Neyveli Lignite Corporation (NLC) for allocation of lignite blocks and it has been decided that henceforth lignite blocks would be identified in consultation with NLC and would be placed in the list of blocks identified for allocation. These could then be circulated to State Governments / Central Ministries or advertised for allocation through Screening Committee as the case may be. Once this exercise is carried out there would be no need for the State Government companies to obtain NOC from NLC separately. The above information was given by Dr. Dasari Narayana Rao, Minister of State for Coal in a written reply in the Lok Sabha today.

2812. (29-8-2007) NEW DELHI : Modernization of coal mines is a continuous process and Coal India Limited (CIL) has been taking initiatives in modernizing their mines. There are 468 mines in CIL of which 283 are underground mines, 149 are opencast mines and 36 are mixed mines having both underground and opencast operations. All 149 opencast mines are mechanized and out of 283 underground mines 197 are mechanized. Of the remaining 86 underground mines, 66 mines have been identified for mechanization in next five years. Opencast mines of Mahanadi Coalfields Limited (MCL) are already mechanized with modern technology. MCL has proposals to modernize operation of underground mines. In underground mines manual coal loading has been replaced by loading machines like Side Discharge Loaders (SDLs)/Load Haul Dumpers (LHDs) in conjunction with belt conveyors. Continuous Miner Technology has been adopted in 3 of the underground mines namely, HBI mine, Orient Mine No.1 and Orient Mine No.2. Man riding systems have been ordered for installation in four underground mines of MCL to reduce travel time of miners.

2813. (29-8-2007) NEW DELHI : The Mid-Day scheme is implemented to cover children studying in classes I-V of Government, Local Body and Government aided schools, and centres run under the Education Guarantee Scheme (EGS) and Alternative & Innovative Education (AIE) across the country. Under this scheme, children are served hot cooked meal of 450 calories and 12 grams of protein per school day. Central assistance to States/UTs is allocated/released only after adjusting unspent balance out of pervious releases. Details of funds released to States during the last three years is given in Annexure-1. The number of students benefited under the scheme during 2006-07 is given in Annexure-2 This was stated by the Minister of State for Human Resource Development, Shri M.A.A.Fatmi in a written reply to a question raised by Sh. M.V. Mysura Reddy in Rajya Sabha today.

2814. (29-8-2007) NEW DELHI : The performance of Indian Railways in respect of loading has gone up from 233.21 Million Tonnes during April-July 2006 to 247.05 Million Tonnes during April-July 2007, registering an increase of 5.93 per cent. Freight earnings have also gone up from Rs. 13145.87 crore during April-July 2006 to Rs.14297.74 crore during April-July 2007, registering an increase of 8.76 per cent. Passenger earnings have gone up from Rs. 5521.89 crore during April-July 2006 to Rs.6216.57 crore during April-July 2007, showing an increase of 12.58 per cent. The Integral Coach Factory (ICF) produced 91 coaches during July 2007. Chitranjan Locomotive Works (CLW), Diesel Locomotive Works (DLW) and Rail Coach Factory (RCF) produced 14 electric locomotives, 19 diesel locomotives and 76 coaches respectively. Rail Wheel Factory (RWF) produced 11764 wheels and 5334 axles during the same period. The punctuality percentage of mail/express trains was 93.9 per cent in Broad Gauge and 99.3 per cent in Metre Gauge during July 2007 compared to 93.7 per cent and 98.4 per cent respectively during the same period last year.

2815. (29-8-2007) NEW DELHI : In a Writ Petition (C) No. 10836 of 2005, the Government has submitted before the High Court of Orissa that the Government is taking follow up action for implementation of the announcement made by the Prime Minister on 28.8.2006 regarding setting up of a National Institute of Science Education and Research (NISER) at Bhubaneswar under the Department of Atomic Energy and that it is proposed to start the academic session from August, 2007. Taking cognizance of this, the Orissa High Court has disposed of the Writ Petition with a direction to the Government to ensure that the NISER is established at Bhubaneswar pursuant to the decision of the Government of India. The Department of Atomic Energy has informed that 300 acres of land has been allotted by the government of Orissa for setting up of NISER. NISER has been registered under the Societies Registration Act and infrastructural facilities are being put in place. In addition, for admission to NISER, an NISER Entrance Screening Test (NEST) followed by interview has been conducted and admission will commence on 10th September, 2007. This was stated by the Minister of State for Human Resource Development Shri M.A.A.Fatmi in a written reply to a question raised by Ms. Pramila Bohidar and Shri B.J. Panda in Rajya Sabha today.

2816. (29-8-2007) NEW DELHI : Some sporadic instances of corporal punishment in schools have been reported in the media recently. National Policy on Education, 1986 as modified in 1992, inter alia, provides that 'corporal punishment will be firmly excluded from the educational system'. Corporal punishment is strictly prohibited in schools run by Kendriya Vidyalaya Sangathan, Navodaya Vidyalaya Samiti and Central Tibetan School Administration, which are under the Ministry of Human Resource Development. Whenever any case of corporal punishment is brought to the notice of autonomous organisations in charge of the school, action is initiated against the persons responsible. Education being a concurrent subject, States follow their own policy in respect of schools under the purview of the State Governments and information on corporal punishment is not centrally maintained.

This was stated by the Minister of State for Human Resource Development Shri M.A.A.Fatmi in a written reply to a question raised by Shri Kalraj Mishra in Rajya Sabha today.

2817. (29-8-2007) NEW DELHI : The issues of quality and standard of education is addressed by the University Grants Commission (UGC) through its various schemes of Development Assistance to eligible Colleges and Universities for improving quality of higher education. The National Assessment and Accreditation Council (NAAC), an Inter-University Centre of the UGC has assessed 140 Universities out of which only 2 Universities are in the lowest bracket having less than 60 marks on a 100 point scale. Improvement of standard is a continuous and ongoing process. While the quality of teaching and research in higher education is ensured by regulating the minimum qualifications for teachers, continuous orientation refresher programmes are organized for teachers through Academic Staff Colleges of UGC. More emphasis is being given on research programmes. The UGC has developed the concept of University and College with potential for excellence, for recognizing and promoting excellence. This was stated by the Minister of State for Human Resource Development Shri M.A.A.Fatmi in a written reply to a question raised by Shri Gireesh Kumar Sanghi in Rajya Sabha today.

2818. (29-8-2007) NEW DELHI : The Chief Minister of Goa has requested the Prime Minister for establishment of Indian Institute of Management (IIM) in Goa. The request would be considered as and when the Government of India initiates the process of setting up of new IIMs in the country. This was stated by the Minister of State for Human Resource Development Shri M.A.A.Fatmi in a reply to a question raised by Shri Shantaram Laxman Naik in Rajya Sabha today.

2819. (29-8-2007) NEW DELHI : According to the information furnished by the University Grants Commission (UGC), at present there are 388 University level Institutions recognized under Scetion 2(f) of the UGC Act, 1956. The National Assessment and Accreditation Council (NAAC), which is an Inter-University Centre of the UGC, has been entrusted with responsibility of assessing and accrediting the Institutions in accordance with the guidelines prescribed for the purpose. The UGC has taken several steps to upgrade the standards of education by providing grants to eligible Universities and Colleges under its various schemes for quality improvement and excellence, such as (i) Universities with Potential for Excellence (ii) Colleges with Potential for Excellence (iii) Special Assistance Programme (SAP) (iv) Assistance for Strengthening of Infrastructure in Science and Technology (ASIST) (v) Assistance for Strengthening of Infrastructure in Humanities and Social Science (ASHISS) (vi) Major and Minor Research Projects (vii) Fellowships for pursuing M.Phil and Ph.D programmes etc. This was stated by the Minister of State for Human Resource Development Shri M.A.A.Fatmi in a reply to a question raised by Sh. V. Hanumantha Rao in Rajya Sabha today.

2820. (29-8-2007) NEW DELHI : Subject to the Plan being finalized, it is proposed to establish 30 new Central Universities during the XIth Plan and the first two years of the XIIth Plan period, and to provide assistance for establishing one college in each district with low Gross Enrolment Ratio (GER) in higher education. Action for establishment, in the first phase, of one Central University, in each of the 16 States which do not have a Central University, so far, namely Bihar, Chhattisgarh, Goa, Gujrat, Haryana, Himachal Pradesh, Jammu and Kasmir, Jharkhand, Karnataka, Kerela, Madhya Pradesh, Orissa, Punjab, Rajasthan, Tamil Nadu and Uttarakhand, has already been initiated. The targeted GER, as against the present level of approximately 10%, is at least 15% by the end of the XIth Plan and 21% by the end of the XIIth Plan. This was stated by the Minister of State for Human Resource Development Shri M.A.A.Fatmi in a reply to a question raised by Smt. N.P.Durga in Rajya Sabha today.

2821. (29-8-2007) NEW DELHI : The Framework for Implementation of Sarva Shiksha Abhiyan (SSA) programme provides for funds sharing in the ratio of 85:15 between the Central Government and States/UTs during IXth plan, in the ratio of 75:25 during the Xth plan and the ratio of 50:50, thereafter. The North Eastern States as special dispensation were allowed funding pattern of 90:10 during 2005-06 & 2006-07 while 15% share in their case was being borne by the Department for Development of North East Region (DoNER). This was stated by the Minister of State for Human Resource Development Shri M.A.A.Fatmi in a reply to a question raised by Ms. Sushila Tiriya in Rajya Sabha today.

2822. (29-8-2007) NEW DELHI : Mumbai Port has carved a unique niche for itself in the Indian commercial geography. The Port is a fully integrated multi-purpose port handling container, dry bulk, liquid bulk and break-bulk cargo. It has extensive wet and dry dock accommodations to meet the normal needs of ships using the Port. There are three enclosed wet dock systems, Prince's, Victoria and Indira docks. There are 45 berths, 4 jetties at Jawahar Dweep to handle crude and POL tankers and an offshore berth at Pir Pau to handle liquid chemicals and some of the POL traffic. The Port has a full-fledged container terminal at BPS in Indira Dock which is equipped with two gantry cranes for ship-to-shore handling of containers and three Rubber-Tyred Cranes for yard operations and two dry docks. Mumbai Port has approximately 7 lakh square meters of open and covered accommodation for storing uncleared goods and hazardous cargo. Container Freight Stations have been set up at Manganese Ore Depot, Timber Pond, and Frere Basin. Rail Container Depot has been shifted inside the Indira Dock near 2 ID-5 ID in the vicinity of the berths to facilitate loading/unloading of ICD containers, avoiding double handling. The Port owns and operates its own railway, which is connected to the broad gauge main lines of Central and Western Railways at its Interchange Railway Yard at Wadala. It has a full fledged cruise terminal with 'Super Star Libra' home-ported there. Mumbai Port is the new hub for automobile export from India. During the year 2006-07, Mumbai Port handled 52.36 million tonnes of cargo, registering a growth of 18.50% over the previous year. This is also 6.86% over the target of 49 million tonnes fixed by the Ministry of Shipping, Road Transport & Highways. The cargo handled comprises of 31.09 million tonnes of imports and 21.27 million tonnes of exports. The Port has achieved double-digit growth during the last four years and almost doubled the cargo throughput from 26.8 million tonnes during 2002-03 to 52.4 MT during 2006-07.

2823. (29-8-2007) NEW DELHI : As per the latest data available from Department of Industrial Policy & Promotion (DIPP), Ministry of Commerce & Industry, the total cumulative inflow of Foreign Direct Investment (FDI) from various countries into the textiles sector during the 10th Plan period (from April 2002 to March 2007) was Rs.1473.23 crore. This information was given by the Minister of State for Textiles, Shri E.V.K.S. Elangovan in the Rajya Sabha today, in a written reply to a question by Shri Ravula Chandra Sekar Reddy. This accounts for 1.24 percentage share in the total cumulative inflow of FDI in the country, which stood at Rs.118562.09 crore during the same period. The Minister further informed the house that to take the advantage of the growing Indian Capital Market, Foreign Institutional Investors (FIIs) are investing in the economy. At present, the Indian Capital Market is buoyant with a strong regulatory framework conducive to attract larger long term FII participation, he added.

2824. (29-8-2007) NEW DELHI : Thirty-two out of thirty five States and Union Territories have published their State of Environment Reports. The overall objective of the SOE reporting is to highlight the linkages of various economic activities and house-hold and Government functions with the environmental issues creating baseline data. This involves systemic data collection, compilation, analysis along with networking with various Government Departments and other Organisations. Inaugurating the National Workshop on State of Environment today, Shri Siddharth Behura, Special Secretary in the Ministry of Environment and Forests, said, it is very satisfying to learn about the progress of 32 reports. Arunachal Pradesh, Jammu and Kashmir and Lakshdweep Islands have yet to fulfill this requirement of National Planning by mainstreaming environment in policy making and strategy formulation. The Ministry will continue its efforts to convince them to prepare this report, he added. The SOE reporting is initiated during Tenth Plan with the financial help of Central Government and technical support with the help of National Host Institutions. During the Tenth Plan a network of Institutions at State level for providing the required information has been developed. SOE reports will become important document for planning formulation and distribution of financial resources from the Planning Commission. During Eleventh Plan efforts will be made to achieve the objective of making their information similar and statistically consistent as well as comparable in concepts definitions and norms. Giving key-note address, Shri Sudhir Mittal, Joint Secretary, Ministry of Environment and Forests, said that it was anticipated that through the SOE reports, State Governments and UT Administrations will be able to integrate environmental dimension in their social, economic and sustainable development planning. Four National Host Institutes viz. The Energy and Resources Institute, New Delhi; The Development Alternatives, New Delhi; The Administrative Staff College of India, Hyderabad and The Environment Protection Training Research Institute, Hyderabad, were engaged for sensitizing, capacity building and Assistant States and Union Territories in preparation of SOE reports. Representatives from State Governments and Union Territories and Officers from Ministry of Environment and Forests and TERI are participating in the Workshop.

2825. (29-8-2007) NEW DELHI : The Minister of State for Textiles, Shri E.V.K.S. Elangovan, informed the Rajya Sabha today, in a written reply to a question by Dr. K. Malaisamy that the Action Plan for the growth of the Textiles & Garments was recently considered by the High Level Committee on Manufacturing (HLCM) under the Chairmanship of the Prime Minister. The HLCM, inter alia, deliberated over the following issues: On the issue of availability of textiles machinery, it has been decided to visit few countries having major textile machinery manufacturers to explain them about the opportunities of investment in India. As there are only six major textile machine manufacturers in the world, they can be easily targeted to attract Foreign Direct Investment. Regarding the issue of rupee appreciation along with high interest rates that has led to a deceleration in the garment exports, it has been decided to form a small group to look into the causes for recent deceleration in exports including rupee appreciation and other macro economic policies on the competitiveness of the industry and suggest measures to address the issue expeditiously. In addition, the Employment-linked Skill Development Scheme, known as "NATIJA", prepared by the Ministry of Textiles has been decided to be finalized soon for expeditious implementation. The flagship Schemes of the Ministry, namely Technology Upgradation Fund Scheme (TUFS) and the Scheme for Integrated Textiles Parks (SITP) have been decided to be continued with adequate funds in the Eleventh Plan.

2826. (29-8-2007) NEW DELHI: The Bharatiya Janata Party's stand on the nuclear deal with the United States stands and there are "no differences" on this in the party, the top leadership asserted here on Tuesday. While party president Rajnath Singh confirmed that ahead of the nuclear debate in Parliament, the central leadership decided to meet once again to discuss in detail the stand on the deal and fine-tune it. On August 31, the party's core group is scheduled to meet and the deal is likely to dominate the session. Immediately after the text of the 123 agreement was made public, senior leaders Yashwant Sinha and Arun Shourie articulated the party's view on the basis of a consensus arrived at a meeting at the former Prime Minister Atal Bihari Vajpayee's residence. A party statement on August 4 said the BJP was "unable to accept this [nuclear] agreement as finalised," as it was "an assault on our nuclear sovereignty."

2827. (29-8-2007) NEW DELHI : The Department of Biotechnology has proposed to strengthen virus research in the country with emphasis on viral diseases like

Hepatitis 'C' and 'E', Avian Influenza, Japanese Encephalitis, Dengue and other emerging viruses like Chikungunya. The goal of this programme is to establish Virus Research Centres and R&D Networks in order to develop broad comprehensive biomedical research programme for viral diseases in India. The Department has invited proposals through advertisements in the national dailies. The proposals are evaluated and selected programmes shall be implemented during the 11th Plan period. This information was given by the Union Minister for Science & Technology and Earth Sciences Shri Kapil Sibal in the Rajya Sabha.

2828. (29-8-2007) NEW DELHI : The Government propose to set up a National Silkworm Seed Regulatory Authority. This information was given by the Minister of State for Textiles, Shri E.V.K.S. Elangovan in a written reply to a question by Shri Rajkumar Dhoot in the Rajya Sabha today. The Minister further informed the House that as per the provisions of Central Silk Board (Amendment) Act, 2006, Central Silkworm Seed Committee has been constituted vide Notification dated 10.8.2007.

2829. (29-8-2007) NEW DELHI : Uttar Pradesh Government has reported release of 3,15,972 electricity connections to Below Poverty Line (BPL) Households during last three years under Rajiv Gandhi Grameen Vidyutikaran Yojana (RGGVY) as on 17-08-2007. Funds under RGGVY are released in installments commensurating with the progress reported by the Implementing agencies. There is no provision for State-wise allocation of funds under RGGVY. U.P. State has availed an amount of Rs.2,357.01 crores under RGGVY as on 17-08-2007. This information was given by the Union Power Minister Shri Sushilkumar Shinde in the Rajya Sabha.

2830. (29-8-2007) NEW DELHI : According to the Liberhan Commission of Inquiry, its report is expected to be submitted to the Government within its present extended tenure, *i.e.* up to 31st August, 2007. The Government had extended the tenure of the Commission on 40 occasions since its appointment. An Expenditure of Rs.717.66 lakh has been incurred on the Commission till 31st July, 2007. This information was given by the Minister of State for Home, Shri Sriprakash Jaiswal in a written reply to a question in the Rajya Sabha today.

2831. (29-8-2007) NEW DELHI : Rajiv Gandhi Grameen Vidyutikaran Yojana (RGGVY) envisages providing single point light connections free of cost to all Below Poverty Line (BPL) Households in the rural areas of the country. Implementing agencies in Bihar have reported release of 14,855 BPL Household Connections under RGGVY since April, 2005 uptill 17-08-2007 and the State Government so far has availed Rs. 960.79 crore under RGGVY. This information was given by the Union Power Minister Shri Sushilkumar Shinde in the Rajya Sabha.

2832. (29-8-2007) NEW DELHI : The mercy petitions filed before the President of India by the condemned prisoner Mohd. Afzal and others on his behalf are being processed in accordance with the prescribed procedure, for submission to the President. The power under Article 72 of the Constitution does not contain any limitation as to the time, in which the power conferred might be exercised. This information was given by the Minister of State for Home, Shrimati V. Radhika Selvi in a written reply to a question in the Rajya Sabha today.

2833. (29-8-2007) NEW DELHI : The annual strategy for polio eradication is decided on the basis of the recommendation of the Indian Expert Advisory Group (IEAG) consisting of National experts and International experts from World Health Organisation (WHO), United Nation's Children Fund (UNICEF), Centre for Diseases Control (CDC) Atlanta. The IEAG reviews the polio epidemiological situation two times a year and recommend the suitable strategies for the country. The National Polio Surveillance Project (NPSP) of WHO provides technical support for high quality Acute Flaccid Paralysis (AFP) surveillance and assists the Government in microplanning, training and monitoring of polio immunization campaign. During this year as on 24th August 2007, less number of polio cases has been reported in comparison to 2006 as 169 polio cases have been reported compared to 231 upto this week of last year. There has been significant decline in the number of cases caused by the most virulent strain of poliovirus type 1 (P1). This year the number of P1 cases has fallen to 48 as compared to 226 up to this week last year. The endemic region of Western Uttar Pradesh has reported only three type 1 polio cases this year. The core districts of Moradabad and J P Nagar, the epicenter of the outbreak last year, have not had a single case of P1 for the last 8 months. Polio type 1 circulation is continuing in certain district of Bihar and UP due to presence of risk factors like high population density, poor sanitation, flooding and migration. Polio type 1 cases reported in 2007 in Gujarat, Rajasthan, Haryana, Maharashtra and Andhra Pradesh are importations from UP & Bihar. The number of cases caused by other surviving strain of poliovirus-type 3-(P3) has risen this year to 121 from 5 in the corresponding period last year, but the circulation is confined to limited geographical area of Western Uttar Pradesh and Udham Singh Nagar district of Uttarakhand. This rise is consistent with the immunization strategy focusing on P1 through the use of more efficacious monovalent type 1 polio vaccine since April 2005. The immunization strategy has been focusing on curtailing P1 and keeping P3 in check because P1 circulates more widely, has been responsible for international spread and has the propensity to cause large outbreaks.

2834. (29-8-2007) NEW DELHI : Leasing out of existing assets of the Port to private operators for providing port services is permitted under the existing scheme for private sector participation in Major Ports. Selection of the private operators for providing the port services is required to be made through open competitive bidding and the party offering the highest share of gross revenue to the Major Port from the operation of the port facility is to be awarded the licence. The licence period may be for a maximum period of 30 years at the end of which the port related assets will revert back to the port in accordance with the conditions of the licence agreements entered in to by the Major Port with the private operator. This information was given by the Minister of Shipping, Road Transport and Highways, Thiru T.R. Baalu in a written reply in the Lok Sabha today.

2835. (29-8-2007) NEW DELHI : The Indian National Shipowners Association (INSA) has requested the Directorate General of Shipping to allow foreign officers to work on Indian ships in view of acute shortage of Indian officers. In order to overcome the shortage, the Government is considering a proposal to allow foreign officers to work on Indian ships subject to certain conditions. This information was given by the Minister of Shipping, Road Transport and Highways, Thiru T.R. Baalu in a written reply in the Lok Sabha today.

2836. (29-8-2007) NEW DELHI : Various steps including International Cooperation with Nepal have been implemented to protect tigers. The initiatives taken by the Government of India for conservation of wild animals including tiger consists of Legal steps, administrative steps and financial steps. Under Legal steps Amendment of the Wild Life (Protection) Act, 1972 for providing enabling provisions for constitution of the National Tiger Conservation Authority and the Tiger and Other Endangered Species Crime Control Bureau comes into force The punishment in cases of offence within a tiger reserve has been enhanced. The Act also provides for forfeiture of any equipment, vehicle or weapon that has been used for committing any wild life offence. Administrative steps includes. Strengthening of antipoaching activities, including special strategy for monsoon patrolling, by providing funding support to Tiger Reserve States, as proposed by them, for deployment of antipoaching squads involving ex-army personnel / home guards, apart from workforce comprising of local people, in addition to strengthening of communication / wireless facilities. Constitution of the National Tiger Conservation Authority with effect from 4.09.2006, for strengthening tiger conservation by, interalia, ensuring normative standards in tiger reserve management, preparation of reserve specific tiger conservation plan, laying down annual / audit report before Parliament, constituting State level Steering Committees under the Chairmanship of Chief Ministers and establishment of Tiger Conservation Foundation. Constitution of a multidisciplinary Tiger and Other Endangered Species Crime Control Bureau (Wildlife Crime Control Bureau) with effect from 6.6.2007 comprising of officers from Police, Forest, Customs and other enforcement agencies to effectively control illegal trade in wildlife. In principle approval has been accorded for declaring eight new Tiger Reserves. Financial and technical help is provided to the States under various Centrally Sponsored Schemes, viz. Project Tiger and Development of National Parks and Sanctuaries for enhancing the capacity and infrastructure of the States for providing effective protection to wild animals. India has a Memorandum of Understanding with Nepal on controlling trans-boundary illegal trade in wildlife and conservation, apart from a protocol on tiger conservation with China. A Global Tiger Forum of Tiger Range Countries has been created for addressing international issues related to tiger conservation. During the 14th meeting of the Conference of Parties to CITES, which was held from 3rd to 15th June, 2007 at The Hague, India introduced a resolution along with China, Nepal and the Russian Federation, which contains directions to Parties with operations breeding tigers on a commercial scale, for restricting such captive populations to a level supportive only to conserving wild tigers. The resolution was adopted with minor amendments. Further, India made an intervention appealing to China to phase out tiger farming, and eliminate stockpiles of Asian big cats body parts and derivatives. The importance of continuing the ban on trade of body parts of tigers was emphasized. This information was given by the Minister of State in the Ministry of Environment and Forests, Shri S.Regupathy in a written reply to a question by Shri M.Shivanna and Smt. Botcha Jhansi Lakshmi in the Lok Sabha today.

2837. (29-8-2007) NEW DELHI : A study was conducted by UNICEF on children affected by HIV in consultation with Government at the state and national level. The study titled 'Barriers to services for children of HIV positive parents in six high prevalence states' focused on the factors that impede the children from acceptance among the community members, limit their access to services like education, health and social welfare. The study also gathered opinion of key services providers in health, education and social welfare departments for solutions to overcome the stigma and discrimination faced by the children. The 'Policy Framework for Children and AIDS' released by the Government on 31st July 2007 proposes 'universal' access to services for all children including 'children affected by HIV/AIDS'. Instead of providing separate special facilities for these children there is a need to mainstream the children into the regular services of education, health and child welfare. This information was given by the Minister for Health & Family Welfare, Dr. Anbumani Ramadoss in a written reply to a question in the Lok Sabha.

2838. (29-8-2007) NEW DELHI : As per direction of the Delhi High Court, Government of NCT of Delhi have framed guidelines for provision of free treatment facilities to patients of Economically Weaker Section (EWS) category. These guidelines have been sent to 36 hospitals for compliance. Any of these private hospital found to be not complying with these guidelines is to be proceeded against as per the direction of the Hon'ble High Court and such hospital will also be liable for contempt of the Court. However, Mool Chand Khairati Ram Hospital, St. Stephen Hospital and Rajeev Gandhi Cancer Institute and Research Centre have refused to provide free treatment to poor patients stating that they are not covered under the judgement of the Hon'ble High Court. Rajeev Gandhi Cancer Institute & Research Centre have filed an application before the Delhi High Court against the implementation of the judgement. The matter is subjudice. At present, there is no proposal to enact a law for providing for free treatment to the poor people by private hospitals. This information was given by the Minister for Health &

Family Welfare, Dr. Anbumani Ramadoss in a written reply to a question in the Lok Sabha.

2839. (29-8-2007) NEW DELHI : Restructuring of National Highways Authority of India (NHAI) for making it a multi-disciplinary body has been approved by the Government with the following salient features: Selection of the Chairman by a search committee and tenure of Chairman be fixed for at least three years; Increase in the full time Members from five to six and part-time Members from four to six; Creation of additional posts of Chief General Managers (CGMs); Creation of expert units in the areas of finance, legal, safety, quality etc Empowering the NHAI to engage outside experts. This information was given by the Minister of State for Shipping, Road Transport and Highways, Shri K.H. Muniyappa in a written reply in the Lok Sabha today.

2840. (29-8-2007) NEW DELHI : National Highways Development Project (NHDP) Phase-IV is at initial stage of planning wherein two laning with paved shoulder of about 20,000 km of National Highways is envisaged with an estimated cost of Rs. 27,800 crore. NHDP Phase-IV is targeted to be completed by December, 2015. This information was given by the Minister of State for Shipping, Road Transport and Highways, Shri K.H. Muniyappa in a written reply in the Lok Sabha today.

2841. (29-8-2007) NEW DELHI : The new Model Concession Agreement (MCA) for Public Private Partnership has been approved by Committee on Infrastructure (CoI). In the new MCA, certain provisions like capacity augmentation based on the traffic, partial traffic risk sharing, provision for distribution of grant/receipt of premium, out-put based technical requirements, obligation of National Highways Authority of India (NHAI) for pre-construction activities, revision of concession period on variation of traffic growth etc., have been introduced. NHAI is adopting new Model Concession Agreement for implementation of future projects on Build, Operate and Transfer (Toll) mode of funding after getting approval from the Public Private Partnership Appraisal Committee (PPPAC). This information was given by the Minister of State for Shipping, Road Transport and Highways, Shri K.H. Muniyappa in a written reply in the Lok Sabha today.

2842. (29-8-2007) NEW DELHI : Rule 50 of the Central Motor Vehicles Rules, 1989 was amended by the Central Government in 2001 to introduce High Security Registration Plates throughout the country, in respect of all categories of motor vehicles. These plates have certain security features which would make removal, tampering or counterfeiting of such plates difficult. Initially, the scheme was to be implemented by 28th September, 2001, in respect of new vehicles and within two years thereafter, in respect of "in use" vehicles. However, the date of implementation was extended from time to time due to non availability of qualified vendors in the country and a number of cases in various High Courts. The date of implementation was last extended vide notification No. S.O. 883 (E) dated 12th

June, 2006 as per which, the scheme was to be implemented by 31st October, 2006, in respect of new vehicles and within two years thereafter, in respect of "in use" vehicles. Implementation of the scheme is the responsibility of the States/ UTs. As per the information available with this Ministry, none of the States have yet implemented the scheme. The issue relating to non-implementation of the scheme is the subject matter of a Writ Petition (Civil) No. 510 of 2005, filed by Shri M.S. Bitta in the Supreme Court in which all the States/UTs have been made respondents. Hon'ble Supreme Court had asked all the States/U.Ts. to file an affidavit explaining the reason for non-implementation of the scheme and the time period within which the same would be implemented. The matter is sub-judice. This information was given by the Minister of State for Shipping, Road Transport and Highways, Shri K.H. Muniyappa in a written reply in the Lok Sabha today.

2843. (29-8-2007) NEW DELHI : The Consultative Committee of Members of Parliament for the Ministry of Power met today under the Chairmanship of Shri SushilKumar Shinde, Union Power Minister, to discuss the Ultra Mega Power Projects (UMPPs). The Committee was informed that out of the 9 projects, the bidding process in respect of 2 projects being located in Mundra and Sasan has been completed. In addition, the bidding process in respect of 2 more projects, to be located in Krishnapatnam in Andhra Pradesh and Tilaiya in Jharkhand, has been initiated. However for the remaining 5 projects, final clearances from the State Governments are awaited. The State Governments of Maharashtra and Karnataka have been asked to indicate alternative sites for locating the UMPPs, as in both these States the identified sites of Girye and Tadri respectively are facing agitation on environmental grounds. While an early finalization is expected in the case of the project in Orissa, the position is not very clear as yet for the projects proposed to be located in Tamil Nadu and Chattisgarh. Government is actively pursuing the matter with these States through letters and in meetings. UMPPs, each of about 4000 MW capacity, are being developed on a Build, Own & Operate basis through tariff based competitive bidding. The bidding process for identification of the project developer is being carried out by project specific shell companies which have been formed as wholly owned subsidiaries of Power Finance Corporation, the identified nodal agency for this initiative. The Central Electricity Authority (CEA) in consultation with the State Governments had identified nine sites, 4 at pithead and 5 at coastal locations for development of UMPPs. The idenfified sites are : Sasan in M.P., Mundra in Gujarat, Krishnapatnam in A.P., Tilaiya in Jharkhand, Cheyyur in Tamil Nadu, Sundergarh in Orissa, Tadri in Karnataka, Akaltara in Chhatisgarh and Girye in Maharashtra. While appreciating the efforts of the Ministry towards achieving the goal of power for all, Members expressed the need for a uniform rehabilitation policy to streamline the process of land acquisition.

2844. (29-8-2007) NEW DELHI : Shri Koshy Koshy, a 1973 batch IPS officer of Haryana Cadre, has been appointed as Director General of the National Disaster

Response Force & Civil Defence. He is currently working as Additional Director General of CRPF.

2845. (29-8-2007) NEW DELHI : The Union Minister for Micro, Small & Medium Enterprises Shri Mahabir Prasad inaugurated Coir Board's new Display and Information Centre here today. Inaugurating the Centre Shri Prasad said, highly labour intensive and export oriented coir industry was providing livelihood to about half a million poor village artisans, predominately women. Since the raw material used in the industry being the coconut husk, which is considered as a waste after taking the coconut nut, the coir industry epitomizes the concept of 'wealth out of waste'. Considering the increasing national significance of this traditional industry, the Government included coir in the National Common Minimum Programme, the Minister added. Shri Mahabir Prasad said that the Board had already been implementing several programmes for market promotion but the need to establish more centres to expose the vast potential of coir products by arranging attractive display at various strategic locations across the country was badly felt. With this intention the Board opened this new Display cum Information Centre in New Delhi to showcase coir products for foreigners to see and select. Further, by setting up of the Display Centre, the overseas buyers would get an opportunity to see the different varieties of coir and handicrafts products, all the information related to the export, domestic market, exporters directory, catalogues, Board's various schemes etc., the Minister concluded. The Minister of Overseas Indian Affairs, Shri Vayalar Ravi, the Chairman of Coir Board Shri A.C. Jose, Secretary, Ministry of Micro, Small & Medium Enterprises Dr. Chandrapal, Shri Pravir Kumar & Shri Sesh Kumar Pulipaka, Joint Secretaries of the Ministry of Micro, Small & Medium Enterprises and other officials were also present on this occasion.

2846. (29-8-2007) NEW DELHI : Doordarshan has been producing and telecasting various campaigns on issues related to women and children on Doordarshan Network. The progress on social development covers Female Foeticide, Pre-Natal Diagnostic Techniques (PNDT) act, Domestic Violence, Discrimination among genders, Nutrition's Education and all the issues laid down in National Rural Health Mission (NRHM). Various Kendras of Doordarshan also telecast programmes on women and children on regular basis. The campaigns undertaken by Doordarshan are funded by Union Ministries of Health & Family Welfare, Women & Child Development & HRD etc. "Kalyani" is a major campaign of Doordarshan, which is in collaboration with the Ministry of Health & Family Welfare. This programme has covered all aspects of health. However, due to special focus on women and children in the community, "Kalyani' programme was divided into two parts *i.e.* Kalyani I and KalyaniII. Kalyani II has complete focus on reproductive and children health needs of the community. The objective of this programme is to highlight and create awareness of focused interventions of reproductive and child health. A study was conducted to evaluate the impact of these programmes designed and telecast on nine TV channels of Doordarshan. The programme has been found successful in creating a brand out of Kalyani. Over 1,200 Doordarshan Kalyani Health Clubs with over 24,000 members have been established which help improve awareness among the people in the community. It has been found that the programme has communicated desired messages effectively. This programme has helped in increasing immunization also. Various suggestions have also been received for further improvement and reach of this programme among rural folks. This information was given by Minister of Information & Broadcasting and Parliamentary Affairs, Shri P. R. Dasmunsi in written reply to a question in Rajya Sabha today.

2847. (29-8-2007) NEW DELHI : Doordarshan has been producing and telecasting various campaigns on issues related to women and children on Doordarshan Network. The progress on social development covers Female Foeticide, Pre-Natal Diagnostic Techniques (PNDT) act, Domestic Violence, Discrimination among genders, Nutrition's Education and all the issues laid down in National Rural Health Mission (NRHM). Various Kendras of Doordarshan also telecast programmes on women and children on regular basis. The campaigns undertaken by Doordarshan are funded by Union Ministries of Health & Family Welfare, Women & Child Development & HRD etc. "Kalyani" is a major campaign of Doordarshan, which is in collaboration with the Ministry of Health & Family Welfare. This programme has covered all aspects of health. However, due to special focus on women and children in the community, "Kalyani' programme was divided into two parts *i.e.* Kalyani I and KalyaniII. Kalyani II has complete focus on reproductive and children health needs of the community. The objective of this programme is to highlight and create awareness of focused interventions of reproductive and child health. A study was conducted to evaluate the impact of these programmes designed and telecast on nine TV channels of Doordarshan. The programme has been found successful in creating a brand out of Kalyani. Over 1,200 Doordarshan Kalyani Health Clubs with over 24,000 members have been established which help improve awareness among the people in the community. It has been found that the programme has communicated desired messages effectively. This programme has helped in increasing immunization also. Various suggestions have also been received for further improvement and reach of this programme among rural folks. This information was given by Minister of Information & Broadcasting and Parliamentary Affairs, Shri P. R. Dasmunsi in written reply to a question in Rajya Sabha today.

2848. (29-8-2007) NEW DELHI : The growing Indian diaspora around the world has crated a market for Indian films overseas that continues to grow at a rapid rate. As per the Price Waterhouse Coopers Report of 2007 conducted by FICCI, the overseas market is estimated to be worth Rs. 700 crores in 2006 and is expected to grow at a Compound Annual Growth Rate of 18%. It is expected to reach Rs. 850 crores during 2007. In accordance with the feedback received from representatives of Indian Film Industry, markets for Indian film are growing steadily in North Europe, Germany, France and Japan. In China too, there is a huge untapped film market. Recently, the mainstream cable companies in the United States have started a "Video on Demand" for Indian films. Latin America is also considered as a new market for Indian films.

2849. (29-8-2007) NEW DELHI : Import of finished carbon steel during the first four months, April to July 2007, was up by 60.2 per cent over the same period last year. During April to July 2007, the imports stood at 1.45 million tonnes compared to 0.905 million tonnes in 2006. Exports during the same period was up by 7.2 per cent, from 1.632 million tonnes in April-July, 2006 to 1.750 million tonnes this year. Production of finished carbon steel went up by 4.1 per cent during April-July 07 and stood at 15.55 million tonnes as against 14.943 million tonnes in April-July 2006. Production of Pig Iron recorded a rise of 13.8 per cent at 1.602 million tonnes. On the price front, while there was no change in price of Pig Iron and GP Sheets in July compared to the previous month, the price of wire rods rose by 3.33 per cent, HR Coils by 2.94 per cent, CR Coils by 1.32 per cent and plates (12 mm) by 1.45 per cent. Prices of Pencil Ingots/Billets fell by 3.16 per cent while those of TOR/TOT (10 mm) went down by 1.54 per cent and rounds (16 mm) by 1.64 per cent during July 2007 as against June 2007.

2850. (29-8-2007) NEW DELHI : Minister for Agriculture, Consumer Affairs, Food and Public Distribution, Shri Sharad Pawar today informed the Consultative Committee attached to his ministry that the Warehousing (Development & Regulation) Bill has been passed by both the Houses of Parliament. He said that by enabling farmers to raise credit against warehouse receipts, this initiative would bring about a revolution in the farming sector. 'This step of the government will make warehouse receipts a negotiable instrument and enable farmers to seek bank loans against these receipts. It would also encourage farmers to store their agricultural produce in scientific warehouses after harvesting, thereby enabling them to sell their produce at higher prices after storage of produce for reasonable periods of time. It is also expected that it would result in providing considerable benefits both at the macro as well as micro levels and increase the liquidity in the rural areas, encourage scientific warehousing of goods, lower cost of financing, improve supply chain and better price risk', the Minister said. Shri Pawar said that farmers would need to be made aware of the provisions of the ensuing law, through the media and the agricultural extension system. The banking system would also need to come forward to help the farmers in taking advantage of this new initiative. The Consultative Committee discussed the performance of the Central Warehousing Corporation and matters relating to the warehousing sector. Members lauded the fast growth of the Corporation in the last 50 years and the range of diverse activities undertaken by it. They also emphasized that the Corporation needs to provide greater support to the farming sector. Shri Pawar facilitated CWC for evolving from a warehousing company to a total logistic player and also for moving towards supply-chain management of farm produce, not just setting up godowns in rural areas. Ministers of State Shri Taslimuddin and Dr. Akhilesh

Prasad Singh also attended the meeting. The following Members of Parliament attended the meeting: S/Shri A. Sai Prathap, Jai Parkash, Ms. Archana Nayak (Lok Sabha), Jayantilal Barot, Pyarelal Khandelwal and Prof. M.S. Swaminathan (Rajya Sabha).

2851. (29-8-2007) NEW DELHI : The Government is considering various legislation for the protection and empowerment of the women. A comprehensive legislation to check the sexual harassment at the work place is being drafted. This was disclosed by the Minister of Women and Child Development Smt. Renuka Choudhary on the occasion of second anniversary of women protection programme 'Parivartan' being run by Delhi Police. She said that her ministry had requested the Home Ministry to increase the number of women in central security forces as a confidence building measure about their security and protection of women. She said that Government programmes and policies about protection of women could be translated and implemented at the grass root level effectively through police. Hence there is utmost need to sensitize police forces about women issues. Expressing concern over some recent cases of domestic violence, Smt. Renuka Choudhary said that the Government is reviewing the implementation of the concerned act but Government's efforts would not suffice until a campaign is run for the change of mind set in general about the status of the women in society. Congratulating Delhi Police about its programme 'Parivartan' for the protection were welfare of the women, she said that many more such campaigns are required to instill confidence among the women. She asked the Police Commissioner of Delhi to extend the 'Parivartan' programme to other districts from northwest districts of Delhi. The 'Parivartan' a programme started by the Delhi Police in 2005 in twenty police beats of northwest districts aims at combating violence against women. According to police, the programme has helped in curbing incidents of violence in the concerned districts significantly. Under the programme police run door-to-door campaign for sensitization about the protection of girl child. Schools are also involved in the campaign. Self defence training is also provided. On the occasion, the Minister awarded ISO certification to Delhi Police for its outstanding performance of 'Parivartan'.

2852. (29-8-2007) NEW DELHI : Concerned by the loss of means of livelihood and property due to the major fire at the Army's biggest ammunition depot at Khundroo in Anantnag district on August 11, the Ministry of Defence (MoD) has decided on a series of measures to provide compensation and relief to the victims. The decisions to this effect were taken by the Defence Minister Shri AK Antony, last night. As a first step, MoD will release Rs. 10 crores as an interim assistance to the Jammu & Kashmir State Government to provide relief to the people. The amount will be adjusted against the final payment to be made towards compensation to the State Government. MoD has also worked out the compensation norms for the people inhabiting areas adjacent to the Ammunition Depot at Khundroo. Those who have suffered complete loss of their Pucca houses will get a compensation of Rs. 1,50,000 per house while for Kutcha houses the compensation will be Rs. 50,000. This is inclusive of the rent for the period till the houses are reconstructed. For partially damaged houses, the compensation will be Rs. 50,000 per Pucca house and Rs. 25,000 per Kutcha house. The compensation for damages to crops, standing fruit trees, orchards, perennial crops and for cattle and birds killed will be as per the rates specified under norms of assistance from the Calamity Relief Fund as laid down by the Ministry of Home Affairs. The damage will be assessed by the District Administration and an Officer to be nominated for the purpose by the Chief Secretary of the State Government would work out the compensation or assistance payable in individual cases as per the norms. It may be mentioned that the families of the persons killed numbering 16 in the incident are being paid Rs. 2.5 lakh each of which Rs. 1.5 lakh is being given by the Army and Rs. 1 lakh by the State Government.

2853. (30-8-2007) NEW DELHI : The President, Smt. Pratibha Devisingh Patil, has condoled the demise of Shri Ramrao Wamanrao Adik. In a condolence message to his brother Shri Govindrao Adik, the President has said, "I am saddened to learn about the passing away of Shri Ramrao Wamanrao Adik. Shri Ramrao Adik was closely associated with various social and educational institutions and held important positions in the State Government including those of Deputy Chief Minister of Maharashtra in his long public career."

2854. (30-8-2007) NEW DELHI : Lt Gen Tej Kumar Sapru is to be the next General Officer Commanding in Chief (Army Commander) of the Chandimandir (near Chandigarh) based Wesern Command. Lt Gen Sapru who is presently commanding a Corps in terrorism-affected region of J&K, is to replace Lt Gen Daljeet Singh who retires on 31 October 2007. The operational responsibility of the Western Command encompasses the extremely important plains region along the Indo Pak borders. Lt Gen Sapru, was born at Srinagar (J&K). He had his early education at Punjab Public School, Nabha. He joined the National Defence Academy, Kharakwasla and was commissioned in the Indian Army, in the infantry (The First Battalion of Fourth Gorkha Rifles) in June 1969. He is one of the few officers who witnessed action both on the Western Front and in the erstwhile East Pakistan during the 1971 war with Pakistan. Lt Gen Sapru has held various prestigious Instructional, Staff and Command appointments. He was Assistant Military and Air Attache in the Embassy of India in Nepal, Kathmandu. His other staff assignment include the General Staff Officer in Directorate General of Military Operations, Army Headquarters, Colonel General Staff in an active Division in J&K, Deputy Military Secretary in Military Secretary Branch and Additional Director General (Procurement) Master General of Ordinance Branch. He was also the Commander of the Junior Leaders' Wing of the Infantry School at Belguam. He is a graduate of the National Defence College, the Defence Services Staff College, Wellington and has attended the Higher Command Course at the Army War College, Mhow. He has been awarded the Chief of Army Staff

Commendation in 1985 and the Yudh Seva Medal for distinguished service in active operations in 1999. Lt Gen Sapru has a varied command experience at various levels. He commanded an Infantry Battalion in Intense Counter Insurgency Operations, an Infantry Brigade in the Punjab, and another brigade in J&K during Operation VIJAY (1999). He has commanded an active Infanty Division deployed on the Line of Control in J&K. Lt Gen TK Sapru, is presently commanding the 16 Corps, the largest Corps of the Army in J&K.

2855. (30-8-2007) NEW DELHI : The Prime Minister, Dr. Manmohan Singh, has condoled the death of Shri Banarsi Das Gupta, former Chief Minister of Haryana. In a condolence message, the Prime Minister said: "I am deeply saddened to hear of the death of Shri Banarsi Das Gupta. In his passing away, we have lost a senior colleague in the Indian National Congress. He was widely loved and respected, particularly in Haryana, of which he was the Chief Minister for several years. He was an active participant in the Bhoodan Andolan and fought against social evils like dowry system and child marriage. May providence give his family the strength and fortitude to bear this irreparable loss. I pray for the peace of the departed soul."

2856. (30-8-2007) NEW DELHI : The Union Cabinet today extended the validity of the Central Notifications dated 29.08.2006 and 27.02.2007 for another six months from 01.09.2007 to 29.02.2008 on the same terms and conditions by a Central Order under section 3 of the Essential Commodities Act, 1955. This would empower the State Governments to undertake de-hoarding operations and to control the prices of wheat and pulses.

2857. (30-8-2007) NEW DELHI : The Union Cabinet today gave its approval for release of additional instalment of dearness allowance and dearness relief to Central Government employees and pensioners respectively, which became due from 1st July 2007. The Central Government employees and pensioners will become entitled to higher amount of dearness allowance/relief respectively with effect from 1st July 2007. The increase of dearness allowance became due from 1st July 2007. The 12 monthly average of the All India Consumer Price Index for the period ending June 2007, works out to587.62 which constitutes an increase of 91.82% over the base index of 306.33. 50% of DA has been merged with basic pay w.e.from 1.4.2004. The rate of DA from 1.7.2007 will be 41% for all Central Government employees, constituting an increase of 6% over the existing 35%. The rate of dearness relief from 1.7.2007 shall accordingly be 41% for all pensioners/family pensioners of Central Government. The additional financial implications on account of this increase of Dearness Allowance is Rs.2206.86 crore per annum; and Rs.1471.24 crore in the financial year 2007-2008. The additional financial implications on account of this increase of Dearness Relief to pensioners is Rs.1078.08 crore per annum, and Rs.718.72 crore in the financial year 2007-08. The combined impact on exchequer on account of both dearness allowance and dearness relief would be Rs.3284.94 crore in a full year and Rs.2189.96 crore in the financial year 2007-08.

2858. (30-8-2007) NEW DELHI : The Union Cabinet today gave its approval for introduction of official amendments to the Factories (Amendment) Bill 2005 pending in the Lok Sabha since 16.8.2005 to amend section 66 of the Factories Act, 1948. This amendment will provide flexibility in the matter of employment of women during night hours.

2859. (30-8-2007) NEW DELHI : The Cabinet Committee on Economic Affairs today gave its approval to the proposal of Oil India Limited for fresh equity issue of 10% of its paid up capital through Initial Public Officer (IPO) to enable the company to get listed on the Stock Exchanges. CCEA has also approved the proposal for issuing of additional 1% of its paid up capital to the employees of OIL. The price/band/floor price and offer price to be approved by the EGoM constituted to decide the price for the sale of Government shares. In addition to the above, CCEA has approved the divestment of 10% of OIL's paid up capital in favour of the three Oil Marketing Companies (OMCs) viz, IOC, HPCL and BPCL in the ratio of 2:1:1 respectively. The divestment in favour of three OMCs would not only strengthen their existing synergies but would also help them to raise resources by disposing these shares in the open market at an opportune time to tide over their under-recoveries. The fresh issue of 10% of its paid up capital would meet SEBI's requirement of listing of the Company's share on the Stock Exchanges. This would not only make OIL more amenable to market discipline but would also boost the company's image. Besides, it would help OIL to raise resources for its future expansion and growth. The additional 1% allocation for its employees would motivate them towards better performance. The proceeds of divestment of Government holding in favour of IOC, HPCL and BPCL would accrue to the Government and is to be used for meeting the needs of social sector programmes as also for the capital investments needs of revivable CPSEs.

2860. (30-8-2007) NEW DELHI : The Cabinet Committee on Economic Affairs today gave its approval for implementation of the J&K Special Package (Phase-II) for improvement of services of both All India Radio and Doordarshan comprising the following components at an estimated cost of Rs.299.87 crore: (i) Generation of software from diverse sources for the DD Kashir Channel-Rs.267.70 crore (2007-08:127.75 cr; 2008-09:Rs.139.95 cr.) (ii) Purchase of equipment and related works-Rs.32.17 crore (2007-08:Rs.25.12 cr.; 2008-09: Rs.7.05 cr.) The special package would enable the DD Kashir channel to improve its viewership by providing wholesome programmes to its viewers in the State and to effectively counter the influence of propaganda from PoK and across the border. It would also help in generating high quality programme content and streamline and strengthen the terrestrial broadcast infrastructure in the State.

2861. (30-8-2007) NEW DELHI : Lt Gen Noble Thamburaj, presently a Corps

Commander in Punjab is to be the next Army Commander of Pune based Southern Command. He takes over from Lt Gen Aditya Singh who is retiring 30 Sep 2007. Lt Gen Thamburaj is from the Corps of Engineers. Lt Gen Thamburaj had his early education at King George's Military School, Chail and Sainik Schools Amravati and Jamnagar. An alumni of National Defence Academy, he was commissioned into Corps of Engineers (Bombay Sappers) in 1969. He is also an alumni of Defence Service Staff College Wellington. Lt Gen Thamburaj was also nominated for the Higher Command and NDC Courses. He has an M Tech from IIT Delhi and M Phil (Def Studies) from Indore University. Lt Gen Thamburaj holds the unique distinction of being the only Sappers Officer to command a Rashtriya Rifle Sector during Op Vijay and an infantry Division during Op Parakram. A qualified paratrooper, he was also an instructor at Defence Services Staff College, Wellington and Officers Training Academy, Chennai. Lt Gen Thamburaj is recipient of Sena Medal and Chief of the Army Staff Commendation Card, twice in his distinguished career. He has seen action in Indo Pak war of 1971, counter terrorism in J&K and six tenures in counter terrorism in the North East. Lt Gen Thamburaj belongs to the Vellore, Tamil Nadu. He is married to Mrs. Anita Thamburaj.

2862. (30-8-2007) NEW DELHI : Lt Gen JK Mohanty, presently Commandant of Mhow (MP) based Army War College has been appointed as the General Officer Commanding in Chief (Army Commander) of Shimla based Army Training Command. He is to replaced Lt Gen ML Naidu who moves to Army HQ as Vice Chief on 01 October 2007. Lt Gen Mohanty was born in Balasore District of Orissa. He is an alumni of Sainik School, Bhubaneshwar. He joined the National Defence Academy, Kharakvasla and was commissioned to the Dogra Regiment in 1969. Lt Gen Mohanty has been an instructor at Indian Military Team in Bhutan and commanded his battalion in high altitude and counter terrorism area in J&K, where his unit earned the three highest peace time gallantry awards of Ashok Chakra, Kirti Cahkra and Shaurya Chakra in a single operation. He himself was awarded a Sena Medal. He is an alumni of College of Defence Management and National Defence College. He has commanded an infantry and mountain brigades. He has commanded an infantry division along the line of control, and later was Additional Military Secretary in Army HQ. He later commanded a Corps in high altitude region of J&K. He is also the recipient of Vishisht Seva and Uttam Yudh Seva Medals.

2863. (30-8-2007) NEW DELHI : Coal India Limited (CIL) has been encouraging Power Sector and other coal consumers and private entrepreneurs to set up coal washeries on Build-own-operate basis for supply of washed coal to the linked consumers. To encourage setting up coal washeries by consumers/private entrepreneurs, CIL has been providing land and other infrastructural facilities on lease/chargeable basis subject to its availability. CIL has also decided in principle to set up washeries with the State-of-the-art technologies on "Build and Operate"

(BO) basis where Coal India Limited and its subsidiary companies will provide the capital funding and other infrastructure facilities. Private entrepreneurs having core competence in the field will construct and operate the washeries. Further, it has been decided that all new opencast projects of more than 2.50 million tones capacity, which are not linked to pit-head power stations should be designed with an integrated washery. The need of the consumers for improved and consistent quality of coal will be satisfied to a large extent through supply of washed coal. Existing non coking coal washing capacity is 103 metric ton per year and it is expected that additional 149 metric tone per year additional washing capacity would be added in XI Plan. The above information was given by Dr. Dasari Narayana Rao, Minister of State for Coal in a written reply in the Rajya Sabha today.

2864. (30-8-2007) NEW DELHI : Shri Murli Deora, Minister of Petroleum & Natural Gas informed the Lok Sabha in a written reply today that production activities in Block RJ-ON-90/1 in Rajasthan will be carried out by the contractor company, namely, Cairn Energy India Pty. Limited. Government has nominated Mangalore Refinery & Petrochemicals Limited (MRPL), a subsidiary of Oil and Natural Gas Corporation Limited (ONGC) as its nominee to receive crude oil produced form the Block RJ-ON-90/1, as per the provisions of Production Sharing Contract. He further underlined that consequent to de-licensing of refinery sector since June, 1998, a refinery may be set up anywhere in India by a Private or Public Sector Enterprise depending on the promoter's assessment of its viability. Therefore, it is not the Government but the Private/Public Sector Enterprise, which has to decide on setting up of refinery based on commercial considerations. Regarding setting up a refinery at Barmer in Rajasthan, Shri Deora said that the proposal is under consideration of ONGC, which is a Navratna company.

2865. (30-8-2007) NEW DELHI : India has been pursuing the import of natural gas from Iran through the Iran-Pakistan-India transnational gas pipeline. For this purpose, two sets of separate Secretary-level bilateral Joint Working Groups (JWGs) have been set up with Pakistan and Iran. Three meetings of India-Iran Special JWG (SJWG) have been held, the last meeting being on December 28 & 29, 2005. Five meetings of India-Pakistan JWG have been held; the last meeting was held on June 27 & 28, 2007 in New Delhi. A tripartite Joint Working Group (JWG) of Iran, Pakistan and India has been formed. Six meetings of the trilateral JWG have been held so far, the last meeting being held in New Delhi on June 28&29, 2007. At the 4th tripartite meeting held in Tehran on January 24 & 25, 2007, a gas pricing formula regarding pricing of gas at Iran-Pakistan border was agreed between Iran and Pakistan sides, subject to approval from the respective Governments. The Indian side agreed to respond to the pricing formula. India conveyed to the Iranian side, vide letter dated 28.2.2007, that the total price payable for the gas at India-Pakistan border would also depend on transportation cost and transit fees payable by India to Pakistan for passage of gas through

Pakistan; as there was no clarity on these, it was not possible for India to decide regarding the final price. Subsequently, Iran demanded introduction of provision for a price revision, in the 5th Tripartite JWG meeting held at Tehran during May 27-30, 2007, which both India and Pakistan disagreed with. The sixth Tripartite meeting was held in New Delhi on June 28 & 29, 2007. The issue of gas price review clause was interalia discussed amongst the participating countries. It was decided to carry forward the discussions to the next round of meetings for resolution of this and other important issues. During the 5th India-Pakistan JWG meeting held in New Delhi on June 27 & 28, 2007, the issue of transportation tariff for passage of gas through Pakistan was discussed. It was agreed that it should be based on cost of service to be achieved through International Competitive Bidding (ICB). However, there is no agreement yet on the transit fees to be payable by India to Pakistan for the passage of natural gas through Pakistan. This information was given by Shri Murli Deora, Minister for Petroleum & Natural Gas in the Lok Sabha in a written reply today.

2866. (30-8-2007) NEW DELHI : The Union Minister for Railways Shri Lalu Prasad said that whether it is Railways or Sports (Rail ho ya Khel), it is our endeavor that India should figure among the leading nations in the world. Speaking at the closing ceremony of the 54th Senior National (Men) Boxing Championship organized by Railway Sports Promotion Board (RSPB) here today, the Minister said that while on the one hand there has been a historic turnaround of the Indian Railways and at the same time Railways have taken all possible steps to promote sports. The Minister said that RSPB is a leading institution to develop sportspersons of national and international repute. Besides offering appointments to the meritorious sportspersons in the Railways, RSPB maintains a close liaison with about 30 national sports federations. He said that sportspersons should not underestimate their participation in national events, as these are the events, which work as ladder for success in international events. He appreciated RSPB for representing Indian Railways in USIC, an organization of world railways. The Minister hoped that Indian sportspersons would win more and more medals and bring laurels to India in next year's Olympics being held in Beijing and Commonwealth games to be held in Delhi in 2010. Around 600 players/officials across the country took part in this mega national event, held in Delhi from 25th to 30th August 2007. RSPB has been declared the winner of this championship after scoring 61 points and winning six Gold medals. Services have been declared the runners-up team after scoring 46 points and winning three Gold medals.

2867. (30-8-2007) NEW DELHI : The State Sports Academy scheme provides for setting up State Sports Academies in the Public-Private Partnership mode. Under this scheme, projects are to be jointly funded by the Private/Public/NGO sponsor, the Central Government and a State Government in the ratio of 51:25:24, subject to the Central Government contribution not exceeding Rs.218 lakh towards capital costs and Rs.17 lakh per annum towards operational costs for a period of

3 years. The cost of the land is not covered under the scheme and is expected to be provided by the Private/Public/NGO sponsor or the State Government. A minimum of 10 acres is required to set up a State Sports Academy. No Academy has been set up under this scheme till date. Under the scheme only one Sports Academy can be assisted in each State/Union Territory. Further, the academy will have multi-disciplinary facilities, including a Fitness Centre, a Sports Medicine centre, a Hostel and a multipurpose hall. This information was given by Shri Mani Shankar Aiyar, Minister of Panchayati Raj, Youth Affairs & Sports and DoNER in the Lok Sabha in a written reply to a question by Shri Balasaheb Vikhe Patil.

2868. (30-8-2007) NEW DELHI : The Ministry of Panchayati Raj has initiated the Panchayat Mahila Shakti Abhiyan to strengthen the elected women of the PRIs within the overall rubric of the "Chalo Gaon Ki Ore" programme of the National Commission for Women. Core Groups are formed State-wise comprising selected EWRs, activists, academics, etc., nominated by the State Government/Government of India to draft and facilitate a draft women's charter for the EWRs of the State stating therein their particular issues. As a follow up, in the States where Core Groups have been formed and the Committees have framed the draft charter, all women Zila Pramukhs, all women Pradhans of the Intermediate Panchayats and selected women Sarpanches from each district of the State, as well as Core Group members and some eminent personalities are invited to a two-day conference of Panchayat Women. A women's charter comprising all the major points distilled from the discussions with the women representatives of the PRIs is then finalized.

2869. (30-8-2007) NEW DELHI : Ministry of Panchayati Raj is actively pursuing the lead role suggested by Hon'ble Prime Minister on taking the benefits of rapid economic development to all parts of the country and all sections of the society through RBH initiative. In June 2004, while addressing the very first Conference of Chief Ministers on the subject "Poverty Alleviation and Rural Prosperity through Panchayati Raj", the Hon'ble Prime Minister had stated that "Panchayat Raj is the medium to transform rural India into 700 million opportunities. The key instrument for integrating economic reforms with institutional reforms in the country side is Gandhiji's farsighted goal of Poorna Swaraj through "Gram Swaraj". In November 2004, the Ministry of Panchayati Raj organized a national presentation on RBH which was attended by 1000 representatives of Panchayats and 200 representatives of Confederation of Indian Industry(CII). Joint RBH Council under the Co-Chairmanship of Minister of Panchayati Raj and the then President of CII was set up at the national level. Similar Councils have been set up in 15 States. The objective of RBH initiative is to promote RBHs across the country by bringing to the attention of business houses, both in the public and private sectors, the unique products or skills in each development block deriving from local resource endowment. In consultation with State Government and Panchayats, the Ministry of Panchayati Raj has identified local resources and skills in more than 1000 development blocks of the country. The Ministry of Panchayati Raj is thus attempting to develop and promote Public-Private-Panchayat Partnership in which the Panchayats will facilitate convergence of extant schemes of State and Central Government, together with initiatives of Panchayats, financial institutions and promotional bodies. This will help develop a holistic and integrated partnership between decentralized rural production units and larger corporate entities. This model is not directly funded by the Ministry of Panchayati Raj. However, under a Central Sector Scheme, limited resources will be available for availing services of professional facilitators and to bridge the critical gaps in infrastructure. The initiative works on a win-win business relationship between rural producers and members of industry, facilitated by the Panchayats. So far 99 MOUs have been signed across the States of Tamil Nadu (51), Karnataka (27), Uttranchal (11), Rajasthan (4), Haryana (3), Nagaland (2) and Uttar Pradesh(1) in such diverse fields as food processing, power generation and distribution, jatropha plantation, carpet weaving, handicrafts, stone carving, etc. These MOUs are at different stages of implementation. The objective of the RBH scheme is to promote at least one RBH in each development block of the country. To identify, develop and refine models for this, a Central Sector Scheme for dpiloting one RBH in each of the Districts of the country is under way. This information was given by Shri Mani Shankar Aiyar, Minister of Panchayati Raj, Youth Affairs & Sports and DoNER in the Lok Sabha, in a written reply to a question by Shri N.S.V. Chitthan.

2870. (30-8-2007) NEW DELHI : Lt Gen Milan Lalitkumar Naidu, presently Army Commander of Army's Shimla based Training Command is to be the next Vice Chief of Indian Army. He will take over from Lt Gen Deepak Kapoor, who is to be the next Army Chief from 01 Oct 2007. Lieutenant General Naidu had his early education at St Joseph's Convent, Bhopal, and to continue his family tradition, joined the National Defence Academy, Khadakvasla, where he excelled in marksmanship (shooting). Commissioned in the Rajput Regiment in Dec 1967, he has had a long and chequered career having served in all sectors and terrain in India and abroad. As Commanding Officer of 5 Rajput he participated in Op PAWAN in Sri Lanka where he was awarded the Yudh Seva Medal. He has the experience of Commanding a Brigade in the semi desert terrain, a Division in the Plains of Punjab during Op PARAKRAM and a Corps in the High Altitude and Glaciated area. Selected to attend the Defence Services Staff College Course in Canada, Lt Gen Naidu has also attended the Higher Command Course at the Army War College. He also holds a Post Graduate in Environmental and Ecological Sciences. Lt Gen Naidu's forte has been in the field on instruction. Having trained cadets and young officers at the Indian Military Academy and the Infantry School, he has also had the distinction of being the Commandant of Indian Army's premier officers' training establishment for combat-The Army War College. Lt Gen Naidu has had varied operational staff experience at all levels including a stint at the Military Operations Directorate at Army HQs. He was also the Defence Attache in Germany. He is a keen sportsman and formed part of the Services team in the National Skeet Shooting Championship in 1968. He still plays golf, tennis and cricket. His leisure hours are devoted to angling, trekking, reading, photography and music. Lt Gen Naidu is also the recipient of Ati Vishist Seva Medal for distinguished services. Lt Gen Naidu is married to Mrs Neeharika who is an daughter of Lt Col Awasthy, a veteran of World War II and 1962 Operations.

2871. (30-8-2007) NEW DELHI: The Lok Sabha was briefly adjourned on Wednesday following protests over violence in Agra and the Bhagalpur incident of an alleged thief being mercilessly beaten up by a mob and dragged by a motorcycle. Pandemonium broke out soon after question hour, with Rashtriya Janata Dal members threatening to storm the well of the House on the Bhagalpur incident. Asking Speaker Somnath Chatterjee to take up the matter, they alleged that the incident was indicative of the "jungle raj" prevailing in the Janata Dal (United)-Bharatiya Janata Party ruled Bihar.

2872. (30-8-2007) NEW DELHI : Although there have been no fatal accidents of supply vessels which are 25 years and above old, two shipping casualties have occurred viz; Samudrika-10, flag India aged 21 years which sank off Mumbai on 9th July 2007 and Samudra Suraksha, flag India aged 24 years which sank of Mumbai on 2nd August 2005. In the case of Samudrika-10, nine crew members were rescued, six lost their lives and two are still missing. Regarding Samudra Suraksha casualty occurred when the vessel hit Mumbai High North production platform. This resulted in the total loss of the platform. Out of the total of 383 personnel on the platform, 361 were rescued 10 died and 12 are missing. Out of a crew of 84 belonging to Samudra Suraksha, one person died. In both the cases, the Directorate General of Shipping have ordered a preliminary inquiry by Principal Officer, Mercantile Department, Mumbai to investigate the circumstances leading to these casualties. In case of "Samudra Suraksha", a formal investigation to be conducted Judicial Magistrate has also been ordered. As per records maintained by the Directorate General of Shipping on the registration of ships, the average age of Indian registered offshore supply vessels operating in the offshore areas is about 22 years. They are issued with statutory certificates with respect to safety, construction of ships, machinery and equipments for undertaking safe voyages during all weather conditions that include stormy seas and adverse weather conditions. They become vulnerable to storms if not maintained by the ship owner during the currency of validity of statutory certificates. The crew are engaged under the Articles of agreement as per the provisions of the Indian Merchant Shipping Act, 1958. The welfare and security measures including insurance are addressed in the collective Bargaining Agreement entered into by ship owners and Seafarers' trade unions. However, to improve crew safety, structural examination and enhanced Flag State Inspection of all Indian offshore supply vessels of more than 15 years of age has been put in place. This information was given by the Minister of Shipping, Road Transport and Highways, Thiru T.R. Baalu in a written reply in the Rajya Sabha today.

2873. (30-8-2007) NEW DELHI : The Government has approved the proposal of the Mumbai Port Trust to award the contract to set up an Offshore Container Terminal on Build, Operate and Transfer (BOT) basis at the Port to a Consortium led by Gammon India Ltd. who has offered highest share of gross revenue of 35.064% from the planned facility to the Mumbai Port Trust, on the basis of open competitive bidding. Pre-investment studies on the project have established the viability of the project. This information was given by the Minister of Shipping, Road Transport and Highways, Thiru T.R. Baalu in a written reply in the Rajya Sabha today.

2874. (30-8-2007) NEW DELHI : Following is the text of the suo moto statement in the Lok Sabha today by Shri T.R. Baalu, Minister of Shipping Road Transport & Highways on Productivity-Linked-Rewards for Port & Dock workers: "The Port and Dock Workers of Major Ports and Dock Labour Boards are not covered by the Payment of Bonus Act, 1965. They are being paid Productivity-Linked-Reward (PLR) instead. From 1994-95, they were paid PLR on the basis of Memorandum of Settlement dated 8.2.1996 between the Management of Major Port Trusts and Labour Federations of Port and Dock Workers under the Industrial Dispute Act, 1947. Under the scheme, the PLR was paid upto 2001-02. A new PLR scheme was evolved by Indian Ports Association in consultation with Major Federations of Port and Dock Workers. In the new Scheme, there are three parameters *i.e.* Average Turn Round Time of ships with weightage of 30%, Average Ship berth day output with weightage of 35% and unit cost of handling with weightage of 35%. Government approved on 8.2.2007 the new PLR Scheme for the period 2002-03 to 2009-10. A new settlement has also been signed between the Port Management and Federations on the new PLR Scheme on 10.4.2007. The joint reference earlier made to the National Tribunal, Mumbai on the question of payment of PLR on the basis of Port-wise productivity has also been withdrawn. Now, the PLR for the year 2006-2007 is due for payment on or before 1-9-2007. The Indian Ports Association have made the computation of PLR for the year 2006-2007 as per the agreed performance parameters and methodology and the PLR percentage is arrived at 21.38%, subject to the maximum ceiling of 20%. I have pleasure to inform the Hon'ble House that in accordance with the new settlement arrived at between the Port Management and the Major Federations, PLR for the year 2006-07 is being released by the Major Port Trusts and Dock Labour Boards to the Port & Dock workers, employees and officers on schedule. The maximum payment per employee at the rate of 20% will be Rs.6,000/- . This will benefit about 66,000 Port and Dock Workers, employees and Officers and the financial implications will be about Rs. 40 crores. The expenditure on account of PLR shall be met by the Major Port Trusts and Dock Labour Boards from their own resources, without budgetary support from the Government."

2875. (30-8-2007) NEW DELHI : Air India is making arrangements for transportation of 1,10,000 pilgrims under the Government quota besides operating additional scheduled services in case there is need to facilitate the transportation of pilgrims going for Haj through private tour operators. This information was given by Shri Praful Patel, Minister for Civil Aviation in a written reply to a question in the Parliament today, The Haj Committee has received 1,90,000 applications through the State Haj Committees against the Government quota of 1,10,000. Apart from this 47,000 pilgrims would be going for Haj 2007 through Private Tour Operators. The maximum number of pilgrims who propose to travel Haj 2007 are from Uttar Pradesh-29,989 followed by Maharashtra-10016, Kerala 7670, Andhra Pradesh-6820, Jammu & Kashmir-6630, Karnataka-6307, and West Bengal 5819. The number of pilgrims airlifted by Air India, Indian Airlines and Saudi Airlines during the last three years are 81022 in 2005, 100012 in 2006-I and 108872 in 2006-II. The Government provides subsidy in airfare makes arrangements for the transportation of the Haj pilgrims going through the Haj Committee of India and facilitates provision of accommodation and other logistic support for them. In addition of this, the Haj Committee of India provides to the pilgrims information regarding confirmation of their seats, travel documents, transportation, accommodation, medical assistance, release of foreign exchange, information on embarkation points and departure dates etc. Air India allows baggage allowance of 45 kgs. per pilgrim, 10 litre of Zam Zam water free of cost and excess baggage at a subsidized rate.

2876. (30-8-2007) NEW DELHI : As part of Participation of youth in Real-time / field Observation to Benefit Education for the National Capital Region (NCR-PROBE), the Department of Science & Technology (DST) is imparting knowledge regarding weather and climate to children of 50 schools in and around Delhi. The programme aims to generate required knowledge and skills for schoolchildren on meteorological observation, computer use and data utilization; and climate change and impact on society and operation and maintenance of Meteorological observational equipments/instruments.

2877. (30-8-2007) NEW DELHI : The Minister of State for Railways Shri Naran Bhai J. Rathwa has called upon the Railway officers to make use of latest technologies in all fields of Railways for efficient functioning and for meeting the satisfaction level of Rail users. Shri Rathwa was speaking at the two-day Conference of Chief Electrical Engineers of all Zonal Railways and Production Units, which began here today. The Minister said that Indian Railways achieved the higher ever target of freight loading of 728 million tonnes and expressed the hope that the Railways will succeed in achieving the ambitious target of 800 million tonnes during this financial year. Under scoring the importance of electrification in meeting this target, the Minister pointed out that Electrical Department is the backbone of Indian Railways, as it constitutes about 65 per cent of the freight and about 50 per cent of the passenger traffic. Appreciating the efforts and contribution of electrical department, the Minister pointed out that reliability and availability of the electrical assets have improved in a big way and touched an all time high. The Minister said that the performance of electrical assents has further improved by over by 19 per cent during the period April-July 2007, which enabled Railways to haul higher traffic and achieve the target. Underlining the significance of the state-of-the-art three phases electrical locos, the Minister said that the new factory which is coming up at Madheypura for this purpose should be set up early so that the deficit of electrical locomotive is timely met. He said that Indian Railways has planned and initiate action to set up workshop with the state-of-the-art facility at Baroda to undertake periodic over hauling of three-phase locomotives. The Minister also stressed the need to improve the working environment of Railways running staff. He suggested to further improving the cabs of the existing locomotives for better ambiance and stress free working so as to match the international standards. The Minister also suggested that railways should plan to introduce air condition EMU service for Mumbai area as a pilot project and then use the results for future expansion of such services. He said that presently 17811 route kilometres of track has been electrified which constitute about 28 per cent of the total Indian Railways network and efforts should be continued to electrify more tracks in view of the economical and environment friendly nature of electric traction. He urged them to closely monitor the projects of electrification for their timely completion.

2878. (30-8-2007) NEW DELHI: The Lok Sabha was briefly adjourned on Wednesday following protests over violence in Agra and the Bhagalpur incident of an alleged thief being mercilessly beaten up by a mob and dragged by a motorcycle. Pandemonium broke out soon after question hour, with Rashtriya Janata Dal members threatening to storm the well of the House on the Bhagalpur incident. Asking Speaker Somnath Chatterjee to take up the matter, they alleged that the incident was indicative of the "jungle raj" prevailing in the Janata Dal (United)-Bharatiya Janata Party ruled Bihar. Almost at the same time, the Samajwadi Party members trooped into the well protesting against the incidents in Agra, where violence erupted after four persons taking part in a religious procession were run over by a truck on Tuesday night. Since the Speaker had allowed a discussion on the adjournment motion, he asked them to maintain order. But as the din continued, he adjourned the proceedings for 20 minutes. The National Human Rights Commission has issued a notice to the Bhagalpur Superintendent of Police and the Director-General of Police (Bihar) on the issues and sought a reply within four weeks. The Bihar police seem to be living in the old colonial days, with the authorities showing scant regard for the dignity of the people, the commission said. It strongly disapproved of such "despicable behaviour" and described it as a serious issue of violation of human rights. The National Commission for Minorities too has sought a report from the Bihar Government on the incident. A meeting of the commission, chaired by Harcharan Singh Josh, said the accused, Mohammad Aurangzeb, was treated like an "animal and a slave" by the police, who joined the mob in punching, kicking and dragging him down a street. The commission has written to Bihar Chief Secretary, seeking a report on the incident. The CPI's national executive condemned the "barbaric" assault and sought immediate dismissal and arrest of the guilty policemen. One is struck with horror at the brutality of the police, conniving with delivery of instant justice, it said.

2879. (30-8-2007) NEW DELHI : Bhabha Atomic Research Centre (BARC) has developed a technique of long lasting preservation of fruits. Experimental tests on apples from Himachal Pradesh have been conducted and the results are encouraging. Mango was the only fruit among the various food items approved for radiation preservation, under the Prevention of Food Adulteration Act Rules, 1955. However, following a notification approving food irradiation on generic class basis, commercial radiation processing of other fruits is now possible. This information was given by the Minister of State in the Prime Minister's Office, Shri Prithviraj Chavan in the Rajya Sabha today.

2880. (30-8-2007) NEW DELHI : The Public Diplomacy Division of Ministry of External Affairs in association with Research and Information System (RIS), Global India Foundation (GIF) and FICCI is organising a national seminar on "SAARC: Accelerating Cooperation through Connectivity" on September 1-2, 2007 at Kolkata. The seminar will see the participation of academicians, think tanks, representatives of industry, intelligentsia, civil society and senior officials. The Union Minister of External Affairs, Shri Pranab Mukherjee will deliver the keynote address at the inaugural session on September 1, 2007. The Chief Minister of West Bengal, Shri Buddhadeb Bhattacharjee would also grace the inaugural session. The seminar will discuss issues related to: a) Globalisation and Economic Integration: Imperatives for South Asia Regional Economic Cooperation; b) Strengthening Physical Connectivity in South Asia, and c) Fostering People-to-People Connectivity in South Asia. Ever since its creation in April 2006, the Public Diplomacy Division of MEA has been in contact with researchers, think tanks, academia, civil society and industry, both within India and abroad, to highlight the contours of Indian foreign policy, as well as initiate debate and discussion within the wider public about the key foreign policy issues confronting India. It is in furtherance of these objectives that the Public Diplomacy Division is organising this seminar to discuss the opportunities and challenges to accelerating cooperation within SAARC.

2881. (30-8-2007) NEW DELHI : The Government has approved the proposal of the Mumbai Port Trust to award the contract to set up an Offshore Container Terminal on Build, Operate and Transfer (BOT) basis at the Port to a Consortium led by Gammon India Ltd. who has offered highest share of gross revenue of 35.064% from the planned facility to the Mumbai Port Trust, on the basis of open competitive bidding. Pre-investment studies on the project have established the viability of the project. This information was given by the Minister of Shipping, Road Transport and Highways, Thiru T.R. Baalu in a written reply in the Rajya Sabha today.

2882. (30-8-2007) NEW DELHI : The Minister of Tourism and Culture Smt. Ambika Soni has said that no consistently declining trend in foreign tourist visits has been observed in respect of any State/UT during the last three years. In a written reply in the Lok Sabha today she said, the number of foreign tourist visits to different States/UTs, and the percentage change over the previous years, during the years 2004, 2005 and 2006 is given in the Annexure.

2883. (30-8-2007) NEW DELHI : In the rural areas, Government has launched the National Rural Employment Guarantee Scheme (NREGS) in February, 2006. A large number of Districts have been covered under the Scheme. The objective of the Scheme is to enhance the livelihood security of the people in rural areas by generating wage employment through works that develop the infrastructure base of the area. This information was given by the Minister of State for Housing & Urban Poverty Alleviation, Kumari Selja in the Rajya Sabha today, in a written reply to a question by Kumari Nirmala Deshpande.

2884. (30-8-2007) NEW DELHI : Prime Minister Dr. Manmohan Singh presented National Awards to the Micro Small and Medium Entrepreneurs here today. The Awards were in three categories: a) Outstanding Entrepreneurs of Micro & Small Enterprises, Khadi and Village Industries and Coir Industries; b) Special Awards to Women and SC/ST Entrepreneurs and c) Banks for Excellence in Small Enterprises Lending. Total 111 entrepreneurs got awards in various categories. 14 entrepreneurs received awards from the Prime Minister, while Shri Mahabir Prasad, Union Minister for Micro, Small & Medium Enterprises presented awards to the rest of the awardees. Presenting the awards Prime Minister Dr. Manmohan Singh said, "Gone are the days when the business limelight was reserved almost entirely for the captains in the corporate sector and SMEs remained in the shadows. India's SME business leaders now stand proudly on their own feet." Appreciating the commitment and persistent endeavour of the small entrepreneurs, the Prime Minister commented, "Nowhere is this spirit of enterprise, this willingness to take risk and an eagerness to strike out on one's own to seek a fortune more in evidence than in our small and medium enterprises sector. It is this animal spirit which makes the SME sector the most dynamic in our economy and worthy of our support and encouragement." Recognizing the importance of providing social security to the unorganized workers as also to the workers of the SME Sector, Dr. Manmohan Singh said, "Our Government recognizes the importance of extending social security to workers in the micro and small enterprises sector. As a first step in this direction, we have declared our intention to provide an old age pension to all citizens above the age of 65 and living below the poverty line. We will also provide life and disability cover to one earning member in each family so that they and their families can get over the consequences of injury or death. We are also working on a health insurance model so that our poor do not have to bear the high cost of medical care. I am sure these initiatives will benefit all workers in the SME sector in particular. Through these three initiatives, we intend to ensure a minimum level of social safety for all of them."

2885. (30-8-2007) NEW DELHI : There has been some delays in the completion of some contracts under National Highways Development Programme (NHDP), due to problems associated with acquisition of land, shifting of utilities, environment and forest clearances, poor performance of some contractors and termination of some contracts etc. The steps taken by the Government to accelerate the pace of construction of National Highways are given below: (a) The Contracts are regularly monitored at various levels such as by Supervision Consultant, Project Directors, Senior officers of NHAI. Progress reviews are also held at the level of Chairman, NHAI, Secretary, Department of Road Transport & Highways and Minister, Shipping Road Transport & Highways. (b) State Governments have appointed Senior officers as nodal officers for resolving problems associated with implementation of the NHDP such as land acquisition, removal of utilities, forest / pollution / environment clearances etc. These nodal officers hold periodic meetings to review the projects and take action to resolve the problems. (c) A Committee of Secretaries has been constituted under Cabinet Secretary to address inter-ministerial and Centre-State issues such as land acquisition, utility shifting, environment approvals, clearance of Road Over Bridges (ROBs). (d) The procedure of issue of Land Acquisition notifications has now been simplified. (e) To expedite the construction of ROBs an officer of the Railways has been posted to NHAI to coordinate with Ministry of Railways. Memorandum of Understanding (MOU) has also been signed with M/s. IRCON for construction of some of the ROBs. (f) Action has been taken against non-performing contractors and they are not allowed to bid for future projects unless they improve the performance in existing contracts. (g) Steps have been taken to improve cash flow problems of contractors by granting interest bearing discretionary advance at the request of contractor, release of retention money against bank guarantee of equal amount, deferment of recovery of advances (on interest basis) and relaxation in minimum Interim Payments Certificate (IPC) amount. This information was given by the Minister of State for Shipping, Road Transport and Highways, Shri K.H. Muniyappa in a written reply in the Rajya Sabha today.

2886. (30-8-2007) NEW DELHI : The Government propose to undertake development of the National Highway 7 Shiridi Ghat section from Shakaleshpur to Mangalore. Three developmental works amounting to Rs. 32.00 crore have been sanctioned for the improvement of NH-48 passing through Shiradi Ghat area (Shakaleshpur-Mangalore section). Out of these, two works have been awarded with twelve month completion period and are likely to be completed by June, 2008. For the third work, revised cost estimate based on tender is under consideration which will be completed after twelve month from the date of award. There has been some delay in the award and execution of sanctioned improvement works due to poor participation by contracting agencies. This information was given by the Minister of State for Shipping, Road Transport and Highways, Shri K.H. Muniyappa in a written reply in the Rajya Sabha today.

2887. (30-8-2007) NEW DELHI : The Government accorded approval for undertaking six laning of 6,500 km of National Highways comprising 5,700 km of Golden Quadrilateral and balance 800 km on other sections, under National Highways Development Project (NHDP) Phase-V. As per the approved implementation mechanism for NHDP Phase-V, stretches of 100 km or more that have been completed at least two years ago and contractual actions on previous contracts have been completed, are being included in the year-wise programme. Where the distance between two cities is less than 100 km, such stretches are also being included as exception cases. Cost per km has been estimated as Rs. 6.34 crore.

2888. (30-8-2007) NEW DELHI : Kandla to Mundra Port stretch of NH 8A (Extension) has been included in National Highway Development Project (NHDP) Phase III. The stretch of NH 8A from Kandla to Gandhidham is already 4-lanned. The consultancy work for preparation of Detailed Project Report (DPR) for 4-lanning from Gandhidham to Mundra Port has been recently awarded by National Highways Authority of India (NHAI) and feasibility study is targeted to be completed by March 2008. Bids for the civil work shall be invited after completion of DPR. The road portion from Mundra to Mundra Port is, however, at present not a National Highway. This information was given by the Minister of State for Shipping, Road Transport and Highways, Shri K.H. Muniyappa in a written reply in the Rajya Sabha today.

2889. (30-8-2007) NEW DELHI : 4-laning of Patna-Hajipur-Muzaffarpur section of NH-19 and NH-77 in the state of Bihar has been included under NHDP Phase IIIA on Build Operate Transfer (BOT) basis. Patna-Hajipur section of NH-19 is already four lane. Bids were invited on BOT (Toll) mode for 4-laning of Hajipur-Muzaffarpur section of NH-77, but no bid has been received till last date of submission of bid *i.e.* 20.08.2007 This information was given by the Minister of State for Shipping, Road Transport and Highways, Shri K.H. Muniyappa in a written reply in the Rajya Sabha today.

2890. (30-8-2007) NEW DELHI : A Committee under the chairmanship of Shri S. Sundar, former Secretary, Ministry of Surface Transport was set up to deliberate and make recommendations for creation of a dedicated body on Road Safety and Traffic Management. The committee submitted its report on 20.02.2007 which among other things, recommend creation of a National Road Safety and Traffic Management Board through an Act of Parliament. A note for Committee of Secretaries in this regard has been prepared and has been circulated to concerned Ministries/Departments for their comments. This information was given by the Minister of State for Shipping, Road Transport and Highways, Shri K.H. Muniyappa in a written reply in the Rajya Sabha today.

2891. (30-8-2007) NEW DELHI : National Highways Development Project (NHDP) Phase-IV is at initial stage of planning wherein two laning with paved shoulder of 20,000 km of National Highways is envisaged with an estimated cost of Rs. 27,800 crore. NHDP Phase-IV is targeted to be completed by December, 2015. This information was given by the Minister of State for Shipping, Road Transport and Highways, Shri K.H. Muniyappa in a written reply in the Rajya Sabha today.

2892. (30-8-2007) NEW DELHI : The Ministry of Textiles is organizing TEX Summit 2007, the conference to deliberate upon areas of concern for textile sector to further boost productivity & export, and to realize the potential of the sector in generating employment. The two day summit with the theme "Exploring Growth Paradigms" will be inaugurated by Shri Kamal Nath, Minister for Commerce & Industry, here tomorrow. Shri Shankarsinh Vaghela, Minister of Textiles, Shri Oscar Fernandes Minister of State for Labour & Employment (I/C) and Shri C. Rangarajan, Chairman, Economic Advisory Council to the Prime Minister will also address the inaugural session. It need not be reiterated that the textile industry in India has carved a niche for itself in world market and provides the maximum employment only next agriculture in our country. The sector has re-positioned itself as a 'sunrise industry' during the recent past. Recognizing the need to build on the strengths like large production base, easy access to raw materials, present across the entire value chain, availability of skilled workforce and expertise in designs and motifs, the Tex Summit 2007 proposes to address variety of issues concerning these areas. To address these issues in cohesive manner four working groups covering Textile Inputs-physical framework, Human Resource Development, Policy Framework and Role of Government and Market Development have been constituted. The Working Groups will consist of leading members of trade and industry, economists, academicians, experts, financial analysts who will deliberate the various issues arising in these areas and suggest the policy framework as roadmap for further growth of sector. The deliberations of all the four Working Groups and their recommendations would be summarized and announced before the summit moved for its valedictory session. The valedictory session will be addressed by the Prime Minister Dr. Manmohan Singh on 1st September 2007 (Saturday). In the valedictory session the recommendations of all the Working Groups will be presented to Hon'ble Prime Minister. It may further be recalled that the competitiveness of the industry had suffered in recent months on account of the steep appreciation of the rupee. Other factors like high transaction cost, power cost, technological obsolescence, local levies had also had their impact. The recent steps taken to address the impact of the rising rupee on exports like revision of the duty draw back and DEPB rates for exporters would provide some relief to them. Government was open to consider further steps to mitigate the impact of the rising rupee on exports. With these measures the Government was confident that exporters would be able to realize the targets of US $ 25.2 billion set for this sector for the year 2007-08. The Technology Upgradation Fund was being extended with the higher allocation, the details of which are likely to be announced shortly. The Industry expects the integrated and holistic view of the policy requirement to be favourably responded by the Government in TEX Summit 2007.

2893. (30-8-2007) NEW DELHI : The Government of National Capital Territory of Delhi (GNCTD) had invited applications from Societies/Associations of unauthorized colonies existing as on 31.3.2002 seeking regularization and received 1432 applications. Further, 107 applications have been received by the GNCTD in response to a later advertisement. GNCTD has informed that processing of these applications has been taken up. This information was given by Shri Ajay Maken, Minister of State in the Ministry of Urban Development in the Rajya Sabha today in a written reply to a question by Shri V.Narayanasamy.

2894. (30-8-2007) NEW DELHI : Delhi Development Authority has informed that the land use of the piece of land surrounded by DDA MIG green flats, Rajouri Garden and road of WZ-106, Rajouri Garden Extension is earmarked for Senior Secondary School to be allotted to Education Department and hence the land cannot be developed as a park. This information was given by Shri Ajay Maken, Minister of State in the Ministry of Urban Development in the Rajya Sabha today in a written reply to a question by Shri Kamal Akhtar.

2895. (30-8-2007) NEW DELHI : Department of Information Technology has received 17 Mission Mode Projects. Out of these, 11 pertain to State MMPs as approved under NeGP and 6 State specific MMPs have been submitted by the Kerala Government. The Capacity Building DPRs (Detailed Project Reports) have been received from various States/UTs including Kerala, and a comprehensive Capacity Building Scheme covering all States/UTs has been formulated for Human Resource and Training initiatives under NeGP. This scheme is currently being processed for approval of the competent authority. The proposal of State Government of Kerala cannot be considered at this state since the Scheme has not been approved by the competent authority. This information was given by Dr.Shakeel Ahmad, Minister of State in the Ministry of Communications and Information Technology in the Rajya Sabha today in a written reply to a question by Shri A.Vijayaraghavan.

2896. (30-8-2007) NEW DELHI : Telecom Regulatory Authority of India has given its recommendations on spectrum for Broadband Wireless Services. The guidelines for allotment of Broadband Wireless Access spectrum are to be formulated taking into account all relevant aspects, including these TRAI recommendations. This information was given by Dr.Shakeel Ahmad, Minister of State in the Ministry of Communications and Information Technology in the Rajya Sabha today in a written reply to a question by Shri Uday Pratap Singh and Shri Amar Singh.

2897. (30-8-2007) NEW DELHI : The Master Plan for Delhi-2021 provides for Multi-storeyed in-situ up-gradation of the land pockets of slum and JJ clusters, which are not required for public/priority use, as the first option for provision of affordable housing for rehabilitation of squatters. This information was given by Shri Ajay Maken, Minister of State in the Ministry of Urban Development in the Rajya Sabha today in a written reply to a question by Shri V.Narayanasamy.

2898. (30-8-2007) NEW DELHI : Railways monitor the availability of reservation on day to day basis. Based on waiting list, additional coaches are attached to clear the rush wherever feasible. Augmentation of trains is an ongoing process subject to traffic pattern, operation feasibility and availability of resources. In addition to this Railways also introduce new trains, increase the frequency of trains, extend the run of trains to take care of the growing demand. Railways also run special trains to clear the seasonal rush of traffic. Different category of coaches are provided in the composition of a train keeping in view the traffic demand in the sector and patronisation of particular type of coaches. Popular trains are augmented to 24 coach length and it is an ongoing process. At present 56 pair of trains are running with 24 coaches. This information was given by the Minister of State for Railways Shri R.Velu in written reply to a question in the Lok Sabha today.

2899. (30-8-2007) NEW DELHI : All out efforts are made by the ticket checking and other staff to curb entry of unauthorized passengers in reserved coaches. Unauthorized persons, found travelling in reserved coaches, are penalized as per provisions of law and detrained with the help of Railway Protection Force/ Government Railway Police. Ticket Collectors are posted at the entry and exit gates at important stations for checking the entry of ticketless/unauthorized passengers into platforms. However, Airport-like checking is not possible due to numerous porous points, which are difficult to be sealed for making entry foolproof. Apart from regular and surprise checks, the minimum penalty for ticketless/ irregular travel has been increased from Rs.50/- to Rs.250/- with effect from 1.7.2004. This information was given by the Minister of State for Railways Shri R.Velu in written reply to a question in the Lok Sabha today.

2900. (30-8-2007) NEW DELHI : An agreement for running of passenger train service between Sealdah and Jamuna Bridge was signed in 2001 and during the visit of Minister of External Affairs to Dhaka on February 19, 2007, Bangladesh agreed for early operationalisation of Sealdah (Kolkata)-Joydevpur (Dhaka) passenger train service. This was reiterated by both sides in the Inter-Governmental Railway meeting held in Dhaka in March 2007. In the Inter-Governmental Meeting held on July 9-10, 2007 in Dhaka, both sides expressed their willingness to commence the commercial operation of the passenger train as early as possible subject to other relevant related concerns being addressed to mutual satisfaction. On 8th July, 2007, the Indian side conducted a trial run of the passenger train and Bangladesh side also conducted their trial run service on July 29, 2007. However, regular traffic is yet to commence. This information was given by the Minister of State for Railways Shri R.Velu in written reply to a question in the Lok Sabha today.

2901. (30-8-2007) NEW DELHI : There are 27000 numbers of encroachments covering an area of approximately 40 hectare of railway land. These encroachments have come up over various years. Various steps have been taken for removal of encroachments, which also include action under Public Premises (Eviction of Unauthorised Occupants) Act, 1971. In the National Capital Territory of Delhi, Railways have agreed to bear part cost of relocation of Pre-1998 encroachers located on Railway land in 'Safety Zone' and on land required for execution of sanctioned projects, as per the Resettlement & Rehabilitation policy of Delhi Government, which has the approval of the Ministry of Urban Development. Northern Railway have deposited over Rs.11 crore with the Government of Delhi on this account, for relocating 'Jhuggies/ Jhopries', to get encroachments removed from railway land. Regular chasing and meetings are done by Railway officials with Delhi Government officials. All efforts are made by Railway towards proper co-ordination with the Government of Delhi including seeking assistance of local police and Magistrate as eviction of encroachers often lead to law and order problems. In the process of removal of encroachers, Railways have to depend on the State Government for Police/Magistrate, and for survey and resettlement of encroachers. Depending on the cooperation of the State Government Railways will continue to make all possible efforts to remove all the encroachers. This information was given by the Minister of State for Railways Shri R.Velu in written reply to a question in the Lok Sabha today.

2902. (30-8-2007) NEW DELHI : The Ministry of Railways has given powers to General Managers of all Zonal Railways to sanction Limited Height Sub-ways depending upon site conditions, costing up-to Rs. 45 lakhs each. Replacement of Unmanned Level Crossing by Limited Height Subways are based on criteria of safety, closure of nearby level crossing, local road user's requirement etc. All Zonal Railways have been advised to identify the level crossings which could be replaced by Limited Height Subways and sanction them for their replacement. As on 31.07.2007, Zonal Railways have identified 446 level crossings for replacement by Limited Height Subways. Out of this, 181 level crossings are located over Southern Railway. This information was given by the Minister of State for Railways Shri R.Velu in written reply to a question in the Lok Sabha today.

2903. (30-8-2007) NEW DELHI : Railtel Corporation of India Limited (RCIL) under the Ministry of Railways proposes to switch over from Bharat Sanchar Nigam Limited (BSNL) network to the Railways' Optical Fibre Cable (OFC) network for its Passenger Reservation System (PRS) in a phased manner as Railways have created their own OFC network spanning 31,000 Route Kilometres connecting 2896 towns/cities across India. Therefore, it will not only economical to run the PRS on Railways' OFC network resulting in considerable saving on rental, but it will also enhance the reliability. However, BSNL's network will also be utilized wherever there is unavailability of Railways' own network or as a standby network for important PRS locations. This information was given by the

Minister of State for Railways Shri R.Velu in written reply to a question in the Lok Sabha today. In reply to another question, the Minister said that RailTel has built a nationwide Wide Area Network (WAN), which can be used by corporate world for exchanging the information from their remotely located plants. This is based on VPN (Virtual Private Network) technology, which provides cost effective network connectivity to the user. The connectivity can be extended to large number of places along the RailTel's OFC network, thus making this facility available in remote, rural and semi urban areas apart from large cities. This will generate revenue for Railways by utilizing the surplus capacity on its Telecommunication network.

2904. (30-8-2007) NEW DELHI : Lok Sabha The surcharge such as busy season surcharge, supplementary surcharge for Mini-rakes and two point rakes are not applicable in lean season, which extends from July to September in the current year. The Ministry of Railways has withdrawn 10 per cent supplementary surcharge on commodities having classification above Class-130 when transported in Mini-rakes and two point rakes from 20.5.2007 till further advice. Ministry of Railways have launched various schemes like Incentive Scheme for Incremental Traffic, Long term Special Incentive Scheme, Incentive for Traditional Empty Flow Direction, Incentive Scheme for freight Forwarders, Incentive Scheme for two Leg Traffic, Incentive Scheme for Loading Bagged Consignments in BOXN, to improve its revenue through carriage of goods. This information was given by the Minister of State for Railways Shri R.Velu in written reply to a question in the Lok Sabha today.

2905. (30-8-2007) NEW DELHI : Railways are establishing a captive power plant of 1000 Mega Watt (MW) capacity at Nabinagar of Aurangabad district, Bihar in collaboration with National Thermal Power Corporation (NTPC) Limited. This has been included in Railway Budget for the year 2007-08. A new Company namely 'Bhartiya Rail Bijlee Company Limited' will be set up for the said purpose. Total estimated cost of the project is Rs. 5352.50 crore with mega status. The debt equity ratio of this project will be 70:30. The equity participation of NTPC will be 74% (Rs. 118.26 crore) & 26% (Rs. 417.5 crore) by Railways. Nabinagar of Aurangabad district in Bihar has been identified as suitable site for setting up of this power plant. This information was given by the Minister of State for Railways Shri R.Velu in written reply to a question in the Lok Sabha today.

2906. (30-8-2007) NEW DELHI : Railways have undertaken plans to recycle and prevent wastage of water at major locations where there is water scarcity and heavy demand of water for domestic & non-domestic purposes. Water Recycling Plants (WRP) have been planned to be installed at important locations. At New Delhi railway station, Water Recycling Plant is planned to be installed for which consultancy contract has been awarded to Tata Energy Research Institute. One Water Recycling Plant each is proposed to be installed at Jabalpur (20 lakh litre/

day), Katni (15 lakh litre/day), Satna (10 lakh litre/day), Bhopal (10 lakh litre/day), Itarsi (08 lakh litre/day), Udaipur (2.4 lakh litre/day), Jodhpur (1.5 litre/day), Puri (05 lakh litre/day), Waltair (10 lakh litre/day), New Delhi (under finalization), Secunderbad (05 lakh litre/day), Hubli (1.8 lakh litre/day), Bangalore (10 lakh litre/day), Yashwantpur (04 lakh litre/day) and Mysore (03 lakh litre/day). The expenditure likely to be incurred on installation of Water Recycling Plants at above mentioned location is Rs. 10.81 crore except the cost of WRP proposed to be installed at New Delhi which is under finalization. This information was given by the Minister of State for Railways Shri R.Velu in written reply to a question in the Lok Sabha today.

2907. (30-8-2007) NEW DELHI : Shri A.Raja, Minister of Communications and Information Technology launched the India Post Freighter for North East at Guwahati yesterday. Shri Raja said this service would give a great fillip to Government of India's efforts to put North East at the heart of economic development. Department of Posts has always been an integral part of the life of the people. And it has constantly developed products and services that met the merging need of different segments of people, Shri Raja said. Recently, it introduced the Instant Money Order service, which allows citizens to send and receive money in a matter of few minutes all across the country. This would enable parents to send money to their children studying in other cities, as also to receive and send money for any emergent need. The Department has reduced rates for Local Speed Post, as also introduced One India One Rate for Speed Post to be sent anywhere in India. These and several other measures taken by the Department, have been greatly appreciated by customers. The Minister said that to effect a long term solution and to remove imperfections in meeting this challenge, Department of Posts has taken a landmark decision to have its own air freight operations in North East. A Boeing 737-200 has been chartered from Indian Airlines, for one year to begin with, to operate on Kolkata-Guwahati-Imphal-Agartala-Kolkata sector. It is a historic event as this is the very first time that they are introducing a freighter, and launching Air India cargo service in India.

2908. (30-8-2007) NEW DELHI : The President, Smt. Pratibha Devisingh Patil has congratulated the Indian Football team on its maiden Nehru Cup title victory. In her messages to the team led by Baichung Bhutia and to Shri P.R. Dasmunshi, Union Minister for Information and Broadcasting who is also the President of the All India Football Federation (AIFF), Smt. Patil has said that the nation is proud of the team's achievement, team spirit, skills and spirit of sportsmanship. She has also sent her hearty greetings to N.P. Pradeep for his magnificent performance in the final match. The President has also said that the victory was possible due to the unstinted support provided by the AIFF.

2909. (30-8-2007) NEW DELHI : Profit margins of drug manufacturers, wholesalers and retailers are included in the maximum retail price (MRP) printed on the medicines being sold in the country. Government has made it mandatory to print MRP inclusive of all taxes on medicines manufactured indigenously after 2.10.2006 and 1.3.2007 for imported medicines vide its notification SO No. 946(E) dt. 26.6.2006. The MRP also includes the taxes levied by the Central as well as State Governments. The Central Government has levied 16% Excise duty on medicines. Almost all State Government have levied 4% VAT except Assam & Meghalaya who have levied 6% VAT on medicines. As a result no Pharma company can charge any additional tax after MRP. The maximum percentage of profit margin allowed is 100% of manufacturing price of medicines on the scheduled formulations to take care of post manufacturing expenses and profit margins of manufacturers, wholesalers and retailers. This is in accordance of para 7 of Drugs (Prices Control), Order, 1995 (DPCO, 95). No percentage of profit is fixed for Non-Scheduled formulations under DPCO, 95. The Draft National Pharmaceutical Policy, 2006 proposes to streamline the system of trade margins. In respect of Generic medicines trade margin of 35% to retailers and 15% to wholesalers is proposed while in case of branded Generic medicines it is 20% for retailers and 10% for wholesalers. For Scheduled drugs, it is proposed that the trade margins would be 16% to retailers and 8% to wholesalers. The Cabinet considered the Draft National Pharmaceutical Policy in its meeting held on 11.1.2007 and referred it to the Group of Ministers (GOM). The first meeting of the GOM was held on 10.4.2007. No time frame has been set for finalizing the National Pharmaceuticals Policy This information was given by the Minister of State for Chemicals & Fertilisers Shri B.K. Handique in a written reply in the Lok Sabha today.

2910. (30-8-2007) NEW DELHI : Steel Authority of India Ltd. (SAIL) has planned to set up two greenfield plants, one each in the States of Jharkhand and Chattisgarh. The plant in Jharkhand, envisages to achieve a capacity of 6 million tonne per annum by 2012-13 and 12 million tonne per annum by 2019-20. The plant in Chattisgarh also envisages to have a capacity of 4 million tonne per annum and would be joint venture with RINL and NMDC. The time by which the greenfield plants will be set up would depend upon the feasibility reports including site selection report for the respective projects. This information was given by the Minister of State for Steel, Dr. Akhilesh Das in a written reply in the Lok Sabha today. He said SAIL is also trying to takeover few existing sick units like Malvika Steels Ltd. in U.P.which is one of them. In reply to another question the Minister said, the Government is working on various measures to improve the steel production capacity in India which inter-alia includes large scale capacity addition by the Public Sector Steel Plants. For effective coordination and monitoring of all issues concerning major steel investments in the country, an Inter Ministerial Group has been set up under the Chairmanship of Secretary (Steel). A Steel Price Monitoring Committee has also been constituted to monitor, analyses and discuss the price movements of steel commodities. To improve the reach of steel products, Steel Public Sector Undertakings (PSUs) have taken up the appointment of district dealers in every district in the country. The steel PSUs have also made arrangements to transport the materials to the dealers' premises and the cost of transportation is borne by the producers.

2911. (30-8-2007) NEW DELHI : The Appointment Committee of the Cabinet has approved the following appointments/extension: Shri Wilfred Lakara, IAS (CG:73), presently Managing Director, TRIFED, as Secretary, National Commission for Scheduled Tribes. Shri Samirendra Chatterjee, IAS (AM:76), presently in the cadre, as Member Secretary, National Commission for Women, in the rank and pay of Additional Secretary, on the retirement of Shri N.P. Gupta, IAS (TN:72) on 31st August, 2007. Shri N. Bala Baskar, IAS (HY:75), presently in the cadre, as Additional Secretary and Financial Adviser in the Ministry of External Affairs in the vacancy of Smt. Sheela Bhide, IAS (AP:73). Extension of tenure of Shri V.P. Raja, IAS (MH:74), Additional Secretary, Department of Atomic Energy for a period upto 30st September, 2008 or until further orders, whichever is earlier.

2912. (30-8-2007) NEW DELHI : The Minister of Tourism and Culture Smt. Ambika Soni has said that Archaeological Survey of India (ASI) undertakes major conservation works in the centrally protected monuments as per the archaeological norms, departmentally through its own manpower resources. In addition to implementing its annual programme, ASI has to honour the requests from State Governments to carry out conservation works in the State protected monuments as deposit works and has to handle projects abroad as part of the bilateral agreements. Coping with an increasing workload, and accomplishing the tasks in a timely manner, is an ongoing challenge.

2913. (30-8-2007) NEW DELHI : The Minister of Tourism and Culture Smt. Ambika Soni has said that no cracks have developed in Sanchi Stupa. During the extensive conservation carried out during the years 1912 to 1919, about 200 weep holes were provided to drain out percolated rainwater. Seepage through the weep holes is a normal process and part of conservation measure to relieve water pressure inside the structure. In a written reply in the Lok Sabha today she said, further, water tightening of the stupa was carried out during 2005-06 and 2006-07 which included grouting, recess pointing. There is no danger to the structural stability of the stupa.

2914. (30-8-2007) NEW DELHI : The Prime Minister, Dr. Manmohan Singh gave away National Awards for Micro, Small and Medium Enterprises at a function here today. Following is the text of the speech of the Prime Minister on the occasion: "I take this opportunity to congratulate all the winners of National Awards a this function today. I commend my colleague Shri Mahabir Prasadji, and his Ministry, for instituting these awards. A few months back, I was at an award ceremony for small and medium enterprises (SMEs) in Mumbai and I was greatly impressed by the tremendous achievements of those award winners as well. I hope awards like these will encourage more and more of our entrepreneurs to strive harder and contribute to our country's economic and social development. The nominations for today's awards and for the earlier Mumbai awards demonstrate that the small and medium enterprises sector in India has truly come into its own. Gone are the days when the business limelight was reserved almost entirely for the captains in the corporate sector and SMEs remained in the shadows. India's SME business leaders now stand proudly on their own feet. I affirm our Government's solemn commitment to their growth and progress in years to come. Micro and small enterprises provide employment to almost 41 million people in our country. Including the handloom and handicraft sector, the total employment provided by them is over 60 million. Hence, from the point of view of our people's livelihood and well-being this sector is of tremendous importance. The fact that SMEs are widely dispersed across the entire country also makes them highly important from a regional developmental perspective and as a means to promote balanced and equitable growth all over the country. The SME sector has contributed to the growth of new industries as well as new industrial centres. There is no doubt that Governmental and institutional support provided to this sector through incentives, infrastructural facilities and other assistance has helped. But what has really made a difference is the spirit of enterprise and creativity of our entrepreneurs in this sector. Nowhere is this spirit of enterprise, this willingness to take risk and an eagerness to strike out on one's own to seek a fortune more in evidence than in our small and medium enterprises sector. It is this animal spirit which makes the SME sector the most dynamic in our economy and worthy of our support and encouragement. Our Government has shown a consistent commitment to the growth and welfare of small and medium enterprises. A significant contribution of our Government is the enactment of the 'Micro, Small and Medium Enterprises Development Act'. It aims to improve the competitiveness of these enterprises and contribute to their healthy growth. I hope the provisions of this Act will benefit all your firms in your business ventures. Our Government has also announced a comprehensive Package for the Promotion of Micro and Small Enterprises. This should also contribute to the realization of this objective. Our government has charted a new strategy based on Cluster Development that offers a holistic and integrated approach to SME sector's development. We have also taken up skill development as a high priority area. I have recently announced our decision to set up a National Mission on Vocational Education and Skill Development, and we intend to fund more polytechnics and ITIs to address the growing demand for skilled manpower of our enterprises.

2915. (30-8-2007) NEW DELHI : The details of competition and training venues finalized for each discipline along with the agencies responsible for establishing the required infrastructure for the Commonwealth Games, 2010 is placed at Annex.I and Annex II respectively. The Games Village near Akshardham Temple is being developed by Delhi Development Authority on the public-private-partnership mode for housing all Indian/foreign accredited athletes, coaches, etc. For augmentation of hotel accommodation, Delhi Development Authority,

Government of Uttar Pradesh, Government of Haryana etc. are taking necessary steps which is being monitored by the Ministry of Tourism. Government has approved project proposals of Sports Authority of India for an amount of Rs.1000 crores (± 10%) for upgradation/creation of sports venue infrastructure; upgradation of Tennis venue by All India Tennis Association at a cost of Rs.30 crores (± 15%) and expenditure budget of Organizing Committee on a revenue neutral basis of Rs.767 crores (± 15%) for 'Conduct of the Games'. The Expenditure Finance Committee has recommended the proposal of the Delhi Development Authority for Rs.325.00 crores (± 25%) for the International Zone etc. in the Games village (which is being developed on Public Private Partnership Mode) and sports infrastructure.

2916. (31-8-2007) NEW DELHI : Shri K. C. Jena, an officer of 1971 batch of Indian Railway Traffic Service, has taken over as the new Chairman, Railway Board and ex-officio Principal Secretary to the Government of India, Ministry of Railways, here today. His ascendancy to the Railway Board comes at a time when the Indian Railways is witness to an unprecedented turnaround and is on the throes of an order-of-magnitude change. Prior to this he has been holding the post of Member (Staff), Railway Board since 31st July 2006. Shri Jena has risen to the highest office in the Indian Railways, after having held important operational management assignments on the South Eastern Railway including that of the Chief Freight Traffic Manager. Known by his dynamic leadership and pro-active approach to challenges, he joined the Railway Board initially as Executive Director (Safety) and then took over as Executive Director (Coaching). He also served as the Chief Commercial Manager (Passenger Services) and thereafter as Chief Operating Manager, Western Railway. During this tenure, he received the prestigious Zonal Efficiency Shield for Excellency in Operations for the year 2004-05. His stint as Division Railway Manager, Vadodra saw path-breaking initiatives in the field of passenger amenities and in pioneering the concept of Special Purpose Vehicle as the future to modernization and expansion of Indian Raillways. Shri Jena was elevated to the post of Additional General Manager, Central Railway and thereafter, took over the dual charge of the posts of General Manager, North Central Railway, Allahabad and General Manager, East Central Railway, Hajipur. Later, he continued as General Manager, East Central Railway. He brings to the office his erudite knowledge and scholarship, imbibed in the course of his study, among others, at the Madras Christian College, Chennai and the Indian Institute of Technology, Kanpur. He joined the Indian Railway Traffic Service in the year 1971. Shri Jena travelled extensively, both within and outside the country whereby he could glean the challenges and opportunities for the Indian Railways. He has received training in U.K. on Inter-modal traffic at the University College of Cardiff, on Management Information Systems in Sweden, Germany and the USA and on Management Essentials for High Potential Executives at STERN School of Business, New York, USA. Shri Jena was elected as the National Chairman of the Chartered Institute of Logistics and Transport (CILT), India, headquartered in U.K. in March 2007.

He has been the recipient of the prestigious Rajiv Gandhi Sadhbhawana Award for the year 2007 from Rajiv Gandhi Foundation. AKS/HK

2917. (31-8-2007) NEW DELHI : Government of India have announced the sale (re-issue) of "8.20 per cent Government Stock, 2022 for a notified amount of Rs. 4,000 crore (nominal) through a priced based auction using multiple price method. Government of India have also announced the sale (re-issue) of "8.33 per cent Government Stock, 2036" for a notified amount of Rs. 3,000 crore (nominal) through a price based auction using multiple price method. The auctions will be conducted by the Reserve Bank of India, Mumbai Office, Fort, Mumbai on September 7, 2007 (Friday). Up to 5% of the notified amount of the sale of both the stocks will be allotted to eligible individuals and Institutions as per the Scheme for Non-Competitive Bidding Facility in the Auction of Government Securities. Bids in the prescribed form obtainable from the Regional Director, Reserve Bank of India, Mumbai Office (Public Debt Office), Fort, Mumbai-400 001 and RBI website www.rbi.org.in should be submitted to that Office on September 7, 2007. The NDS members should submit competitive as well as non-competitive bids in electronic format using Primary Market Operation (PMO) module of NDS. All bids should be submitted by 12.30 P.M. The result of the auctions will be announced on September 7, 2007 and payment by successful bidders will be during banking hours on September 10, 2007 (Monday).

2918. (31-8-2007) NEW DELHI : The Scheme for Financial Support to Public Private Partnerships in Infrastructure (Viability Gap Funding (VGF) Scheme) to accelerate and increase PPs in infrastructure was announced in August, 2005 by Government of India. In order to be eligible for funding under the Scheme the project must be developed, financed, constructed, maintained and operated during the project term by an entity with at least 51% private equity. The total VGF under the scheme is ordinarily limited to 20% of the project cost. The Government or statutory entity that owns the project may, if it so decides, provide additional grants out of its budget up to further twenty percent of the total project cost. The exact VGF support to be given would however be decided on the basis of competitive bidding. The sectors eligible under the Scheme are roads and bridges, railways, seaports, airports, inland waterways, power, urban transport, water supply, sewerage, solid waste management and other physical infrastructure in urban areas, infrastructure projects in Special Economic Zones, International convention centres and other tourism infrastructure projects.

2919. (31-8-2007) NEW DELHI : The Vice President of India Mohd. Hamid Ansari has said that gaps in human development should be bridged for peace, security and progress of all. Innovative approaches such as Participatory banking and finance should be adopted in plugging such gaps. He was addressing the Conference on "Participatory Banking for all as a business proposition" here today.

2920. (31-8-2007) NEW DELHI : As part of the Composite Dialogue between India and Pakistan, the delegations of the two countries met in New Delhi on 30-31 August 2007 for discussions on the Wullar Barrage/Tulbul Navigation Project. The Indian delegation was led by Mrs. Gauri Chatterji, Secretary, Ministry of Water Resources, Government of India and the Pakistan delegation was led by Mr. Muhammad Ismail Qureshi, Secretary, Ministry of Water and Power, Government of Pakistan. The talks were held in a cordial and constructive atmosphere. The two sides further discussed their respective positions on the project and had a better appreciation of each other's views. They reaffirmed their commitment to the Indus Waters Treaty of 1960. The two sides emphasized the need for an early and amicable resolution of the issue in accordance with the provisions of the Indus Waters Treaty of 1960 for the socio-economic development of the peoples of the two countries. The Secretaries agreed to hold discussions including at technical level on mutually acceptable dates. Both sides looked forward to the next round of talks under the Composite Dialogue with a view to resolving the issue at an early date. The Pakistan delegation also called on Prof. Saifuddin Soz, Minister for Water Resources Government of India.

2921. (31-8-2007) NEW DELHI : It has come to the notice of Ministry of Information & Broadcasting that some private FM radio channels are airing news snippets and current affairs in violation of rules for FM radio operators. These violations have been viewed very seriously by the Ministry. As per the policy, news and current affairs are not allowed to be broadcast by private FM channel in any manner. The carriage of news snippets and current affairs violates the provisions, which have been incorporated in clause 1.4 and 23.4 of Grant of Permission Agreement signed by private operators with the Government. It is, therefore, advised that all concerned parties refrain from any such activities, which are in violation of terms and conditions of FM license. Ever since the implementation of private FM Radio Policy in July 2005, over 100 FM stations became operational within a year and around 150 FM stations are likely to be operational by the year-end.

2922. (31-8-2007) NEW DELHI : The All India Consumer Price Index Number for Industrial Workers (CPI-IW) (base 2001-100) during July 2007 increased by two points to stand at 132 (one hundred and thirty two) points. The Rise/Fall in index varied from centre to centre. The index recorded an increase of 8 points in Bhilai centre and 7 points in Bhavnagar centre, 6 points each in Siliguri and Ranchi-Hatia centres, 4 points in 7 centres, 3 points in 13 centres, 2 points in 21 centres and 1 point in 25 centres.

2923. (31-8-2007) NEW DELHI : National Foundation for Teachers' Welfare is organizing on Monday a voluntary Fund Collection Drive on the eve of Teachers' Day. The funds collected on the occasion will be utilized for the welfare of teachers. It will be followed by a cultural function at Shastri Bhawan, New Delhi.

Secretary, School Education & Literacy (SE&L) will be Chief Guest of the function. The Fund Collection Drive will be carried out with the help of students and teachers from Kendriya Vidyalaya, Sector-II, R.K. Puram and Laxman Public School, Hauz Khas, from 9.00 A.M. to 10.30 A.M. After the Fund Collection Drive, the students from the above schools will present a cultural programme from 12.00 Noon to 1.00 P.M. at Reading Hall of Central Secretariat Library, Shastri Bhawan. The National Foundation for Teachers' Welfare was set up in 1962 with the main objective to provide financial assistance to teachers in indigent circumstances. The Foundation is operating various schemes like Financial Assistance for the Construction of Shikshak Sadans, Financial Assistance to Teachers Suffering from Serious Ailments, Paid Holiday to Eminent Teachers who have rendered meritorious services, Support for Professional Education of Children of School Teachers, etc. for the welfare of teachers all over India. The Foundation celebrates Teachers' Day to mark the birthday of Dr.S. Radhakrishnan, former President, noted educationist and philosopher.

2924. (31-8-2007) NEW DELHI : Keeping in view the extreme conditions of farmers in 31 debt stressed districts in four state of Maharashtra (06), Andhra Pradesh (16), Karnataka (06) and Kerala (03), a relief package was announced for farmers by the Government. It provides for waiver of the entire interest on overdue loans as on 01.07.2006. At the time of finalisation of the scheme, it was estimated to waive Rs. 2720.93 crore as overdue interest in the 31 identified districts. However, as on 27.07.2007 an amount of Rs. 3732.96 crore as overdue interest has been waived in these districts. The special package also provides for reschedulement of overdue loans of the farmers as on 01.07.2006 over a period of 3-5 years with a one year moratorium. The estimated amount of loan to be rescheduled was Rs. 9051.81 crore, whereas an amount of Rs. 10967.98 crore of loan has been rescheduled as on 27.07.2007. This information was given by Shri Pawan Kumar Bansal, Minister of State for finance in reply to a question raised by Shri Pratik P. Patil in Lok Sabha today.

2925. (31-8-2007) NEW DELHI : The proceeds from disinvestments of Government's equity in Central Public Sector Enterprises would be channelised into the National Investment Fund (NIF). The corpus of NIF will be of a permanent nature. NIF would be professionally managed to provide sustainable returns to the Government, without depleting the corpus. Selected Public Sector Mutual Funds are to be entrusted with the management of the corpus of NIF. 75% of the annual income of NIF will be used to finance selected social sector schemes, which promote education, health and employment. The residual 25% of the annual income of NIF will be used to meet the capital investment requirements of profitable and revivable CPSEs that yield adequate returns, in order to enlarge their capital base to finance expansion/diversification. This information was given by Shri S.S. Palanimanickam, Minister of State for finance in reply to a question raised by Shri L. Rajagopal in Lok Sabha today.

2926. (31-8-2007) NEW DELHI : Central Board of Excise and Customs (CBEC), Department of Revenue issued Notification no. 90/2007-Cus (N.T), here today, notifying tariff values of edible oils and brass scrap (all grades) as shown in the Table below. The tariff values of six palm group oils and crude soyabean oil remain unchanged. However, tariff value of brass scrap (all grades) has been lowered.

2927. (31-8-2007) NEW DELHI : Report No. 514 on "Household Consumer Expenditure Among Socio-Economic Groups: 2004-2005" based on the seventh quinquennial survey on Household Consumer Expenditure carried out during the NSS 61st round (July, 2004-June, 2005) by the National Sample Survey Organisation (NSSO) in the Ministry of Statistics and Programme Implementation has been released. This is the last report in the series of seven reports planned to be brought out on the basis of the survey. The report is based on the information on socio-economic characteristics of the households viz, social group, household type ascertained on the basis of means of livelihood, land possessed by the households in rural areas and the commodity-specific data on household consumption collected from the sample households. Four social groups, viz., Scheduled Tribes (ST), Scheduled Castes (SC), Other Backward Classes (OBC) and the residual class (Others) were considered for the collection of the information on social group. It is important to note that the social group reported for head of the household was taken to be the social group of all members of that household and the information recorded in this regard was based entirely on the response of the informant and not ascertained from any official list of social groups. All the data are provided separately for rural and urban sectors of each State and UTs of India. Like all regular NSS surveys, the present survey covered practically the whole of the Indian Union. All States and Union Territories were covered under the survey except some interior areas of Nagaland, Andaman & Nicobar Islands, and Ladakh and Kargil districts of Jammu & Kashmir. The survey was spread over 7999 villages and 4602 urban blocks covering 79298 rural and 45346 urban households respectively.

2928. (31-8-2007) NEW DELHI : There is no shortage in the aggregate number of doctors and nurses in the country. As per information furnished by Medical Council of India (MCI), at present there are 6,83,682 allopathic registered doctors in the country. Besides, 30,922 doctors pass out from 269 medical colleges every year adding to the strength of doctor in the country. In addition, there are more than 6 lakh practitioners of Indian Systems of Medicine and Homoeopathy in the country. However, there is an imbalance in the availability of doctors in the rural and urban areas of the country. As regard nurses, according to the Report of the National Commission on Macroeconomic and Health, around 3.25 lakh nurses would be required by 2015. There are 1597 Graduate Nursing Midwifery (GNM) Schools functioning in the country with an intake capacity of 80000 students (approximately) per year. In order to expand the facilities of Medical Education and Health related services, under Pradhan Mantri Swasthya Suraksha Yojana

(PMSSY) the Government has decided to set up six AIIMS like institutions in under served-states and also to upgrade 13 existing Government Medical College / Institutions in ten States. Further, the Government encourages setting up of new medical college in the Government as well as private sector and also in increase in intake capacity of medical stundents. Under National Rural Health Mission (NRHM), all PHC's are envisaged to be strengthened by upgrading single doctor PHC to 2 doctors PHC by posting of Ayush practitioner and skilled nurses at PHC level. The States are encouraged to appoint doctors, specialists and paramedics on contractual basis. Multi-skill training of doctors and in-service training of ANMs/Nurses is done. The States have been requested to strengthen their nursing cadre. Requirement of funds for establishment / strengthening of nursing and ANM schools, as incorporated in the PIP of some States under NRHM (2006-07) has been approved.

2929. (31-8-2007) NEW DELHI : The Government has decided to support the Public Health Foundation of India (PHFI) in setting up world class Institutes of Public health in India through contribution of upto Rs. 65 crore as one-time grant to the initial Rs. 200 crore PHFI corpus. The representatives of the Government are also there in the Governing Board of PHFI. PHFI is an autonomous Public-Private partnership and besides Government of India, the Bill & Melinda Gates Foundation, Deshpande Foundation, Amar Foundation and other high net worth corporates/individuals, both from within India and abroad, are contributing to the PHFI corpus fund. PHFI is an initiative to bridge the gap between the requirement and availability of trained personnel in public health and to effectively promote public health management. It will not only train health professionals, but will also assist in strengthening the existing institutions in the public health sector, create a pool of excellent faculty, act as a think tank for the Government providing inputs for policy initiatives and set standards for public health education. The research programmes of PHFI would be geared to facilitate policy and programme development in public health through inter-disciplinary studies. PHFI has decided to establish Institutes of Public health in Hyderabad, Andhra Pradesh and Gandhinagar, Gujarat. The institutes will be fully operation by 2009, although short and medium term education and training programmes are expected to start from year 2008 itself. This information was given by the Minister of State for Health & Family Welfare, Smt. Panabaka Lakshmi in a written reply to a question in the Rajya Sabha.

2930. (31-8-2007) NEW DELHI : The Minister of State for Housing & Urban Poverty Alleviation, Kumari Selja informed the Lok Sabha today, in a written reply to a question by Shri Girdhari Lal Bhargava that Projects to improve urban slums with foreign assistance are undertaken as part of broad sectoral programmes in the sphere of land assembly and development, water supply, transport, sanitation & sewerage, drainage and provision of basic services to the urban poor. The relevant details are annexed.

2931. (31-8-2007) NEW DELHI : There have been several reports recently in the newspapers regarding poor product quality of Chinese made goods including toys. According to Indian Council of Medical Research (ICMR), an NGO Toxies Link had conducted a study in 2006, which examined toys from Delhi, Mumbai and Chennai, and reported high levels of cadmium & lead in PVC used in soft toys. Most of the toys in Chennai and Mumbai were being imported from China. Lead is a known neuro and hematological toxin which can lead to delayed development and lower IQs in children. Cadmium is one of the heavy metals which has its primary effect on kidneys.

2932. (31-8-2007) NEW DELHI : The area coverage of kharif crops as compared to 30th August last year has gone up considerably as per data compiled by Agriculture Ministry. The total coverage of kharif rice has gone up to 337 lakh ha as compared to 334.18 lakh hectare at this time last year, the weekly Crop Weather Watch Group meeting of the Ministry of Agriculture was informed here today. The sowing of rice is at ending stage in the states of Gujarat, Haryana and Rajasthan. In rest of the states transplanting is at peak. Total coarse cereals have covered an area of 207.42 lakh ha as compared to 195.87 lakh ha at this time last year. Cotton has been sown in 90.2 lakh ha as compared to 86.14 lakh ha last year. Out of this, 53.33 lakh hectare is under Bt cotton. Sugarcane coverage is reported to be 51.04 lakh hectare compared to 48.32 lakh ha last year, and jute 7.89 lakh hectare (last year 8.18 lakh ha.). The total coverage of oilseeds so far has been 170.15 lakh ha as compared to 156.42 lakh ha on August 30, last year. Soyabean has been sown in 9 % and groundnut in 14% higher area as compared to that in 2006. Pulses cover an area of 115.3 lakh ha against 108.3 lakh ha up to this time last year.

2933. (31-8-2007) NEW DELHI : In order to regulate the conduct of doctors, the Medical Council of India (MCI) with the approval of the Central Government, has notified Indian Medical Council (Professional Conduct, Etiquette and Ethics) Regulations, 2002. These regulations prescribe various acts of commission and omission on the part of a physician, which are construed as misconduct and unethical. The MCI or the appropriate State Medical Councils have been empowered to take disciplinary action against a physician for violation of the provisions or the regulations. As and when complaints are received by the Government against the violation of code of ethics of doctors, MCI is advised to inquire into such violations and take strict action against violators. This information was given by the Minister of State for Health & Family Welfare, Smt. Panabaka Lakshmi in a written reply to a question in the Rajya Sabha.

2934. (31-8-2007) NEW DELHI : There is no system of banning drugs globally by any organization or regulation. The safety and efficacy of a drug is ascertained as per Schedule Y of Drugs and Cosmetics Rules before market approval in the country. Even after market approval is given for any drug, the safety and efficacy is continuously examined on the basis of information received through Pharmoco-vigilance, Post-Marketing Surveillance and information reported from other countries. In order to examine such information, the Drug Technical Advisory Board under Drugs & Cosmetics Act has constituted a Sub-committee, consisting of experts on the subject who examine the information received from the sources mentioned above and take a final view as to whether the prohibit the manufacture, sale and distribution of drugs or restrict its use for specific population and accordingly recommend to the Government to make suitable amendment in the market authorization or prohibit manufacture, sale and distribution and drugs under Section 26A of the Drugs & Cosmetics Act which empowers the Central Government to prohibit the manufacture, sale or distribution of such drug or cosmetics. No information has been received in the Directorate General of Health Services (DGHS) regarding availability in the market of drugs banned in the country under Section 26A of the Drugs & Cosmetics Act. This information was given by the Minister for Health & Family Welfare, Dr. Anbumani Ramadoss in a reply to a question in the Rajya Sabha.

2935. (31-8-2007) NEW DELHI : Climate change due to rising levels of Carbon dioxide in the atmosphere is one of the most serious environmental concerns of our time. General expansion of economic activity, increased population and use of fossil fuels are responsible for man-made emission of Green House Gases (GHG). To address the problem posed by Climate Change the International community has set up the United Nations Framework Convention on Climate Change (UNFCCC) in 1992, based on the principle of "common but differentiated responsibilities and respective capabilities of countries". The objective of UNFCCC is to stabilize GHGs concentration in the atmosphere to prevent dangerous anthropogenic interference with the climate system. Later in the year 1997, Parties adopted the Kyoto Protocol which sets legally binding targets for GHG reductions by industrialized countries during "first commitment period", 2008-2012, totalling 5.2% below their aggregate 1990 emissions.

2936. (31-8-2007) NEW DELHI : Railways' ambitious project to connect Kashmir valley to rest of India through Udhampur-Srinagar-Baramulla railway track is going to cost more than what was estimated earlier. The rough estimated cost at the time of preparation of project report was assessed as Rs. 3077 crore. Now the cost has been estimated as Rs. 11,270 crore after completion of detailed engineering survey. Earlier, estimate was prepared on the basis of topo sheets and aerial photographs as detailed survey could not be completed due to highly difficult inaccessible terrain and adverse conditions/situation of the area. An outlay of Rs. 1700 crore has been proposed as an additonality during 2007-08 and an expenditure of Rs. 3836 crore has been incurred upto March 2007.

2937. (31-8-2007) NEW DELHI : Shri Kamal Nath, Minister for Commerce and Industry has said that in view of the large growing domestic market and to face the challenges in the International market, it is essential for the country to create international "Home-grown Brand" in the textile sector. Shri Kamal Nath said this while inaugurating the two-day "Tex Summit 2007", here today. The inaugural function was attended by Shri Shankersinh Vaghela, Minister of Textiles, Shri Oscar Fernandes, Minister of State (Independent Charge) for Labour and Employment, Shri E.V.K.S. Elangovan, Minister of State for Textiles, Dr. C. Rangarajan, Chairman, Economic Advisory Council to the Prime Minister, Shri Jagdish Narayan Rai, Minister, Department of Handloom and Silk, Government of Uttar Pradesh besides leading industrialist from textile sector, academicians, economists and several senior officers of the Government of India. In his inaugural address Shri Kamal Nath said that for building 'home-grown brand' internationally, the Commerce Ministry can support the textile Ministry from its India Brand Equity Fund. In order to face challenges, Shri Kamal Nath said that we have to think about the strategy for bringing agricultural sector into the folds of commercial sector. For this, it will be appropriate to impart training to the agricultural workers to facilitate their migration to the textile sector. He further stated that as India globalises there would be challenges from the new competitors like Bangladesh, Cambodia and Central American countries. Both the industry and government have to introspect with a view to face new competition. He also stated that we have great advantage of our large and growing domestic market and the target of achieving 10 per cent of the global trade is achievable. Regarding anti-dumping duties, Shri Kamal Nath said the government would continue follow pro-actively and in a transparent manner.

2938. (31-8-2007) NEW DELHI : The average annual requirement of electricity of the Railways for the year 2005-06 was 12,705 million units approximately. The average charges of electricity for operation of trains (traction) for the year 2005-06 was 422 paisa per unit and the average charges of electricity for other than train opeation was 424 paisa per unit. Railways are establishing a captive power plant 1000 Mega Watt capacity at Nabinagar of Aurangabad district in Bihar in collaboration with NTPC Ltd. This has been included in Railway Budget for the year 2007-08. Ten per cent power from this power plant will be earmarked to other users. This information was given by the Minister of State for Railways Shri R.Velu in written reply to a question in the Rajya Sabha today.

2939. (31-8-2007) NEW DELHI : All possible steps are undertaken on a continuing basis by Indian Railways to prevent accidents. These measures include timely replacement of over-aged assets, installations of weighbridges to check overloading of wagons, adoption of suitable technologies for up-gradation and maintenance of track, rolling stock, signalling and interlocking systems, safety drives and inspections at regular intervals to monitor and educate staff for observance of safe practices: As a result, there has been a decline in the number of accidents from 234 in 2004-05 to 195 in 2006-07. Continuous efforts are made to check overloading of wagons. Frequency and speed of trains are increased only when suitable infrastructure is available. This information was given by the Minister of State for Railways Shri R.Velu in written reply to a question in the Rajya Sabha today.

2940. (31-8-2007) NEW DELHI : Continuing its noble tradition of extending assistance to the families of those who laid down their lives for the cause of the nation, the Ministry of Railways has offered job to Shri Jamil Alam, grandson of Martyr Abdul Hameed, one of the heroes in the 1965 Indo-Pak war. Hawaldar Abdul Hameed was posthumously awarded the Param Vir Chakra for his defiant valour in that war. The Minister of Railways Shri Lalu Prasad here today handed over the appointment letter to Shri Jamil Alam for the post of Electric Signal Maintainer (ESM), a Group 'C' post in Northern Railways. Also present on the occasion were the Union Minister for Corporate Affairs, Shr Prem Chand Gupta, the widow of Martyr Abdul Hameed and Smt. Rasoolan Bi. The Railways have earlier also helped the family when it gave job to Shri Juned Alam, son of Martyr Abdul Hameed, six years ago. The spirit of the assistance is to boost the morale of our brave army men so as to assure them that their families will ever be looked after by the nation. Last month, the Ministry of Railways had offered jobs to two unemployed daughters of under privileged Shri Vinayak Rao Tope, the descendents of Martyr Tantya Tope, the hero of India's first war of independence (1857). The Minister said that Railways will continue to extend all possible assistance to similar noble cause.

2941. (31-8-2007) NEW DELHI : In order to make TPDS more focused and targeted towards the poorest of the poor families in the country, the Antyodaya Anna Yojana (AAY) was launched in December, 2000 to cover one crore such families amongst the BPL families. Subsequently, this scheme has been expanded during 2003-2004, 2004-2005 and 2005-2006, to add 50 lakh AAY households each time. Thus, the target of the Government is to cover 2.50 crore families under this scheme. Against the target, various State/UT Governments have so far identified about 2.40 crore families (more than 12 crore persons) and issued distinctive ration cards to them. The Central Government is allocating foodgrains for these 2.4 crore AAY families at the scale of 35 kg. per family per month under TPDS. Rice and wheat are being distributed to them at Rs. 3/- per kg. and Rs. 2/- per kg. since December, 2000.

2942. (31-8-2007) NEW DELHI : The Union Minister for Rural Development, Dr. Raghuvansh Prasad Singh has assured the Members of Parliament that demand of compliance to their suggestions to district/ State authorities regarding implementation of Rural Development Schemes and having a say in the block/ district/state level Vigilance and Monitoring Committee will be taken care of and the State Governments will be contacted to ensure this. Interacting with a group of Members of Parliament from Gujarat, Uttarakhand and Union Territories in the present chain of such meetings about the various Rural Development Schemes launched by his Ministry here yesterday Dr. Singh laid emphasis on the monitoring of schemes at district level so that the schemes are implemented properly. He asked the elected representatives to ensure the holding of quarterly village, district and state level Vigilance and Monitoring Committee meetings at regular intervals. This will pave the way for people's participation, close monitoring, transparency and accountability for the successful implementation of Rural Development programmes, Dr. Singh added. The MPs emphasized for the need of a proper mechanism of awareness for the check on irregularities and fraudulent practices in implementation of the programmes and asked for the removal of technical bottlenecks coming in the way of smooth implementation process. The interactive sessions with the Members of Parliament by the Rural Development Minister are currently being organized so as to apprise the MPs of various rural development schemes, their implementation and their suggestions are taken for the better implementation of schemes like National Rural Employment Guarantee Programme (NREGA), SGSY (Sampoorana Gramin Swarozgar Yozana), PMGSY (Pradhan Mantri Gram Sadak Yozana), ARWSP (Accelerated Rural Water Supply Programme), IWDP (Integrated Wasteland Development Programme) and TSC (Total Sanitation Campaign).

2943. (31-8-2007) NEW DELHI : On attaining the age of superannuation Maj Gen Harwant Krishan, Director General Resettlement, Ministry of Defence, retired today after rendering 38 years of illustrious service. During this span he achieved fame in planning and opening of the Srinagar-Muzaffarabad Road at the international level. Being at the helm of affairs he set an enviable example in disaster management by organising the relief and rehabilitation of the earthquake victims in Oct 2005 in the Baramulla-Uri Sector. General Krishan took over the appointment of Director General Resettlement on 01 Mar 2006. During his tenure of 18 months as DGR, he took charge of resettlement and welfare of over 25 lakh ex-servicemen (ESM) and widows by exploring possibilities of their re-employment in the corporate sector. The magnitude of the problem could be guessed from the fact that this population is growing on an average, at the rate of 65,000 personnel who retire every year at an age when they are still left with useful and active life by civil standards. General Krishan undertook this gigantic task by establishing contacts with renowned industrial houses in the country and by creating awareness in the corporate sector about the availability of this vast, trained disciplined force which could be employed by latter for mutual benefit. A special mention needs to be made of the DGR for his untiring efforts in organizing placement oriented training courses in esteemed business schools in the country and other useful courses like 'Retail Management Course', Heavy Earthmoving Equipment operation course, Hospitality Industry related courses etc. He was also instrumental in creating employment opportunities for Personnel Below Officer Rank (PBOR) by organizing career transition capsules in the Regimental/Corps Centres throughout the country where prospective employers are taken to pick up personnel and offer jobs to them on the spot.

2944. (31-8-2007) NEW DELHI : The Prime Minister, Dr. Manmohan Singh dedicated two reactors to the Nation at a function in Tarapur, Mumbai today.

Following is the text of the speech of the Prime Minister on the occasion: "I am truly honoured to be here today for the dedication of Units 3 and 4 of the Tarapur Atomic Power Station to the Nation. Tarapur is where India's quest for developing nuclear energy began in 1969. Tarapur is a shining example that India can do it; that we can overcome hurdles. It, therefore, holds special significance for our country's journey towards the building of a strong and self-reliant economy. Tarapur stands as a tribute to the visionary leadership of Pandit Jawaharlal Nehru and Dr. Homi Bhabha and to all those nuclear scientists and engineers who have helped to translate that magnificent vision into reality. Their hard work has today earned us a place among the leading nations of the world in the area of nuclear technology. On behalf of a grateful nation, I salute all the scientists and engineers for this great national effort. I would particularly like to compliment the Nuclear Power Corporation of India and all those in the Department of Atomic Energy, Indian industry, our R&D facilities and Universities who have made the development of TAPS 3 and 4 possible. It is truly an outstanding effort, achieved in the face of adverse circumstances and challenges of the last few decades. I congratulate each and every one of you. This is a moment of pride for all Indians. The development of our indigenous capability in the area of nuclear power generation demonstrates that where there is a will there is a way. Starting from humble beginnings in the 1960s, the country today has seventeen power reactors, largely Pressurized Heavy Water Reactor plants. Those that we have developed are state-of-the-art facilities. As we move forward on development of fast breeder reactors and thorium reactors, I have no doubt that we would in the future exercise global leadership in these technologies. There can be no greater tribute to our capabilities than the fact that Units 3 and 4 of TAPS have been commissioned ahead of schedule and well within the sanctioned cost.

2945. (31-8-2007) NEW DELHI : Increased public awareness in environmental issues and their linkages with economic and social issues has led to increased demand for a better environment by the public at large. This has resulted in the need to generate authentic information, which can be used by policy makers for decision making to improve the environment. The Ministry of Environment and Forests with the help of Planning Commission started this process of developing environmental indicators in 2002, which are easily understandable by the environmental community, policy planners, business houses, general public, environmental NGOs and stakeholders since last five years. 35 States started the process of collecting data covering three aspects, natural resources base, utilization of natural resources and socio-economic aspects of population. Natural resource base included geographical profile, land use, mineral resources, forest resources, wild life, water resources, wetlands, animal husbandry, grazing land and pastures. Under utilization of natural resources, agriculture, horticulture, industrial development, energy, bio-diversity, pollution and transportation has been covered. The third aspect *i.e.* socio-economic aspect of population took care of culture and archaeology, housing, transportation, tourism, women and environmental education and natural disaster. 32 States out of 35 States have prepared these reports, which have mixed outputs where some of the processes adopted and products developed on their own which are pioneering. The States have also contributed to policy and decision making within the country and also reporting to the global system. Several Indian Institutions have often been called upon to take a leadership role in regional and global SoE reporting processes. But they give environmental indicators for respective states. The scheme of preparation of State of Environment Reports was launched with a total outlay of Rs.6 crores as a Plan Scheme in the Tenth Five Year Plan. It started in October 2002 and included a more streamlined data collection and collation system, appropriate consultative process, reporting system through a range of static and interactive media. Based on the experience and suggestions from All India Workshop on State of Environment which concluded recently for reporting during 11th Plan also will be planned for future course.

2946. (31-8-2007) NEW DELHI : Shri Kamal Nath, Union Minister of Commerce and Industry, has expressed hope that the bilateral trade between India and Thailand would take a growth trajectory that would take trade relations between the two countries to a new height. He hoped that the FTA negotiations that are underway covering trade in goods, services and investments, including issues such as Rules of Origin, trade facilitation, Anti-dumping and safeguard measures, Dispute Settlement Mechanism would benefit the two countries. He stated this while welcoming Mr. Kosit Panpiemras, Deputy Prime Minister and Minister of Industry of Thailand during the Indo-Thailand bilateral talks here today. Senior Officials from both the countries were also present during the talks. The Trade between India and Thailand has grown significantly during 1992 to 1997 from a level of US$ 399.8 million in 1992 to US$ 896.4 million in 1997. Bilateral trade crossed the US$ 1 billion mark during the year 2000 (US$ 1,122.6 million), a significant increase of 40.2% compared to 1999 (US$ 800.2). The Bilateral trade has shown an impressive growth rate in the last few years. Bilateral trade volume increased by 29% over previous year, to touch US$ 2,286 million in 2005-06 (exports US$ 1,075 million; imports US$ 1,211 million) and had touched US$ 1,509 million by September 2006. India's exports to Thailand were US$ 1075 million in 2005-06, an increase of 19% over the previous year. In 2006-07 (April-Sept), India's exports to Thailand were US$ 697 million. India's imports from Thailand were US$ 1,211 million in 2005-06, a growth of about 40% over the previous year. The figure for 2006-07 (April-Sept) was US$ 812 million. India's major exports to Thailand are Gemstones, mainly diamonds and emeralds; other metal ores, metal waste scrap and products; chemicals; iron, steel and products; vegetables and vegetable products; machinery and parts; medicinal and pharmaceutical products; yarn and fibres; vehicle parts and accessories; fresh aquatic animals, chilled, frozen and instant; fertilizer and pesticides; animal and animal products; plastic products; metal manufacturers. The Major imports of India from Thailand are Polymers of ethylene, propylene etc. in primary forms; radiobroadcast receivers, television receiver and parts thereof; iron and steel and their products; motor cars, parts and accessories; machinery and parts thereof; automatic data processing machines and parts thereof; chemical products; air-conditioning machine and parts thereof; aluminium products; plastic products.

2947. (31-8-2007) NEW DELHI : The Kumaon and Naga Regiments launched a mountaineering expedition to Nanda Devi East peak from Ranikhet, today. This expedition is to commemorate 13th Reunion of Kumaon and 7th Reunion of Naga Regiments and Tri Services affiliation ceremony. Nanda Devi East lies in the Kumaon Himalaya at a height of 7434M. The expedition to it involves some very technical climbs that have attracted mountaineers from around the world. Famous Mountaineer Tenzing Nogray was asked which had been his most difficult climb ever, expecting him to say Mount Everest. He surprised his mountaineers by saying Nanda Devi. The Nanda Devi East Massif has been named amongst the most beautiful mountains in the world by some of the famous international climbers and explorers. It also enjoys the status of a revered deity as Goddess Nanda Devi amongst the people of Kumaon and Garhwal. The expedition, led by Major Shyamal Sinha comprises twenty five climbers from the Regiment and from affiliated Units of the Parachute Regiment, Mechanized Infantry and INS Khanjar. The team plans to complete the expedition in approx 40 days. The expedition was flagged off today by Lt Gen Satyavir Yadav, Colonel of the Kumaon and Naga Regiments and the Kumaon Scouts.

2948. (31-8-2007) NEW DELHI : Maj Gen P Mohapatra is to be the next Colonel Commandant of the Corps of Signals. He takes over this appointment on 01 September from Lt Gen A K Saini who is retiring from service. Born in Mayurbhanj District of Orissa, Maj Gen Mohapatra had his early education at Sainik School, Bhubaneswar. He then joined the National Defence Academy for his pre commission training. Maj Gen Mohapatra was commissioned in 1971 and immediately thereafter he participated in the Indo-Pak war in the Northern Sector. He is also an alumnus of Defence Services Staff College and Higher Command Course at Army War College and has attended prestigious National Defence College. During the Higher Command Course he was awarded the Commandants Medal for the best research study. Maj Gen Mohapatra has held a number of important appointments to include command of an Armoured Division Signal Regiment and Chief Signal Officer of a Strike Corps during Op PARAKRAM. He has operated in counter terrorism environment in J&K and Nagaland. He has also been on staff of Military Operations Directorate in the Army HQ. He is presently Additional Director General and Assistant Chief of Integrated Defence Staff (Signal Intelligence). A voracious reader, he was the Editor of Defence Technology Journal at the Army War College. As Colonel Commandant he will oversee various ceremonial and human resources aspects of Corps of Signals.

2949. (31-8-2007) NEW DELHI : IMD operates a network of 10 stations across the country where rain water samples are collected and are analysed for the last 26 years. The analysis carried out suggests that rain water samples collected in

Nagpur have shown acid content in the last 10 years since 1997. However, samples of 2006 have shown a remarkable recovery at Nagpur. Rain water samples over Pune have remained by and large in safe range. The introduction of ultra low sulphur rules for vehicles and automobiles, that has been extended all over the country by the Government, will help in arresting the identified acidification trends considerably. This information was given by the Union Minister for Science & Technology and Earth Sciences Shri Kapil Sibal in the Lok Sabha today in a written reply to a question regarding high acid contents found in rain water in Nagpur and Pune.

2950. (31-8-2007) NEW DELHI : The Union Minister of Shipping, Road Transport and Highways, Thiru T. R. Baalu, has been elected the Chairperson of the first meeting of the South Asian Association for Regional Cooperation (SAARC) Transport Ministers in New Delhi today. The countries which participated in the conference are Afghanistan, Bangladesh, Bhutan, India, Maldives, Nepal, Pakistan and Sri Lanka. This Meeting was preceded by the 2nd Meeting of the Technical Committee on Transport (August 29, 2007) and 2nd Meeting of the Intergovernmental Group on Transport (August 30, 2007).

2951. (31-8-2007) NEW DELHI : The Ministry of Agriculture has launched a Central Sector Capital Investment Subsidy Scheme for promoting public as well as private sector investment in the country for creation of scientific storage capacity with allied facilities in rural areas. This scheme aims at meeting the requirement of farmers for storing farm produce, processed farm produce and consumer articles/ agricultural inputs; and promoting grading, standardization and quality control of agricultural produce to improve their marketability. This measure seeks to prevent distress sales immediately after harvest by providing the facility of pledge financing/ marketing credit. It is also strengthening the agricultural marketing infrastructure in the country by paving way for the introduction of a national system of warehouse receipts in respect of agricultural commodities stored in such godowns and reversing the declining trend of investment in agriculture sector by encouraging private and cooperative sector to invest in the creation of storage infrastructure in the country. The capital investment subsidy available under the Scheme is @ 25% of the capital cost with an upper ceiling of Rs.37.50 lakh for farmers, agricultural graduates and public agencies and @ 15% for other individuals and companies/ corporations with an upper ceiling of Rs.22.50 lakh. For North-East States and hilly areas and in the cases of entrepreneurs belonging to SCs/ STs, the rate of subsidy has been kept as 33.33% of the capital cost of the project with an upper ceiling of Rs.50.00 lakh for each project. Under the scheme, the entrepreneur including Panchayats and Mandals, are free to construct or encourage godowns at any place, as per their commercial judgment except for the restriction that it would be constructed only outside the limits of Municipal Corporation area. The godown constructed under the Scheme shall be properly ventilated, shall have well fitted doors, windows and ventilators and shall be waterproof (for control of moisture from floor, walls and roof etc.). The godown structure shall have protection from rodents. The godown shall have protection from birds also. By the end of March, 2007, 12,704 new rural godown projects and 1,664 projects for renovation of godowns have been sanctioned under the Scheme involving the creation of total storage capacity of 158.40 lakh MTs and 23.78 lakh MTs respectively. This information was given in the Rajya Sabha today by the Minister of State for Agriculture, Shri Kanti Lal Bhuria in a written reply.

2952. (31-8-2007) NEW DELHI : A centrally sponsored Integrated Scheme of Oilseeds, Pulses, Oil palm & Maize (ISOPOM) is under implementation in 14 major pulses producing states to enhance the production and productivity of pulses. Further, with a view to enhancing the production of pulses in the country and achieve self-sufficiency, Government has proposed to launch a National Food Security Mission (NFSM) comprising rice, wheat and pulses in major growing states/districts during XI Plan. An area expansion of 2.47 million ha through intercropping with pigeon pea, cereals, cotton, sugarcane, oilseeds, replacement of rainfed upland paddy during kharif and another 2.0 million ha by utilizing rice follows in major rice growing states (in rabi) has been targeted during XI Five Year Plan under NFSM-Pulses. The requirement of pulses in the country is continuously increasing and the domestic production of pulses, despite various efforts has been unable to keep pace with the demand. In 2006-07 the production of pulses was 14.23 million tonnes against the requirement of 17.71 million tonnes. The newly released high yielding varieties/hybrids of pulses developed by Indian Council of Agriculture Research/State Agriculture Universities system and International Crops Research Institute for Semi Arid Tropics (ICRISAT) are being popularized through seed minikits. Further, Production technologies such as application of micronutrients (sulphur, zinc, boron etc.) in deficient soils, nutrition through bio-fertilizers, Integrated Pest Management (IPM), sprinkler irrigation, soil amelioration through application of gypsum/lime etc. are being promoted under ISOPOM for increasing the per ha yield and production of pulses to reduce import dependence. This information was given in the Rajya Sabha today by the Minister of State for Agriculture, Shri Kanti Lal Bhuria in a written reply.

2953. (31-8-2007) NEW DELHI : Following is the text of Prime Minister, Dr. Manmohan Singh's address at the Graduation function of the 50th Batch of BARC Training School in Mumbai today: "It gives me great pleasure to be here in the midst of some of our brightest scientists and engineers. For any young man or woman, a graduation ceremony is always a defining moment in his or her life. It becomes particularly poignant when you belong to the 50th graduating class. No words are enough to express our gratitude to the hard work put in by the faculty of the BARC Training School over these fifty years. They have single-handedly contributed to the training of over 7,500 graduates during this period. It is these scientists and engineers who have laid the building blocks of self-reliance in the field of nuclear science and technology and of India's emergence as a knowledge economy. Today, we have honoured some of them. The Training School has evolved into a model institute, which is recognised internationally as a school of excellence. It is because of your collective efforts that India is ranked among the top few countries to have mastered the entire Nuclear Fuel Cycle. I am specially glad that the Homi Bhabha National Institute has successfully started its academic programmes. The creation, and successful operation of a wide variety of institutes of high quality fully conforms to our government's belief that education and human resource development is the best investment we can make for the future of our country. I have approved the setting up of five new Indian Institutes of Science Education and Research, eight new Indian Institutes of Technology, seven new Indian Institutes of Management, and twenty new Indian Institutes of Information Technology. On the 15th of August I said from the ramparts of the Red Fort that our nation is today ready for a New Revolution in Education. We seek a quantum leap in the availability of educational opportunities for our children and our youth at all levels of the pyramid of knowledge and training. We have effected a major increase in elementary and secondary education. We are now increasing the capacity of our higher education and research system. It is not just a quantitative leap forward that I seek in education, but also a qualitative leap forward.

2954. (31-8-2007) NEW DELHI : The President, Smt. Pratibha Devisingh Patil will be travelling to Sriperumbudur on her first domestic tour to a state. The President shall arrive in Chennai late this evening and travel to Sriperumbudur tomorrow where she will deliver the Foundation Day Address at the Rajiv Gandhi National Institute of Youth Development. The President will also unveil the Institute's Logo as well as launch the Institute's websites. Smt. Patil shall also be paying her tributes at the Rajiv Gandhi Memorial. The President returns to the capital tomorrow afternoon after the function.

2955. (31-8-2007) NEW DELHI : India and Nepal have agreed, under the 1996 Mahakali Treaty, to jointly develop the Pancheshwar Multipurpose Project (5600 Mw) on the Mahakali river. The two Governments are engaged in finalizing the Detailed Project Report (DPR) of the Pancheshwar Project. Further, a Joint Project Office has been established in Nepal with Indian assistance to carry out field investigations for preparation of the DPR for Sun-Kosi Sapta Kosi Project (around 3300 MW). Preliminary discussions have also been held on the feasibility of Naumure hydroelectric project. This information was given by the Union Power Minister Shri Sushilkumar Shinde in the Lok Sabha today.

2956. (31-8-2007) NEW DELHI : The PFC has sanctioned loan amount of Rs.165.48 crore for Lakwa Waste Heat Recovery Project (1x37.2 MW) of Assam Power Generation Corporation Ltd. (APGCL) in December, 2006. Out of this an amount of Rs.40.45 crore has been disbursed upto 31.07.2007. Another loan proposal for Namrup Gas Based Combined Cycle Power Project, Phase-I (100 MW) of APGCL has been received by PFC. The financial sanction and disbursement depends upon the detailed appraisal and request received from the concerned State. This information was given by the Union Power Minister Shri Sushilkumar Shinde in the Lok Sabha today.

2957. (31-8-2007) NEW DELHI : As per the existing delegation of powers applicable to Navaratna Companies including NTPC Ltd., the ceiling on equity investment to establish financial joint ventures and wholly owned subsidiaries in India or aboard shall be 15% of the net worth of the Public Sector Enterprise (PSE) in one project limited to Rs.1000 Crore and the overall ceiling on such investment in all projects put together shall be 30% of the net worth of the PSE. NTPC Ltd. had approached Ministry of Power for waiver of ceiling of Rs.1000 Crore for equity investment by NTPC Ltd. to establish financial joint venture for the purpose of participating in the bidding of Ultra Mega Projects being established at the initiative of Ministry of Power. Government had approved the proposal of waiver of ceiling of Rs.1000 Crores for equity investments by NTPC Ltd. to establish financial joint ventures and wholly owned subsidiaries in India or abroad for the purpose of participating in the bidding of ultra mega projects. However, the ceiling of 15% of the net worth of NTPC in one project and the overall ceiling of 30% of the net worth of the NTPC Ltd. in all such projects of NTPC Ltd. put together shall remain. This information was given by the Union Power Minister Shri Sushilkumar Shinde in the Lok Sabha today.

2958. (31-8-2007) NEW DELHI : On the request of Government of Tamil Nadu and Karnataka during January 2001, National Hydroelectric Power Corporation Ltd. (NHPC) had been entrusted with the work of preparation of the Detailed Project Reports (DPRs) of 4 Hydroelectric Projects (HEP) in the Cauvery Basin, viz. the Hogenekkal HEP (120 MW) and Rasimanal HEP (360 MW) in Tamil Nadu and Shivasamudram HEP (270 MW) and Mekadatu HEP (400 MW) in Karnataka. Preparation of DPRs for these projects could not be taken up by NHPC due to the differences between the Government of Tamil Nadu and Karnataka on the 'draft tripartite agreement' to be signed between the two State Governments and NHPC. Government of Karnataka have, however, now informed that since the two projects of Shivasamudram and Mekadatu are exclusively within the territory of Karnataka, the State proposes to forthwith execute the project through Karnataka Power Corporation Ltd. (KPCL). Government of Karnataka have further informed that KPCL has already initiated preliminary works like survey, Geo-Technical Investigation, Soil Investigation and preparation of DPR as per the pattern of downstream releases ordered by the Cauvery Water Disputes Tribunal. This information was given by the Union Power Minister Shri Sushilkumar Shinde in the Lok Sabha today.

2959. (31-8-2007) NEW DELHI : The Department of Science & Technology is implementing the National Mission on Bamboo Applications (NMBA) to develop, validate and demonstrate technologies for Value Added Products using Bamboo as raw material. As part of this mission, gasifiers using bamboo as raw material have been developed for generation of electricity. These gasifiers can use Bamboo waste and other biomass. All the States where Bamboo is available in plenty can use these gasifiers for generation of electricity. Examples being all the States in the North East, Karnataka, Andhra Pradesh, Chattisgarh, Madhya Pradesh, Orissa etc. The Government has no plans to set up Power Generation Units in all the States. However, the States, if interested, can use the technology. This information was given by the Union Minister for Science & Technology and Earth Sciences Shri Kapil Sibal in the Lok Sabha today.

2960. (31-8-2007) NEW DELHI : Biotechnology industry in 2006-07 is estimated to have touched around Rs. 8,500.00 crores (over $2 billion) in revenues, registering a 30 per cent growth, over the previous year's (2005-06) estimated revenues of Rs. 6,500.00 crores. The Government has taken special measures to promote the biotechnology industry and to facilitate increase in turnover of biotech sector. Initiatives have been taken to provide an enabling environment for industrial growth such as streamlining regulatory procedures; exemption of biotech sector from compulsory licensing; permitting 100 per cent FDI; reducing the area of SEZ to bring it at par with IT sector; providing fiscal incentives to recognized in-house R&D of industries in terms of exemption of custom duty on capital goods, reduction in import duty and 150 per cent weighted deduction against expenditure incurred on R&D. To encourage public-private partnerships for joint R&D and technology development, Ministry of Science and Technology is implementing schemes through Technology Development Board (TDB) and Pharmaceutical Research and Development Support Fund (PRDSF) under Department of Science & Technology (DST) as well as New Millennium Indian Technology Leadership Initiative (NMITLI) Scheme under Council for Scientific and Industrial Research (CSIR). To further accelerate industrial R&D in biotechnology, recently, the Department of Biotechnology has also launched a novel public-private scheme "Small Business Innovative Research Initiative" for providing grant and soft loan to small and medium biotech industries for strengthening R&D and product development even at pre-proof-of concept and post-proof-of concept stage. This information was given by the Union Minister for Science & Technology and Earth Sciences Shri Kapil Sibal in the Lok Sabha today.

2961. (31-8-2007) NEW DELHI : Trained to be only winners in battles, nearly five thousand military personnel from 89 nations across the globe on the last count will compete with each other at the biggest multi-sport International event of 2007 on the world stage-the fourth edition of the 'Conseil International du Sport Militaire's' (CISM) Military World Games (MWG), being hosted at Hyderabad and Mumbai from October 14-21, in India. The ambassadors of the armed forces of the participating nations will sportingly achieve the underlying CISM mission-promote peace through friendship, set against the backdrop of the CISM motto-'friendship through sport', adopted in 1948. But that may not just yet take away the highly competitive element of the games that will be fiercely contested just as in any competitive sports for the 1076 medals, albeit in a spirit of military excellence, camaraderie and espirit-de-corps. But even as military athletes the world over prepare to compete at the select playfields of Hyderabad that are to be the sporting battlefields of the ensuing games, the MWG organizers of the Indian Armed Forces, led by none less than the Vice Chief of the Army Staff, Lieutenant General Deepak Kapoor are approaching the conduct of the event with a game plan that is no less in measure, magnitude and scale than any elaborate war plan of a successful conquest. The planning and execution so far bears the ubiquitous stamp of military precision, procedures and doggedness, all in pursuit of the successful conduct of the event. "We are very happy with the procedures and progress of the organization," expressed President CISM, Brigadier General Gianni Gola from Italy, clearly impressed with the arrangements and preparations after the final preparatory meet visit to the games venues, at Hyderabad and Mumbai in the third week of August. "It is for the first time in the history of CISM that a new member country has been able to construct new infrastructures for the games," he further stated thanking the host nation India for that. Usually a host country organizing an event of the scale of Olympic normally gets into the preparatory act 8-10 years preceding the event. The 4th MWG being conducted here being next only in scale, proportion and participation to the Olympics, comes about in a period of less than two years. "In a short span of less than two years we have achieved a great deal," informs Commodore SC Joshi, Secretary General of the MWG Organising Committee.

2962. (31-8-2007) NEW DELHI : The Mayor of London has invited the Minister for Tourism & Culture Smt. Ambika Soni to the Regent Street 'India Now' Festival on 2nd September 2007 and the Minister has accepted the invitation. She is leaving for a two-day visit to London on early morning on 2nd September, 2007 and will return to India on 4th September, 2007. 'India Now' an event being coordinated by the office of the Mayor of London, is being held in London from July to September 2007. This event comprises a series of India-centric events and activities showcasing India's contribution to world culture, its rich tradition and more importantly, contemporary India and new Indian trends across art, film, theatre, food, music and fashion. Over 150 cultural organizations from London are participating in this event. It is the biggest festival of India to be staged in the UK, with activities planned across London for the entire season. It is expected that at least 1 million Londoners and visitors to London will participate in the event and there has been extensive media coverage as well. One of the main highlights of the 'India Now' event is the Regent Street Festival, to be held on the 2nd September 2007, when London's premier shopping street will be transformed into an Indian streetscape with music, food and artisans. Regent Street is one of the world's most prestigious streets and home to some of the very best retail brands and flagship stores. Activities on the day will include cultural performances of music and dance, a food quarter with three restaurant areas on Regent Street serving Indian cuisine, Indian market stalls selling spices/herbs/silks/arts and crafts, in-store promotions, competitions, food sampling and many more activities. UK is one of the most important source markets for India, with over 7 lakh tourists from UK visiting India during 2006, an increase of 12.8% as compared to the previous year. Tourists from UK account for over 16% of the total tourist traffic to India. Various promotional activities are being undertaken to further tap the immense potential of this market and to augment tourist arrivals to the country from UK. One of the major promotional activities is advertising through various media to ensure greater visibility of "Incredible India" in the market. With a view to having an effective presence of Incredible India in London, during the "India Now" event and to benefit from the reach it would offer amongst visitors at the event, the Ministry of Tourism, Govt. of India has undertaken an extensive Media Campaign in the print and electronic media as well as on buses, taxis and outdoor panels in Central London, during the 3 month period (July to September 2007). As part of the campaign some of the Buses and Taxis plying along the main routes in Central in London have a vibrant look with "Incredible India" colours. Outdoor panels at prominent locations in Central London highlight London's landmarks through "Incredible India" visuals and the print campaign focuses on the close links between India and UK, with the by-line "India is closer than you think". This media campaign has generated a lot of interest in London and has invited significant attention, with celebrities including Shahrukh Khan, Shilpa Shetty and members of the Indian Cricket Team being photographed with the "Incredible India" banners put up in London.

2963. (31-8-2007) NEW DELHI : The Government approved setting up of Serious Fraud Investigation Office (SFIO) on 9th January, 2003. However, it started functioning from 1st October, 2003. A Coordination and Monitoring Committee (CMC), co-chaired by Secretary, (then) Ministry of Company Affairs (MCA) and Chairman, SEBI was set up in March, 1999 to settle the policy issues regarding the delinquent companies/promoters and to monitor the progress in regard to action against vanishing companies. Out of the companies that came out with the IPOs during 1992-98, a total of 229 companies were originally identified as vanishing companies. With the continuous efforts of CMC, 116 companies have been traced back, resulting in the number of Vanishing Companies being reduced to 113. Subsequently, the Task Forces have also undertaken a similar exercise in respect of the companies that came out with IPOs during 1998-2001. As a result of this exercise, 9 companies have been identified as vanished. Thus, the total number of vanishing companies as of now stands at 122. The Serious Fraud Investigation Office (SFIO) has no role to play with regard to the monitoring of action taken against Vanishing Companies. This information was given by the Minister of Corporate Affairs Shri Prem Chand Gupta in written reply to a question in Lok Sabha today.

2964. (31-8-2007) NEW DELHI : India and Australia have agreed to undertake a joint feasibility study into the benefits of a free trade agreement (FTA) between both countries. Trade and investment links between Australia and India have grown rapidly in recent years. It is expected that the study would provide a timely opportunity to examine the potential for benefits which might flow from a bilateral FTA. India is emerging as one of the key drivers for global economic growth and its economic rise will be increasingly critical to world economic development. Australia's established economic strength and competencies make it a significant trading partner for many countries, including India. The study will examine the potential benefits of FTA for both countries. In particular, the study will focus on the impact a FTA could have on promoting economic growth in both countries, bilateral trade in good and services, as well as investment and other commercial linkages. The Governments will initially hold bilateral meetings to discuss the terms of reference for the FTA feasibility study. The study will commence in late 2007 and is expected to be completed in 2009. Two-way trade in goods and services between Australia and India reached US$ 7.76 billion in 2006-07.

2965. (31-8-2007) NEW DELHI : The Prime Minister, Dr. Manmohan Singh has expressed satisfaction over the implementation of the Jawaharlal Nehru National Urban Renewal Mission and said that the single largest initiative for urban development has been benefiting large number of people. Speaking at a function in Mumbai, after handing over the Rs 400 crore cheque for the Brihan Mumbai Storm Water Drainage project, he said, Maharashtra has been a frontrunner in the urban renewal field with 46 projects amounting to Rs 6,112 crores. In Mumbai alone, there are 10 JNNURM projects being implemented at a cost of Rs 2,732 crores, covering water supply, sewerage, drainage and urban transport. He called for creative process of urbanizing to ensure better quality of life. The Brihan Mumbai Storm Water Drainage or the BRIMSTOWAD, as it is commonly known, is an ambitious Rs 1,800 crore rupee project to improve the storm drainage facility in Mumbai, which was put in place by the British 150 years ago. The system was designed to handle 25 mm of rain per hour, while the current requirement is 50 mm per hour. BRIMSTOWAD includes widening, deepening of nalla and river systems and provision of eight storm water pumping stations. The project, facing funding problems, was submitted to the Centre to take up the balance work worth Rs 1,200 crores. The centre accepted the proposal and agreed to disburse funds in three installments. The first instalment of Rs 400 crores was received today by the Mayor of Mumbai, Smt. Shubha Raul. The Maharashtra Governor, Shri S M Krishna, Chief Minister, Shri Vilasrao Deshmukh, Union Agriculture Minister, Shri Sharad Pawar, Petroleum Minister, Shri Murli Deora, Minister of State in PMO, Shri Prithviraj Chavan were among the dignitaries present. It may be recalled that inadequate drainage in Mumbai, home to 18 million people, had caused wide spread flooding after the deluge of July 26, 2005.

2966. (1-9-2007) NEW DELHI : The Minister of Petroleum & Natural Gas Sh. Murli Deora has appealed the dealers of petroleum products in Maharashtra not to resort to protest closure of retail outlets as proposed by them on Monday. He has emphasized that such strike will cause avoidable difficulties to the people. The Minister further said that the demand of the dealers to be provided with marker testing kit is not justified as the new system of marking Kerosene has been started with the objective of preventing adulteration of petroleum products. This position also has been upheld by various High Courts. Marker has been introduced by oil companies to detect adulteration of petroleum products and marker testing kits are used by them for this purpose so that pure and quality products are supplied to consumers.

2967. (1-9-2007) NEW DELHI : The impact of television advertisements on tender minds of children is deep to the extent that their choices are greatly driven by these ads. This is the theme of the book brought out by Publications Division recently, which was released in the 13th Delhi Book Fair in Pragati Maidan, New Delhi today. As part of inauguration of Publications Division's stall at the Delhi Book Fair, the book 'Mayamrig' authored by Ms. Ruchi Kashyap was released by Shri Liladhar Mandloi, Director General, Doordarshan, Delhi who was the Chief Guest in the function. On the occasion Shri Mandloi said that initially television in India had a definite role in the development of the society and had a limited reach. Since then it has transformed into mass media in true sense. He said that there was a need to bring out a book in Hindi on this important subject, which was partly fulfilled by this book. The author Ms. Ruchi Kashyap said that the society has been witness to three revolutions in the last three decades-television as a mass medium, advertisements occupying important place in our day-to-day lives and unprecedented increase in the size of the middle class. She explained that these have changed lifestyle of the people significantly. The manuscript of this book has won her the prestigious Bhartendu Harishchandra Award for excellent journalistic writing from the Government of India. The Chief Editor of monthly magazine 'Yojana', Shri Anurag Mishra presided over the function. 'Yojana' is brought out by the Publications Division in 13 languages simultaneously. Publications Division is a unit under the Ministry of Information and Broadcasting, Government of India that brings out authentic, informative and affordable books on a spectrum of subjects related to national life. The Division has been among the firsts in publishing industry to visualize the potential of e-publishing. Recently it has released an audio CD of Division's celebrated book '1857 ka Swatantrata Sangram' for the visually challenged persons as a social welfare initiative. Publications Division is participating in the book fair in a big way with its books and journals for readers in all age groups.

2968. (1-9-2007) NEW DELHI : The Prime Minister, Dr. Manmohan Singh, has called upon the Textile Industry to look far into the future and invest for the coming two decades and not for the next season. He said the textile industry must show aggression and spirited enterprise like in other sectors of automobiles, steel and pharmaceuticals. He emphasised that the textile sector must graduate from being low cost, low value supplier to high volume, high value supplier. Side by side, it must also develop internationally known brands and labels with global footprint and global ambitions. For this, the Government and the industry must work in true spirit of partnership to make this happen. The Prime Minister said this today while addressing the concluding session of the two-day Tex Summit being held here. In his valedictory address, Dr. Manmohan Singh assured that the Government would pay the closest attention to the recommendations of the four working groups to devise appropriate strategies to further promote the growth and competitiveness of the textile sector. He said that he would direct the Ministries of Finance, Commerce and Textiles as well as the National Manufacturing Competitiveness Council to sit together and find out a durable, productive and pragmatic solution to the problems of the textile industry. Recognising the strategic role of textile sector in industrial economy, the Prime Minister said that this sector could act as a vehicle for nationwide industrial modernisation and revitalisation of traditional skills and designs. The sector can generate large scale employments, especially in rural areas. Being the second largest employer after agriculture, the growth and all-round development of textile industry has a direct bearing on our ability to make our growth process more socially inclusive. Dr. Singh further said that the Government was willing to step in and help the industry, especially if it can address the challenge of generating more employment. Keeping in view the inherent potential and historical roots of textile industry in our country, the Prime Minister said that the textile ministry should work with the industry to take advantage of its existing core competencies to ensure that the textile sector grows at 15 per cent per annum in the next decade.

2969. (1-9-2007) NEW DELHI : Muhammad Ismail Qureshi, Secretary, Water and Power, Government of Pakistan along with a delegation called on Prof. Saifuddin Soz, the Union Minister of Water Resources here last evening. The Pakistan delegation was here for a two day meeting to discuss the problems with regard to Wullur Barrage/Tulbul Navigation Project with their Indian counterparts. The Indian delegation was led by Mrs. Gauri Chatterji, Secretary, Ministry of Water Resources and the Pakistan delegation was led by Muhammad Ismail Qureshi, Secretary, Water & Power, Government of Pakistan. The Delegation Heads conveyed to Prof. Soz that the meeting spread over two days, was held in a cordial atmosphere and both sides presented their view points. They expressed the hope that this would lead to better atmosphere and finally to the solution of various issues. Prof. Soz expressed satisfaction over the cordial atmosphere in which the two sides deliberated upon various issues and said that this should continue for creation of an atmosphere of goodwill and understanding between the two countries. A 'Joint Statement' was issued at the end of the two day meeting.

2970. (1-9-2007) NEW DELHI : The Central Office bearers of the BJP and the Prabharis of different states met at New Delhi today. The office bearers and the prabharis discussed the political situation of the country and the organisational preparedness to deal with this situation. The BJP believes that there is a national drift under the UPA Government. An indecisive Government, a weak leader and a government which is callous towards India's security are the hallmark of the UPA rule. Events of the past few days have convinced the BJP that the UPA government is divisive in its policies and its continuation will hurt the country. While addressing the meeting, Party President Shri Rajnath Singh first evaluated the progress made on various issues and committees constituted at the last National Executive meeting of the party in Delhi. Shri Rajnath Singh thereafter stressed that the next one year is a year of challenges and elections, and in this context the party has to gear up to effectively deal with all of them. The party is now in election mode and needs to project effectively itself as the alternate. He pointed out that the national situation is delicate and the nation is at crossroads. As a nationalist party, the BJP has to shoulder the responsibility of providing the people of the country with a stable, secure and responsive government. The BJP President spoke at length about that the Action Taken Report on the Justice Sachar panel's recommendation that leaves none in doubt that the UPA's lust of vote bank politics will result in creating an atmosphere of distrust and divisiveness in the country. From religion based job reservation, we all are now moving towards communal based development expenditure and communal budgeting. Shri Rajnath Singh said that the UPA government is trying to communally divide the country. The BJP will not tolerate this and announced the formation of a committee under Shri M Venkaiah Naidu to launch a countrywide agitation and mobilise national opinion against the implementation of this report. Poverty cuts across religion. All Indians need jobs and development irrespective of their mode of worship. The Sachar recommendations are a case of reverse discrimination which the BJP will vehemently oppose and organise a national opinion against this. The meeting also deliberated on other issues including the Hyderabad blasts where many innocents lost their lives as a result of cross-border terrorism being perpetuated by an out sourced wing of the Al-Quaida on one hand and weak-kneed policies of the UPA Government on the other hand.

2971. (1-9-2007) NEW DELHI : The minister of Tourism and Culture Smt. Ambika Soni has called upon the Tour operators to sustain boom in tourism through effective planning and coordination within the industry. She was speaking after inaugurating the Silver Jubilee Celebrations of the Indian Association of Tour Operators (IATO) here today. Smt. Soni said, the tourism sector is having multiplier effect on the Economy and its contribution to the GDP is one of the highest and its ability to generate employment is perhaps bigger than that of the IT sector. She said as per Tourist Satellite Account System the sector has generated about 50 million jobs directly or indirectly in last three years. Referring to the recent achievements of the ministry Smt. Soni said, the recently notified tax abatement upto 75% and the signing of the Ordinance on 'Bed & Breakfast' by Lt. Governor of Delhi are major achievements to encourage growth in the Tourism Sector. The minister said, the tour operators should take cognizance of the need for maintaining ecological balance while pursuing Eco, Adventure and Wildlife Tourism. She also urged them to support Ministry of tourism campaign for clean environment and anti-graffiti at monuments. She said, the industry's feed back will help us to better understand the issues that are crucial to the growth of the sector. Delhi's Lt. Governor Sh. Tejendra Khanna and Tourism ministers from several States also spoke on the occasion.

2972. (1-9-2007) NEW DELHI : The National Highways Authority of India (NHAI) has signed the Concession Agreement for 4/6-laning of Zirakpur-Parwanoo Section of NH-22 including Pinjore-Kalka-Parwanoo Bypass, in the States of Punjab (2 km), Haryana (21 km) and Himachal Pradesh (6 km) on Build Operate & Transfer (BOT) basis under National Highways Development Project (NHDP) Phase III. The Agreement was signed last evening by NHAI in the presence of Dr. Jivtesh Singh Maini, Chairman NHAI with M/s Jaiprakash & Associates. The Concession Period for this project is 20 years including construction period of 30 months. The total project cost is Rs. 295 crores. The work has been awarded with viability gap funding of Rs. 117.00 crores. The project involves 4-laning of 28.690 km including 6-lane structures *i.e.* bridges, grade separators/flyovers, under-passes etc. Out of this, 11.250 km are on new alignment for a combined bypass for very congested towns of Pinjore & Kalka in Haryana and Parwanoo in Himachal Pradesh. This should provide a great relief to road users going towards Solan and State Capital Simla. It may be recalled that the Government had approved upgradation and four laning of 12,109 km of National Highways on BOT basis under NHDP Phase III at an estimated cost of Rs 80,626 Crores. Out of this, 30 Projects costing Rs. 11,627 Crores covering 1941 km have already been awarded. Another 3000 km are proposed to be awarded during current financial year. The remaining length will be awarded in a phased manner before March, 2010.

2973. (1-9-2007) NEW DELHI : Following is the Text of the Prime Minister, Dr. Manmohan Singh's address at the Valedictory Session of Texsummit 2007 here today. "I am delighted to have this opportunity to listen to some of the problems at the Textiles Industry faces and this Valedictory Session of the Textiles Summit 2007 has served that purpose very well. I listen with great interest to the findings of the all working groups and I will ask the Ministry of Finance the Ministry of Commerce and Ministry of Textiles with the Manufacturing Competitive Council to sit together and to find durable productive pragmatic solutions to the various problems that the textiles industry faces in our country. I therefore, compliment Shri Shankersinh Ji and the Ministry of Textiles for organizing this two-day summit to discuss the problems and prospects of the textile sector. You have organized this conference at an opportune time when global opportunities for textiles are opening up rapidly and there is a need to exploit these to the fullest. There are great opportunities with the dismantling the Multi-Fiber Agreement, there are immense opportunities the quota regime everywhere are going to end or have ended but there are also immense challenges that we have countries in

East Asia, South-Asia and country like China which are aggressively planning to take full advantage of these New opportunities.

2974. (1-9-2007) NEW DELHI : I am pleased to be visiting the Rajiv Gandhi National Institute of Youth Development to deliver this Foundation Day Address and to inaugurate this beautiful Auditorium and the Logo of the Institute. Rajivji was a young man with a dream of building a modern India, but in the midst of his high promise, he was snatched cruelly from us. Rajivji had great faith in the youth of India and believed in their empowerment. He took the significant decision of reducing the voting age from 21 years to 18 years, and this resulted in almost 50 million youth getting the right to participate in elections. Rajivji always extolled the youth to come to the forefront with creative ideas for taking India ahead. Speaking in 1988, he said, and I quote, "we are one of the world's oldest civilizations and one of the youngest nations. Our country's demographic profile has undergone a major revolution. Now, there is a preponderance of youth. This is a decisive factor in determining our nation's destiny." Unquote. Between his 1988 speech and this Inaugural address, India has grown younger still. Today, the average age of India's population is below 25 years. Approximately, 77 crore of our people, or about 70 percent of the population, fall below the age of 35 and, thus, within the ambit of our National Youth Policy. It is likely that all through the first half of the 21st century, India will maintain this exceptionally young demographic profile while all of the developed world, and also China, are expected to grow older and older. This opens up for us the possibility of a demographic dividend. It is potentially the single most important comparative advantage we enjoy which could be leveraged to catapult India to the front ranks of human civilization.

2975. (2-9-2007) NEW DELHI : The Vice President of India, Shri Mohammad Hamid Asari has congratulated the space scientists and technologists involved in the successful launch from Sriharikota of the Geosynchronous Satellite Launch Vehicle, GSLV-F04 that has lifted the high-powered INSAT-4CR communication satellite into space. He noted that this successful launch further validates the immense economic and strategic importance of the country's space programme.

2976. (2-9-2007) NEW DELHI : BJP President Shri Rajnath Singh today convened a meeting of the various All India Cells of the BJP at the party central office in New Delhi. The meeting was attended by the Convenors and Joint Convenors of all the party Cells in the presence of senior party leaders Shri M Venkaiah Naidu, Dr. Murli Manohar Joshi, Prof Bal Apte, Shri Ramlal, Shri Gopinath Munde, Shri Vijay Goel, Shri Ravi Shankar Prasad and Shri Prakash Javadekar. While addressing the meeting, Shri Rajnath Singh said that the Cells need to act as a bridge between the party and various segments of society. He pointed that unfortunately today a situation is developing across the country where political parties and politicians are facing a serious crisis of credibility and particularly among the professionals in society who want to maintain a distance from them. This is an unfortunate development since besides being a social, economic and cultural entity, human beings are also political entities as representative government in a civilized society is incapable of functioning without the active participation of people, he said. The BJP President said while carrying the message of the party to various segments in society, it also needs to be highlighted that no other political party in the history of independent India has been able to establish a higher stature than the Congress Party and successfully demolish the hegemony of a single party rule. Shri Rajnath Singh said that the Cells should also highlight the party's distinct ideology of Integral Humanism which seeks the comprehensive and integrated development of human beings. This approach has been nationally and internationally appreciated. In this context, the Cells can act as LIVE contact in conveying the message of the party to the people and in turn sensitizing the party about their problems and concerns, he added. In his address Shri M Venkaiah Naidu said that Cells can help create opinion among the opinion makers of society. He emphasized the importance of the Cells to study the needs and problems of the people, help organize them and thereafter enable to solve the problem even by agitation is required. However, in this process, care should be taken so as not to create confrontation with other sections of society, he added. Prof Bal Apte while initiating a discussion of the various Cells and their priorities and programmes, said that each Cell should put in place a concrete action plan with specific targets and activities that need to be completed in a time bound manner. Dr. Murli Manohar Joshi while addressing the Cells said that they can play an important role in making the party's functioning more effective. The Cells can provide focused inputs to the party on crucial matters and in the process sharpen the party's policy initiatives and response on important issues. Such focused and researched issues can also be raised by the party at appropriate forums. BJP General Secretary (Orgn) Shri Ramlal briefed the Cells on organizational issues to be kept in mind and how to make their functioning more meaningful and effective.

2977. (2-9-2007) NEW DELHI : The Minister of Petroleum & Natural Gas Sh. Murli Deora has appealed the dealers of petroleum products in Maharashtra not to resort to protest closure of retail outlets as proposed by them on Monday. He has emphasized that such strike will cause avoidable difficulties to the people. The Minister further said that the demand of the dealers to be provided with marker testing kit is not justified as the new system of marking Kerosene has been started with the objective of preventing adulteration of petroleum products. This position also has been upheld by various High Courts. Marker has been introduced by oil companies to detect adulteration of petroleum products and marker testing kits are used by them for this purpose so that pure and quality products are supplied to consumers.

2978. (2-9-2007) NEW DELHI : Shri Kamal Nath, Union Minister of Commerce and Industry has accorded the approval to the Pitampura-Dhar-Mhow industrial region in "Delhi Mumbai Industrial Corridor" Project. In his communication to the Chief Minister of Madhya Pradesh, here today, Shri Kamal Nath has expressed confidence that with this approval, the state of Madhya Pradesh would join other front line states in developing the state-of-the-art Industrial infrastructure and investment environment in the country. The inclusion of Pitampura-Dhar-Mhow industrial region in "Delhi Mumbai Industrial Corridor" Project follows the relentless efforts made by Shri Kamal Nath during the past several months to ensure that Madhya Pradesh becomes the favourite investment centre of scores of Japanese and other International infrastructure firms who are looking for quality investment opportunities. The efforts made by Shri Kamal Nath, who pursued the matter with several coordinating Ministries finally brings the State of Madhya Pradesh as an important stakeholder in this prestigious project. Shri Kamal Nath has also informed that the Investment regions of Pitampura-Dhar-Mhow and Industrial Area of Neemuch-Nayagaon will have requisite industrial infrastructure like industrial estates, knowledge hubs, agro-processing hubs, IT/ ITES hubs, logistics hubs and physical infrastructure (feeder roads/ rail lines, ports, airports, power etc.) The Project proposes to leverage the rail connectivity offered by Delhi-Mumbai Dedicated Rail Freight Corridor and road connectivity by the National Quadrilateral developed under National Highway Programme. Shri Kamal Nath hoped that after completion of the project youths in all the states including Madhya Pradesh would have the benefit of jump in doubling the employment potential, tripling industrial output and quadrupling exports in five years.

2979. (3-9-2007) NEW DELHI : The President Smt. Pratibha Devisingh Patil has congratulated the scientists, engineers, technologists and all others of Indian Space Research Organisation involved with the successful launch of the INSAT-4CR communication satellite into orbit from Sriharikota yesterday. In a congratulatory message to Shri G. Madhavan Nair, Chairman of ISRO, the President has said, "I congratulate you on the successful launch of the INSAT-4CR communications satellite into orbit form Shriharikota yesterday. This satellite is another significant milestone for further development of our indigenous communication systems. Millions of our citizens will be its beneficiaries. Kindly convey my heartiest greetings to the hardworking team of scientists, engineers, technologists and all others involved in the mission, which is another important step in the progress of our space programme."

2980. (3-9-2007) NEW DELHI : Air Marshal JN Burma AVSM, VSM has flagged off first ever Inter Command Air Force Schools Sports Championship at New Delhi today. The champion is scheduled from 03 Sep 07 to 06 Sep 07 as a part of Platinum Jubilee celebrations of the IAF. Besides six command teams, Air HQ team comprising of the children of air Force Schools located in New Delhi will be competing in each event. The championship is being organized by the Directorate of Education under the aegis of IAF Educational and Cultural society, New Delhi. The championship is being conducted in five disciplines, namely;

Cricket, Football, Basketball, Table Tennis and Badminton for the boys and Badminton & Table Tennis events for the girls. The participants represents various unit run AF Schools and have won in their respective Intra command tournament which were held to select the command team in each discipline. The aim of this championship is to inculcate spirit-de-corps among the children and to encourage and groom potential players for higher level of competitions. A total of 392 participants, including 56 girls are competing for the champion's trophy in each discipline and also vying for the overall best team championship trophy during the week long tournament scheduled to be held at different venues in Delhi. Cricket championship will be held at Air Force Station Palam, cricket ground, Football & Basketball championships at Air Force Station Race Course and Tennis & Badminton championships at Air Force Golden Jubilee Institute, Subroto Park. The inauguration ceremony of the championship was followed by a football match played between Air HQ and Training Command team.

2981. (3-9-2007) NEW DELHI : The meeting of the full Planning Commission scheduled to be held tomorrow (04.09.2007) under the chairmanship of the Prime Minister has been postponed. New date will be intimated later. Inconvenience caused is regretted.

2982. (3-9-2007) NEW DELHI : Prof. Saifuddin Soz, the Union Minister for Water Resources has announced that "National Ground Water Congress" will be held in New Delhi on September 11, 2007 to discuss the strategies for sustainable and equitable use of ground water and to promote water literacy. Addressing a Press Conference here today Prof. Soz said that the Congress will evaluate role of ground water in national food security and water security, promote more crop and income per drop of water and evolve pro-nature, pro-poor and pro-woman sustainable ground water security system. The Prime Minister Dr. Manmohan Singh will inaugurate the Congress and the President Smt Pratibha Devisingh Patil will address the valedictory session of the Congress. The technical papers will be presented during the technical sessions. The first meeting of Ground Water Advisory Council on Afritifical Recharge held in July 2006 recommended holding up National Ground Water Congress. The main objective of Advisory Council is to popularise concept of artificial recharge among stakeholders. Prof. Soz also announced that the Government instituted, first time, the National Water Award and Bhumijal Samvardhan Award to encourage NGOs Gram Panchayats/Urban Local Bodies for adopting innovative practices of ground water augmentation through people's participation. One National Award of Rs 10 Lakh and 18 Bhumijal Samvardhan Puraskars of Rs 1 Lakh each with a plaque and a citation will be presented. These awardees have been selected by a four member committee set up under the chairmanship of Prof. M.S. Swaminathan, MP and nominations were invited through state governments. 55 nominations were received and the committee recommended 1 National Award and 14 Puraskars. The Minister also announced the launching of Farmer's Participatory Research Programme in 5000 villages in different agro-climatic reasons of the country with the help of 50 Agriculture Universities and Research Institutes to produce more crop and income per drop of water.

2983. (3-9-2007) NEW DELHI : Lt Gen Sree Kumar, the Signal Officer-in-Chief flagged off a high altitude trek at India Gate here today. To commemorate its Diamond Jubilee celebrations of raising, 1 Army Headquarters Signal Regiment has organised a unique 20 days high altitude trekking expedition in the enchanting and picturesque area of Garhwal Himalayas. As per Colonel Vivek Dogra, the team leader and an experienced mountaineer, this expedition aims to promote awareness with respect to the multifaceted activities of the Corps of Signals amongst the local populace of the far flung remote mountain hamlets, through which the trekking route will pass. One of the oldest Signal Regiments of the Indian Army, 1 Army Headquarters Signal regiment was born on 15 August 1947 and since then has been doing a yeoman service in provisioning of communications to army headquarters located at Delhi and public address cover for national functions to include those Republic Day and Independence Day. The Regiment has always been in the forefront of other activities also, especially those which encourage the spirit of adventure. This expedition would involve cross-country movement in high altitude terrain along some of the most beautiful and challenging surroundings of the Himalayas. During this trek, the team is going to cover more than 210 Kms of mountainous stretch by trekking. The trekking team consists of volunteers who have shown keen interest to pursue their love for adventure. Naib Subedar Jagmail Singh a para and commando qualified Junior Commissioned Officer who had lost his left foot in a brave and daring operation in Sri Lanka will also be a team member. He already has the enviable credit of climbing fiery heights of Brahma-II (6700 M) in spite of being an amputee. The expedition will start from picturesque ski resort of Auli and terminate at an equally beautiful place in the heart of Garhwal Himalayas called Gwaldam.

2984. (3-9-2007) NEW DELHI : UGC launches a new scheme for D S Kothari Post-Doctoral Fellowships (PDFs) from the academic session 2007-08 to commemorate the birth centenary of Prof. D S Kothari, an eminent educationist and scientist and former Chairman of UGC. UGC's initiative to launch a prestigious PDF scheme, named after an illustrious scientist, is one of the important and timely step which fills a widely felt void in availability of high quality research personnel in the country. An MOU was signed in this context between UGC and Pune University, today, which has been identified as the nodal university for launching the scheme. The selection process under the scheme would be open all the year round and not restricted by any specified deadlines as thesis submission and award of Ph.D degree are open ended processes. There would be a rolling advertisement on the UGC website; other institutions and UGC affiliates would be encouraged to replicate it on theirs. Applications would be submitted electronically on forms that can be downloaded from the web and the entire process would be carried out on-line. A standing peer group would evaluate the applications. Since this is a promotional scheme to inculcate post-doctoral research culture, emphasis during the review process/selection would be on an appropriate mix of the candidate's accomplishment at Ph. D level and the professional standing of mentor and institution where the post-doctoral research is to be carried out. There could be up to 500 such awards every year, making it to about 1000 at its peak. Candidates who have either received a Ph. D degree or submitted their Ph. D thesis are eligible to apply. When selected, those holding the Ph. D degree will be directly awarded the named PDF. Those who have submitted their Ph. D thesis may be awarded a 'bridging fellowship' (with marginally reduced stipend) until they are formally awarded the Ph. D degree. The fellowship will be awarded on a yearly basis with renewal/termination clause on the basis of PDF mentor/peer group appraisal. However, the maximum duration of the PDF award would be 3 yrs. Candidates should give an undertaking while availing the award, along with the endorsement of the research mentor, that they would stay in place for a minimum of six months. He stipend for these awards would be Rs.18,000-22,000 per month with annual increase of Rs.1000 per month. The 'bridging fellowship' stipend would be Rs.16,000 per month. The PDFs award would carry a contingency grant of Rs.50,000 per annum.

2985. (3-9-2007) NEW DELHI : Air Marshal JN Burma AVSM, VSM flagged off first ever Inter Command Air Force Schools Sports Championship at New Delhi today. The champion is being held from 03 Sep 07 to 06 Sep 07 as part of Platinum Jubilee celebrations of the IAF. Besides six command teams, Air HQ team comprising of the children of Air Force schools located in New Delhi will be competing in each event. The championship is being organized by the Directorate of Education under the aegis of IAF Educational and Cultural society, New Delhi. The championship is being conducted in five disciplines, namely; Cricket, Football, Basketball, Table Tennis and Badminton for the boys and Badminton & Table Tennis events for the girls. The participants represents various unit run AF Schools and have won in their respective Intra command tournament which were held to select the command team in each discipline. The aim of this championship is to inculcate spirit-de-corps among the children and to encourage and groom potential players for higher level of competitions. A total of 392 participants, including 56 girls are competing for the champion's trophy in each discipline and also vying for the overall best team championship trophy during the week long tournament scheduled to be held at different venues in Delhi. Cricket championship will be held at Air Force Station Palam, cricket ground, Football & Basketball championships at Air Force Station Race Course and Tennis & Badminton championships at Air Force Golden Jubilee Institute, Subroto Park. The inaugural ceremony of the championship was followed by a football match played between Air Headquarters and the Training Command team.

2986. (3-9-2007) NEW DELHI : In a daredevil night rescue operation by the

IAF on 02 September 2007, the MI-17 Helicopter crew from the Jodhpur based 107 Helicopter Unit rescued Shri Dilip Kumar, a reveller who was washed away in the flash floods while saving others from his group. The group was enjoying the weekend at the gorges at Bhawarkund, a picnic spot on the banks of Chambal river near Kota town in Rajasthan. On receiving request from DC Jodhpur at 1800 hrs, the Air Officer Commanding, Jodhpur air base, Air Commodore J Kumbhat launched a MI-17 Helicopter fitted with NVG (Night Vision Goggles) within the shortest possible time. The Helicopter was airborne by 1940 hrs and reached the spot which was surrounded by high tension cables with extra size poles. The captain of the Helicopter, Wing Commander Sameer Pendse with his co pilot Squadron Leader Rosa used night vision goggles to track Dilip Kumar who was there since the last 5 to 6 hours. The pilots hovered for almost 20 minutes over the spot, criss-crossed by high tension cables. A winch and monkey belt was sent below for rescue, but Dilip Kumar refused to come up as he was either tired or he was scared. The captain then sent the third pilot Squadron Leader Pranay who volunteered to go down. The courageous pilot came down under winch and held Shri Dilip Kumar and pulled him up. The complete operation which took 40 minutes of hovering and operations in the night without lights was a tedious task for the pilots. "Wing Commander Mathur, the Commanding Officer of the Kota based Air Squadron NCC was of a great help. Being a local pilot, he gave me the general description of the high tension wires and topography of the area from the Air Traffic Control. He also helped me communicate to the state authorities to switch off all the ground lights available at the site so that they could effectively used the NVG's" stated Wing Commander Pendse. Landing back with Dilip Kumar at Kota Airfield was also a difficult task. The Kota airfield did not have any night landing facility. Four trucks were positioned with lights on at the tarmac of Kota Airfield so as to make the MI 17 land.

2987. (3-9-2007) NEW DELHI : Lt Gen SPS Dhillon, GOC Desert Corps, released the new edition of "Customs & Etiquette in the Services "at a well attended ceremony at Jodhpur today. "Customs & Etiquette in the Services" is written by Maj Gen RK Arora and Col HR Roach and is considered the Bible of Etiquette amongst armed forces officers. The book was first published in 1956 and has been updated with every edition. The 216 page attractive book, published by Dehra Dun based Natraj Publishers, deals with customs of the Army, Navy and the Air Force is a semi-official treatise on how an officer is expected to conduct himself not only when on parade, but more importantly when off parade. Paying of compliments, the dress code, the esoteric art of table manners, the procedures to be followed during Dinner and Regimental Guest Nights, the Officers dress Code, and a host of customs and rituals, which have since time immemorial acted as a unifying and driving force amongst the Services, have been encapsulated in language easily understandable by the professional soldier as well as the layman. This latest edition also contains a chapter on etiquette for the Lady Officers and another on etiquette on the Golf Course. This book should also be of immense interest to a wide. Maj Gen Arora is the GOC of the Battle Axe Division. He has also written a number of books on military history. His last book "The Trishakti Corps : A Saga of Success" was released in September last year. Col Roach was an instructor at the Indian Military Academy, Dehra Dun, when the book was first written. He has since retired from service. The book has a foreword by Adjutant General of the Army, Lt Gen Thomas Mathew. As per Lt Gen Mathew, the book is appropriate for people in all walks of life.

2988. (3-9-2007) NEW DELHI : The existing rules 31A and 31AA of the Income-tax Rules, 1962 require only a Government office and a company to furnish quarterly statements of deduction/collection of tax at source electronically. The said rules 31A and 31AA have been amended vide Notification No. 238/2007 [S.O. 1484(E)] dated 30th August, 2007 to provide that in addition to the existing two categories, quarterly statements of TDS/TCS shall also have to be furnished electronically in the following cases:- (i) Where the deductor/collector is a person required to get his accounts audited under section 44AB of the Income-tax Act in the immediately preceding financial year. (ii) The number of deductees'/collectees' records in a quarterly statement for any quarter of the immediately preceding financial year is equal to more than fifty. Failure to furnish quarterly statements of TDS and quarterly statements of TCS shall, under the provisions of section 272A of the Income-tax Act, 1961, render the defaulter liable for a penalty of Rs.100/- for every day during which the default/failure continues. The notification has come into effect from 1st day of September, 2007. Accordingly, quarterly statement for the quarter ending 30th September, 2007 shall have to be mandatorily filed electronically by Government and corporate deductors/collectors and by the deductors/collectors falling in the aforementioned two categories.

2989. (3-9-2007) NEW DELHI : Reports have been appearing in a section of the Press that the Government is considering taking steps not be allow the use mobile phones by children below 16 years of age. The reports are factually incorrect. The facts are as under: The draft guidelines for complying with limits for human exposure to Electromagnetic Fields (Base Station antennas and Mobile Telephones/Radio Terminals) are under preparation by an Expert Group involving experts from all stakeholders including Ministry of Health, Department of IT, Indian Council of Medical Research (ICMR), SAMEER, Telecom Service Providers, BSNL, MTNL, Telecom Associations like COAI, AUSPI, TEMA etc. The views expressed during discussions as well as the inputs provided by the Expert Group have been merely compiled and it is in the form of a draft for discussion in future meetings. TEC has not given any recommendation on the subject as on date.

2990. (3-9-2007) NEW DELHI : The Conseil International du Sport Militaire's (CISM) 4th Military World Games (MWG) to be held at Hyderabad and Mumbai from October 14-21 by the Ministry of Defence, Government of India is the biggest multi-sport International event to be conducted anywhere around the globe this year concedes the CISM President, Brigadier General Gianni Gola of Italy.

Considered next only to the conduct of Olympics, the statistics of the Games is indeed staggering. And if any doubts remain, then sample this statistics taken on the last official count. This year's MWG will see the participation of 4581 military personnel from 89 countries. Of these 3006 are athletes (2272 men and 734 women) and 1575 team officials. This does not include the 1300 technical officials who along with the organizing committee members add up to a sizable sum. The total participation of women is about 18 per cent. A total of three military sports – military pentathlon, shooting, parachuting; eight individual/team events – football, handball, volleyball, sailing, triathlon, athletics, swimming and diving; three combat events – boxing, judo and wrestling will see these 3227 athletes compete for 1076 medals (341 Gold, 341 Silver, 394 Bronze). The medals mentioned are all inclusive of the team events. The maximum medals to be won are in the track and field games, 28 and 26 each of gold, silver and bronze by men and women athletes respectively. Next in order comes swimming with 28 and 23 each in similar categories. Sailing is the only event in which the medals in the mixed category will be awarded. The medals are being made at the Government Mint at Mumbai. The top three countries in the last WMG held at Catania (Italy) in 2003 were China (31 G-15 S-12 B), Russia (25 G-34 S-33 B) and Italy (20 G-14 S-19 B). India is yet to make a debut in the medal tally of the WMG as yet. There are 3377 civilian and military volunteers, 17400 security personnel from the Andhra Pradesh State Police and 2600 home guards who will substantially add up the total tally to about 35000 persons involved with the Games, one way or the other. Apart from the invites there would also be the significant presence of both the national and the world media covering the WMG. In the previous three editions of the WMG at Rome (Italy) in 1995, Zagreb (Croatia) in 1999 and Catania (Italy) in 2003, the total number of countries that participated were 93, 82 and 87 figuring 17, 20 and 11 disciplines with 4017, 6734 and 3406 athletes respectively. CISM officials hoped that this year the participation could reach the highest at 100 countries. But the figure now rests officially at 89. The maximum participation is in the track and field events. 67 countries are fielding a total of 858 participants comprising 516 men and 141 women athletes with 191 men and 10 women as team officials respectively.

2991. (3-9-2007) NEW DELHI : 192 MW Grid Interactive Renewable Power has been commissioned against the target of 1500 MW for the year 2007-08. 55 MW of Wind Power Capacity was commissioned during last month. In the field of biomass power capacity 17.5 MW was commissioned last month taking the achievement in the sector to 54.5 MW against a target 275 MW for 2007-08. In the field of small hydro power 5 MW capacity was commissioned during the same period. 12 MW biomass (non-bagasse) cogeneration capacity for captive use of a paper mill was commissioned during the last month taking the achievement in the sector to 12 MW against a target of 20 MW for 2007-08 and cumulative achievement in the sector to 57.80 MW. More than 3000 villages and 830 hamlets have been electrified under remote village electrification programme so far, where

36 villages were covered under this scheme during last month. 5 Test Projects on Village Energy Security were commissioned during June and July 2007-08 taking cumulative achievement under the programme to 13 test projects. Indian Renewable Energy Development Agency (IREDA) disbursed Rs.12.44 crore as loan during last month. The Ministry has target of Rs. 550 crore for 2007-08, out of which Rs. 156.26 crores disbursement has been achieved.

2992. (3-9-2007) NEW DELHI : Shri Kamal Nath, Union Minister of Commerce and Industry while welcoming Mr. Sten Tolg-fors, Swedish Minister of Foreign Trade has appreciated the Swedish Government's desire for enhanced engagement with India and welcomed Sweden's strong interest to deepen and diversify relations with India in the area of trade and commerce. Shri Kamal Nath was speaking at the bilateral meeting during the visit of Mr. Sten Tolg-fors, Swedish Minister of Foreign Trade here today. The meeting was attended by senior officials from both the sides as well. Observing that the relations between India and Sweden are stable, friendly and multidimensional with visible signs of an enhanced desire on both sides to deepen the level of engagement in all areas, Shri Kamal Nath expressed satisfaction that the bilateral trade between the two countries has increased by 55% during 2006-07 as compared to trade in 2005-06. While India's export to Sweden has increased by 19%, Swedish export to India has shown a growth of 65%. On FDI and investments, the Commerce and Industry Minister noted that while investment flows from Sweden are encouraging and even though Sweden is 12th largest investor in India, there is considerable room for larger investments in India, particularly in areas such as infrastructure and renewable energy. "Sweden with its large number of MNCs has had a long history of presence in India. There has been traditional reluctance on the part of the Swedish small and medium industries to come forward to invest in India but in recent years these industries are also exploring India due to inherent advantages of cost benefits and a growing market. We, as governments, must do our best to help the SME sector engage bilaterally", Shri Kamal Nath, stated. India's main imports from Sweden are in the areas of electronic goods, computer software in physical form, machinery and gold. India's main exports to Sweden are readymade garments cotton including accessories, manufacturers of metals, cotton yarn, fabrics and carpets, etc. The percent share of India's exports of ten principal commodities to Sweden constitutes 65%.

2993. (3-9-2007) NEW DELHI : The exports during July 2007 were valued at US $ 12494.11 million, which was 18.52 % higher than the level of US $ 10542.14 million during July 2006. In rupee terms, exports touched Rs. 50493.57 crore, which was 3.10% higher than the value of exports during July, 2006. Cumulative value of exports for the period April-July 2007 was US$ 46797.61 million (Rs. 191824.22 Crore) as against US$ 39586.71 million (Rs. 181139.67 Crore) during the same period last year. The Imports during July 2007 were valued at US $ 17508.63 million representing an increase of 20.40 % over the level of imports valued at US $ 14542.21 million in July 2006. In Rupee terms, imports increased by 4.74 %. Cumulative value of imports for the period April-July, 2007 was US$ 72417.47 million (Rs. 297080.57 Crore) as against US$ 55427.93 million (Rs. 253545.49 Crore) during the same period last year. The Oil imports during July, 2007 were valued at US $ 5048.33 million which was 8.75% higher than oil imports valued at US $ 4642.31 million in the corresponding period last year. Oil imports during April-July, 2007 were valued at US$ 19878.52 million, which was 5.33% higher than the oil imports of US$ 18873.12 million in the corresponding period last year. Non-oil imports during July, 2007 were estimated at US $ 12460.30 million which was 25.86% higher than growth on non oil imports of US$ 9899.90 million in July, 2006. Non-oil imports during April-July, 2007 were valued at US$ 52538.95 million which was 43.73% higher than the level of such imports valued at US$ 36554.82 million in April-July, 2006.

2994. (3-9-2007) NEW DELHI : The Prime Minister, Dr. Manmohan Singh has congratulated scientists and technicians of ISRO for the successful launch of GSLV-F04. In a message the Prime Minister said. "I am happy to learn that the 5th launch of India's Geosynchronous Satellite Launch Vehicle, GSLV-F04, has successfully placed the latest communication satellite, INSAT-4CR in orbit from the Satish Dhawan Space Centre at Sriharikota in Andhra Pradesh. The spectacular launch of the GSLV-F04 has been witnessed by the whole nation. The nation is justly proud of the scientific and technological capabilities of our space scientists. With this launch we have reaffirmed our capabilities to not only build state-of-the-art communication satellites, but also to launch them using an indigenously designed and developed launch vehicle. I am happy that ISRO has been able to overcome the problem faced in the last mission within the shortest possible time. I congratulate all the scientists and technicians associated with the launch and wish them even greater successes in the future."

2995. (3-9-2007) NEW DELHI : President Smt. Pratibha Devisingh Patil will give away National awards on Teachers' Day to accord public recognition to meritorious teachers of primary and secondary schools. This year, the awards are being given for the year 2005-06 to 314 teachers, which includes 88 lady teachers, 11 Sanskrit teachers, 3 Arabic/Persian teachers, and 12 teachers for promoting education of children with disabilities. The Award carries a Silver Medal, a Certificate and a cash award of Rs. 25,000/-. There are 366 awards out of which 20 awards have been earmarked for Sanskrit, Persian and Arabic teachers. Each State Government and Union Territory Administration has an earmarked quota based on the number of teachers in their respective States/UTs. The Scheme also covers teachers of Sainik Schools, Navodaya Vidyalaya Samiti (NVS), Kendriya Vidyalaya Sangathan (KVS), schools affiliated to Central Board of Secondary Education (CBSE) & Council for the Indian School Certificate Examination (CISCE), Central Tibetan Schools Administration (CTSA) and schools run by the Atomic Energy Education Society. 33 'Special Awards' have been earmarked for teachers who have engaged themselves in the inclusive education of children with special needs. The teachers with disabilities working in regular schools are also considered for the award in this category. In order to be eligible for the award, a class-room teacher should have at least 15 years of continuous service on the date of consideration. For Principals and Headmasters the eligibility is 20 years. For the special awards, minimum continuous experience for eligibility is 10 and 15 years for teachers and Principal of the school & that for Special Awards is 10 & 15 years respectively. The process of selection begins at the District level under a Committee of District Education Officer/District Inspector of Schools. Based on their recommendations, a State Award Committee under the Director of Education/Public Instructions is held to examine the District Awardee lists and based on the number of quota allotted, recommends the nominations to the Central Government. In the said Committee, inter-alia, a Central Government representative is also represented. The cases are examined at the Ministry level and based on the Vigilance clearance given by the State Governments, the list of awardees is processed. The teachers will also call on the Prime Minister on 4th September, 2007. National Award to teachers, instituted in 1958, is celebrated in our country as Teachers 'Day in honour of Dr. S. Radhakrishnan, former President of India, a philosopher and a great teacher. From mid-60s, 5th September has been the date of investiture. .....

2996. (3-9-2007) NEW DELHI : Central Water Commission (CWC) under Ministry of Water Resources is monitoring storage position of 81 important reservoirs spread all over the country, of which as many as 31 reservoirs have significant hydro-power benefits with installed capacity of more than 60 MW each. The combined live storage in these 78 reservoirs at the beginning of monsoon *i.e.* 1st June, 2007 was 25 per cent of their designed capacity and stood at 70 per cent of the designed capacity as on 30th August 2007. The present storage is 92 per cent of the last year's storage and 122 per cent of last 10 years average storage during the same period. Out of these 71 reservoirs there are presently 10 reservoirs where this year's storage is 80 per cent or less than the average of previous 10 years and in the remaining 71 reservoirs the storage is more than 80 per cent of the average of previous 10 years. In order to derive the best possible benefits from the available water, Central Water Commission is keeping in touch with the Department of Agriculture and Cooperation and providing information of the weekly storage position to the Crop Weather Watch Group for evolving suitable crop strategies and also apprising the situation to various Departments and Ministries involved in Water Resources Planning.

2997. (3-9-2007) NEW DELHI : The Vice President, Mohd. Hamid Ansari has greeted the people of our country on the auspicious occasion of Janmashtami which is celebrated across the country with religious fervour and enthusiasm. In his greetings, the Vice President said that the festival reminds us of the birth, simplicity and heroic deeds of the young Lord Krishna who is immortalized in our popular consciousness. We must derive inspiration from the life and teachings of Lord Krishna. The Vice President said that on this occasion let us rededicate ourselves to the teachings of Lord Krishna and work for the creation of a just and peaceful society.

2998. (3-9-2007) NEW DELHI : The total approximate earnings of Indian Railways on originating basis during the period 11th August – 20th August 2007 were Rs. 1707.94 crore compared to Rs. 1491.75 crore during the same period last year, registering an increase of 14.49 per cent. The total goods earnings have gone up from Rs. 997.81 crore during 11-20 August 2006 to Rs. 1169.03 crore during 11-20 August 2007, showing an increase of 17.16 per cent. The total passenger revenue earnings during the period 11–20 August 2007 were Rs. 487.49 crore compared to Rs. 430.96 crore during the same period last year, an increase of 13.12 per cent. The revenue earnings from other coaching amounted to Rs. 38.82 crore during this period compared to Rs. 50.41 crore during the same period last year. The total sundry earnings have gone up from Rs. 12.57 crore during 11-20 August 2006 to Rs. 12.60 crore during 11-20 August 2007, showing an increase of 0.24 per cent. The total approximate number of passengers booked during the period 11–20 August 2007 were 181.08 million compared to 165.94 million during the same period last year, showing an increase of 9.12 per cent. In the suburban and non-suburban sectors, the number of passengers booked during 11-20 August 2007 were 104.46 million and 76.62 million compared to 92.90 million and 73.04 million during the same period last year, registering an increase of 12.44 per cent and 4.90 per cent respectively.

2999. (3-9-2007) NEW DELHI : Shri Sontosh Mohan Dev, Minister for Heavy Industries & Public Enterprises will present the SCOPE Meritorious Awards in Specialized Fields for the year 2005-06 on 5th September 2007 in New Delhi. The Standing Conference of Public Enterprises (SCOPE) has instituted six awards in the fields of Environmental Excellence and Sustainable Development; Research & Development and Innovation; Best Practice in Human Resource Management; Corporate Social Responsibility & Responsiveness; Good Corporate Governance; and, Best Managed PSE set up under Section 25. SCOPE Meritorious Awards are presented to recognize significant achievements of member public enterprises in various fields leading to business excellence and competitive advantage; to encourage and motivate them; to achieve higher goals of excellence; and, to reward those enterprises which have demonstrated extra ordinary skills and have made a mark in chosen fields which have been primarily responsible for growth/ turnover of the enterprise. Shri Dev will also inaugurate the "3rd Directors Certification Programme on Corporate Governance." Dr. R.C. Panda, Secretary, Heavy Industries & Public Enterprises will deliver the Key Note address, while Shri Sarthak Behuria, Chairman SCOPE will preside over the function. Dr. S.M. Dewan, Director General SCOPE will give welcome address.

3000. (3-9-2007) NEW DELHI : The Ministry of Petroleum & Natural Gas over the years has been making concerted efforts to accelerate exploration and production of oil and natural gas in India. As the demand has far outstripped the domestic production of oil and gas, Government has successfully encouraged Oil PSUs led by ONGC Videsh to acquire equity oil/gas acreages abroad. Another significant development in the sector in recent years has been a landmark turn around in the refining sector with country turning a major exporter of value added (refined) petroleum products from a major product importer. Government has also initiated a number of other initiatives for development of oil and gas infrastructure in the country for supplying latest grade fuels to the consumers in different sectors of economy.

3001. (3-9-2007) NEW DELHI : The President, Smt. Pratibha Devisingh Patil in her message on the occasion of Janmashtami, which is being celebrated tomorrow, has said:-"On the auspicious occasion of Janmashtami, I extend my greetings and good wishes to all my fellow citizens. Signifying the triumph of virtue and righteousness, the life and teachings of Lord Krishna have a universal message. Lord Krishna in his message has preached duty without thought of reward. May this festival inspire all of us to follow the path of virtue and righteousness in thought, word and deed".

3002. (3-9-2007) NEW DELHI : The Prime Minister, Dr. Manmohan Singh, has greeted citizens in India and abroad on the auspicious occasion of Janamashtami, which is being celebrated tomorrow. In a message, the Prime Minister said, "Janamashtami reminds us of Lord Krishna's eternal message of performing one's duty without any expectation of reward. Let us follow the divine teachings of Lord Krishna and pledge to rededicate ourselves to the welfare of the people and of our country. May the festival herald peace, prosperity and happiness for all", the Prime Minister added.

3003. (3-9-2007) NEW DELHI : The Union Ministry of Tourism has launched a Scheme to classify fully operational rooms of Home Stay Facilities as "Incredible India Bed & Breakfast (B&B) Establishment". The basic idea is to provide a clean and affordable place for foreigners and domestic tourists alike, including an opportunity for foreign tourists to stay with an Indian family to experience Indian customs and traditions and relish authentic Indian cuisine. 81 Establishments have been registered in this Scheme in Delhi, out of which 23 are in the Gold category and 58 are in the Silver category. The total number of rooms registered under the Scheme is 221. The number of establishments registered in the National Capital Region (NCR) is 94. In view of the positive response received by this Scheme and the potential it has to create additional accommodation, the Govt. of NCT of Delhi has passed the 'National Capital Territory of Delhi (Incredible India) Bed & Breakfast Establishment (Registration and Regulation) Ordinance, 2007". This Ordinance extends to the whole of National Capital Territory of Delhi and exempts Bed & Breakfast Establishments from levy of Luxury Tax and Value Added Tax. Earlier the owners of these establishments had to pay 12.5% Luxury Tax.

3004. (4-9-2007) NEW DELHI : The President, Smt. Pratibha Devisingh Patil has condoled the passing away of the husband of the Rajya Sabha, Member of Parliament, Dr. Najma Heptulla. In a condolence message, the President has said she is saddened to learn about the passing away of Shri Akbarali A. Heptulla and conveyed her condolences to Dr. Heptulla and the other members of the family.

3005. (4-9-2007) NEW DELHI : The govt. first rejected the tender which offered wheat @ $263 per MT in June citing the reason of prices being too high. Suddenly, after 10 days govt. changed its mind and ordered import of 5.7 lakh tonnes of wheat @ $325 per MT. This wheat is yet to arrive. But the govt. called for 3 rd tender and has placed order for nearly 8 lakh tonnes at whopping rate of $390 per MT. This is daylight robbery. The govt. has given many reasons to cancel the first tender @ $263. Main of them being, prices being too high, expectation of new arrival and softening of prices by end September in international markets. Bharatiya Janata Party asks the prime Minister to intervene and stop the costly imports, as it is fraud on nation and heist on national exchequers. How can govt. justify cancelling the first tender @ $263 per MT and within days place order @ $325 and now @ $390 per MT? BJP appeals to vigilance agencies and courts to take so-moto pro-active action in face of such a fraud if govt. is not accepting our demand for CBI enquiry. Indian farmers stands betrayed in the process. The UPA govt. paid only Rs. 850/- per quintal and now paying Rs. 1600/- per quintal to foreign farmers. This is adding insult to Indian farmer's injury, which were demanding only Rs. 1100/- per quintal. The govt.'s argument of building up required buffer stock also do not hold two reasons. First, it govt. would have offered Rs. 1100/- per quintal, enough procurement would have taken place. Second, this year's production is more by 50 lakh tonnes than last year, thus raising no distress signals. The Prime Minister also must explain how costly imports of wheat of unacceptable quality will help stabilize the price lime on one hand and deliver justice to Indian farmers on the other. BJP has already launched agitation on wheat import scam. Now, BJP will take the message of UPA's fraud on nation and betrayal of farmers to the nook and corner of the country in its national campaign.

3006. (5-9-2007) NEW DELHI : The Prime Minister, Dr. Manmohan Singh has released a postage stamp commemorating Dr. J.P.Naik, an eminent educationist, on the occasion of Teacher's Day here today. Following is the Text of the Prime Minister's remarks on the occasion: "I am delighted that on the occasion of Teachers' Day we are paying our respects to an outstanding teacher and great educationist by releasing a postage stamp in his honour. The Late Shri J.P.Naik was a great educationist, a revered teacher and a true and great institution builder. Above all, he was a nationalist and a Gandhian, admired by his students and well-wishers all over the country. His professional life began as a teacher in a primary school and culminated in his role as an outstanding educational planner. It is a happy coincidence that he shared his birthday with another great educationist and teacher, our former Rashtrapathiji, Dr. Sarvepalli Radhakrishnan. It gives me great pleasure that we honour two of our great educationists today. Dr. Naik was a great institution builder. Among the many institutions he built was the Indian Council of Social Science Research (ICSSR). ICSSR has played a foundational role in the development of social science research across our country. Dr. Naik helped build world-class research institutions in various State capitals, including at Thiruvananthapuram, Kolkata, Bangalore, Jaipur, Lucknow, Patna and Ahmedabad. He played an extremely important role in promoting educational reforms. I have been told that he took a token salary of one rupee and in return, gave our nation a priceless record of service to our education system. The outstanding quality of his work greatly influenced generations of educationists both inside and outside our country. He was honoured by UNESCO which placed his name in the Honour Rolls of World Educators. Dr. Naik was a true product of our freedom movement. He was deeply influenced by the ideas and ideals of Mahatma Gandhi. The ideas he elaborated continue to have relevance for educational reforms and societal reforms even today. In our effort to vastly improve the educational standards of our people we need to pay heed once again to visionaries and institution builders like the late Shri J.P. Naik. In the scheme of educational reforms advocated by Dr. Naik, social justice was seen as an important objective, if not a more important one, as compared to merit and the promotion of excellence. His view that selection procedures for admission to educational institutions must be based both on merit and on the principles of social justice show his equal commitment to enlarging access and promoting excellence in education. Dr. Naik also showed keen interest in our health care system.

3007. (5-9-2007) NEW DELHI : The Working Group on Power for XI Plan (2007-12) has projected fund requirement of about Rs. 1,23,790 crore for State Sector generation projects. According to the proposed capacity addition programme during the XI Plan, in the State Sector, 73 generation projects aggregating to about 27950 MW have been envisaged. As per the current status of projects, out of the proposed capacity addition during the XI Plan, 50 projects aggregating to about 15840 MW are under execution in the State Sector.

3008. (5-9-2007) NEW DELHI : The Ministry of Power had launched an initiative for the development of coal based Ultra Mega Power Projects (UMPPs), each of about 4000 MW capacity. These projects are being developed on a Build, Own and Operate basis, and the project developer is selected through a tariff based competitive bidding process initiated/to be initiated by project specific shell companies which have been formed as wholly owned subsidiaries of Power Finance Corporation, the identified nodal agency for this initiative.

3009. (5-9-2007) NEW. DELHI : Smt. Pratibha Devisingh Patil, President of India has said that the education system needs to strengthen the values of secularism, democracy, inclusiveness and pluralism. She was giving away National Awards to teachers, here, today. She further said, 'These are the great values enshrined in our Constitution and traditionally developed by our civilization. These values give strength and sustenance not only to our diverse multi-cultural society but also to our country'. 314 teachers received national awards for the year 2005-06. On the occasion, the President underlined the need to upgrade teachers' knowledge, skills and competencies through professional preparation. "Teacher training programmes need to reflect critically the multiple contexts in which schools function and come out with specific solutions relevant to teaching in schools located in urban areas, rural areas, tribal areas and located in disadvantaged regions. The models of pre-service and in-service teacher preparation require critical review. In pre-service teacher education programmes, there is a need for integration between, theory and practices and between subject content and pedagogy", she said. She also emphasised need to develop vocational skills and the role of women in promoting our education objectives. Shri Mohd. Ali Ashraf Fatmi, MOS, HRD said that a good teacher teaches best through his/her own example. He appreciated the dedication, professional competence and services rendered by the teachers for the cause of building the future of the nation. He said, 'The 'National Award' is a token of recognition for your dedication and services rendered towards education. We expect you to play the leadership role in striving towards quality education for all children'. He underlined the need to reduce drop-out rates at various levels, improve the learning outcomes and prepare the students for higher stages of education with adequate skill.

3010. (5-9-2007) NEW DELHI : The construction of the Scorpene class submarine has started since December 2006. The first submarine is scheduled to be delivered in December 2012 and thereafter one each every year till December 2017. M/ s. Mazagon Dock Ltd (MDL) is at present the only defence public sector undertaking in the country undertaking construction of submarines. The submarine production line at MDL remained under-utilized for some time till commencement of construction of the Scorpene submarines. This information was given by the Defence Minister Shri AK Antony in a written reply to Shri Ravi Prakash Verma and others in Lok Sabha today. ACQUISITION OF HELICOPTERS FOR ARMY The US Government has conveyed their concern over the disqualification of M/ s Bell Helicopter Company in the case of procurement of a replacement helicopter for the Cheetah/Chetak helicopters of the Indian Army. No issues have been raised about the bona-fides of the firm by the US Government. The helicopter offered by the Bell Helicopter Company was not found technically qualified as per General Staff evaluation made by the Army based on field trials. No settlement has either been reached or proposed with the firm This information was given by the Defence Minister Shri AK Antony in a written reply to Shri Jyotiraditya M Scindia in Lok Sabha today.

3011. (5-9-2007) NEW DELHI : The construction of Indigenous Aircraft Carrier (IAC) is progressing with the scheduled "launch" of the ship in 2010 at Cochin

Shipyard Ltd (CSL). However, the final delivery of the ship may be delayed from the earlier likely delivery in 2012. The delay is due to size and complexities in construction of an aircraft carrier, being designed and built indigenously for the first time at Cochin Shipyard Ltd. Besides, delay has also occurred due to delay in receipt of some critical materials such as steel from abroad. Principal design has been completed and specialist design inputs outsourced are progressing as per schedule. Contractor for Phase-1 has been concluded with CSL in May 2007 and the construction of hull and ordering of equipment is progressing as per the contracted schedule. Adequate funds required at this stage as per contract, have been provided to CSL for procurement of various material, equipment and towards yard-effort as per shipbuilding schedule, as also for infrastructure augmentation. The project is being reviewed at various levels to remove impediments, if any, expeditiously. This information was given by the Defence Minister Shri AK Antony in a written reply to Shri Ravi Prakash Verma in Lok Sabha today.

3012. (5-9-2007) NEW DELHI : Renowned journalist and author Shri Ramsharan Joshi released the Publications Division's book titled-'Ye Karwan Hamara' today. In his remarks, Shri Joshi said, in today's market driven world, it is all the more important to make children aware of the meaning of freedom and the pain people had to bear to win it. This function was organised by Publications Division, Ministry of Information and Broadcasting, as part of the ongoing 13th Delhi Book Fair. This is the Hindi translation of renowned writers Ms/s. Surekha Panandikar, Ira Saxena and Neelima Sinha's celebrated book 'Together we Marched' also published by the Division. Ms. Shashi Jain has done the translation. This book is a collection of small inspiring stories of common men who silently contributed in India's freedom struggle. Since the first war of independence in 1857 till the time when our country won freedom in 1947, youth across the religions and states participated in freedom movements. This book tells stories of their bravery and martyrdom woven around these movements. Talking about the book, Ms. Surekha Panandikar said that they have tried to put human values forward through incidents without preaching about them. She said that children need more such books and hoped that the Division would publish more such books specially when the country is commemorating 150 years of the first war of independence, 100 years of satyagraha and birth centenary of Bhagat Singh, all in the same year. Publications Division is a unit under the Ministry of Information and Broadcasting Government of India that brings out authentic and informative books on a spectrum of subjects at affordable prices. It has close to 8000 titles to its credit till now. Started small in 1941, Publications Division today is one of the biggest publishing organizations in India. With a mandate to publish books on matters of national importance, the Division brings out books in Hindi, English and all major regional languages.

3013. (5-9-2007) NEW DELHI : Ministry of Food Processing Industries (MFPI) has been providing financial assistance in the form of grant-in-aid for Technology Upgradation /Establishment/Modernization of food processing industries upto

25% of the cost of plant and machinery and technical civil works subject to a maximum of Rs. 50 lakh in general areas and upto 33.33% in difficult area subject to a maximum of Rs. 75 lakh to various implementing agencies for the overall development of Food Processing Sector. The Ministry does not set up food processing industries of its own. The Ministry has approved financial assistance of Rs. 24.16 crore for the State of Uttar Pradesh during the last three year *i.e.* 2004-05, 205-06, 2006-07. Under the Cold Chain component of 10th Plan Scheme, assistance upto 25% of the cost of plant and machinery and technical civil works in general areas and 33.33% in difficult areas with a common ceiling of Rs. 75 lakh was admissible to all implementing agencies. The assistance under the scheme was limited to cold storages for non-horticulture produces, special type of cold storages with controlled/modified atmosphere technology, cold storages as integral part of processing units or as a common facility in food parks. Besides, other agencies of Government of India like National Horticulture Board (NHB), Agriculture and Processed Food Products Export Development Authority (APEDA), National Cooperative Development Corporation (NCDC) and State Government also provide assistance under their respective schemes. The budget allocation utilized by the Ministry on infrastructure development including cold storages during 2004-05, 2005-06 and 2006-07 was Rs. 11.82 crore, Rs. 15.65 crore and Rs. 13.21 crore respectively. Two cold storages have also been approved in Uttar Pradesh so far. Although MFPI does not set up food testing laboratories of its own, it provides financial assistance for setting up/upgradation of food testing laboratories under its Plan Scheme to various stakeholders such as Central/State Government organizations, IITs, Universities, private sector organisations. MFPI has approved financial assistance to five organizations in Uttar Pradesh under its Plan Scheme amounting to Rs. 9. 48 crore. The MFPI provides financial assistance for establishment of food parks. It does not set up Food Parks on its own. The Ministry has approved financial assistance for five food parks in Uttar Pradesh *i.e.* Ghaziabad, Kharkion (District Varanasi), Kushalipur (District Saharanpur), Shahajanwa (District Gorakhpur), and Kursi Road (District Barabanki) and released an amount of Rs. 2.71 crore, Rs. 2 crore, Rs. 3 crore, Rs. 0.81 crore and Rs. 4 crore respectively for establishment of these Food Parks. Of these, Ghaziabad Food Park is under review and other four Food Parks are operational. This information was given by Shri Subodh Kant Sahai, Minister of State for Food Processing in reply to a Question raised by Shri Amir Alam Khan in Rajya Sabha today.

3014. (5-9-2007) NEW DELHI : As per the provisions of the Mines and Minerals (Development & Regulation) Act, 1957, the rates of royalty can be enhanced only once in three years. Since the rates of royalty were last revised on 14.10.2004, further revision in royalty rates is possible only after 13.10.2007. A Study Group has accordingly been constituted in the Ministry of Mines to review the royalty rates. This was stated by Shri Sis Ram Ola, Minister of Mines in the Rajya Sabha today while reply to a question about demand from the States for enhancing royalty on minerals. Responding to another query, he informed the House that State Governments have sought to give preference to such applicants in grant of mineral concession who are willing to do value addition of the minerals within the State. A National Mineral Policy, which also covers this issue, is under consideration of the Central Government.

3015. (5-9-2007) NEW DELHI : National Co-operative Consumers' Federation of India Limited (NCCF), a multi state cooperative society, was allocated coal, on the recommendation of the Ministry of Consumer Affairs, Food and Public Distribution, with the objective of distributing coal to small and tiny consumers who do not have linkage or sponsorship and find it difficult to approach directly coal companies to meet their requirements of coal.

3016. (5-9-2007) NEW DELHI : The Chief Ministers of the State Governments of Orissa, Chattisgarh, Jharkand, Rajasthan and Karnataka had raised concerns on dilution of powers of the State Governments in the National Mineral Policy, 2007. These issues were discussed with the Governments of chief mineral producing States and based on the resolution achieved with them, a draft National Mineral Policy is under consideration of the Government. The Group of Ministers has considered the National Mineral Policy. This was stated by the Minister of Mines Shri Sis Ram Ola in a written reply in the Rajya Sabha today.

3017. (5-9-2007) NEW DELHI : The Lower Pen Ganga Project was earlier received in Central Water Commission (CWC) in August 1982. This project was sent back to project authorities in July 1987 due to non compliance of observations of CWC. Subsequently, the Government of Maharashtra submitted a fresh preliminary report on the project to CWC in November 2006. This preliminary report was examined in CWC and the comments on various aspects were sent to the project authorities in March 2007 for compliance, which is still awaited from the State Government of Maharashtra. This information was given by the Minister of State of the Ministry of Water Resources Shri Jai Prakash Narayan Yadav in a written reply in the Lok Sabha.

3018. (5-9-2007) NEW DELHI : Land erosion along the rivers is a natural phenomenon and occurs especially in alluvial plains. Due to erosion bank lines of the river keep moving on either side at different places. Being a continuous process, no account is available on land loss from the state governments. Flood Management being State subject, the flood control schemes are planned, investigated and implemented by the State Governments with their own funds. The assistance rendered by the Central Government is technical, catalytically and promotional in nature. However, the Central Government has been providing financial assistance to the flood affected States under various plan schemes in order to enable them to take up flood management works in critical areas. Consultations are being held regularly with neighbouring countries on land erosion problem, particularly in Nepal. A Standing Committee on Inundation Problem (SCIP) between India and

Nepal was set up in 1986 for dealing the problem. Last meeting of the committee was held form 30th August to 1st September, 2006 at Patna. This information was given by the Minister of State of the Ministry of Water Resources Shri Jai Prakash Narayan Yadav in a written reply in the Lok Sabha.

3019. (5-9-2007) NEW DELHI : The manuscript of "The History of Azad Hind Fauz (Indian National Army)" written by eminent Historian Late Dr. Praful Chandra Gupta at the behest of the Government of India is presently in the custody of the History Division of the Ministry of Defence. The said manuscript is open for consultation by any person interested in it. There is no proposal before the Government to publish the manuscript. This information was given by the Defence Minister Shri AK Antony in a written reply to Shri Subrata Bose in Lok Sabha today. SALE OF DEFENCE PRODUCTS TO FOREIGN COUNTRIES Encouraging exports of defence products is an on-going exercise and Defence Public Sector Undertakings and Ordnance Factory Board are engaged in sale of Defence products to countries like Nepal, Sri Lanka and Bhutan etc. The Government, through Defence Public Sector Undertakings & Ordnance Factory Boards, has exported defence products amounting to Rs. 428.84 crores during the year 2006-2007. During 2005-2007, proposals for possible purchase of defence products have been received from various countries like Indonesia, Chile, Nepal, Malaysia, Thailand, Vietnam, Israel, Algeria, Botswana, Kenya, Belgium, Cyprus, Turkey, Surinam etc. and these are examined and orders executed in consultation with the Defence Public Sector Undertakings and Ordnance Factory Board and Ministry of External Affairs. This information was given by the Of State for Defence Production Rao Inderjit Singh in a written reply to Shri Subhash Sureshchandra Deshmukh in Lok Sabha today. PILOTLESS AIRCRAFT LAKSHYASo far, 23 Pilotless Target Aircraft Lakshya have been inducted into the defence services. The production cost of one aircraft is Rs. 293.75 lakh. Some countries, like Singapore, Malaysia and Israel have expressed interest for "paid demonstration" of the Lakshya aircrafts as a target. A similar "paid demonstration" was conducted for Israel's Air Force during the year 2002. This information was given by the Defence Minister Shri AK Antony in a written reply to Shri Ramdas Athawale in Lok Sabha today.

3020. (5-9-2007) NEW DELHI : Brahmos supersonic cruise missile has gone through a series of successful flight trials launched from ship and from road mobile launchers for Navy and Indian Army. The system has been inducted in the Indian Navy and Indian Army. The missile, which can be launched from submarine, is also ready and awaiting the necessary platform for trials Indian Navy will soon identify the platform. The development of Air version of the Brahmos missile is also in progress and will be integrated on IL-38 for the Navy and SU-30 MKI for the Air Force. This information was given by the Defence Minister Shri AK Antony in a written reply to Shri Hansraj G. Ahir in Lok Sabha today. PROCUREMENT OF SUKHOI AIRCRAFT A Protocol signed by the Indian side and the Russian side in April 2002 in pursuance of General contract dated 28th December 2000 for licence production of 140 SU-30 MKI aircraft by Hindustan Aeronautics Limited, had determined a net annual escalation rate of 2.55% valid till 2007. Discussions between the two sides to decide the annual escalation rate for the years 2008 to 2012 are in progress. The amounts payable for defence equipment procured from Russian suppliers may increase in case the escalation rate is raised. This information was given by the Defence Minister Shir AK Antony and others in a written reply to Shri Braja Kishore Tripathy and others in Lok Sabha today. ADVANCED LIGHT HELICOPTER The Advanced Light Helicopter (ALH) is the first attempt at indigenous production. Teething problems occurred in the initial stages. The Serviceability of ALH has show improvement over a period of time with extensive product support provided by M/s. Hindustan Aeronautics Limited (HAL) in the areas of supply of spares, tools & other equipment and also technical & logistics support at operational bases. In order to support the ALH in a full integrated manner, HAL has set up a new division for maintenance and overhaul of all critical systems including engines, avionics, transmission system etc. fitted on ALH. The ALH was inducted in the Armed Forces in 2001-2002. A total of 61 ALHs have been produced so far. Production programme is in accordance with the requirement of the Armed Forces. This information was given by the Defence Minister Shri AK Antony in a written reply to Shri Anandrao V. Adsul and Shri Adhalrao Patil in Lok Sabha today.

3021. (5-9-2007) NEW DELHI : The Ministry of Shipping, Road Transport & Highways is primarily responsible for the development and maintenance of National Highways (NHs). No assessments have been made regarding the impact of conditions of NHs and increasing traffic thereon on the development of the Indian Economy. The Government has taken several steps for enhancing the funds for the development of National Highways by imposing the cess on petrol and diesel and has taken decision for implementing the projects under National Highways Development Project (NHDP) –Phase-III onwards primarily on Build-Operate-Transfer (BOT) basis through Public-Private-Partnership. This information was given by the Minister of State for Shipping, Road Transport and Highways, Shri K.H. Muniyappa in a written reply in the Lok Sabha today.

3022. (5-9-2007) NEW DELHI : Union Government has received any proposal from the State Government of Madhya Pradesh regarding four-laning of the National Highways passing through the State under "Bharat Jodo Pariyojana".

3023. (5-9-2007) NEW DELHI : The safety of road users is primarily the responsibility of the concerned State Government. However, this department has taken several steps to improve road safety for road users which are as under: i) It is ensured that road safety is the integral part of road design at the planning stage for National Highways/Expressways. ii) Various steps to enhance road safety such as road furniture, road markings/road signs, introduction of Highway Traffic

Management System using Intelligent Transport System, enhancement of discipline among contractors during construction, road safety audit on selected stretches, have been undertaken by National Highways Authority of India (NHAI). iii) Refresher training to Heavy Motor Vehicle drivers in the unorganized sector by Department of Road Transport and highways. iv) Involvement of NGOs for road safety activities by Department of Road Transport and Highways and NHAI. v) Setting up of Model Driving Training School in the country. vi) Publicity campaign on road safety awareness through audio-visual-print media. vii) Institution of National Award for voluntary organizations/individual for outstanding work in the field of road safety. viii) Tightening of safety standards of vehicles. ix) Providing cranes and ambulances to various State Governments/NGOs under National Highway Accident Relief Service Scheme. National Highways Authority of India also provides ambulances at a distance of 50 Km. on each of its completed highways under its Operation & Maintenance contracts. x) Widening and improvements of National Highways from 2 lanes to 4 lanes and 4 lanes to 6 lanes etc. Apart from the above, following measures are being taken by the NHAI on Delhi-Gurgaon section of NH 8 to check the increasing number of accidents and the problem faced by the people:- i) Segregation of slow moving traffic from high speed traffic. ii) Provision of adequate pedestrian crossings. iii) Provision of fencing work along the median. This information was given by the Minister of State for Shipping, Road Transport and Highways, Shri K.H. Muniyappa in a written reply in the Lok Sabha today.

3024. (5-9-2007) NEW DELHI : The Nehru Yuva Kendra Sangathan organized various programmes at school level, village level, village cluster level, district level and also at the State level in all States, including Rajasthan. The programmes *inter alia* included seminars, debates, essay writing, prabhat pheris, cycle rallies etc. All these programmes had "1857" as their theme. At the national level, the Nehru Yuva Kendra Sangathan participated in the inaugural function of the national celebration to commemorate the 150th year of the First War of Independence by organizing a National Youth Rally from Meerut to Delhi from 7-10 May 2007, which culminated in a major function at the Red Fort, Delhi, attended by the President, Vice President, Prime Minister, Chairperson UPA and other high dignitaries.

3025. (5-9-2007) NEW DELHI : Even as the Parliament was fully seized of the Indo-US Nuclear Agreement and was awaiting a full discussion on it the Government constituted a parochial and partisan committee, outside the Parliament, to examine fully the implications of both the Henry J. Hyde US-India Atomic Energy Cooperation Act of 2006, and the commonly called 123 Nuclear Cooperation agreement. This is a deliberate and blatant violation of the Parliament's rights, prerogatives and privileges. This setting up of a private committee is a total negation of the opposition's rights and role in Parliament. It triviliases the high importance of a vital national issue impacting on our national security and the country's strategic autonomy for the next half century. The Government has voluntarily handed over decision making to the CPI (M) and the Left Front. There is now apparently no Central Government effectively holding the reins of office; the Communists have been handed over power to decide the future of India but without any responsibility. This abdication by the Government, of its responsibility is a betrayal of their oath. The NDA cannot accept this. Even now the Government must recognize the perilous path on which they are obstinately set. The NDA demands that our voice in Parliament must be paid heed to. The NDA's demand of a JPC on the issue must be accepted. This is what we expect.

3026. (5-9-2007) NEW DELHI : Government of India in April, 2005 introduced "Rajiv Gandhi Grameen Vidyutikaran Yojana" a scheme of Rural Electricity Infrastructure and Household Electrification with the aim of electrifying all the balance un-electrified villages (except remote villages to be covered by the Ministry of New and Renewable Energy) by the year 2009.

3027. (5-9-2007) NEW DELHI : A Constitutional Amendment Bill for the transfer of the entry of sports from the State List to the Concurrent List was introduced in the Rajya Sabha on 24.11.1988, but was not pursued although it was indicated to cabinet that a majority of State Governments had approved the proposal. The draft Comprehensive National Sports Policy reiterates the need to transfer the subject of "Sports" from the State List to the Concurrent List in the Seventh Schedule of the Constitution of India. The draft is in the consultative process. Detailed discussions are at present underway with all stakeholders, including State Governments. This information was given by Shri Mani Shankar Aiyar, Minister of Panchayati Raj, Youth Affairs & Sports and DoNER in the Lok Sabha today in a written reply to a question by Shri Bhartruhari Mehtab.

3028. (5-9-2007) NEW DELHI : Government are conscious of the need to ensure proper planning and timely preparation for the Commonwealth Games, 2010 and to this end a number of institutional arrangements have been made. These include a Core Group of Ministers (GoM) under the co-Chairmanship of the Minister for Human Resource Development and the Home Minister for coordinating the various works related to the conduct of the Games; an Apex Committee headed by the Minister for Youth Affairs and Sports to oversee preparations; an Organizing Committee (OC) headed by the President, Indian Olympic Association for the conduct of the Games; and a Committee of Secretaries headed by Cabinet Secretary which is responsible for monitoring the implementation of the decisions of the GoM and taking decisions on other related matters. In addition to these arrangements at the Central level, there is a sub-committee under the Chief Minister of Delhi to take decisions in respect of all matters pertaining to infrastructure and other preparations for the Games within the jurisdiction of the Government of NCT of Delhi. The Lt. Governor Delhi has been entrusted with the overall responsibility for matters coming under DDA and with specific reference to security and law and order. Locations for the various competitions/training venues and International Broadcasting Centre (IBC)/Main Press Centre (MPC) have been agreed among the stakeholders. All stakeholders have indicated specific time-lines with reference to key milestones, viz., finalization of detailed designs and estimates, commencement of the tendering process, award of the work, commencement of the work, completion of the work; and handing over to OC. It is expected that work on all the major sports venue infrastructure projects will commence before December, 2007 and the venues will be handed over to the OC by the end of 2009. An Empowered Committee has been set up under the chairmanship of Chief Secretary, GNCTD, with representatives from all the agencies/authorities concerned to facilitate speedy clearances in respect of Games-related projects. Another Committee has been set up by under Secretary, Ministry of Urban Development to facilitate clearances pertaining to the Delhi Urban Arts Commission (DUAC).

3029. (5-9-2007) NEW DELHI : The Minister of State for Textiles, Shri E.V.K.S. Elangovan, informed the Rajya Sabha today, in a written reply to a question by Shri Tapan Kumar Sen and Shri Mohammed Amin that the Jute Advisory Board has been reconstituted vide Order dated 14th May, 2007 for a period of two years. The Minister further informed the House that at present, the Jute Advisory Board has 2 Government official members from non-jute growing States, 8 government official members from jute growing States, 10 non-official members from jute growing States and 11 non-official members from non-jute growing States. Thus, out of the total 31 members of the Board, 18 are from jute growing States.

3030. (5-9-2007) NEW DELHI : The Minister of State for Textiles, Shri E.V.K.S. Elangovan, informed the Rajya Sabha today, in a written reply to a question by Smt. Supriya Sule that on the recommendation of the Working Group constituted by the Planning Commission for the 11th Five Year Plan on Textile and Jute industry the Government has proposed a scheme for the development and growth of technical textiles which is in the process of being approved the competent authority. The Technical Textiles industry is also covered under the centrally sponsored financial assistance schemes like Technology Upgradation Fund Scheme (TUFS) and Scheme for Integrated Textiles Park (SITP).

3031. (5-9-2007) NEW DELHI : Shri Sontosh Mohan Dev, Minister for Heavy Industries & Public Enterprises presented the SCOPE Meritorious Awards in Specialized Fields for the year 2005-06 here today. Presenting the awards, Shri Dev said, "the 11th Plan growth targets, though looked ambitious, are very much in the realm of attainability. In this context, the onerous responsibility of developing infrastructure like power, roads, ports, railways etc. is largely on the public sector. The public sector is considered as growth engine for the economy". The Minister also announced that four more companies-National Aluminum Company Ltd., National Mineral Development Corporation Ltd., Power Grid Corporation of India Limited and Rural Electrification Corporation Limited would also be conferred the Navratna status once they fulfil the criterion of requisite number of non-official directors on their boards. The Standing Conference of Public Enterprises (SCOPE) has instituted six awards in the fields of Environmental Excellence and Sustainable Development; Research & Development and Innovation; Best Practice in Human Resource Management; Corporate Social Responsibility & Responsiveness; Good Corporate Governance; and, Best Managed PSE set up under Section 25.

3032. (5-9-2007) NEW DELHI : Smt. Kanti Singh, Minister of State for Heavy Industries and Public Enterprises inaugurated a three-day International Conference on Industrial Safety and Socio-Economic Growth titled 'Safety Convention, 2007' here today. Inaugurating the conference, the Minister said, "apart from the large industries, even the small industries should also focus on occupational and health safety for improving country's growth and competitiveness in the global market". Expressing concern over the decline of industries in urban India, Smt. Kanti Singh said ' Number of big factories in urban areas has declined from 85,516 to 83,230 between year 2000 and 2005. The major jobs which have come up in recent years is in service sector, followed by construction and transport". More than 300 leading engineers, architects, town planners, designers, building material manufacturers and administrators are taking part in the three-day convention.

3033. (5-9-2007) NEW DELHI : In conformity with the letter and spirit of Part IX of the Constitution, read with Article 243 ZD and the Eleventh Schedule, Centrally Sponsored Schemes (CSS) covering the 29 subjects listed in the Eleventh Schedule of the Constitution are to be planned and implemented by Panchayati Raj Institutions functioning as "institutions of local self-government". While the guidelines in respect of some CSS provide for the centrality of Panchayati Raj Institutions (PRIs), there are other CSS where the PRIs are yet to be assigned a central role. In order to clarify and ensure the role of the PRIs in all CSS, consultations are being held with the Central Ministries concerned by a Review Committee under the aegis of the Cabinet Secretariat, co-chaired by Secretary, Panchayati Raj and Secretary (Coordination & Public Grievances), Cabinet Secretariat. This information was given by Shri Mani Shankar Aiyar, Minister of Panchayati Raj, Youth Affairs & Sports and DoNER in the Lok Sabha today in a written reply to a question by Shri Braja Kishore Tripathy.

3034. (5-9-2007) NEW DELHI : A committee was established vide Cabinet Secretary's Office order No.563/9/2/2007-CA.IV dated 16.8.2007 under the co-chairmanship of Secretary, Panchayati Raj and Secretary(Coordination & Public Grievances) in the Cabinet Secretariat to review the progress in implementing the directions of the Cabinet Secretary dated 8th November, 2004 to all Union Ministries concerned to restructure Centrally Sponsored Schemes to provide for the role of Panchayats in planning and implementation in conformity with the relevant Constitutional provisions. These consultations are likely to be completed with the Ministries concerned by the end of September 2007. This information was given by Shri Mani Shankar Aiyar, Minister of Panchayati Raj, Youth Affairs & Sports and DoNER in the Lok Sabha today in a written reply to a question by Shri Hemlal Murmu.

3035. (5-9-2007) NEW DELHI : No decision has been taken by the Union Government to allocate funds directly to Gram Panchayats. However, one of the goals set by the Government in the National Common Minimum Programme is to ensure that funds going to the Panchayats are neither delayed nor diverted. In pursuance of this goal, a Committee in the Ministry of Panchayati Raj went into this issue in detail and submitted its report in May, 2005. In pursuance of the recommendations of this Committee, the Ministry of Panchayati Raj supports the position that financial inflows meant for Panchayats should first flow into the Consolidated Fund of State Governments, but should then be speedily transferred direct to the Panchayats "without delay or diversion". Releases of funds on the basis of recommendations of the Twelfth Finance Commission and under the BRGF Programme conform to this pattern of fund flow. This information was given by Shri Mani Shankar Aiyar, Minister of Panchayati Raj, Youth Affairs & Sports and DoNER in the Lok Sabha today in a written reply to a question by Shri Harisinh Chavda.

3036. (5-9-2007) NEW DELHI : According to Maharashtra State Electricity Distribution Company Limited (MSEDCL), they are purchasing power from other States through power traders at higher rate. NTPC proposes to set up the Mauda Thermal Power Project (2x500 MW) in Mauda Tehshil of Nagpur District, Maharashtra. Action has been initiated for obtaining necessary clearances including from the State Pollution Control Board (SPCB) and acquisition of land. Public hearing for NOC from SPCB (Maharashtra) has been held on 18th June, 2007. Action has also been initiated for obtaining Environmental clearance from Ministry of Environment & Forests. The project is expected to be commissioned during the 11th Plan period. Maharashtra State Power Generation Company Ltd. (MSGPCL) proposes to add 3,675 MW by way of new capacity addition and replacement of existing units which have completed more than 30 years of operation. MSGPCL is in the process of tying up of basic inputs and obtaining statutory clearances required for these projects. According to the Maharashtra State Electricity Distribution Company Ltd., power traders have sourced power for Maharashtra mainly from West Bengal, Orissa, Sikkim, Kerala, at higher rate. This information was given by the Union Power Minister Shri Sushilkumar Shinde in a written reply to a question in the Rajya Sabha.

3037. (5-9-2007) NEW DELHI : According to the Report of the 17th Electric Power Survey of India, the all India peak demand in the year 2009-10 is estimated to be 1,31,413 MW and the energy requirement is expected to be 848.39 billion units. To meet the growing demand, in addition to other measures such as increasing the inter-regional transmission capacity of the National grid, a generation capacity addition to the tune of over 37,000 MW has been envisaged during the period 2007-08 to 2009-10. Out of this, as on 30th August, 2007, 2265 MW has already been commissioned.

3038. (5-9-2007) NEW DELHI : In Uttarakhand, out of total 15,761 revenue villages, 15199 (96.4%) are electrified. Balance 562 villages are to be electrified by grid (357) and non-grid (171). Out of 11.85 lakhs rural households, 6.87 lakhs rural households are electrified. Out of balance 4.98 lakhs unelectrified households, Uttarakhand Government intends to cover 3.57 lakhs rural household under RGGVY. Ministry of Power has already sanctioned projects for all the 13 districts of Uttarakhand with an outlay of Rs.643.89 crore. The State has reported that works have been carried out in 968 un-electrified and 2332 electrified villages as also release of 38424 rural household connections including 37,016 BPL household connections as on 24th August, 2007. Uttarakhand has so far availed Rs.355.61 crore under RGGVY. The State has reported that the Schedule Tribe villages are also covered in this scheme. However, 171 villages which are far away from grid line and are situated in forest area are meant to be electrified by non-conventional energy sources. Ministry of Power as also Rural Electrification Corporation have been regularly conducting the review meeting and impressing upon the State Govt./state power utility for timely attainment of the sanctioned targets in the State. This information was given by the Union Power Minister Shri Sushilkumar Shinde in a written reply to a question in the Rajya Sabha.

3039. (5-9-2007) NEW DELHI : Department of Science & Technology (DST) is planning to establish a specialized research centre at the national level for initiating holistic studies on Himalayan Glaciology including the effective monitoring all important glaciers to work out options to effectively deal with the emerging situation with increased snow melts in the future. Glaciers in general, including the Himalayan glaciers, are receding. Geological Survey of India (GSI) has been conducting studies on the recession of the Gangotri glacier since 1935. In the eastern Himalayas, which sit in the Ganga basin, glacier melts have been reported. The rate of shrinking of 30.2 km-long Gangotri Glacier in the last three decades has been found to be more than the rate during the earlier decades. Average recession for this period is about 25 meter/year (83 feet/year). Wadia Institute of Himalayan Geology (WIHG) is studying the melting of Himalayan Glaciers in the Garhwal Himalaya, namely, Dokriani and Chorabari glaciers. The Dokriani and Chorabari glaciers have been receding at an average rate of 17.5 m/year between 1991 and 2005, and 10 m/year between 2003 and 2006 respectively. This information was given by the Union Minister for Science & Technology and Earth Sciences Shri Kapil Sibal in a written reply to a question in the Rajya Sabha.

3040. (5-9-2007) NEW DELHI : India is one of the partner countries to the efforts of International Coffee Genome Network (KCGN). ICGN is a worldwide network of scientists from research organizations, universities, industry within the coffee producing and consuming countries. The first founding meeting was held at Paris on 4th to 5th April 2005 which was attended by 27 scientists from 12 countries and 3 other International research organizations including 2 scientists from Coffee Board and one from Centre for Cellular and Molecular Biology (CCMB), Hyderabad. As on today there are 49 individual members and 5 Institutional members. The national funding for the Indian component is being provided by Department of Biotechnology to six institutes. The major efforts of the ICGN concentrate on use and conservation of coffee genetic resources through the application of genetic tools. A coffee genome database has been created by ICGN which is an open source database on coffee genomics and includes comprehensive information on the coffee specific mocrosatelites, ESTs and other bioinformatic tools. The network would facilitate information and resource sharing within the scientific community and will help breeders by providing molecular tools and know-how for precision breeding. The major objectives of ICGN are development of trait specific molecular markers in coffee, formulation of a global and coordinated strategy for coffee genomics, enhancing the inter-institutional commitment to work jointly for value addition by avoiding repetition and to promote opportunities to fund common research. This information was given by the Union Minister for Science & Technology and Earth Sciences Shri Kapil Sibal in a written reply to a question in the Rajya Sabha.

3041. (5-9-2007) NEW DELHI : A Memorandum of Understanding among the Governments of the Republic of India, the Federative Republic of Brazil and the Republic of South Africa on cooperation in the field of Public Administration and Governance is slated to be signed by the respective governments. The main objectives of the cooperation under the proposed MoU are as follows: (i) To consolidate IBSA initiatives and collaboration at regional and global level for promoting good governance. (ii) To promote social and economic development of the people of their respective countries through efficient, accessible, transparent and accountable public service, by resorting to joint efforts and collaboration in the field of Public Administration and Governance. (iii) To strengthen South – South cooperation amongst the three countries and promote trilateral cooperation in the field of Public Administration and Governance in seeking to achieve Millennium Development Goals and sustainable development. The salient features of the proposed MoU are as follows: (i) Cooperation in the field of Public Administration and Governance in the following areas:· Integrated monitoring and evaluation; · E-governance; · Human resources development; · Citizen oriented service delivery; · Anti-corruption and ethics; and · Accountability and transparency. (ii) Working Group on Public Administration set up by the three sides would be responsible for implementation of the MoU. (iii) The Working Group would finalize a programme of action for implementation of the MoU by identifying specific activities for each area of cooperation. (iv) The Working Group would review the progress of implementation of the programme of action and submit a report to the respective competent authorities. The above information was given by the Minister of State in the Ministry of Personnel, Public Grievances and Pensions and Minister of State in the Ministry of Parliamentary Affairs, Shri Suresh Pachouri in written reply to a question in the Lok Sabha today.

3042. (5-9-2007) NEW DELHI : India-Meteorological Department (IMD) is expanding rainfall monitoring network in its modernization plan by adding 1350 Automatic Rain Gauges (ARGs). This is in addition to specific networks set up by States and Central Water Commission (CWC). IMD generates river basin scale quantitative precipitation estimates (QPF) in short range (24-72 hrs) which is utilized by the CWC. Currently, daily Monsson Watch carried out with the rainfall records manually received from States and CWC (from 945 stations covering 62 river basins) are used for assessment of monsson rainfall scenario. This information was given by the Union Minister for Science & Technology and Earth Sciences Shri Kapil Sibal in a written reply to a question in the Rajya Sabha.

3043. (5-9-2007) NEW DELHI : Global System for Mobile Communications based Cellular Mobile Telephone Service being provided by BSNL in the rural areas of Uttar Pradesh (East) Telecom Circle including Sidharth Nagar, Deoria, Basti, Gonda, Dumariaganj Station and Azamgarh districts is working satisfactorily at present. Base Transceiver Station (BTS) – cellsite at Thekma Exchange in Azamgarh has been optimized so as to ensure that the same serves as the primary BTS for the said area. BSNL has also planned to install three new BTSs in adjoining areas of Thekma Exchange in Azamgarh during the current financial year. The cellular mobile network of BSNL is also continuously optimized for its performance and monitoring of the network has been strengthened by BSNL to ensure performance as per the Quality of Service parameters prescribed by Telecom Regulatory Authority of India. This information was given by Dr. Shakeel Ahmad, Minister of State in the Ministry of Communications and Information Technology in the Lok Sabha today in a written reply to a question by Shri Mohd. Mukeem.

3044. (5-9-2007) NEW DELHI : Department of Posts along with NABARD has been disbursing rural credit in select post offices in Tamilnadu State through a pilot project. Department of Posts has been training its staff on operative procedures while NABARD has been providing on identification of Self Help Groups. Remuneration earned is as a percentage of the interest collected on the loan disbursed and not as a fixed sum. This information was given by Dr. Shakeel Ahmad, Minister of State in the Ministry of Communications and Information Technology in the Lok Sabha today in a written reply to a question by Shri Iqbal Ahmed Saradgi.

3045. (5-9-2007) NEW DELHI : The Government has decided to issue a single licence for provision of Internet services including Internet telephony and facility to establish Internet Gateway stations to companies registered under Indian Companies Act, 1956. Foreign Direct Investment ceiling in the Licensee Companies is 74 per cent. This information was given by Dr. Shakeel Ahmad, Minister of State in the Ministry of Communications and Information Technology in the Lok Sabha today in a written reply to a question by Shri Eknath M.Gaikwad and Smt. Nivedita Mane.

3046. (5-9-2007) NEW DELHI : Representations are received from time to time from ex-servicemen of less than 14 years of service, demanding pensionary benefits. Recently, Ex-Servicemen Welfare Society, Kannur has requested for grant of pension to those Ex-Servicemen who have put in less than 14 years of service. The minimum qualifying service required to earn service pension is 20 years for Commissioned Officers and 15 years for Personnel Below Officer Rank. No change in the existing policy is presently contemplated by the Government. This information was given by the Defence Minister Shri AK Antony in a written reply to Shri Subrata Bose in Lok Sabha today.

3047. (5-9-2007) NEW DELHI : Indian Navy is in the process of acquiring the aircraft carrier (ex-Admiral Gorshkov) and three stealth frigates from Russia. Warships are inducted in the Navy as replacement for de-commissioned platforms and for augmenting the strength of the Force. This is a continuous process based on the threat perception and international security environment according to which modernisation plans of the Navy are formulated. A detailed exercise is undertaken to identify appropriate platform. This information was given by the Defence Minister Shri AK Antony in a written reply to Shri Hansraj G Ahir in Lok Sabha today.

3048. (5-9-2007) NEW DELHI : Smt. Pratibha Devisingh Patil, President of India has said that the education system needs to strengthen the values of secularism, democracy, inclusiveness and pluralism. She was giving away National Awards to teachers, here, today. She further said, 'These are the great values enshrined in our Constitution and traditionally developed by our civilization. These values give strength and sustenance not only to our diverse multi-cultural society but also to our country'. 314 teachers received national awards for the year 2005-06. On the occasion, the President underlined the need to upgrade teachers' knowledge, skills and competencies through professional preparation. "Teacher training programmes need to reflect critically the multiple contexts in which schools function and come out with specific solutions relevant to teaching in schools located in urban areas, rural areas, tribal areas and located in disadvantaged regions. The models of pre-service and in-service teacher preparation require critical review. In pre-service teacher education programmes, there is a need for integration between, theory and practices and between subject content and pedagogy", she said. She also emphasised need to develop vocational skills and the role of women in promoting our education objectives. Shri Mohd. Ali Ashraf Fatmi, MOS, HRD said that a good teacher teaches best through his/her own example. He appreciated the dedication, professional competence and services rendered by the teachers for the cause of building the future of the nation. He said, 'The 'National Award' is a token of recognition for your dedication and services rendered towards education. We expect you to play the leadership role in striving towards quality education for all children'.

3049. (5-9-2007) NEW DELHI : Defence Research and Development Organisation (DRDO) has developed many systems and sub-systems, which have been accepted by the Armed Forces and are in use by them. Apart from excellent contributions to the strategic programmes, it has developed missiles, radars, sonars, an advanced weapon system, unmanned aircrafts, command and control system, NBC reconnaissance vehicle, logistic systems, like Armoured Engineer Reconnaissance Vehicle, Multi-span Mobile Bridging system, etc. Projects on Electronic Warfare, Airborne Early Warning and Control (AEW&C) have made commendable progress. Few of the projects have been delayed for genuine technological and field trials and evaluation reasons. Against a set target of Rs. 12072 crore, projects totalling to Rs.11385 crore has been taken up, during X Plan. The project for development of Main Battle Tank, Arjun was completed in March 1995 with a total expenditure of Rs.305.60 crore, with delivery of 12 prototypes and 15 pre-production series of Arjun Tanks. Army has placed an indent of 124 MBT Arjun on Ordnance Factory Board/Heavy Vehicle Factory, and deliveries commenced. Light Fighter Plane, Tejas is in Initial Operational Clearance phase. Expenditure incurred in Full Scale Engineering Development (FSED) Phase-I was Rs.2188 crore and in phase-II is Rs.2195.76 crore. IAF has already placed order for one squadron of Aircraft to Initial Operational Clearance standards. Army has evaluated the MBT in field trials and accepted it. A few minor defects were noticed during field evaluation of production tanks, which were analysed jointly by DRDO and Army. These production defects were rectified by DRDO and HVF and clearance for production of MBT Arjun has been given by Army. This information was given by the Defence Minister Shri AK Antony in a written reply to Shri Surendra Lath in Rajya Sabha today.

3050. (5-9-2007) NEW DELHI : At the meeting of the 14th ASEAN Regional Forum (ARF) in Manila on 2 August, 2007, India offered assistance to ARF member states in building capacity to ensure the safety and security of sea-lanes passing through the region. India will design and conduct a training module on maritime security specifically for the ARF Member States, on the themes of anti-piracy, search & rescue, offshore and port security, anti-smuggling and narcotics control and anti-poaching operations. The above information was given by the External Affairs Minister, Shri Pranab Mukherjee in written reply to a question in the Lok Sabha today.

3051. (5-9-2007) NEW DELHI : The Bill for setting up the Airport Economic Regulatory Authority (AERA) was introduced in the Lok Sabha today by the Minister for Civil Aviation Shri Praful Patel. Following is the Statement of Objects and Reasons tabled along with the Bill: Most of the civil airports, including civil enclaves at Defence Airports, are presently controlled by the Airports Authority of India (Airports Authority) in the Ministry of Civil Aviation. The Airports Authority, with the approval of the Central Government, fixes the aeronautical charges for the airports under its control, prescribes the performance standards of all airports and monitors the same. The Airport Infrastructure Policy formulated in 1997 provides for the private sector participation for improving quality, efficiency and increasing competition. As a result of this initiative, Greenfield airports are now coming up at Bangalore and Hyderabad in Public-Private-Partnership. A private airport is already fully operational at Cochin. Delhi and Mumbai Airports are also being restructured through the Joint Venture route for modernization and development. The trends indicate growing competition and a requirement of level playing field amongst different categories of airports in future.

3052. (5-9-2007) NEW DELHI : The 10th annual meeting of the National Oil Spill Contingency Plan will be held in New Delhi on 07 September, 2007 to review the preparedness for national oil spill and disaster contingencies and coordination in the implementation stage. The meeting will be chaired by the DG Coast Guard Vice Admiral R F Contractor and is likely to be attended by representatives from about 50 government departments, ports, oil industry, oil exploration units and state pollution control boards. The meeting will offer a forum to resolve issues pertaining to organizations involved in pollution response and procedures involving more than one agency. The delegates will also review the progress made in developing upto 700 tonnes Tier-1 oil spill response facility by various stakeholders. The protection of marine environment against oil spill is a challenge confronting the country in the backdrop of growing trade through sea and increase in shipping traffic. The oil transported along the Indian coast amounts to 70% of the world's oil traffic. Over the years the Coast Guard, in coordination with other resource agencies, has checked 65 oil spills, averting a hazard to marine environment. Deliberations on ways and means of preventing oil spills by bringing in strict legislations and punitive actions for defaulting agencies will also be pursued during the meeting. The availability of new technology like pollution response software, consultancy, pollution response cum dredging vessels available at national/ international level will also be discussed. Presentations on "Environment Risk Analysis – An Overview" and "Marine pollution by highly noxious substances" have also been arranged during the meeting.

3053. (5-9-2007) NEW DELHI : The Ministry of Tribal Affairs has set up Eklavya Model Residential Schools (EMRSs) to provide quality education to Scheduled Tribes students from class VI to XII in different States and in order to enable them to avail of higher and professional level educational courses as well as better job opportunities. This was stated by Shri P.R. Kyndiah, Minister for Tribal Affairs in a reply to a question by Dr. Gyan Prakash Pilania in Rajya Sabha. He further stated that in the State of Rajasthan, seven EMRSs have been set up in the districts of Udaipur (1), Banswara (2), Dungarpur (1), Sirohi (1),

Tonk (1) and Baran (1). Two more EMRSs have been sanctioned to the State Government of Rajasthan during the current financial year. He further stated that in these schools the teacher pupil ratio is 1:30 and classroom pupil ratio is 1:50. The State Government of Rajasthan has reported that during the academic session 2006-07, average results for the class X board examination have been 42.58%. Shri Kyndiah informed that to improve the EMRSs in the country the recurring grant per school has already been enhanced from Rs. 30.00 lakh to Rs. 72.50 lakh.

3054. (5-9-2007) NEW DELHI : The Ministry of Women and Child Development is implementing the Swadhar Scheme which provides holistic and integrated services to abandoned and widow women including shelter, food, clothing and care. The objective of the scheme is to rehabilitate them socially and economically. But, Ministry of Women and Child Development has no separate scheme to provide pension to such women. This was stated by Smt. Renuka Chowdhury, Minister for Women and Child Development in a reply to a question by Dr. Gyan Prakash Pilania in Rajya Sabha. She further stated that the Ministry of Women and Child Development has advised the State Governments to formulate a time bound programme to establish Swadhar Shelter Homes in urban, rural and remote areas for women in difficult circumstances who are without any social or economic support, on the basis of number of widows/divorced/separated women of different ages, in rural and urban, she added.

3055. (5-9-2007) NEW DELHI : The Government has taken a number of steps to increase the effectiveness of the delivery of services under ICDS scheme. These include: a) The scheme has been expanded twice in the year 2005-06 and 2006-07 during the Tenth Five Year Plan. b) The Government has doubled the financial norms for supplementary nutrition from Rs. 1 to Rs. 2/- per beneficiary per day. c) From the year 2005-06, 50% cost of supplementary nutrition is also being shared with the States/UTs.d) A Central Monitoring Unit (CMU) has been set up at National Institute of Public Cooperation and Child Development (NIPCCD) to monitor the scheme through independent profession organization, institution in each State/UT. This would be in addition to the monitoring mechanism in place at present.e) A National Level Monitoring Committee has also been constituted under the chairpersonship of MOS (WCD) to oversee the entire functioning of the Scheme and to ensure that the services are deleivered to the Target groups in an effective manner and the objectives of the scheme are fulfilled within the overall framework of the ICDS scheme. f) Constant emphasis on regular supply of supplementary nutrition as per schematic norms and ensure effective convergence of health, nutrition, education and safe drinking water services under various programmes. This was stated by Smt. Renuka Chowdhury, Minister for Women and Child Development in a reply to a question by Shri Datta Meghe in Rajya Sabha.

3056. (5-9-2007) NEW DELHI : The Government has approved construction of 27 road links along the India-China border at an estimated cost of Rs. 912 crore.

The Government has simultaneously initiated action for obtaining forest and environmental clearances wherever required. Upgradation of infrastructure along borders is continuously reviewed. These road link projects are expected to be completed by 2012-13. An amount of Rs. 3.16 crore has been released to the executing agencies for the preliminary works. This information was given by the Minister of State for Home, Smt. V.Radhika Selvi in written reply to a question in the Rajya Sabha today.

3057. (5-9-2007) NEW DELHI : The Unorganised Sector Workers Social Security Bill and formulation of social security scheme for unorganised workers are under active consideration and all efforts are being made to introduce the Bill during the current Session of Parliament. The modalities of the scheme and coverage thereof are being examined. This information was given in the Rajya Sabha today by Shri Oscar Fernandes, the Minister of State (Independent Charge) of Labour and Employment, in a written reply to a question by Smt. N. P. Dugra.

3058. (5-9-2007) NEW DELHI : Under the provision of the Minimum Wages Act, 1948, the State Government of Orissa has notified the rates of minimum wages for unskilled beedi workers at Rs. 70/- per day with effect from May 1, 2007 as applicable throughout the State. This information was given in the Rajya Sabha today by Shri Oscar Fernandes, Minister of State (Independent Charge) of Labour and Employment, in a written reply to a question by Ms. Pramila Bohidar.

3059. (5-9-2007) NEW DELHI : The matter regarding rate of interest for the year 2006-07 was placed before the Central Board of Trustees, Employees' Provident Fund in its 179th meeting held on March 10, 2007. However, the matter was deferred as it required more discussions at various levels. Subsequently, the Board in its special meeting held on July 23, 2007 recommended the rate of interest for the year 2006-07 as 8.5 per cent. As per the provisions of the Employees' Provident Fund Scheme 1952, interest is required to be credited to the account of each member at such rate as may be determined in such a manner that there should be no overdrawal on the Interest Suspense Account as a result of debit thereto of the interest credited to members' accounts. This information was given in the Rajya Sabha today by Shri Oscar Fernandes, Minister of State (Independent Charge) of Labour and Employment, in a written reply to a question by Shri Rajkumar Dhoot.

3060. (5-9-2007) NEW DELHI : There has been a growing demand for relay and transmission of Punjabi programmes. Prasar Bharati have informed that w.e.f. 5.8.2000 Regional Language Satellite channel DD-Punjabi is available all over India beaming Punjabi serials and programmes. Punjabi language programmes are being telecast on DD-1 in regional platform from 3.00 p.m. to 8.00 p.m. for Punjab State which are also available on satellite channel in the entire country. Besides this, round the clock transmission on DD-Punjabi is in Punjabi language. This information was given by Minister of Information & Broadcasting and Parliamentary Affairs, Shri P. R. Dasmunsi in written reply to a question in Rajya Sabha today.

3061. (5-9-2007) NEW DELHI : The statutory inquiry by Commissioner of Railway Safety, Eastern Circle, Kolkata (Ministry of Civil Aviation, Government of India) into collision of 288 Dn Katwa-Barddhaman (NG), Passenger train with a truck No. WMK-1856 at unmanned level crossing No. 5-D at km 4/4-5 between Kamnara Halt and Barddhaman Railway Stations on Katwa-Barddhaman, Narrow Gauge, Single Line, Non – Electrified Section of Howrah Division of Eastern Railway at about 09.33 hours on 05.08.2007 has revealed that the accident had occurred due to failure of person other than Railway Staff.One person was killed, five grievously injured and thirteen others had suffered simple injuries as a result of this accident.

3062. (5-9-2007) NEW DELHI : Finance Minister, Shri P. Chidambaram has approved 17 Foreign Direct Investment proposals recommended by Foreign Investment Promotion Board (FIPB) in its meeting held on 31st August, 2007. The approval amounts to Rs. 284.7695 crore. The proposals are related to Ministries /Departments, namely,Agriculture & Cooperation, Chemicals & Petro-chemicals, Commerce, Consumer Affairs, Heavy Industry, Information & Broadcasting, Telecommunications and Economic Affairs.

3063. (5-9-2007) NEW DELHI : National Knowledge Commission (NKC) has recommended that while the role of University Grants Commission (UGC) would be re-defined to focus on the disbursement of grants to and maintenance of, public institutions in higher education, the entry regulatory functions of the AICTE, the Medical Council of India and Bar Council of India would be performed by the Independent Regulatory Authority for Higher Education (IRAHE), so that their role would be limited to that of professional associations. However, recommendations of the NKC are in the public domain for wider debate among all stake-holders. A proposal to set up a 'National Commission on Higher Education' is under consideration in the light of the observations of various concerned stake-holders. This information was given by the Minister of State for Human Resource Development Smt. D. Purandeswari in a written reply to a question raised by Sh. B.K. Hariprasad in Rajya Sabha today.

3064. (5-9-2007) NEW DELHI : The Sarva Shiksha Abhiyan has made considerable progress in enhancing access to elementary education. From 4.4 crore children who were out of school in 2001, the number of out of school children has now come down to 75.97 lakhs as on March, 2007. Education Cess @ 2% on major Central Taxes was levied through Finance (No.2) Act, 2004.

3065. (6-9-2007) NEW DELHI : The Cabinet Committee on Economic Affairs today gave its approval for: (i) Sanctioning of Jallaram Shaft project (2.285 Million tones per annum) of Singareni Collieries Company Ltd. (SCCL) for a net capital requirement of Rs.467.78 crore and total outlay of Rs.512.87 crore including an Interest During Construction (IDC) of Rs.14.35 crore.(ii) For flexibility in the implementation stage within the approved cost estimates to respond to improvements in technology and equipments which would result in improved profitability and productivity parameters. Upon completion of the project, 2.285 Mtpa of coal would be produced and will cater to the demand of NTPC Ramagundam and other cement units. Singareni Collieries Company Ltd. is a Public Sector company owned by Government of Andhra Pradesh (GOAP) with equity sharing of 51:49 between GOAP and Government of India (GOI). At present, SCCL has 45 Underground and 12 Opencast operating mines and the Company produced 37.71 million tones (Mt) of coal in the year 2006-07. Jallaram Shaft Project is located in Karimnagar District of Andhra Pradesh.

3066. (6-9-2007) NEW DELHI : The Cabinet Committee on Economic Affairs today gave its approval for continuation of Centrally Sponsored Scheme of Post Matric Scholarship to students belonging to Scheduled Castes in its existing form, with an anticipated expenditure of Rs.5000 crore, during the 11th five-year plan (2007-08 to 2011-12) with modifications to the extent that (a) in case of professional courses it is available to only those students who are admitted against 'free seats' whether in government or private institutions and (b) in case of private institutions where admission is only the basis of 12th standard examination marks, there shall be a bench mark of 60% for availing the scholarship. CCEA also approved the enhancement of 10th Five Year Plan Outlay from Rs.1558 crore to Rs.1822.45 crore. The Post Matric Scholarship Scheme is an open-ended scheme. All the SC students, whose parents annual income does not exceed Rs.1.00 lakh, will be benefited.

3067. (6-9-2007) NEW DELHI : The Cabinet Committee on Economic Affairs today gave its approval for continuation of the Rural Employment Generation Programme (REGP) in its present form, beyond 31 March, 2007 till 31st March 2008 so that the employment generation through encouragement of entrepreneurs to set up units which are in full swing in the rural areas, goes on uninterruptedly. CCEA also gave its approval for an expenditure of Rs.445 crore towards REGP during the year. The continuation of the REGP would result in generation of 7.04 lakh additional employment opportunities in the rural areas during the year.

3068. (6-9-2007) NEW DELHI : The Union Cabinet today gave its approval for launching of the Health Insurance Scheme for the Workers in the Unorganized Sector. The said Scheme would facilitate health insurance cover to the workers in the unorganized sector. The Scheme will be launched in a phased manner for BPL workers / families in the unorganized sector. The scheme will be formally launched on 2nd October, 2007 when States will be asked to formulate projects. The following would be the criteria of eligibility under this scheme : Unorganised sector workers belong to BPL category and their family members (a family unit of five) will be the beneficiaries. It shall be the responsibility of the implementing agencies to verify the eligibility of the unorganized sector workers and his family members who are proposed to be benefited. The beneficiaries will be issued smart cards for the purpose of identification.

3069. (6-9-2007) NEW DELHI : The Union Cabinet today gave its approval for introduction of the revised 'Unorganized Sector Workers' Social Security Bill, 2007 in Parliament. The proposal would facilitate formulation of social security schemes for the unorganized sector workers.

3070. (6-9-2007) NEW DELHI : The Union Cabinet today gave its approval for establishment of National Institute of Science Education and Research (NISER) at Bhubaneswar at an estimated cost of Rs. 823.19 crore and also creation of 761 posts in academic, scientific, technical, administrative and auxiliary categories. NISER will start functioning initially from the campus of Institute of Physics (IOP) and its academic programme will start from September, 2007. The said institute will conduct the following programmes in science education for bright and meritorious students selected on all-India basis : a) An integrtated 5 year M.Sc. programme in the core and emerging branches of Basic Sciences to students after their 10+2 Higher Secondary schooling. This in turn will be integrated with Ph.D. programme on the one hand and employment in various R&D organizations and industry in the country on the other. b) Integrated m.Sc. + Ph.D after B.Sc from other Universities. c) Ph. D. programme after M.Sc. from other universities.

3071. (6-9-2007) NEW DELHI : The Union Cabinet today gave its approval for constitution of Council for Promotion of Overseas Employment (CPOE) by a resolution of the Government. The Council will perform the following functions : i) Study, monitor, research and analyze employment potential in the world manpower market. ii) Initiate, Institute and monitor skill development programmes and standardize skill certification, by coordinating with concerned agencies / organizations in Government & Private Sector.

3072. (6-9-2007) NEW DELHI : It's a matter of very deep concern that the Department of Personnel & Training (DOPT), Government of India, has issued a directive to all the State Governments and U.T. to ensure that Muslim Policemen be posted in Police Stations and posts with large Muslim population and there should be more Muslim teachers and health personnel in Muslim dominated areas . This directive apart from its serious constitutional vulnerability has very dangerous and sinister implications for the unity and integrity of India . In fact this directive is reminiscent of the frequent demand which the Muslim league used to raise during the pre-partition days. After India became free the framers of the Constitution, who were great leaders though, took steps for preservation of linguistic, cultural, educational rights of minorities as also freedom of religion; they specifically turned down the demand for communal employment, communal policing, communal budgeting, and communal electorate. There were demands for these but as leaders of foresight they knew that this would create foundations for further division and weaken the unity and integrity of the Country. The BJP strongly believes in justice for all and appeasement of none and that minorities including Muslims should be given good education training and scientific knowledge. This is to be noted that in the sixty years of India's independence the Congress Party has ruled at the Centre directly or, indirectly for fifty two years with the shallow claim of secular politics and the vote of Muslims and if the condition of these minorities are not satisfactory they have to do a lot of explanation themselves. However, it is self evident that the present dangerous and divisive circular is the by-product of compensatory politics being a fallout of the self created mess of the UPA government pertaining to the Nuclear deal with USA. It is very disturbing to note that the Congress Party has not learnt any lessons from the dangerous consequences of compensatory politics in spite of the Shahbano issue of the 1980s. Is it just fair reasonable and in national interest at all to presume that even after sixty years of India's independence, a non Muslim police officer cannot protect Muslims. What message are we giving, more particularly when India is facing an all out attack from terrorist and their patrons inside and outside. Would it not openly encourage terrorist to boldly demand that all investigation against them is farce because the investigating team did not had Muslim officers or, that they would not face the trial unless there is a Muslim Judge. The mute voices which we hear in this regard now would only become louder and stronger. What happens if other communities also start making similar demands that they should be policed by officers of their own community. The very idea of India governed by rule of law and constitutional norms would become a casuality. This is wholly unacceptable and the BJP would oppose it with all the might at its command. It would also appeal to all the right thinking Indians to raise in one voice against this sinister design against India.

3073. (6-9-2007) NEW DELHI : The Union Cabinet today gave its approval for signing of a Bilateral Investment Promotion and protection Agreement with Uruguay and the ratification thereof. The said Agreement will increase investment flow between India and Uruguay.

3074. (6-9-2007) NEW DELHI : The Union Cabinet today gave its approval to the following proposals : i) To establish Translational Health Science and Technology Institute under the Department of Bio-Technology as an autonomous institution, with a total cost of Rs. 98.00 crore ii) To set up an extramural centre which will over a period of seven years generate revenue for meeting 50% of the recurring expenditure excluding salaries and infrastructure upgradation. The Translational Health Science and Technology Institute will facilitate development, optimization and evaluation of technologies for public health in respect of bio-technologies by concerted work through an inter-disciplinary team.

3075. (6-9-2007) NEW DELHI : Congress Spokespeson Shri Abhishek Singhvi said that the NDA obviously converted itself into the "Never Do Anything" Opposition. They are an Opposition who comes, who disrupts and departs. Yesterday, it was Sachar. The NDA is the "Never Do Anything" Opposition. It is an Opposition, which comes, which disrupts and which departs. Yesterday, it was a national issue of the Sachar report. Today it is another issue of equal national importance the nuclear issue, the civilian energy cooperation issue. Issues don't matter. What matters is that national issues of pressing national importance are like cannel fodder in the game of political one upmanship which the NDA believes in. It obviously does not matter to them as to whether a NSG security agreement is good for India if so how good in what way it is good it doesn't matter to them to discuss and debate and understand whether the Hyde Act overrides the 123 agreement. It does not matter to them to discuss whether the agreement is the national interest or not. None of these things matter because friends you have before you the "National Disruptive Alliance". You have before you "Naturally Destructive Alternative". Unfortunately it appears that they have become habitual offenders in this regard. The Congress feels concern and calls upon them to stop this repeated established practice if parliament is to have continued relevance as a national institution. We call ourselves rightly and proudly a Parliamentary democracy and that Parliamentary democracy has now been reduced to half at best only a "democracy". The people who do this have to stop, they have to face the nation, they have to provide answers as to what why are they apprehensive even about the debate. To a question on whether the house should be adjourned sine die, Shri Singhvi said it is for them to answer. We have been making all the efforts. Even today we were ready for the nuclear debate. You will get an answer to this question when you will see the conduct of the Opposition in the House. We cannot answer this in advance. You must ask the Opposition as to how many times or for how long they will continue to do this. If the Opposition continues to disrupt the proceedings of the Parliament then it will a natural death of the Parliament. No need to ask this question as the House is being adjourned daily sine die. The Opposition with its behaviour is adjourning the House daily sine die. To another question, he said so put premiums on disruption, put a premium on doing something unprecedented and give in ridiculous demands.

3076. (6-9-2007) NEW DELHI : The Union Cabinet today gave its approval for signing the Agreement between India and Egypt on foreign convicted prisoners to be transferred to their home countries. This decision would enable the prisoners to be near to their families and would help in the process of their social rehabilitation.

3077. (6-9-2007) NEW DELHI : The Union Cabinet today gave its approval for signing the Treaty between India and united Mexican States on Mutual Legal Assistance in Criminal Matters. Similar Treaties / Agreements on Mutual Legal Assistance in Criminal Matters have been signed with Switzerland, Turkey, United Kingdom, Canada, Russian Federation, France, Kyrgyzstan, Kazakhstan, united Arab Emirates, Uzbekistan, Mongolia, Tajikistan, Ukraine, United States of America, South Africa, Bahrain, Thailand, Kuwait, South Korea, Singapore, Belarus, Mauritius and Spain. The Treaty aims at providing an effective bilateral framework in matters of investigation, prosecution and suppression of crime through cooperation and mutual legal assistance in criminal matters.

3078. (6-9-2007) NEW DELHI : The Union Cabinet today gave its approval for signing the Extradition Treaty between India and united Mexican States and also ratification the same. The Treaty would provide a legal framework for seeking extradition of terrorists and other criminals from and to the United Mexican States.

3079. (6-9-2007) NEW DELHI : The Union Cabinet today gave its approval to the following proposals :-1. Outsourcing of front-end activities of passport issuance through an open bidding process to a Service Provider(s), setting up of 68 Passport Facilitation Centres and use of the current Passport Offices as Passport Back-Offices. 2. Outsourcing of dispatch of passports to India post. 3. Upgradation of information Technology, with uniform procedures, in use in passport issuance system, setting up of a Central Printing unit and online links with concerned police authorities. 4. Permit the Service provider(s) to levy a fee, to be decided through an open bidding process, over and above the Government fee for each service so as to enable him recover his costs. 5. improvement in the working conditions in Passport Back-Offices at a cost of Rs. 8 crores. 6. Setting up of a Project Management Unit for implementation of the project. 7. Establishing a Special Purpose Vehicle (SPV) at an appropriate time for the management, supervision and monitoring of the project. The Passport Seva project will result in delivery of passport-related services to the citizens in a timely, transparent, more accessible and reliable manner and in a comfortable environment through streamlined processes and a committed, trained and motivated workforce. The Project will be implemented over a period of 19 months by the Ministry of External Affairs.

3080. (6-9-2007) NEW DELHI : The Union Cabinet today gave its approval for construction of the Chancery, residences and common community facilities for the Embassy of India in Kathmandu within the India house Estate at a revised cost estimate of Rs. 188.22 crores including refundable VAT. Presently, The Embassy offices are located in old barrack type, dilapidated structures scattered all over the India House Estate in an unplanned manner. These structures, besides being totally inadequate for meeting the current space requirements of the Embassy, are in a state of severe deterioration. There is an urgent need to replace these as they also pose potential security risks. The present condition of the offices and many of the residences is very poor, reflecting adversely on India's image. There is also a need to utilize the vacant land available on the India House Estate for constructing residences for the officers and staff living in hired accommodation to save on rentals. This decision will facilitate to construct a Chancery complex in Kathmandu that is imperative. It will meet the present space requirements of the Mission and commensurate with India's high profile presence in Nepal.

3081. (6-9-2007) NEW DELHI : The Union Cabinet today gave its approval for signing the Bilateral Cooperation Agreement between India and Mongolia in the field of Health and medical Science for a period of three years. The said Agreement shall facilitate cooperation between India and Mongolia in the field of Health and Medical Science on the basis of equality, reciprocity and mutual benefit.

3082. (6-9-2007) NEW DELHI : The Union Cabinet today gave its approval to the MoU signed between India and Italy on February 15, 2007 on Indo-Italian Renewable Energy cooperation. The MoU will establish New and Renewable Energy Cooperation between Italian and Indian entities with the aim of developing new and renewable energy technologies.

3083. (6-9-2007) NEW DELHI : Prof. Saifuddin Soz, the Union Minister of Water Resources has said that Ground water is a very important and vital resource in our drinking water supply, agricultural and industrial water needs. This resources has, however, come under stress due to its over-exploitation in many areas of the country. Addressing at a function on "Demonstration of Rain Water Harvesting and Artificial Recharge of Ground Water", Prof. Soz expressed his concern that Delhi is one of the States where ground water level has fallen considerably. The ground water in this area and in its vicinity was about 6.50 meters below ground surface in the year 2001. It is now fallen to a level of 10 to 12 meters blow ground surface. This clearly establishes the decline in the level of ground water as per data of Central Ground Water Board. There are in fact many areas in Delhi which are facing ground water over-exploitation and decline in the level of ground water.

3084. (6-9-2007) NEW DELHI : The journey of Civil Aviation in India began in 1932 when J.R.D. Tata flew the first weekly mail service from Karachi to Mumbai en-route to Chennai. By 1947, private airlines were carrying 2,50,000 passengers in India. However, this was not enough. The air transport sector was nationalized in 1953. Our national carriers, Air India and Indian Airlines were allowed monopoly over the skies. A vast network of airports and airstrips was created. The monopoly regime in the public sector, while was suitable for initial growth, gave rise to various systematic inefficiencies. High tariff regime kept aviation out of the reach of a vast majority of our population. A large number of airports/air strips remained unused. On the other hand, the airports at major stations were unable to handle traffic. The need for greater liberalization was felt in 1989 itself when a new policy was enunciated. The monopoly of national carriers was dismantled in 1994 and a large number of private carriers entered the domestic skies. The increased competition led to greater connectivity, better services and higher growth. Despite occasional hiccups such as the 9/11 aftermath and SARS scare in South East Asia, Civil Aviation has shown a healthy growth.

3085. (6-9-2007) NEW DELHI : Shri Vayalar Ravi, Minister of Overseas Indian Affairs, has made a statement in the Lok Sabha today on Emigration Clearance Requirement Suspension (ECRS). Following is the text of his statement: "I rise to share with the members of this house an important reform measure under the Emigration Act that I propose to implement for the benefit of a large number of poor people. Under the Emigration Act, 1983 a person holding a passport as Emigration Check Required (ECR) is required to obtain emigration clearance from the Protector of Emigrants (POE) before leaving the country for overseas employment. This is a statutory requirement. The Emigration Act does not cover

ECR passport holders who travel overseas for visits other than for employment. However, for the last two decades administrative instructions have been in force requiring them to obtain Emigration Clearance Requirement Suspension or what is commonly referred to as ECRS. Sir, the ECRS system has no statutory basis. No other country imposes such restrictions on International travel. The ECRS system has led to considerable inconvenience and harassment to passengers. It has resulted in corruption in POE offices and a nexus between unscrupulous recruiting agents and middleman resulting in the exploitation of a large number of poor people. Sir, the last year over 5.5 lakh people who travelled overseas for purposes other than employment had to obtain ECRS. The ECRS system, which has no statutory basis is retrograde.

3086. (6-9-2007) NEW DELHI : An Indian Air Force contingent comprising 29 Air Warriors alongwith an IL-76 aircraft would be participating in joint Indo-Russian Indra 07 Exercise from 11 Sep 07 till 20 Sep 07 at Pskov in Russia. Ex Indra 07 is an airborne exercise in which there would be joint participation between the airborne forces of Russia, Indian Army and the Indian Air Force. The Indian Air Force team, led by Gp Capt SRK Nair, would be participating in paradrop and other exercise manoeuvres at Pskov near St Petersburg in Russia. This 10 day coy level exercise is based on the theme of counter terrorism. Exercise Indra 07 would give boost to the bilateral defence cooperation between India & Russia. The exercise is also very important from training point of view as the Indian Air Force would familiarize with Russian training aspects and understand the counter terrorism doctrine of the host Nation. The exercise also provides an opportunity to practice free fall technique with highly experienced diving team in the world. It may be recalled that in Oct 2005 Exercise Indra 05 was held in India in which three IL-76 from Russia along with their airborne forces had participated. During exercise Indra 05 heavy drops and combat training and training was done between participants. Exercise Indra 07 poses unique challenges for flying. The accuracy of drops is an absolute necessity to success of such operations. The IAF crew would be maintaining accurate flying parameters while negotiating unknown terrains and changing weather conditions for the success of the operations.

3087. (6-9-2007) NEW DELHI : The Union Minister for Water Resources, Prof. Saifuddin Soz has assured West Bengal that the Centre would extend full assistance to the State in tackling various flood management, anti-erosion and irrigation problems confronting the State. Prof. Soz who had a long discussion in his office with an All Party delegation of West Bengal comprising Ministers and MLAs, assured them that West Bengal Government's proposals would be processed immediately as and when these are received. The West Bengal delegation, which was led by Dr. Surya Kanta Mishra, Panchayat, Rural Development, ESI and Biotechnology Minister comprised about two dozen MLAs and 3 Ministers including Mr. Sailen Sarkar, Minister for Parliamentary Affairs and Environment Departments,

Shri Subhas Naskar, Minister for Irrigation and Water Ways Department and Smt. Rekha Goswami, Minister for Self Help Group and Self Employment Department. The delegation submitted a memorandum to the Union Minister incorporating their demands. Prof. Soz told the delegation that Teesta river is being considered as a national project, against a scientific criteria, alongwith other rivers, but no decision has been taken as yet. Problems pertaining to Farrakha and Teesta were also discussed in detail. SK/BS.

3088. (6-9-2007) NEW DELHI : Under the Scheme of Non-Lapsable Central Pool of Resources (NLCPR) the State Governments of the North Eastern Region submit prioritized project proposals annually to the Ministry for the Development of the North Eastern Region (MDONER). These lists are available on the website of MDONER under the head of 'NLCPR'. State-wise they can be seen under sub head : "b. *Priority List of Projects*". These details are also available on the Ministry's website under the head of "NLCPR" and State-wise sub head: "d. *Retained Projects*". Almost all the projects sanctioned under NLCPR are implemented by the State Governments concerned. In order to enhance the pace of implementation of these projects by the North-Eastern States, the Ministry is using following mechanism/processes: i) Project-wise progress of implementation is reviewed on the basis of Quarterly Progress Reports (QPR). ii) Chief Secretaries of the State Governments are required to hold quarterly meetings to review the progress of implementation of on-going projects under NLCPR. iii) States are required to carry out project inspections periodically. iv) A nodal officer for each project is made responsible for project implementation and monitoring. v) Field inspections are carried out by officers of the Ministry of DONER. Where the slow implementation of a project causes concern, State Governments are reminded through letters from various levels, including the Minister for the Development of the North-Eastern Region. We have recently introduced monthly reviews through video-conferences with officers of State Governments. In addition, for closer monitoring, the data base of NLCPR projects has been computerized and officers in the Ministry of DONER, as well as officials concerned in the States, have been trained for online data entry as well as retrieval. This information was given by Shri Mani Shankar Aiyar, Minister of Panchayati Raj, Youth Affairs & Sports and DoNER in the Rajya Sabha today in a written reply to a question by Shri Matilal Sarkar.

3089. (6-9-2007) NEW DELHI : Railways have budgeted for a 'cash surplus of Rs.16082 crore after dividend' in the current year. This cash surplus is utilized to finance the Railways' Plan for augmentation of track & rolling stock and replacement & renewal of the Railway infrastructure. At present, around Rs.218 crore have been sanctioned for various works costing above Rs.50 lakh to bring about improvement in sanitary conditions of service buildings (including station buildings), Railway colonies and improving the condition of coaches including provision of green toilets. In the current year's Plan, an amount of Rs.23 crore (*i.e.*, 0.14% of the above cash surplus) has been provided for undertaking these works. Works valuing less than Rs.50 lakh are undertaken by zonal railways under their powers. Apart from above, about Rs.800 cr is to be spent on the sanitation of service buildings (including stations), residential colonies & welfare buildings and the coaches from out of the working expenses of the Railways which are incurred before arriving at the above surplus. A special campaign has been launched to mark the year 2007 as 'cleanliness year'. Frontline staff are being imparted 'on the job customer care training' besides the class room training for a period of one year or so. A number of stations have been selected on Indian Railways for developing them as Clean Train Stations. Railways are also making special efforts to improve the standards of cleanliness and hygiene in trains with special emphasis on rake cleaning in the depots during maintenance by going in for mechanized cleaning arrangements, enroute cleaning at Clean Train Stations wherever commissioned, cleaning during terminal attention at the other ends, comprehensive cockroach and rodent control in trains etc. This information was given by the Minister of State for Railways Shri R.Velu in written reply to a question in the Lok Sabha today.

3090. (6-9-2007) NEW DELHI : Automatic Ticket Vending Machines (ATVMs) have not yet been installed on Indian Railways for disbursing journey tickets. However, Platform Ticket Vending Machines are functional at Patna, Muzaffarpur, Gaya, Bangalore city, Bangalore Cantt., Mysore, Yeshwantpur and Krishnarajpuram stations of Indian Railways. Provision of approximately 6000 ATVMs at approximately 1400 locations has been sanctioned. These are proposed to be installed through 'Public Private Partnership' model subject to successful implementation of pilot project. Yes, Sir. A pilot project for installation of approximately 300 smart card based ATVMs in suburban stations of Central and Western Railways in Mumbai area will be undertaken by the end of year 2007. This information was given by the Minister of State for Railways Shri R.Velu in written reply to a question in the Lok Sabha today.

3091. (6-9-2007) NEW DELHI : The Railways have taken following steps to upgrade the security at sensitive stations:- 1. Unauthorized entry / exit points are being reviewed for closure. 2. Close Circuit Television and Cameras have been installed at important railway stations and trained staffs are put to monitor suspicious movements or persons on the platforms and other station areas. 3. At main entry points to the platforms, Door Frame Metal Detectors have been installed. 4. Public address system is being used at all important railway stations cautioning the passengers about precautions to be taken. 5. Strength of Dog Squad is being augmented. 6. Constant drives are being conducted against unauthorized passengers/ undesirable elements in trains and railway premises. 7. Railway Protection Force personnel have been briefed thoroughly for keeping effective vigil on the suspects boarding and alighting the trains at the stations. In addition to these measures modern security gadgets are being procured. Efforts are also being made to fill-up the vacancies in RPF and further augment the strength. All passengers holding valid tickets for journey and platform ticket holders are allowed to enter the platforms. Regular checks are conducted in association with police to check the entry of unauthorized persons on platforms.

3092. (6-9-2007) NEW DELHI : The sales of CFLs in India has grown from about 20 million in 2003 to more than 90 million in 2006. This has been provided by Bureau of Energy Efficiency, Ministry of Power. The Government of India is promoting the use of Compact Fluorescent Lamps (CFLs) as they, use 75% less energy, thereby reducing green house gas emissions that contribute to global climate change and lasts 6 times longer than incandescent bulbs. This information was given by the Minister of State in the Ministry of Environment and Forests, Shri Namo Narayan Meena in a written reply to question by Shri C. Perumal in the Rajya Sabha today.

3093. (6-9-2007) NEW DELHI : It has been decided to establish an Energy Security Division in the Ministry of External Affairs. The main objectives of the new Division are the following: i.) To serve as a nodal point in MEA for Energy Security. The Unit would sensitize and assist our Missions abroad in identifying possible opportunities for Indian companies. ii.) To maintain close coordination with the concerned Ministries and support their international engagement through appropriate diplomatic interventions. iii.) To support efforts of our corporate entities, in acquiring energy assets overseas, and in building strategic partnerships with foreign companies. iv.) To promote the transfer of new and emerging energy technologies to India; and v.) To interface with leading energy security think tanks and experts in India and abroad on energy-related issues. Energy Security has been an integral part of our bilateral discussions with several of the energy resource rich countries. Our Missions have taken active interest in identifying the emerging opportunities in the energy sector and are keeping Indian companies and concerned Ministries continuously informed of developments in this regard. Government of India and Indian oil companies have concluded several arrangements including investment agreements with many countries for the supply of oil and its derivatives to India, and in most of the cases delivery has begun. In addition, the possibility of bilateral cooperation in the areas of oil, natural gas, petrochemicals, hydrocarbons, non-conventional energy, and joint ventures are also constantly being explored with various countries including Iran, Kuwait, Saudi Arabia, Yemen, United Arab Emirates, Oman, Brazil, Colombia, Mexico, Venezuela, Ecuador and Myanmar.

3094. (6-9-2007) NEW DELHI : Numaligarh Refinery Ltd. (NRL) has signed an agreement with M/s. Oil India Ltd. (OIL) for supply of 1.0 million metric standard cubic metre per day (MMSCMD) of natural gas for its Refinery. A new natural gas pipeline is being laid for transporting natural gas from Duliajan to Numaligarh. The proposed natural gas pipeline is expected to be completed by October, 2008 at an estimated cost of Rs. 318 crore. Above information was given by the Minister of State for Petroleum & Natural Gas Shri Dinsha Patel in a written reply in the Lok Sabha today.

3095. (6-9-2007) NEW DELHI : The 5% Ethanol Blended Petrol (EBP) programme has been notified by the Ministry of Petroleum and Natural Gas in September 2006 keeping in view the under-mentioned benefits:- (i) Use of ethanol blended petrol will reduce the country's dependence on import of crude oil, (ii) Ethanol is environment friendly as it enhances combustion of petrol resulting in lower hydrocarbon emissions, (iii) Ethanol being an agricultural by-product, will give boost to farmers' income and (iv) It is a renewable natural fuel. The landed cost of ethanol is compared with benchmark price of landed cost of petrol at a particular location, including transportation, all taxes and duties paid etc. At present, Oil Manufacturing Companies (OMCs) are procuring ethanol at a basic price of Rs. 21500 per kilo litre. At current prices of petrol and at 5% of ethanol blend, the difference between landed cost of ethanol and landed cost of petrol is Re. 0.25 at Delhi. Against this margin, OMCs are incurring an estimated under recovery of Rs. 4.92/- per litre at Retail Selling Price on Motor Spirit at Delhi. Above information was given by Shri Murli Deora, Minister for Petroleum & Natural Gas in a written reply in the Lok Sabha today.

3096. (6-9-2007) NEW DELHI : The Special Incentive Package Scheme to encourage investments for setting up Semiconductor Fabrication and other micro and nano technology manufacture industries in India, has been announced by the Government vide Gazette Notification No. 78, part I, Section I dated 21st March, 2007.

3097. (6-9-2007) NEW DELHI : Realizing the seriousness of rapidly growing problem of urban transportation, Government has formulated National Urban Transport Policy (NUTP) in April, 2006. The Policy provides guidelines and incentives to the States/cities to design their urban transport strategies. The Government is providing Central financial assistance for urban transport planning and for taking up urban transport projects through various schemes like Jawaharlal Nehru National Urban Renewal Mission (JNNURM), Scheme of Ministry of Finance for financial support to Public Private Partnership in Infrastructure and budgetary support, etc. Government have not conducted any study or survey with regard to the effect of growth in real estate industry on the Public Transport. This information was given by Shri Ajay Maken, Minister of State in the Ministry of Urban Development in the Rajya Sabha today in a written reply to a question by Shri Ajya Singh Chautala.

3098. (6-9-2007) NEW DELHI : As per STPI (Software Technology Parks of India) during the Financial Year 2007 more than 7000 STP units are operating. As per NASSCOM (National Association of Software and Services companies) top 20 IT companies contribute about 6-65 per cent of the IT exports. As per ESC (Electronics and Computer Software Export Promotion Council) there is no special incentives to small companies of which big industries are deprived of. However, companies having their turnover upto Rs.15 crore in the preceding year are eligible for financial assistance for their export promotion activities, under the MDA scheme of Department of Commerce and similar other scheme run by the Ministry of SSI. This information was given by Dr. Shakeel Ahmad, Minister of State in the Ministry of Communications and Information Technology in the Rajya Sabha today in a written reply to a question by Shri Raj Mohinder Singh Majitha and Dr.Murli Manohar Joshi.

3099. (6-9-2007) NEW DELHI : Department of Posts will lay the foundation stone for the construction of a Post Office Building at a vacant plot at Prasad Nagar, New Delhi area tomorrow. The foundation stone will be laid by Smt. Anju Das Gupta, Member (I&FS), Postal Services Board. Smt. Krishna Tirath, Member of Parliament will preside over the function in the presence of Shri Raghav Lal, Principal Chief Postmast General, Delhi Circle. Shri Ramakant Goswami area MLA will attend the function as a Special Guest. The plot measures 600 sq.mts. and the construction is likely to be completed within six months. When complete this Post Office will cater to the needs of Karol Bagh, Prasad Nagar and East Patel Nagar localities. Now the residents of this area use the Post Offices at Karol Bagh and Patel Nagar. The Post Office will be of selection grade status and will be fully computerized Post Office.

3100. (6-9-2007) NEW DELHI : According to Fourth Assessment Report of the three Working Groups of the Inter-governmental Panel on Climate Change, the global atmospheric concentration of carbon dioxide has increased at the rate of 2.5 parts per million (ppm) by volume per year since the year 2000. The atmospheric concentrations of carbon dioxide during three years, viz. 2005, 2004 and 2003, were 379 ppm, 376.5 ppm and 374 ppm respectively. The country-wise estimates of atmospheric concentration are not recorded. The updated 100 years linear trend of increase of average global surface air temperature is 0.74 degree Celsius. The Government of India is a Party to the Kyoto Protocol to the United Nations Framework Convention on Climate Change (UNFCCCC) and has set up the National Clean Development Mechanism Authority to accord Host Country Approvals (HCA) to eligible Clean Development Mechanism (CDM) projects. India also has the largest number of projects under the CDM of the Kyoto Protocol, which reduce net emissions of greenhouse gases. Further, even though India as a developing country does not have any mitigation commitments, nevertheless, a sustainable development path is being followed through a range of policies and programmes to mitigate climate change: (i) ensuring energy conservation and improved energy efficiency in various sectors as well as setting up of Bureau of Energy Efficiency (ii) promoting use of renewable energy (iii) power sector reforms and active renewable energy programme (iv) use of cleaner and lesser carbon intensive fuel for transport (v) fuel switching to cleaner energy (vi) afforestation and conservation of forests (vii) promotion of clean coal technologies (viii) reduction of gas flaring (ix) encouraging Mass Rapid Transport systems (x) environmental quality management for all sectors This information was given by the Minister of State in the Ministry of Environment and Forests, Shri Namo Narayan Meena in a written reply to question by Shri Abu Asim Azmi in the Rajya Sabha today.

3101. (6-9-2007) NEW DELHI : The Ministry of Communication and Information Technology has prepared a draft policy on setting up of Information Technology Investment Regions which would be endowed with excellent infrastructure and investor friendly policy environment. No final view on the policy has yet been taken. It is envisaged that the State Governments may propose the locations of any ITIRs. At this stage, this Ministry has not identified places for setting up of Integrated Townships in the country. While the Ministry has not identified places for ITIRs in the State of Andhra Pradesh, the Government of Andhra Pradesh had separately requested, in November 2005 to announce Hyderabad as the location of proposed Mega Fab City. This information was given by Dr. Shakeel Ahmad, Minister of State in the Ministry of Communieations and Information Technology in the Rajya Sabha today in a written reply to a question by Shrimati N.P. Durga.

3102. (6-9-2007) NEW DELHI : Chief Minister of Andhra Pradesh Shri Y.S. Rajasekhara Reddy has submitted proposal for inclusion of Warangal and Tirupati cities under JNNURM. Decision to keep number of cities covered under the Jawaharlal Nehru National Urban Renewal Mission (JNNURM) around 60 was taken with the approval of Government. However, cities which are not covered under the JNNURM have been covered under another scheme of the Ministry, namely, Urban Infrastructure Development Scheme for Small and Medium Towns (UIDSSMT). This information was given by Shri Ajay Maken, Minister of State in the Ministry of Urban Development in the Rajya Sabha today in a written reply to a question by Shri M.V.Mysura Reddy.

3103. (6-9-2007) NEW DELHI : The Joint Forest Management strategy has been adopted by all the 28 States and 2 Union Territories. As per the information furnished by the State Forest Departments there are more than one lakh village level Joint Forest Management Committees (JFMCs) managing approximately 22 million hectare of forest area. As per the provisions of National Forest Policy, 1988 Government of India has issued guidelines to States on June 1, 1990 to involve village communities in regeneration and protection of forest areas under the Joint Forest Management Programme.. This information was given by the Minister of State in the Ministry of Environment and Forests, Shri S.Regupathy in a written reply to question by Kumari Nirmala Deshpande :in the Rajya Sabha today.

3104. (6-9-2007) NEW DELHI : Government of India provides financial and technical assistance to State/UT Governments for wildlife protection under the various Centrally Sponsored Schemes – Development of National Parks and

Sanctuaries, Project Tiger and Project Elephant. During the current financial year, *i.e.* 2007-08, Government of Maharashtra has submitted proposals worth Rs. 15.75 crores to Government of India for wildlife conservation. The funds under the Schemes-Development of National Parks and Sanctuaries, Project Tiger and Project Elephant are released after scrutiny of the proposals received from the State/UT Governments and also subject to the availability of funds and fulfilment of procedural requirements. This information was given by the Minister of State in the Ministry of Environment and Forests, Shri S.Regupathy in a written reply to question by Shri Balvant Pate and Shri Vinay Katiyar in the Rajya Sabha today.

3105. (6-9-2007) NEW DELHI : The Ministry of New and Renewable Energy proposes to create SEZ for production of equipments required for renewable energy. The States of Tamil Nadu, Andhra Pradesh, Maharashtra, Jharkhand have offered to give land for this purpose. Inaugurating the National Conference on Renewable Energy, Shri Vilas Muttemwar, Minister of State for New and Renewable Energy disclosed that acquisition of land and other facilities as well as details are under discussion. All the remote villages in the country will get minimum 1 Unit electricity during the Eleventh Plan *i.e.* by March 2012 under renewable energy. Declaring this target the Minister said that 4000 remote villages and hamlets have been covered under the rural electrification under Rajiv Gandhi Gramin Vidutikaran Yojana through Renewable Energy so far. The Ministry is working on such electrification to cover another 2700 villages. Giving the details of progress during the Tenth Plan, he said it was quite encouraging. The Renewable power electricity addition has been around 25 per cent of the total installed capacity during this period. Wind power ranks 4th globally despite low and moderate wind regimes are endowed with. Our wind resource potential utilization is 16 per cent in comparison with less than 2 per cent for Europe and less than 1 per cent for the United States. Our wind resource potential is based on a lower threshold wind power density of 200 watts per sq. meter as against 300 watts adopted elsewhere. Regarding high electricity potential, Shri Muttemwar said it lies in our North East Region which by and large remain unexploited. He appealed to work together to realize this potential to the best advantage of the Nation.

3106. (6-9-2007) NEW DELHI : Steel Authority of India Ltd. (SAIL) is undertaking ambitious modernization and expansion plans to increase production of hot metal from present level of 14.6 million tonnes per annum (2006-2007) to 26 million tonnes per annum by the year 2010-2011 at an indicative cost of Rs.49,000 crores. The expenditure involved in these programmes is proposed to be funded by SAIL itself from its own internal resources and supplemented by market borrowings, as required. SAIL has taken various steps to rationalize its cost of production, which includes 100% production of steel through Basic Oxygen Furnace (BOF) route, 100% processing of steel through continuous casting, value addition by reduction of semi finished steel, auxiliary fuel injection system in all the blast furnaces (BF), state of art process control computerization/automation, debottlenecking and productivity improvement schemes, secondary refining and augmentation of production facility at coal and iron ore mines. SAIL plans to develop area adjoining the Salem Steel Plant into a steel sector Special Economic Zone (SEZ). The proposed SEZ will have units that would be setting up manufacturing facilities in different areas such as utensils, kitchen and hospital wares, machines and equipments for food processing, chemicals and pharmaceutical sectors, pipes and tubes manufacturers etc. These processing units would be set up by companies other than SAIL. SAIL will provide customized steel input to the processing units in the proposed SEZ. The details of the project will be known only after formulation of project contours such as master planning, Detailed Feasibility Report, Utility Planning and Market Study. The scheme is currently in planning stage. This information was given by the minister of state for Steel Dr. Akhilesh Das in Lok Sabha today.

3107. (6-9-2007) NEW DELHI : The National Highways Authority of India (NHAI) has awarded 518.46 crore rupee contract for design, construction, development, finance, operation and maintenance of Km 230.000 (Islamnagar) to Km 278.000 (Kadtal) of Nagpur-Hyderabad Section on NH-7 in Andhra Pradesh including strengthening of the existing 2 lanes on Build, Operate and Transfer (BOT) Annuity basis. The project is a part of North-South Corridor under NHDP Phase-II. The Agreement was signed yesterday evening by NHAI with M/s Patel KNR Heavy Infrastructure Private Limited (an SPV formed by M/s. Patel – KNR JV). The Concession period would be 20 years including construction period of 24 months. The work has been awarded with semi annuity amount of Rs 44.37 crores payable to the Concessionaire by NHAI. The project will have adequate provisions for construction of Bridges, Flyovers, Underpasses, Service Roads, Truck Lay-byes etc.

3108. (6-9-2007) NEW DELHI : The new Model Concession Agreement (MCA) for Public Private Partnership has been approved by the Committee on Infrastructure (CoI). In the new MCA, certain provisions like capacity augmentation based on the traffic, partial traffic risk sharing, provision for distribution of grant/receipt of premium, out-put based technical requirements, obligation of National Highways Authority of India (NHAI) for pre-construction activities, revision of concession period on variation of traffic growth etc., have been introduced. Under Build, Operate and Transfer (BOT) (Toll) projects, concerned State has to execute State Support Agreement as per provision of the Concession Agreement. No other counter guarantee from the concerned State is required under BOT (Toll) Projects. This information was given by the Minister of State for Shipping, Road Transport and Highways, Shri K.H. Muniyappa in a written reply in the Rajya Sabha today.

3109. (6-9-2007) NEW DELHI : The concession for 2 projects for widening of National Highway No. 8 to six lane between Vadodara to Bharuch and Bharuch to Surat having total length of 148 km has been signed in July, 2006 on Built,

Operate and Transfer (BOT) basis. The project is targeted for completion by July, 2009. This information was given by the Minister of State for Shipping, Road Transport and Highways, Shri K.H. Muniyappa in a written reply in the Rajya Sabha today.

3110. (6-9-2007) NEW DELHI : The National Highways Authority of India has commissioned a feasibility study for the Ring Road around Bangalore city which is expected to be submitted in January, 2008. Based on the outcome of the study, the said ring Road project would be considered under National Highway Development Projects Phase-VII. State Government could also consider the feasibility of implementing the project under the Viability Gap Funding (VGF) Scheme. This information was given by the Minister of State for Shipping, Road Transport and Highways, Shri K.H. Muniyappa in a written reply in the Rajya Sabha today.

3111. (6-9-2007) NEW DELHI : Major Port Trusts, except Visakhapatnam, Tuticorin and Paradip, are facing shortage of pilots affecting the pilotage of vessels. Some of the pilots working with the Major Port Trusts are being attracted away to work in the privately operated Ports in India, foreign Ports and shipping lines on competitive terms and conditions. Indian Ports Association (IPA) has constituted a committee to propose model terms and conditions for hiring retired pilots as well as pilots to be employed on contract basis in the Major Ports. Government has also constituted a Pay Revision Committee to review the pay and service conditions of the employees of Major Port Trusts including pilots. This information was given by the Minister of Shipping, Road Transport and Highways, Thiru T.R. Baalu in a written reply in the Rajya Sabha today.

3112. (6-9-2007) NEW DELHI : The Tourism and Culture Minister Smt. Ambika Soni has said that her Ministry had sanctioned a Mega Project to India Tourism Development Corporation (ITDC) for Illumination of 13 Archaeological Survey of India (ASI) monuments in National Capital Territory of Delhi for a total amount of Rs.2375.09 lakh in the year 2006-07. In a written reply in the Lok Sabha today she said, the ASI monuments covered under the project are –Purana Quila, Sher Shah Gate and Masjid, Safdarjung Tomb, Sabz Burj, Kotla Feroze Shah, Khan-e-Khana, 12 Khamba at Nizamuddin, Lal Darwaja area at Delhi Gate, Chhoti Ghumati at Green Park, Sikari Ghumati at Green Park, Biran Ka Gumbad at Green Park, Dadi Poti ka Gumbad at Green Park, Najaf Khan's Tomb at Jorbagh.

3113. (6-9-2007) NEW DELHI : The Tourism and Culture Minister Smt. Ambika Soni has said that the objectives of the duty free shops of ITDC are sale of handlooms, handicraft products and imported general merchandise. In a written reply in the Lok Sabha today she said, the ITDC is presently running duty free shops at airports in the following places:- 1. Mumbai (Maharashtra) 2. Bangalore (Karnataka) 3. Calicut (Kerala) 4. Goa Smt. Soni said, the setting up of duty free shops at SEZs and seaports is at the initial stage of discussion with the authorities concerned for taking over the requisite space.

3114. (6-9-2007) NEW DELHI : The Minister of State for Housing & Urban Poverty Alleviation, Kumari Selja informed the Rajya Sabha today, in a written reply to a question by Smt. Jaya Bachchan that the Government has launched the Jawaharlal Nehru National Urban Renewal Mission (JNNURM) to assist cities and towns in taking up housing and infrastructural facilities for the urban poor in 63 cities in the country under the Basic Services to the Urban Poor (BSUP) Programme. For other cities, for taking up housing and slum upgradation programmes, the Integrated Housing and Slum Development Programme (IHSDP) has been launched with the objective to strive for holistic slum development, with a healthy and enabling environment by providing adequate shelter and basic infrastructure facilities to the slum dwellers. Both BSUP and IHSDP are under implementation since December-2005. The duration of JNNURM would be seven years beginning from the year 2005-06.

3115. (6-9-2007) NEW DELHI : The Government, with a view of providing interest rate subsidy for housing loans availed by Urban poor categorized as Economically Weaker Section (EWS) and Low Income Group (LIG) people has made a Budget provision of Rs.30 crore for the financial year 2007-08. This information was given by the Minister of State for Housing & Urban Poverty Alleviation, Kumari Selja in the Rajya Sabha today, in a written reply to a question by Shri Sanjay Raut.In response to a question about hike in interest rates for housing loan leading to a large number of people especially poor and middle class family deprived of having their own homes, the Minister informed that the interest rates on housing loans are decided by the managements of various Primary Lending Institutions (PLIs) after taking into account the cost of funds, transaction/ operation expenses and the general interest rate scenario in the country emerging from various monetary/ credit/fiscal policies announced from time to time.

3116. (6-9-2007) NEW DELHI : The Tourism and Culture Minister Smt. Ambika Soni has said that details of the World Heritage Cultural sites from India inscribed on the UNESCO World Heritage list are at Annexure 'A'. In a written reply in the Lok Sabha today she said, the UNESCO World Heritage Committee during its 31st session held at Christchurch (New Zealand) from 23rd June to 2nd July, 2007, has updated the World Heritage List and has inscribed Red Fort Complex, Delhi, India on the World Heritage list due to its outstanding universal value represented by flourishing Mughal architecture built upon local traditions, as a symbol of power since the reign of Shahjahan, and as the place where Indian Independence was first celebrated and is still celebrated today.

3117. (6-9-2007) NEW DELHI : The Tourism and Culture Minister Smt. Ambika Soni has said that the State Government of Maharashtra has planned a number of projects and programmes at a total cost of Rs. 817 crore (pre-revised) for commemoration of Tercentenary of Gur-ta-Gaddi at Nanded. These projects are being funded mainly under Jawahar Lal Nehru Urban Renewal Mission of the Urban Development Ministry of Government of India, contribution from Nanded

Waghala City Muncipal Corporation, State Government of Maharashtra, etc. The important components include (i) Development of City infrastructure; (ii) Gurudwara related developments; and (iii) event infrastructure developments. In a written reply in the Lok Sabha today she said, the Government of India have also constituted a National Committee with Shri Shivraj V. Patil, Union Home Minister as Chairperson and the Chief Minister of Maharashtra as Co-Chairperson to approve policies, plans and programmes and supervise and guide the commemoration of Gur-ta-Gaddi celebrations at Nanded to be held in 2008.

3118. (6-9-2007) NEW DELHI : The Tourism and Culture Minister Smt. Ambika Soni has said that the first phase of Pushpa Gujaral Science City comprising of, amongst others, Large Format Film Project System, Flight Stimulator/ Time Machine, Virtual Reality Centre (3-D Show), Indoor Laser Show, Exhibits on Space, Dynamotion Gallery, Health Gallery, Kids Park and Boating Facility have been completed and open to public w.e.f 20th March, 2005. In a written reply in the Lok Sabha today she said, the second phase of the project comprising of, amongst others, Evolution Gallery (Dinosaurs Park), Digital Planetarium, Upgradation of Space Gallery, Upgradation of Health & Biotechnology Gallery, Upgradation of Gallery on Dynamotion (Fun Science Gallery), Virtual Reality Gallery and Cyber Space, Science of Sports and Development of Park, is under progress. So far, Government of India have released Rs. 65.01 crore and State Government of Punjab have releases Rs. 22.36 crore for this project. The entire project is likely to be completed by September, 2008.

3119. (6-9-2007) NEW DELHI : The Minister of Tourism and Culture Smt. Ambika Soni has said that the Nehru Memorial Museum and Library have prepared a detailed project for modernisation at a total cost of Rs.20 crores. The proposal includes a component for digitisation of precious collection of private institutional papers kept in the Nehru Memorial Museum and Library at a total cost of Rs.10 crores. The digitisation proposal takes into account the latest techniques being followed presently by the leading Archives and Libraries in the World. In a written reply in the Lok Sabha today she said, the Ministry of Finance have provided a sum of Rs.20 crores to fund the project in the first batch of Supplementary Demands for Grants for the year 2007-08.

3120. (6-9-2007) NEW DELHI : As a follow up action to the Sachar Committee Report, the Ministry of Minority Affairs has constituted two Expert Groups (a) one to recommend an appropriate diversity index to promote diversity in living, educational and work spaces (b) the other to examine and determine the structure and functions of an Equal Opportunity Commission for the minority communities in the country. Notifications to this effect have been issued by the Ministry recently. The first Expert Group will recommend an appropriate diversity index for promoting diversity in living, educational and workspaces. This group will have Prof. Amitabh Kundu as Chairman and Prof. Sugata Marjit, Prof. Md. Abdul

Kalam, Dr. Ashwini Deshpande and Dr. Hasib Drabu as Members. The terms of reference of this Expert Group will be to develop and devise a transparent and acceptable index to measure diversity in the areas of education, government and private employment and housing; to suggest an appropriate structure of incentives & disincentives; to suggest a suitable mechanism for operationalising the diversity index and monitoring its implementation and to make any other recommendations relevant to the above. The second Expert Group to examine and determine the structure and functions of an Equal Opportunity Commission will have Prof. (Dr.) N.R. Madhava Menon as Chairman and Prof. Javeed Alam, Prof. Satish Deshpande, Prof. Yogendra Yadav and Prof. Gopal Guru as Members. The terms of reference of this Expert Group will be to recommend the structure, scope and functions of the proposed Equal Opportunity Commission; to advise on an appropriate legislative framework for such a Commission and to make any other recommendations relevant to the above. The Expert Groups will submit their reports within a period of three months.

3121. (6-9-2007) NEW DELHI : Finance Minister has urged the Members of Parliamentary Consultative Committee attached to his Ministry to persuade their State Governments to mainstream Public Private Partnership (PPP) in infrastructure development and to take full benefits of the various schemes and initiatives of the Ministry of Finance. Addressing the Consultative Committee Meeting, here today, Shri P. Chidambaram said, since many of the State Governments have not caught up with the PPP idea and most of the projects are confined to a few States only, help can be taken from a panel of 11 expert Transaction Advisors. He stated that the PPP issue has been discussed in detail at the two national and four regional level conferences organized by Ministry of Finance. Shri Chidambaram said that India's economic performance in the past few years-particularly in the last three years-has been commendable on many counts. Economic growth has accelerated and we are now averaging an annual growth in excess of 8%. As per the revised estimates released by CSO on May 31, 2007, GDP at factor cost at 1999-2000 prices was estimated at Rs 28,482 billion. National income aggregates in net terms had a higher rate of growth (9.4) in 2006-07. Alternate measures of national income at current prices yielded a growth of 15.2 to 15.8 per cent in 2006-07. The Finance Minister stated that our infrastructure deficiencies have become more visible because of high growth. The most visible indicators of overstretched infrastructure are India's congested highways, airports and ports. He added that traffic at Ports has grown over 2005-06 at 13%; Air Passenger movement (25%) and Air Cargo (10%) growth over the last 2 years has exceeded expectations; Railways has clocked a growth of 9% in freight, 8% in passenger traffic over the last 3 years.

3122. (6-9-2007) NEW DELHI : Union Power Minister, Shri Sushilkumar Shinde has called upon the young technocrats to use their talent and energy to take India forward. Inaugurating the Induction Programme of NTPC's Executive Trainees-2007 Batch in New Delhi today, he expressed confidence in the young human resource of the country which is ready to accept challenges and achieve the goal of making India a global power. Welcoming the new entrants to the power sector, Shri Shinde told them to carry forward the rich tradition of nation building that NTPC has been following for the last 32 years. Earlier, in his keynote address Secretary Power, Shri Anil Razdan congratulated the young entrants for choosing power sector which is poised for an unprecedented growth as their career option and for joining NTPC, one of the best organizations in the public sector. Observing that the NTPC is growing from strength to strength, he expressed hope that the young team would further strengthen the roots of the organization. Chairperson CEA, Shri Rakesh Nath; Chairman and Managing Director, NTPC, Shri T. Shankarlingam also spoke on the occasion. Shri Shinde presented the Gold Medal to Shri Amod Kumar Singh and Silver Medal to M. Balaji in Engineering disciplines and Gold Medal to S.K. Upadhayay in HR discipline. A total of 423 Executive Trainees in Engineering have joined NTPC, out of 45.423 applicants. The Selection Process consists of an All India Written Test, Group Discussion followed by Personal Interview. Since the inception of the Executive Trainee Programme in 1977, thirty-one batches of Executive Trainees have been inducted. So far 6304 Engineer Trainees have been inducted. The total number of Finance and HR Trainees inducted so far is over 400. This comprises more than half the total executive strength of the company.

3123. (6-9-2007) NEW DELHI : Shri K.C.Jena, Chairman Railway Board has also taken over as Chairman, International Union of Railways (UIC). Shri Jena will be Chairman of UIC till December 2008. The Chairman Railway Board of Indian Railways had taken over as the first non-European Chairman of UIC for two-Year term in January 2007. Indian Railways have been actively associated with the organization since 1998 and has played an important role in its restructuring to transform it to a truly global institution. As part of the restructuring, six regional units of UIC have been formed and UIC-Asia will be headquartered at New Delhi. Indian Railways will facilitate the setting up of UIC-Asia regional Units. Indian Railways will also provide all assistance for the International Railway Strategic Management Institute (IRSMI) that would come up at Chanakyapuri, New Delhi. International Union of Railways (UIC) is an international association of rail operators and organizations established in 1922 with headquarters in Paris having 224 members worldwide. The organization provides a forum to different Railway organization in the world to undertake joint research projects, develop strategies for implementation of international projects like inter-continental freight corridors, and high speed rail. It also enables Railway Managers across the globe to develop skills through its International Railway Strategic Management Institute. The priority areas for UIC would be to have increased worldwide investments in rail transport. UIC's focus is to establish rail transport as the key link in the global logistics chain.

3124. (6-9-2007) NEW DELHI : Direct tax collections recorded a growth of 42% for the five-month period ending August 2007. Net tax collections stood at Rs.61,030 crore, up from Rs.42,980 crore during the same period last fiscal. Corporate tax recorded a growth of 49.49% at Rs.33,766 crore, up from Rs.22,587 crore during the previous fiscal. Personal income tax (including FBT, STT and BCTT) grew by 33.76% at Rs.27,206 crore, up from Rs.20,340 crore. The growth in Securities Transaction Tax (STT) was 35.16% and Banking Cash Transaction Tax (BCTT) was 79.73%. During the fiscal 2007-08, direct tax collections have consistently maintained a growth of over 40%, reflecting continued buoyancy in the economy, better tax compliance and improved tax administration.

3125. (7-9-2007) NEW DELHI : The Tourism and Culture Minister Smt. Ambika Soni has said that promotion of domestic tourism will further strenthen national integration and social unity in the country. She was speaking here today after releasing a book 'SAFAR SUHANA DUNIYA KA' written by Shri Alok Mehta, Editor Outlook (Hindi). Smt. Soni said the country is witnessing a boom in tourism sector and more than 4.45 million Tourists arrived in the country in the last year. She said, the book written by Shri Mehta will be helpful in developing better understanding about the world for common traveller. Smt. Soni said, valuable inputs given in the book may be used as ready reference by stakeholders in the tourism sector. The 464 page book narrates travel experiences of Shri Alok Mehta in more than 35 countries.

3126. (7-9-2007) NEW DELHI : The Chief Justice of India Sh. Justice K.G.Balakrishnan has called for implementing serious recommendation of various Law Commissions. He was speaking at function after releasing a book entitled " Legislative Drafting: Shaping the Law for the New Millennium" here this evening. Justice Sh.Balakrishnan said that the laws should be drafted depending upon the needs of the people. Asserting that our laws are inferior to none, the Chief Justice of India said that the law should be for greatest happiness to greatest number of people. Presiding over the function, the Minister for Law and Justice Sh.H.R.Bhardwaj said that the country's legal system is moving towards fast track. He said that there is demand for legislation of which we never thought of earlier like meeting the challenge of terrorism. He said that his ministry has decided to poll all resources in meeting the emerging challenges in legislation drafting. Sh. Bhardwaj said that we have maintained the independence of judiciary and of the institutions. The Law Secretary Sh.T.K. Viswanathan who has revised and updated the book " Legislative Drafting: Shaping the Law for the New Millennium", said legislative drafting is discipline which needs continuous training. Observing that ordinary citizen was affected by the laws from cradle to grave, the Law Secretary said, " With the legislative machinery churning out of a steady mass of legislation, it becomes necessary for the stakeholders to understands the law making process." He said the law Ministry is aspiring to produce drafters of international standards. The Minister for Law and Justice, Shri H. R. Bhardwaj released the digitized version of the general of Indian Law Institute containing articles published during the last 49 years.

3127. (7-9-2007) NEW DELHI : Countrywide census of the number of persons suffering from AIDS is not technically viable. Annual sentinel surveillance is carried to estimate trends in HIV prevalence. The 2006 estimates released recently by the National AIDS Control Organisation are based on an expanded sentinel surveillance system and use of multiple data sources including National Family Health Survey-3. As per the results of the survey the estimated prevalence is 0.36% and the number of HIV infected persons between 2 million to 3.1 million.

3128. (7-9-2007) NEW DELHI : Following is the remarks of Prime Minister, Dr. Manmohan Singh on the occasion of the release of a book in honour of Dr. Balram Jakhar 'Abhinandan Granth – Kalpavraksh' by the President, Smt. Pratibha Devisingh Patil here today: "I deem it a great privilege in joining this distinguished gathering here in greeting Dr. Balram Jakhar on the occasion of his 85th birth anniversary. Dr. Jakhar is one of our tallest leaders in public life-in more senses than one! He has long been admired for his deep and sincere commitment to the cause of the Indian farmer. He is a scholar, a first rate administrator, a farmers' leader and above all a deeply secular and patriotic Indian. Jakharji has been described by his admirers as Pandit Balram Jakhar because of his deep knowledge of agriculture. It is not often that one encounters a person with varied talents in the world of politics. It is a measure of his commitment to public life and to the world of ideas that he has been able to combine both. I had the privilege and the pleasure of interacting with him both when I was the Governor of the Reserve Bank and as Deputy Chairman of the Planning Commission and later on as Finance Minister. I had the privilege of serving as Finance Minister when Dr. Jakhar was the Union Minister of Agriculture. His wisdom, his knowledge and his vast experience are truly a great national asset. I recall the keen interest he showed in planning for agriculture and in promoting our farmers' welfare. He has a deep understanding of the problems of farmers and always championed their cause at a time when the farming community looked for leadership. Today's generation does not know how deep was the crisis in Indian agriculture and our food economy in the 1960s.

3129. (7-9-2007) NEW DELHI : Kantakabi Lakshmikanta Mohapatra was a leading freedom fighters and a nationalist poet of rare caliber. His powerful patriotic songs were a perennial source of inspiration during freedom struggle of India and separate state-hood movement. Lakshmikanta, popularly known as 'Kantakabi' by the people of Orissa, occupies a unique place in the socio-political-cultural life of the State. Kantakabi was a versatile genius, who tried his hand in drama, parody, poetry, short-story, novel with a flair nationalistic fervour and incredible craftsmanship in satire. He was one of the few writers who made significant contributions to Oriya literature, when the very existence of Oriya language was threatened. A creator and a critic rolled in one, Kantakabi's caustic critism of erring politicians and despot feudal chiefs earned him an awful reputation. As a musician and actor he has also contributed enormously to the rich tradition of performing arts in Orissa. So it would be proper to say that Kantakabi a distinguished man of letters, has left behind his indelible foot-prints in various fields of Oriya literature.Kantakabi's popular patriotic songs like *Bande Utkala Janani, Koti Koti Kanthe Aji, Udaee Nisana Bajai Veri* had thrilled the souls of millions of Oriya's during freedom struggle and separate state-hood movement. His composition *Bande Utkala Janani* was adopted as the welcome song for Balasore Session of Utkal Sammilani, the organization which sphere-headed the separate Orissa state movement. This song has assumed the status of state song of Orissa and immortalized him. Apart from his bountiful contributions to Oriya literature, Kantakabi's family had also participated in the freedom struggle to a great extent. His sisters Janhavi Devi and Kokila Devi, younger brother Kamalakanta and two sons Nityananda and Gour Chandra joined the national movement and courted arrest time and again in different phases of the struggle. His father Bhagabat Prasad Samantaray Mohapatra, though an advocate by profession, was a great nationalistic leader, Bhagabat Prasad represented Bihar-Orissa Legislative Council for four times and served as its deputy speaker for two terms. As a social reformer, Bhagabat Prasad's role in eradication of dowry system and reduction of wedding expenses are memorable. Sister Janhavi Devi and Kokila Devi mobilized women for Civil Disobedience movement and especially enlightened the rural illiterate women about various programmes of freedom struggle.

3130. (7-9-2007) NEW DELHI : Vision Document 2015 on Food Processing Industries has been finalized by the Ministry of Food Processing Industries (MFPI), which envisages trebling the size of the processed food sector by increasing the level of processing of perishables from 6% to 20%, value addition from 20% to 35% and share in global food trade from 1.5% to 3% by 2015. To realize the vision, an estimated investment of Rs. 2.00 lakh crore will be required, out of which ten percent would be from Government and the remaining would come equally from financial institutions and private investors/FDI. The Cabinet has approved the integrated strategy for promotion of agribusiness-Vision, Strategy and Action Plan for the Food Processing Sector, based on the recommendations made by the Group of Ministers (GOM) for growth of Food Processing Sector. The thrust areas identified for strategic intervention are establishment of Mega Food Parks in identified clusters with appropriate backward and forward linkages, creation of integrated cold chains/value addition and preservation infrastructure, modernization of abattoirs, upgradation of hygienic and quality street food and food streets, establishment and upgradation of quality control laboratories, restructuring and strengthening of MFPI, rationalizing tax structure, incentivising FDI and private investment in infrastructure, undertaking capacity building of small and unorganized sector, liberalized wine and beer policy, launching a major promotional campaign for the food processing sector and need for larger public investment for creation of critical rural infrastructure in food processing sector. In the 11th Plan, the Ministry proposes to implement various schemes to attract private sector investment in the food processing sector.

3131. (7-9-2007) NEW DELHI : The Supreme Court of India has passed an order to provide maintenance allowance to Muslim women from their husbands under Section 125. The Apex Court in its judgement dated05.06.2007 in Iqbal Bano Vs. State of UP & anrs. has held as follows: 1. A Muslim husband is liable to make reasonable and fair provision for the future of the divorced wife which obviously includes her maintenance as well. Such a reasonable and fair provision extending beyond the iddat period must be made by the husband within the iddat period in terms of Section 3(i) of Muslim Woman (Protection of Rights on Divorce) Act, 1986. 2. Liability of the Muslim husband to his divorced wife arising under Section 3(i)(a) of the Act to pay maintenance is not confined to the iddat period. 3. A divorced Muslim woman who is not remarried and who is not able to maintain herself after the iddat period can proceed as provided under Section 4 of the Act against her relative who are liable to maintain her in proportion to the properties which they inherit on her death according to Muslim law for such divorced woman including her children and parents. If any of her relative being unable to pay maintenance, the Magistrate may direct the State Waqf Board established under the Act to pay maintenance. 4. The provisions of the Act do not offend Article 14,15 and 21 of the Indian constitution. Government does not propose to take any steps in this regard since the Supreme Court has not given any directions to the Central Government in the matter. This was stated by the Minister of State of Law and Justice, Shri K. Venkatapathy in a written reply in Lok Sabha today.

3132. (7-9-2007) NEW DELHI : The Transparency International's Global Corruption Report, 2007 has come to the notice of the Government which inter-alia states that 77 per cent of the general public has stated the Indian judicial system to be corrupt. The Government, however, does not agree with the said perception. The Government has already introduced Judges (Inquiry) Bill, 2006 in the Lok Sabha on December 19, 2006. The Bill seeks to devise a suitable legislative framework for empowering a judicial forum to deal with complaints against judges of the Supreme Court and High Courts. As far as the District and Subordinate Courts are concerned, the respective High Courts are empowered to take cognizance of complaints against the members of the lower judiciary. This was stated by the Minister of Law and Justice, Shri H. R. Bhardwaj in a written reply in Lok Sabha today.

3133. (7-9-2007) NEW DELHI : The then Chief Minister of Gujarat had in September 2000 conveyed that the State Government felt that Circuit Benches of the Gujarat High Court be established at Surat and Rajkot. The matter was examined in consultation with the Chief Justice of the High Court who informed that it would not be in the interest of the Institution to have a Circuit Bench either at Surat or at Rajkot. The Chief Minister of Gujarat was informed accordingly in May 2001. Thereafter, no proposal has been received from the Government of Gujarat, in consultation with the Chief Justice for the establishment of Benches of the Gujarat High Court either at Surat or at Rajkot. This was stated by the Minister of Law and Justice, Shri H. R. Bhardwaj in a written reply in Lok Sabha today.

3134. (7-9-2007) NEW DELHI : The Government do not propose any amendment to the Constitution regarding international treaties and agreements to come into effect only after they are ratified by the Parliament. The Union Government with the approval of the Cabinet conclude all treaties and agreements with foreign countries. Legislature's approval is required for any implementing legislation, wherever necessary. Regarding implementation of the recommendations of M.N. Venkatachalaiah Committee on Constitutional Reforms action lies with the Ministries/Departments of the Government of India, which are administratively concerned with the subject matter of the recommendations. Copies of the report have already been forwarded to the Ministries/Departments. This was stated by the Minister of State in the Ministry of Law and Justice, Shri K. Venkatapathy in a written reply in Lok Sabha today.

3135. (7-9-2007) NEW DELHI : As per extant policy Foreign Direct Investment (FDI) upto 100% under the automatic route is allowed for construction development projects, including housing commercial premises, resorts, educational institutions, recreational facilities, city and regional level infrastructure township, subject to conditions laid down in Press Note No. 2 (2005 series). This information was given the Minister of State for Housing & Urban Poverty Alleviation, Kumari Selja in the Lok Sabha today, in a written reply to a question by Shri Ramdas Athawale.

3136. (7-9-2007) NEW DELHI : As such the administrative reporting system generates data for those individuals that have availed the facilities provided in the health institutions. The data for those not availing these services is captured through periodic large-scale surveys like the District Level Household Surveys (DLHS) and the National Family Health Surveys (NFHS). According to the District Level Household Survey-II, (2002-2004) 26.6% of mothers had not availed of any antenatal check-up services during the survey period.

3137. (7-9-2007) NEW DELHI : The Cabinet Committee on Economic Affairs (CCEA), in its meeting on 16.3.2006, has approved the setting up of six AIIMS-like institutions. In so far as AIIMS, Jodhpur in Rajasthan, the State Government has provided 100 acres land. The boundary wall around the site has already been completed. WAPCOS, a Government of India organization has completed Environmental Impact (EIA) Study and pre-construction survey. The State Government has been requested to provide facilities for water, power and sewage connectivity. The bid process for selection of Project Consultant in 2006 was unresponsive. Likewise, the offer to short listed Architectural Design Consultant for preparing enlarged concept design was rejected due to the exorbitantly high price quoted by them. The whole process has been initiated de novo. The construction of housing complex (houses & hostels) is proposed through a turnkey developer for EPC (Engineering, Procurement and Construction). The Request for proposal has been issued in May 2007 to short listed bidders. The bids for the selection of EPC Developer were opened on 16.8.2007. Bids are being evaluated. Likewise, the process of selection of Design-DPR Consultant for preparing the detailed project report of medical college and hospital complex has been initiated. The Request for Proposals has been issued to short listed bidders in May 2007 and last date for receipt of bids is 24.9.2007. It is expected that the civil construction work would start by early 2008 and be completed in 2009 (for housing/hostel) and in 2010-11 (for hospital/medical college complex). This information was given by the Minister of State for Health & Family Welfare, Smt. Panabaka Lakshmi in a written reply to a question in the Rajya Sabha.

3138. (7-9-2007) NEW DELHI : The Ministry of Rural Development is vigorously implementing Total Sanitation Campaign (TSC). The sanitation coverage has now gone up to 46 per cent, which was merely 1 per cent in the year 1981, and 21 per cent in 2001. In last three years more than 3 crore households have been provided with household latrines, apart from school toilets, Anaganwadi toilets and sanitary complexes. The Ministry has sanctioned project for 573 districts of the country to construct 11.60 crore individual household latrines, 10.16 lakh school toilets, 3.70 lakh Anaganwadi latrines and 27,900 sanitary complexes. The Ministry is monitoring its implementation on regular basis and releasing comparative performance of States in implementation of TSC in physical and financial terms.

3139. (7-9-2007) NEW DELHI : Outbreak of diseases especially water-borne and vector-borne diseases may occur after floods. Cholera, viral hepatitis, enteric fever and acute diarrhoeal diseases are the main water borne diseases caused by contamination of water with virus and bacteria, whereas diseases caused by mosquitoes, which mainly breed in water, are dengue, malaria, filariasis, viral encephalitis etc. Health is a State subject and primarily, the State Government is responsible for the management of waterborne and other diseases in wake of the floods. The Government of India supplements the efforts of the State Governments/ Union Territories by providing technical support and material supplies to the State Governments on their request or when the extent of the outbreak is beyond the coping abilities of the State. Prior to the onset of monsoon season, guidelines and the action required to be taken by the State Governments for prevention and control of various diseases, which may arise due to floods, are circulated to all the States. These guidelines elaborate on likely public health risks, stepping up of surveillance to detect early warning signs, ensuring safe drinking water and instituting public health measures to prevent outbreak of diseases. The Government of India provides financial assistance to the State affected by natural calamities as per norms of Calamity Relief Fund (CRF) shared by the Centre and the State on 75:25 basis. If the calamity is of severe nature, additional funds are also made available from National Calamity Contingency Fund (NCCF). The requirement of the additional funds is assessed by Ministry of Home Affairs, which is the nodal Ministry for the fund. The CRF and NCCF norms include assistance for provision of medicines, disinfectants, insecticides for prevention and outbreak of epidemics. In addition, a comprehensive National Vector Borne Disease Control Programme (NVBDCP) is implemented through the States for prevention and control of vector borne diseases caused by mosquitoes. The strategies for control of vector borne diseases include disease management through early case detection and treatment, epidemic preparedness and rapid response. An integrated approach has been initiated with Department of Drinking Water Supply to provide the technical support to monitor the quality of drinking water in different states so as to prevent occurrence of water borne diseases.

3140. (7-9-2007) NEW DELHI : The Rules notified under Tobacco control legislation enacted in 2003 discourages consumption of tobacco in the country through various measures, which includes: (i) Prohibition of smoking in a public place; (ii) Prohibition of direct and indirect advertisement; (iii) Prohibition of sale of tobacco products to minors; (iv) Prohibition of sale of tobacco products within 100 yards of educational institutions; (v) Depiction of pictorial warning indicating ill effects of Tobacco Product for educating the masses. The State Governments are the implementing agencies, and they are being repeatedly impressed upon to effectively enforce the provisions of the Act/Rules framed there under. National Tobacco Control Programme has been launched for effective enforcement of the tobacco control legislation with a focus on; (i) Building awareness about ill effects of tobacco at the community level. (ii) Building enforcement capacity of the State Governments. This information was given by the Minister of State for Health & Family Welfare, Smt. Panabaka Lakshmi in a written reply to a question in the Rajya Sabha.

3141. (7-9-2007) NEW DELHI : The Government has formulated several schemes for providing health services to citizens specially those who are below the poverty line. These include programmes for providing Reproductive and Child Health (RCH) Services, control of communicable and non-communicable diseases, providing curative as well as preventive/promotive care through a chain of primary, secondary and tertiary care health institutions. Government has also launched the National Rural Health Mission (NRHM) throughout the country with special focus on 18 states which have relatively poor health indicators/infrastructure. {These include 8 Empowered Action Group States (Bihar, Jharkhand, Madhya Pradesh, Chhattisgarth, Uttar Pradesh, Uttaranchal, Orissa and Rajasthan), 8 NE States, Himachal Pradesh and Jammu & Kashmir}. The main aim of NRHM is to provide accessible, affordable, accountable, effective and reliable primary health care facilities, especially, to the poor and vulnerable sections of the population. The NRHM envisages improvements in range and quality of hospital care, decentralization of programme to district level to improve intra and inter-sectoral convergence and effective utilization of resources. The NRHM further aims to provide overarching umbrella to the existing National programmes of Health & Family Welfare including RCH-II, Malaria, Blindness, Iodine deficiency, Filaria, Kala Azar, T.B., Leprosy and Integrated Disease Surveillance. Further, it addresses the issue of health in a sector-wide manner addressing sanitation and hygiene, nutrition and safe drinking water as basic determinants of good health. The initiatives under NRHM are benefiting the weaker sections including the poorer and minority community. The Government has finalized a detailed framework for implementation of NRHM, which provides the road map for operationalisation of various strategies. While the improved health services are envisaged to be available to all the citizens, special provisions are made for the underprivileged persons and persons living in underserved areas. This information was given by the Minister for Health & Family Welfare, Dr. Anbumani Ramadoss in a reply to a question in the Rajya Sabha.

3142. (7-9-2007) NEW DELHI : As per information available, there are a total of 4745 posts sanctioned in the Central Health Service out of which 3491 posts were filled up as on 1.1.2007. In respect of State Governments, as per the National Health Policy profile 2006 brought out by the Central Bureau of Health Intelligence, there were 73549 allopathic doctors. Additionally, under NRHM there are 3673 doctors and 3163 specialists are working on contractual basis as on 1.6.2007. The Central Govt had noted the increasing trend of Govt doctors especially the Specialists seeking Voluntary Retirement or Resigning due to the attractive financial compensation and other generous service benefits in foreign assignments/domestic private sector. The Govt had constituted an Expert Committee under the Chairmanship of Shri Javid Choudhury, former Secretary (Health) to suggest measures/disincentives that should be introduced to arrest the outflow of doctors and changes in the terms and conditions of service. The Committee has made a number of recommendations to improve the lot of these doctors. Amongst the steps taken by the Govt (i) the age of retirement of specialists in the three sub-cadres of Teaching, Non-teaching and Public Health has already been increased from 60 to 62 years (ii) the period of study leave has also been increased from two years to three years in respect of CHS doctors. This information was given by the Minister of State for Health & Family Welfare, Smt. Panabaka Lakshmi in a written reply to a question in the Rajya Sabha.

3143. (7-9-2007) NEW DELHI : Government of India is implementing Antiretroviral Treatment (ART) Programme for eligible persons with HIV/AIDS since April 2004 with first line ARV drugs. Treatment with second line ARV drugs is not part of the programme at present.

3144. (7-9-2007) NEW DELHI : The Prevention of Food Adulteration Act, 1954 and Rules, 1955 have been enacted to prevent adulteration in foodstuffs and to save consumers from frauds and deceptions. The standards of various food articles have been prescribed in Appendix 'B' of the said rules. Food articles sold in the markets are required to conform to the specifications laid down under PFA Rules, 1955. The implementation of the PFA Act, 1954 & Rules, 1955 is entrusted with the Food (Health) Authorities of the States/U.Ts. The enforcement staff of the States/U.T. draw random samples of various food articles from time to time to check adulteration in food commodities and action is taken against the offenders where the samples do not conform to the prescribed standards or do not conform to various provisions of the PFA Act, 1954 & Rules, 1955. There is no provision in PFA Act, 1954 and Rules, 1955 to compensate for loss of lives and properties. Action is taken under Section 16 of the PFA Act, 1954 where samples are not found to be conforming to the PFA standards, against all persons found responsible for conduct of business of a company or the person nominated under section 17(2) of the PFA Act, 1954. The offenders are awarded punishment by the courts ranging from six months to life imprisonment with fine depending upon the gravity of offence. This information was given by the Minister of State for Health & Family Welfare, Smt. Panabaka Lakshmi in a written reply to a question in the Rajya Sabha.

3145. (7-9-2007) NEW DELHI : Based on the recommendations of the Dental Council of India, the Central Government has granted permission to Rungta College of Dental Sciences & Research, at Bhilai, in the state of Chhattisgarh with reduced intake capacity of 50 seats against the original intake of 100 seats. Permission has not been granted permission to two dental colleges in the State of Chhattisgarh, namely, New Horizon Dental College & Research Institute, Bilaspur and Chhattisgarh Dental College & Research Institute, Rajnandgaon due to deficiencies including teaching faculty as per DCI norms for the academic session 2007-08.

3146. (7-9-2007) NEW DELHI : The Minister for Civil Aviation, Shri Praful Patel today met the Chief Minister of West Bengal, Shri Buddhadeb Bhattacharjee in Kolkata today. They held discussions on the modernization of the Netaji Subash Chandra Bose International Airport at Kolkata. A presentation was also made to the Chief Minister in this regard. Some of the important upcoming infrastructure at Kolkata Airport will be an Integrated Passenger Terminal Building at an area measuring more than 180 thousand Sq.mt. with 104 Check-in counters, 22 immigration counters for Arrival and 22 for Departure, 25 Security Gates-9 for international and 16 for domestic passengers, 5 conveyer belts and 15 Aerobridges. It may be recalled that on 18 April 2007, the Committee on Infrastructure (COI) headed by the Prime Minister decided that the Kolkata Airport would be developed by the Airports Authority of India (AAI) from its own resources and an Inter-Ministerial Group (IMG) formed under the Chairmanship of the Secretary, Ministry of Civil Aviation, would finalize an Action Plan for the development of Kolkata Airport. Following the decision of the COI, Letter of Intent was issued to the consultants on 30 May 2007 and 1 June 2007. The AAI received detailed Project

Report (DPR) from the consultants on 30th June, which was considered by the Ministry of Civil Aviation and approved by the AAI Board on 3rd August 2007. The PIB note in this regard is under the consideration of the Ministry of Civil Aviation. The consultants appointed for the modernization of Kolkata Airport are: M/s. Sikka Architect and Associates with consortium partner RMJM (Hong Kong) and Virendra Khanna and Associates with consortium partners ADPI (Paris). At present the Kolkata Airport has a passenger handling capacity of 0.73 million international passengers annually and 4.7 million domestic passengers annually which is likely to saturate by year 2008-09 and 2006-07 respectively. AAI has recently added cargo-handling capacity to the Airport, which is sufficient to cater to the demand up to 2015-16. In 2006-07 there were 65687 aircraft movements of which 9414 were international and 56273 domestic. The passenger traffic in 2006-07 was 5993058 of which 805191 were international (registering a growth of 12%) and 5187867 was domestic (registering a growth of 20%). In view of these facts, the decision has been taken to develop a modern Integrated Passenger Terminal Building to handle 20 million passengers, which will be sufficient to meet the demand up to 2015-16. Work is already in progress for 9 domestic bays. Three cargo bays and 11 additional parking bays will be constructed along with the new Integrated Terminal Building. Automation will be introduced in the CNS/ATM operation and a new control tower will be built. The Project of modernizing the Kolkata Airport envisages an investment of Rs. 2000 crore.

3147. (7-9-2007) NEW DELHI : Under village electrification programme, 6000 villages have been provided electricity through non-conventional energy sources. Out of this 3000 villages during 2004-05, 2000 villages during 2005-06 and 1000 villages have been provided electricity during 2006-07 respectively. Under the remote village electrification programme, 381 villages have been completed during 2004-05, 293 during 2005-06 and 1017 villages have been completed during 2006-07. During 2006-07, Jharkhand has completed maximum *i.e.* 234 villages followed by Tripura with 205 villages and West Bengal 135 villages. This information was given by the Minister of State in the Ministry of New and Renewable Energy, Shri Vilas Muttemwar in a written reply to question in the Lok Sabha today.

3148. (7-9-2007) NEW DELHI : The New and Renewable Energy has been implementing a broad based programme covering research, development, demonstration and utilization of various renewable energy sources like bio-energy, solar energy, wind energy, small hydro and other emerging renewable sources of energy for more than two decades. The renewable sources of energy are 'Green' as they are either carbon neutral or carbon free. Technologies for utilisation of some of the Renewable energy sources have really matured and are in early phases of commercialization. The use of ethanol, a form of bio fuel, for blending with petrol on a limited scale has already been introduced in the country. However, technologies for utilisation of bio diesel, hydrogen, geo thermal energy and tidal energy are presently under different stages of research, development and demonstration in the country. An amount of Rs.1500 crores as budgetary support has been proposed by the Ministry of New and Renewable Energy for research and development on various renewable sources of energy during 11th Plan period. The increase of new and renewable sources of energy would reduce our dependence on fossil fuels, reduces emission of green house gases and ultimately provide energy security to the country. This information was given by the Minister of State in the Ministry of New and Renewable Energy, Shri Vilas Muttemwar in a written reply to question :in the Lok Sabha today.

3149. (7-9-2007) NEW DELHI : Most of the commonly used renewable energy system and equipments are being manufactured indigenously. The Indian companies are also exporting some of the renewable energy system and equipments. The Government is providing several financial and fiscal incentives to encourage domestic production and make renewable energy available at cheaper rates. These incentives include capital subsidy on some of the systems, soft loan to manufacturers and users, concessional or nil duty on import of some of the equipments, raw materials and components, excise duty exemption and 80 per cent accelerated depreciation in first year. The import of various renewable energy equipments is permitted under open general licence (OGL); therefore, no data on import of all renewable energy equipments are maintained by the New and Renewable Energy. This information was given by the Minister of State in the Ministry of New and Renewable Energy, Shri Vilas Muttemwar in a written reply to question :in the Lok Sabha today.

3150. (7-9-2007) NEW DELHI : Bihar Rural livelihoods Project" has been signed with the World Bank on 9th August, 2007 for an IDA credit amounting to Special Drawing Rights (SDR) 41.4 million or about US$63 million. The objective of the project is to enhance social and economic empowerment of the rural poor in Bihar. The credit amount will be utilised for social, economic and infrastructure activities including group based income generating activities, small infrastructure investments, including access to public services and improving skills and organisation. The projects on rural livelihood already under implementation with World Bank assistance are in the States of Andhra Pradesh, Chhattisgarh, Madhya Pradesh, Rajasthan and Tamil Nadu. Similar projects for the States of Orissa and Madhya Pradesh (Phase-II) have been sent to the World Bank for consideration. This information was given by Minister of State for Finance, Shri Pawan Kumar Bansal in reply to a question raised by Shri Adhir Chowdhury and Shri Nikhil Kumar in Lok Sabha today.

3151. (7-9-2007) NEW DELHI : A total of 29,25.698 Self Help Groups (SHGs) have been Credit Linked under the Bank Linkage Programme till June 2007 involving a bank loan of Rs. 18,051.74 crore. Reserve Bank of India (RBI) has deregulated the rate of interest on advances above Rs. 2 lakh in respect of commercial banks. However, for loans upto Rs. 2.00 lakh, RBI has stipulated that the rate of interest charged by the commercial banks should not exceed the Benchmark Prime Lending Rate (BPLR). Banks are, therefore, free to determine the rate of interest they charge from groups or members of groups. The rates of interest charged by different banks on their loans to SHGs vary from 9.5% to 11.5% per annum. The policies of the Government regarding SHGs are directed towards providing financial services to the poor and thus achieve maximum financial inclusion. To provide a formal statutory framework for the promotion, development and regulation of the micro finance sector, the Government has introduced a bill in Lok Sabha on 20.03.2007 entitled "The Micro Financial Sector (Development and Regulation) Bill, 2007". This information was given by Minister of State for Finance, Shri Pawan Kumar Bansal in reply to a question raised by Shri K.S. Rao in Lok Sabha today.

3152. (7-9-2007) NEW DELHI : A consensus had been arrived at between he Centre and the States that the CST should be phased out in 4 steps, *i.e.*, reducing the CST rate from 4% to 3% w.e.f. 01.04.2007, from 3% to 2% w.e.f. 01.04.2008, from 2% to 1% w.e.f. 01.04.2009 and eventually abolishing the tax on 31.03.2010. A package of compensation to the States for revenue loss on account of phasing out of the CST has also been agreed upon between the States and the Central Government. As per the agreed package, the states shall be compensated through a combination of non-monetary and monetary measures. During 2007-08, such measures to be taken to compensate the states for CST reduction from 4% to 3% include abolition of Form-D, levy of VAT on Tobacco @12.5% by States and transfer of total proceeds of tax on identified services to the States. In case these measures prove inadequate to fully cover the loss, budgetary support shall be given. In order to give effect to the above decisions the Taxation Laws (Amendment) Act, 2007 has been enacted, whereby the CST Act, 1956 and the Additional Duties of Excise (Goods of Special Importance) Act, 1957 have been amended, inter alia, resulting in the reduction of rate of CST on inter-State sale to registered dealers (against Form-C) from 4% to 3% w.e.f. 01.04.2007, the withdrawal of the facility of inter-State purchases by Government Departments at concessional CST rate against Form-D and the enabling of the states to levy VAT on Tobacco. Further, a provision of Rs.2,500 crores has been made in the Department of Revenue Budget for 2007-08 for releasing CST Compensation to the States. This information was given by Minister of State for Finance, Shri S.S. Palanimanickam in reply to a question raised by Shri Hansraj G. Ahir in Lok Sabha today.

3153. (7-9-2007) NEW DELHI : Jammu and Kashmir will have 1000 Micro Hydro Projects for increased electricity access. The implementation of this project started in 2005-06 after a component under the reconstruction plan for Jammu and Kashmir announced by the Prime Minister in November 2004. The implementation of this project is being done through the Army. 967 Projects have been completed so far, of which 893 have been handed over to the village community or State administration. The Ministry of New and Renewable Energy supports the deployment of small hydro projects, *i.e.* upto 25 MW station capacity for which it provides central finance assistance. This information was given by the Minister of State in the Ministry of New and Renewable Energy, Shri Vilas Muttemwar in a written reply to question :in the Lok Sabha today.

3154. (7-9-2007) NEW DELHI : During Eleventh Plan period 2100 MW capacity addition is proposed from bio power comprising 500 MW bio-mass power, 1200 MW baggasse and 400Mwe energy power from industrial and municipal waste. In addition 100 Mwe of distributed renewable generation for power and heat has been proposed which include bio-mass resources. Apart from preferential tarrif in most potential States, central financial assistance (CFA) for setting up bio energy/power projects is available. Due to Court Orders, Municipal solid waste projects has been kept in abeyance. An estimated employment of about 17 million mandays per annum is likely to generated in various States during Eleventh Plan period, as a result of deploying bio-mass projects. This information was given by the Minister of State in the Ministry of New and Renewable Energy, Shri Vilas Muttemwar in a written reply to question by S/shri Anandrao V. Adsul, Adhalrao Patil Shivajirao and Ravi Prakash Verma :in the Lok Sabha today.

3155. (7-9-2007) NEW DELHI : Accelerated Urban Water Supply Programme has been subsumed in Urban Infrastructure Development Scheme for Small and Medium Towns w.e.f. 3rd December, 2005. Proposal have not been received under AUWSP during the years 2006-07 and 2007-08. For the ongoing projects (sanctioned upto 2004-05) under AUWSP Scheme, amounts released during 2006-07 and 2007-08 (upto August, 2007) are Rs.47.63 crore and Rs.10.93 crore respectively. This information was given by Shri Ajay Maken, Minister of State in the Ministry of Urban Development in the Lok Sabha today in a written reply to a question by Shri Braja Kishore.

3156. (7-9-2007) NEW DELHI : Shri K.C.Jena, Chairman Railway Board has also taken over as Chairman, International Union of Railways (UIC). Shri Jena will be Chairman of UIC till December 2008. The Chairman Railway Board of Indian Railways had taken over as the first non-European Chairman of UIC for two-Year term in January 2007. Indian Railways have been actively associated with the organization since 1998 and has played an important role in its restructuring to transform it to a truly global institution. As part of the restructuring, six regional units of UIC have been formed and UIC-Asia will be headquartered at New Delhi. Indian Railways will facilitate the setting up of UIC-Asia regional Units. Indian Railways will also provide all assistance for the International Railway Strategic Management Institute (IRSMI) that would come up at Chanakyapuri, New Delhi.International Union of Railways (UIC) is an international association of rail operators and organizations established in 1922 with headquarters in Paris having 224 members worldwide. The organization provides a forum to different Railway organization in the world to undertake joint research projects, develop strategies for implementation of international projects like inter-continental freight corridors, and high speed rail. It also enables Railway Managers across the globe to develop skills through its International Railway Strategic Management Institute. The priority areas for UIC would be to have increased worldwide investments in rail transport. UIC's focus is to establish rail transport as the key link in the global logistics chain.

3157. (7-9-2007) NEW DELHI : Union Rural Development Minister Dr. Raghuvansh Prasad Singh has emphasized on the importance of the District Vigilance & Monitoring Committees in taking stock of the progress of implementation of various programmes launched by the Ministry of Rural Development. Addressing the ninth interactive session with the MPs from Andhra Pradesh and Maharashta held here yesterday, Dr. Singh urged the Members of Parliament to play a major role as Chairmen of such committees and also to take out field visits for ascertaining ground level realities in implementation of the schemes like the flagship programme Bharat Nirman and schemes like NREGA, PMGSY, IAY, Sanitation and Drinking Water Supply. The eighth such session was held with the MPs from Uttar Pradesh on Wednesday. The MPs urged Dr. Singh to give directions that their suggestions regarding the implementation of Centrally sponsored Rural Development Schemes to be given priority by the implementing agencies working under the State/ district authorities. The members expressed concern over the reported instances of irregularities and fraudulent practices and apprised the minister of their field experiences during the verification process conducted by them for the schemes run under NREGA, TSC, SGSY and Area Development Programmes like HARYALI, DPAP and IWDP. They also raised the issues such as fake muster rolls, lesser payment to labourers, use of inferior quality material and willful selection of work sites by the local authorities. Dr. Singh assured the MPs of an appropriate and timely action in this regard. Smt. Surya Kanta Patil and Sh. Chandra Shekhar Sahu, both the Minister of State in the Ministry of Rural Development were also present on the occasion. The objective of these group meetings is to apprise the MPs about different provisions of the rural development schemes, the status of implementation of various programmes in the concerned State and also to get their valuable feedback/suggestions based on their Review meetings as Chairman of District Vigilance & Monitoring Committees. The last such meeting in this series with the MPs of Bihar and Jharkhand is scheduled on 13th of this month.

3158. (7-9-2007) NEW DELHI : Three registered brands are being used by the Khadi and Village Industries Commission (KVIC), exclusively for products under the purview of KVI sector: (a) Khadi Brand: Mainly for premium and export oriented products, (b) Sarvodaya Brand: Products for consumption of middle and lower income group & (c) Deshi Aahar: For organic food items. KVIC takes part in international trade fairs and exhibitions where, branded products, including khadi items, are widely exhibited. Delegations of Export oriented Units/Institutions registered with KVIC/State/Union Territory Khadi and Village Industries Boards (KVIBs) are also provided financial assistance to participate in the international exhibitions. During 2006-07, KVIC took part in 5 such exhibitions. For promotion of export of khadi and village industry products, KVIC provides cash incentives to the registered exporting institutions and individual entrepreneurs at the rate of 5 per cent of the 'free on board' (FOB) value of exported items. KVIC has launched 'Mission Khadi' to convert the khadi fabric into ready-made garments of latest designs and the help of National Institute of Fashion Technology (NIFT), Chennai (Tamilnadu) and NIFT, Kolkata (West Bengal) is being taken for identification and procurement of appropriate machinery for projects under 'Mission Khadi', recommendation of expert designers required for the units, training of people engaged in such projects, etc. This information was given by the Minister of Micro, Small & Medium Enterprises, Shri Mahabir Prasad in a written reply to a question in Rajya Sabha today.

3159. (7-9-2007) NEW DELHI : The Director General, Coast Guard has advocated penalties for ships and vessels that spread pollution in the Indian waters. Presiding over a meeting on fighting oil spills in New Delhi today, Vice Admiral RF Contractor called for stringent implementation of pollution control measures in harbours and ports on the Indian coastline. Admiral Contractor also expressed concern over the operation of ageing vessels that posed a threat to marine environment in Indian waters. As many as 18 ships have either sunk or been grounded along the Indian coast so far this year alone. He said the Indian Coast Guard would soon acquire three specialised, indigenously built pollution control vessels to tackle oil spills and other threats to marine ecology. About 70 delegates from various Government departments, Ports, Oil Industry and Exploration Units and State Pollution Control Boards participated in the 10th National Oil Spill and Disaster Contingency Plan (NOSDCP) and Preparedness Meeting. It deliberated on working out synergies between various agencies and port authorities to build capacities to fight Oil spills of upto 700 tonnes. The Indian Coast Guard is the central coordinating agency for implementation of the NOSDCP. The Coast Guard has been holding regular exercises with various agencies to simulate Oil Spill Contingencies.

3160. (7-9-2007) NEW DELHI : Biotechnology Parks set up in Lucknow (Uttar Pradesh), Pune (Maharashtra) and Hyderabad (Andhra Pradesh) are functional. A Biotechnology Park is being set up at Vadodara (Gujarat). Projects for setting up Biotechnology Incubation Centres have been supported in the States of Andhra Pradesh, Himachal Pradesh, Kerala and Karnataka. A proposal has just been received from the Government of Tamil Nadu for strengthening the TICEL Bio Park. Another proposal has just been received from the Government of Gujarat for establishment of a Marine Biotech Incubator. These would be processed and considered by the Expert Committee constituted for the purpose. A decision on these is expected to be taken by early 2008. This information was given by the

Union Minister for Science & Technology and Earth Sciences Shri Kapil Sibal in a written reply to a question in the Lok Sabha today.

3161. (7-9-2007) NEW DELHI : A 3-Member team of scientists from GSI (Northern Region), Office, Lucknow have been constituted to study the reported cracks in Bundelkhand area of Uttar Pradesh and the team has already left on 5/9/2007 to study the affected area. Ground fissures have developed in some of the areas in Bundelkhand particularly in Hamirpur District of Uttar Pradesh and also in Badrinath area of Uttarakhand State. In Hamirpur district of Bundelkhand area, the fissures are reported to have developed in Maudha Tehsil where it is around 800 m in length and 60 cm wide. In Uttarakhand State, cracks have been reported from Neelkhanth Parvat in Badrinath area. This information was given by the Union Minister for Science & Technology and Earth Sciences Shri Kapil Sibal in a written reply to a question in the Lok Sabha today.

3162. (7-9-2007) NEW DELHI : The Government is setting up a National Early Warning System for Tsunami and Storm Surges in Indian Ocean and the system is scheduled to be operational by the end of September 2007. An interim warning centre is already working at Indian National Centre for Ocean information Services, Hyderabad, Andhra Pradesh on a 24x7 basis. The National Cyclone Risk Mitigation Project (NCRMP) has been drawn up with a view to address cyclone hazard risks in 13 cyclone prone coastal States/UTs, including Tamil Nadu. The cyclone warning system is already functional and cyclone warnings are being provided by India Meteorological Department for all the coastal regions of the country. This information was given by the Union Minister for Science & Technology and Earth Sciences Shri Kapil Sibal in the Lok Sabha today in response to a question related to reported sea water ingress into the coastal villages of Tamil Nadu following the Tsunami in 2004.

3163. (7-9-2007) NEW DELHI : This is a proposal to set up an institute to study the impact of global warming/climatic changes etc. Based on the discussions of a Brainstorming meeting, held on June 1, 2007 organized by the Ministry of Earth Sciences (MoES), involving experts working on climate change and representatives from all the concerned Ministries, Non-governmental organizations, and academic and scientific institutions, a coordinated research programme on climate change shall be launched to study all associated science aspects of climate change viz. Carbon and Nitrogen cycles; Asian Brown Cloud (ABC). As part of climate change programme, there is a proposal for the establishment of a dedicated Centre to undertake research on Science aspects of climate change at Indian Institute of Tropical Meteorology (IITM), Pune. This information was given by the Union Minister for Science & Technology and Earth Sciences Shri Kapil Sibal in a written reply to a question in the Lok Sabha today.

3164. (7-9-2007) NEW DELHI : Delay in supply of critical equipment has emerged as one of the reasons for slippages in executing the power projects in the recent past. The proposed capacity addition of 16,335 MW for the current year includes a number of thermal projects aggregating approximately 4,275 MW which were originally scheduled to be commissioned in the previous year 2006-07, but have not yet been commissioned. To avoid the slippages of the Eleventh Plan targets, inter alia, quarterly progress review of the capacity addition programme is being carried out with the Central Electricity Authority and the Central Public Sector Undertakings. Expansion of BHEL's capacity as well as development of manufacturing capacity by generating CPSUs, or private players alone, or through joint ventures are possible options to augment the manufacturing capacity in line with the generation capacities being planned for the Eleventh Plan and beyond. In addition, import of equipment is also permissible The working of Bharat Heavy Electricals Limited (BHEL), which is the major manufacturer of plant and equipment in the public sector, is being regularly reviewed by the Ministry of Heavy Industry and Public Enterprises; furthermore, BHEL is augmenting its capacity to 10,000 MW by December, 2007 and further to 15,000 MW by December, 2009. This information was given by the Union Power Minister Shri Sushilkumar Shinde in a written reply to a question in the Lok Sabha today.

3165. (7-9-2007) NEW DELHI : A total number of 165 executives have resigned from NTPC in the year 2006-07. The attrition percentage for the year 2006-07 is 1.55% which is not high. The reasons cited by these executives for resigning from NTPC are career enhancement, more pay and perks, academic pursuits etc. The Government has declared NTPC as a Navaratna Public Sector Undertakings with a vision of making it a global power company having autonomy in decision making. Accordingly, NTPC has been pursuing Human Resource Development (HRD) initiatives to enhance organizational performance by institutionalizing an objective and open performance management system; to align individual and organizational needs and develop business leaders by implementing a career development system; to enhance commitment of employees by recognizing and rewarding high performance; to build and sustain a learning organization of competent world –class professionals; and to institutionalize core values and create a culture of team-building, empowerment, equity, innovation and openness which would motivate employees and enable achievement of strategic objectives. This information was given by the Union Power Minister Shri Sushilkumar Shinde in a written reply to a question in the Lok Sabha today.

3166. (7-9-2007) NEW DELHI : Satluj Jal Vidyut Nigam Limited(SJVNL) is taking several steps to deal with the heavy silt content in river Satluj. These include: i) A comprehensive Catchment Area Treatment (CAT) Plan with a proposed outlay of Rs. 29.57 crores is being implemented by the State Forest Department. The period of implementation is 10 years w.e.f. 2002-03. ii) SJVNL has carried out an extensive exercise and prepared a Detailed Report on bank protection and landslides protection works for an estimated cost of Rs. 94 crores to reduce the silt contents in the river. The report has been submitted to State Forest Department and Central Electricity Authority for their perusal and approval in November, 2006. iii) For preparation of base line data / record of vulnerable area of Satluj Catchment, SJVNL has awarded a work on 'Preparation of Comprehensive CAT Plan of Satluj basin (within Indian territory)' so that a detailed GIS and Remote Sensing map based vulnerable erosion prone areas, land slide prone areas, Nallahas, geological sensitive area etc. be identified for appropriate treatment as suggested. The Work is scheduled to be completed in October, 2007. iv) Nallahs contributing high quartz laden silt in the river water upstream of the dam axis have been identified for treatment and are being treated. v) The underwater turbine parts of the plant have been coated with Tungsten Carbide Coating by High Velocity Oxygen Fuel (HVOF) to improve abrasion resistance to silt. vi) SJVNL is carrying out regular flushing of reservoir at Nathpa Dam to reduce the silt load. (vii) Dam height has been increased for increased pondage and settling of silt. As per information available, the Nathpa Jhakhri Power Plant during the current year 2007-08 has been halted for 7.87 days on account of high silt in the river Satluj and for 1.44 days on account of periodic reservoir flushing. Whenever the silt concentration in the river water exceeds the permissible limit of 4000 Parts Per Million (PPM), the plant has to be shut down to avoid erosion to underwater parts of the turbine. A provision has, therefore, been made in the generation target in the Memorandum of Understanding for closure of plant upto 16 days in a year to accommodate the loss in generation due to excessive silt in river waters and also for reservoir flushing operations. Reservoir flushing is a technical requirement for sediment management.

3167. (7-9-2007) NEW DELHI : The Delhi Electricity Regulatory Commission (DERC) has not permitted the Distribution Companies including BSES to raise power tariff in Delhi as the distribution companies are required to file their tariff petitions under Multi Year Tariff Regulations before DERC. This information was given by the Union Power Minister Shri Sushilkumar Shinde in a written reply to a question in the Lok Sabha today. Determination of power tariffs to be charged by the distribution licensees is the statutory function of the State Electricity Regulatory Commissions (SERCs). In doing so SERCs are guided by the provisions contained in the Electricity Act 2003 which, inter alia, include the factors that would encourage competition, efficiency, economical use of resources, safeguarding of consumers interests and at the same time ensure recovery of cost of electricity in a reasonable manner, reduction of cross subsidies, the National Electricity Policy and the Tariff Policy. The SERCs are required to determine tariff in a transparent way after hearing various stakeholders.

3168. (7-9-2007) NEW DELHI : Section 11 of the Companies Act, 1956 provides that no company, association or partnership consisting of more than 10 persons (more than 20 persons in case of other than those which are doing the business of banking) shall be formed for the purpose of carrying on the business unless it is registered as a company under Companies Act, 1956 or is formed in pursuance of some other Indian Law. However, no specific time frame for registration under Companies Act, 1956 has been provided. Necessary legal action is initiated under section 11(4) & (5) of the Companies Act, 1956 as and when contravention of section 11(1) & (2) of the Companies Act comes to notice. This information was given by the Minister of Corporate Affairs, Shri Prem Chand Gupta in written reply to a question raised in Lok Sabha today.

3169. (7-9-2007) NEW DELHI : The Ministry of Corporate Affairs has implemented an e-Governance Project called 'MCA21' with a view to improve the speed and certainty in delivery of MCA services in a transparent manner. This improvement is ensured primarily through the mechanism of secure electronic filing (e-filing) and easy online payment for all the services provided by the Registrar of Companies. It is, therefore, a significant step towards an end-to-end paperless delivery of the Government services with widespread use of Digital Signature to carry out e-filing in a secure manner in conformity with the Information Technology Act, 2000. Starting with the launch of the first pilot on February 18, 2006 from Coimbatore and the major launch of the second pilot from Delhi by the Hon'ble Prime Minister on March 18, 2006, the programme was rolled out at all the ROC locations in a phased manner by September 4, 2006. Electronic filing, using Digital Signatures, was made compulsory from September 16, 2006 with the amendment in the Companies Act, 1956. The facility for online payment through Credit Card and Internet Banking has also been provided on the portal through a secure payment gateway, to ensure prompt recognition of payment and delivery of services. A total of 25.32 lakh documents have been filed online since the launch of this project and a significant improvement has been achieved in reduction of time in delivery of service. The stakeholders can now file their documents on-line at any time and from anywhere in a 24 X 7 X 365 time frame from the comfort of their offices or homes without physically visiting the ROC offices. This information was given by the Minister of Corporate Affairs, Shri Prem Chand Gupta in written reply to a question raised in Lok Sabha today.

3170. (7-9-2007) NEW DELHI : Railways always endeavour to provide and maintain required facilities in the Railway quarters and colonies as per entitlement of the employees. However required facilities may not be available in some quarters/colonies. Corporate Welfare Plan for 10 years at a cost of Rs. 5000 crore has also been approved to pay special attention towards maintenance and improvement of staff quarters with particular emphasis on substandard quarters lacking basic amenities and replacement of old and dilapidated quarters on Railways. In the current year sanctions have been given for additional works of Rs. 344 crore. This information was given by the Minister of State for Railways Shri R.Velu in written reply to a question in the Rajya Sabha today.

3171. (7-9-2007) NEW DELHI : Indian Railways have improved the tracks structure & designed new wagons, which has enabled running of some freight trains at 100 KMPH. Investment in wagon design & tracks structure will help in improving rail efficiency & prove to be economical in the long run. National Transport Policy Committee observed that the speed differential between the mail/ express & freight trains adversely affects the line capacity utilization. The committee felt that if freight trains could be run at speeds of 90 KMPH it will reduce turnround time & wagon requirement. This information was given by the Minister of State for Railways Shri R.Velu in written reply to a question in the Rajya Sabha today.

3172. (7-9-2007) NEW DELHI : A consortium comprising of M/s Terry Farrel & Partners, Hong Kong, Ove Arup and Partners, Hong Kong and SMEC International Pvt. Ltd., Gurgaon have been engaged as Consultants for re-development of only New Delhi railway station as world class station. Other 21 stations identified for development as World Class station are – Pune, Chhatrapati Shivaji Terminus (Mumbai), Howrah, Anand Vihar (Delhi), Bijwasan (Delhi), Lucknow, Amritsar, chandigarh, Varanasi, Chennai, Thiruvananthapuram, Secunderabad, Ahmedabad, Patna, Gaya, Bhubaneswar, Mathura, Agra, Bangalore, Bhopal and Jaipur. This information was given by the Minister of State for Railways Shri R.Velu in written reply to a question in the Rajya Sabha today.

3173. (7-9-2007) NEW DELHI : Necessary infrastructure is provided for handling of cargo as per the offering of traffic at railway stations. All possible steps are taken to prevent avoidable damages and loss to the cargo. The application for filing a claim for compensation is accepted at the railway station(s), who forward the same to the concerned Divisional/ Zonal Railway head quarter. The Station Managers of selected important stations have also been empowered to settle claims for compensations upto Rs. 400/- in each case. This information was given by the Minister of State for Railways Shri R.Velu in written reply to a question in the Rajya Sabha today.

3174. (7-9-2007) NEW DELHI : Minister of State for Finance, Shri Pawan Kumar Bansal affirmed in Lok Sabha today that some de-mat accounts have been freezed in the absence of Permanent Account Number (PAN), this year. The value of holdings in frozen accounts with the Depositories as on August 31, 2007 was Rs.95,769 crore. 18.86 lakh demat accounts have been released by the depositories since January 1, 2007 after submission of PAN details by the account holders. Shri Bansal this in a written reply to a question raised by Shri Dharmendra Pradhan and Shri Kiren Rijiju.

3175. (7-9-2007) NEW DELHI : The national level programme is being organised in the main hall of Vigyan Bhawan. The President of India Smt. Pratibha Devisingh Patil will be the Chief Guest. Minister of Human Resource Development, Shri Arjun Singh will preside over the function. The function will be attended in large number by volunteers and learners of Adult Education Programme, school children, senior officials of the Government of India, diplomats and representatives of international organizations and NGOs. Several special publication brought out by the National Literacy Mission will be presented to the Hon'ble President of India. A 10 ½ minute documentary film on literacy 'The Marquee Effect' will also be screened on this occasion.

3176. (7-9-2007) NEW DELHI : Shri Murli Deora, Minister for Petroleum & Natural Gas introduced the Rajiv Gandhi Institute of Petroleum Technology Bill 2007 in Rajya Sabha today to declare the institution known as the Rajiv Gandhi Institute of Petroleum Technology to be an institution of national importance and to provide for its incorporation and matters connected therewith. This marks a major step towards setting up of Rajiv Gandhi Institute of Petroleum Technology at Jias, Rai Bareli District, Uttar Pradesh as 'Institute of National Importance' under an Act of Parliament. The Rajiv Gandhi Institute of Petroleum Technology (RGIPT) is envisaged to serve as the fountainhead for the nurturing of world class technical human resources capable of serving as the leaders and innovators of tomorrow in the field of Petroleum Technology. To start with the Institute will commence its academic operations by admitting students in basic undergraduate courses from the academic year 2008-09, from a rented campus. The institute will become fully operational in 2015-16. On its becoming fully operational the Institute would have 7 B. Tech, 6 Integrated Masters Degrees, 8 M.Tech/MBA and 12 PGD and Ph.D programmes. The total estimated capital cost of the project is Rs.435 crores which would be met partially through budgetary support of Rs. 285 crores and Rs. 150 crores from Oil Industry Development Board. The total estimated recurring expenditure of Rs. 260.58 crores would be met from the accrual of interest on Endowment Fund of Rs. 250.00 crores to be created with the contribution of Oil Public Sector Undertakings (PSUs), student fees, donations and other earnings of the Institute through Research & Development, consultancies, students' placement fees, etc. The Institute is envisaged to be self sufficient and self-reliant by the year 2015-16. It is important to note that Government had come out with the New Exploration Licensing Policy in 1999 and with the passage of time this policy has been made more and more attractive to foreign companies as well as Indian private and public sector companies. As on date, only 30% of the sedimentary basins in India has been explored and there is still a vast potential in terms of acreages that are to be explored. The Government is committed to increase the exploration coverage to an extent of 100% by the year 2015. In a recent study conducted by consultant Price Waterhouse Coopers for Petrofed, the gap between the availability and requirement of trained manpower in India is projected to be about 36000 by the year 2019 and the existing institutes may not be adequate to meet the increasing requirement of technical manpower in the petroleum sector. The proposed Rajiv Gandhi Institute of Petroleum Technology is expected to meet this shortfall to a significant extent.

3177. (7-9-2007) NEW DELHI : The Government has decided to select the best performing Central Public Sector Enterprises (CPSEs) group wise. Accordingly, from this year the total number of MoU Excellence Awards will be twelve (one from each of ten Syndicates, one from the listed CPSEs, one from amongst the turnaround sick and loss making enterprises). All other excellent performing CPSEs will get MoU excellence certificates. This was stated by Shri Sontosh Mohan Dev, Minister for Heavy Industries & Public Enterprises at the Consultative Committee meeting attached to his Ministry here last night. The top ten MoU Excellence Awards have so far been given based on the composite scores vis-a-vis their performance during the year achieved by CPSEs. This did not differentiate between different kinds of CPSEs, the Minister said. Shri Dev said, it was also decided to introduce the MoU system in the State level Public Sector Enterprises. Some states already have such a system but most of the states do not have any performance contract for their state level Public Sector Enterprises. The Ministry of Heavy Industries & Public Enterprises would organize a workshop for the state governments and state level public sector enterprises shortly, the Minister added. Some of the members suggested that more autonomy should be given to non-Navratna and non-Miniratna companies as well and that the CPSEs should lend a helping hand towards sick units that are engaged especially in the infrastructure development projects. The Minister assured the Members that the government was taking all necessary steps to revive sick units that are potentially viable. In certain cases there had been a tremendous turnaround for sick CPSEs. Smt. Kanti Singh, Minister of State for Heavy Industries & Public Enterprises and Dr. R.C. Panda, Secretary, Ministry of Heavy Industries & Public Enterprises also spoke on this occasion. Dr. Panda, in a presentation explained to the Members the importance, objectives and scope of the MoU system. He said that in 2006-07, 114 CPSEs signed MoUs with the Government and in 2007-08, 145 CPSEs would be covered under the MoU system.

3178. (7-9-2007) NEW DELHI : The Prime Minister said here today that it is a matter of great pleasure to be present at this function organized to felicitate D. Balram Jakhar on his 85th Birthday and to release the Abhinandan Granth, titled "Kalpa Vriksha". Dr. Jakhar is a towering personality, known to be a man of principles and as an outstanding leader, whose contribution to Parliament and commitment to the welfare of the farming community in particular are well known. Dr. Balram Jakhar began his distinguished legislative career in 1972, when he was elected to the Punjab Legislative Assembly and appointed the Deputy Minister for Cooperation, Irrigation and Power. He was re-elected in, 1977 to the Assembly and became the Leader of the Opposition. In these capacities, he proved himself to be an outstanding leader and an able administrator. In 1980, Dr. Jakhar entered the Lok Sabha from the Ferozepur constituency, and had the unique distinction of being elected as Speaker of the Lok Sabha in his very first term as a Member of Parliament. It was an onerous task and a great responsibility, full of challenges. With his characteristic down-to-earth approach, he took on this challenge and conducted the proceedings of the House with great dignity and impartiality, earning the support and goodwill of Parliamentarians, across party lines. During times of heated debate he sought to calm tempers and to change a confrontational debate into a discussion during which varied points of view were shared, thus enriching understanding of issues. Therefore, on his re-election to Parliament in 1985 from Sikar constituency, he was unanimously elected as Speaker of the Lok Sabha for the second time, a testimony to the enormous confidence that Members had on his ability to preside over the business of the House. Dr. Jakhar's diplomacy was not limited only to the House. It was during his tenure that the Parliament of India developed strong ties of cooperation with other national Parliaments and also with international parliamentary bodies, including the Commonwealth Parliamentary Association and the International Parliamentary Union. This enhanced the profile of the Indian Parliament and the country as a whole in the global arena. During his entire life, Dr. Jakhar has been a tireless champion of farmers and their causes. Himself a farmer, he introduced several innovative ideas for the development of orchards and for improved farming. As Agriculture Minister, Dr. Jakhar worked relentlessly to improve the lot of the rural areas. He has always maintained that an Economic Policy cannot be complete without an Agricultural Policy. This is a sound economic inter-linkage. In our country more than 70 percent of the population resides in rural areas and, therefore, sustained development of our country requires growth in the rural sector. Farmers need to be provided better and easier access to credit and marketing facilities.

3179. (8-9-2007) NEW DELHI : The Centre has asked the States that the implementation of smart card based project for issuance of Driving Licence and Registration Certificate needs to be completed by 31st March next year by all the States and UTs. At a meeting of State Road Transport Secretaries/Commissioners of all the States held here today, it was also decided that the computerization of all Road Transport Offices (RTOs) of the States should be completed by 31st March 2008 and linking of these offices to their respective State Head Quarters should also be completed by that time. Later on the State Head Quarters could be linked to Central Level to create National Register of motor vehicle data which would provide lateral connectivity amongst RTOs. The National Informatics Centre (NIC) would be the nodal agency for providing the national connectivity, who are in the process of formulating the project. All the participating States agreed that there was a need for immediate reforms in the road transport sector. There was also unanimity amongst the States for the need to have rationalized tax structure for motor vehicles. The Centre impressed upon the States that they should evolve a mechanism to have unified check posts at single entry point at inter-state borders to ensure barrier free movement of both goods and passenger vehicles across the country. The identification of points on National Highways where such check posts are to be created/set up should have the clearance from the concerned Transport Commissioner and the concerned Chief Engineer, National Highways. The States were urged to take effective enforcement measures to check the menace of overloading and to ensure that the order of Hon'ble Supreme Court is implemented in the right earnest. The States were also urged to strictly enforce various traffic laws enshrined in the Motor Vehicles Act, 1988 and rules made there under to improve road safety scenario in the country. At the meeting Competition Commission of India had made a presentation on their recent study findings concerning State Policies affecting competition on "Passenger Road Transport Sector" to advocate institutional reform to engender greater competition in the Passenger Road Transport Sector. It was decided that recommendations made in the study will be examined by the States to imbibe greater competition in passenger transport services.The meeting was presided over by the Secretary, Road Transport and Highways Shri Brahm Dutt.

3180. (8-9-2007) NEW DELHI : The President of India, Smt. Pratibha Devisingh Patil has said that it is a matter of concern that the male-female gap in literacy rates continues to be unacceptably high. This divide is sharper in rural areas. Women's literacy and education has to be made a priority. She was speaking as the Chief Guest at the celebrations organised on the occasion of International Literacy Day, here, today. She also said, 'Specific education programmes, with targets, should be launched for education of girls'. Referring to Millennium Development Goals set in the Summit held in New York in 2000, the President observed, ' 2015 is only 8 years away. Globally, there are still 77 million primary school age children who are not enrolled in schools and 771 million adults who do not have basic literary skills. The proportion of women who are not literate is very high. Concerted action will be required if the Millennium Development education targets are to be reached by 2015'. 'As we enter the 11th Plan period we need to take stock of the literacy rates in the country. We have made tremendous progress in literacy in the last century. In 1901, India had an abysmally low literacy rate of 5.35 percent, at the time of Independence literacy had risen to only 18.33 percent but in 2001, the literacy rate had risen substantially to 64.84 percent. This is considerable progress, but there are still millions in our country without basic literary skills,' the President added. The Minister of Human Resource Development, Shri Arjun Singh who presided over the function recalled that our Late Prime Minister Rajiv Gandhi set up the National Literacy Mission in 1988 as one of the five technology missions but with one aim, to create a resurgent India with a literate human resource, inclusive society and empowered individuals. He appreciated the fact that though the figures in literacy elude us, the enthusiasm is catching, which is necessary for us to succeed. He mentioned that the challenges before the NLM still remain, he felt that there is urgent need to bridge the gender gap between male and female literacy and bring the disadvantaged sections of society into the fold of literacy. He further added that the churning in the literacy movement must result in mass awakening and the literacy and life long learning must take on the character of a mass movement which can whip up excitement, enthuse people, raise people's aspirations and make the programme community owned. As a result of new initiatives of the Ministry, most of the districts would transit to the Continuing Education (CE) phase in 11th Plan.

3181. (8-9-2007) NEW DELHI : The 35th Annual Conference of the Prosthodontic Society was inaugurated here today. This conference is being held under the aegis of the Army Dental Corps and under the stewardship of The President Indian Prosthodontic Society, Lt Gen Paramjit Singh, Director General Dental Services and the dynamic organizing secretary Brig Vimal Arora from 06th to 11th Sep 2007 at the prestigious India Habitat centre. Conference was inaugurated by the Director General Armed Forced Medical Services Lt Gen Yogendra Singh, Senior Colonel Commandant Army Medical Corps, at the Air force Auditorium. Prosthodontics over its long history, has proven to be a remarkably adaptable and innovative branch of dentistry as it has evolved and responded to expanding and ever more sophisticated patient needs and new technologies. It was the first specialty involved in reconstruction, a departure from the ablative approach of early dentistry. Over a period of time, it has changed considerably and it possesses a unique set of characteristics that have shaped much of dentistry what it is today. This conference will be attended by over 1200 delegates which includes national and international delegates. The conference will show case the latest developments in the field of Prosthodontics, which will include CAD-CAM technology that is being used in developed countries for the fabrication of various restorations from crowns and bridges to maxillofacial prosthesis. Dentistry has witnessed a revolutionary change in the use of Implants for replacement of missing teeth. The delegates will get an opportunity to upgrade their knowledge in this field as well as other latest developments in Prosthodontics. The theme of the conference' Treatment Modalities for the Partially Edentulous' will be vigorously deliberated during this 4 day conference. 11 pre-conference courses on various aspects of Prosthodontics were conducted which mainly include Dental implants, Cad-Cam restorations, full mouth rehabilitation, maxillofacial Prosthodontics and Aesthetic dentistry. There will be approximately 600 scientific paper presentations, poster presentations and table clinics, which will benefit all the prosthodontists and a large number of student delegates attending this conference. The conference also has a tremendous participation from the dental industry from India and abroad. An massive trade fare has been organized with approx 100 stalls where dental dealers from all over the world will show their products and machinery.

3182. (8-9-2007) NEW DELHI : A Three day special 'Experience Sharing Program' for member countries of the 'Association of Government Accounts Organisations of Asia' (AGAOA) begins here on Monday. The programme, organised by the Institute of Government Accounts & Finance (INGAF), the training arm of the Controller General of Accounts, Ministry of Finance is expected to strengthen the process of information sharing in issues related to accounting reforms, internal audit and training needs of the member countries. India is a founder member of AGAOA along with Pakistan, Sri Lanka, Nepal, Bangladesh, Bhutan, Myanmar and Maldives. It aims at promoting 'professional understanding and technical cooperation among member institutions through exchange of ideas and experiences in the fields covered by Government Accounts Organisations to ensure transparency, accountability and good governance.' Its member-countries have agreed to collectively foster applied research, training and capacity building initiatives for human resource development and to meet the demands of a modern technology driven accounting and financial environment.

3183. (8-9-2007) NEW DELHI : The President of India said here that we have gathered here today to celebrate the International Literacy Day and to reaffirm our commitment to the goal of eradication of illiteracy. I congratulate all those who have won awards for their excellent implementation of the literacy advancement programmes. The many teachers, scholars, NGOs and volunteers in our country who are making substantial contributions to education also deserve our appreciation. In the ancient world, with an oral tradition, the mode of transmission of knowledge was through discourses and discussions. However, in the modern world, literacy skills are fundamental to informed decision making, personal empowerment, and participation in the local and global community. Literacy is an indispensable component of human resource development. There is a phrase in Marathi which means that you will survive only if you read. Basic education, within which literacy is the key learning tool, was recognized as a human right in the Universal Declaration of Human Rights over 50 years ago. At the Millennium Development Summit held in New York in 2000, world leaders agreed on a global partnership to work collectively for eradicating poverty, hunger, disease, ignorance and improving the lives of people. They adopted specific goals. One of the Millennium Development Goals is the achievement of universal primary education by 2015 and within the context of the goal on gender equality, the target is to eliminate gender disparity in education. 2015 is only 8 years away. Globally, there are still 77 million primary school age children who are not enrolled in schools and 771 million adults who do not have basic literacy skills. The proportion of women who are not literate is very high. Concerted action will be required if the Millennium Development education targets are to be reached by 2015. India is home to some of the best engineering and management institutions in the world. Every year at least 30 lakh graduates and 7 lakh post-graduates are added to its knowledge capital. India has one of the largest manpower of computer specialists and also one of the largest body of English speaking IT professionals in the world. However, on the other hand, India is home to the world's largest number of illiterates and this is a matter of great concern. India accounts for 20 percent of the world's out-of-school children and 35 percent adult illiterates.

3184. (10-9-2007) NEW DELHI : Lalit Kala Akademi (National Academy of Art), New Delhi today honoured thirteen eminent art personalities by conferring Lalit Kala Ratna on them. Speaker of the Lok Sabha Shri Somnath Chatterjee conferred the awards at a glittering function here in the presence of eminent artists, academicians and theatre personalities. Minister for Culture and Tourism Smt. Ambika Soni presided over the function. Those who were honoured by conferring the Lalit Ratna Awards by the Lok Sabha Speaker include S/Shri Bal Chhabda (Maharashtra), B.N. Arya (U.P.), Devi Prasad (New Delhi), Dinkar Kowshik (West Bengal), K. Rajaiah (A.P.), Kekoo Gandhy (Mumbai), Krishna Reddy (New York),

L.Munuswamy (Tamil Nadu), Laxman Pai (Delhi), M.V. Krishnan (Kerala), Piraji Sagara (Gujarat), P.N. Choyal (Rajasthan) and Sobha Brahma (Assam). A Portfolio containing the works of the honoured artists was also released on the occasion. A flute recital by Pt. Hariprasad Chaurasia was also presented on the occasion.

3185. (10-9-2007) NEW DELHI : Both the Houses of the Parliament have passed Competition (Amendment) Bill-2007. The Bill was introduced by the Minister of Corporate Affairs, Shri Prem Chand Gupta on 29th August, 2007. After the Presidential Assent is received, the Govt will notify the Rules under the Act and other steps will be taken for operationalization of the Competition Commission of India (CCI). This will require new Selection Rules to be notified and appointments of Chairperson and Members. The Commission will then prepare its Regulations for conduct of its business.

3186. (10-9-2007) NEW DELHI : The president of Mexico H.E Felipe Calderon Hinojosa inaugurated the Exhibition "Dressing Like Gods" here this evening. The Minister of Culture and Tourism Smt. Ambika Soni presided over the inaugural function held at the National Museum.The exhibition presents 58 choicest art objects from the National Institute of Anthropology and History, Mexico, in various forms and materials of the pre-Colombian world and intends to show the richness of dressing the human body, which is a continuous art form from the time immemorial. The use of fabrics, feathers, and ornaments has its own significance to express the ideal of beauty in Mexican Art, the origin of which is divine, as has been the case in India. The visitors will notice a combination of realism, symbolism and the perfection in style that was in vogue in Mexican traditional societies, reflecting the hierarchical positions of the persons. Most important as has been the head to manifest the ideals of beauty, hairdressing witnessed the highest refinement, some with inter-weaving hair, while others with ornaments of natural fibers or half coiffure, and some times representing tufts, shaved heads and stylized shaved. Hence, the fineness in hairdressing was so strong that it continues even today in some indigenous communities. The art objects on display speak very high of both the masculine and feminine beauty, as some sculptures wear short skirts made with bits and shells, others wearing plumes in a variety of styles, and the feminine ones wearing complicated head-dresses leaving on the visitors a magical impact for the delicacy of the lines, elegant attitude and her social status in the Mexican society. The exhibits show a unique richness of the dressing sense and reveal the worldview of the societies in the pre-Columbian world on one hand and on the other define the idealism of beauty at its best, the activity or the importance of the persons and their relationship with the Gods. The exhibition accompanies an exhibition catalogue with illustrations in full colour and is organized by the National Museum in collaboration with the National Institute of Anthropology and History, Mexico and the Ministry of Foreign Affairs of Mexico. The exhibition will remain open till November 10, 2007 at the National Museum from 10.00 AM to 5.00 P.M. daily (except Mondays).

3187. (10-9-2007) NEW DELHI : Dr. Raghuvansh Prasad Singh, Union Minister for Rural Development will inaugurate the SARAS – 2007, a fortnight long event at Dilli Haat, New Delhi tomorrow. Organised jointly by the Ministry of Rural Development and Council for Advancement of People's Action and Rural Technology (CAPART), this fair will continue till 24th of this month. The fair aims at facilitating the SGSY beneficiaries, rural artisans, Craftsmen, SHGs and NGOs to exhibit and sell their products and provide them the opportunity for additional income and exposure and interaction on a large scale. This exhibition-cum-sales fair under the brand name of SARAS will display a wide range of products manufactured by the rural artisans, Craftsmen and beneficiaries of Self Help Groups from all over the country. It creates a unique platform for developing linkages with the buyers and customers and also provides opportunity to deal directly with the buyers avoiding the middlemen. Around 190 Stalls and 500 Swarojgaries from 20 States from all over India will be participating in the fair. Some of special attractions for this SARAS are Metal work products from Madhya Pradesh, Sambalpur, Saris from Orissa, Wood-works from Tamil Nadu, Bamboo Craft from Tripura, Madhubani paintings from Bihar, Terracotta's from Chattisgarh and Shawls & Carpets from Jammu and Kashmir etc. Another major attraction of the mega event is the presentation of divergent cultural programmes of different States throughout the fair. Organizing SARAS fair at Dilli Haat and at the India International Trade Fair (IITF) by the Ministry of Rural Development is an annual feature. The Ministry also organizes a number of regional SARAS fairs at State capitals and other major cities throughout the country. During the year 2006-07, 23 Regional SARAS fairs were organized besides IITF SARAS fair.

3188. (10-9-2007) NEW DELHI : The Vice President of India Mohd. Hamid Ansari has said that the sheer necessity has propelled thinking to bring into focus two new paradigms of politics and security – the first, at the sub-national and micro-level, is the concept of human security; the second, at the supra-national and macro level, is the quest for solutions to problems of human security that transcend national boundaries and thus necessitate regional cooperation and structures imperative for its realisation. Delivering inaugural address at a Seminar on "Politics and Security" being held as part of Indo-Bangladesh dialogue here today, he said that we have to admit that the traditional paradigm of politics and security has reached an impasse. The imperative of survival calls for an alternate approach. He called upon the participants in the seminar to respond to the challenge – for the common good of the people of Bangladesh and India?Following is the text of the Vice President's address:"I deem it a privilege to be invited to inaugurate today's seminar on "Politics and Security", it being the third theme of the Indo-Bangladesh Dialogue. The dialogue itself has been in progress now for over a decade; more importantly, it has retained its autonomous character and has brought together persons of diverse political persuasions and intellectual backgrounds. It is a credible manifestation of civil society interaction between two countries.

3189. (10-9-2007) NEW DELHI : The matter of setting up of a Bench of Supreme Court in other parts of the country was taken up again with the Supreme Court for its reconsideration. The Supreme Court informed that after reconsideration of the matter, the Full court, in its meeting held on August 7, 2007 found no justification for deviating from its earlier resolution on the subject and did not favour setting up of Benches of the Supreme Court outside Delhi. The Government do not propose to bring an amendment to the Constitution. This was stated by the Minister of Law and Justice, Shri H. R. Bhardwaj, in a written reply in Rajya Sabha today.

3190. (10-9-2007) NEW DELHI : The Delimitation Commission could not complete its work by the scheduled time because of the following intervening circumstances: In June 2003, Parliament passed Constitution (Eighty-seventh Amendment) Act, 2003 which provides that the Delimitation of the Assembly and Parliamentary Constituencies should be done on the basis of 2001 census figures. As a consequence the work done by the Commission till June 2003 on the basis of 1991 census figures became non-est and the Commission started afresh. These figures were made available to the Commission much later. The Delimitation Commission, in terms of the Constitutional provisions, can base its work, only on the published census figures. The 2001 census figures were published as late as on December 31, 2003. Thereafter in march, 2004 the Lok Sabha was dissolved. Fresh elections were held and the Fourteenth Lok Sabha was constituted. The Associate Members of the Delimitation Commission were nominated by the Lok Sabha Speaker in July 2004. The Gauhati High Court stayed the delimitation exercise in respect of the State of Arunachal Pradesh, Assam, Nagaland and Manipur on the grounds of disputed census figures. The Delimitation Commission was constituted under section 3 of the Delimitation Act, 2002 vide Government of India Gazette Notification dated July 12, 2002. Initially, the Delimitation Commission was given a term of two years from the date of publication of Notification dated July 12, 2002. Subsequently, its term was extended on year to year basis. Vide the Government of India Notification number S.O. 1064 (E), dated the July 2, 2007 its present term has been extended up to July 31, 2008. So far the Delimitation Commission has completed its exercise in respect of 25 State. The Delimitation exercise was respect to the remaining States and Union Territories is yet to be completed. The new delimitation will take effect from the date to be specified by the President of India under the second proviso to article 82 and second proviso clause (3) of article 170 of the Constitution.This was stated by the Minister of State of Law and Justice, Shri K. Venkatapathy, in a written reply in Rajya Sabha today.

3191. (10-9-2007) NEW DELHI : With a view to check the increasing number of pending cases, the Government have taken the following measures, inter-alia, to facilitate speedy disposal of cases in the courts:¨ Review of the Judge strength in High Courts from time to time and prompt action for filling the vacancies.¨

The term of 1562 Fast Track Courts, which were functional in the States as on March 31, 2005 has been extended for another five years *i.e.* upto March 31, 2010." With a view to ensuring expeditious disposal of civil cases, the Civil Procedure Code has been amended which, inter-alia, limits the number of adjournments which can be granted to a party to three." With a view to ensuring speedy disposal of criminal cases, appropriate changes have been made in the Code of Criminal Procedure through Code of Criminal Procedure (Amendment) Act, 2005, inter-alia, introducing the concept of plea bargaining." Modernization of the judicial infrastructure through computerization of courts. Further, with a view to make quick and less expensive justice accessible to the common man at the grass root level, Government has introduced a Bill to establish Gram Nyayalalyas in the rural areas. A large number of disputes have already been settled and are being settled regularly through Lok Adalat system. The people in general are being made aware of the utility and advantage of resolution of disputes through Lok Adalats. This was stated by the Minister of Law and Justice, Shri H. R. Bhardwaj, in a written reply in Rajya Sabha today.

3192. (10-9-2007) NEW DELHI : The Unorganised Sector Workers Social Security Bill 2007 was introduced in the Rajya Sabha today by the Minister of State (Independent Charge) for Labour and Employment, Shri Oscar Fernandes. It provides legislative backing to all the social security schemes. These include the 'Aaam Admi Bima Yojana', National Old Age Pension Scheme and the Health Insurance Scheme. These Schemes were earlier announced by the Prime Minister on August 15 this year and are a part of the Schedule having 11 schemes to the proposed legislation. Addressing a Press Conference, Shri Fernandes said that the Health Insurance Scheme has been formulated for BPL workers and will cover 6 crore families progressively in the next 5 years. In all, more than 30 crore workers will be benefitted. A provision has been made for issuing smart card, carrying a unique identification number, to each of these families. Both public and private health facilities will be utilised for providing medical services and there would be cashless transactions to ensure that there is no harassment of the beneficiaries. Each family would be entitled to health care worth Rs. 30,000/- per annum. Under the scheme, during the first year, an expenditure of about Rs. 700 crore is estimated and this will go upto more than Rs. 3500 crore at the end of five years when all the six crore BPL families would be covered. The Minister said that the National Old Age Pension Scheme will be extended to all the persons Below Poverty Line above the age of 65 years. A pension of Rs. 200/- per month will be provided and States will be requested to add another Rs. 200/- to this scheme. An amount of more than Rs. 4000 crore per annum will be spent under the scheme which will be administered by the Ministry of Rural Development. Under the 'Aaam Admi Bima Yojana', all the rural landless households in the country will be provided life and disability insurance cover. This cover will be for Rs. 75,000/- on death due to accident and permanent disability due to accident. In case of partial disability due to accident, the insurance cover would be

Rs. 37,500/-. Upon death of a member, prior to terminal date, Rs. 30,000/- is the insurance amount. The premium to be charged under the scheme will be Rs. 200 per annum per member of which 50 per cent will be contributed by the Central Government and remaining by the State Governments.

3193. (10-9-2007) NEW DELHI : The process of consultation on the recommendations made by the Expert Group on agricultural indebtedness has been initiated. The Expert Group was constituted by the Government under the Chairmanship of Prof. R. Radhakrishna, Director, Indira Gandhi Institute of Development Research, Mumbai to look into the problems of agricultural indebtedness. The Report of the Expert Group focuses on institutions and instruments that would strengthen the credit delivery mechanism for the farm community in particular and for rural India in general. While doing so, it takes cognizance of the imperatives of addressing the credit absorption and demand-side issues. Policy interventions and institutional reforms essential for resolving the farm crisis, which go beyond the credit delivery system, also form part of this Report. In the long-term interest of the financial system, a positive repayment culture for bank loans deserves to be actively promoted.

3194. (10-9-2007) NEW DELHI : According to the 17th Electric Power Survey of India, published by the Central Electricity Authority (CEA), the estimates of electricity demand for the State of Tamil Nadu at the end of the 11th Plan (2011-12), in terms of peak demand and energy requirement, are projected to be 14,224 MW and 87,222 million units respectively. An all-India generation capacity addition of 78,577 MW has been envisaged for the 11th Plan to meet the projected All-India demand, consisting of projects in the Central, State and private sectors. Under the State sector in Tamil Nadu, a capacity addition of 1,152 MW has been proposed. Tamil Nadu will also have a share in the Central sector projects likely to yield benefits during 11th Plan in the Southern region. However, in addition to the proposed generation capacity addition, the inter-State transmission capacity is also being augmented by the Central Government to enable inter-State transfer of power. This information was given by the Union Power Minister Shri Sushilkumar Shinde in a written reply to a question in the Rajya Sabha today.

3195. (10-9-2007) NEW DELHI : The Central Leather Research Institute (CLRI), Chennai has developed two collagen based products along with drug delivery system for wound dressing. The collagen based dressing for controlled delivery of Silver Sulphadiazine has been developed to address infection during healing process. The preparation of collagen scaffold impregnated with silver sulphadiazine (SSD) loaded alginate micropheres is capable of delivering the drug in a controlled manner, thus, reducing frequency of dressing change and making wound assessment and management easier. Another product is collagen based wound dressing material to deliver ciprofloxacin, an antibiotic. This information was given by the Union Minister for Science & Technology and Earth Sciences Shri Kapil Sibal in a written reply to a question in the Rajya Sabha today.

3196. (10-9-2007) NEW DELHI : The statutory inquiry by Commissioner of Railway Safety, Northern Circle, New Delhi (Ministry of Civil Aviation, Government of India) into collision of 2716 Down Amritsar-Nanded Express with a road vehicle at Manned (Engineering) Level Crossing gate No. 93 C-Class located at Km 168/14-12 between Dhola Mazara and Dhirpur railway stations on Delhi-Ambala double line electrified section of Delhi Division of Northern Railway at 10.55 hours on 16.07.2007 has revealed that the accident had occurred due to failure of Railway staff and failure of person other than Railway Staff. One train passenger died and four were grievously injured as a result of this accident. The Commissioner, Railway Safety has made the following main recommendations:· In the gate working instructions failure of lifting barrier should be elaborated to include failure of locking arrangements and action to be taken thereafter.· This level crossing gate No. 93C-Class should be interlocked with signals and kept open to road traffic as TVUs of October 2006 is 134207.· Format regarding the opening and closing the level crossing gates should be approved by the Railway Administration and printed registers with this format should be given to the gatemen on duty for recording the opening and closing of the level crossing gates. The register should be containing pages for recording the failure of level crossing gates. Details of failure and rectification of failure should be recorded on the similar pattern as done in signal failure register kept with SM/ASMs in their rooms. The Commissioner has sent his preliminary report for the consideration of the Central Government.

3197. (10-9-2007) NEW DELHI : An independent survey was commissioned by the Government of India and conducted by Social and Research Institute, a unit of International Marketing Research Bureau (SRI-IMRB) in July-August, 2005 with the aim of assessing the number of out-of-school children across the country. As per the findings of the survey, the number of out of school children in Bihar and Uttar Pradesh was 31.77 lakhs and 29.95 lakhs and 29.95 lakhs respectively. This number has now reduced to 21.20 lakhs in Bihar and 7.86 lakhs in Uttar Pradesh as per State Reports as of March, 2007. Context specific interventions for children who are "hard to reach" such as bridge courses, learning centres with flexible timings, seasonal hostels, home based education, mobile schools, have been taken up under the Sarva Shiksha Abhiyan Programme. The Government of India has undertaken 19 orientation and capacity building workshops with States/ UTs with illustrative case studies of good practices, to encourage State/Districts to do such context specific interventions. This information was given by the Minister of State for Human Resource Development Shri M.A.A. Fatmi in a written reply to a question raised by Shri Kalraj Mishra in Rajya Sabha today.

3198. (10-9-2007) NEW DELHI : An independent survey was commissioned by the Government of India and conducted by Social and Research Institute, a unit of International Marketing Research Bureau (SRI-IMRB) in July-August, 2005 with the aim of assessing the number of out-of-school children across the country.

As per the findings of the survey, the number of out of school children in Bihar and Uttar Pradesh was 31.77 lakhs and 29.95 lakhs and 29.95 lakhs respectively. This number has now reduced to 21.20 lakhs in Bihar and 7.86 lakhs in Uttar Pradesh as per State Reports as of March, 2007. Context specific interventions for children who are "hard to reach" such as bridge courses, learning centres with flexible timings, seasonal hostels, home based education, mobile schools, have been taken up under the Sarva Shiksha Abhiyan Programme. The Government of India has undertaken 19 orientation and capacity building workshops with States/ UTs with illustrative case studies of good practices, to encourage State/Districts to do such context specific interventions. This information was given by the Minister of State for Human Resource Development Shri M.A.A. Fatmi in a written reply to a question raised by Shri Kalraj Mishra in Rajya Sabha today.

3199. (10-9-2007) NEW DELHI : As per the information provided by the University Grants Commission (UGC), the Commission has issued a letter to all the applicant Trusts/Societies/Institutions to get the institution/courses accredited from the National Assessment and Accreditation Council (NAAC) and National Board of Accreditation, as the case may be, depending upon the courses offered by them. The Central Government is empowered by the UGC Act, 1956 to declare an institution of higher education, other than a University, as Deemed to be a University, on the advice of the UGC. The UGC has laid down guidelines for consideration of proposals for declaring an institution as deemed to be a university. The proposals received for conferment of status under Section 3 of the UGC Act, 1956 are examined as per the provisions of these guidelines. The UGC evaluates the proposal by deputing an Expert Committee to the applicant institution that inspects and makes an on the spot assessment of the applicant institution and the facilities available there, including those of the infrastructure and faculty, and submits a report to the Commission. The UGC considers the report in its meeting before making its recommendations to the Central Government. This information was given by the Minister of State for Human Resource Development Smt. D. Purandeswari in a written reply to a question raised by Ms. Sushila Triya in Rajya Sabha today.

3200. (10-9-2007) NEW DELHI : Under Article 30(1) of the Constitution, minorities have the right to establish and administer institutions of their choice. In exercise of the Constitutional right, the minorities in each State have established educational institutions. An educational institution is recognized as a minority educational institution by the authority of the Central Government or the State Government, under whose, jurisdiction such institutions are established. The Central Government has so far recognized three institutions deemed to be universities and one Central University (Aligarh Muslim University) as minority educational institutions. The recognition granted to the Aligarh Muslim University is Sub-judice in the Supreme Court of India. Information in respect of educational institutions falling under the jurisdiction of States is not maintained centrally. The

National Commission for Minority Educational Institutions (NCMEI) is also competent under Section 12B and 12C of the (NCMEI) Act, 2004 to decide on the minority status of an educational institution.

3201. (10-9-2007) NEW DELHI : The Minister of Overseas Indian Affairs Shri Vayalar Ravi said that his Ministry is developing the policy framework and institutional arrangements to best serve the Overseas Indian Workers over the medium to long term. Inaugurating the second annual conference of Heads of Indian Missions of six GCC countries, Malaysia, Jordan, Libya and Yemen in New Delhi today, he said the ECR suspension system for those travelling on visit visa is being done away with. It will benefit about 5-6 lakh international travellers from India resulting in a saving of about Rs 100 crore. The conference is being organized by the Ministry of Overseas Indian Affairs (MOIA). The Minister said that a Council for Promotion of Overseas Employment (CPOE) will soon be established by the Ministry. It will function as a think tank for conducting international labour market research and devising strategies for enabling Indian workers to avail the employment opportunities overseas. He further stated that the proposal for the amendment to the Emigration Act has been finalized and is expected to be placed before the Cabinet shortly. The Amendment will give Indian Missions a statutory role in the protection and welfare of the workers and also provide stringent actions against the unscrupulous recruiting agents and those who are involve in Human Smuggling. Shri Ravi informed that several important decisions have been taken for the protection and welfare of Household Service Workers (HSWs), which need effective implementation and follow-up with the cooperation of Indian Missions. The emigration process is being revamped to make it simple, efficient and transparent by introduction of e-governance. The MOIA has planned a nation wide awareness campaign to educate the potential emigrants about the dangers of illegal/irregular migration through unscrupulous agents. He also informed that the Ministry has signed MoUs with Government of UAE and Kuwait for the protection and welfare of Indian workers. Similar MOUs are proposed to be signed with Malaysia, Bahrain, Oman and Yemen. The MOIA has also implemented an elaborate Orientation-cum-Training scheme for potential emigrant workers in partnership with State Governments and Apex Industry Associations, he added. The Minister also appreciated the contribution of the Indian diplomatic missions in protecting the rights of Indian emigrants and addressing their problems in the host countries. He said that management of emigration needs sensitivity and empathy on the part of all authorities working in the field of emigration as there is no substitute for "governance with a human face". He called upon all participants to deliberate on all issues during the Conference and suggest effective measures for protection and welfare of emigrants. Earlier Shri Nirmal Singh, Secretary, the Ministry of Overseas Indian Affairs and Shri N. Ravi, Secretary (East), the Ministry of External Affairs also addressed the participants.

3202. (10-9-2007) NEW DELHI : India is keen to share its expertise with Africa in the fields of industry, trade and investment, Shri Kamal Nath, Minister of Commerce and Industry, said while underlining the country's commitment to promoting South-South cooperation at the inaugural session of the first International Conference on "India-Africa Cooperation in Industry, Trade and Investment", organized by the United Nations Industrial Development Organisation (UNIDO) in cooperation with Government of India here today. Known as the Sanjay Lall Memorial Conference, the five-day event is organized under the banner of the recently established UNIDO Centre for South-South Industrial Cooperation (UCSSIC), and is being attended by 42 delegates from 13 African countries – Cameroon, Ethiopia, Ghana, Kenya, Madagascar, Mozambique, Nigeria, Senegal, South Africa, Sudan, Tanzania, Uganda and Zambia. "India's trade in goods and services will be in the region of 500 billion dollars this year. Our foreign exchange reserves are 230 billion dollars. The size of our economy has crossed 1 trillion dollars. But all this has not come easily to us. India has achieved this by dint of hard work. We would like to continue to share our experience, our expertise, our technology with our brothers and sisters from Africa", the Minister said, adding that India had as much to learn as to teach. Shri Ajay Shankar, Secretary, Department of Industrial Policy and Promotion (DIPP), spoke of the special bond between India and Africa, and said the conference was a timely initiative which would help in carrying the south-south development process forward. Mr. J. Vinanchiarachi, Principal Adviser to the Director-General/UNIDO, described the late Professor Sanjaya Lall as a development-minded practical thinker, who contributed a lot to the work of international organizations. His concepts on R & D and innovation-induced products as the drivers of global trade helped UNIDO in framing its industrial performance and capabilities index, Mr. Arachi added. Mr. Anthony de Sa, Director, UCSSIC, said the Centre would develop projects on leather, cotton, auto components, hand tools, low-cost building materials, renewable energy, pharmaceuticals and IT applications in industry.

3203. (10-9-2007) NEW DELHI : Independent monitors have been appointed after consultation with the Central Vigilance Commissioner, as required under the provisions of the Pre-Contract Integrity Pact to be signed with bidders in defence procurement cases of estimated value exceeding Rs. 100 crore. The independent monitors so appointed are S/Shri TR Prasad, former Cabinet Secretary, Government of India, PC Rawal, former Secretary Government of India, and Hemendra Kumar, former Special Secretary, Government of India. This information was given by the Defence Minister Shri AK Antony in a written reply to Shri Adhir Chowdhury and others in Lok Sabha today.

3204. (10-9-2007) NEW DELHI : As per reports received from the Army, there were two incidents of sale of liquor by Army personnel to unauthorized persons in the last seven years. In these cases, army officers involved in sale of liquor to unauthorized personnel were given exemplary punishment involving rigorous imprisonment and cashiering from service. As and when a case is reported, it is investigated thoroughly and strict action is taken against involved army personnel irrespective of the rank they hold. Besides this surprise checks in the canteens are carried out periodically by a board of officers. Constant vigil is also maintained by Military Police and Military Intelligence units on unauthorized sale of liquor. Smart cards have been issued to defence personnel regulating the sale of liquor from unit run canteens as per entitlement.

3205. (10-9-2007) NEW DELHI : The incidence of HIV positive cases in the Armed Forces during the last 5 years has shown declining trend from 501 cases in the year 2001 to 377 cases in 2006. The Armed Forces Medical Services have an elaborate HIV /AIDS control programme, which includes the following: (a) Health education of the troops and their families. (b) Surveillance of High Risk Groups such as blood donors, patients of sexually transmitted diseases, tuberculosis patients, ante natal cases, personnel proceeding abroad in peace keeping missions and returning from there. (c) Hundred percent screening of all ante natal cases. (d) Hundred percent screening of all blood / blood products of HIV, Hepatitis B, Hepatitis C, Syphilis and Malaria. (e) Encouraging voluntary counselling and testing. (f) Spreading awareness about HIV/AIDS through audio-visual means. The Armed Forces Medical Services are running a comprehensive prevention and control programme of HIV / AIDS is close coordination with the National AIDS Control Organisation and United Nations AIDS Programme. This information was given by the Defence Minister Shri AK Antony in a written reply to Shri Bansagopal Choudhury and Shri Sunil Khan in Lok Sabha today.

3206. (10-9-2007) NEW DELHI : India signed a Double Taxation Avoidance Agreement (DTAA) with Mexico for the avoidance of double taxation and for the prevention of fiscal evasion with respect to Taxes on Income, here today. This Agreement shall enter into force on a date to be notified in due course. The Agreement also aims at promoting economic cooperation between the two countries. The Agreement was signed by Shri P. Chidambaram, Union Minister of Finance on behalf of the Government of India and Ms.Patricia Espinosa Cantellano, Foreign Minister of Mexico on behalf of the Government of the United Mexican States. The DTAA between India and Mexico will cover in the case of India, income-tax including any surcharge thereon and in the case of Mexico, the federal income-tax. The DTAA provides for taxation of dividend, interest, royalties and fees for technical services-both in the country of residence as well as the country of source. However, the rate of tax in the country of source shall not exceed ten percent of the gross amount of payment in case the beneficial owner of the payments is a resident of the other Contracting State.The DTAA provides that capital gains from alienation of shares of a company shall be taxable in the country where the company is a resident. The incidence of double taxation shall be avoided by one country giving credit for taxes paid by its residents in the other country. There is a provision for exchange of information in cases which are under investigation in either of the two countries. Both countries shall assist each other in collection of revenue claims. There is also a provision for limitation of benefits under the DTAA to prevent misuse of the provisions of the DTAA. The Agreement will further stimulate the flow of capital, technology and personnel between the two countries. It will also contribute to the tax stability and reduce any obstacles in providing mutual cooperation.

3207. (10-9-2007) NEW DELHI : The Government has initiated a scheme to provide one time financial assistance of Rs. 12.3 crore for establishment of 65 new polytechnics in the country and also by providing financial assistance for upgradation of infrastructural facilities in 77 existing polytechnics. The All India Council for Technical Education (AICTE) has permitted double shifts in those diploma level institutions where adequate infrastructure, faculty and other facilities are available. AICTE has also relaxed the norms for land requirement for establishment of diploma level institutes by fifty percent. In order to meet the shortage of teachers in the polytechnics, the faculty student ratio has been reduced from 1:15 to 1:20. This information was given by the Minister of State for Human Resource Development Smt. D. Purandeswari in a written reply to a question raised by Smt. Shobhana Bhartia in Rajya Sabha today.

3208. (10-9-2007) NEW DELHI : The State Government of Andhra Pradesh has submitted a proposal for financial assistance of Rs. 243.27 lakhs for modernization of madarsas and a separate proposal for the appointment of 2874 number of Urdu language teachers. The proposal, being recent, can only be considered when the Grants-in-Aid Committee meets next. The proposal of Urdu teachers in under-examination. This information was given by the Minister of State for Human Resource Development Smt. D. Purandeswari in a written reply to a question raised by Shri C. Ramachandraiah in Rajya Sabha today.

3209. (10-9-2007) NEW DELHI : The Indian Armed Forces, despite heavy internal commitments, remain battle ready to take on multiple external security commitments, beyond borders, in various regions and terrains across the globe, in collaboration with friendly forces of many nationalities. The Indian Army would be engaging in Joint military manoeuvres with its British counterparts in the glacial heights of Ladakh (Ex Himalayan Warrior) as well as with the crack Russian Airborne forces in the chillingly cold riverine plains of Pskov, South East of St Petersburg (Ex Indra 07). Indra-07 is the next edition of joint military manoeuvres between Russia and India, which began with the first ever-joint Airborne Exercise (Indra-05) conducted between the two armies in Oct 2005, in the deserts of Rajasthan. The theme of Indra-07 is Counter-Terrorism during which, the special airborne forces of the two countries would be jointly planning and conducting air and ground manoeuvres to neutralize concentration of international terrorists in a third country, under a UN mandate. The joint training, planning and tactical manoeuvres will commence in Pskov on 11 Sep 07 and will continue for next ten days. The manoeuvres will be conducted under the aegis of Russian 76 Airborne Division and will involve over 400 airborne special forces troops of the two countries; plethora of state-of-art battle equipment as well as a large number fixed and rotary wing aircrafts; the UAVs and the aircrew. The manoeuvres will be conducted in three phases culminating in a realistic simulated joint operational exercise involving surveillance, acquiring and assessing of intelligence; joint planning; multi-directional mass airborne insertion and tactical paradrop; regrouping into joint task forces and joint teams; followed by a series of counter-terrorist operations. The manoeuvres will involve cross-country movement over approx 100 km post air insertion; assault crossing of a river obstacle; destruction of terrorist hides; extrication from the target area into neutral territory. The exercise has been structured so as to enhance interoperability and maximize mutual learning from each others rich combat experiences. The Indian airborne forces from the Parachute Regiment will not only get an opportunity to showcase their combat skills but will also enrich themselves from the experiences, operational concepts and tactical designs and methodologies of their Russian counterparts. Joint command & control at all levels will also help the two forces in refining processes, procedures and drills so as to enhance inter-operability. All this will lead to maximizing operational effectiveness. The Indra-07 will pave way for further up-scaling of military cooperation in terms of scope, content and enhanced participation in the years to come.

3210. (10-9-2007) NEW DELHI : The Government of India has set up three Indian Institutes of Science Education and Research (IISERs), at Pune, Kolkata and Mohali. Two more IISERs are being set up at Bhopal and Thiruvananthapuram. These Institutes have been/are being set up on the recommendations of the Scientific Advisory Council to the Prime Minister (SAC-PM). The total estimated project cost of each IISER is Rs. 500.00 crores which includes Rs. 241.00 crores fro construction of building and other infrastructural facilities and Rs. 259.00 crores as recurring expenditure, spread over a period of 7 years. This information was given by the Minister of State for Human Resource Development Smt. D. Purandeswari in a written reply to a question raised by Shri Ravula Chandra Sekar Reddy in Rajya Sabha today.

3211. (10-9-2007) NEW DELHI : The expenditure on Higher Education including Technical Education was 0.44 percentage of GDP during 2005-06. The Central Government is aware of the fact that our public expenditure per student is low as compared to several other countries Efforts have been made by the Central Government by increasing the budgetary provision for higher education, including technical education substantially since 2004-05 resulting in the creation of new Central Universities and other higher educational institutions. The strategy being followed is to expand capacity as well as increase opportunities of access to all sections of the society, while maintaining standards. There is no bar on private not-for-profit initiatives in the field of higher and technical education. This information was given by the Minister of State for Human Resource Development Smt. D. Purandeswari in a written reply to a question raised by Shri Vijay J. Darda in Rajya Sabha today.

3212. (10-9-2007) NEW DELHI : For filling up the forthcoming vacancies of Directors of Indian Institutes of Management at Ahmedabad, Bangalore and Kolkata, the Government had also invited applications through advertisements to ensure broad based and transparent procedure. In addition, letters were also written to eminent educationists, industrialists, heads of Institutes etc. to recommend suitable persons for the post of Director for consideration of the Search-cum Selection Committees constituted for this purpose. Though certain concerns were raised in the media and a section of faculty of these Institutes over the inviting of applications through press advertisements, the Government has clarified that there has been no change in the established procedure of selection of the Director and the Search-cum-Selection Committee can consider and recommend the name of any suitable candidate for the post of Director of Indian Institute of Management and such a candidate need not have necessarily applied against the open press advertisement. The Director of Indian Institutes of Management (IIMs) is appointed by the appointments Committee of the Cabinet (AAC) on the basis of recommendation of the Search-cum-Selection Committee constituted for this purpose. This information was given by the Minister of State for Human Resource Development Smt. D. Purandeswari in a written reply to a question raised by Shri Amar Singh in Rajya Sabha today.

3213. (10-9-2007) NEW DELHI : The Ministry of Tribal Affairs grants funds to State Governments on 50:50 basis towards the cost of construction under the scheme of Establishment of Ashram Schools in TSP areas. This was stated by Shri P.R. Kyndiah, Minister for Tribal Affairs in a reply to a question by Miss Anusuiya Uikey in Rajya Sabha today. He further added that the proposals have been received from State Governments of Madhya Pradesh, Gujarat, Chhattisgarh and UT Administration of Dadra and Nagar Haveli for release of grant under the scheme during current financial year. An amount of Rs. 273.81 lakh has already been released to State Government of Madhya Pradesh under the scheme, during current financial year. The receipt of proposals from State Governments/UT Administrations for release of grants-in-aid for construction of Ashram Schools is a continuous process. The grant-in-aid is released only if the proposal is complete in all respects *i.e.* availability of land free of cost, confirmation about availability of 50% State share, Utilization Certificate and physical progress reports in respect of proposals sanctioned in previous years and the availability of funds.

3214. (10-9-2007) NEW DELHI : Apart from legislative changes in the relevant Acts, instructions have been issued to the State Governments/Union Territory Administrations to effectively enforce legislation relating to crimes against women and monitor the enforcement and to give more focused attention to improving the administration of criminal justice system and to take such measures as are necessary for the prevention of crime against women and other vulnerable sections of society. This was stated by Smt. Renuka Chowdhury, Minister for Women and Child Development in a reply to a question by Shri B.J. Panda in Rajya Sabha today.

3215. (10-9-2007) NEW DELHI : NTPC Limited and BHEL shall form a Joint Venture Company for carrying out Engineering Procurement and Construction (EPC) activities in the power sector on mutually beneficial terms. An MoU to this effect was signed in New Delhi today in the presence of Shri A.K.Puri, CMD BHEL and Shri T. Sankaralingam, CMD, NTPC. Senior officials from both the companies were present on the occasion. The Joint Venture Company shall be jointly owned by NTPC and BHEL on the basis of 50:50 equity participation. The post of CMD of the proposed Joint Venture Company shall be rotated amongst the senior officials of NTPC and BHEL National Thermal Power Corporation (NTPC) a premier Power Utility having an operating capacity of over 27,900 MW is looking for business synergy in order to expand its business activities. Over the years, NTPC has developed world class technology and skills in design, engineering, construction, project management, Operations & Maintenance and Renovation & Modernization of Power Projects. With 20% of all India's installed capacity it contributes around 29% of country's power generation. NTPC is now emerging as an integrated power major with plans to become a 75000 MW plus Company by 2017. Bharat Heavy Electricals Ltd. (BHEL) is the largest engineering and manufacturing enterprise in India in the energy related infrastructure sector and is having specialization, expertise in manufacturing power plant equipment like thermal, hydro, gas and nuclear turbine generators, transformers, capacitors, reactors, circuit breakers, switchgears, insulators, manufacturing equipment and systems for industries viz. captive power plants, industrial steam turbines, industrial boilers, development of rolling stock and traction propulsion systems and technology for exploiting non-conventional and renewable sources of energy etc.

3216. (10-9-2007) NEW DELHI : The Prime Minister Dr. Manmohan Singh will inaugurate the National Ground Water Congress – 2007 and the President of India Smt. Partibha Devisingh Patil will address the valedictory session of the Congress and will present 'National Water Award and Bhoomijal Samvardhan Purskars'at a function here tomorrow (11th September'07). Prof. Saifuddin Soz, the Union Minister for Water Resources, Shri Jai Prakash Narayan Yadav, the Union Minister of State for Water Resources, Dr. M.S. Swaminathan, M.P and renowned water experts will address the Congress. The Congress will be attended by Government, Non-Governmental agencies and various stake holders. Technical papers on ground water issues will be presented in the Congress. The main objectives of National Ground Water Congress are : To develop strategies for sustainability and equitable use of ground water to mitigate water and create awareness: evaluate the role of ground water in national food and water security and promoting more crop and income per drop of water. National Water Award and Bhoomijal Samvardhan Purskars are given for innovative practices of ground water augmentation through rain water harvesting and artificial recharge. National Water Award consists of a cash award of Rs. 10 lakh and a plaque with citation. The National Water Award shall be given for the best innovative practice of ground water augmentation through rain water harvesting and artificial recharge from amongst 18 award winners of the Bhoomijal Samvardhan Puraskar. The Bhomijal Samvardhan Purskar consists of a cash award of Rs. 1 lakh each and a plague with citation. There are 18 Puraskars in total. One each shall be given for the three different categories *i.e.* NGO, Gram Panchayat and Urban Local Body in six zones. There will be two Technical Sessions – First session on the theme of "Awareness of Opportunities for Sustainable management of ground water through Rain Water Harvesting and Water Conservation" and "Role of different Panchayati Raj Institutes, Agricultural Universities, Rural Institutes, Women Institutes and Private Sector in Ground Water Conservation and Sustainable and Equitable use and the Second session on the theme of "More Crop and Income Per Drop of Water".

3217. (10-9-2007) NEW DELHI : The Minister of Tourism & Culture Smt. Ambika Soni is leaving for Japan on 11th September, 2007. She will lead the delegation from India for the JATA World Travel Fair, Tokyo. During her stay there, she will also deliver the keynote address at the 'Incredible India' Seminar and will address the Japanese travel trade and media during the Road Show. Smt. Soni is scheduled to return to Delhi on 14th September, 2007.Japan is one of the leading tourist generating markets for India, with approximately 1.2 lakh tourists from Japan visiting India during 2006, an increase of over 15.5% as compared to the previous year.During the visit of the Hon'ble Prime Minister of India to Japan in December 2006, a Joint Statement designating the year 2007 as the 'India-Japan Tourism Exchange Year', was signed between the two countries for cultural exchanges and to increase the two way flow of tourism. The Ministry of Tourism has, accordingly, organized a number of promotional activities in Japan to showcase and promote India as a tourist destination in the Japanese market and has also dovetailed many of its activities with the events being organized by ICCR during the year. As part of the Joint Statement issued, it was decided that India would participate in events including the JATA World Travel Fair, being held in Tokyo, Japan.

3218. (10-9-2007) NEW DELHI : While filing applications and making payments online, it has been observed that exporters/ importers face technical problems on account of non-availability of relevant documents, malfunctioning of system etc. For attending to these technical problems, DGFT has set up a Helpdesk. The trading community can access the Help Desk by dialing the toll free number 1800 111 550 or by e-mail at dgftedi@nic.in. The help desk will be available between 10.00 AM to 7.00 PM on all working days. A complaint number may be provided by helpdesk if an issue remains unresolved. The complaint number may be quoted for all future reference. For e-mails, complaint Numbers may be conveyed on the next working day, if the complaint is unresolved. Directorate General of Foreign Trade (DGFT), Ministry of Commerce & Industry, New Delhi.

3219. (11-9-2007) NEW DELHI : Press Note: Rescheduling the Programme of Bye-election to the Council of States from Uttar Pradesh to fill up the Vacancy Occurring due to Resignation of sitting member Miss. Mayawati on 5th July, 2007.

3220. (11-9-2007) NEW DELHI : The President of India, Smt. Pratibha Devisingh Patil has said that we should undertake an extensive awareness campaign to make our people aware of the need to use water wisely. As they say "drop by drop is the mighty ocean made". Our efforts to save every drop of water, by using it sensibly, would go a long way in improving water availability. Delivering valedictory address at the "National Ground Water Congress – 2007" here today she said that from the very beginning we should make our children "water-literate" so that they understand that water is a valuable commodity and should be used carefully. Water pollution is yet another important issue that requires our immediate attention. We need to maintain cleanliness of rivers, ponds, water reservoirs, wells and other water bodies in our country. The President said that India is gifted with extensive river systems and receives substantial annual precipitation but water continues to be a limited resource and under considerable pressure. Water resource management is going to be vitally important to sustain the needs of our population. In fact, one of the key determinants of our ability to continue on the path of growth and prosperity will depend on whether we are able to optimally utilize our water resources. Our efforts should be to augment our water reserves and to adopt water conservation practices to ensure that there is no water wastage. The President expressed her concern that in situations of water scarcity, it is always the poor, marginalized and the women who are severely affected. Therefore, access to water supply should be an integral part of poverty eradication and women welfare programmes. Such holistic policies and practices will make it possible for water resources to be used more efficiently, effectively and equitably. The President also presented the "National Water Award" and Bhoomijal Samvardhan Puraskars" on the occasion.